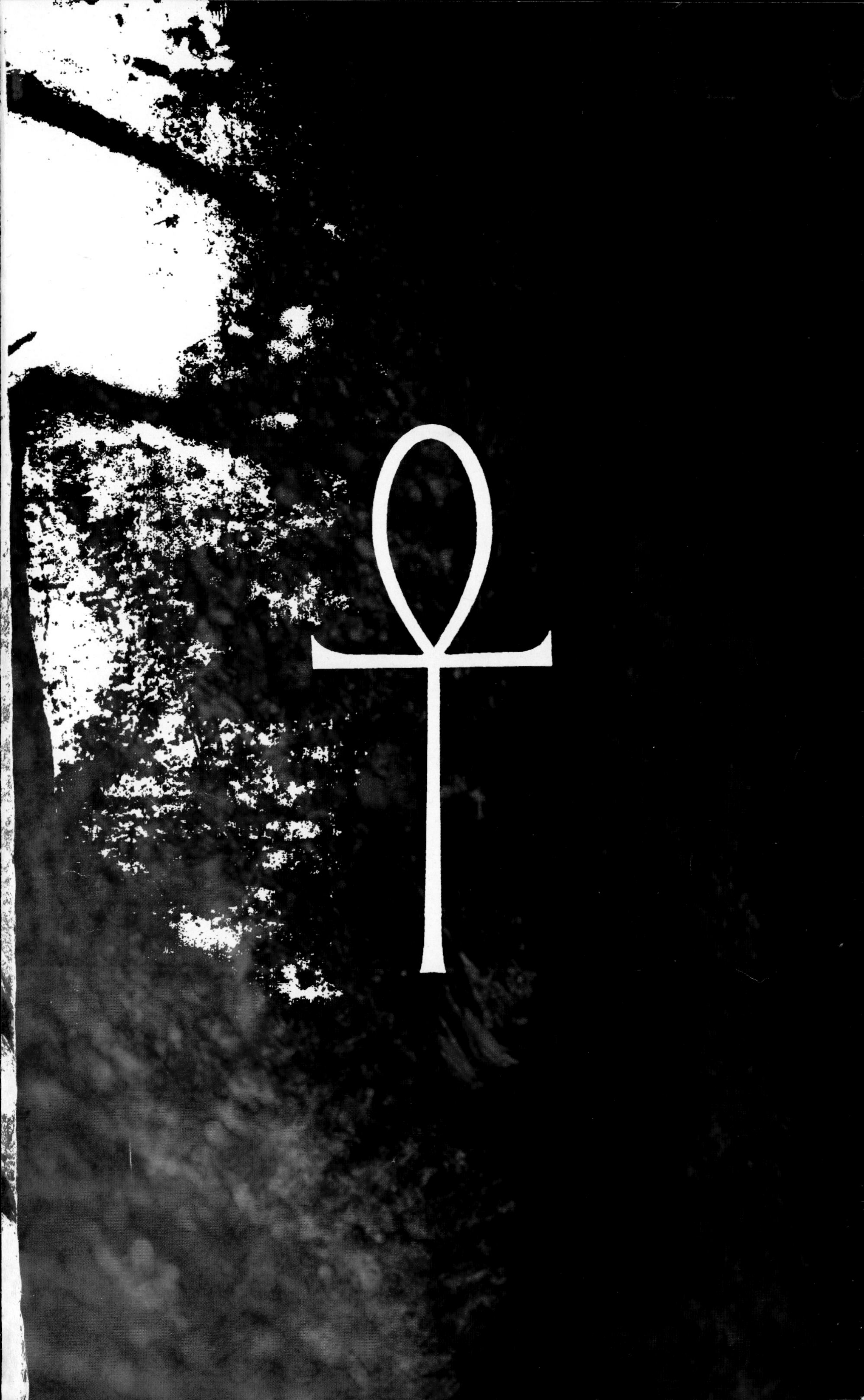

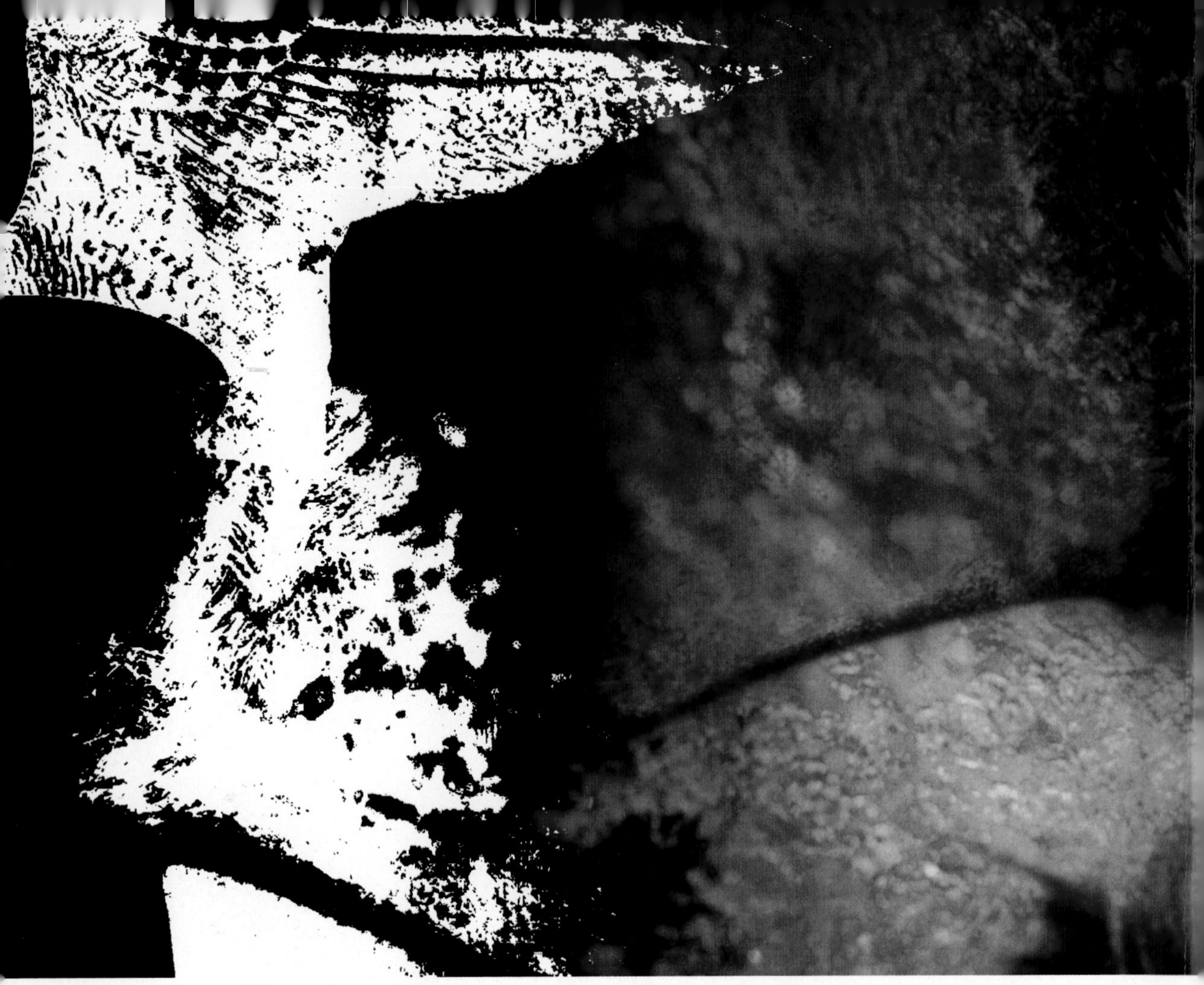

Written by Neil Gaiman

Illustrated by Chris Bachalo Mark Buckingham Mike Dringenberg Colleen Doran
P. Craig Russell Malcolm Jones III Mark Pennington Dave McKean Jeffrey Jones

Colored by Steve Oliff Matt Hollingsworth Daniel Vozzo Lovern Kindzierski Jon J Muth Alex Bleyaert Rob Ro

Lettered by Todd Klein Jeffrey Jones

Cover Art and Original Series Covers by Dave McKean

Featuring characters created by Neil Gaiman, Sam Kieth and Mike Dringenberg

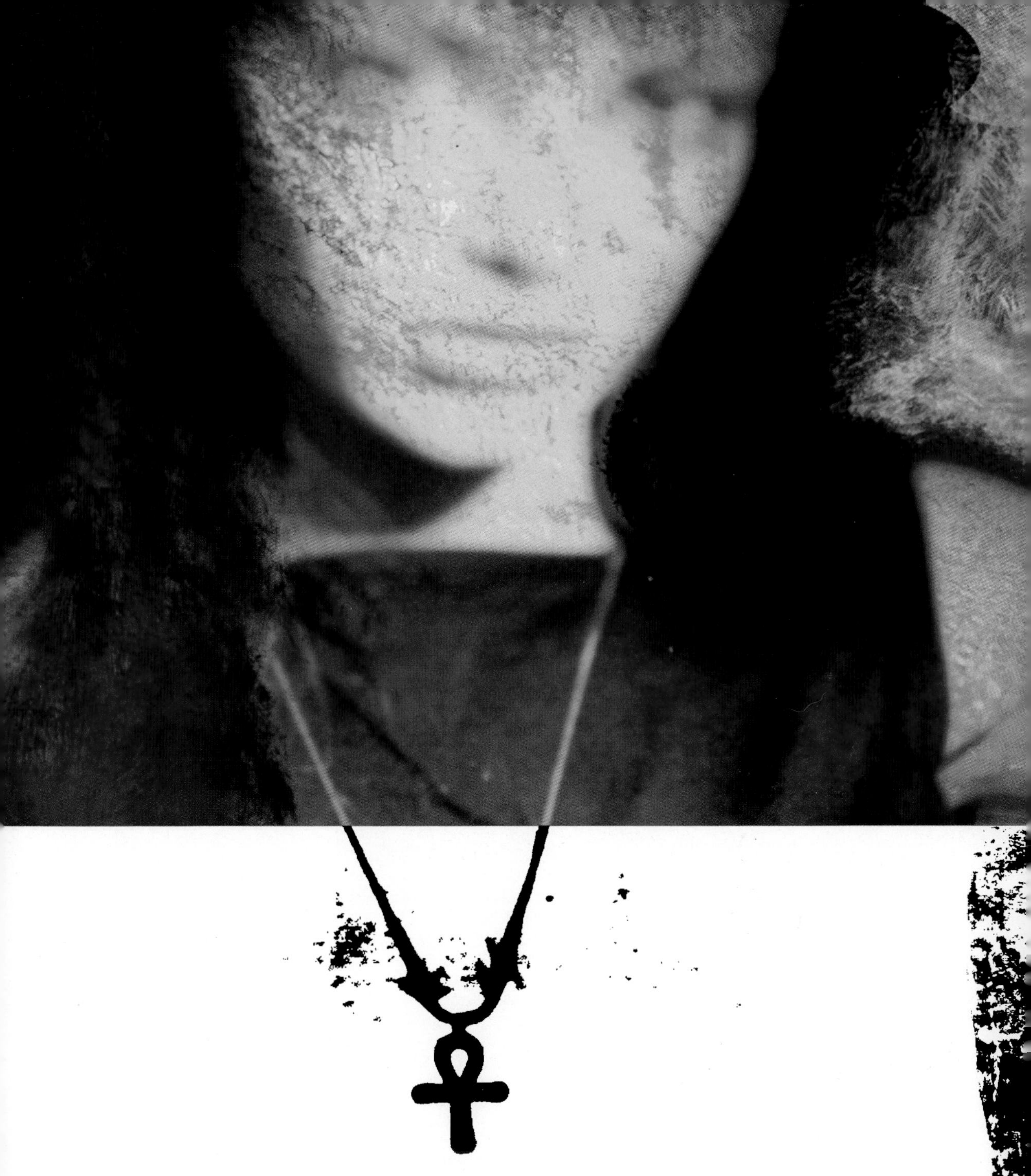

DEATH: THE DELUXE EDITION

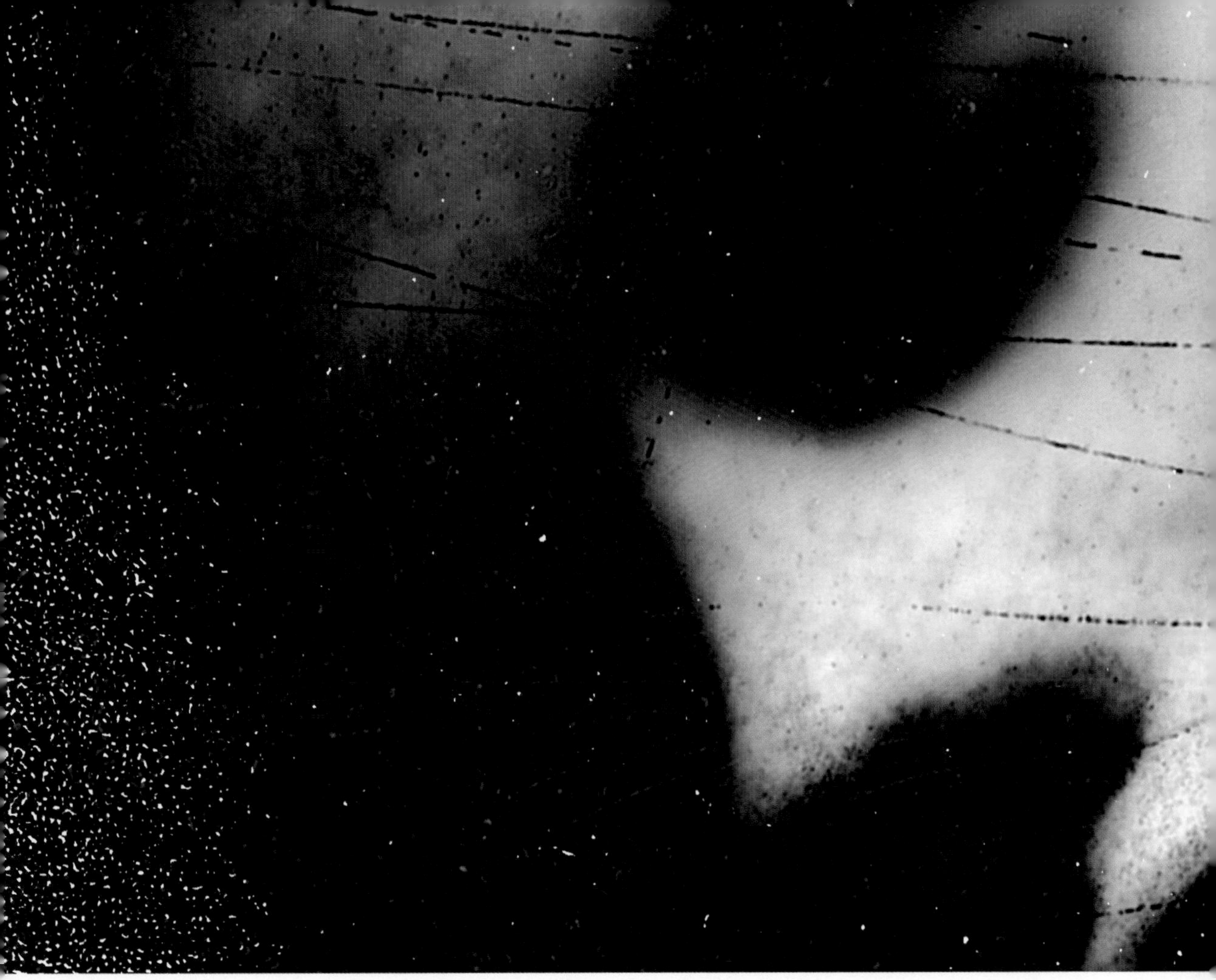

Karen Berger Shelly Roeberg Editors – Original Series
Lisa Aufenanger Alisa Kwitney Shelly Roeberg Jennifer Lee Mariah Huehner Assistant Editors – Original Series
Scott Nybakken Editor Robbin Brosterman Design Director – Books Louis Prandi Publication Design

Karen Berger Senior VP – Executive Editor, Vertigo Bob Harras VP – Editor-in-Chief

Diane Nelson President Dan DiDio and Jim Lee Co-Publishers Geoff Johns Chief Creative Officer
John Rood Executive VP – Sales, Marketing and Business Development Amy Genkins Senior VP – Business and Legal Affairs
Nairi Gardiner Senior VP – Finance Jeff Boison VP – Publishing Operations Mark Chiarello VP – Art Direction and Design
John Cunningham VP – Marketing Terri Cunningham VP – Talent Relations and Services Alison Gill Senior VP – Manufacturing and Operations
Hank Kanalz Senior VP – Digital Jay Kogan VP – Business and Legal Affairs, Publishing Jack Mahan VP – Business Affairs, Talent
Nick Napolitano VP – Manufacturing Administration Sue Pohja VP – Book Sales Courtney Simmons Senior VP – Publicity Bob Wayne Senior VP – Sales

DEATH: THE DELUXE EDITION

DC Comics, 1700 Broadway, New York, NY 10019
A Warner Bros. Entertainment Company.
Printed in the USA. First Printing. ISBN: 978-1-4012-3548-2

Library of Congress Cataloging-in-Publication Data

Gaiman, Neil.
Death, deluxe edition / Neil Gaiman.
p. cm.
"Originally published in single magazine form in Death: The High Cost Of Living 1-3, Death: Time Of Your Life 1-3, The Sandman 8, 20, The Sandman: Endless Nights, Death Talks About Life, Death Gallery, 9-11, Vertigo: Winter's Edge 2."
ISBN 978-1-4012-3548-2
1. Death (Fictitious character : Gaiman)--Comic books, strips, etc. 2. Graphic novels. I. Title.
PN6737.G3D43 2012
741.5'942--dc23

2012022443

SUSTAINABLE FORESTRY INITIATIVE
Certified Chain of Custody
At Least 25% Certified Forest Content
www.sfiprogram.org
SFI-01042
APPLIES TO TEXT STOCK ONLY

Table of Contents

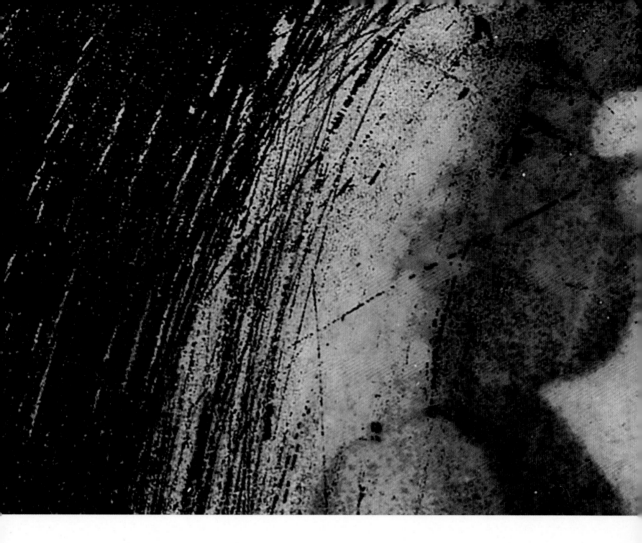

It's funny but on good days I don't think of her so much.

In fact never. I never just say hi when the sun is on my tongue and my belly's all warm. On bad days I talk to Death constantly, not about suicide because honestly that's not dramatic enough. Most of us love the stage and suicide is definitely your last performance and being addicted to the stage, suicide was never an option — plus people get to look you over and stare at your fatty bits and you can't cross your legs to give that flattering thigh angle and that's depressing.

So we talk. She says things no one else seems to come up with, like let's have a hot dog and then it's like nothing's impossible.

She told me once there is a part of her in everyone, though Neil believes I'm more Delirium than Tori, and Death taught me to accept that, you know, wear your butterflies with pride. And when I do accept that, I know Death is somewhere inside of me. She was the kind of girl all the girls wanted to be, I believe, because of her acceptance of "what is." She keeps reminding me there is change in the "what is" but change cannot be made till you accept the "what is."

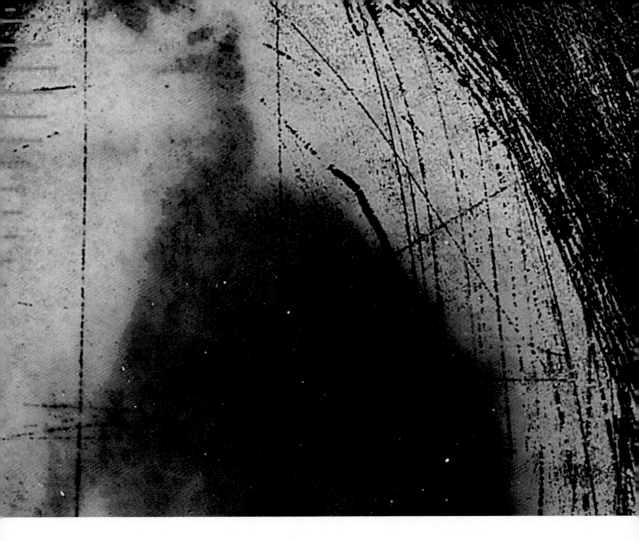

Like yesterday, all the recording machines were breaking down again. We almost lost a master take and the band leaves tomorrow and we can't do any more music till we resolve this. We're in the middle of nowhere in the desert and my being wants to go crawl under a cactus and wish it away. Instead, I dyed my hair and she visited me and I started to accept the mess I'm in. I know that mess spelled backwards is ssem and I felt much better armed with that information. Over the last few hours I've allowed myself to feel defeated, and just like she said if you allow yourself to feel the way you really feel, maybe you won't be afraid of that feeling anymore.

When you're on your knees you're closer to the ground. Things seem nearer somehow.

If all I can say is I'm not in this swamp, I'm not in this swamp then there is not a rope in front of me and there is not an alligator behind me and there is not a girl sitting at the edge eating a hot dog and if I believe that, then dying would be the only answer because then Death couldn't come and say Peachy to me anymore and after all she has a brother who believes in hope.

— Tori Amos
1994

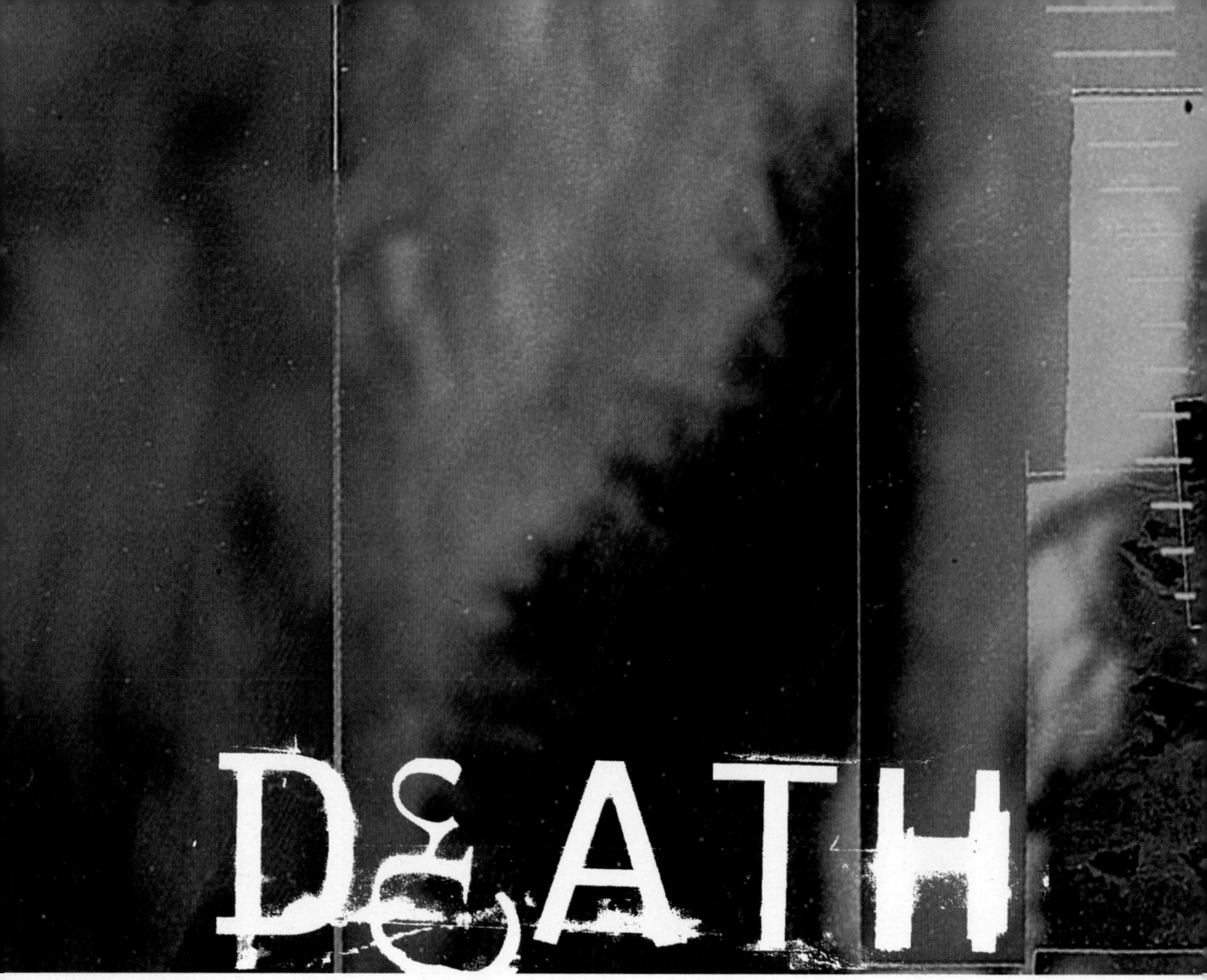
DEATH

THE DELUXE EDITION

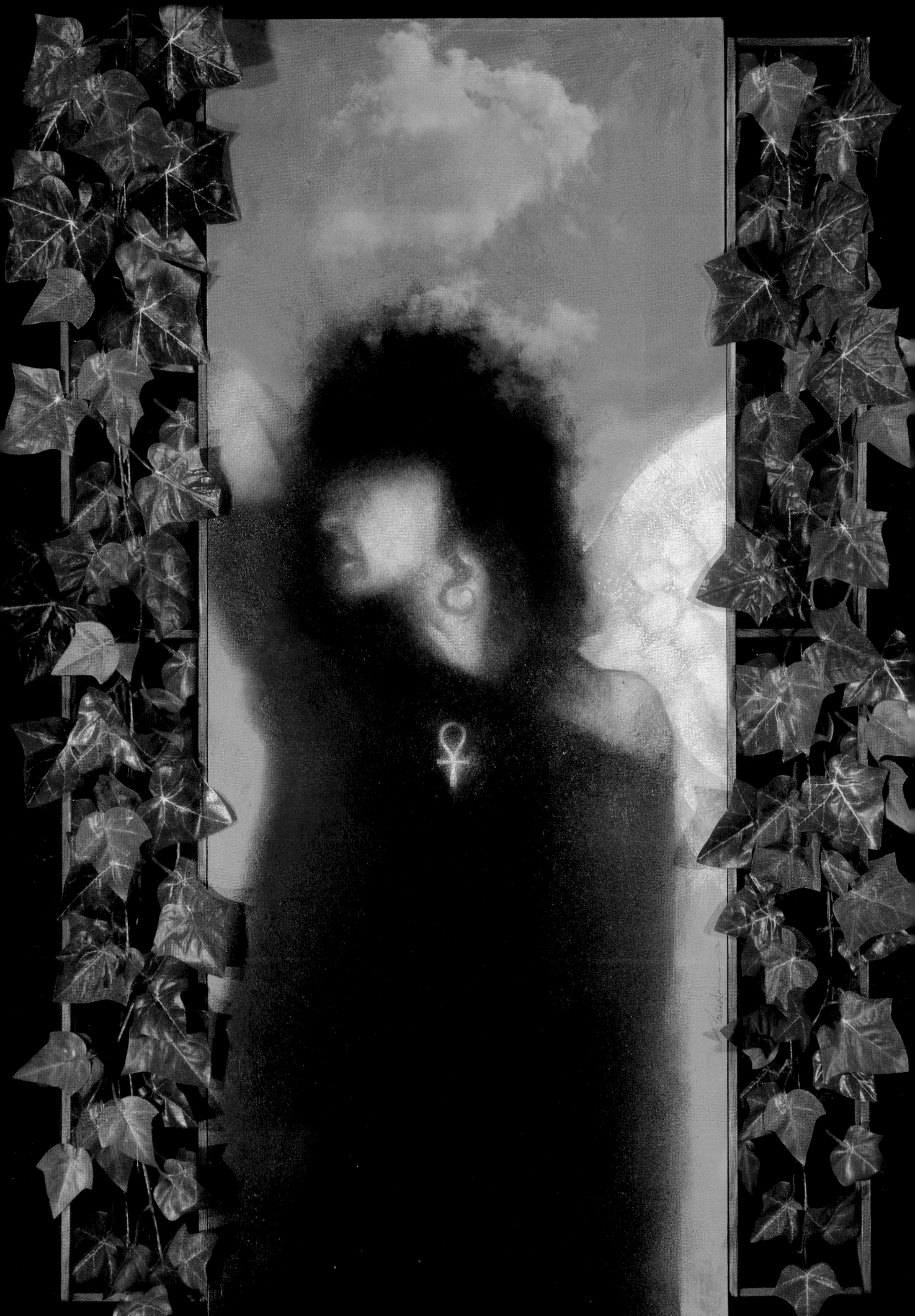

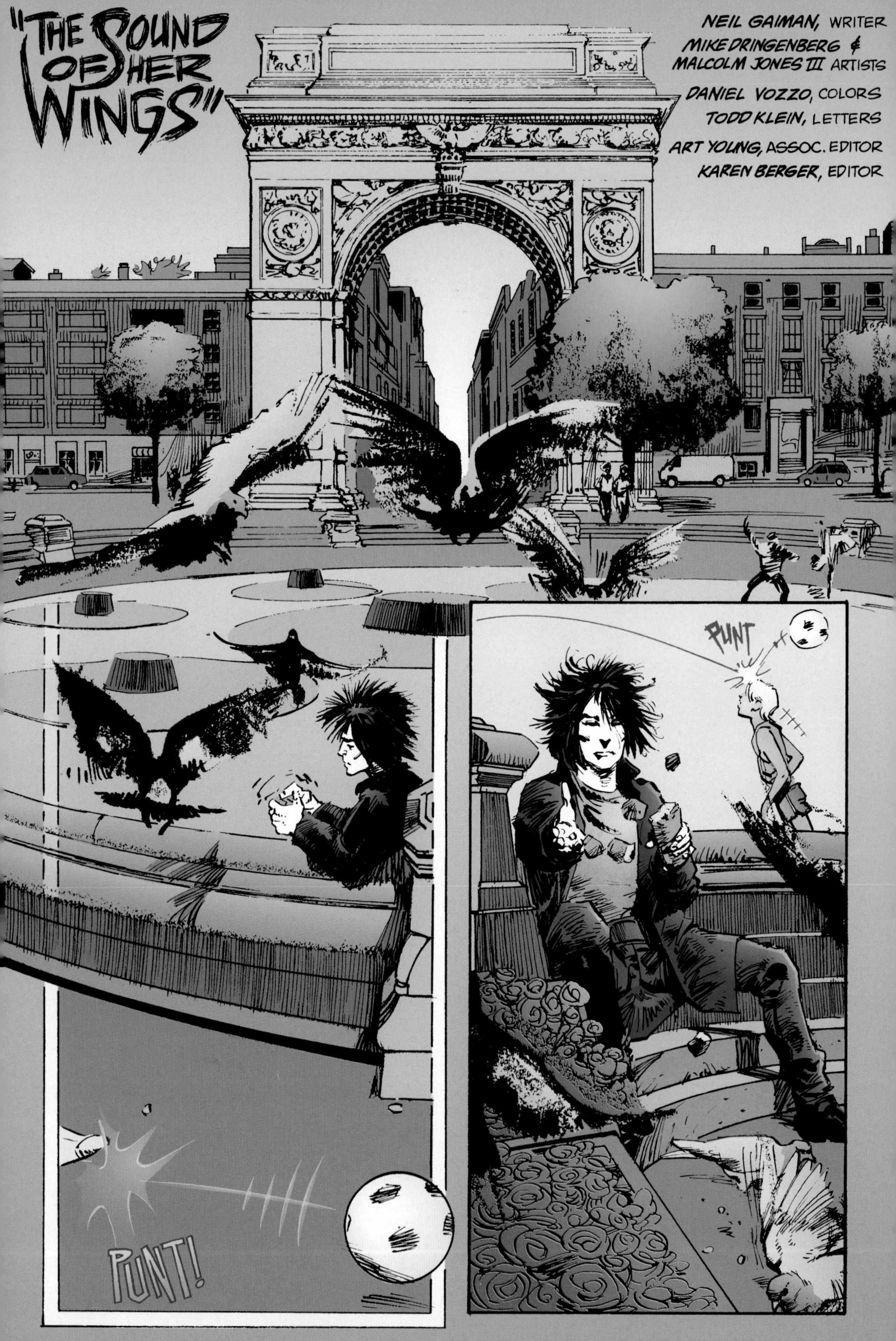
"THE SOUND OF HER WINGS"
NEIL GAIMAN, WRITER
MIKE DRINGENBERG & MALCOLM JONES III ARTISTS
DANIEL VOZZO, COLORS
TODD KLEIN, LETTERS
ART YOUNG, ASSOC. EDITOR
KAREN BERGER, EDITOR
PUNT!
PUNT

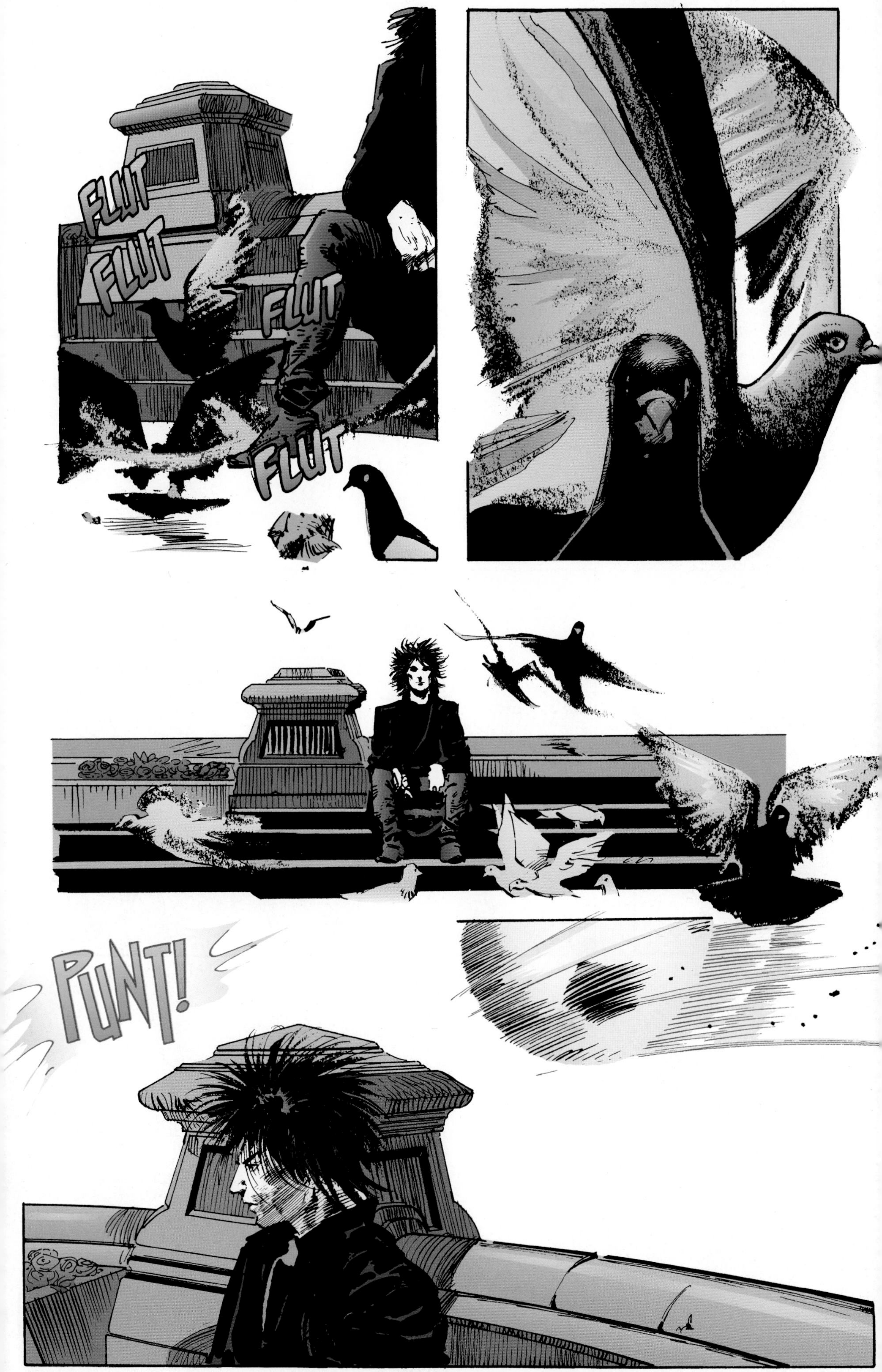
FLUT
FLUT
FLUT
FLUT
PUNT!

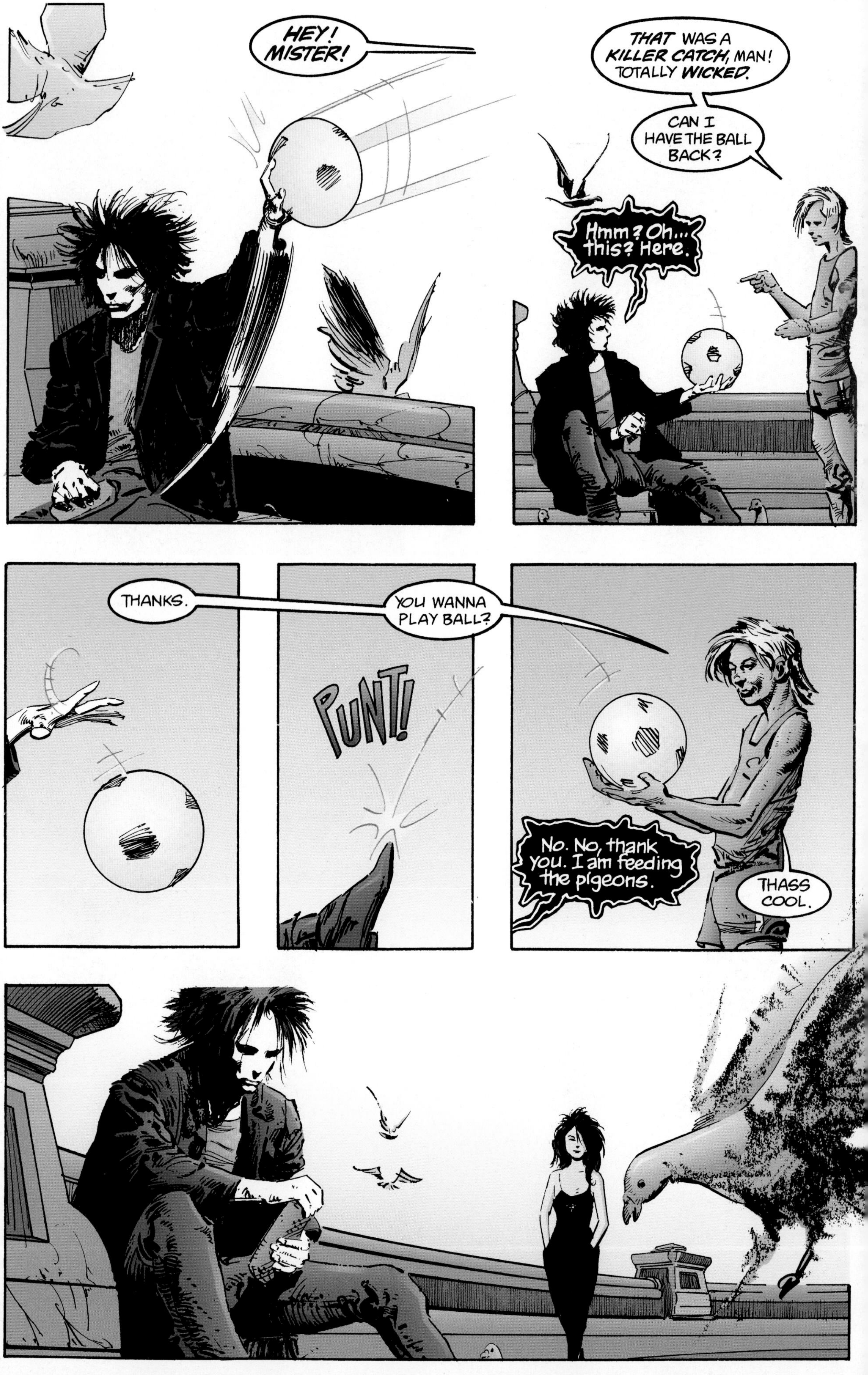
HEY! MISTER!
THAT WAS A KILLER CATCH, MAN! TOTALLY WICKED.
CAN I HAVE THE BALL BACK?
Hmm? Oh... this? Here.
THANKS.
YOU WANNA PLAY BALL?
PUNT!
No. No, thank you. I am feeding the pigeons.
THASS COOL.

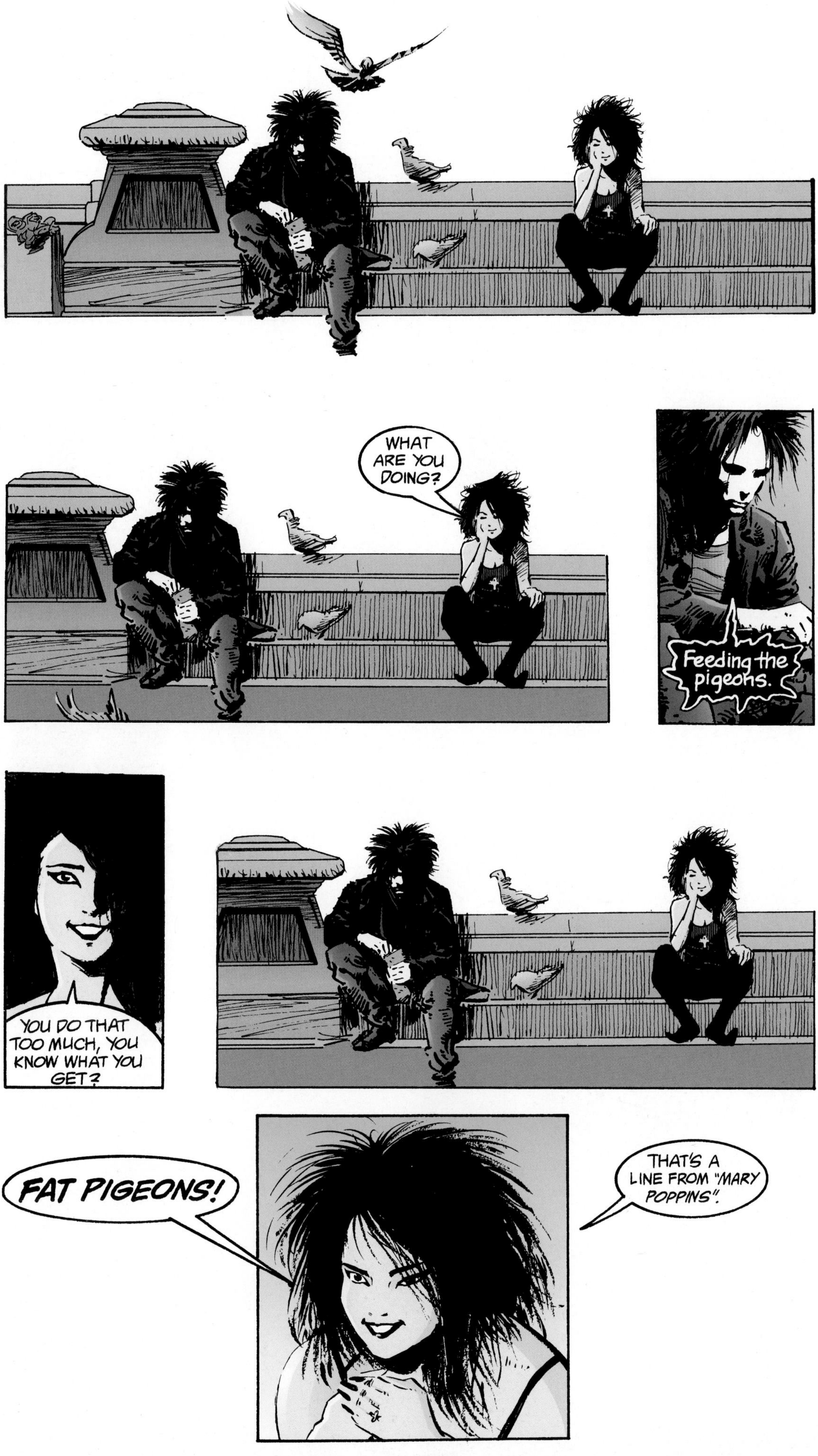
WHAT ARE YOU DOING?
Feeding the pigeons.
YOU DO THAT TOO MUCH, YOU KNOW WHAT YOU GET?
FAT PIGEONS!
THAT'S A LINE FROM "MARY POPPINS".

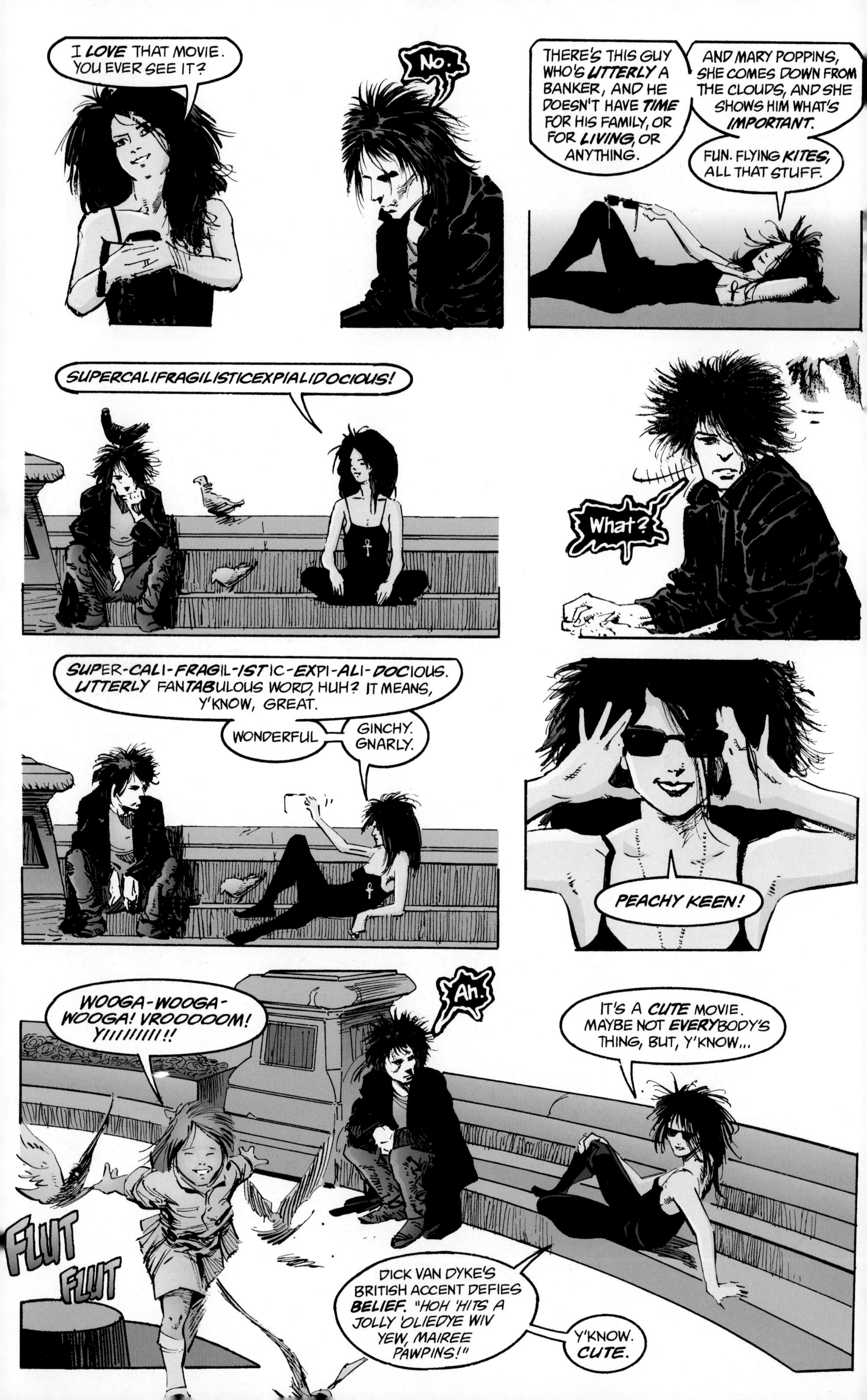
I LOVE THAT MOVIE. YOU EVER SEE IT?
No.
THERE'S THIS GUY WHO'S UTTERLY A BANKER, AND HE DOESN'T HAVE TIME FOR HIS FAMILY, OR FOR LIVING, OR ANYTHING.
AND MARY POPPINS, SHE COMES DOWN FROM THE CLOUDS, AND SHE SHOWS HIM WHAT'S IMPORTANT.
FUN. FLYING KITES, ALL THAT STUFF.
SUPERCALIFRAGILISTICEXPIALIDOCIOUS!
What?
SUPER-CALI-FRAGIL-IST-IC-EXPI-ALI-DOCIOUS. UTTERLY FANTABULOUS WORD, HUH? IT MEANS, Y'KNOW, GREAT.
WONDERFUL
GINCHY. GNARLY.
PEACHY KEEN!
WOOGA-WOOGA-WOOGA! VROOOOOM! YIIIIIIII!!
Ah.
IT'S A CUTE MOVIE. MAYBE NOT EVERYBODY'S THING, BUT, Y'KNOW...
FLUT
FLUT
DICK VAN DYKE'S BRITISH ACCENT DEFIES BELIEF. "HOH 'HITS A JOLLY 'OLIEDYE WIV YEW, MAIREE PAWPINS!"
Y'KNOW. CUTE.

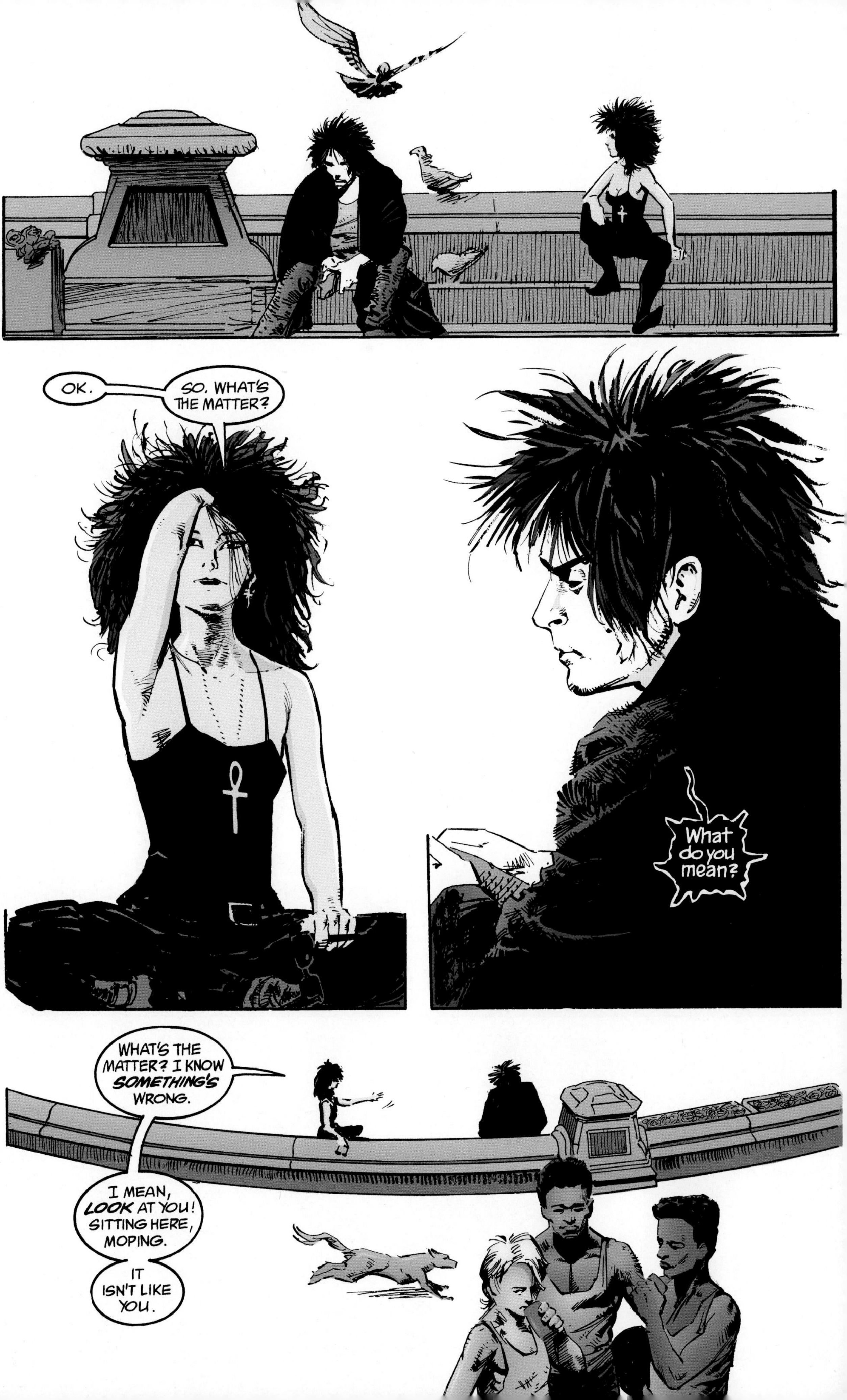
OK.
SO, WHAT'S THE MATTER?
What do you mean?
WHAT'S THE MATTER? I KNOW **SOMETHING'S** WRONG.
I MEAN, **LOOK** AT YOU! SITTING HERE, MOPING.
IT ISN'T LIKE YOU.

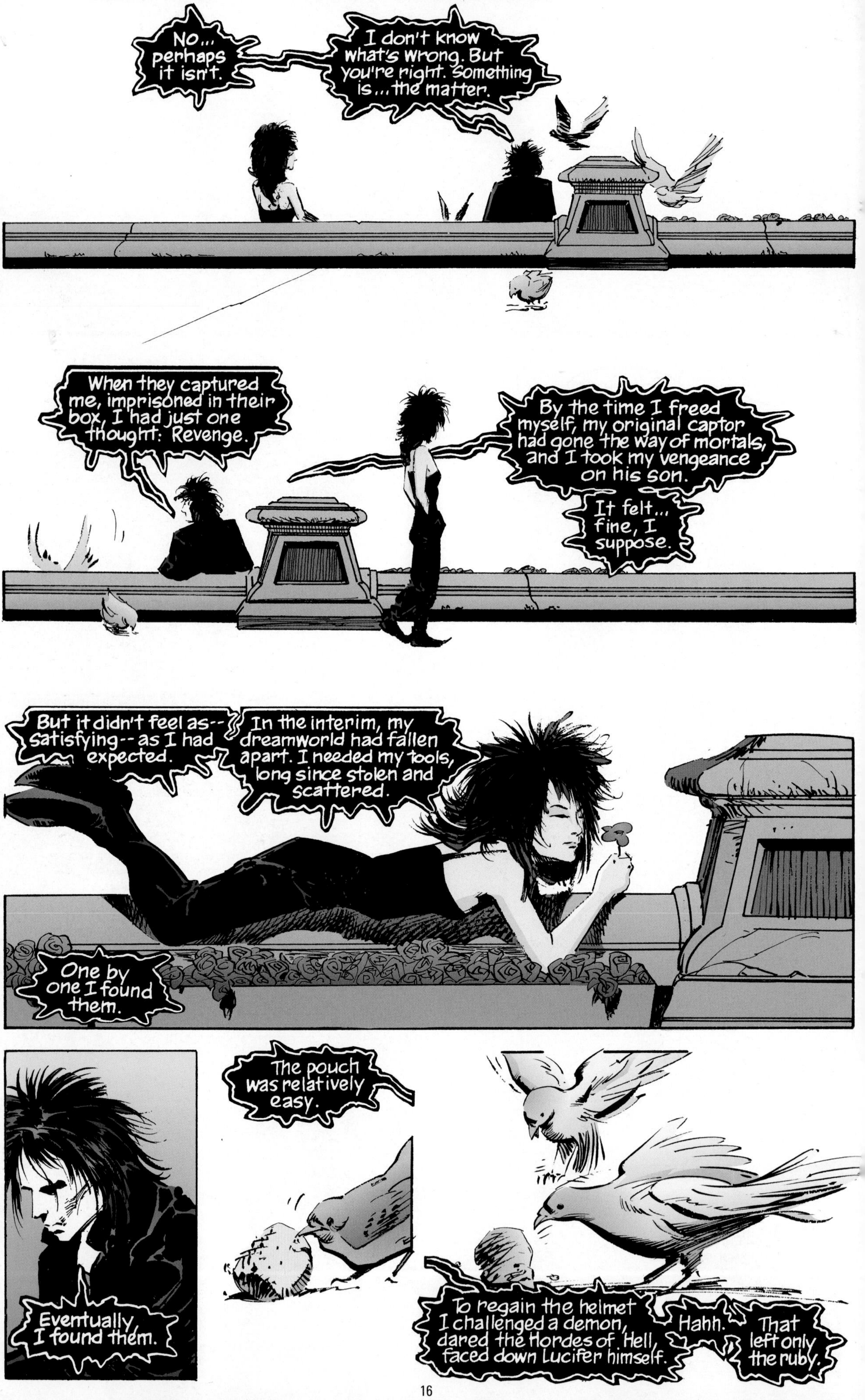
No... perhaps it isn't.
I don't know what's wrong. But you're right. Something is... the matter.
When they captured me, imprisoned in their box, I had just one thought: Revenge.
By the time I freed myself, my original captor had gone the way of mortals, and I took my vengeance on his son.
It felt... fine, I suppose.
But it didn't feel as-- satisfying-- as I had expected.
In the interim, my dreamworld had fallen apart. I needed my tools, long since stolen and scattered.
One by one I found them.
Eventually, I found them.
The pouch was relatively easy.
To regain the helmet I challenged a demon, dared the Hordes of Hell, faced down Lucifer himself.
Hahh.
That left only the ruby.

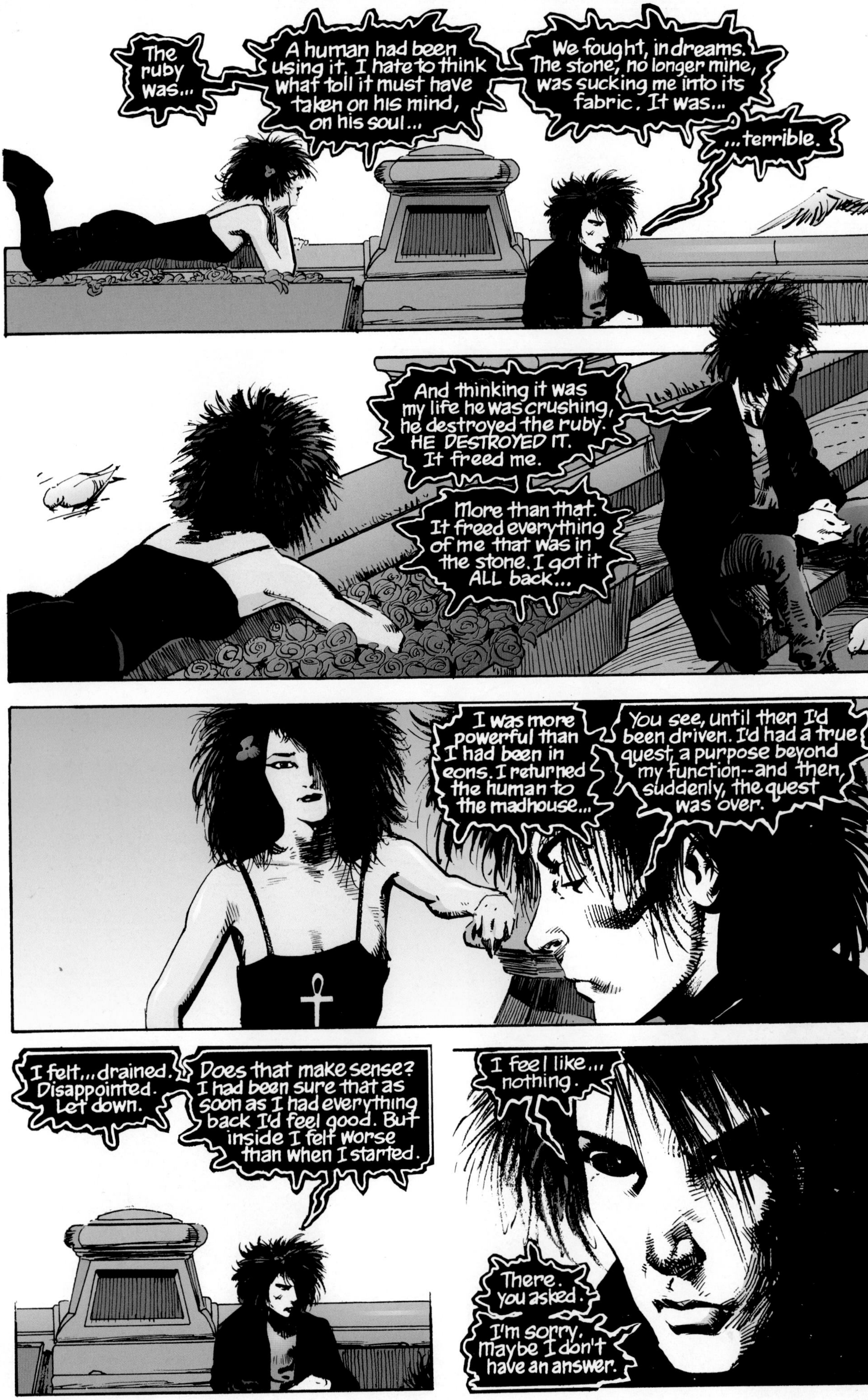
The ruby was...
A human had been using it. I hate to think what toll it must have taken on his mind, on his soul...
We fought, in dreams. The stone, no longer mine, was sucking me into its fabric. It was...
...terrible.
And thinking it was my life he was crushing, he destroyed the ruby. HE DESTROYED IT. It freed me.
More than that. It freed everything of me that was in the stone. I got it ALL back...
I was more powerful than I had been in eons. I returned the human to the madhouse...
You see, until then I'd been driven. I'd had a true quest, a purpose beyond my function--and then, suddenly, the quest was over.
I felt... drained. Disappointed. Let down.
Does that make sense? I had been sure that as soon as I had everything back I'd feel good. But inside I felt worse than when I started.
I feel like... nothing.
There. You asked.
I'm sorry. Maybe I don't have an answer.

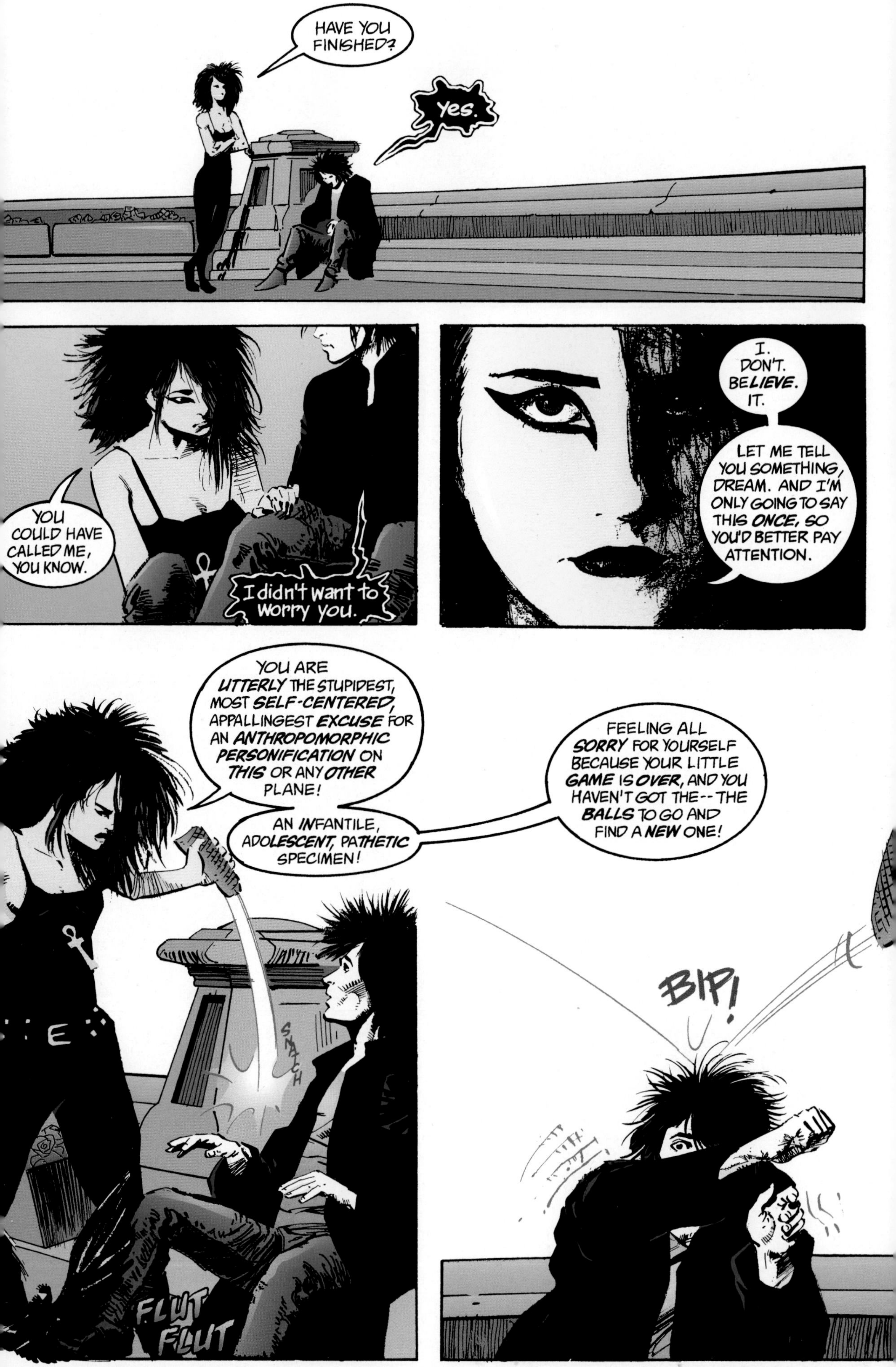
HAVE YOU FINISHED?
Yes.
YOU COULD HAVE CALLED ME, YOU KNOW.
I didn't want to worry you.
I. DON'T. BELIEVE. IT.
LET ME TELL YOU SOMETHING, DREAM. AND I'M ONLY GOING TO SAY THIS ONCE, SO YOU'D BETTER PAY ATTENTION.
YOU ARE UTTERLY THE STUPIDEST, MOST SELF-CENTERED, APPALLINGEST EXCUSE FOR AN ANTHROPOMORPHIC PERSONIFICATION ON THIS OR ANY OTHER PLANE!
AN INFANTILE, ADOLESCENT, PATHETIC SPECIMEN!
FEELING ALL SORRY FOR YOURSELF BECAUSE YOUR LITTLE GAME IS OVER, AND YOU HAVEN'T GOT THE-- THE BALLS TO GO AND FIND A NEW ONE!
SNATCH
FLUT FLUT
BIP!

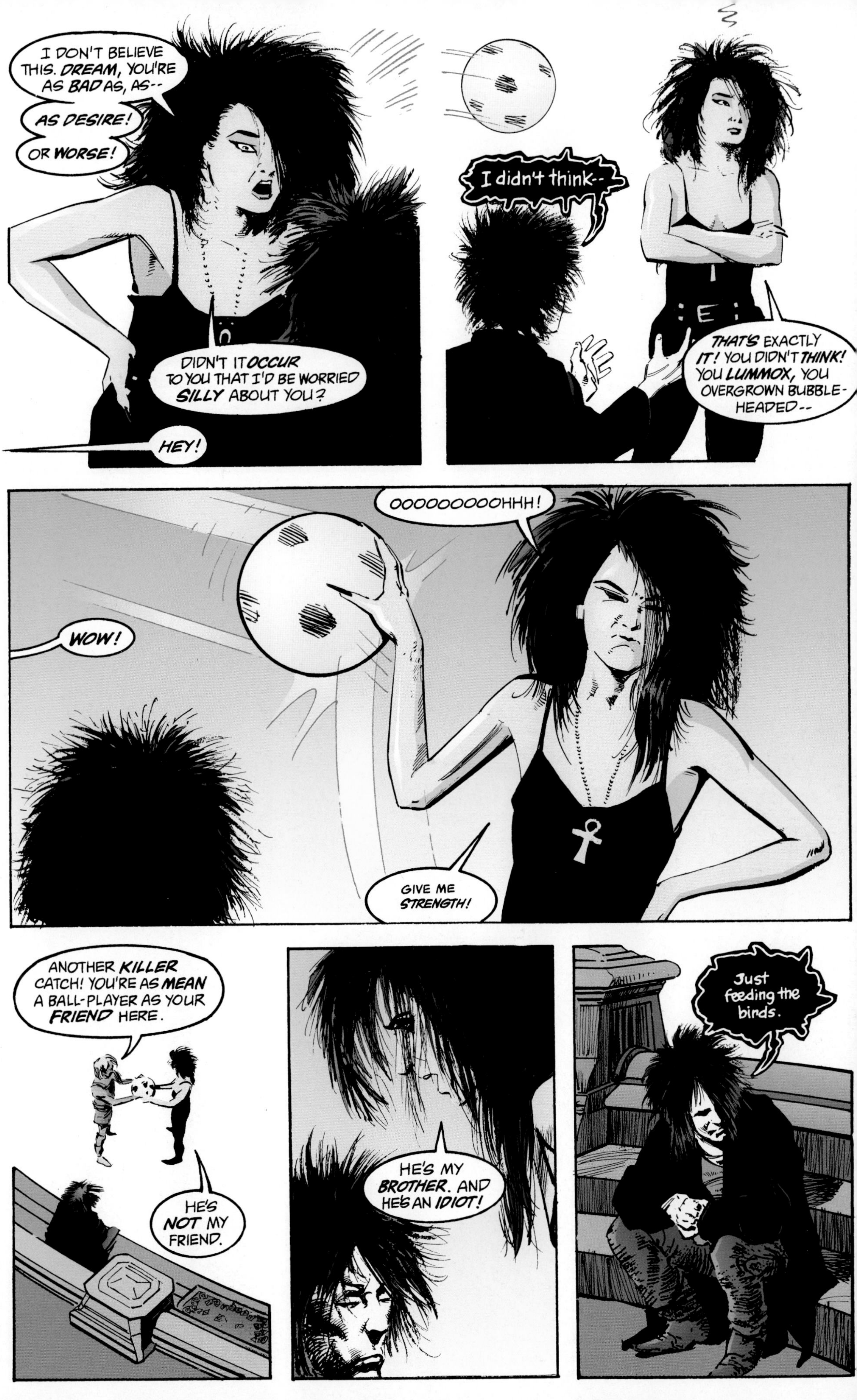
I DON'T BELIEVE THIS. DREAM, YOU'RE AS BAD AS, AS--
AS DESIRE!
OR WORSE!
DIDN'T IT OCCUR TO YOU THAT I'D BE WORRIED SILLY ABOUT YOU?
HEY!
I didn't think--
THAT'S EXACTLY IT! YOU DIDN'T THINK! YOU LUMMOX, YOU OVERGROWN BUBBLE-HEADED--
OOOOOOOOOHHH!
WOW!
GIVE ME STRENGTH!
ANOTHER KILLER CATCH! YOU'RE AS MEAN A BALL-PLAYER AS YOUR FRIEND HERE.
HE'S NOT MY FRIEND.
HE'S MY BROTHER. AND HE'S AN IDIOT!
Just feeding the birds.

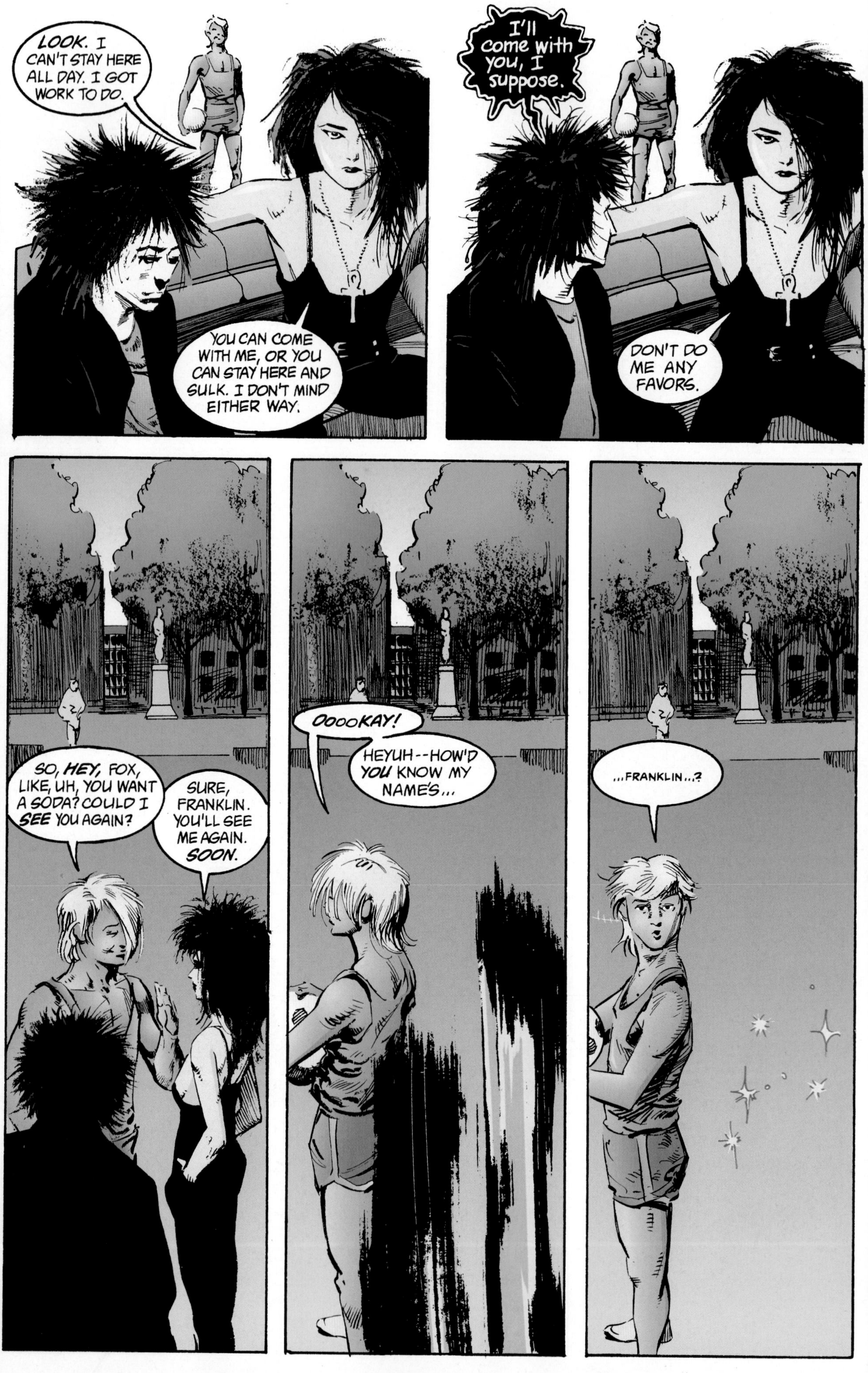

LOOK. I CAN'T STAY HERE ALL DAY. I GOT WORK TO DO.
YOU CAN COME WITH ME, OR YOU CAN STAY HERE AND SULK. I DON'T MIND EITHER WAY.
I'll come with you, I suppose.
DON'T DO ME ANY FAVORS.
SO, HEY, FOX, LIKE, UH, YOU WANT A SODA? COULD I SEE YOU AGAIN?
SURE, FRANKLIN. YOU'LL SEE ME AGAIN. SOON.
OOOOKAY!
HEYUH--HOW'D YOU KNOW MY NAME'S...
...FRANKLIN...?

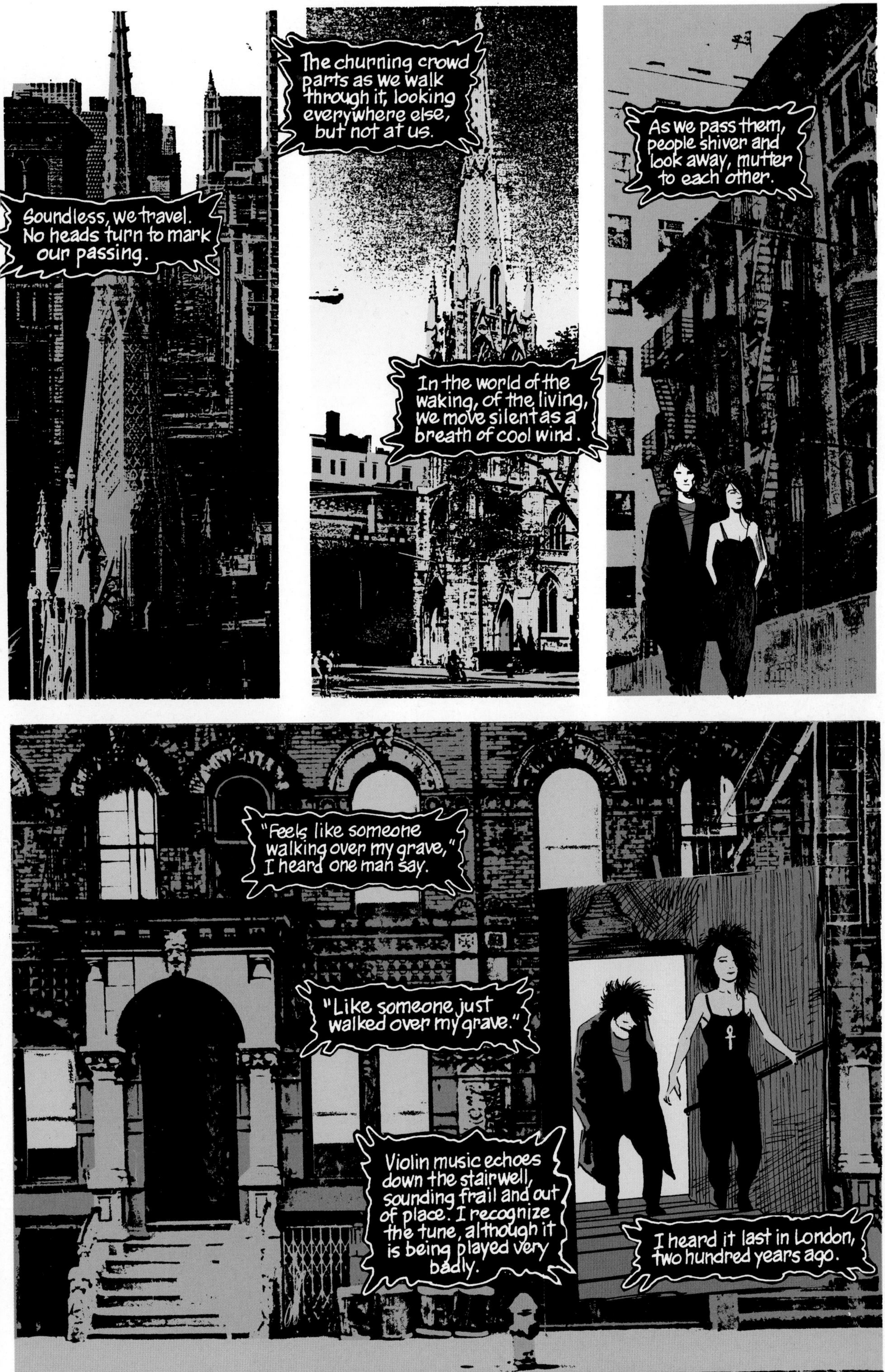
Soundless, we travel. No heads turn to mark our passing.
The churning crowd parts as we walk through it, looking everywhere else, but not at us.
In the world of the waking, of the living, we move silent as a breath of cool wind.
As we pass them, people shiver and look away, mutter to each other.
"Feels like someone walking over my grave," I heard one man say.
"Like someone just walked over my grave."
Violin music echoes down the stairwell, sounding frail and out of place. I recognize the tune, although it is being played very badly.
I heard it last in London, two hundred years ago.

CAN YOU ROCKER ROMANY? CAN YOU PATTER FLASH? ♪ ♪ ♪ ♪ ♪

CAN YOU ROCKER ROMANY? CAN YOU FAKE A BOSH? ♪ ♪ ♪ ♪ ♪

YES. I CAN PATTER ROMANY, HARRY. CAN YOU?

HUNH? I DIDN'T HEAR NOBODY COME IN...

CAN I PATTER ROMANY?

NOT SO GOOD. BUT I CAN FAKE A BOSH. MEANS T' PLAY THE FIDDLE. I'M NOT REAL ROMANY...

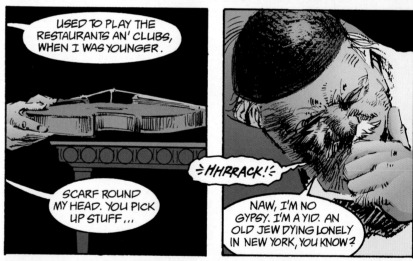

USED TO PLAY THE RESTAURANTS AN' CLUBS, WHEN I WAS YOUNGER.

SCARF ROUND MY HEAD. YOU PICK UP STUFF...

⟨HHRRACK!⟩

NAW, I'M NO GYPSY. I'M A YID. AN OLD JEW DYING LONELY IN NEW YORK, YOU KNOW?

YES, I KNOW WHO YOU ARE, HARRY. DO YOU KNOW WHO I AM?

YOU? YOU'RE... NO! NOT YET! ...PLEASE?

YEAH, I KNOW WHO YOU ARE.

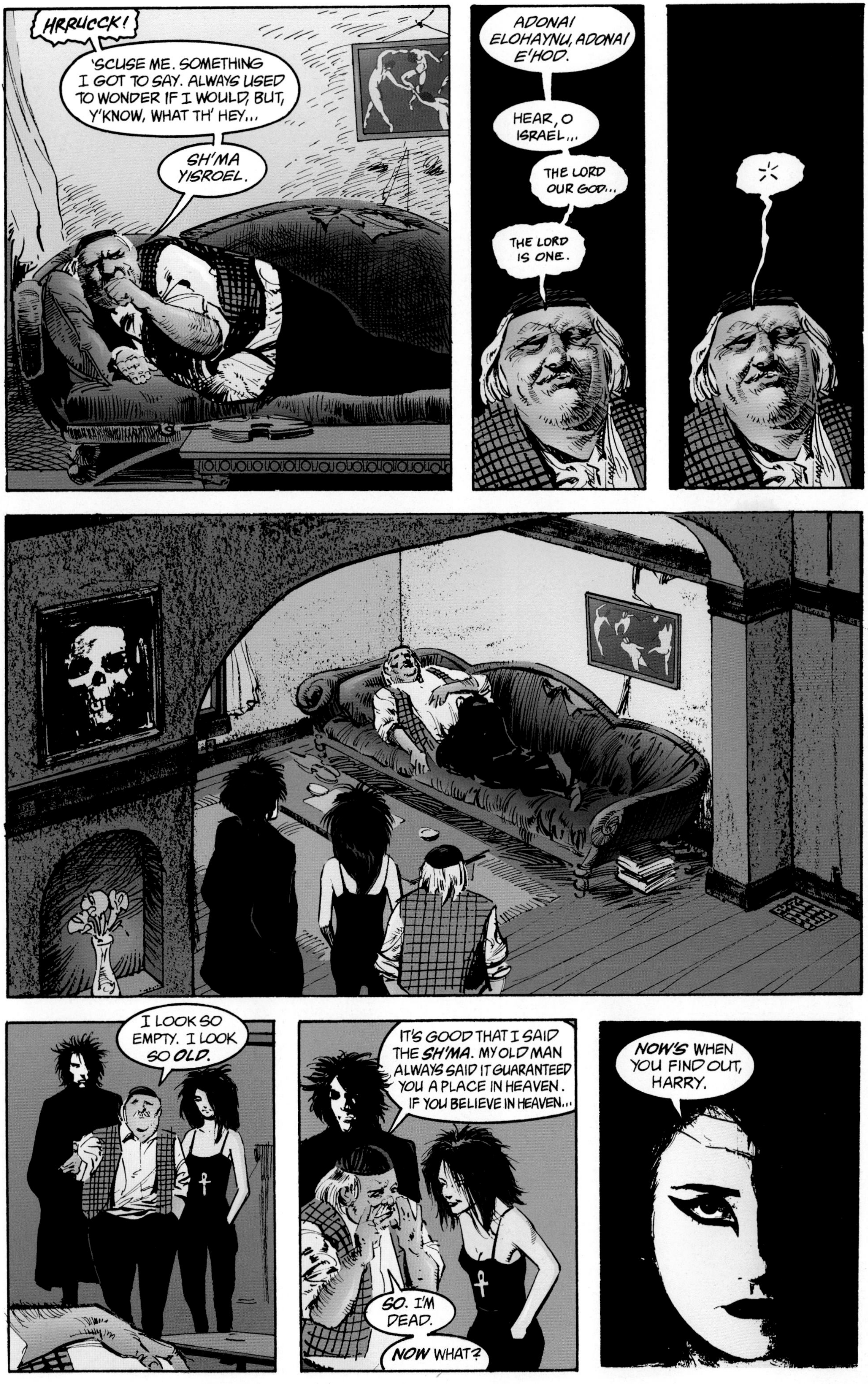
HRRUCCK!
'SCUSE ME. SOMETHING I GOT TO SAY. ALWAYS USED TO WONDER IF I WOULD, BUT, Y'KNOW, WHAT TH' HEY...
SH'MA YISROEL.
ADONAI ELOHAYNU, ADONAI E'HOD.
HEAR, O ISRAEL...
THE LORD OUR GOD...
THE LORD IS ONE.
I LOOK SO EMPTY. I LOOK SO OLD.
IT'S GOOD THAT I SAID THE SH'MA. MY OLD MAN ALWAYS SAID IT GUARANTEED YOU A PLACE IN HEAVEN. IF YOU BELIEVE IN HEAVEN...
SO. I'M DEAD.
NOW WHAT?
NOW'S WHEN YOU FIND OUT, HARRY.

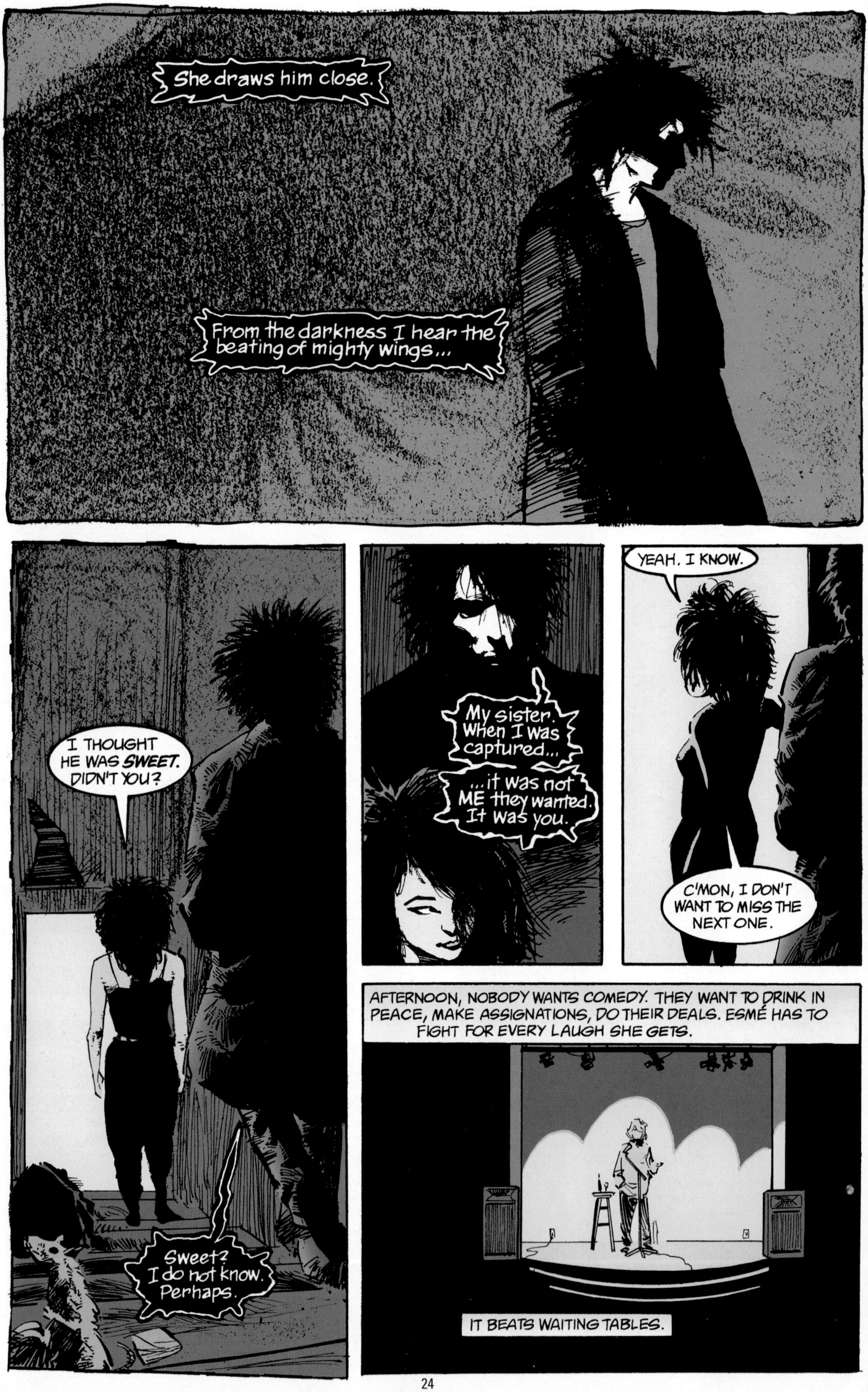
She draws him close.
From the darkness I hear the beating of mighty wings...
I THOUGHT HE WAS SWEET. DIDN'T YOU?
Sweet? I do not know. Perhaps.
My sister. When I was captured...
...it was not ME they wanted. It was you.
YEAH. I KNOW.
C'MON, I DON'T WANT TO MISS THE NEXT ONE.
AFTERNOON, NOBODY WANTS COMEDY. THEY WANT TO DRINK IN PEACE, MAKE ASSIGNATIONS, DO THEIR DEALS. ESMÉ HAS TO FIGHT FOR EVERY LAUGH SHE GETS.
IT BEATS WAITING TABLES.

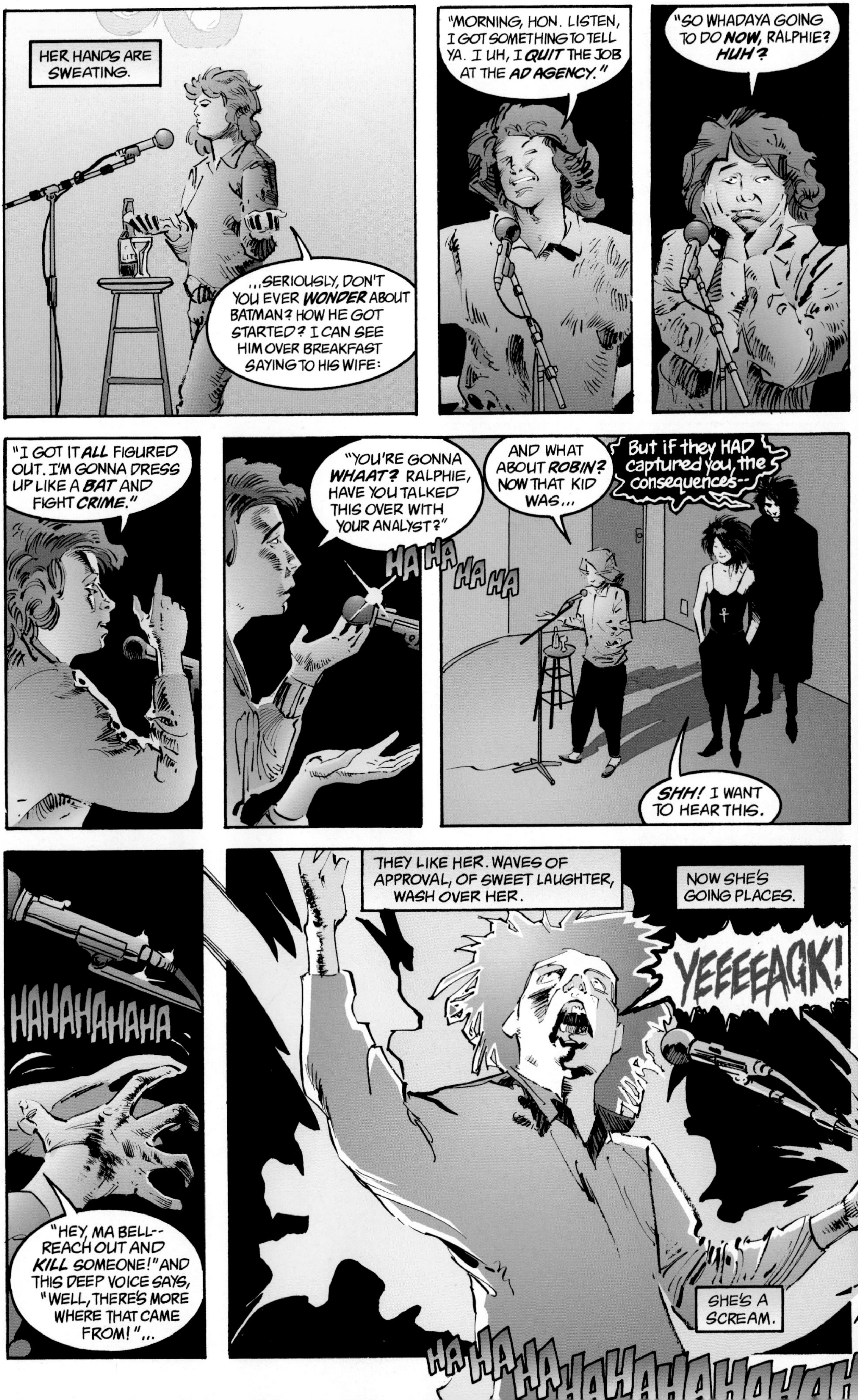
HER HANDS ARE SWEATING.
...SERIOUSLY, DON'T YOU EVER WONDER ABOUT BATMAN? HOW HE GOT STARTED? I CAN SEE HIM OVER BREAKFAST SAYING TO HIS WIFE:
"MORNING, HON. LISTEN, I GOT SOMETHING TO TELL YA. I UH, I QUIT THE JOB AT THE AD AGENCY."
"SO WHADAYA GOING TO DO NOW, RALPHIE? HUH?
"I GOT IT ALL FIGURED OUT. I'M GONNA DRESS UP LIKE A BAT AND FIGHT CRIME."
"YOU'RE GONNA WHAAT? RALPHIE, HAVE YOU TALKED THIS OVER WITH YOUR ANALYST?"
HA HA HA HA
AND WHAT ABOUT ROBIN? NOW THAT KID WAS...
But if they HAD captured you, the consequences--
SHH! I WANT TO HEAR THIS.
HAHAHAHAHA
"HEY, MA BELL-- REACH OUT AND KILL SOMEONE!" AND THIS DEEP VOICE SAYS, "WELL, THERE'S MORE WHERE THAT CAME FROM!"...
THEY LIKE HER. WAVES OF APPROVAL, OF SWEET LAUGHTER, WASH OVER HER.
NOW SHE'S GOING PLACES.
YEEEEAGK!
SHE'S A SCREAM.
HA HA HAHAHAHAHAHAHAH

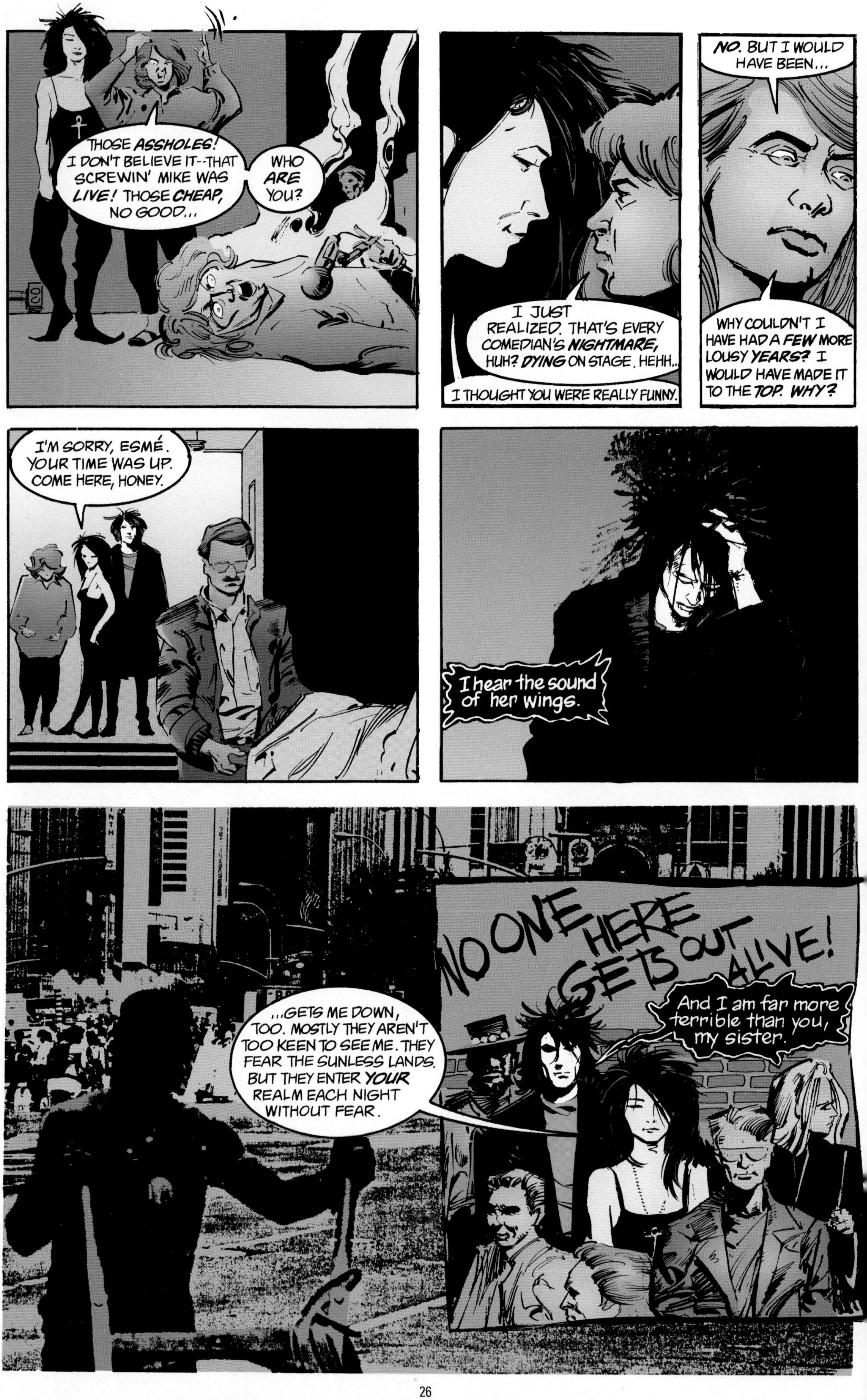
THOSE ASSHOLES! I DON'T BELIEVE IT--THAT SCREWIN' MIKE WAS LIVE! THOSE CHEAP, NO GOOD...
WHO ARE YOU?
I JUST REALIZED. THAT'S EVERY COMEDIAN'S NIGHTMARE, HUH? DYING ON STAGE. HEHH...
I THOUGHT YOU WERE REALLY FUNNY.
NO. BUT I WOULD HAVE BEEN...
WHY COULDN'T I HAVE HAD A FEW MORE LOUSY YEARS? I WOULD HAVE MADE IT TO THE TOP. WHY?
I'M SORRY, ESMÉ. YOUR TIME WAS UP. COME HERE, HONEY.
I hear the sound of her wings.
NO ONE HERE GETS OUT ALIVE!
...GETS ME DOWN, TOO. MOSTLY THEY AREN'T TOO KEEN TO SEE ME. THEY FEAR THE SUNLESS LANDS. BUT THEY ENTER YOUR REALM EACH NIGHT WITHOUT FEAR.
And I am far more terrible than you, my sister.

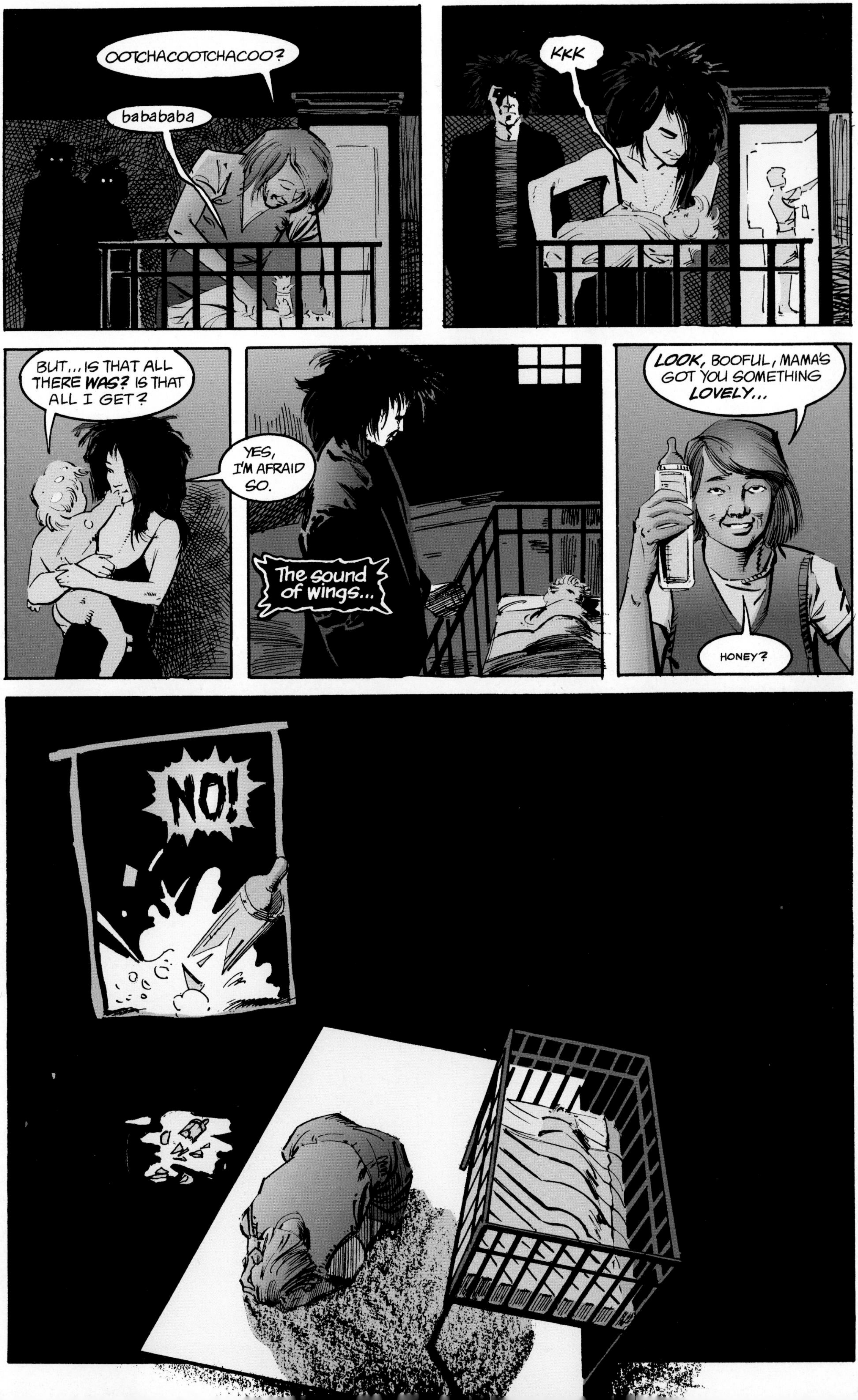
OOTCHACOOTCHACOO?
babababa
KKK
BUT... IS THAT ALL THERE WAS? IS THAT ALL I GET?
YES, I'M AFRAID SO.
The sound of wings...
LOOK, BOOFUL, MAMA'S GOT YOU SOMETHING LOVELY...
HONEY?
NO!

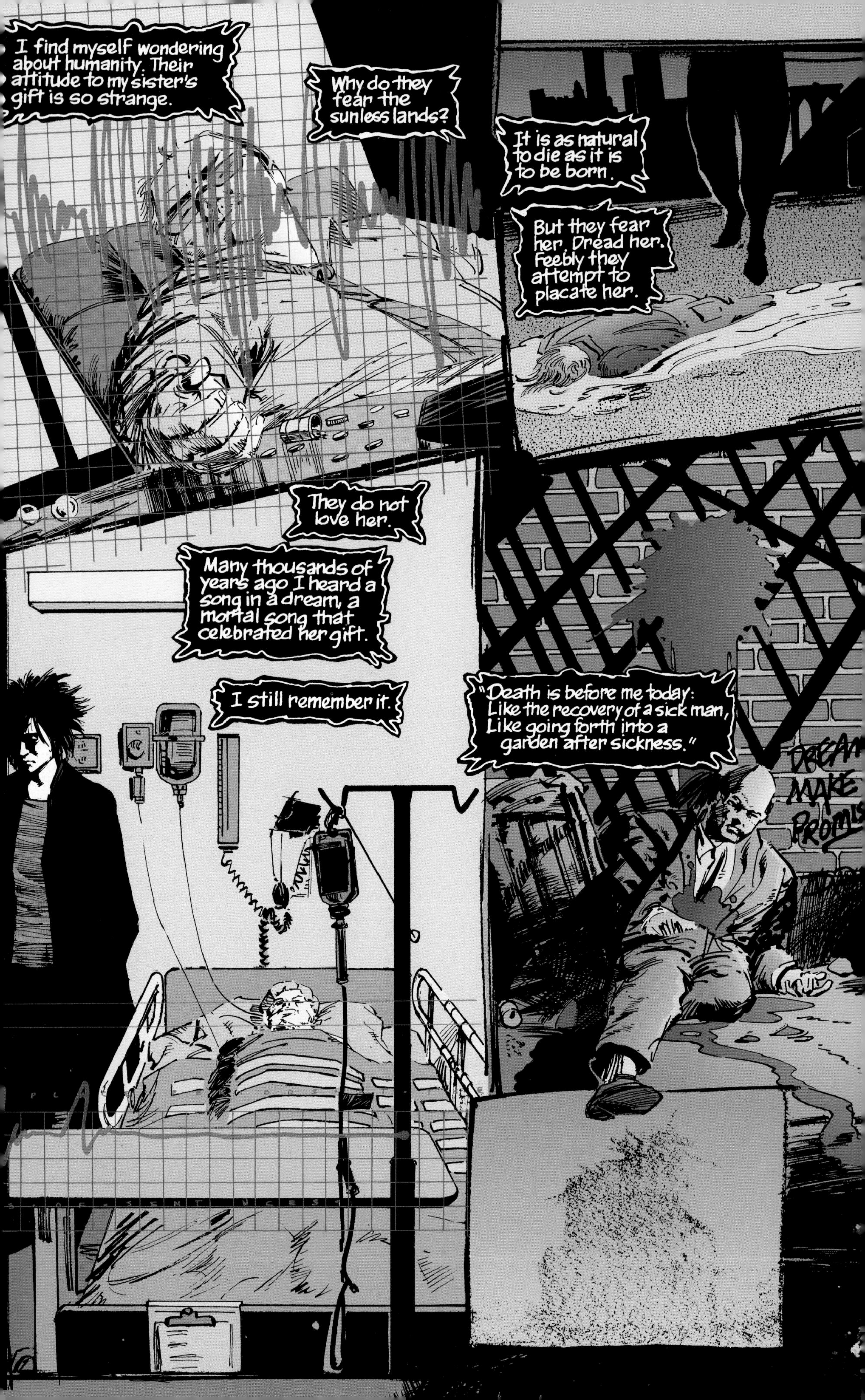
I find myself wondering about humanity. Their attitude to my sister's gift is so strange.
Why do they fear the sunless lands?
It is as natural to die as it is to be born.
But they fear her. Dread her. Feebly they attempt to placate her.
They do not love her.
Many thousands of years ago I heard a song in a dream, a mortal song that celebrated her gift.
I still remember it.
"Death is before me today: Like the recovery of a sick man, Like going forth into a garden after sickness."

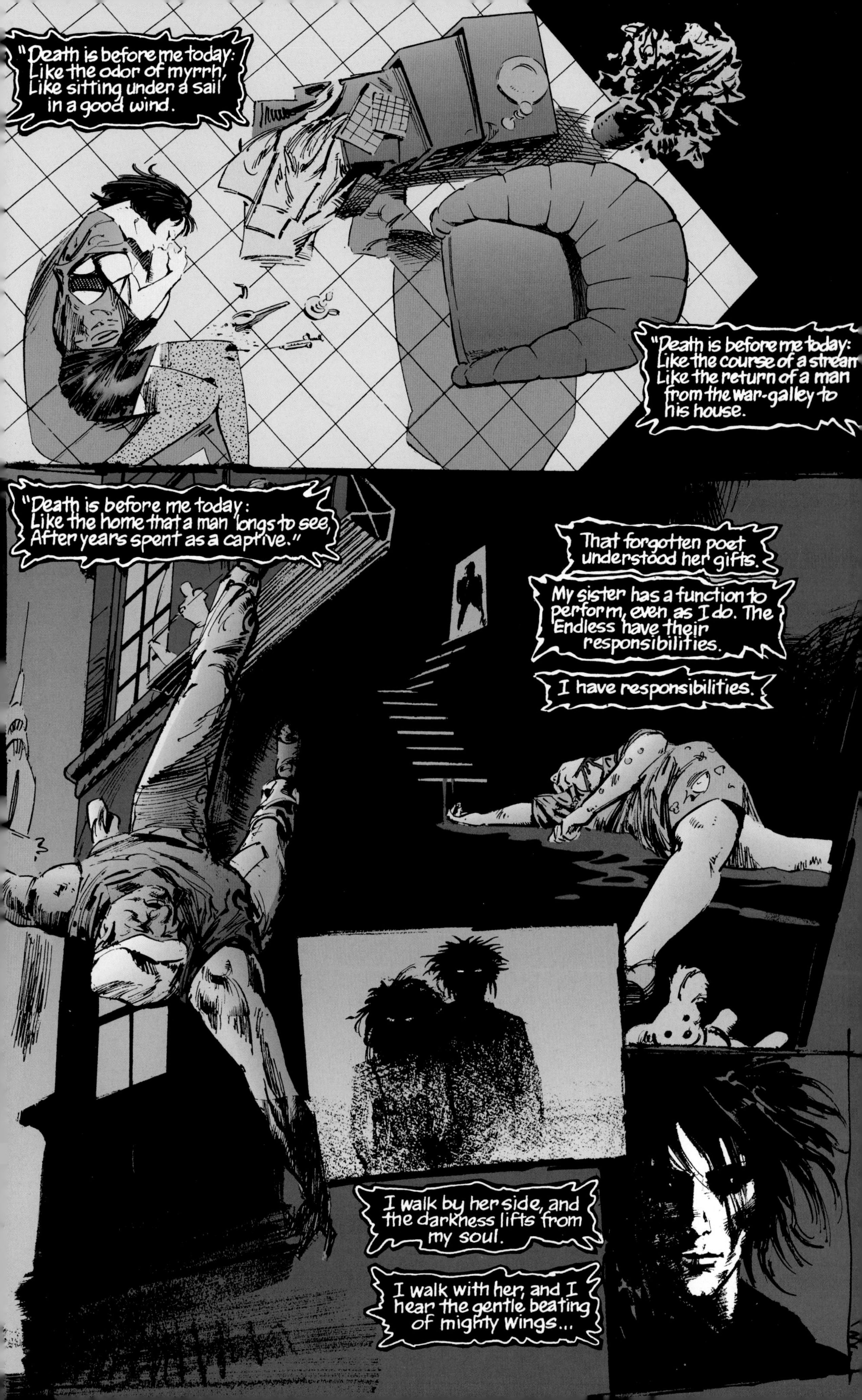
"Death is before me today: Like the odor of myrrh, Like sitting under a sail in a good wind.
"Death is before me today: Like the course of a stream Like the return of a man from the war-galley to his house.
"Death is before me today: Like the home that a man longs to see, After years spent as a captive."
That forgotten poet understood her gifts.
My sister has a function to perform, even as I do. The Endless have their responsibilities.
I have responsibilities.
I walk by her side, and the darkness lifts from my soul.
I walk with her, and I hear the gentle beating of mighty wings...

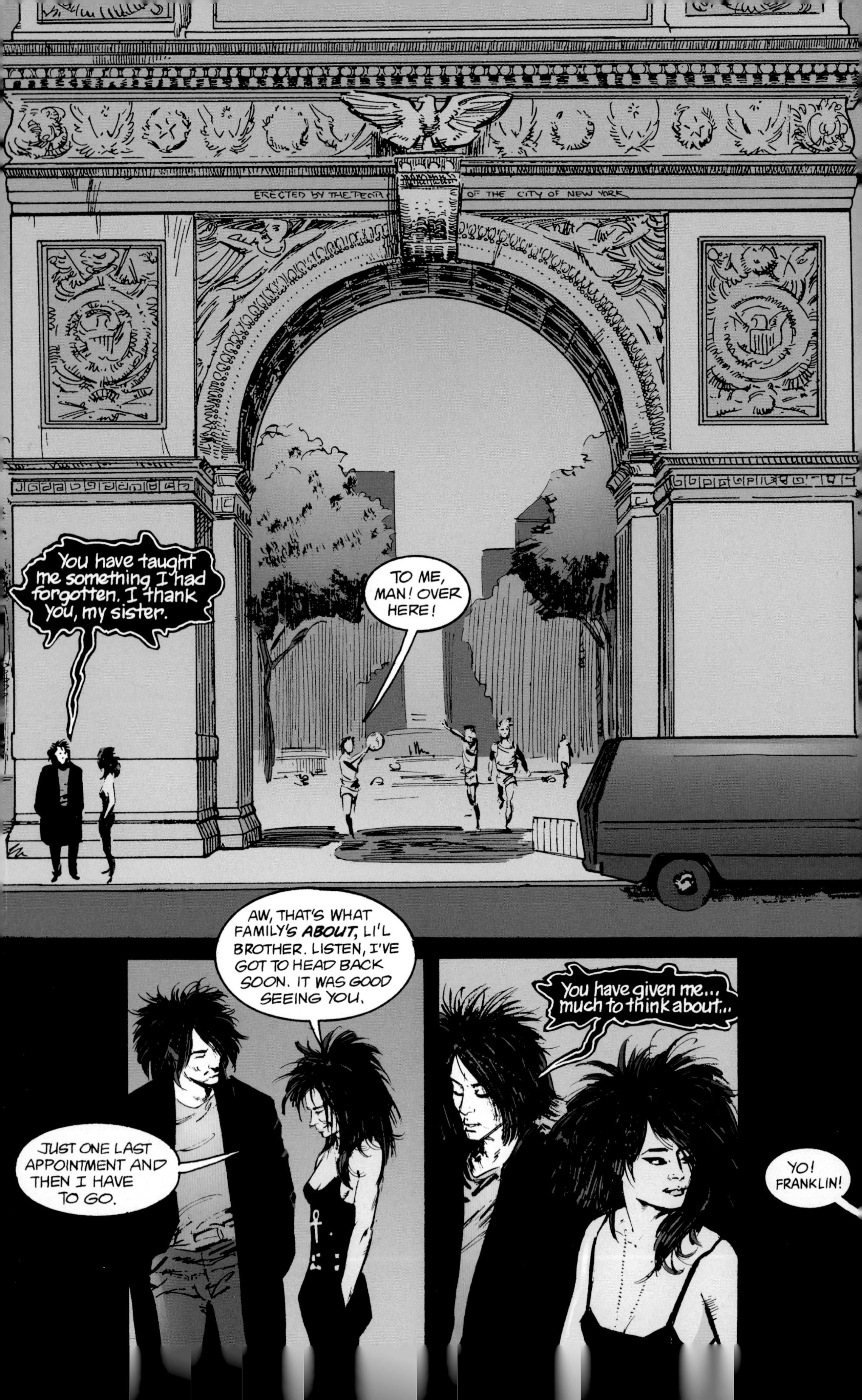
ERECTED BY THE PEOPLE OF THE CITY OF NEW YORK
You have taught me something I had forgotten. I thank you, my sister.
TO ME, MAN! OVER HERE!
AW, THAT'S WHAT FAMILY'S **ABOUT**, LI'L BROTHER. LISTEN, I'VE GOT TO HEAD BACK SOON. IT WAS GOOD SEEING YOU.
JUST ONE LAST APPOINTMENT AND THEN I HAVE TO GO.
You have given me... much to think about...
YO! FRANKLIN!

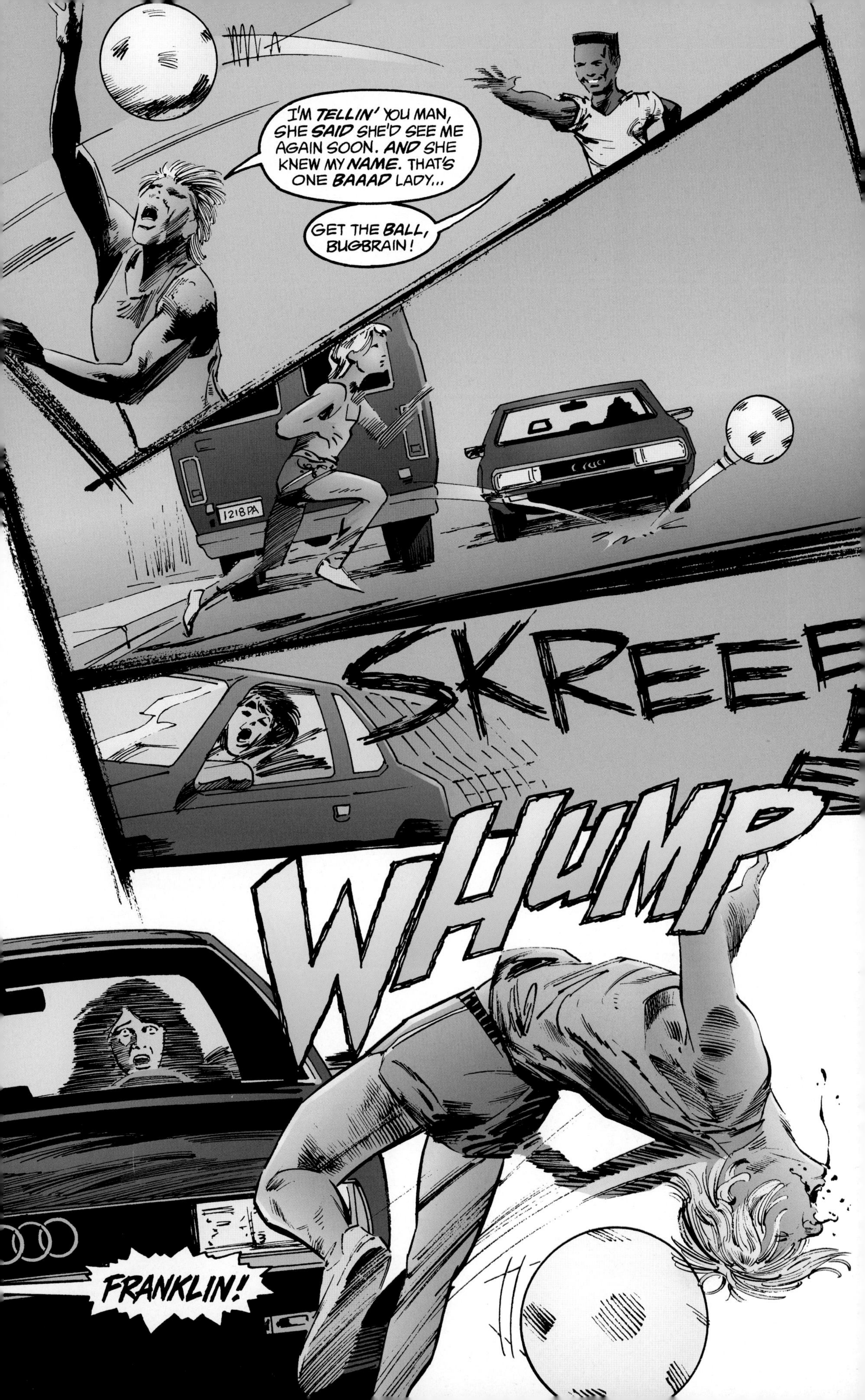
I'M TELLIN' YOU MAN, SHE SAID SHE'D SEE ME AGAIN SOON. AND SHE KNEW MY NAME. THAT'S ONE BAAAD LADY...
GET THE BALL, BUGBRAIN!
1218 PA
SKREEE
WHUMP
FRANKLIN!

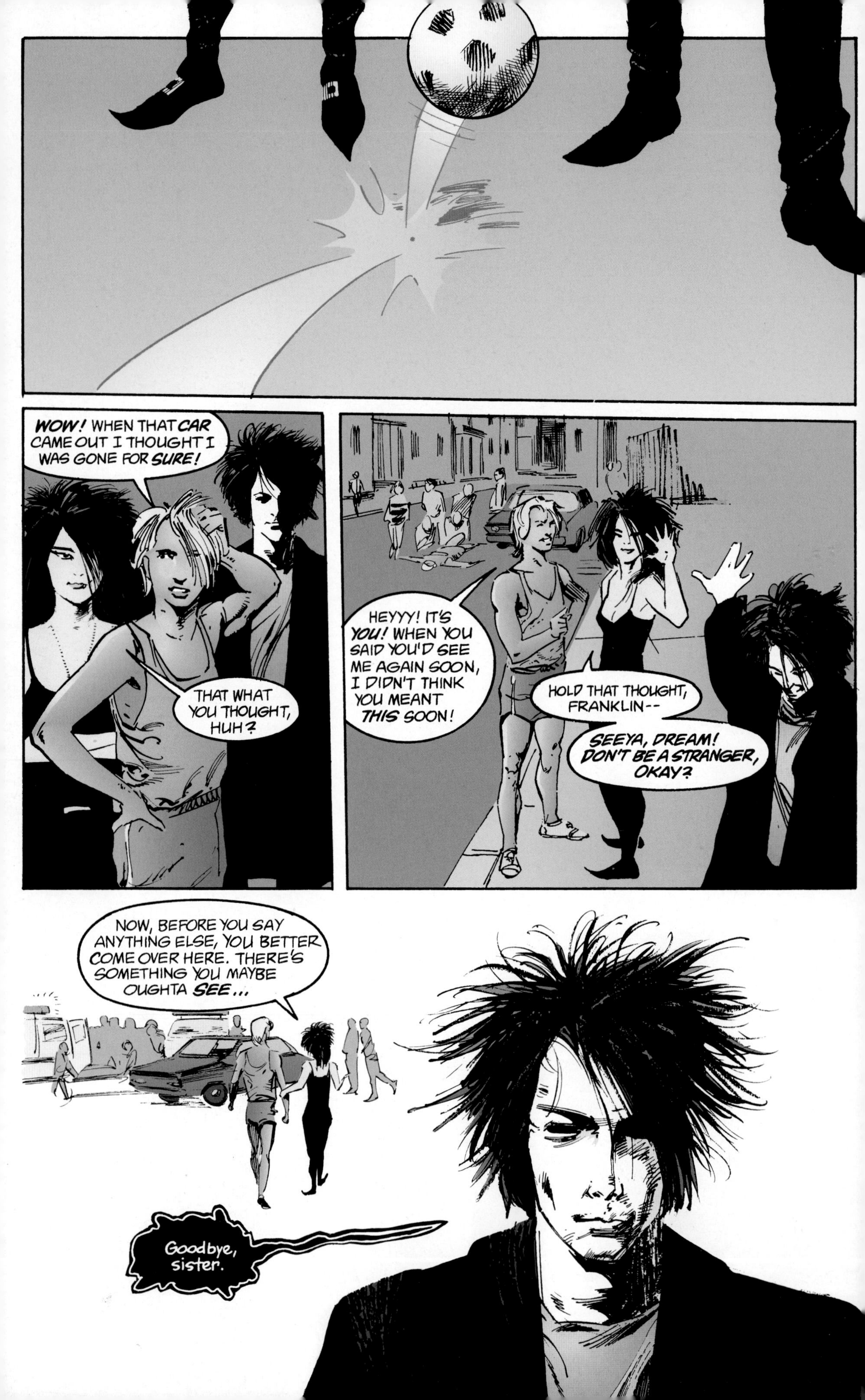
WOW! WHEN THAT CAR CAME OUT I THOUGHT I WAS GONE FOR SURE!
THAT WHAT YOU THOUGHT, HUH?
HEYYY! IT'S YOU! WHEN YOU SAID YOU'D SEE ME AGAIN SOON, I DIDN'T THINK YOU MEANT THIS SOON!
HOLD THAT THOUGHT, FRANKLIN--
SEEYA, DREAM! DON'T BE A STRANGER, OKAY?
NOW, BEFORE YOU SAY ANYTHING ELSE, YOU BETTER COME OVER HERE. THERE'S SOMETHING YOU MAYBE OUGHTA SEE...
Goodbye, sister.

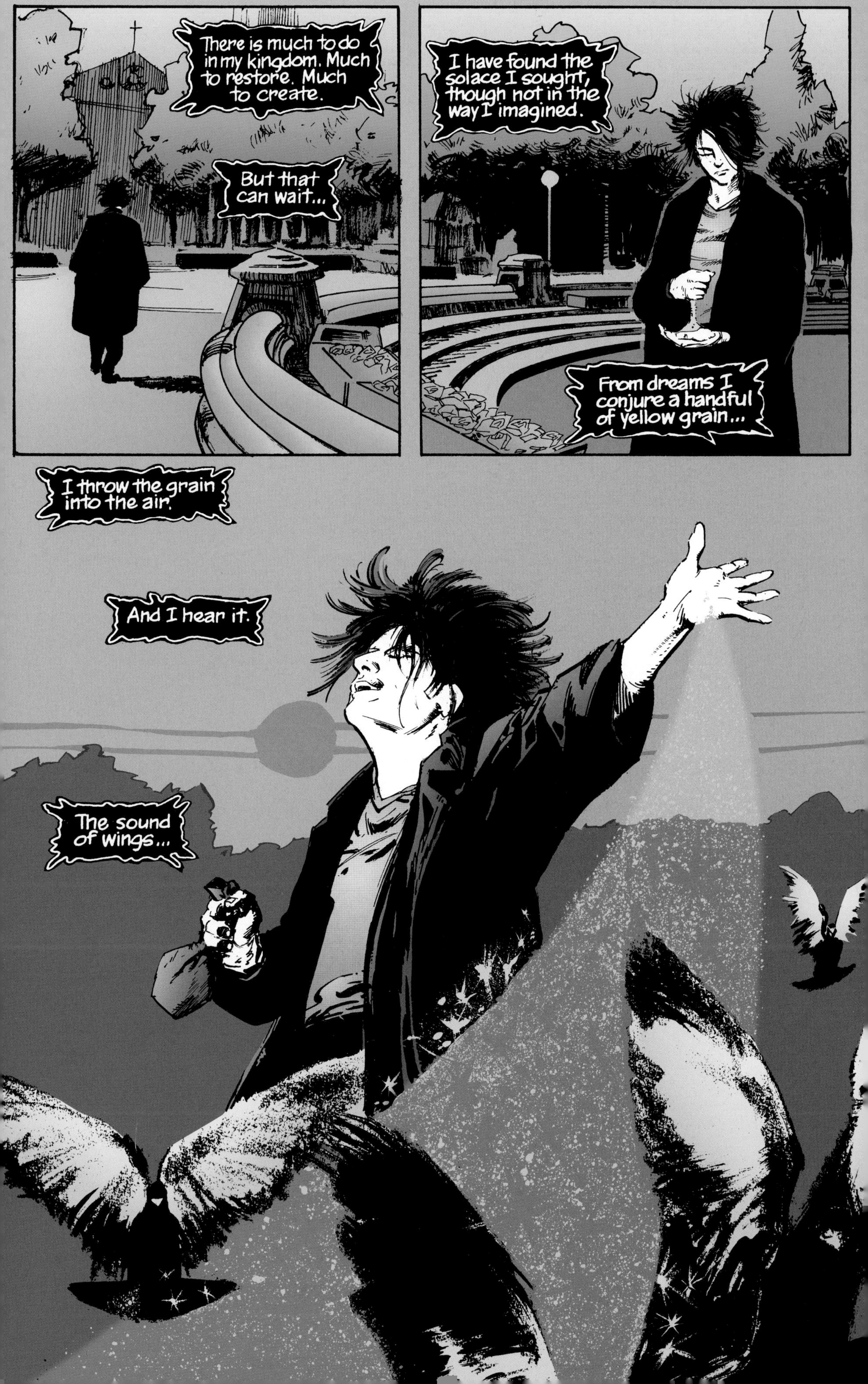
There is much to do in my kingdom. Much to restore. Much to create.
But that can wait...
I have found the solace I sought, though not in the way I imagined.
From dreams I conjure a handful of yellow grain...
I throw the grain into the air.
And I hear it.
The sound of wings...

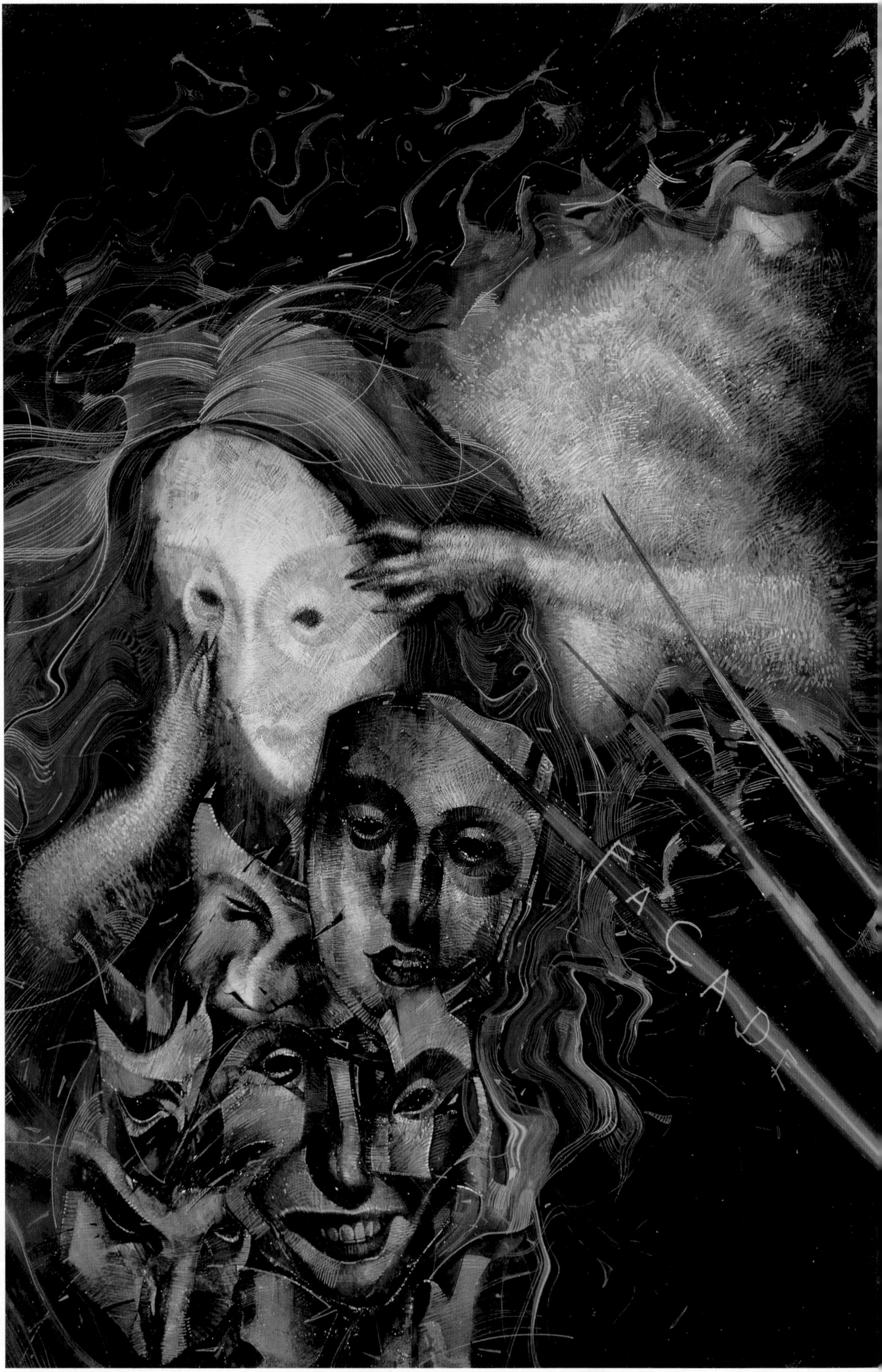
FAÇADE

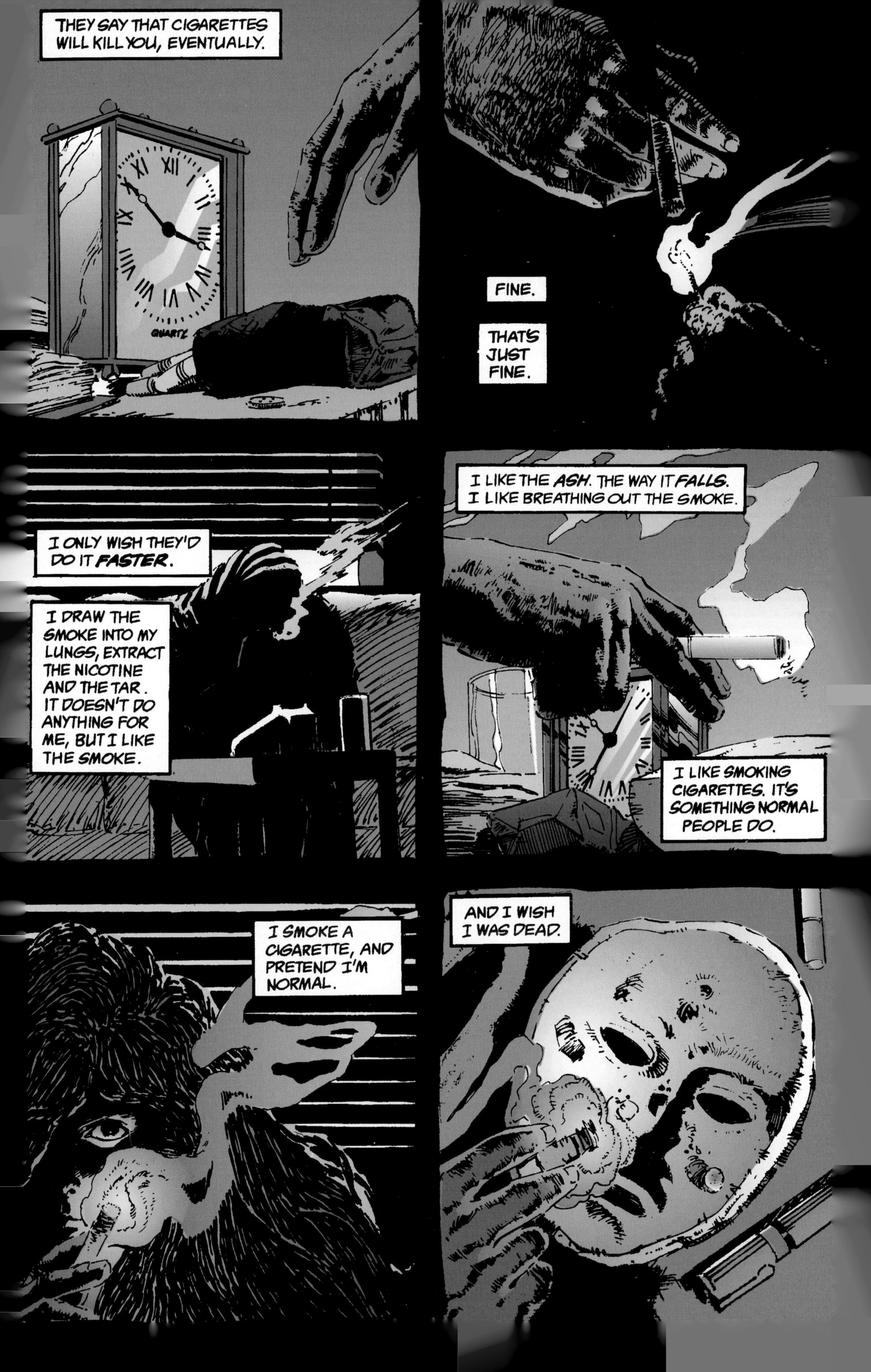
THEY SAY THAT CIGARETTES WILL KILL YOU, EVENTUALLY.
FINE.
THAT'S JUST FINE.
I ONLY WISH THEY'D DO IT FASTER.
I DRAW THE SMOKE INTO MY LUNGS, EXTRACT THE NICOTINE AND THE TAR. IT DOESN'T DO ANYTHING FOR ME, BUT I LIKE THE SMOKE.
I LIKE THE ASH. THE WAY IT FALLS. I LIKE BREATHING OUT THE SMOKE.
I LIKE SMOKING CIGARETTES. IT'S SOMETHING NORMAL PEOPLE DO.
I SMOKE A CIGARETTE, AND PRETEND I'M NORMAL.
AND I WISH I WAS DEAD.

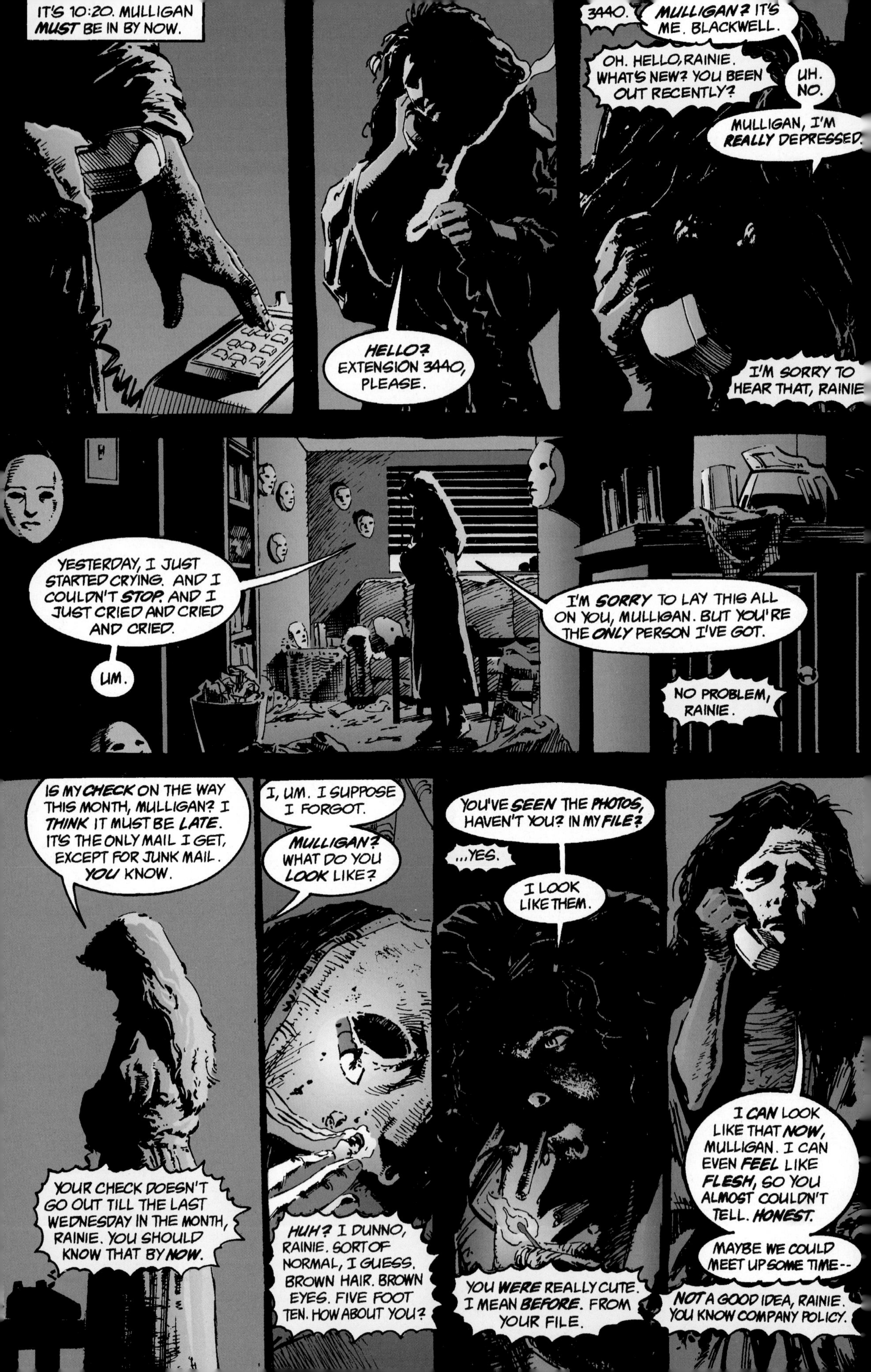
IT'S 10:20. MULLIGAN MUST BE IN BY NOW.
HELLO? EXTENSION 3440, PLEASE.
3440.
MULLIGAN? IT'S ME. BLACKWELL.
OH. HELLO, RAINIE. WHAT'S NEW? YOU BEEN OUT RECENTLY?
UH. NO.
MULLIGAN, I'M REALLY DEPRESSED.
I'M SORRY TO HEAR THAT, RAINIE.
YESTERDAY, I JUST STARTED CRYING. AND I COULDN'T STOP. AND I JUST CRIED AND CRIED AND CRIED.
UM.
I'M SORRY TO LAY THIS ALL ON YOU, MULLIGAN. BUT YOU'RE THE ONLY PERSON I'VE GOT.
NO PROBLEM, RAINIE.
IS MY CHECK ON THE WAY THIS MONTH, MULLIGAN? I THINK IT MUST BE LATE. IT'S THE ONLY MAIL I GET, EXCEPT FOR JUNK MAIL. YOU KNOW.
YOUR CHECK DOESN'T GO OUT TILL THE LAST WEDNESDAY IN THE MONTH, RAINIE. YOU SHOULD KNOW THAT BY NOW.
I, UM. I SUPPOSE I FORGOT.
MULLIGAN? WHAT DO YOU LOOK LIKE?
HUH? I DUNNO, RAINIE. SORT OF NORMAL, I GUESS. BROWN HAIR. BROWN EYES. FIVE FOOT TEN. HOW ABOUT YOU?
YOU'VE SEEN THE PHOTOS, HAVEN'T YOU? IN MY FILE?
...YES.
I LOOK LIKE THEM.
YOU WERE REALLY CUTE. I MEAN BEFORE. FROM YOUR FILE.
I CAN LOOK LIKE THAT NOW, MULLIGAN. I CAN EVEN FEEL LIKE FLESH, SO YOU ALMOST COULDN'T TELL. HONEST.
MAYBE WE COULD MEET UP SOME TIME--
NOT A GOOD IDEA, RAINIE. YOU KNOW COMPANY POLICY.

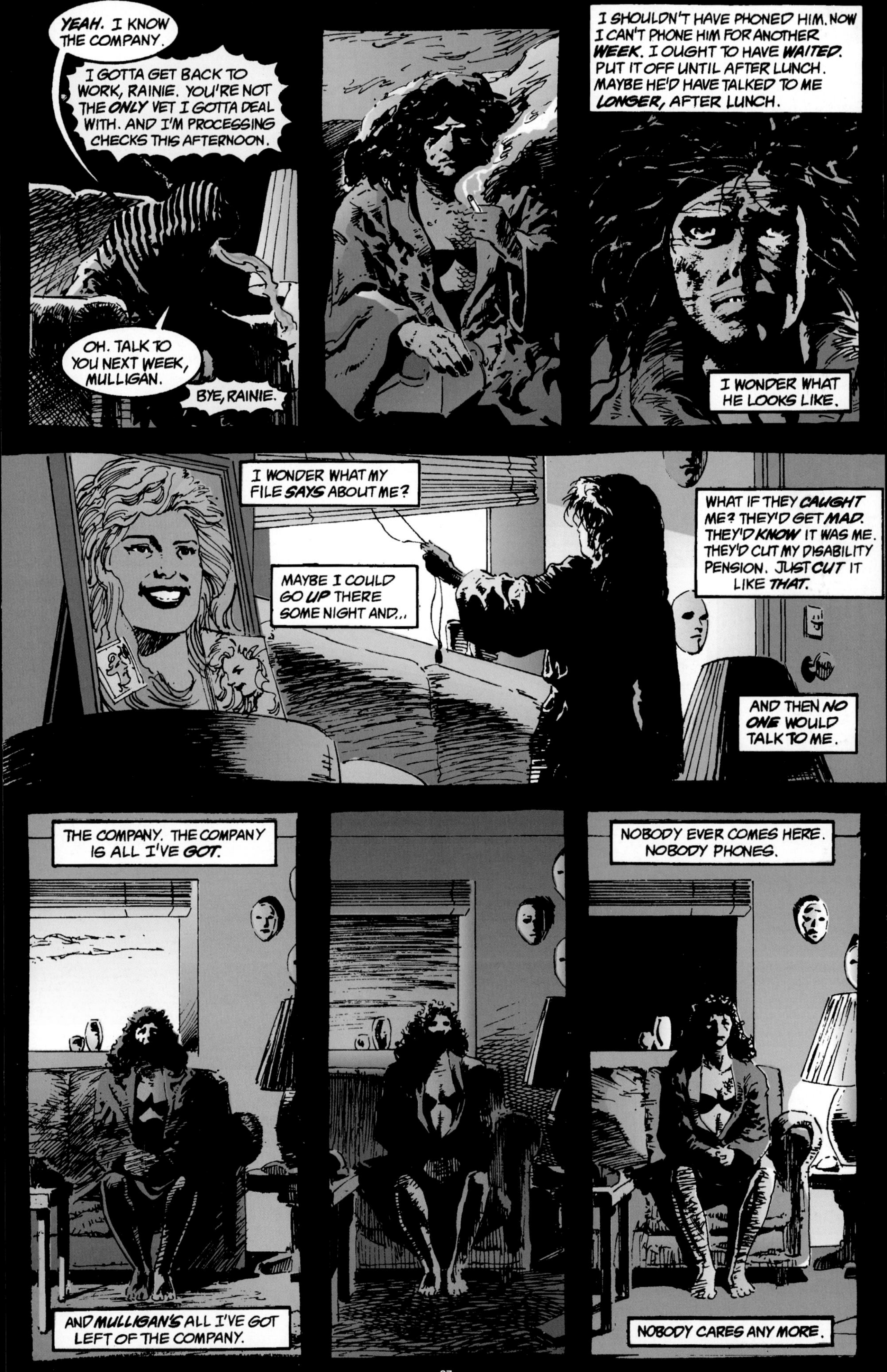
YEAH. I KNOW THE COMPANY.
I GOTTA GET BACK TO WORK, RAINIE. YOU'RE NOT THE ONLY VET I GOTTA DEAL WITH. AND I'M PROCESSING CHECKS THIS AFTERNOON.
OH. TALK TO YOU NEXT WEEK, MULLIGAN.
BYE, RAINIE.
I SHOULDN'T HAVE PHONED HIM. NOW I CAN'T PHONE HIM FOR ANOTHER WEEK. I OUGHT TO HAVE WAITED. PUT IT OFF UNTIL AFTER LUNCH. MAYBE HE'D HAVE TALKED TO ME LONGER, AFTER LUNCH.
I WONDER WHAT HE LOOKS LIKE.
I WONDER WHAT MY FILE SAYS ABOUT ME?
MAYBE I COULD GO UP THERE SOME NIGHT AND...
WHAT IF THEY CAUGHT ME? THEY'D GET MAD. THEY'D KNOW IT WAS ME. THEY'D CUT MY DISABILITY PENSION. JUST CUT IT LIKE THAT.
AND THEN NO ONE WOULD TALK TO ME.
THE COMPANY. THE COMPANY IS ALL I'VE GOT.
AND MULLIGAN'S ALL I'VE GOT LEFT OF THE COMPANY.
NOBODY EVER COMES HERE. NOBODY PHONES.
NOBODY CARES ANY MORE.

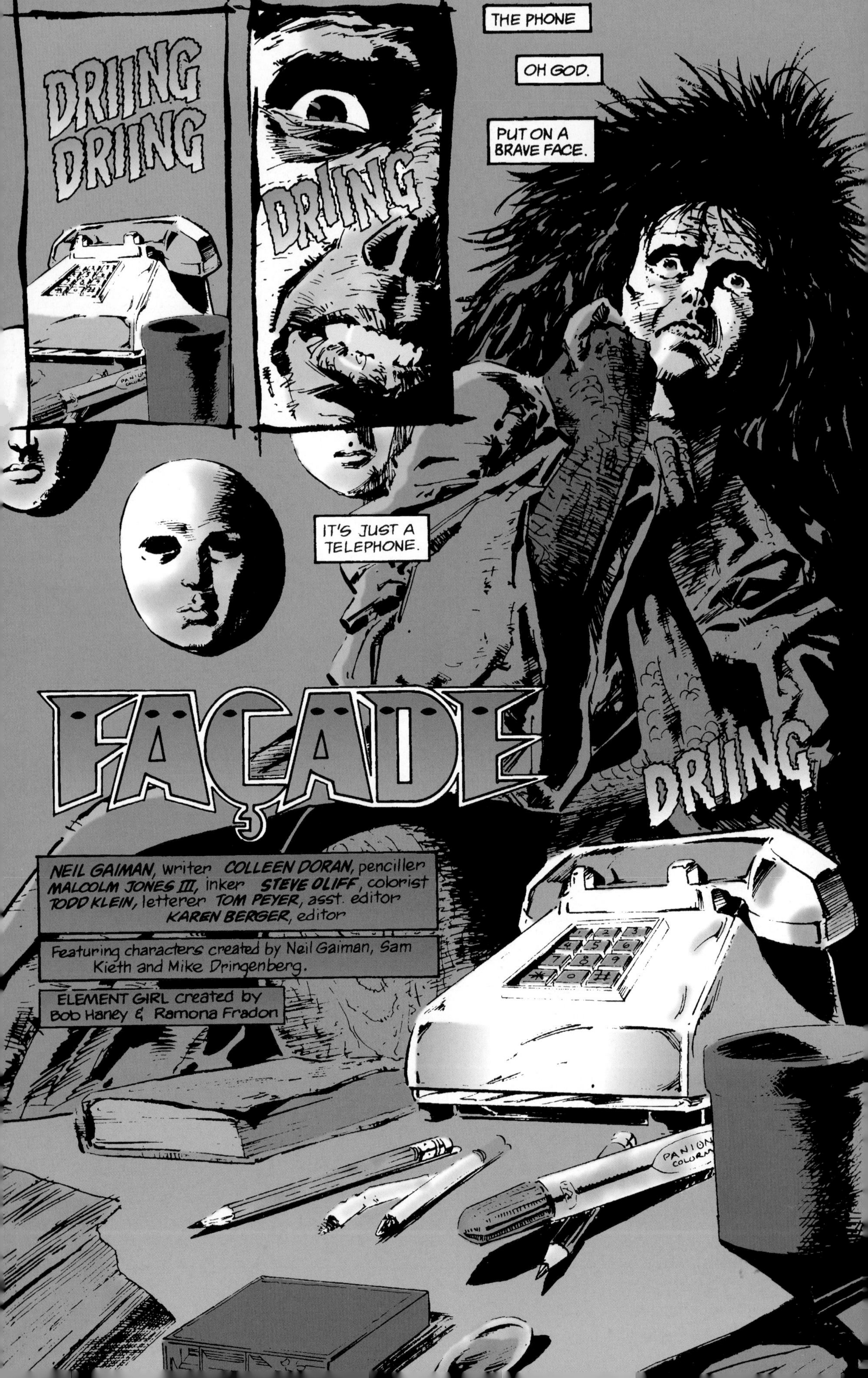
DRIING
DRIING
DRIING
THE PHONE
OH GOD.
PUT ON A BRAVE FACE.
IT'S JUST A TELEPHONE.
FAÇADE
DRIING
NEIL GAIMAN, writer COLLEEN DORAN, penciller
MALCOLM JONES III, inker STEVE OLIFF, colorist
TODD KLEIN, letterer TOM PEYER, asst. editor
KAREN BERGER, editor
Featuring characters created by Neil Gaiman, Sam Kieth and Mike Dringenberg.
ELEMENT GIRL created by Bob Haney & Ramona Fradon

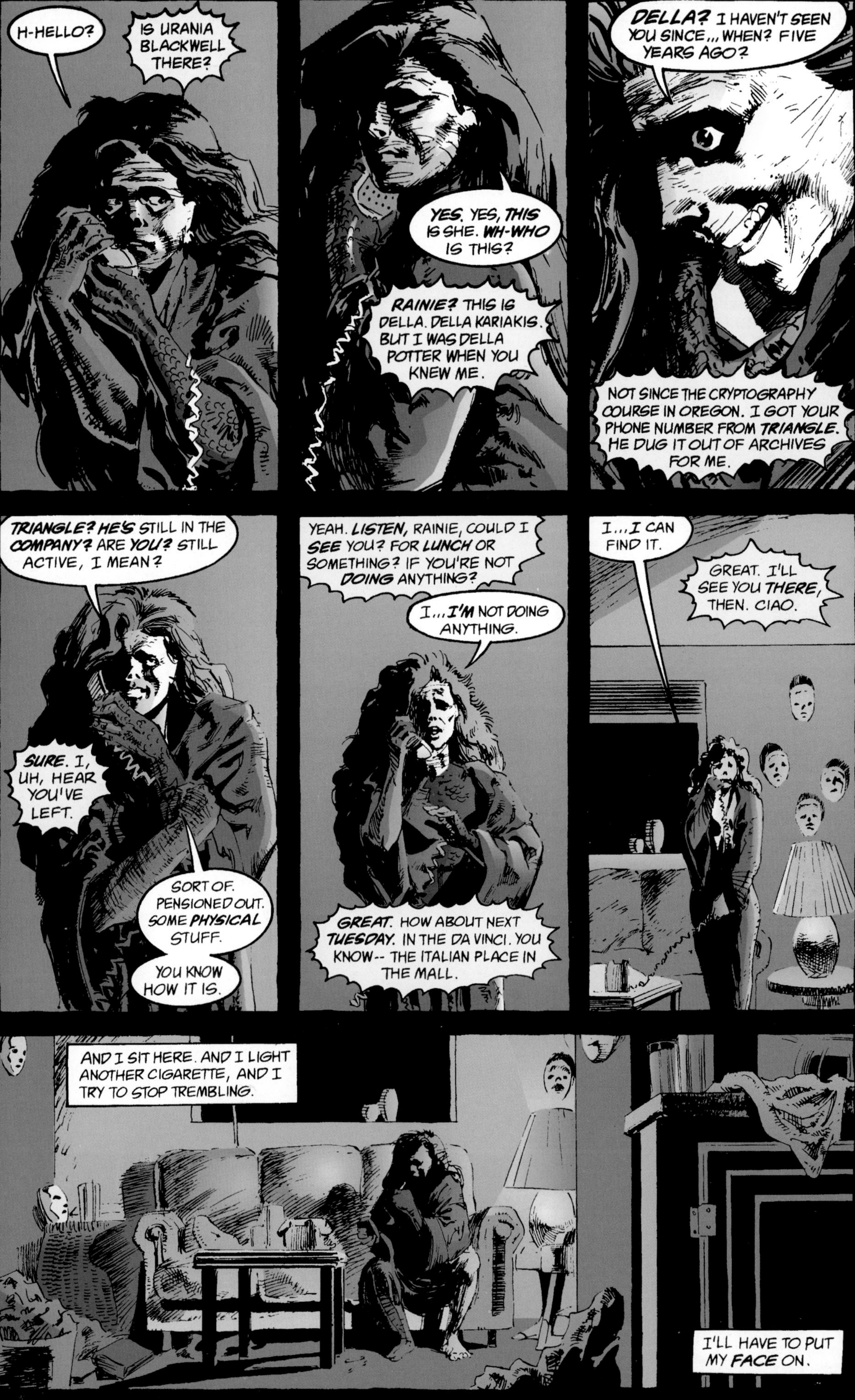
H-HELLO?
IS URANIA BLACKWELL THERE?
YES. YES, THIS IS SHE. WH-WHO IS THIS?
RAINIE? THIS IS DELLA. DELLA KARIAKIS. BUT I WAS DELLA POTTER WHEN YOU KNEW ME.
DELLA? I HAVEN'T SEEN YOU SINCE... WHEN? FIVE YEARS AGO?
NOT SINCE THE CRYPTOGRAPHY COURSE IN OREGON. I GOT YOUR PHONE NUMBER FROM TRIANGLE. HE DUG IT OUT OF ARCHIVES FOR ME.
TRIANGLE? HE'S STILL IN THE COMPANY? ARE YOU? STILL ACTIVE, I MEAN?
SURE. I, UH, HEAR YOU'VE LEFT.
SORT OF. PENSIONED OUT. SOME PHYSICAL STUFF.
YOU KNOW HOW IT IS.
YEAH. LISTEN, RAINIE, COULD I SEE YOU? FOR LUNCH OR SOMETHING? IF YOU'RE NOT DOING ANYTHING?
I... I'M NOT DOING ANYTHING.
GREAT. HOW ABOUT NEXT TUESDAY. IN THE DA VINCI. YOU KNOW-- THE ITALIAN PLACE IN THE MALL.
I... I CAN FIND IT.
GREAT. I'LL SEE YOU THERE, THEN. CIAO.
AND I SIT HERE. AND I LIGHT ANOTHER CIGARETTE, AND I TRY TO STOP TREMBLING.
I'LL HAVE TO PUT MY FACE ON.

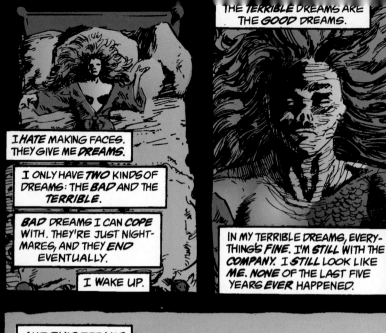

I *HATE* MAKING FACES. THEY GIVE ME *DREAMS*.

I ONLY HAVE *TWO* KINDS OF DREAMS: THE *BAD* AND THE *TERRIBLE*.

BAD DREAMS I CAN *COPE* WITH. THEY'RE JUST NIGHT-MARES, AND THEY *END* EVENTUALLY.

I WAKE UP.

THE *TERRIBLE* DREAMS ARE THE *GOOD* DREAMS.

IN MY *TERRIBLE* DREAMS, EVERY-THING'S *FINE*. I'M *STILL* WITH THE *COMPANY*. I *STILL* LOOK LIKE *ME*. *NONE* OF THE LAST FIVE YEARS *EVER* HAPPENED.

SOMETIMES I'M *MARRIED*. ONCE I EVEN HAD *KIDS*. I EVEN KNEW THEIR *NAMES*. EVERYTHING'S *WONDERFUL* AND *NORMAL* AND *FINE*.

AND THEN I WAKE UP. AND I'M STILL ME.

AND I'M STILL HERE.

AND THAT IS *TRULY* TERRIBLE.

AND *THIS* DREAM?

RAINIE, IN *THAT* TOMB'S THE DOOHICKEY THAT TURNED REX MASON INTO A *SUPER-MAN*.

YOU'RE GOING *IN* THERE A *TOP* COMPANY OFFICER. BUT YOU'RE GOING TO COME *OUT* AN *AMERICAN SUPER-WOMAN*. FOR UNCLE SAM.

I NEVER *HAD* ANY UNCLES, TRIANGLE. *DID* I?

IN MY DREAM THE TOMB DOESN'T SMELL OF ANYTHING.

THE LAST TIME I CAME DOWN HERE IT SMELLED OF DUST, AND OF DEATH.

THAT'S THE ORB OF RA.

COME TO ME, DAUGHTER.

I AM RA. I AM THE SUN, WHO IS LIFE. I AM HE WHO IS BORN A CHILD EVERY MORN, AND DIES, AN OLD MAN, AT NIGHTFALL.

FROM MY *SENILE* SPITTLE AND FROM THE DUST, HUMANKIND WAS CREATED TO WALK THE EARTH, AND TO WORSHIP THE GODS.

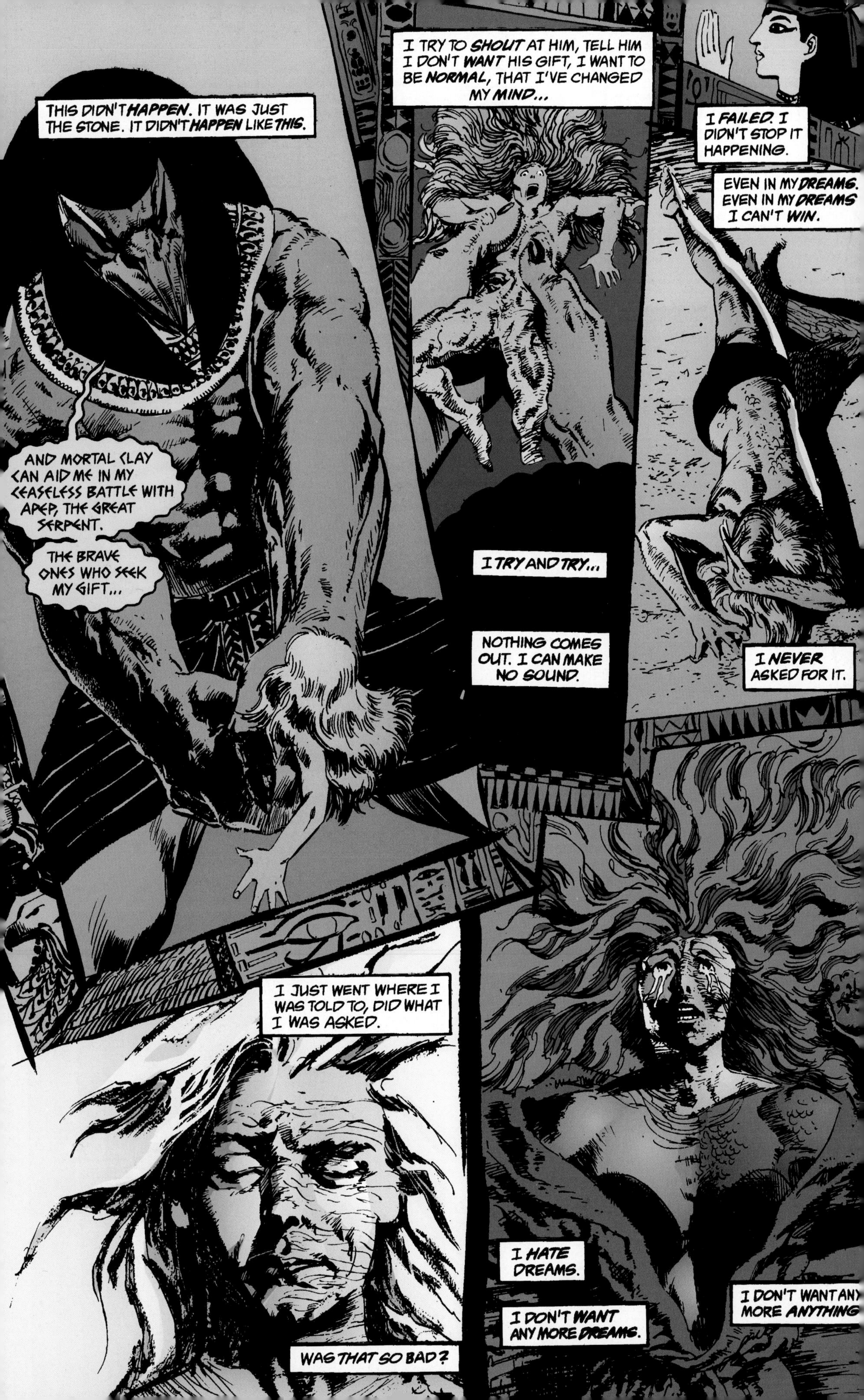

THIS DIDN'T HAPPEN. IT WAS JUST THE STONE. IT DIDN'T HAPPEN LIKE THIS.
AND MORTAL CLAY CAN AID ME IN MY CEASELESS BATTLE WITH APEP, THE GREAT SERPENT.
THE BRAVE ONES WHO SEEK MY GIFT...
I TRY TO SHOUT AT HIM, TELL HIM I DON'T WANT HIS GIFT, I WANT TO BE NORMAL, THAT I'VE CHANGED MY MIND...
I TRY AND TRY...
NOTHING COMES OUT. I CAN MAKE NO SOUND.
I FAILED. I DIDN'T STOP IT HAPPENING.
EVEN IN MY DREAMS. EVEN IN MY DREAMS I CAN'T WIN.
I NEVER ASKED FOR IT.
I JUST WENT WHERE I WAS TOLD TO, DID WHAT I WAS ASKED.
WAS THAT SO BAD?
I HATE DREAMS.
I DON'T WANT ANY MORE DREAMS.
I DON'T WANT ANY MORE ANYTHING.

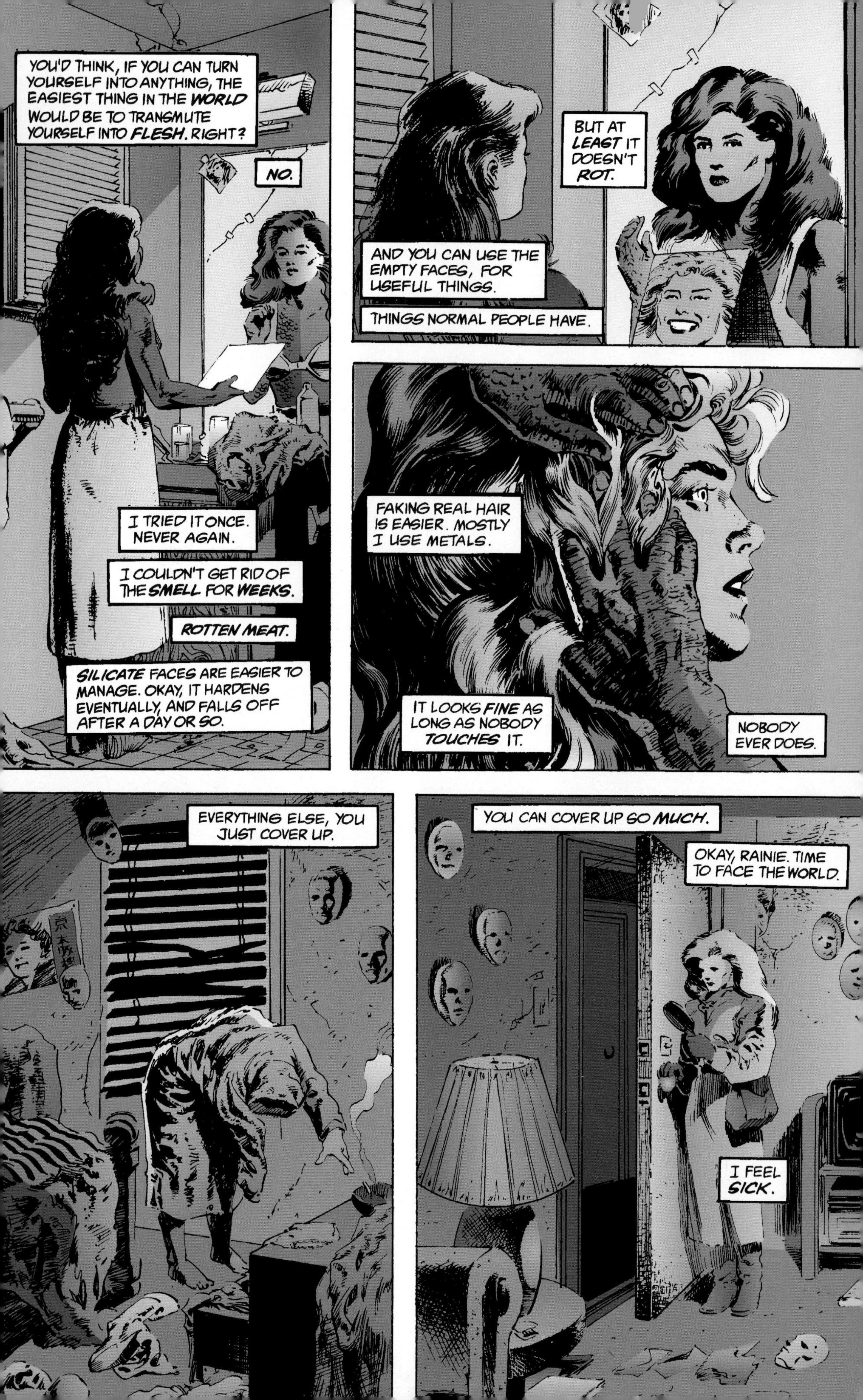
YOU'D THINK, IF YOU CAN TURN YOURSELF INTO ANYTHING, THE EASIEST THING IN THE WORLD WOULD BE TO TRANSMUTE YOURSELF INTO FLESH. RIGHT?
NO.
I TRIED IT ONCE. NEVER AGAIN.
I COULDN'T GET RID OF THE SMELL FOR WEEKS.
ROTTEN MEAT.
SILICATE FACES ARE EASIER TO MANAGE. OKAY, IT HARDENS EVENTUALLY, AND FALLS OFF AFTER A DAY OR SO.
BUT AT LEAST IT DOESN'T ROT.
AND YOU CAN USE THE EMPTY FACES, FOR USEFUL THINGS.
THINGS NORMAL PEOPLE HAVE.
FAKING REAL HAIR IS EASIER. MOSTLY I USE METALS.
IT LOOKS FINE AS LONG AS NOBODY TOUCHES IT.
NOBODY EVER DOES.
EVERYTHING ELSE, YOU JUST COVER UP.
YOU CAN COVER UP SO MUCH.
OKAY, RAINIE. TIME TO FACE THE WORLD.
I FEEL SICK.

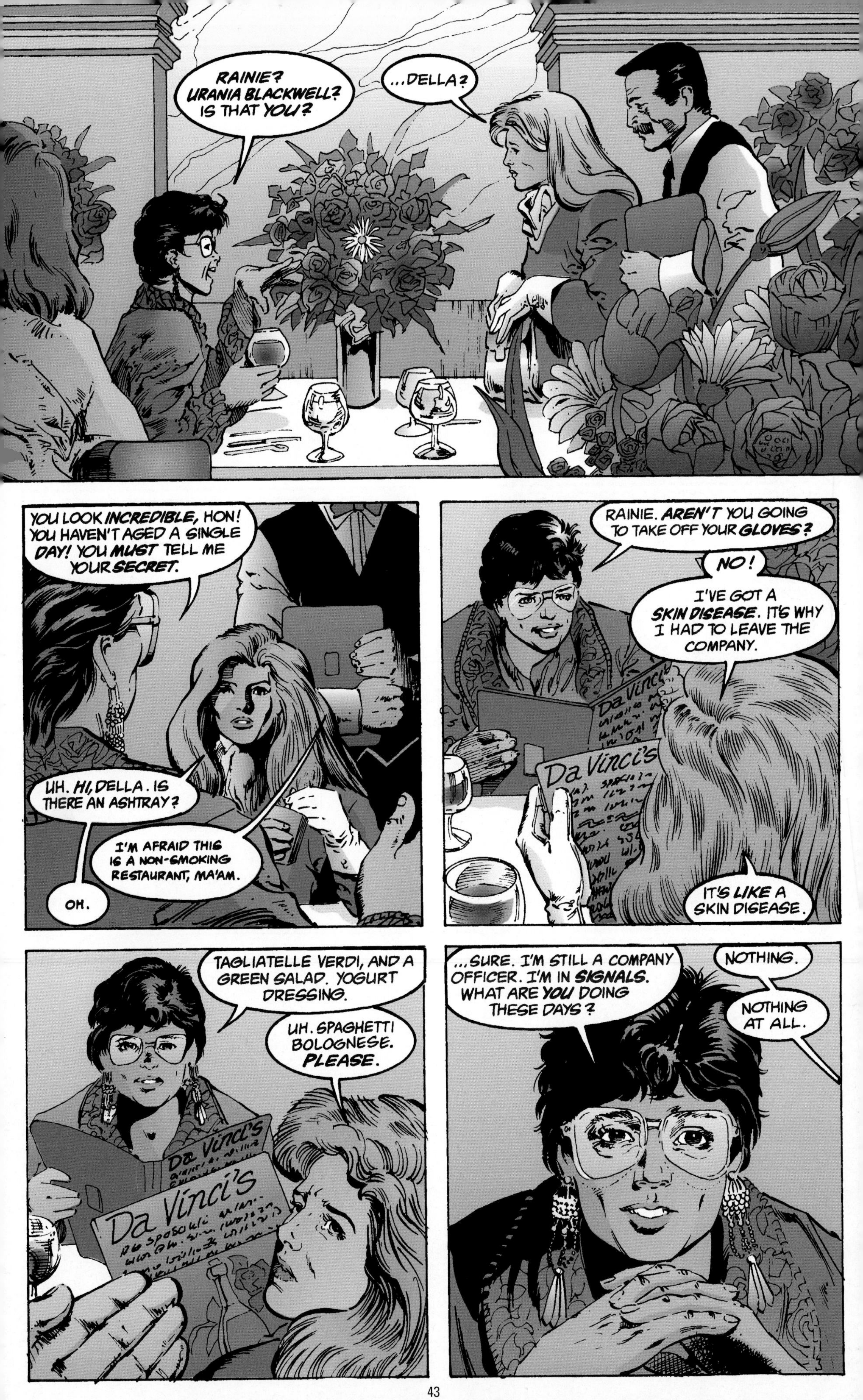
RAINIE? URANIA BLACKWELL? IS THAT YOU?
...DELLA?
YOU LOOK INCREDIBLE, HON! YOU HAVEN'T AGED A SINGLE DAY! YOU MUST TELL ME YOUR SECRET.
UH. HI, DELLA. IS THERE AN ASHTRAY?
I'M AFRAID THIS IS A NON-SMOKING RESTAURANT, MA'AM.
OH.
RAINIE. AREN'T YOU GOING TO TAKE OFF YOUR GLOVES?
NO!
I'VE GOT A SKIN DISEASE. IT'S WHY I HAD TO LEAVE THE COMPANY.
IT'S LIKE A SKIN DISEASE.
Da Vinci's
TAGLIATELLE VERDI, AND A GREEN SALAD. YOGURT DRESSING.
UH. SPAGHETTI BOLOGNESE. PLEASE.
...SURE. I'M STILL A COMPANY OFFICER. I'M IN SIGNALS. WHAT ARE YOU DOING THESE DAYS?
NOTHING.
NOTHING AT ALL.

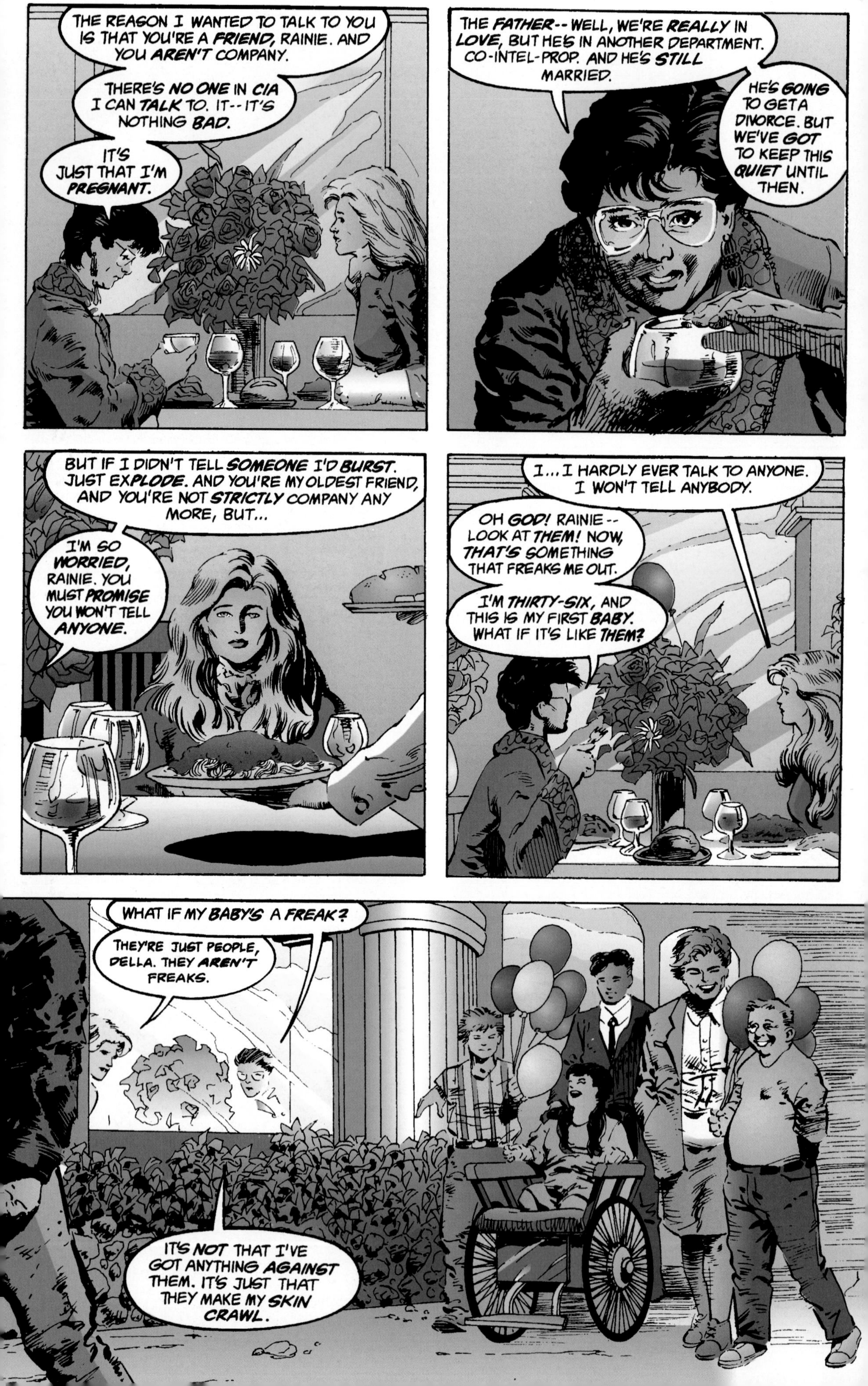
THE REASON I WANTED TO TALK TO YOU IS THAT YOU'RE A FRIEND, RAINIE. AND YOU AREN'T COMPANY.
THERE'S NO ONE IN CIA I CAN TALK TO. IT--IT'S NOTHING BAD.
IT'S JUST THAT I'M PREGNANT.
THE FATHER-- WELL, WE'RE REALLY IN LOVE, BUT HE'S IN ANOTHER DEPARTMENT. CO-INTEL-PROP. AND HE'S STILL MARRIED.
HE'S GOING TO GET A DIVORCE. BUT WE'VE GOT TO KEEP THIS QUIET UNTIL THEN.
BUT IF I DIDN'T TELL SOMEONE I'D BURST. JUST EXPLODE. AND YOU'RE MY OLDEST FRIEND, AND YOU'RE NOT STRICTLY COMPANY ANY MORE, BUT...
I'M SO WORRIED, RAINIE. YOU MUST PROMISE YOU WON'T TELL ANYONE.
I... I HARDLY EVER TALK TO ANYONE. I WON'T TELL ANYBODY.
OH GOD! RAINIE -- LOOK AT THEM! NOW, THAT'S SOMETHING THAT FREAKS ME OUT.
I'M THIRTY-SIX, AND THIS IS MY FIRST BABY. WHAT IF IT'S LIKE THEM?
WHAT IF MY BABY'S A FREAK?
THEY'RE JUST PEOPLE, DELLA. THEY AREN'T FREAKS.
IT'S NOT THAT I'VE GOT ANYTHING AGAINST THEM. IT'S JUST THAT THEY MAKE MY SKIN CRAWL.

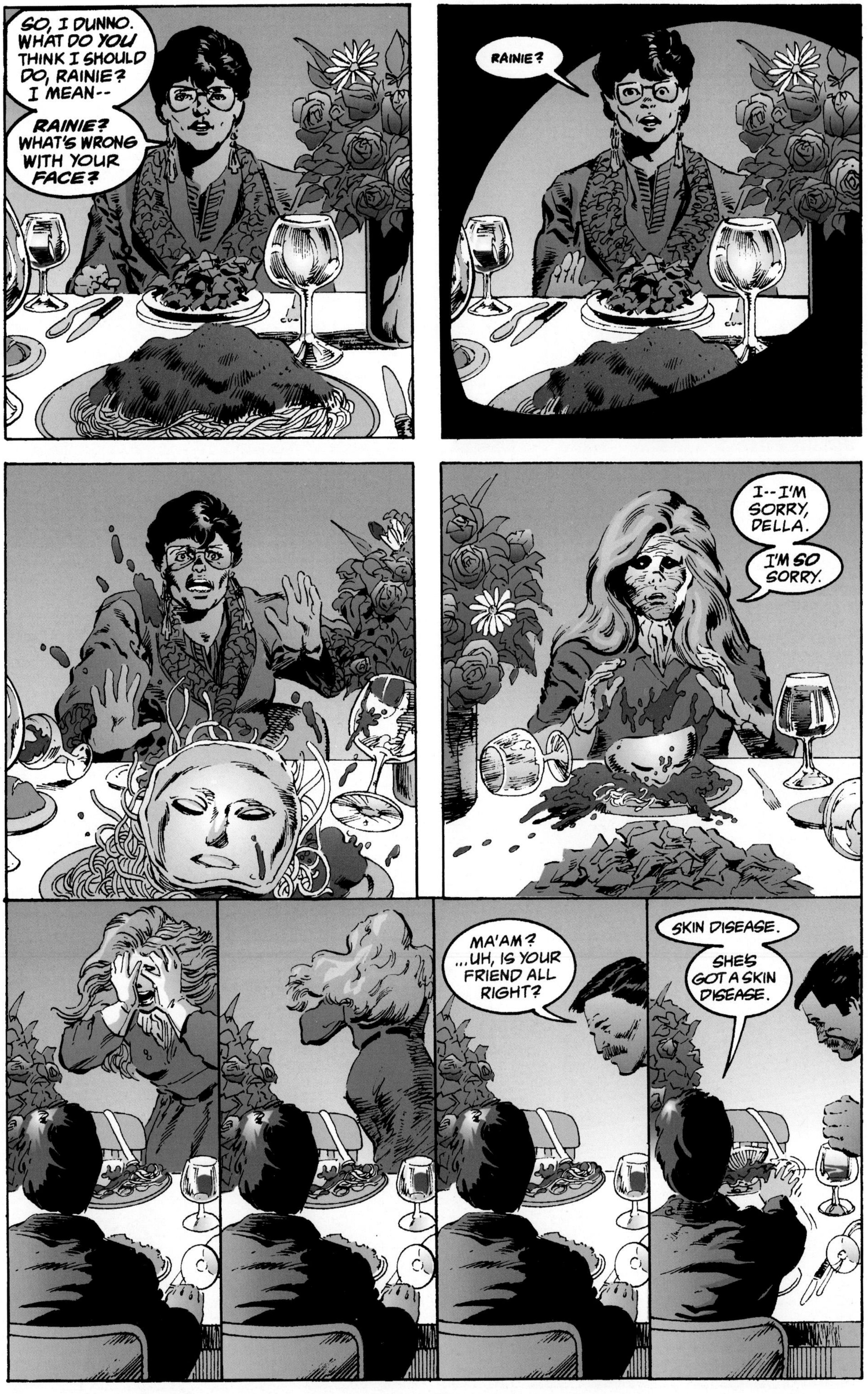
SO, I DUNNO. WHAT DO YOU THINK I SHOULD DO, RAINIE? I MEAN--
RAINIE? WHAT'S WRONG WITH YOUR FACE?
RAINIE?
I--I'M SORRY, DELLA.
I'M SO SORRY.
MA'AM? ...UH, IS YOUR FRIEND ALL RIGHT?
SKIN DISEASE.
SHE'S GOT A SKIN DISEASE.

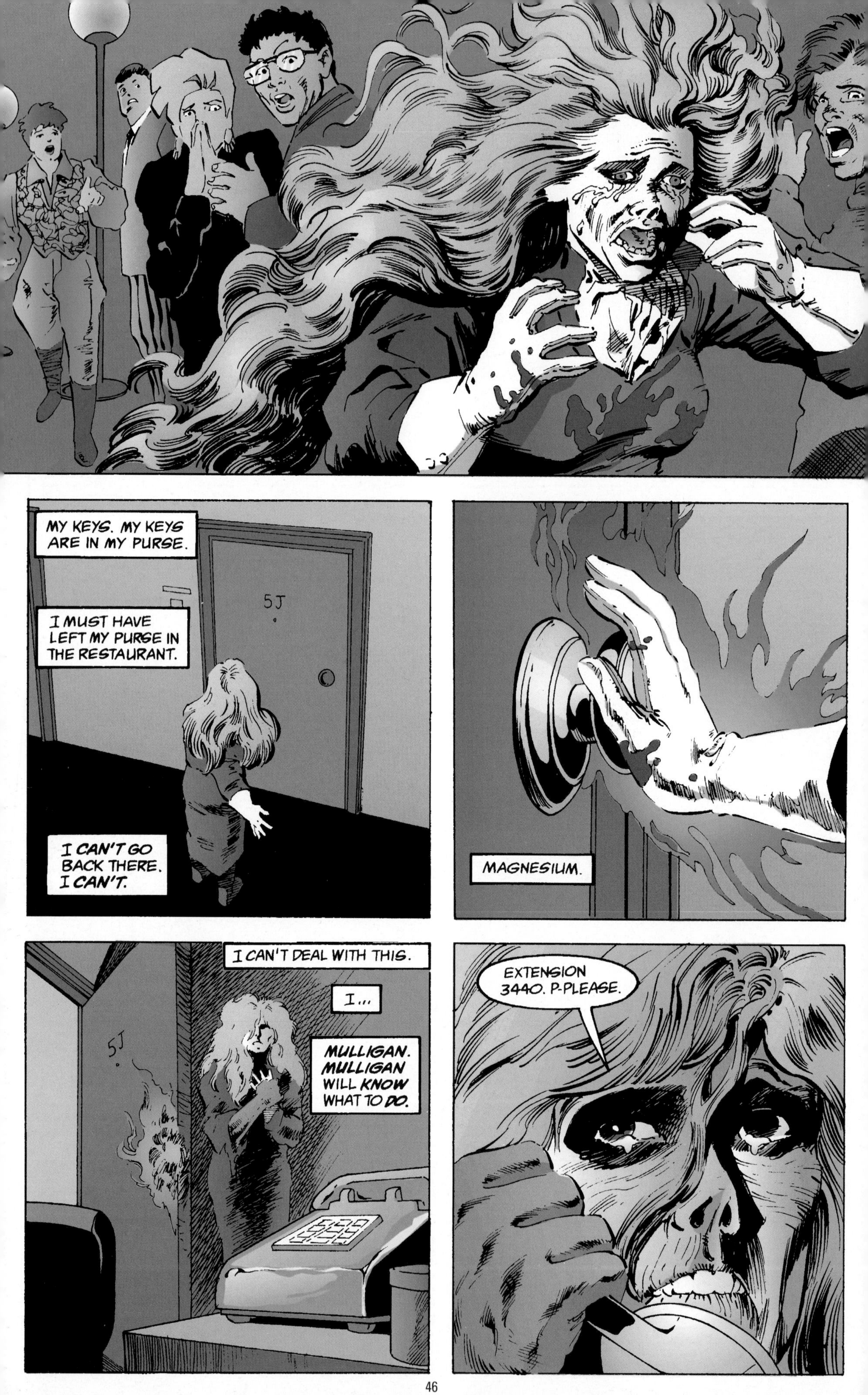
MY KEYS. MY KEYS ARE IN MY PURSE.
I MUST HAVE LEFT MY PURSE IN THE RESTAURANT.
I CAN'T GO BACK THERE. I CAN'T.
MAGNESIUM.
I CAN'T DEAL WITH THIS.
I...
MULLIGAN. MULLIGAN WILL KNOW WHAT TO DO.
EXTENSION 3440. P-PLEASE.

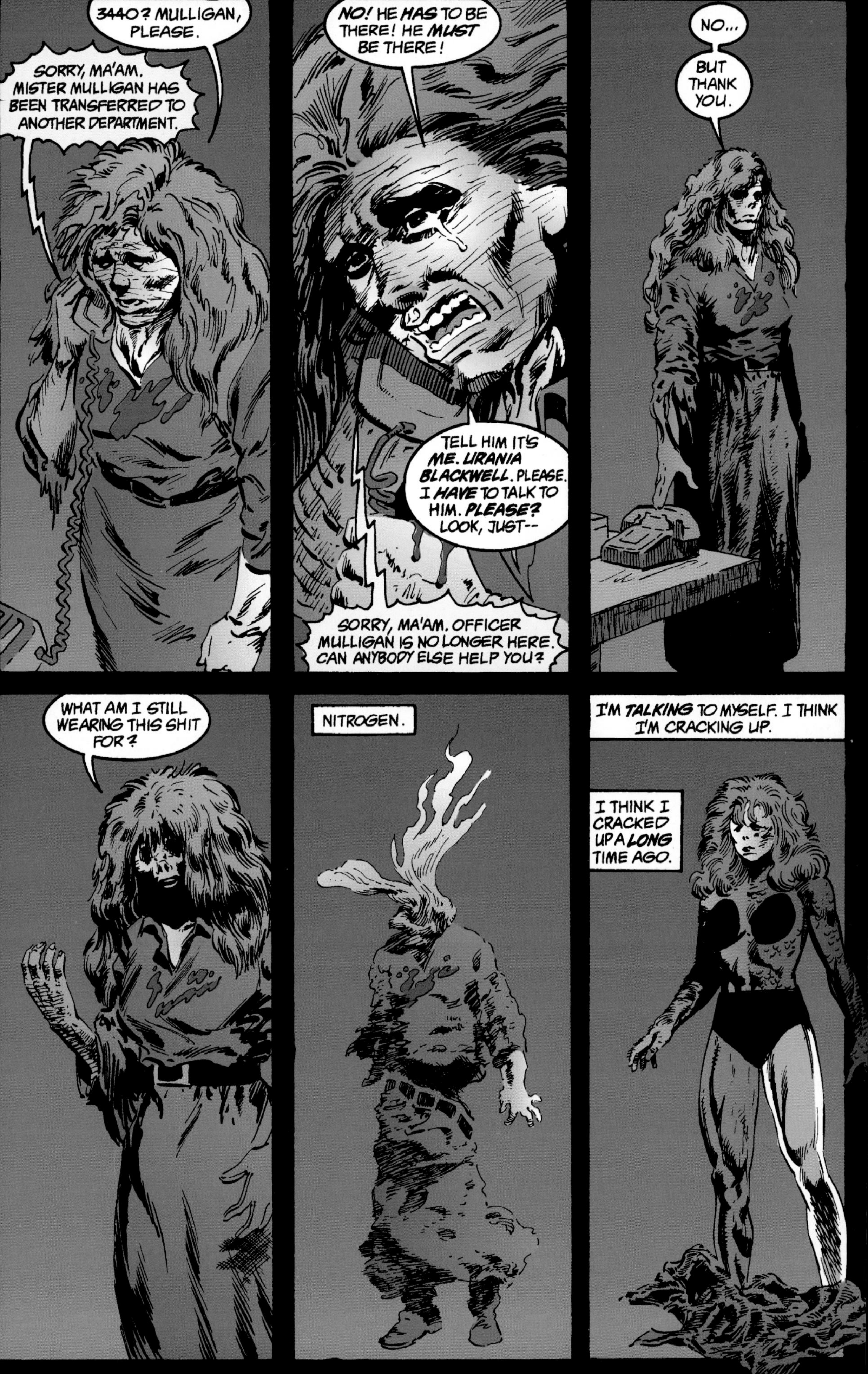
3440? MULLIGAN, PLEASE.
SORRY, MA'AM. MISTER MULLIGAN HAS BEEN TRANSFERRED TO ANOTHER DEPARTMENT.
NO! HE HAS TO BE THERE! HE MUST BE THERE!
TELL HIM IT'S ME. URANIA BLACKWELL. PLEASE. I HAVE TO TALK TO HIM. PLEASE? LOOK, JUST--
SORRY, MA'AM. OFFICER MULLIGAN IS NO LONGER HERE. CAN ANYBODY ELSE HELP YOU?
NO...
BUT THANK YOU.
WHAT AM I STILL WEARING THIS SHIT FOR?
NITROGEN.
I'M TALKING TO MYSELF. I THINK I'M CRACKING UP.
I THINK I CRACKED UP A LONG TIME AGO.

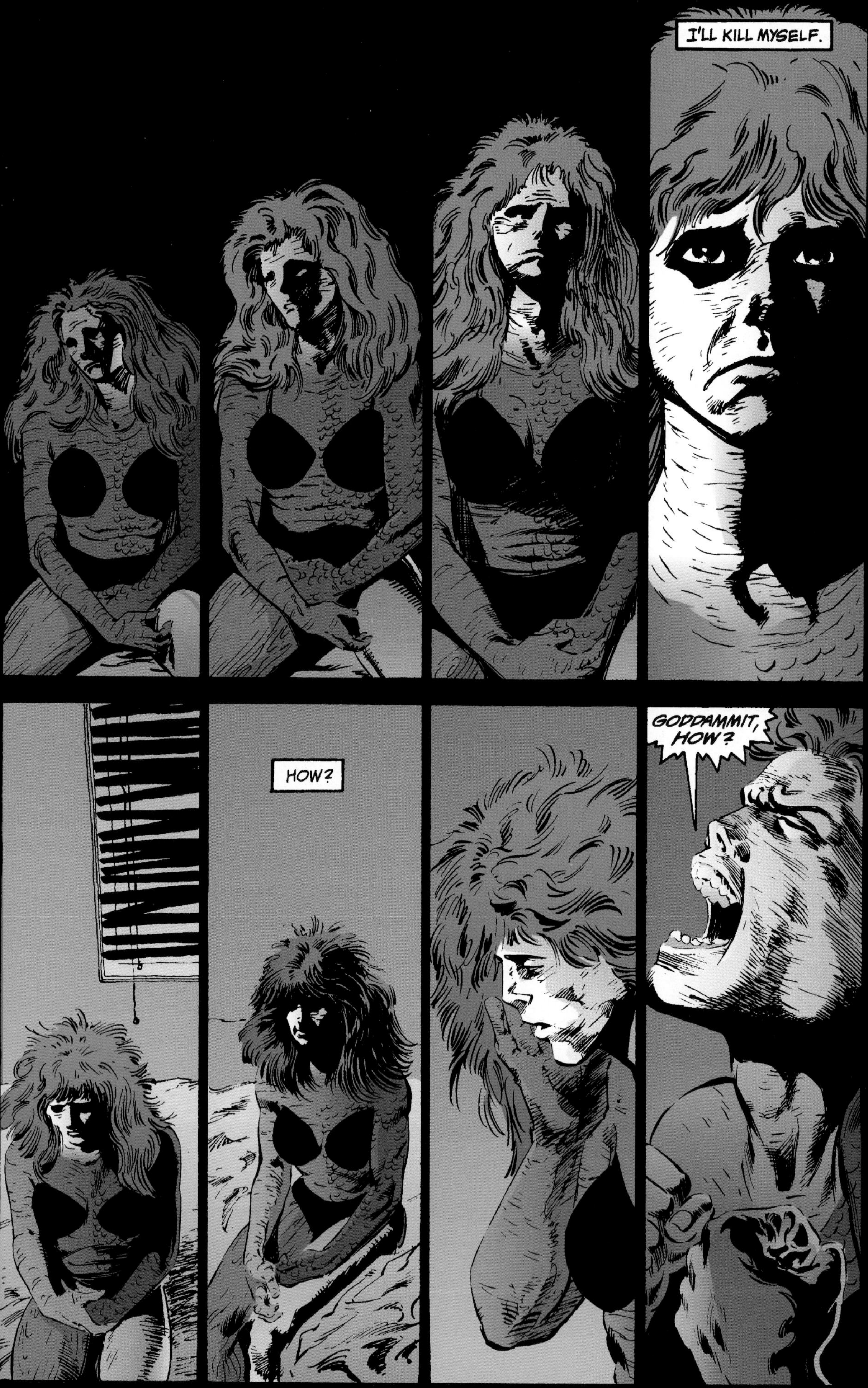
I'LL KILL MYSELF.
HOW?
GODDAMMIT, HOW?

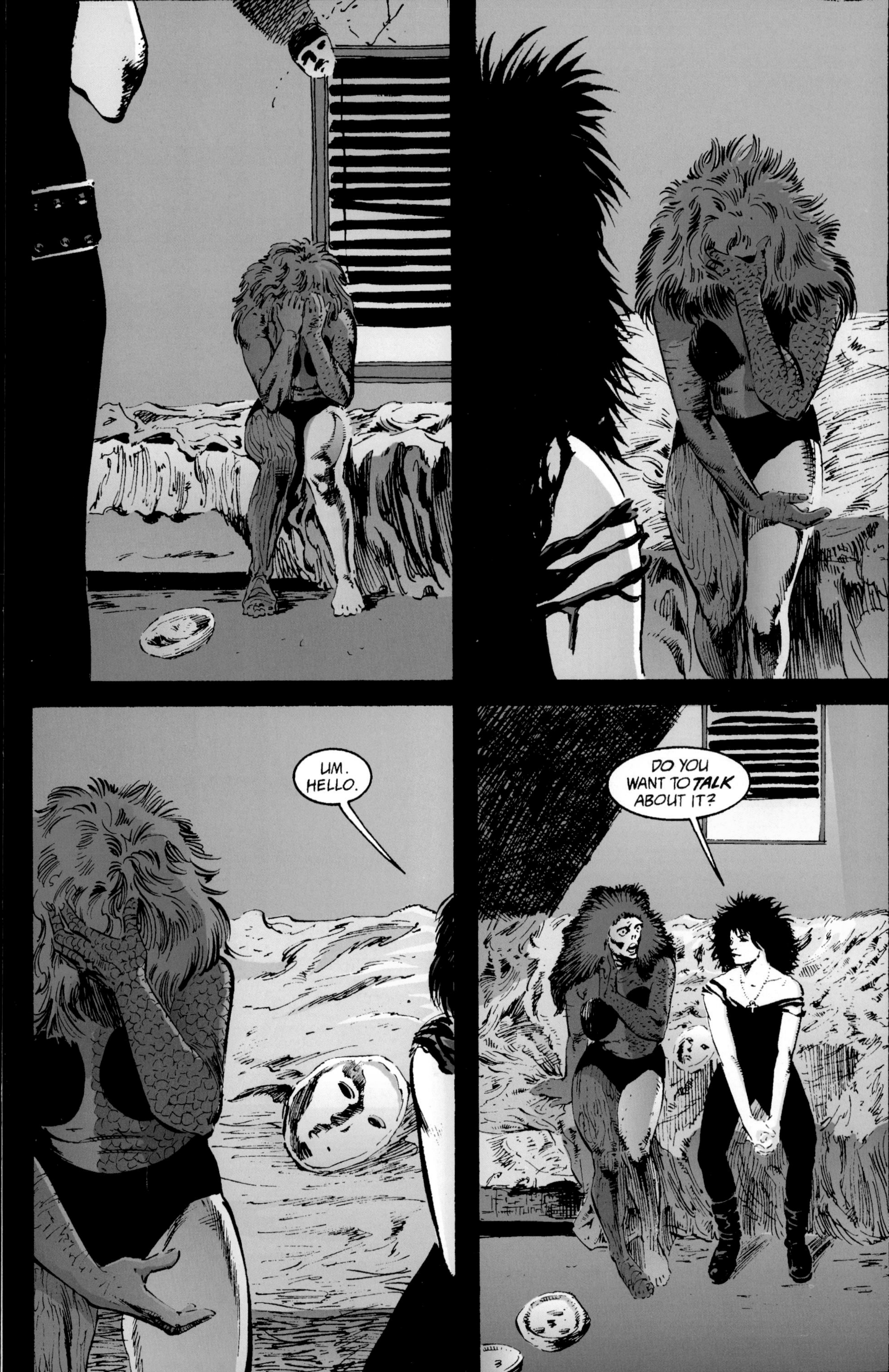
UM. HELLO.
DO YOU WANT TO *TALK* ABOUT IT?

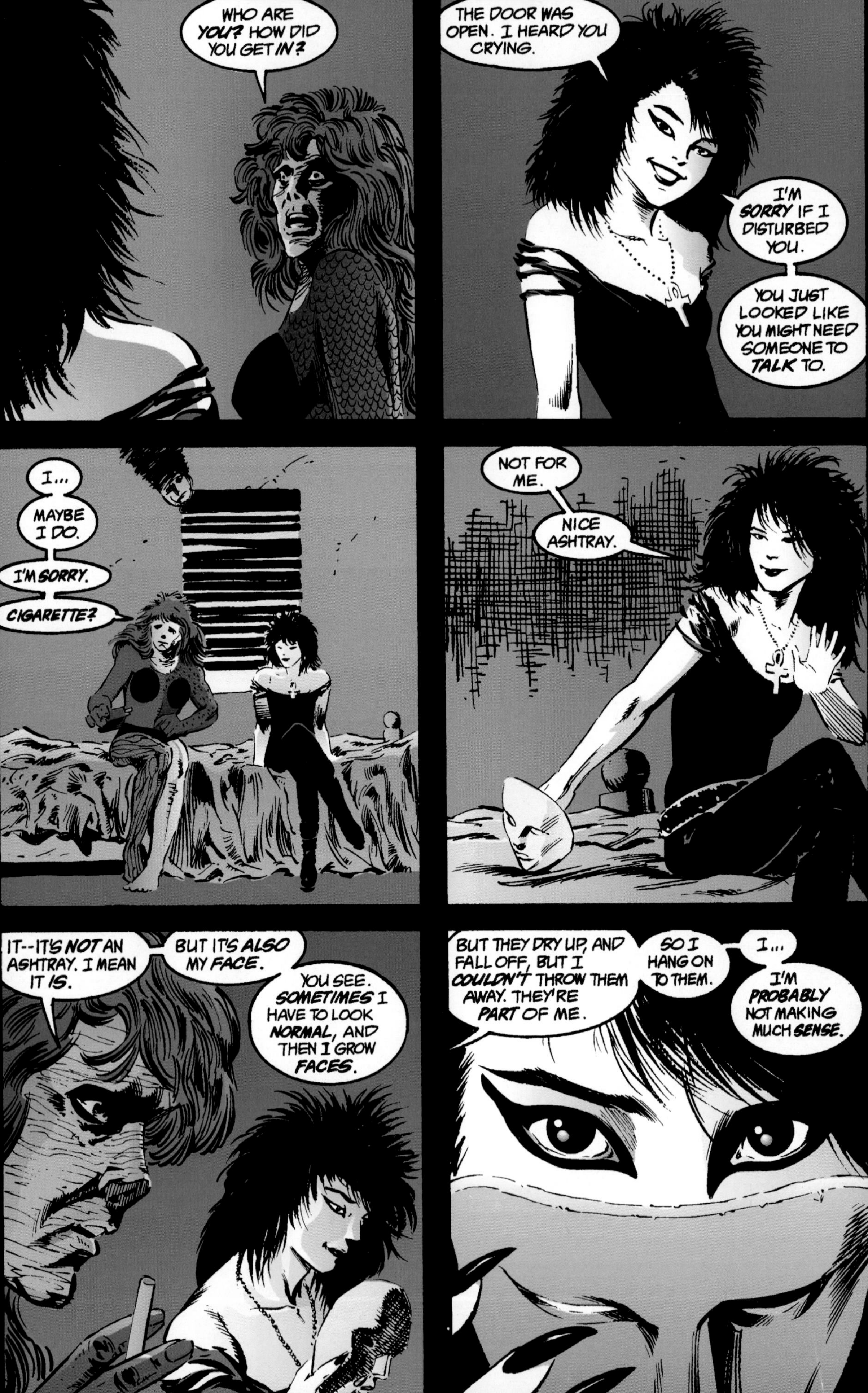
WHO ARE YOU? HOW DID YOU GET IN?
THE DOOR WAS OPEN. I HEARD YOU CRYING.
I'M SORRY IF I DISTURBED YOU.
YOU JUST LOOKED LIKE YOU MIGHT NEED SOMEONE TO TALK TO.
I...
MAYBE I DO.
I'M SORRY.
CIGARETTE?
NOT FOR ME.
NICE ASHTRAY.
IT--IT'S NOT AN ASHTRAY. I MEAN IT IS.
BUT IT'S ALSO MY FACE.
YOU SEE. SOMETIMES I HAVE TO LOOK NORMAL, AND THEN I GROW FACES.
BUT THEY DRY UP, AND FALL OFF, BUT I COULDN'T THROW THEM AWAY. THEY'RE PART OF ME.
SO I HANG ON TO THEM.
I...
I'M PROBABLY NOT MAKING MUCH SENSE.

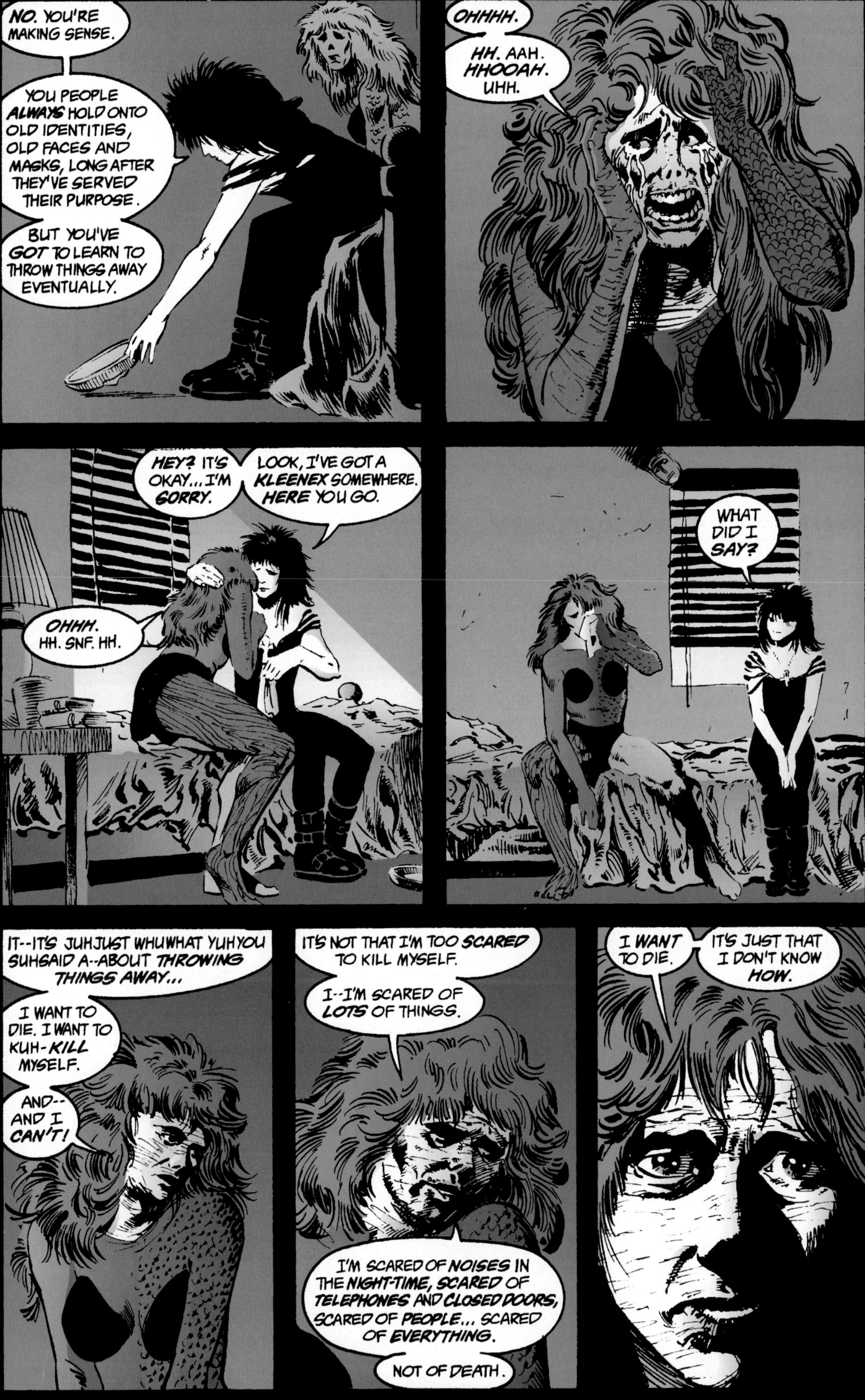
NO. YOU'RE MAKING SENSE.
YOU PEOPLE ALWAYS HOLD ONTO OLD IDENTITIES, OLD FACES AND MASKS, LONG AFTER THEY'VE SERVED THEIR PURPOSE.
BUT YOU'VE GOT TO LEARN TO THROW THINGS AWAY EVENTUALLY.
OHHHH.
HH. AAH. HHOOAH. UHH.
HEY? IT'S OKAY... I'M SORRY.
LOOK, I'VE GOT A KLEENEX SOMEWHERE. HERE YOU GO.
OHHH. HH. SNF. HH.
WHAT DID I SAY?
IT--IT'S JUHJUST WHUWHAT YUHYOU SUHSAID A--ABOUT THROWING THINGS AWAY...
I WANT TO DIE. I WANT TO KUH-KILL MYSELF.
AND--AND I CAN'T!
IT'S NOT THAT I'M TOO SCARED TO KILL MYSELF.
I--I'M SCARED OF LOTS OF THINGS.
I'M SCARED OF NOISES IN THE NIGHT-TIME, SCARED OF TELEPHONES AND CLOSED DOORS, SCARED OF PEOPLE... SCARED OF EVERYTHING.
NOT OF DEATH.
I WANT TO DIE.
IT'S JUST THAT I DON'T KNOW HOW.

I'VE BEEN THINKING ABOUT IT FOR *SO LONG*, NOW. I CAN'T SLASH MY *WRISTS*--I DON'T HAVE ANY *BLOOD*.

WHEN I WAS AT HIGH SCHOOL, A KID SHUT HIMSELF IN A GARAGE, TOOK SLEEPING PILLS, CLIMBED IN THE CAR AND TURNED THE IGNITION.

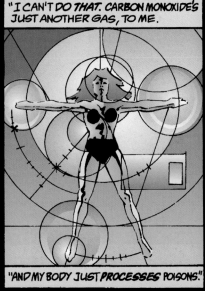

"I CAN'T DO *THAT*. CARBON MONOXIDE'S JUST ANOTHER GAS, TO ME.

"AND MY BODY JUST *PROCESSES* POISONS."

I CAN'T *SHOOT* MYSELF. A BULLET WOULDN'T DO ANY *REAL* DAMAGE.

SO THEN I GET MORE EXTREME.

"MAYBE I COULD SIT AT GROUND ZERO OF A NUCLEAR TEST-- IF I COULD *FIND* ONE.

"BUT I'M *AFRAID* I COULD *SURVIVE* THAT. I *THINK* I WOULD.

"PERHAPS I'D BE RADIOACTIVE FOR ALWAYS...BUT I'D *SURVIVE*."

THEN NO ONE WOULD *EVER* WANT TO TALK TO ME...

"I THOUGHT ABOUT TRANS-MUTING MYSELF TO FREE OXYGEN RADICALS AND JUST MELDING WITH THE *AIR*. OR WITH ADDED HYDROGEN, I COULD BECOME *WATER* AND JOIN MYSELF WITH THE SEA.

"BUT I'D PROBABLY *STILL* BE *CONSCIOUS*. JUST *SPREAD* OUT ALL OVER THE *WORLD*."

I WANT IT TO *STOP*.

I DON'T *KNOW* HOW TO *STOP* IT.

HOW DID THAT *SONG* GO? FROM THAT TV SHOW?

SUICIDE IS ♩ PAINLESS ...IT♪ BRINGS ON MANY CHANGES...AND♪ I CAN TAKE OR♪ LEAVE IT...

ISN'T IT *DUMB?* ALL OVER THE WORLD, PEOPLE RUNNING AROUND, TRYING *NOT* TO *DIE?*

HANGING ON TO LIFE LIKE GRIM DEATH.

AND I *WANT* TO DIE. AND I *CAN'T*.

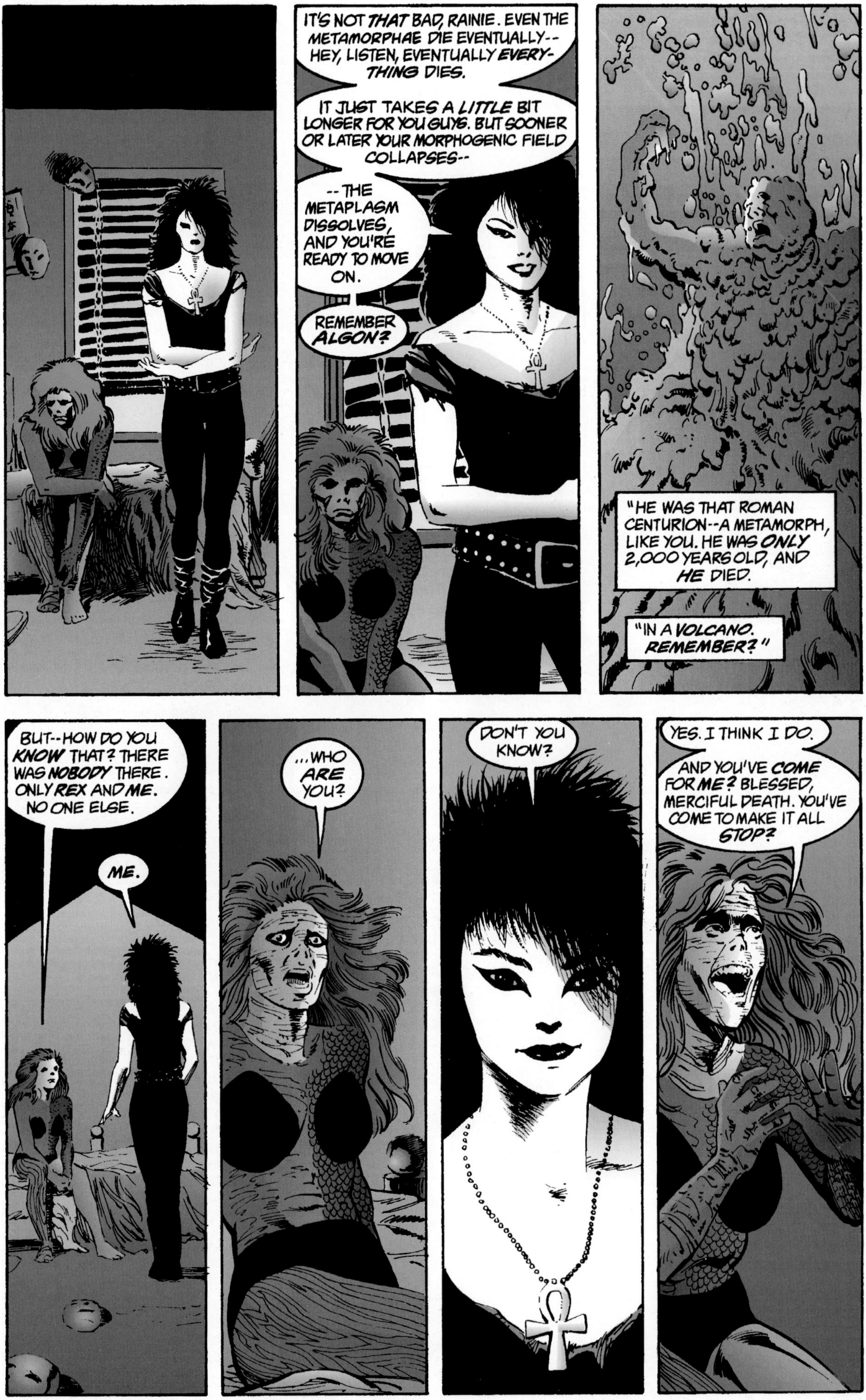
IT'S NOT THAT BAD, RAINIE. EVEN THE METAMORPHAE DIE EVENTUALLY-- HEY, LISTEN, EVENTUALLY EVERYTHING DIES.
IT JUST TAKES A LITTLE BIT LONGER FOR YOU GUYS. BUT SOONER OR LATER YOUR MORPHOGENIC FIELD COLLAPSES--
--THE METAPLASM DISSOLVES, AND YOU'RE READY TO MOVE ON.
REMEMBER ALGON?
"HE WAS THAT ROMAN CENTURION--A METAMORPH, LIKE YOU. HE WAS ONLY 2,000 YEARS OLD, AND HE DIED.
"IN A VOLCANO. REMEMBER?"
BUT--HOW DO YOU KNOW THAT? THERE WAS NOBODY THERE. ONLY REX AND ME. NO ONE ELSE.
ME.
...WHO ARE YOU?
DON'T YOU KNOW?
YES. I THINK I DO.
AND YOU'VE COME FOR ME? BLESSED, MERCIFUL DEATH. YOU'VE COME TO MAKE IT ALL STOP?

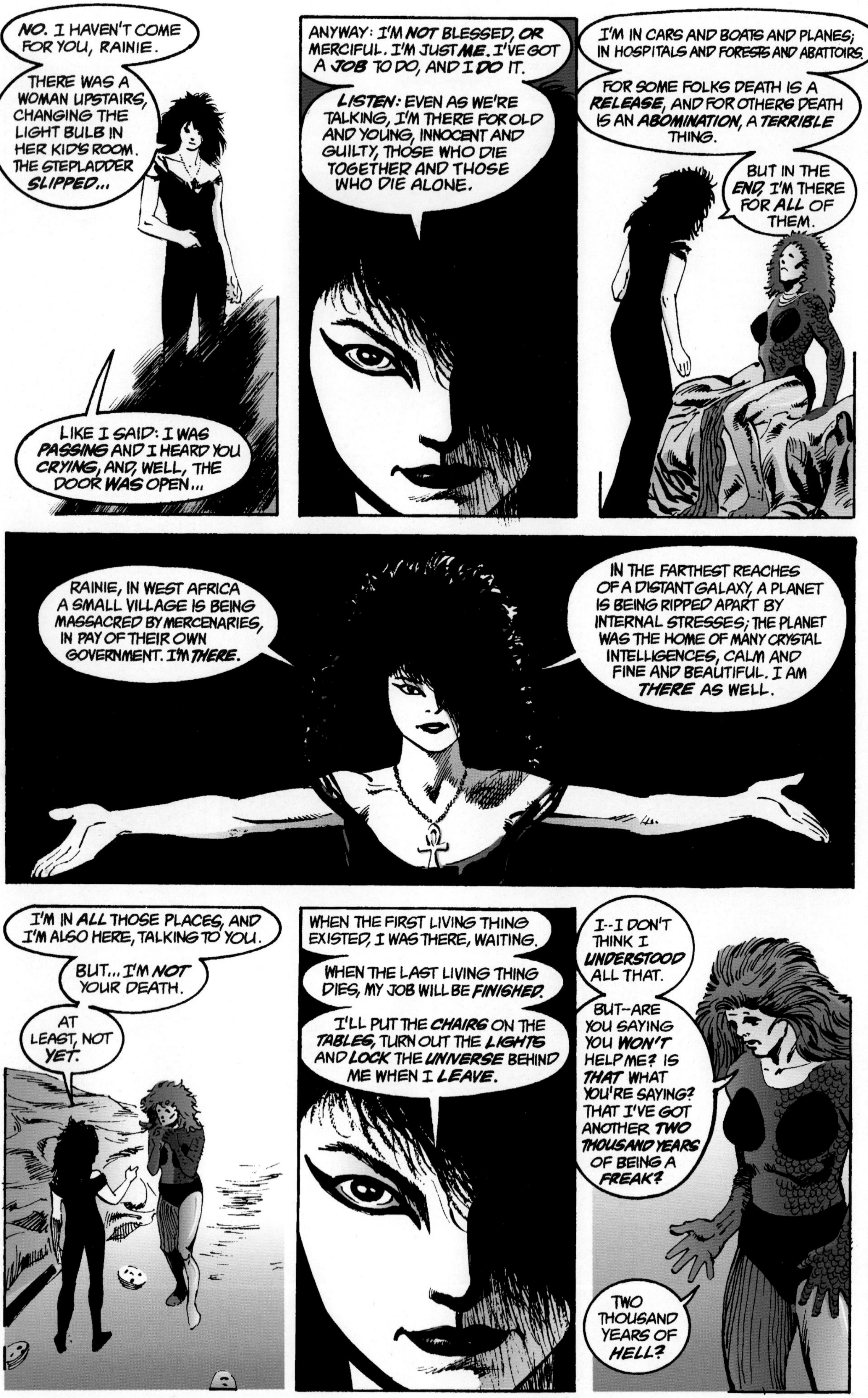
NO. I HAVEN'T COME FOR YOU, RAINIE.
THERE WAS A WOMAN UPSTAIRS, CHANGING THE LIGHT BULB IN HER KID'S ROOM. THE STEPLADDER SLIPPED...
LIKE I SAID: I WAS PASSING AND I HEARD YOU CRYING, AND, WELL, THE DOOR WAS OPEN...
ANYWAY: I'M NOT BLESSED, OR MERCIFUL. I'M JUST ME. I'VE GOT A JOB TO DO, AND I DO IT.
LISTEN: EVEN AS WE'RE TALKING, I'M THERE FOR OLD AND YOUNG, INNOCENT AND GUILTY, THOSE WHO DIE TOGETHER AND THOSE WHO DIE ALONE.
I'M IN CARS AND BOATS AND PLANES; IN HOSPITALS AND FORESTS AND ABATTOIRS.
FOR SOME FOLKS DEATH IS A RELEASE, AND FOR OTHERS DEATH IS AN ABOMINATION, A TERRIBLE THING.
BUT IN THE END, I'M THERE FOR ALL OF THEM.
RAINIE, IN WEST AFRICA A SMALL VILLAGE IS BEING MASSACRED BY MERCENARIES, IN PAY OF THEIR OWN GOVERNMENT. I'M THERE.
IN THE FARTHEST REACHES OF A DISTANT GALAXY, A PLANET IS BEING RIPPED APART BY INTERNAL STRESSES; THE PLANET WAS THE HOME OF MANY CRYSTAL INTELLIGENCES, CALM AND FINE AND BEAUTIFUL. I AM THERE AS WELL.
I'M IN ALL THOSE PLACES, AND I'M ALSO HERE, TALKING TO YOU.
BUT... I'M NOT YOUR DEATH.
AT LEAST, NOT YET.
WHEN THE FIRST LIVING THING EXISTED, I WAS THERE, WAITING.
WHEN THE LAST LIVING THING DIES, MY JOB WILL BE FINISHED.
I'LL PUT THE CHAIRS ON THE TABLES, TURN OUT THE LIGHTS AND LOCK THE UNIVERSE BEHIND ME WHEN I LEAVE.
I--I DON'T THINK I UNDERSTOOD ALL THAT.
BUT--ARE YOU SAYING YOU WON'T HELP ME? IS THAT WHAT YOU'RE SAYING? THAT I'VE GOT ANOTHER TWO THOUSAND YEARS OF BEING A FREAK?
TWO THOUSAND YEARS OF HELL?

YOU MAKE YOUR *OWN* HELL, RAINIE.

OKAY. I'LL HELP YOU. IF THAT'S WHAT YOU WANT.

THAT'S WHAT *I* GET FOR GETTING *INVOLVED.*

YOU'LL *KILL* ME? TAKE MY *LIFE?* GIVE ME *OBLIVION?*

YOUR LIFE IS YOUR OWN, RAINIE. *SO* IS YOUR DEATH.

AND *OBLIVION...?* THAT'S *NOT* AN OPTION, I'M AFRAID.

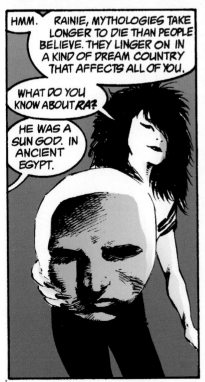

HMM. RAINIE, MYTHOLOGIES TAKE LONGER TO DIE THAN PEOPLE BELIEVE. THEY LINGER ON IN A KIND OF DREAM COUNTRY THAT AFFECTS ALL OF YOU.

WHAT DO YOU KNOW ABOUT *RA?*

HE WAS A SUN GOD. IN ANCIENT EGYPT.

YEAH. THAT'S RIGHT.

HE'S SEEN *BETTER* DAYS. HE *STILL* KEEPS BRINGING THE METAMORPHAE INTO EXISTENCE, EVEN THOUGH THE BATTLE YOUR KIND FOUGHT FINISHED *AGES* AGO.

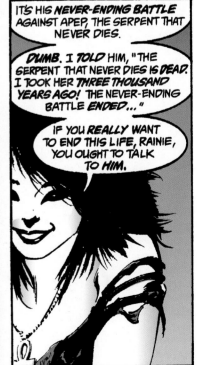

IT'S HIS *NEVER-ENDING BATTLE* AGAINST APEP, THE SERPENT THAT NEVER DIES.

DUMB. I *TOLD* HIM, "THE SERPENT THAT NEVER DIES IS *DEAD.* I TOOK HER *THREE THOUSAND* YEARS AGO! THE NEVER-ENDING BATTLE *ENDED...*"

IF YOU *REALLY* WANT TO END THIS LIFE, RAINIE, YOU OUGHT TO TALK TO *HIM.*

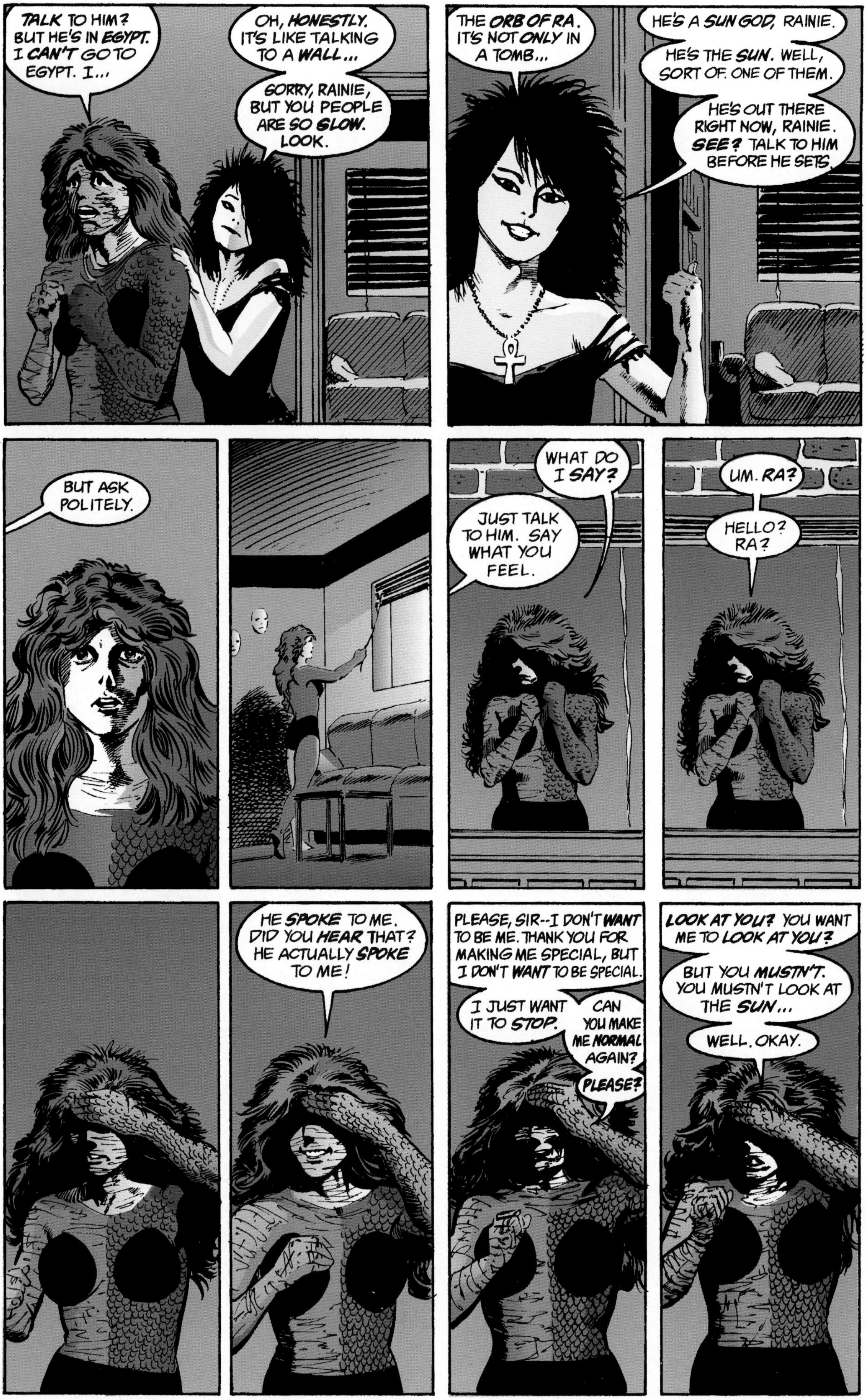
TALK TO HIM? BUT HE'S IN EGYPT. I CAN'T GO TO EGYPT. I...
OH, HONESTLY. IT'S LIKE TALKING TO A WALL...
SORRY, RAINIE, BUT YOU PEOPLE ARE SO SLOW. LOOK.
THE ORB OF RA. IT'S NOT ONLY IN A TOMB...
HE'S A SUN GOD, RAINIE.
HE'S THE SUN. WELL, SORT OF. ONE OF THEM.
HE'S OUT THERE RIGHT NOW, RAINIE. SEE? TALK TO HIM BEFORE HE SETS.
BUT ASK POLITELY.
WHAT DO I SAY?
JUST TALK TO HIM. SAY WHAT YOU FEEL.
UM. RA?
HELLO? RA?
HE SPOKE TO ME. DID YOU HEAR THAT? HE ACTUALLY SPOKE TO ME!
PLEASE, SIR--I DON'T WANT TO BE ME. THANK YOU FOR MAKING ME SPECIAL, BUT I DON'T WANT TO BE SPECIAL.
I JUST WANT IT TO STOP.
CAN YOU MAKE ME NORMAL AGAIN?
PLEASE?
LOOK AT YOU? YOU WANT ME TO LOOK AT YOU?
BUT YOU MUSTN'T. YOU MUSTN'T LOOK AT THE SUN...
WELL. OKAY.

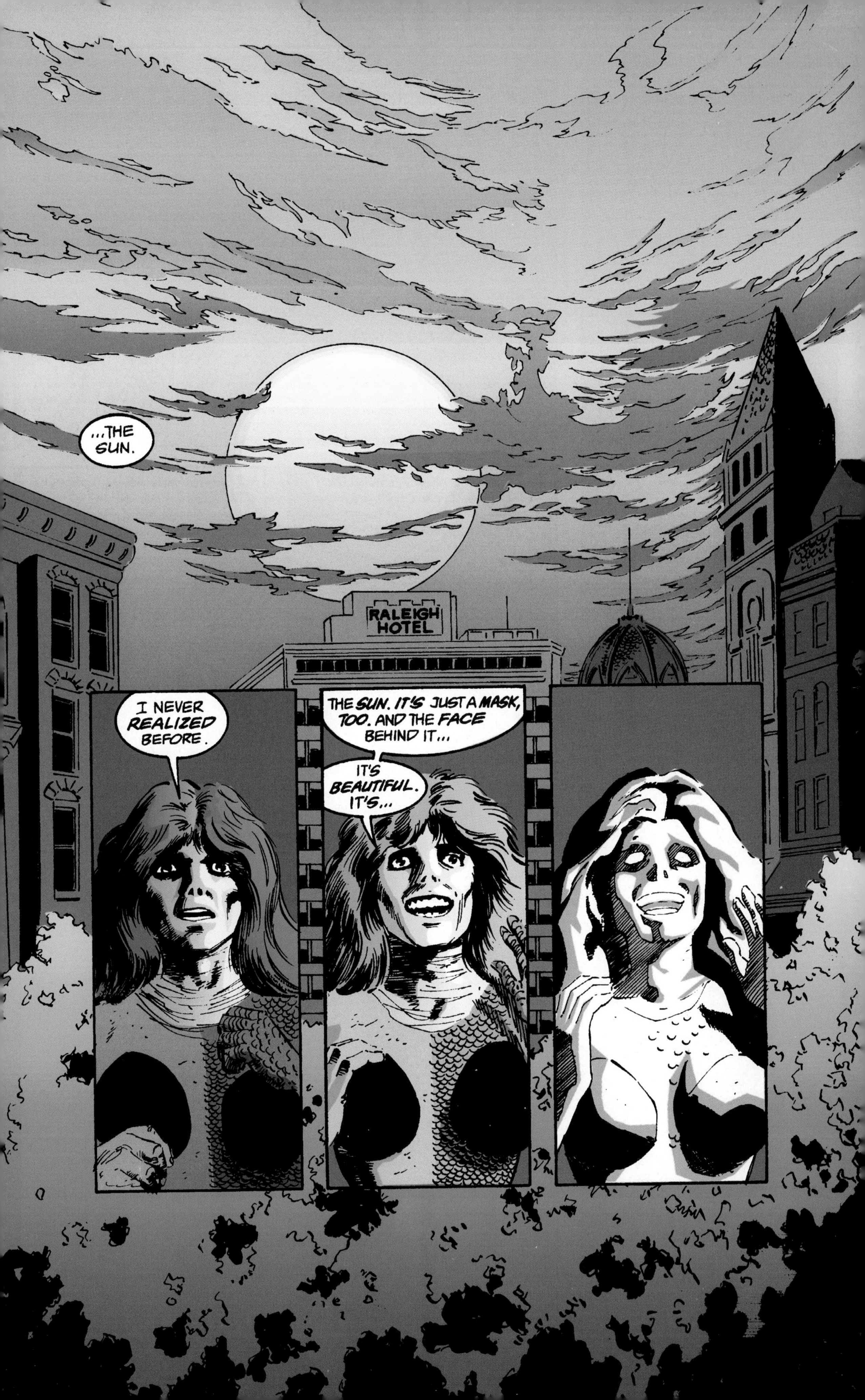
...THE SUN.
I NEVER REALIZED BEFORE.
THE SUN. IT'S JUST A MASK, TOO. AND THE FACE BEHIND IT...
IT'S BEAUTIFUL. IT'S...
RALEIGH HOTEL

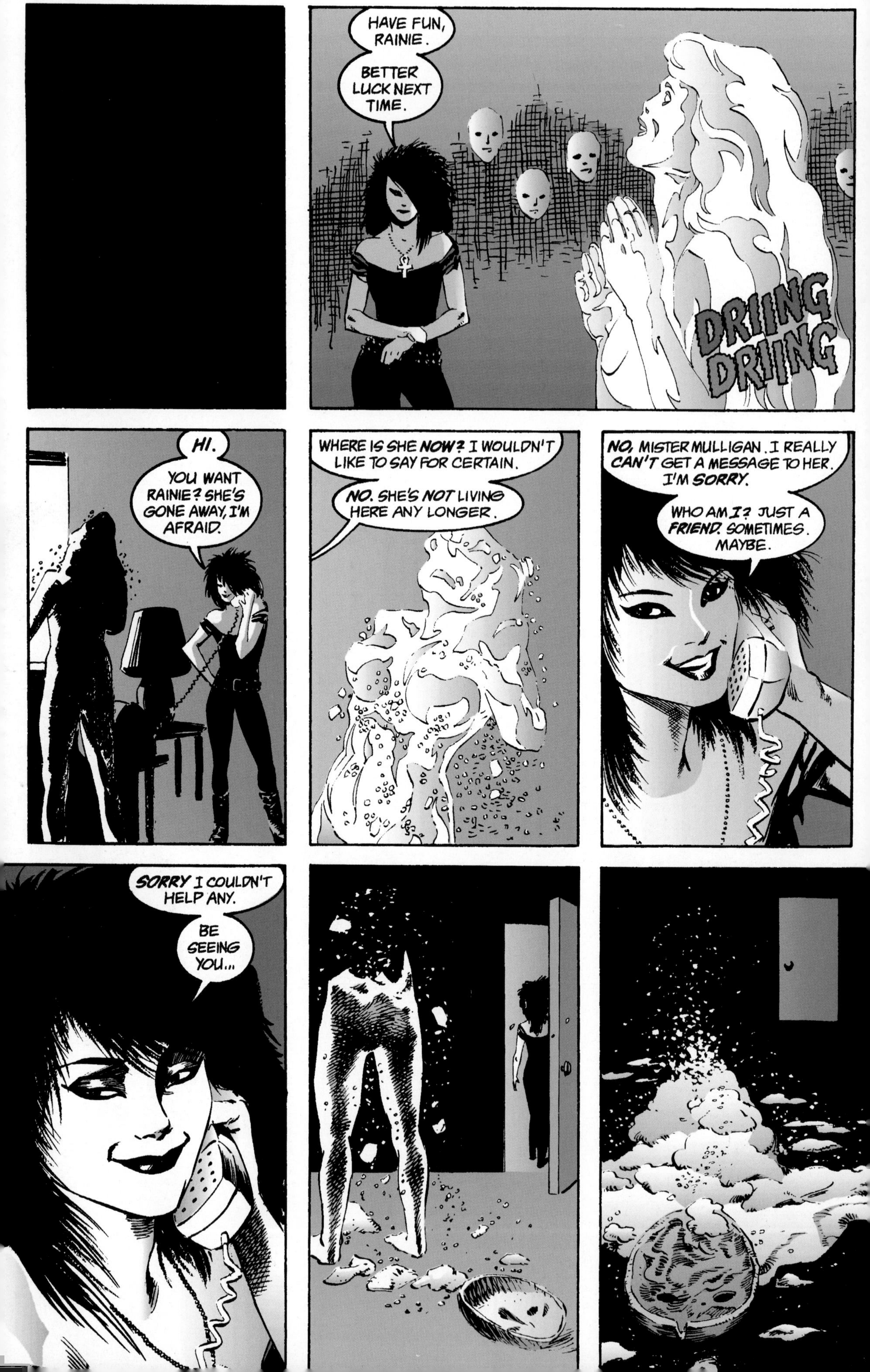
HAVE FUN, RAINIE.
BETTER LUCK NEXT TIME.
DRIING DRIING
HI.
YOU WANT RAINIE? SHE'S GONE AWAY, I'M AFRAID.
WHERE IS SHE NOW? I WOULDN'T LIKE TO SAY FOR CERTAIN.
NO. SHE'S NOT LIVING HERE ANY LONGER.
NO, MISTER MULLIGAN. I REALLY CAN'T GET A MESSAGE TO HER. I'M SORRY.
WHO AM I? JUST A FRIEND. SOMETIMES. MAYBE.
SORRY I COULDN'T HELP ANY.
BE SEEING YOU...

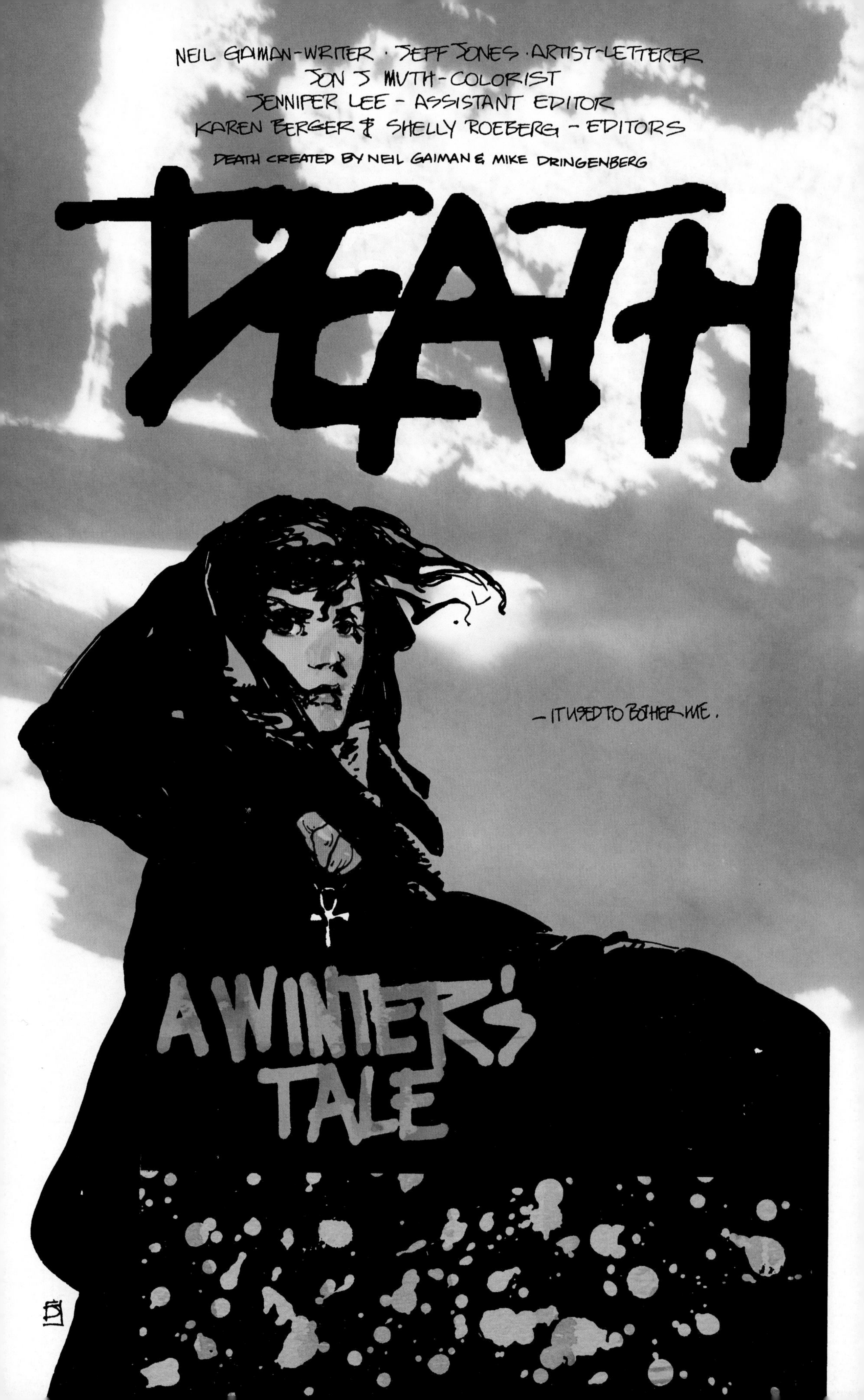
NEIL GAIMAN-WRITER · JEFF JONES · ARTIST-LETTERER
JON J MUTH-COLORIST
JENNIFER LEE - ASSISTANT EDITOR
KAREN BERGER & SHELLY ROEBERG - EDITORS
DEATH CREATED BY NEIL GAIMAN & MIKE DRINGENBERG
DEATH
- IT USED TO BOTHER ME.
A WINTER'S TALE

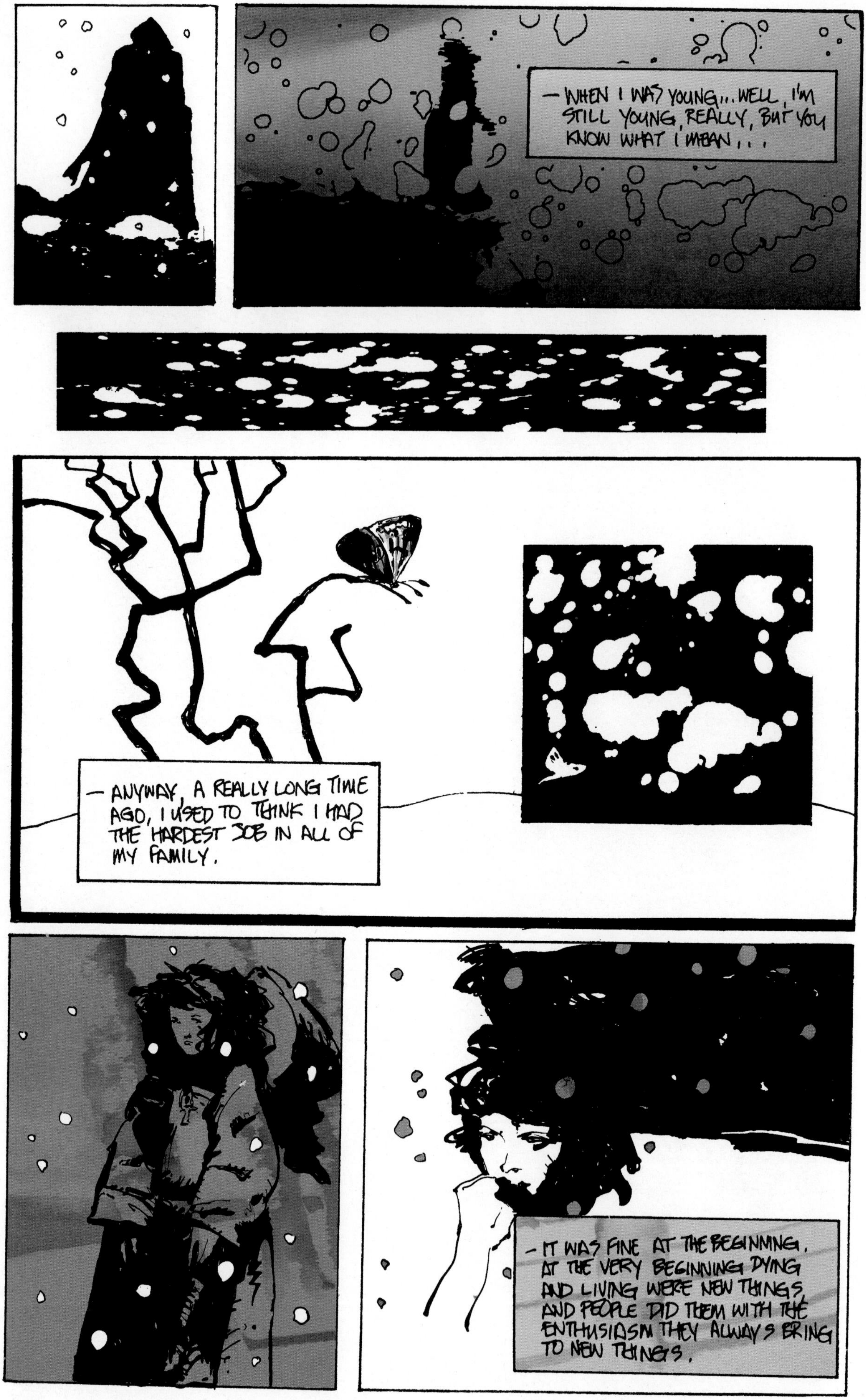
—WHEN I WAS YOUNG... WELL, I'M STILL YOUNG, REALLY, BUT YOU KNOW WHAT I MEAN...
—ANYWAY, A REALLY LONG TIME AGO, I USED TO THINK I HAD THE HARDEST JOB IN ALL OF MY FAMILY.
—IT WAS FINE AT THE BEGINNING. AT THE VERY BEGINNING DYING AND LIVING WERE NEW THINGS, AND PEOPLE DID THEM WITH THE ENTHUSIASM THEY ALWAYS BRING TO NEW THINGS.

— AND THEN, AFTER A BIT, IT GOT HARDER.

— THEY WERE PLEASED TO SEE ME, AT THE BEGINNING, AND AT THE END. THEY'D TELL ME ALL ABOUT IT, YOU KNOW. THE WHOLE LIFE THING.

— THE ONLY PEOPLE WHO GREETED ME WITH RELIEF DID SO AS AN ESCAPE FROM SOMETHING BAD OR INTOLERABLE.

— THE REST OF THEM JUST WISHED I'D GO AWAY, AS IF DYING WERE SOME KIND OF ADMISSION OF FAILURE.

— IT MADE ME SAD. YOU KNOW. I MEAN, I WAS SAD TOO MUCH OF THE TIME. I THOUGHT ABOUT GIVING IT UP — WALKING OUT.

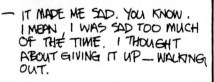

— AND ONE DAY I DID. THIS WAS STILL A LONG TIME AGO, AND LONG BEFORE THIS WORLD.

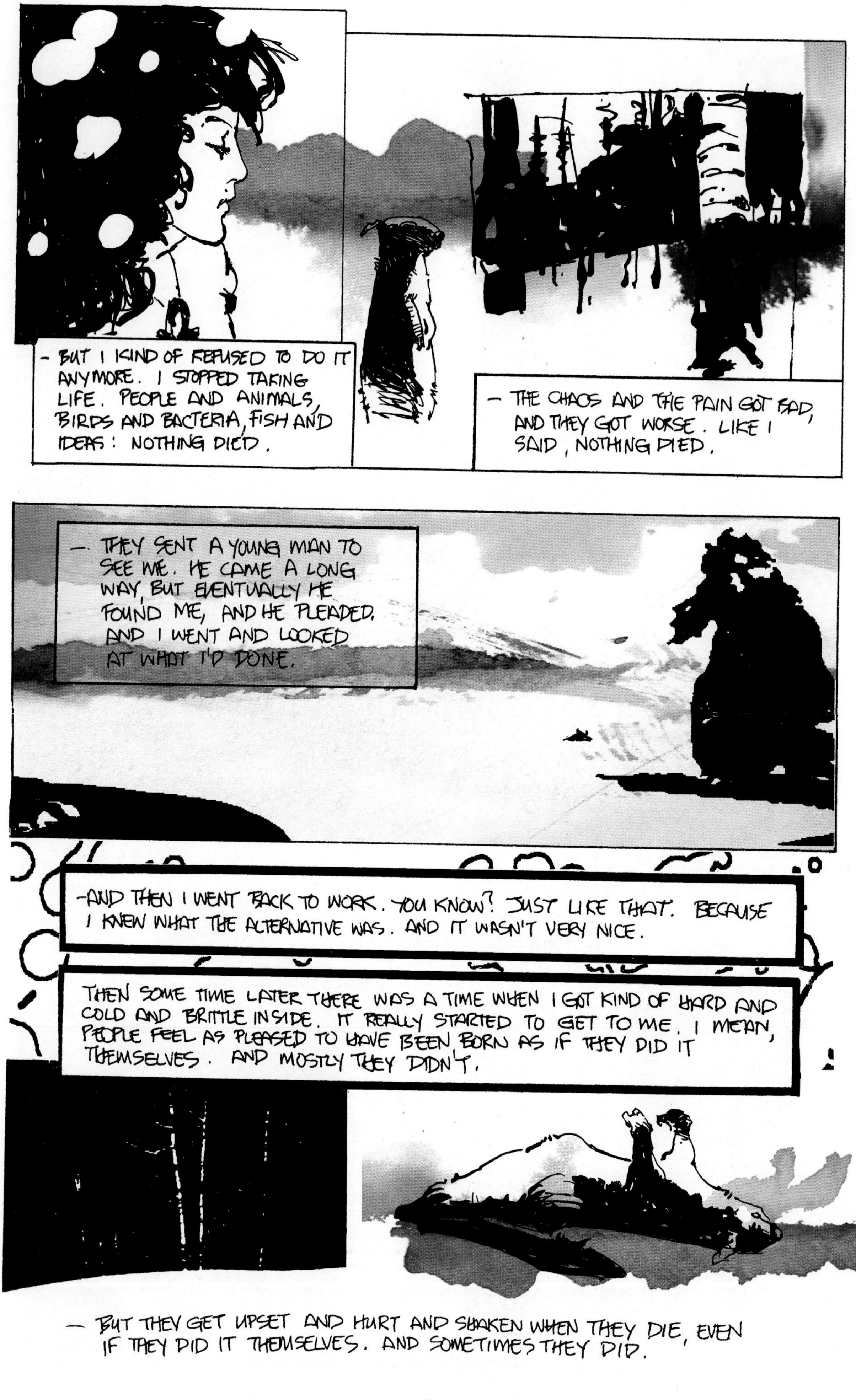

- BUT I KIND OF REFUSED TO DO IT ANYMORE. I STOPPED TAKING LIFE. PEOPLE AND ANIMALS, BIRDS AND BACTERIA, FISH AND IDEAS: NOTHING DIED.
- THE CHAOS AND THE PAIN GOT BAD, AND THEY GOT WORSE. LIKE I SAID, NOTHING DIED.
- THEY SENT A YOUNG MAN TO SEE ME. HE CAME A LONG WAY, BUT EVENTUALLY HE FOUND ME, AND HE PLEADED. AND I WENT AND LOOKED AT WHAT I'D DONE.
-AND THEN I WENT BACK TO WORK. YOU KNOW? JUST LIKE THAT. BECAUSE I KNEW WHAT THE ALTERNATIVE WAS. AND IT WASN'T VERY NICE.
THEN SOME TIME LATER THERE WAS A TIME WHEN I GOT KIND OF HARD AND COLD AND BRITTLE INSIDE. IT REALLY STARTED TO GET TO ME. I MEAN, PEOPLE FEEL AS PLEASED TO HAVE BEEN BORN AS IF THEY DID IT THEMSELVES. AND MOSTLY THEY DIDN'T.
- BUT THEY GET UPSET AND HURT AND SHAKEN WHEN THEY DIE, EVEN IF THEY DID IT THEMSELVES. AND SOMETIMES THEY DID.

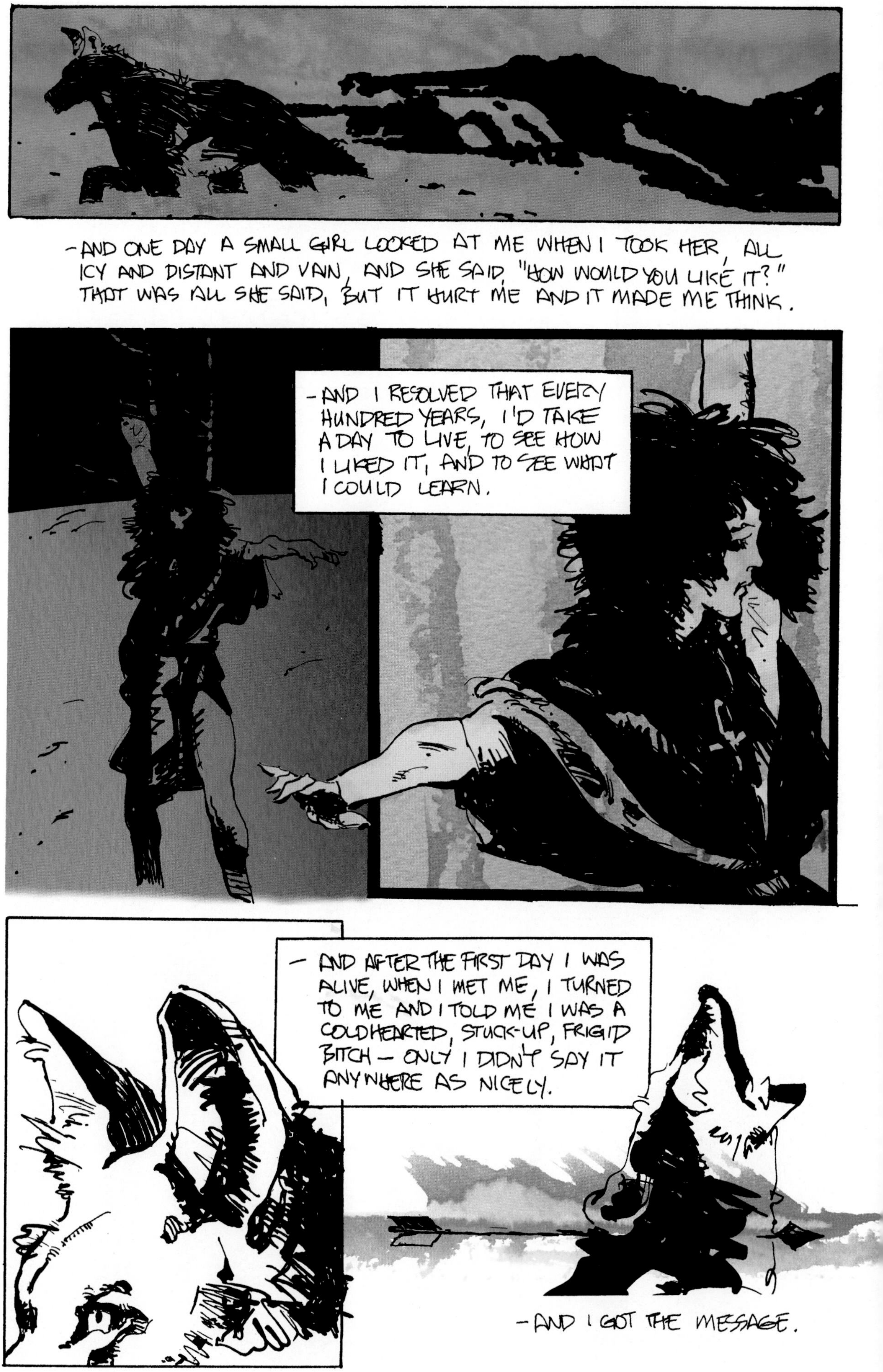
-AND ONE DAY A SMALL GIRL LOOKED AT ME WHEN I TOOK HER, ALL ICY AND DISTANT AND VAIN, AND SHE SAID, "HOW WOULD YOU LIKE IT?" THAT WAS ALL SHE SAID, BUT IT HURT ME AND IT MADE ME THINK.
-AND I RESOLVED THAT EVERY HUNDRED YEARS, I'D TAKE A DAY TO LIVE, TO SEE HOW I LIKED IT, AND TO SEE WHAT I COULD LEARN.
-AND AFTER THE FIRST DAY I WAS ALIVE, WHEN I MET ME, I TURNED TO ME AND I TOLD ME I WAS A COLDHEARTED, STUCK-UP, FRIGID BITCH -- ONLY I DIDN'T SAY IT ANYWHERE AS NICELY.
-AND I GOT THE MESSAGE.

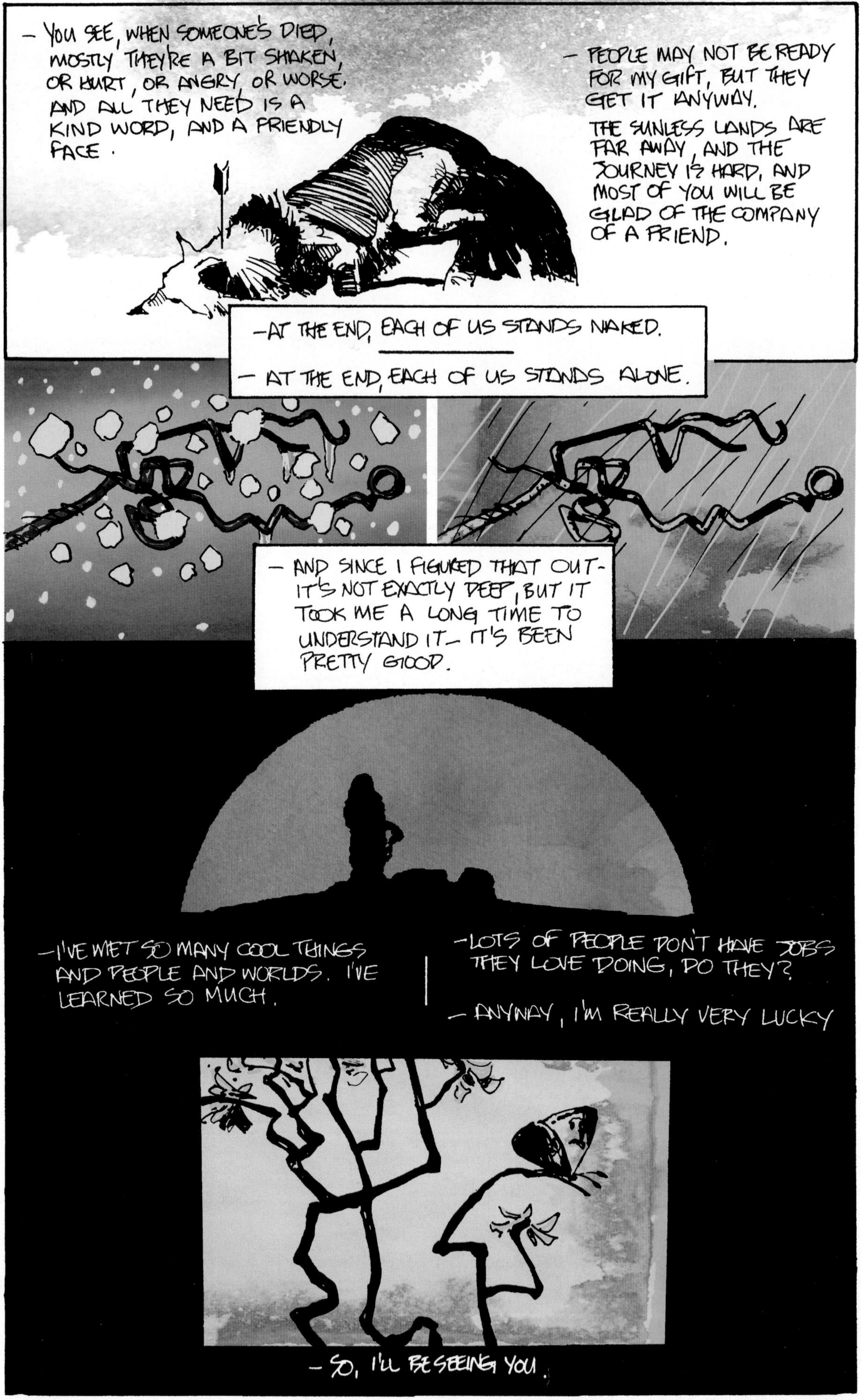

– YOU SEE, WHEN SOMEONE'S DIED, MOSTLY THEY'RE A BIT SHAKEN, OR HURT, OR ANGRY, OR WORSE. AND ALL THEY NEED IS A KIND WORD, AND A FRIENDLY FACE.
– PEOPLE MAY NOT BE READY FOR MY GIFT, BUT THEY GET IT ANYWAY.
THE SUNLESS LANDS ARE FAR AWAY, AND THE JOURNEY IS HARD, AND MOST OF YOU WILL BE GLAD OF THE COMPANY OF A FRIEND.
– AT THE END, EACH OF US STANDS NAKED.
– AT THE END, EACH OF US STANDS ALONE.
– AND SINCE I FIGURED THAT OUT – IT'S NOT EXACTLY DEEP, BUT IT TOOK ME A LONG TIME TO UNDERSTAND IT – IT'S BEEN PRETTY GOOD.
– I'VE MET SO MANY COOL THINGS AND PEOPLE AND WORLDS. I'VE LEARNED SO MUCH.
– LOTS OF PEOPLE DON'T HAVE JOBS THEY LOVE DOING, DO THEY?
– ANYWAY, I'M REALLY VERY LUCKY
– SO, I'LL BE SEEING YOU.

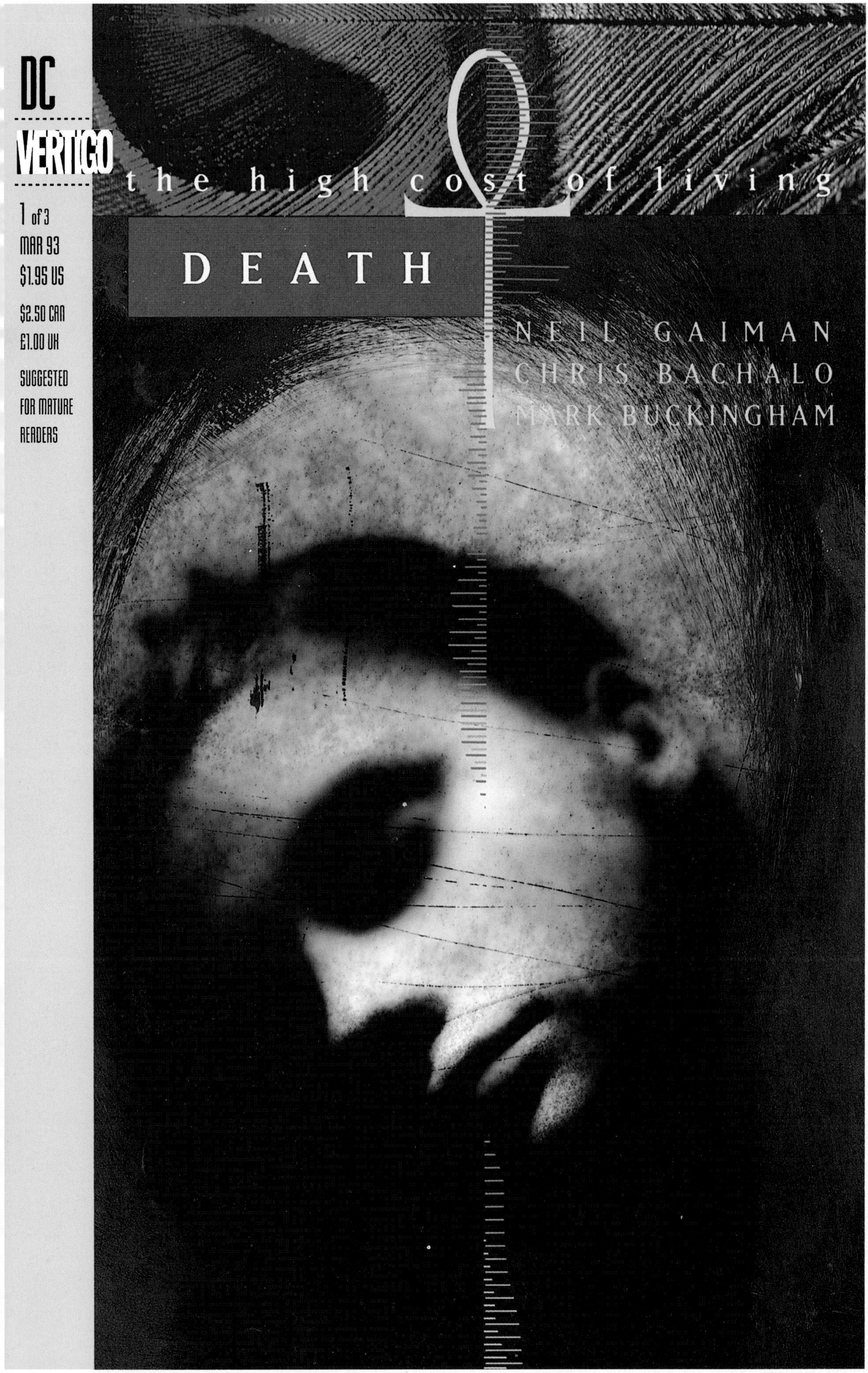
DC
VERTIGO
1 of 3
MAR 93
$1.95 US
$2.50 CAN
£1.00 UK
SUGGESTED FOR MATURE READERS
the high cost of living
DEATH
NEIL GAIMAN
CHRIS BACHALO
MARK BUCKINGHAM

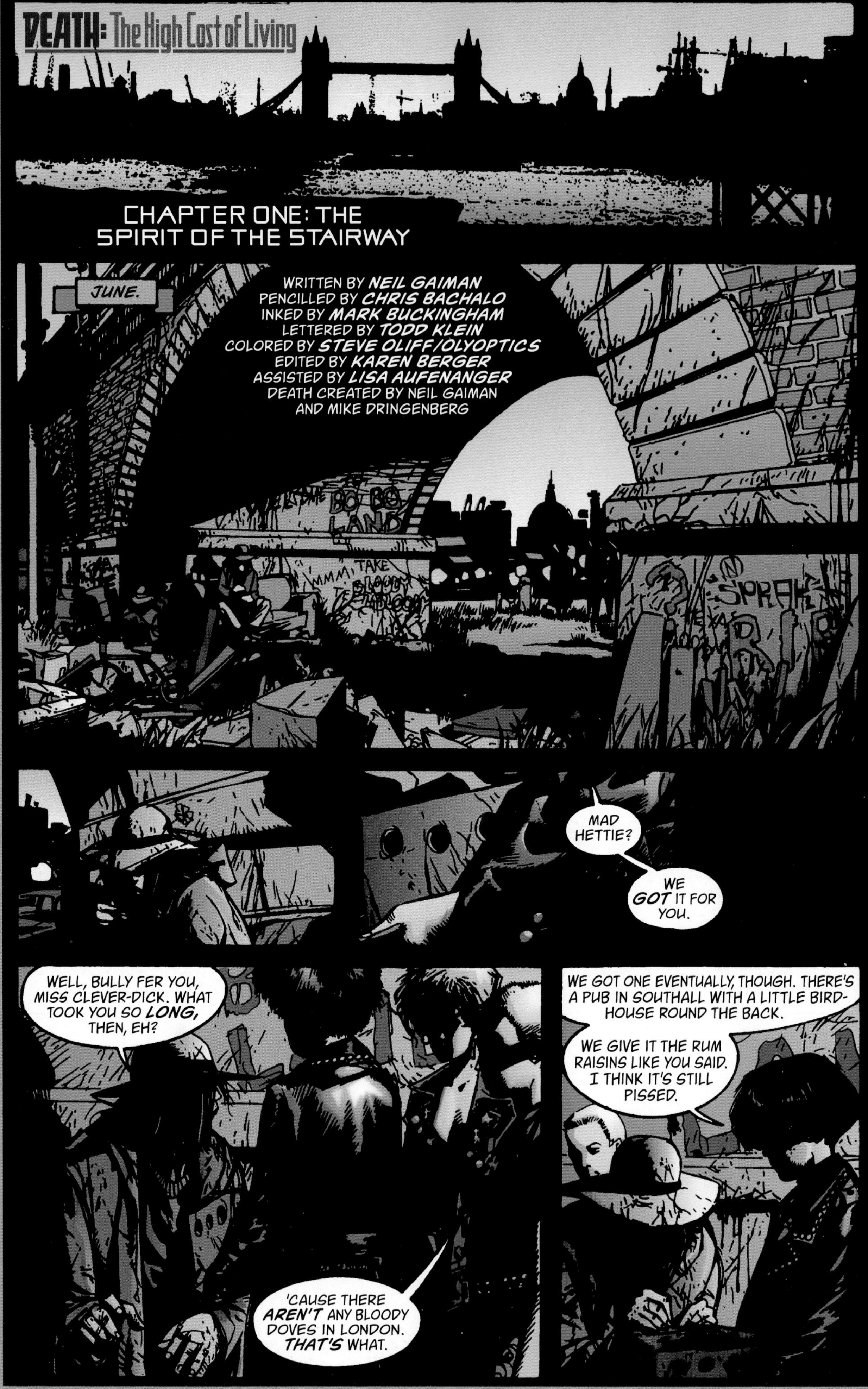

DEATH: The High Cost of Living
CHAPTER ONE: THE SPIRIT OF THE STAIRWAY
JUNE.
WRITTEN BY NEIL GAIMAN
PENCILLED BY CHRIS BACHALO
INKED BY MARK BUCKINGHAM
LETTERED BY TODD KLEIN
COLORED BY STEVE OLIFF/OLYOPTICS
EDITED BY KAREN BERGER
ASSISTED BY LISA AUFENANGER
DEATH CREATED BY NEIL GAIMAN AND MIKE DRINGENBERG
MAD HETTIE?
WE GOT IT FOR YOU.
WELL, BULLY FER YOU, MISS CLEVER-DICK. WHAT TOOK YOU SO LONG, THEN, EH?
'CAUSE THERE AREN'T ANY BLOODY DOVES IN LONDON. THAT'S WHAT.
WE GOT ONE EVENTUALLY, THOUGH. THERE'S A PUB IN SOUTHALL WITH A LITTLE BIRD-HOUSE ROUND THE BACK.
WE GIVE IT THE RUM RAISINS LIKE YOU SAID. I THINK IT'S STILL PISSED.

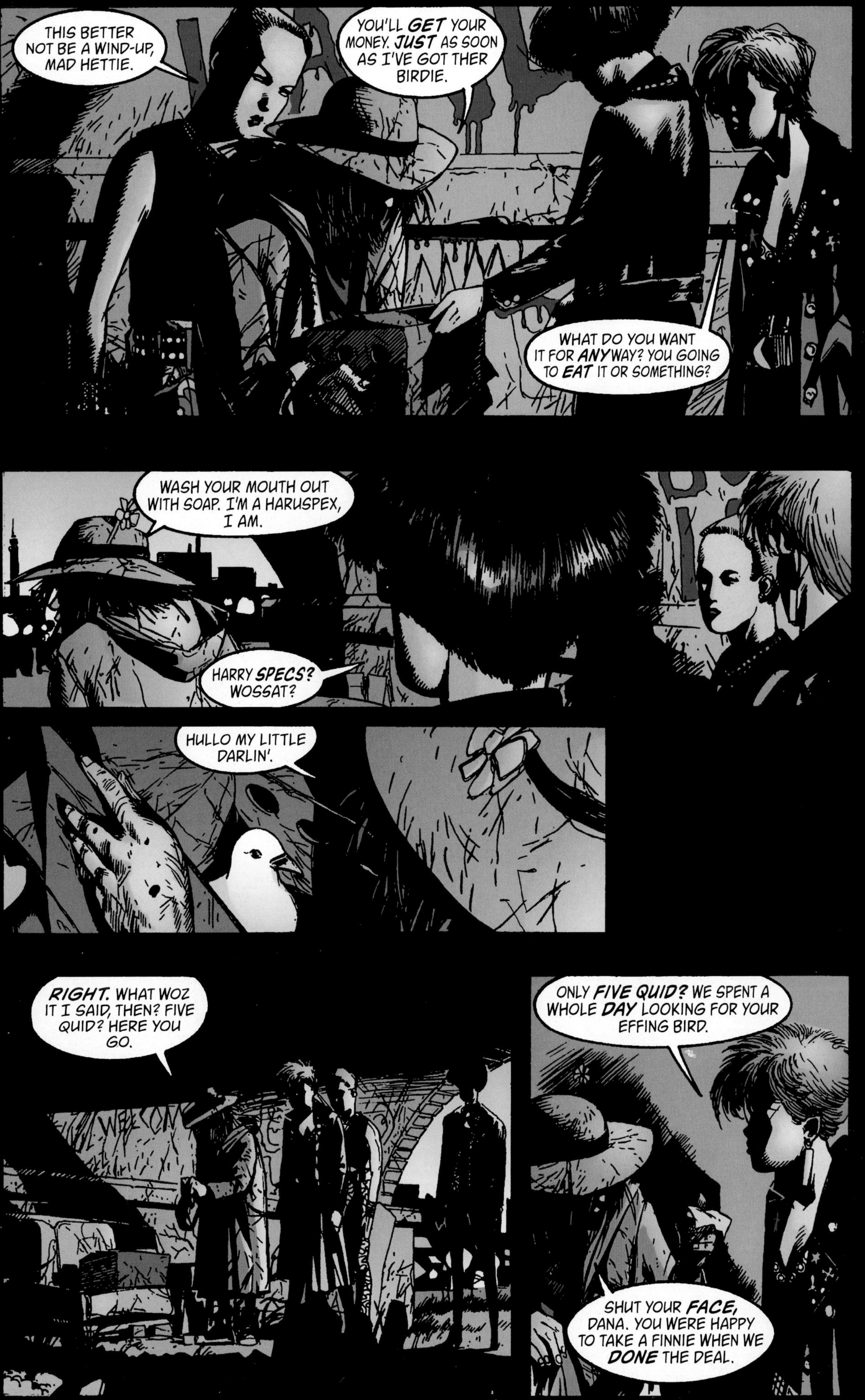

THIS BETTER NOT BE A WIND-UP, MAD HETTIE.
YOU'LL GET YOUR MONEY. JUST AS SOON AS I'VE GOT THER BIRDIE.
WHAT DO YOU WANT IT FOR ANYWAY? YOU GOING TO EAT IT OR SOMETHING?
WASH YOUR MOUTH OUT WITH SOAP. I'M A HARUSPEX, I AM.
HARRY SPECS? WOSSAT?
HULLO MY LITTLE DARLIN'.
RIGHT. WHAT WOZ IT I SAID, THEN? FIVE QUID? HERE YOU GO.
ONLY FIVE QUID? WE SPENT A WHOLE DAY LOOKING FOR YOUR EFFING BIRD.
SHUT YOUR FACE, DANA. YOU WERE HAPPY TO TAKE A FINNIE WHEN WE DONE THE DEAL.

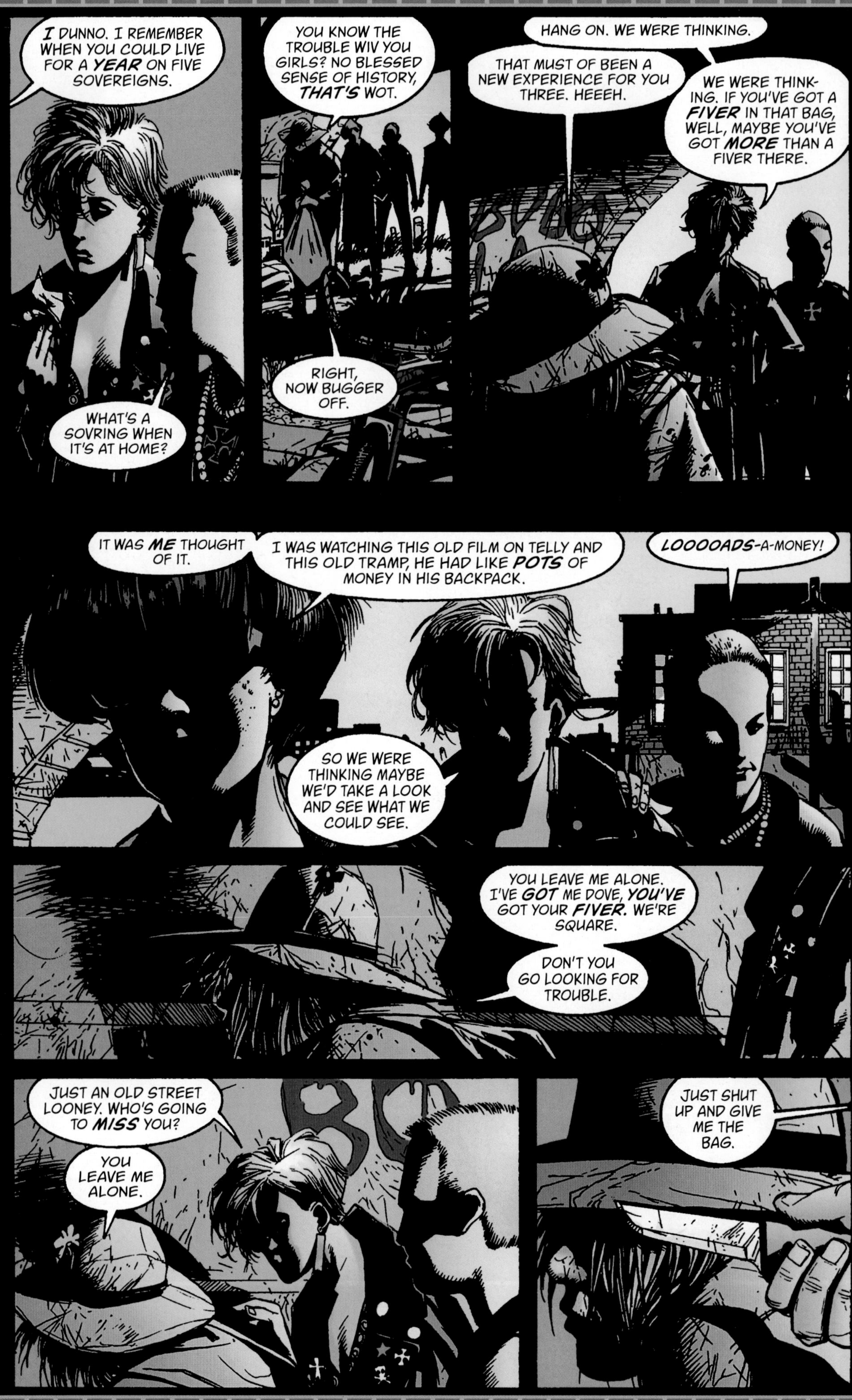
I DUNNO. I REMEMBER WHEN YOU COULD LIVE FOR A YEAR ON FIVE SOVEREIGNS.
WHAT'S A SOVRING WHEN IT'S AT HOME?
YOU KNOW THE TROUBLE WIV YOU GIRLS? NO BLESSED SENSE OF HISTORY, THAT'S WOT.
RIGHT, NOW BUGGER OFF.
HANG ON. WE WERE THINKING.
THAT MUST OF BEEN A NEW EXPERIENCE FOR YOU THREE. HEEEH.
WE WERE THINKING. IF YOU'VE GOT A FIVER IN THAT BAG, WELL, MAYBE YOU'VE GOT MORE THAN A FIVER THERE.
IT WAS ME THOUGHT OF IT.
I WAS WATCHING THIS OLD FILM ON TELLY AND THIS OLD TRAMP, HE HAD LIKE POTS OF MONEY IN HIS BACKPACK.
LOOOOADS-A-MONEY!
SO WE WERE THINKING MAYBE WE'D TAKE A LOOK AND SEE WHAT WE COULD SEE.
YOU LEAVE ME ALONE. I'VE GOT ME DOVE, YOU'VE GOT YOUR FIVER. WE'RE SQUARE.
DON'T YOU GO LOOKING FOR TROUBLE.
JUST AN OLD STREET LOONEY. WHO'S GOING TO MISS YOU?
YOU LEAVE ME ALONE.
JUST SHUT UP AND GIVE ME THE BAG.

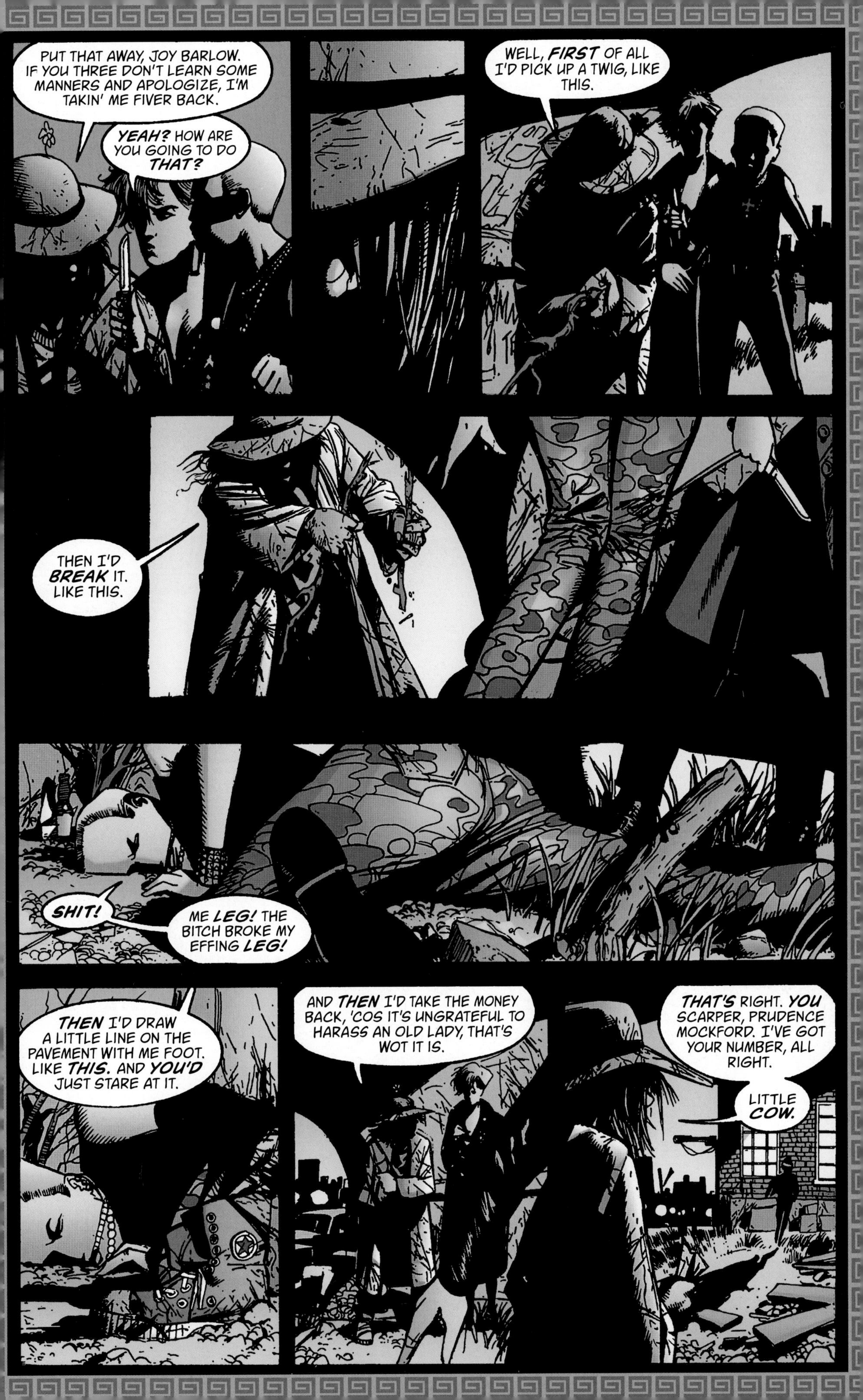
PUT THAT AWAY, JOY BARLOW. IF YOU THREE DON'T LEARN SOME MANNERS AND APOLOGIZE, I'M TAKIN' ME FIVER BACK.
YEAH? HOW ARE YOU GOING TO DO THAT?
WELL, FIRST OF ALL I'D PICK UP A TWIG, LIKE THIS.
THEN I'D BREAK IT. LIKE THIS.
SHIT!
ME LEG! THE BITCH BROKE MY EFFING LEG!
THEN I'D DRAW A LITTLE LINE ON THE PAVEMENT WITH ME FOOT. LIKE THIS. AND YOU'D JUST STARE AT IT.
AND THEN I'D TAKE THE MONEY BACK, 'COS IT'S UNGRATEFUL TO HARASS AN OLD LADY, THAT'S WOT IT IS.
THAT'S RIGHT. YOU SCARPER, PRUDENCE MOCKFORD. I'VE GOT YOUR NUMBER, ALL RIGHT.
LITTLE COW.

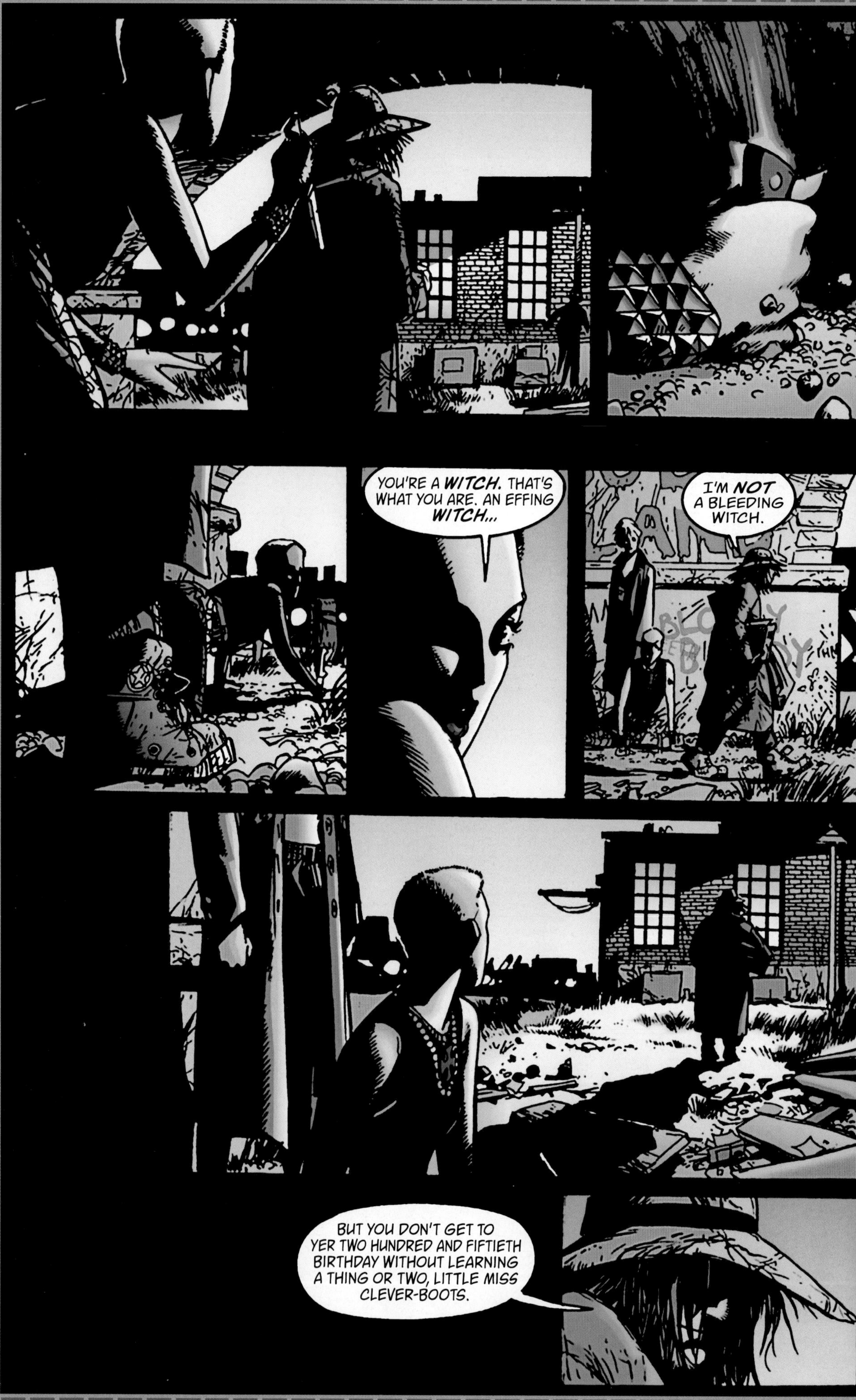
YOU'RE A WITCH. THAT'S WHAT YOU ARE. AN EFFING WITCH...
I'M NOT A BLEEDING WITCH.
BUT YOU DON'T GET TO YER TWO HUNDRED AND FIFTIETH BIRTHDAY WITHOUT LEARNING A THING OR TWO, LITTLE MISS CLEVER-BOOTS.

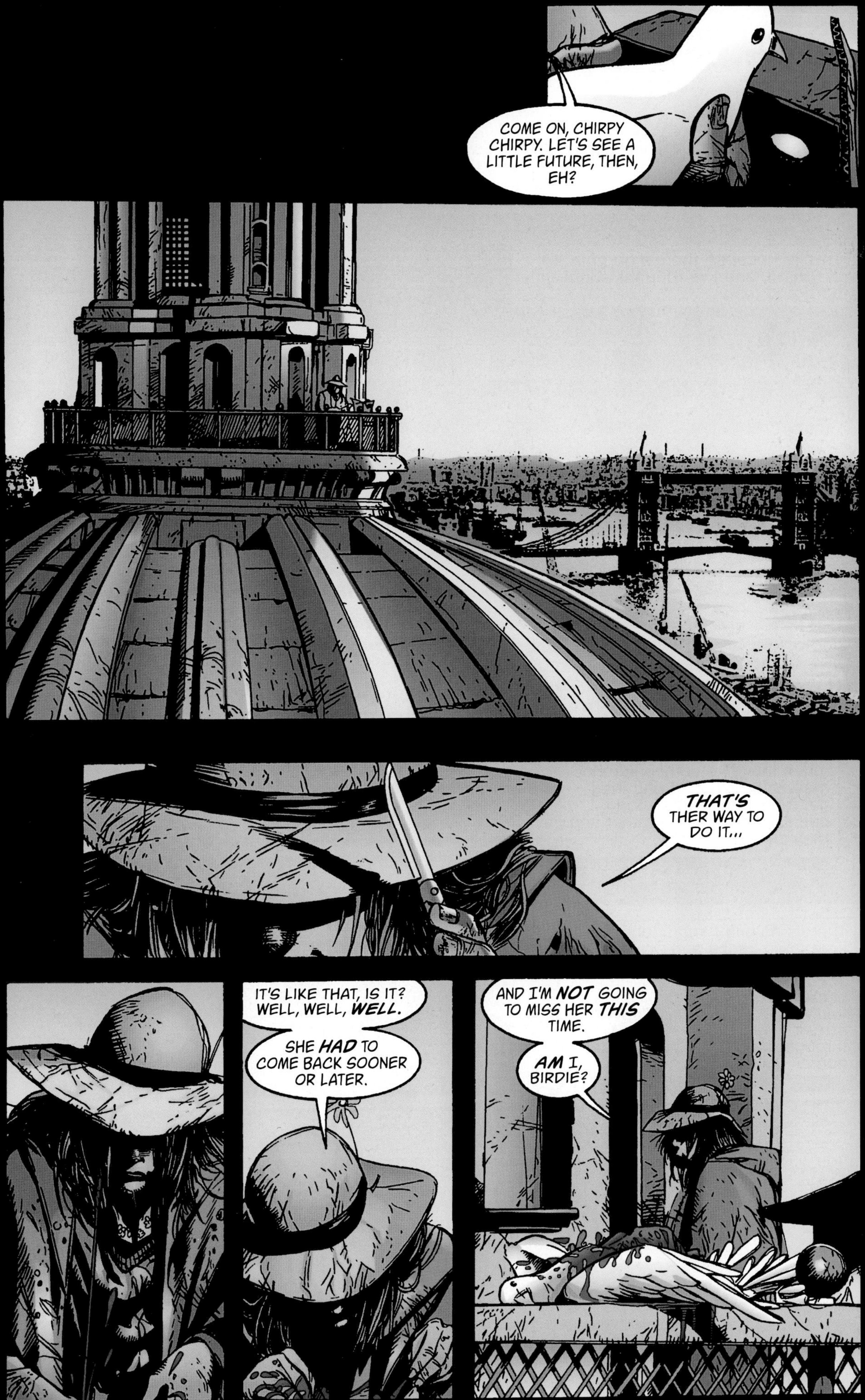
COME ON, CHIRPY CHIRPY. LET'S SEE A LITTLE FUTURE, THEN, EH?
THAT'S THER WAY TO DO IT...
IT'S LIKE THAT, IS IT? WELL, WELL, WELL.
SHE HAD TO COME BACK SOONER OR LATER.
AND I'M NOT GOING TO MISS HER THIS TIME.
AM I, BIRDIE?

My name is Sexton Furnival, but I'm pretty much used to it by now, and this is the last thing I'm ever going to write.

This is because there's no point to anything, and I've thought about this hard and long.

Okay. I figure, I'm mature. I know my own mind. I'm sixteen —almost sixteen and a half. And what have I got to show for it?

For a start I don't have anybody I'm in love with.

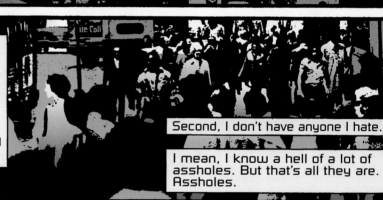

To be honest, I think love is complete bullshit. I don't think anyone ever loves anyone. I think the best people ever get is horny; horny and scared, so when they find someone who makes them horny, and they get too scared of the world outside, they stay together and they call it love.

Second, I don't have anyone I hate.

I mean, I know a hell of a lot of assholes. But that's all they are. Assholes.

There's no one I know who's evil. I mean, in books and movies you get the bad guy, and you know immediately who the bad guy is because, well, he's bad. And you've got the good guy and it doesn't matter what he goes through, he knows who the bad guy is.

And I don't even have a faithful sidekick.

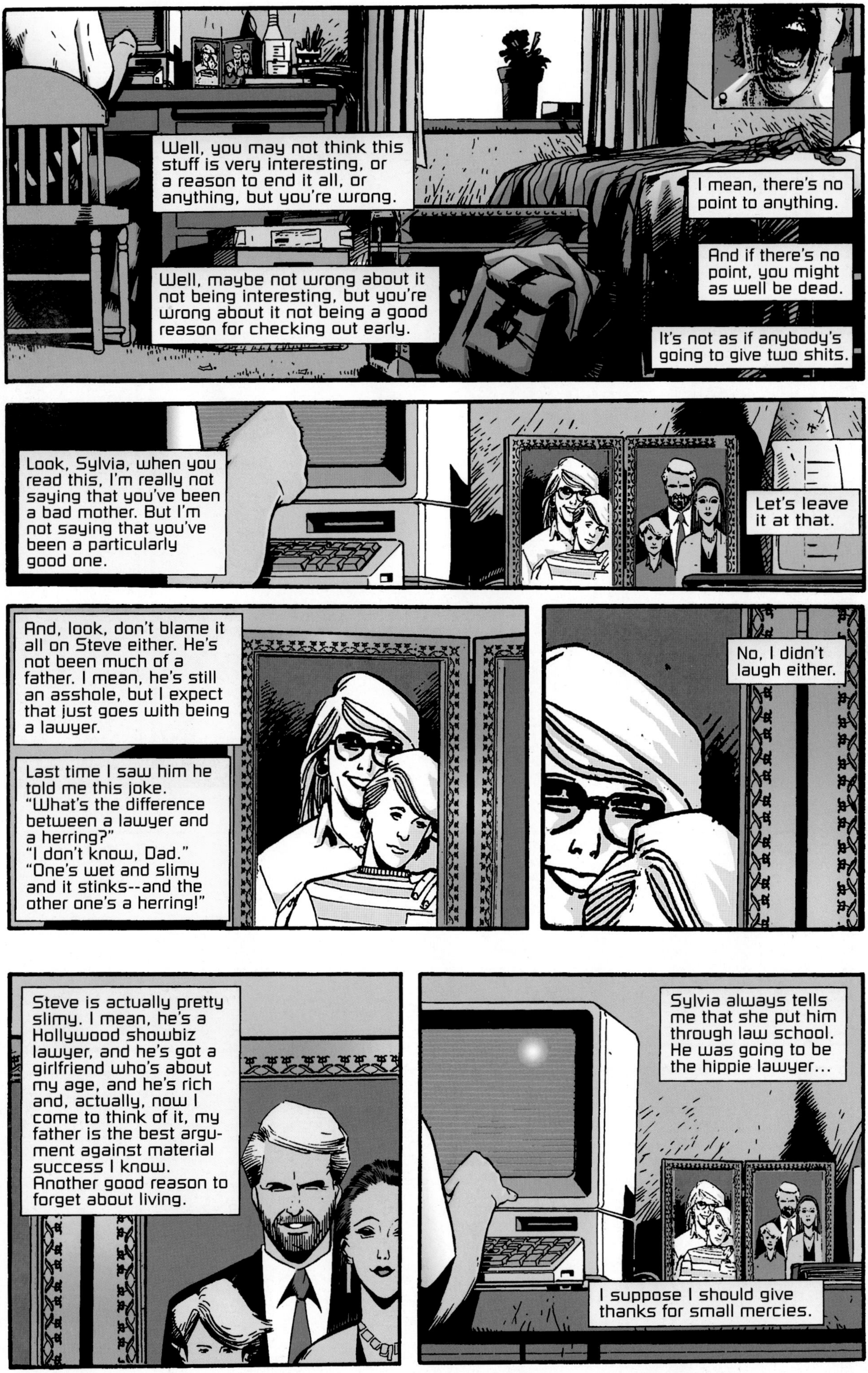

Well, you may not think this stuff is very interesting, or a reason to end it all, or anything, but you're wrong.
Well, maybe not wrong about it not being interesting, but you're wrong about it not being a good reason for checking out early.
I mean, there's no point to anything.
And if there's no point, you might as well be dead.
It's not as if anybody's going to give two shits.
Look, Sylvia, when you read this, I'm really not saying that you've been a bad mother. But I'm not saying that you've been a particularly good one.
Let's leave it at that.
And, look, don't blame it all on Steve either. He's not been much of a father. I mean, he's still an asshole, but I expect that just goes with being a lawyer.
Last time I saw him he told me this joke. "What's the difference between a lawyer and a herring?" "I don't know, Dad." "One's wet and slimy and it stinks--and the other one's a herring!"
No, I didn't laugh either.
Steve is actually pretty slimy. I mean, he's a Hollywood showbiz lawyer, and he's got a girlfriend who's about my age, and he's rich and, actually, now I come to think of it, my father is the best argument against material success I know. Another good reason to forget about living.
Sylvia always tells me that she put him through law school. He was going to be the hippie lawyer...
I suppose I should give thanks for small mercies.

I read somewhere that suicide notes are a cry for help. Well, not this one.

This one's a statement of belief. Or of disbelief. Because there's nothing in the way of adult bullshit I do believe.

Which is another thing I'm different from my mom on, because she believes in everything. I mean, it changes every week, but I figure by now she must have believed in everything.

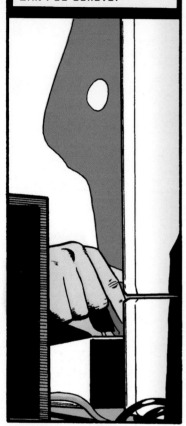 

SEXTON? EVERYTHING OKAY?

HI, MOM. SHOULDN'T YOU BE AT THE RESTAURANT TODAY?

NOPE. I GAVE MYSELF A DAY OFF. WE MADE MARLON PERMANENT CHEF YESTERDAY, SO I FIGURED IT'D BE GOOD TO STAY OUT OF THE **WAY** FOR A DAY.

WHAT'RE YOU DOING?

HOMEWORK.

YOU **WANT** ANYTHING? A **COKE** OR ANYTHING?

NOPE.

That's the other thing. I don't **want** anything.

So I might as **well** be dead. Right?

YOU **REALLY** OUGHT TO TALK TO THEM. EVERYBODY **KNOWS** THAT PLANTS LIKE TO BE TALKED TO.

SYLVIA, WHAT PLANTS LIKE IS **WATER**.

WHEN I WAS A KID YOU'D BUY PLANTS EVERY MONTH. THREE WEEKS LATER I'D WALK AROUND, EVERYTHING WOULD BE BROWN AND DEAD AND I'D GO ROUND AND THROW EVERYTHING OUT. THEN THE NEXT WEEK YOU'D BUY NEW PLANTS AND START AGAIN.

I'M **SURE** IT WASN'T LIKE THAT, DARLING. **PLANTS** ARE OUR LITTLE GREEN **SIS-TERS**.

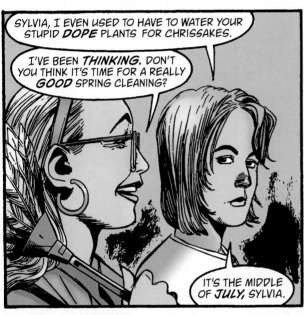

SYLVIA, I EVEN USED TO HAVE TO WATER YOUR STUPID **DOPE** PLANTS FOR CHRISSAKES.

I'VE BEEN **THINKING**. DON'T YOU THINK IT'S TIME FOR A REALLY **GOOD** SPRING CLEANING?

IT'S THE MIDDLE OF **JULY**, SYLVIA.

SPRING CLEANING. I MEAN, JUST **LOOK** AT THIS APARTMENT. IT STINKS.

OH NO.

I THINK MAYBE YOU SHOULD GO **OUT** FOR THE REST OF THE AFTERNOON.

I'M IN **EARTH MOTHER** MODE. THESE LITTLE FINGERS **ITCH** TO CREATE. LIKE THE MOLE AT THE BEGINNING OF WIND IN THE WILLOWS.

HOLD ON. I GOTTA SAVE THIS FIRST.

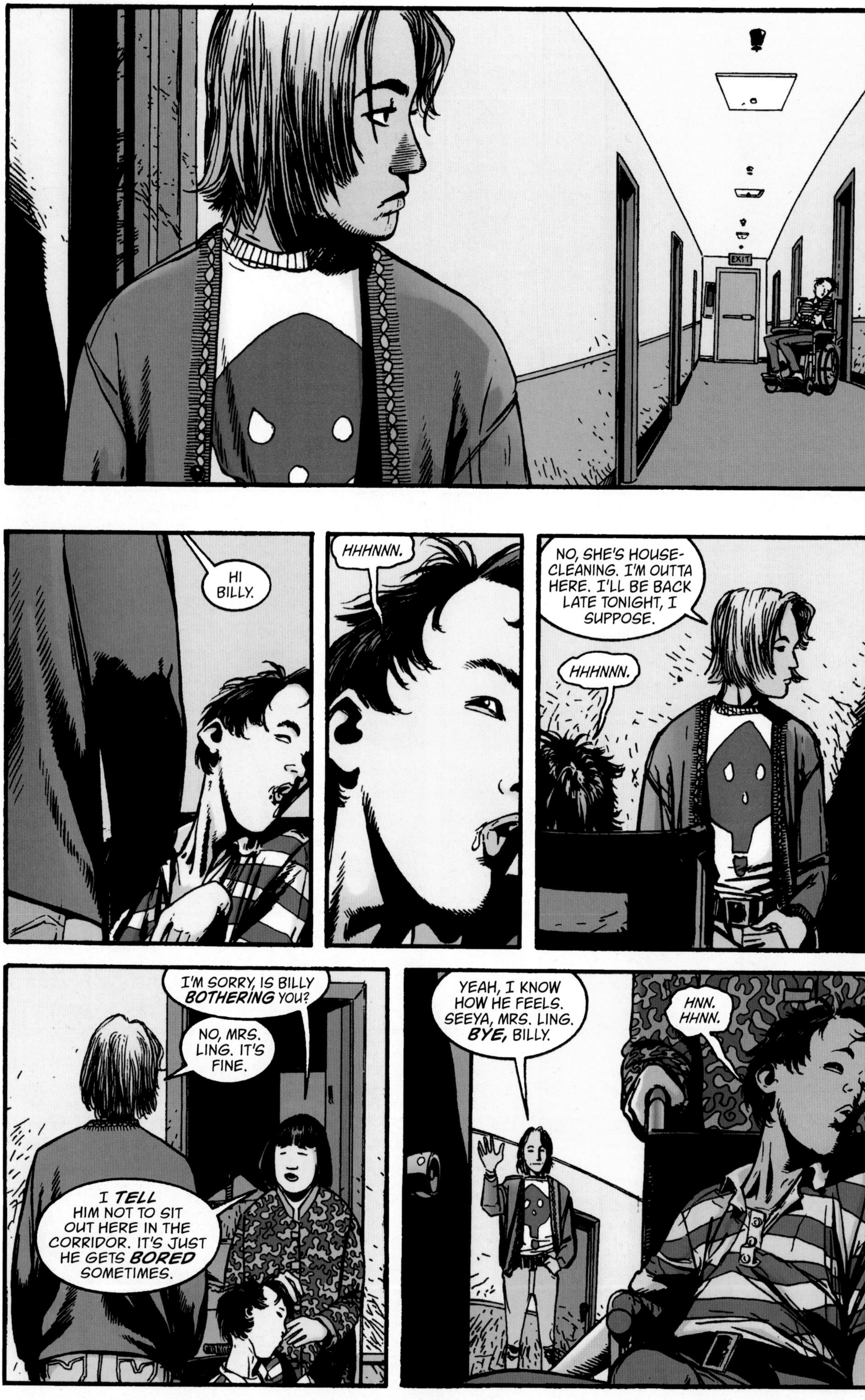

HI BILLY.
HHHNNN.
NO, SHE'S HOUSE-CLEANING. I'M OUTTA HERE. I'LL BE BACK LATE TONIGHT, I SUPPOSE.
HHHNNN.
I'M SORRY, IS BILLY **BOTHERING** YOU?
NO, MRS. LING. IT'S FINE.
I **TELL** HIM NOT TO SIT OUT HERE IN THE CORRIDOR. IT'S JUST HE GETS **BORED** SOMETIMES.
YEAH, I KNOW HOW HE FEELS. SEEYA, MRS. LING. **BYE,** BILLY.
HNN. HHNN.

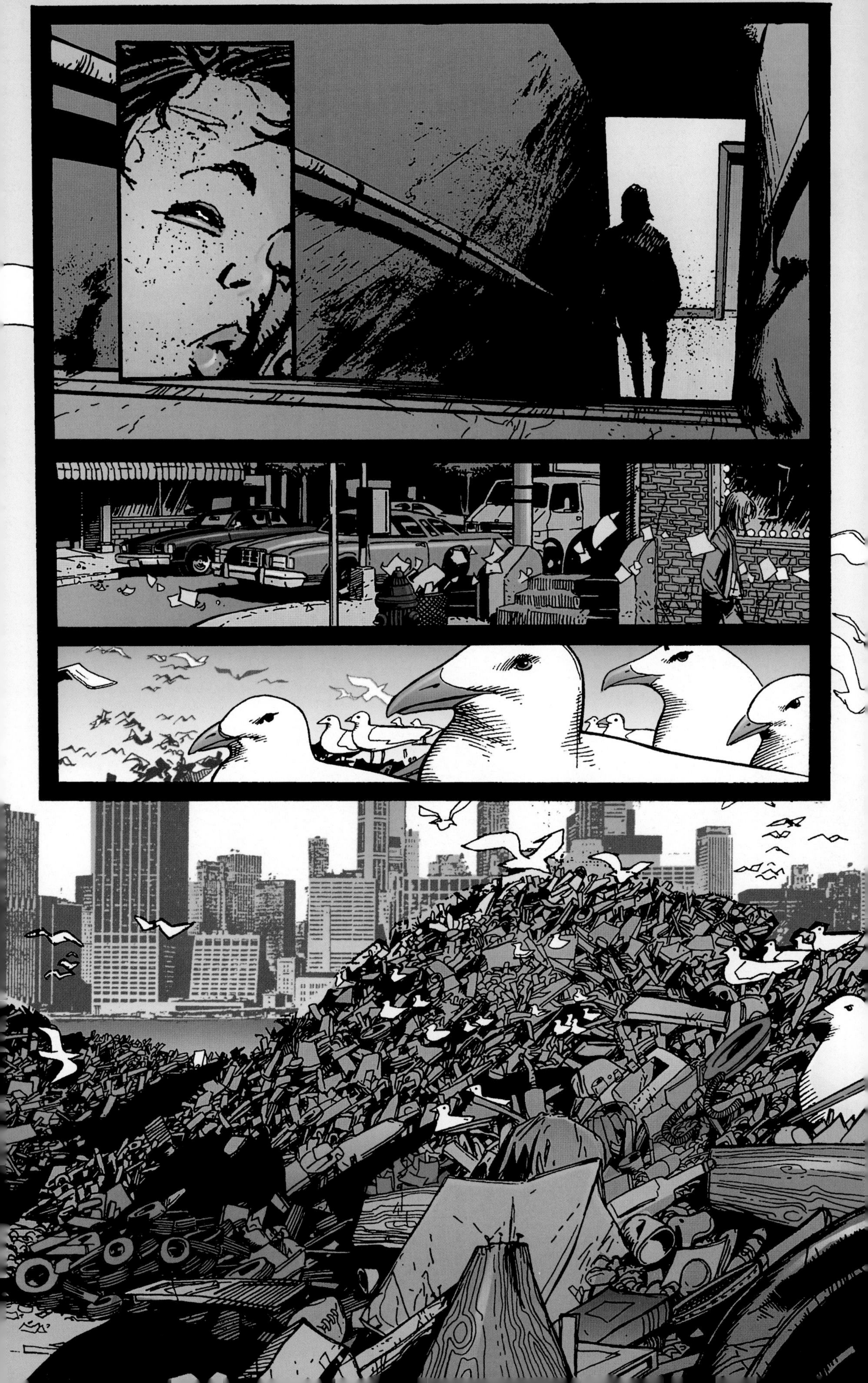

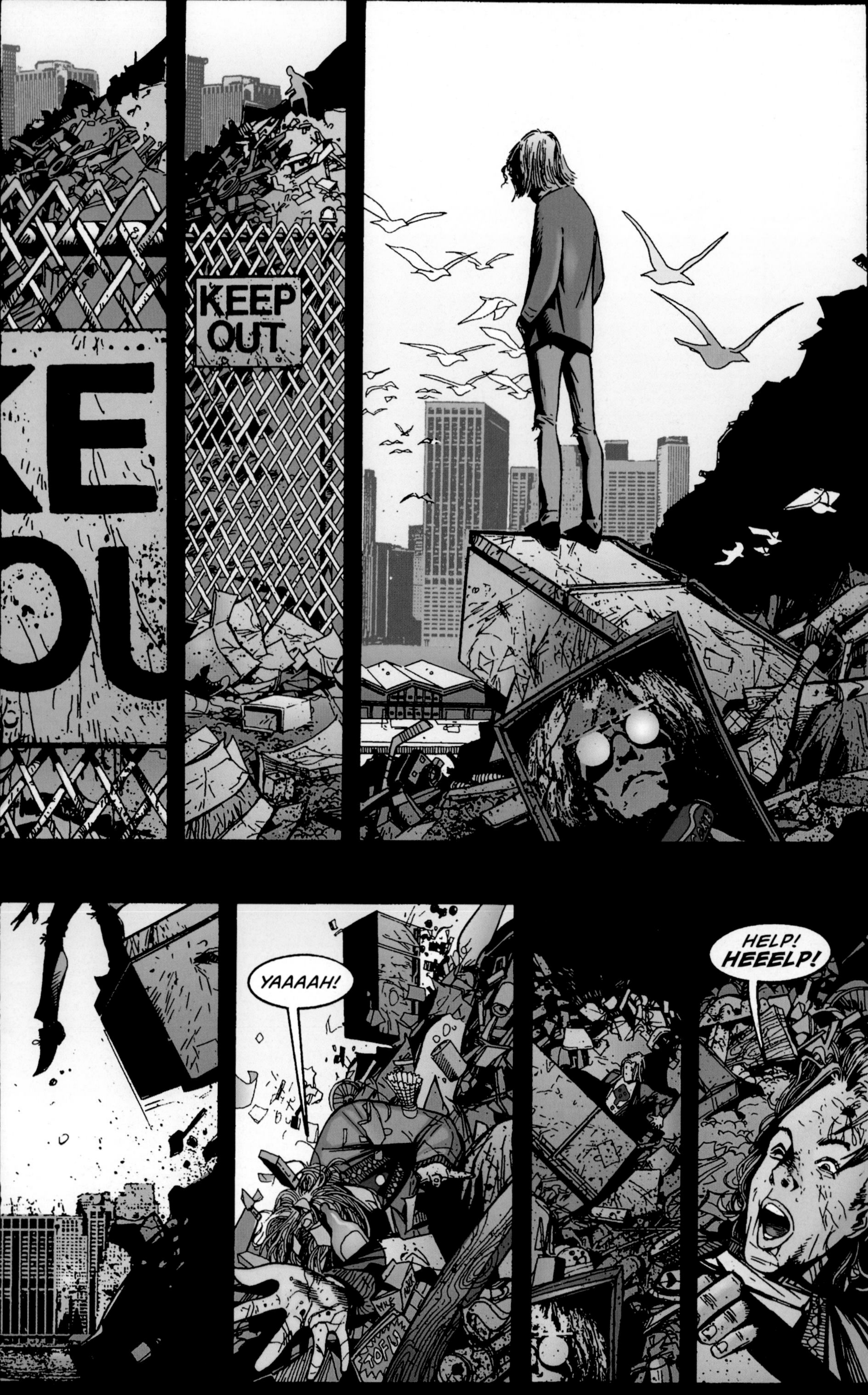
KEEP
OUT
YAAAAH!
HELP!
HEEELP!

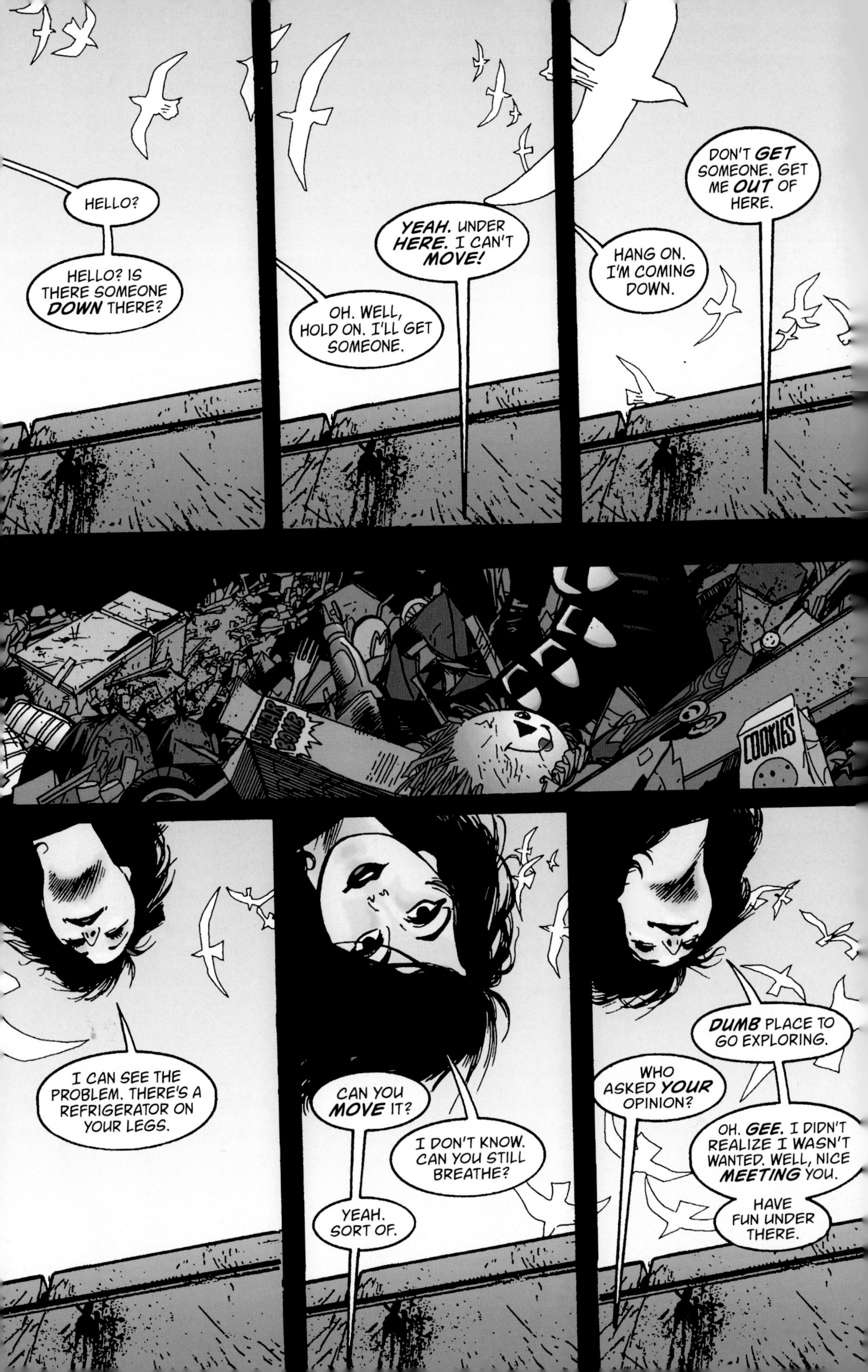
HELLO?
HELLO? IS THERE SOMEONE DOWN THERE?
YEAH. UNDER HERE. I CAN'T MOVE!
OH. WELL, HOLD ON. I'LL GET SOMEONE.
DON'T GET SOMEONE. GET ME OUT OF HERE.
HANG ON. I'M COMING DOWN.
SUGAR BOMB
COOKIES
I CAN SEE THE PROBLEM. THERE'S A REFRIGERATOR ON YOUR LEGS.
CAN YOU MOVE IT?
I DON'T KNOW. CAN YOU STILL BREATHE?
YEAH. SORT OF.
DUMB PLACE TO GO EXPLORING.
WHO ASKED YOUR OPINION?
OH. GEE. I DIDN'T REALIZE I WASN'T WANTED. WELL, NICE MEETING YOU.
HAVE FUN UNDER THERE.

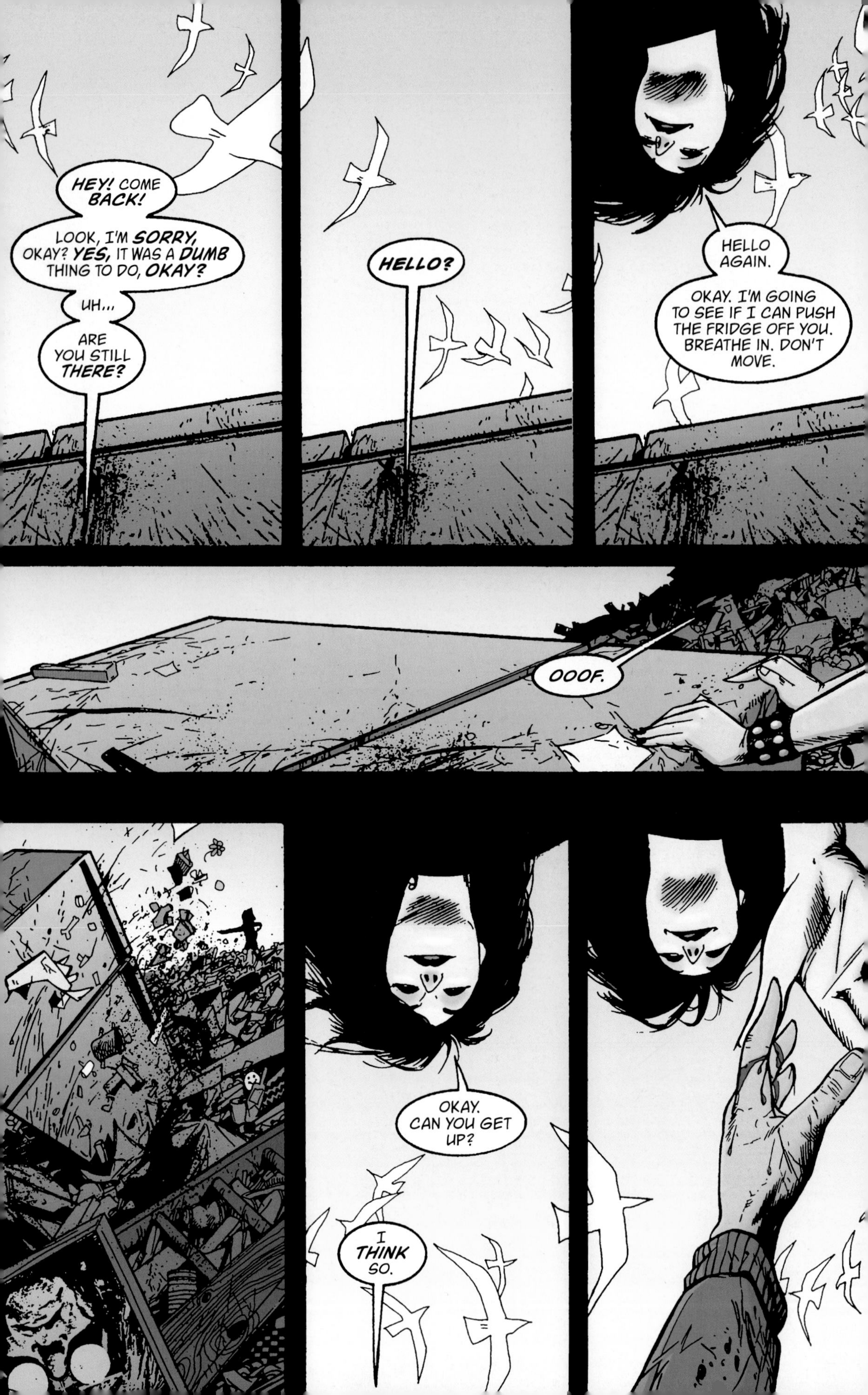
HEY! COME BACK!
LOOK, I'M SORRY, OKAY? YES, IT WAS A DUMB THING TO DO, OKAY?
UH...
ARE YOU STILL THERE?
HELLO?
HELLO AGAIN.
OKAY. I'M GOING TO SEE IF I CAN PUSH THE FRIDGE OFF YOU. BREATHE IN. DON'T MOVE.
OOOF.
OKAY. CAN YOU GET UP?
I THINK SO.

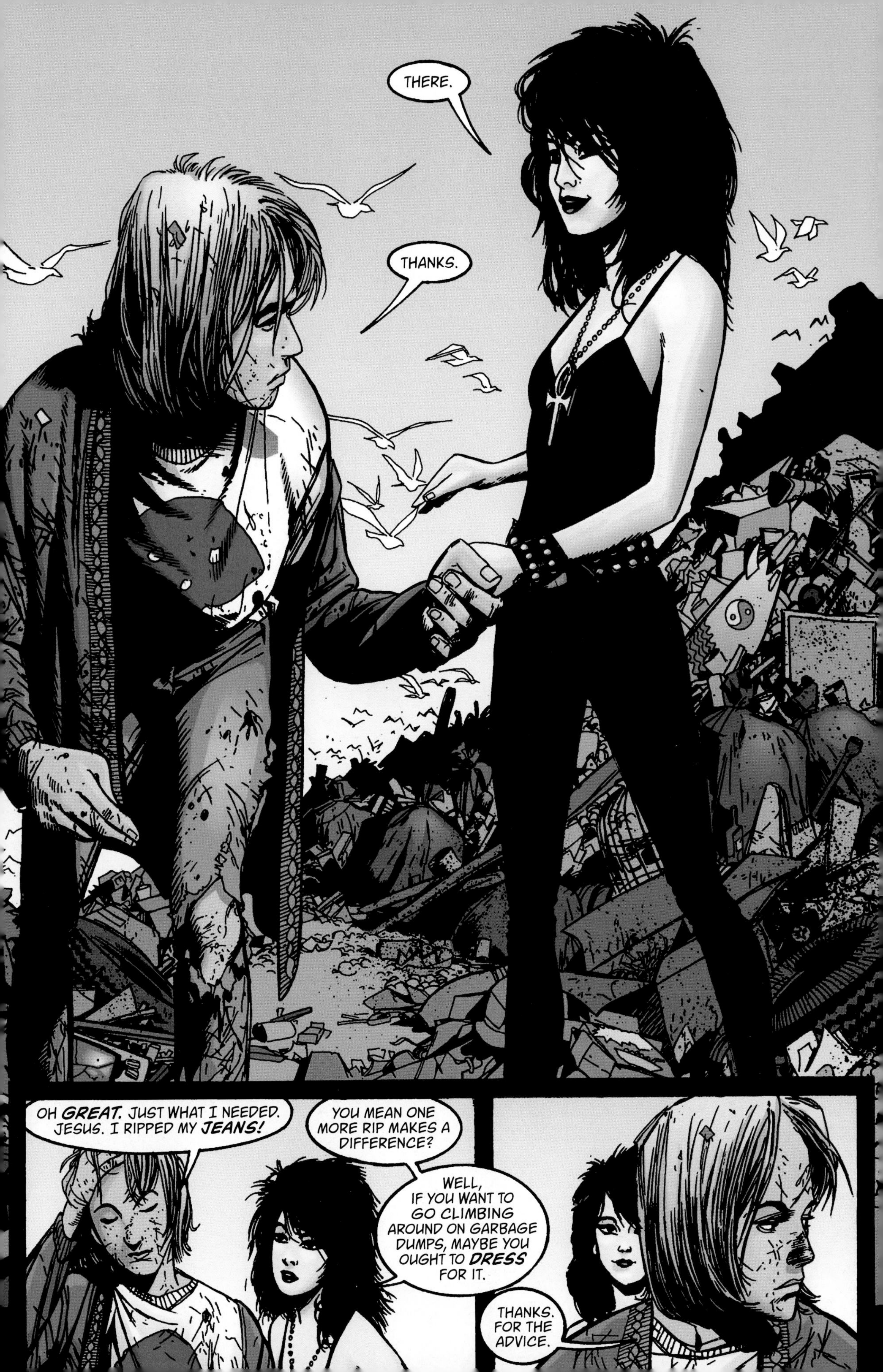
THERE.
THANKS.
OH GREAT. JUST WHAT I NEEDED. JESUS. I RIPPED MY JEANS!
YOU MEAN ONE MORE RIP MAKES A DIFFERENCE?
WELL, IF YOU WANT TO GO CLIMBING AROUND ON GARBAGE DUMPS, MAYBE YOU OUGHT TO DRESS FOR IT.
THANKS. FOR THE ADVICE.

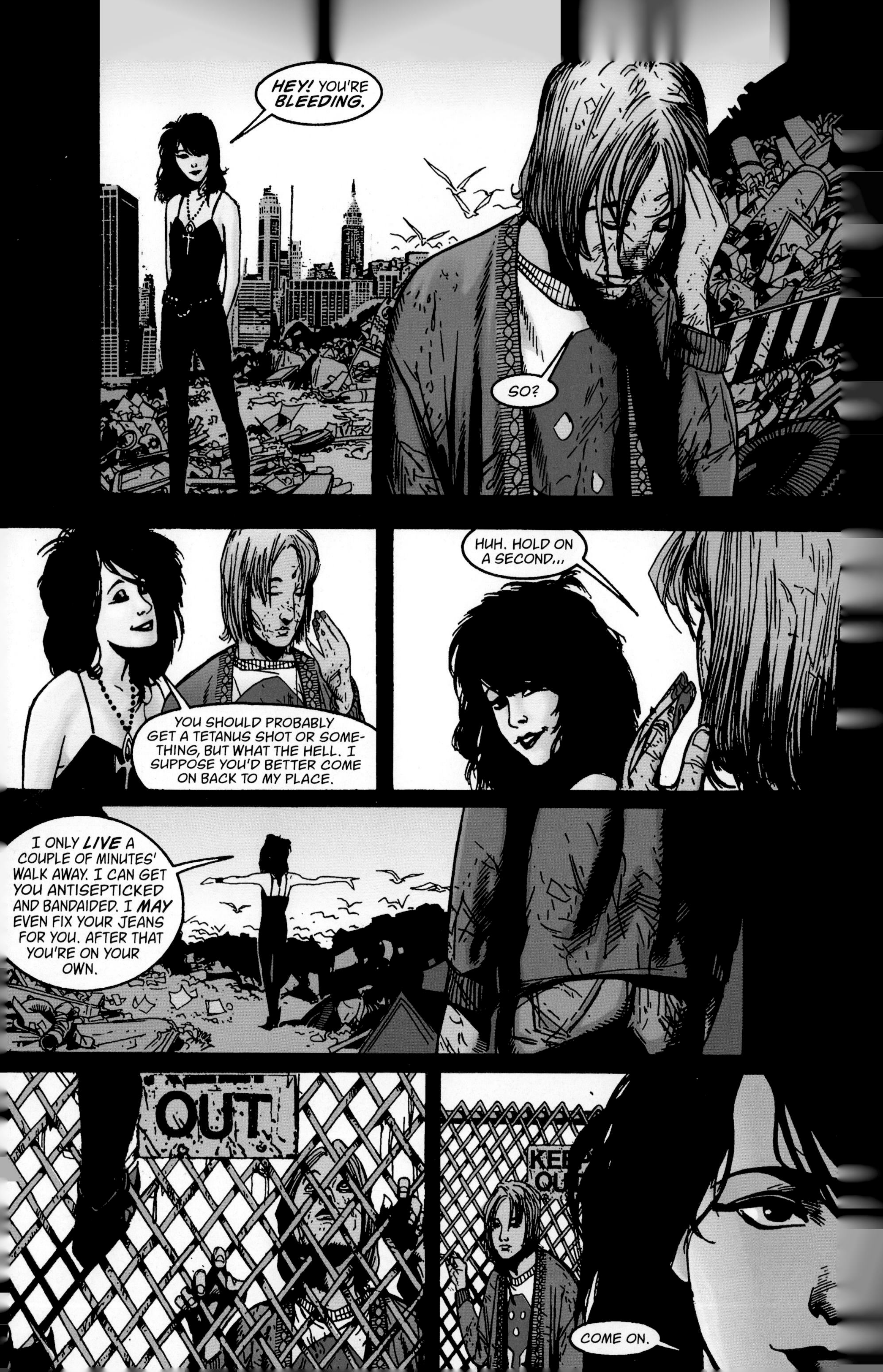
HEY! YOU'RE BLEEDING.
SO?
YOU SHOULD PROBABLY GET A TETANUS SHOT OR SOMETHING, BUT WHAT THE HELL. I SUPPOSE YOU'D BETTER COME ON BACK TO MY PLACE.
HUH. HOLD ON A SECOND...
I ONLY LIVE A COUPLE OF MINUTES' WALK AWAY. I CAN GET YOU ANTISEPTICKED AND BANDAIDED. I MAY EVEN FIX YOUR JEANS FOR YOU. AFTER THAT YOU'RE ON YOUR OWN.
OUT
COME ON.

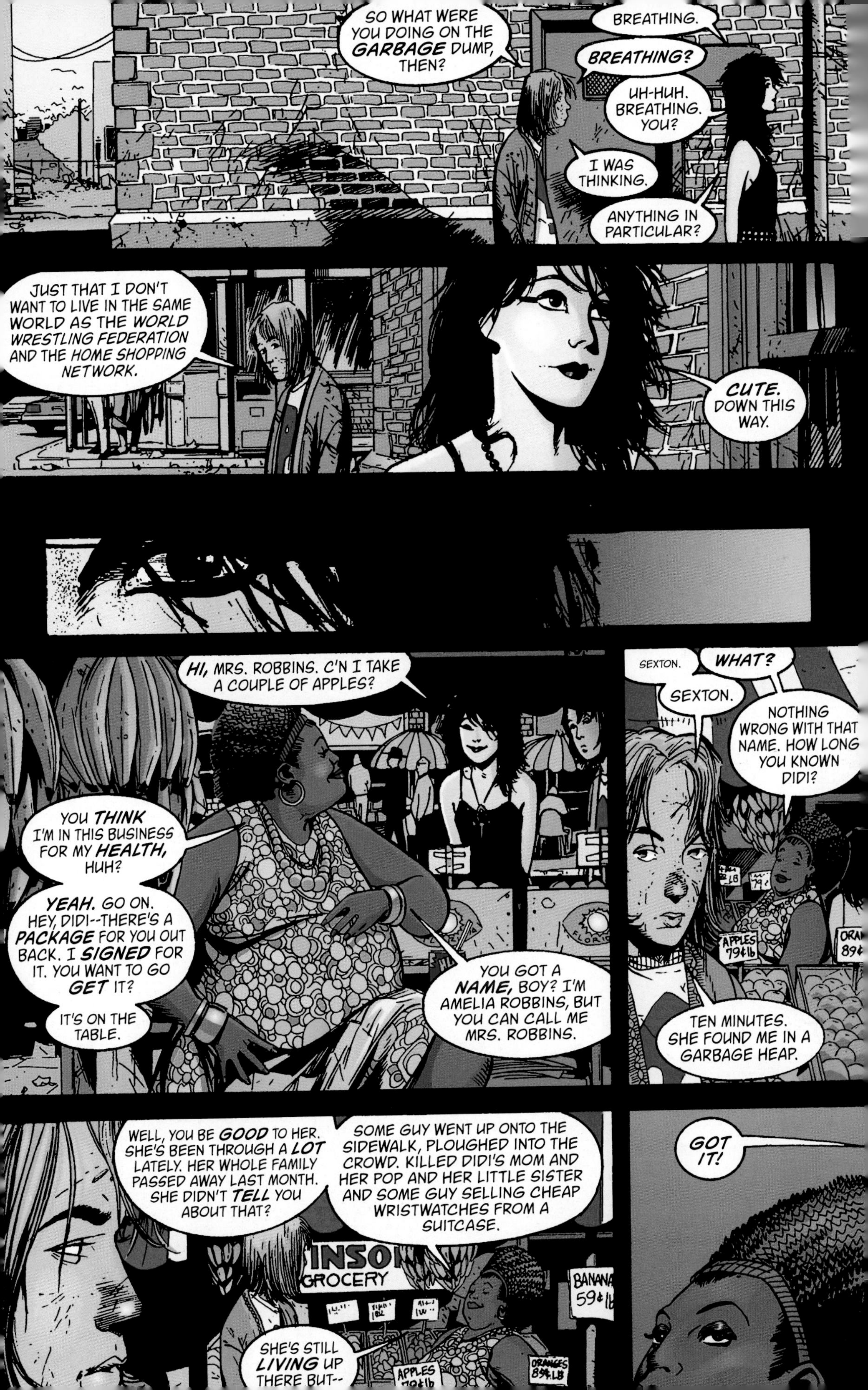
SO WHAT WERE YOU DOING ON THE GARBAGE DUMP, THEN?
BREATHING.
BREATHING?
UH-HUH. BREATHING. YOU?
I WAS THINKING.
ANYTHING IN PARTICULAR?
JUST THAT I DON'T WANT TO LIVE IN THE SAME WORLD AS THE WORLD WRESTLING FEDERATION AND THE HOME SHOPPING NETWORK.
CUTE. DOWN THIS WAY.
HI, MRS. ROBBINS. C'N I TAKE A COUPLE OF APPLES?
YOU THINK I'M IN THIS BUSINESS FOR MY HEALTH, HUH?
YEAH. GO ON. HEY, DIDI--THERE'S A PACKAGE FOR YOU OUT BACK. I SIGNED FOR IT. YOU WANT TO GO GET IT?
IT'S ON THE TABLE.
YOU GOT A NAME, BOY? I'M AMELIA ROBBINS, BUT YOU CAN CALL ME MRS. ROBBINS.
SEXTON.
WHAT?
SEXTON.
NOTHING WRONG WITH THAT NAME. HOW LONG YOU KNOWN DIDI?
TEN MINUTES. SHE FOUND ME IN A GARBAGE HEAP.
APPLES 79¢ lb
WELL, YOU BE GOOD TO HER. SHE'S BEEN THROUGH A LOT LATELY. HER WHOLE FAMILY PASSED AWAY LAST MONTH. SHE DIDN'T TELL YOU ABOUT THAT?
SOME GUY WENT UP ONTO THE SIDEWALK, PLOUGHED INTO THE CROWD. KILLED DIDI'S MOM AND HER POP AND HER LITTLE SISTER AND SOME GUY SELLING CHEAP WRISTWATCHES FROM A SUITCASE.
GROCERY
BANANA 59¢ lb
SHE'S STILL LIVING UP THERE BUT--
GOT IT!

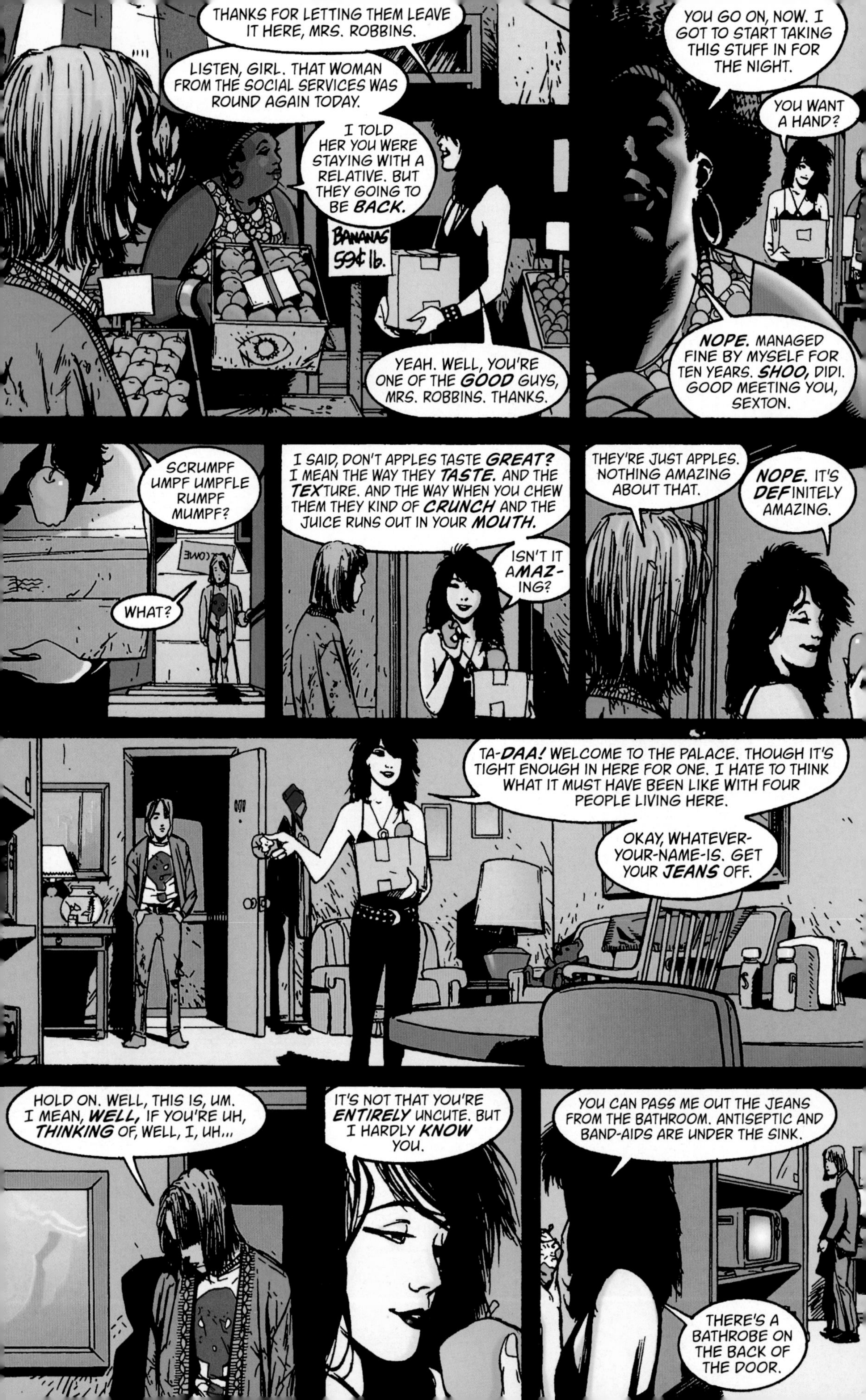
THANKS FOR LETTING THEM LEAVE IT HERE, MRS. ROBBINS.
LISTEN, GIRL. THAT WOMAN FROM THE SOCIAL SERVICES WAS ROUND AGAIN TODAY.
I TOLD HER YOU WERE STAYING WITH A RELATIVE. BUT THEY GOING TO BE BACK.
BANANAS 59¢ lb.
YEAH. WELL, YOU'RE ONE OF THE GOOD GUYS, MRS. ROBBINS. THANKS.
YOU GO ON, NOW. I GOT TO START TAKING THIS STUFF IN FOR THE NIGHT.
YOU WANT A HAND?
NOPE. MANAGED FINE BY MYSELF FOR TEN YEARS. SHOO, DIDI. GOOD MEETING YOU, SEXTON.
SCRUMPF UMPF UMPFLE RUMPF MUMPF?
WHAT?
I SAID, DON'T APPLES TASTE GREAT? I MEAN THE WAY THEY TASTE. AND THE TEXTURE. AND THE WAY WHEN YOU CHEW THEM THEY KIND OF CRUNCH AND THE JUICE RUNS OUT IN YOUR MOUTH.
ISN'T IT AMAZING?
THEY'RE JUST APPLES. NOTHING AMAZING ABOUT THAT.
NOPE. IT'S DEFINITELY AMAZING.
TA-DAA! WELCOME TO THE PALACE. THOUGH IT'S TIGHT ENOUGH IN HERE FOR ONE. I HATE TO THINK WHAT IT MUST HAVE BEEN LIKE WITH FOUR PEOPLE LIVING HERE.
OKAY, WHATEVER-YOUR-NAME-IS. GET YOUR JEANS OFF.
HOLD ON. WELL, THIS IS, UM. I MEAN, WELL, IF YOU'RE UH, THINKING OF, WELL, I, UH...
IT'S NOT THAT YOU'RE ENTIRELY UNCUTE. BUT I HARDLY KNOW YOU.
YOU CAN PASS ME OUT THE JEANS FROM THE BATHROOM. ANTISEPTIC AND BAND-AIDS ARE UNDER THE SINK.
THERE'S A BATHROBE ON THE BACK OF THE DOOR.

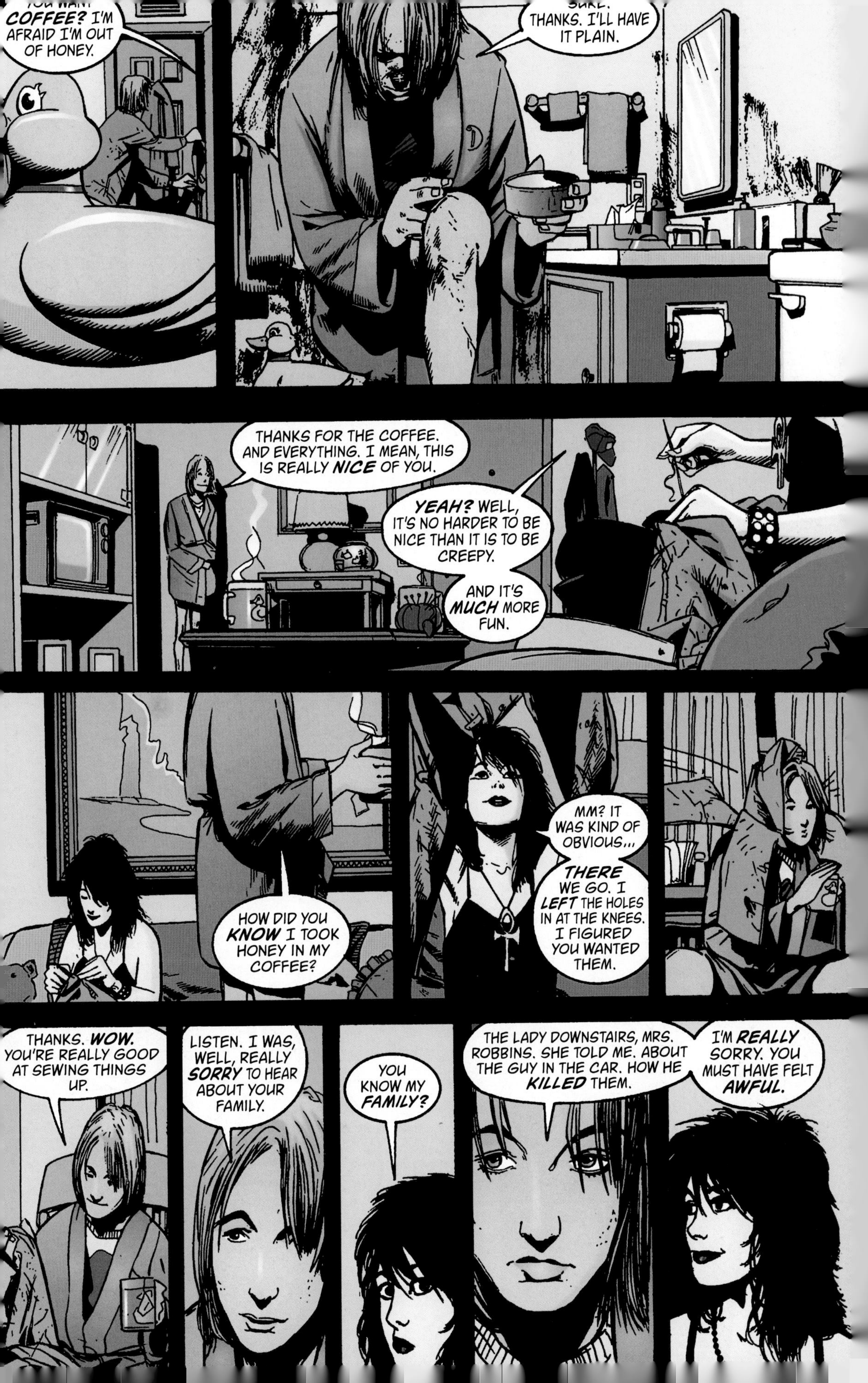

COFFEE? I'M AFRAID I'M OUT OF HONEY.
THANKS. I'LL HAVE IT PLAIN.
THANKS FOR THE COFFEE. AND EVERYTHING. I MEAN, THIS IS REALLY NICE OF YOU.
YEAH? WELL, IT'S NO HARDER TO BE NICE THAN IT IS TO BE CREEPY.
AND IT'S MUCH MORE FUN.
HOW DID YOU KNOW I TOOK HONEY IN MY COFFEE?
MM? IT WAS KIND OF OBVIOUS...
THERE WE GO. I LEFT THE HOLES IN AT THE KNEES. I FIGURED YOU WANTED THEM.
THANKS. WOW. YOU'RE REALLY GOOD AT SEWING THINGS UP.
LISTEN. I WAS, WELL, REALLY SORRY TO HEAR ABOUT YOUR FAMILY.
YOU KNOW MY FAMILY?
THE LADY DOWNSTAIRS, MRS. ROBBINS. SHE TOLD ME. ABOUT THE GUY IN THE CAR. HOW HE KILLED THEM.
I'M REALLY SORRY. YOU MUST HAVE FELT AWFUL.

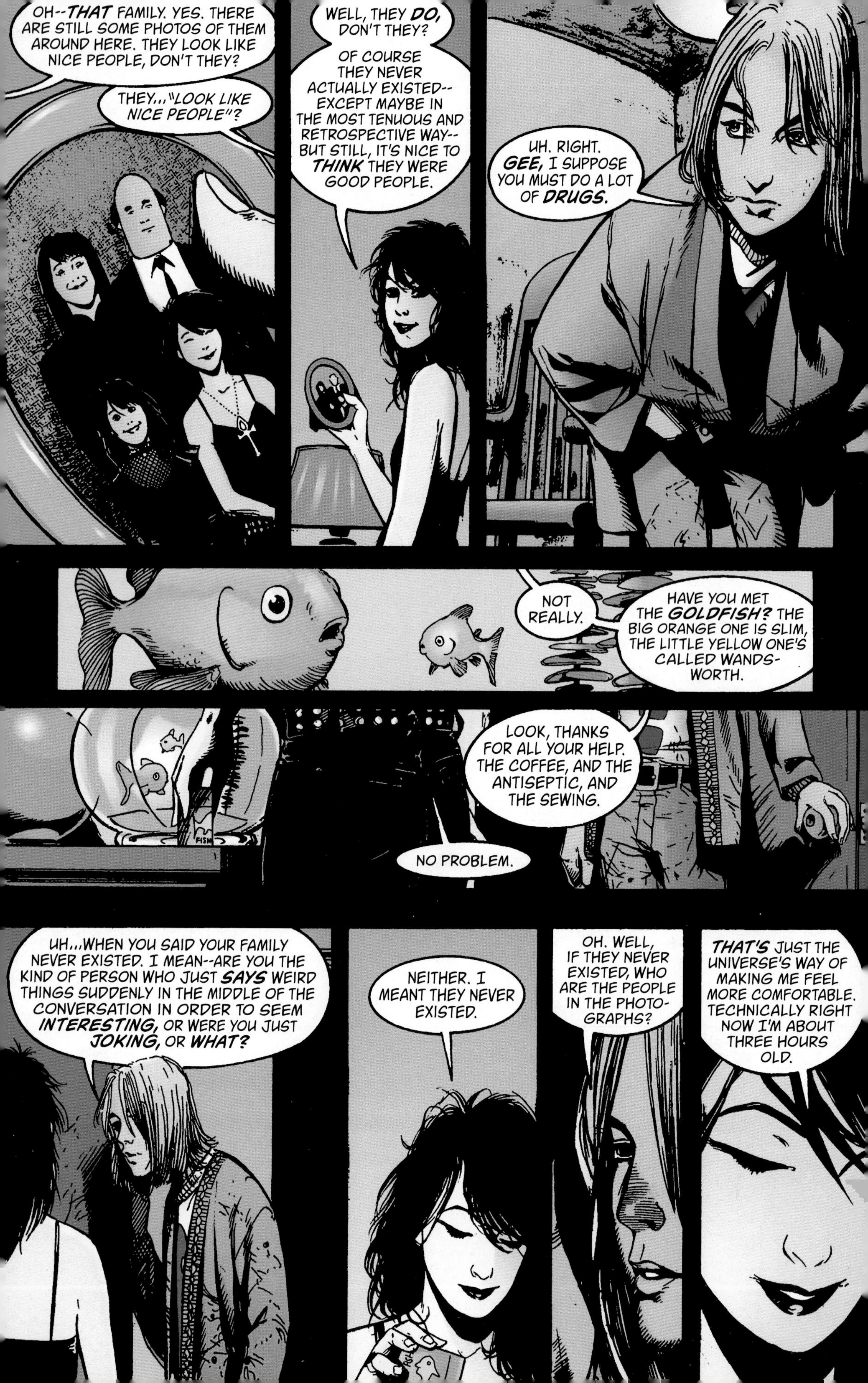
OH--THAT FAMILY. YES. THERE ARE STILL SOME PHOTOS OF THEM AROUND HERE. THEY LOOK LIKE NICE PEOPLE, DON'T THEY?
THEY..."LOOK LIKE NICE PEOPLE"?
WELL, THEY DO, DON'T THEY?
OF COURSE THEY NEVER ACTUALLY EXISTED--EXCEPT MAYBE IN THE MOST TENUOUS AND RETROSPECTIVE WAY--BUT STILL, IT'S NICE TO THINK THEY WERE GOOD PEOPLE.
UH. RIGHT. GEE, I SUPPOSE YOU MUST DO A LOT OF DRUGS.
NOT REALLY.
HAVE YOU MET THE GOLDFISH? THE BIG ORANGE ONE IS SLIM, THE LITTLE YELLOW ONE'S CALLED WANDSWORTH.
LOOK, THANKS FOR ALL YOUR HELP. THE COFFEE, AND THE ANTISEPTIC, AND THE SEWING.
NO PROBLEM.
UH...WHEN YOU SAID YOUR FAMILY NEVER EXISTED. I MEAN--ARE YOU THE KIND OF PERSON WHO JUST SAYS WEIRD THINGS SUDDENLY IN THE MIDDLE OF THE CONVERSATION IN ORDER TO SEEM INTERESTING, OR WERE YOU JUST JOKING, OR WHAT?
NEITHER. I MEANT THEY NEVER EXISTED.
OH. WELL, IF THEY NEVER EXISTED, WHO ARE THE PEOPLE IN THE PHOTOGRAPHS?
THAT'S JUST THE UNIVERSE'S WAY OF MAKING ME FEEL MORE COMFORTABLE. TECHNICALLY RIGHT NOW I'M ABOUT THREE HOURS OLD.

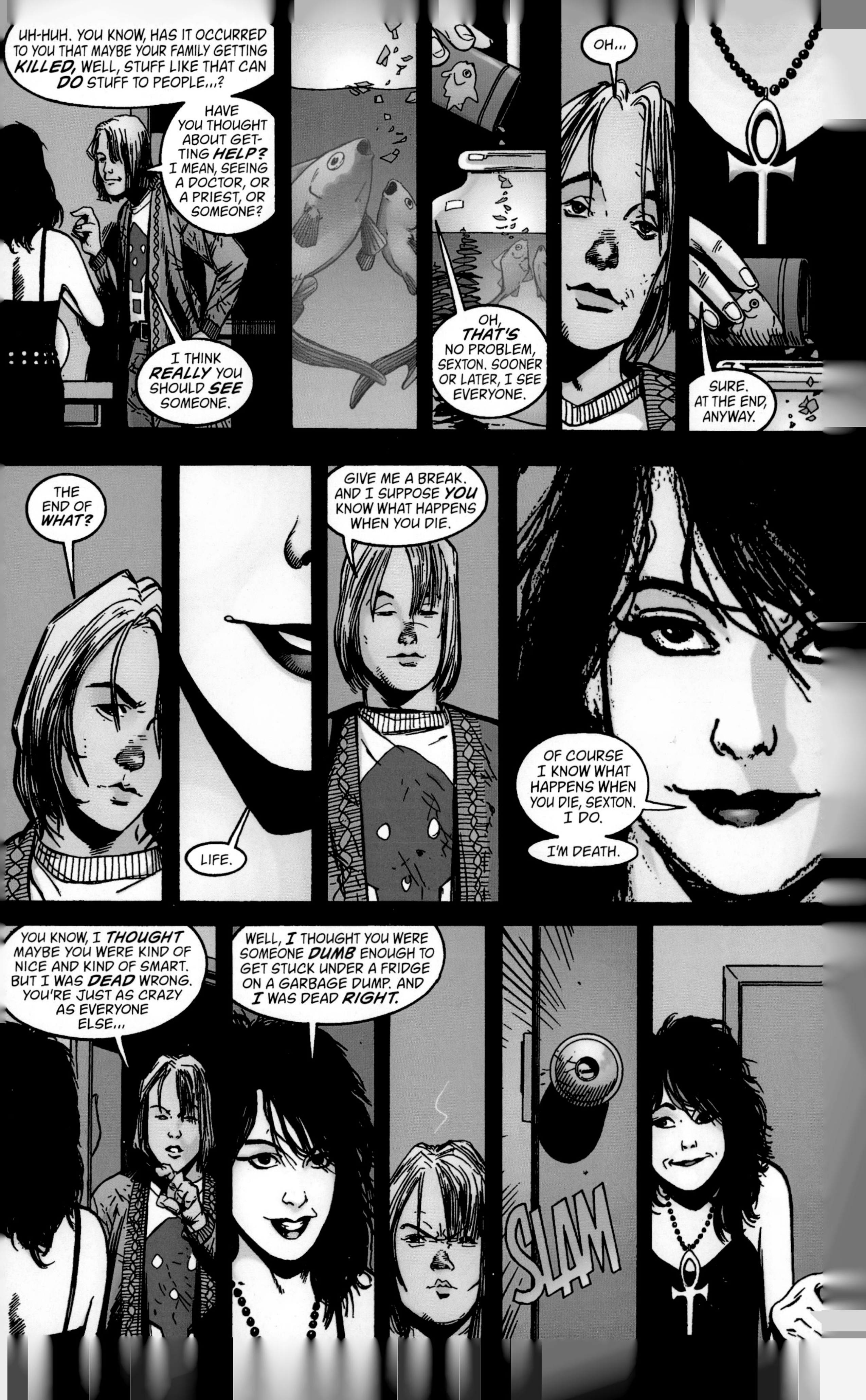
UH-HUH. YOU KNOW, HAS IT OCCURRED TO YOU THAT MAYBE YOUR FAMILY GETTING KILLED, WELL, STUFF LIKE THAT CAN DO STUFF TO PEOPLE...?
HAVE YOU THOUGHT ABOUT GETTING HELP? I MEAN, SEEING A DOCTOR, OR A PRIEST, OR SOMEONE?
I THINK REALLY YOU SHOULD SEE SOMEONE.
OH, THAT'S NO PROBLEM, SEXTON. SOONER OR LATER, I SEE EVERYONE.
OH...
SURE. AT THE END, ANYWAY.
THE END OF WHAT?
LIFE.
GIVE ME A BREAK. AND I SUPPOSE YOU KNOW WHAT HAPPENS WHEN YOU DIE.
OF COURSE I KNOW WHAT HAPPENS WHEN YOU DIE, SEXTON. I DO.
I'M DEATH.
YOU KNOW, I THOUGHT MAYBE YOU WERE KIND OF NICE AND KIND OF SMART. BUT I WAS DEAD WRONG. YOU'RE JUST AS CRAZY AS EVERYONE ELSE...
WELL, I THOUGHT YOU WERE SOMEONE DUMB ENOUGH TO GET STUCK UNDER A FRIDGE ON A GARBAGE DUMP. AND I WAS DEAD RIGHT.
SLAM

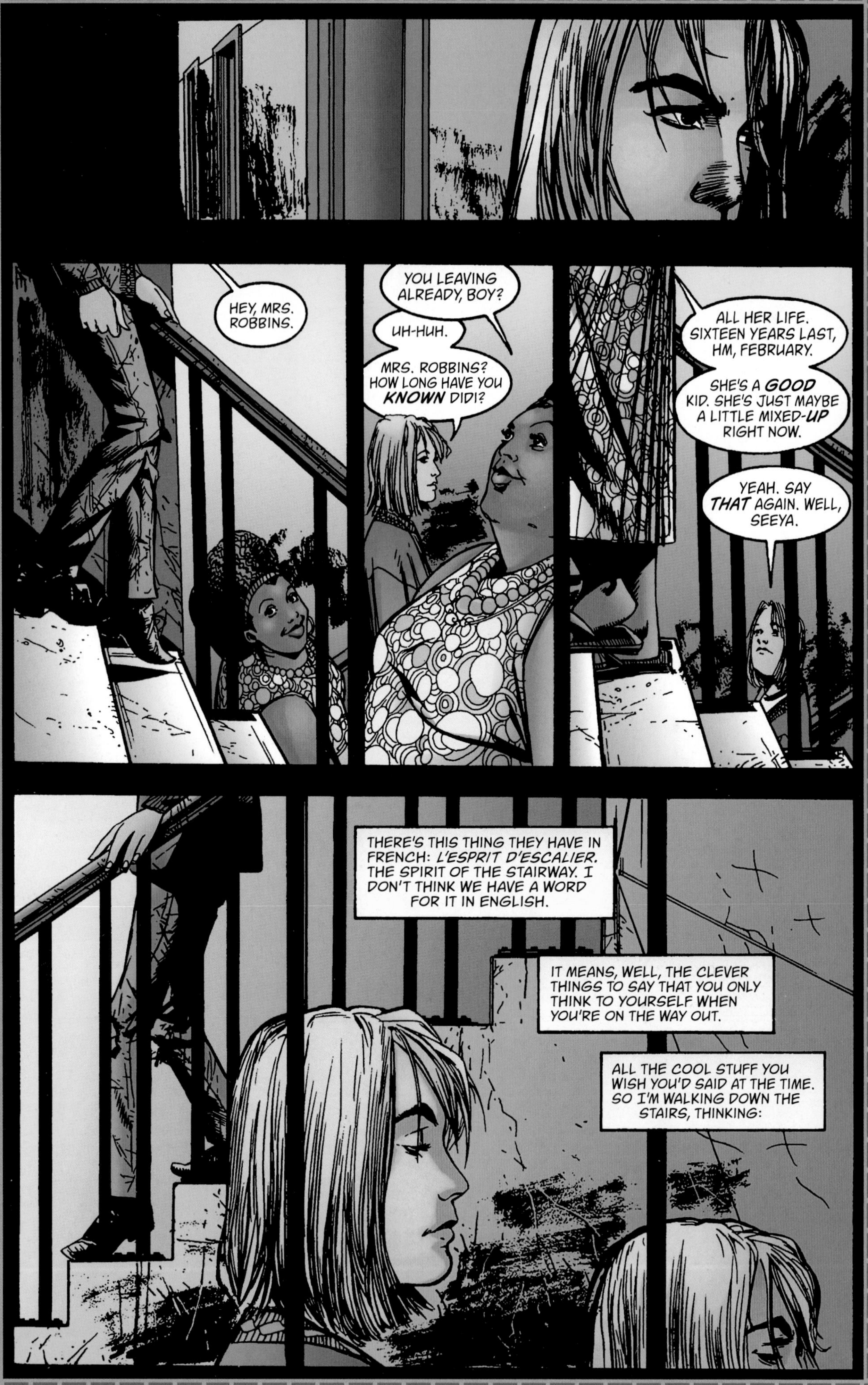

HEY, MRS. ROBBINS.
YOU LEAVING ALREADY, BOY?
UH-HUH.
MRS. ROBBINS? HOW LONG HAVE YOU KNOWN DIDI?
ALL HER LIFE. SIXTEEN YEARS LAST, HM, FEBRUARY.
SHE'S A GOOD KID. SHE'S JUST MAYBE A LITTLE MIXED-UP RIGHT NOW.
YEAH. SAY THAT AGAIN. WELL, SEEYA.
THERE'S THIS THING THEY HAVE IN FRENCH: L'ESPRIT D'ESCALIER. THE SPIRIT OF THE STAIRWAY. I DON'T THINK WE HAVE A WORD FOR IT IN ENGLISH.
IT MEANS, WELL, THE CLEVER THINGS TO SAY THAT YOU ONLY THINK TO YOURSELF WHEN YOU'RE ON THE WAY OUT.
ALL THE COOL STUFF YOU WISH YOU'D SAID AT THE TIME. SO I'M WALKING DOWN THE STAIRS, THINKING:

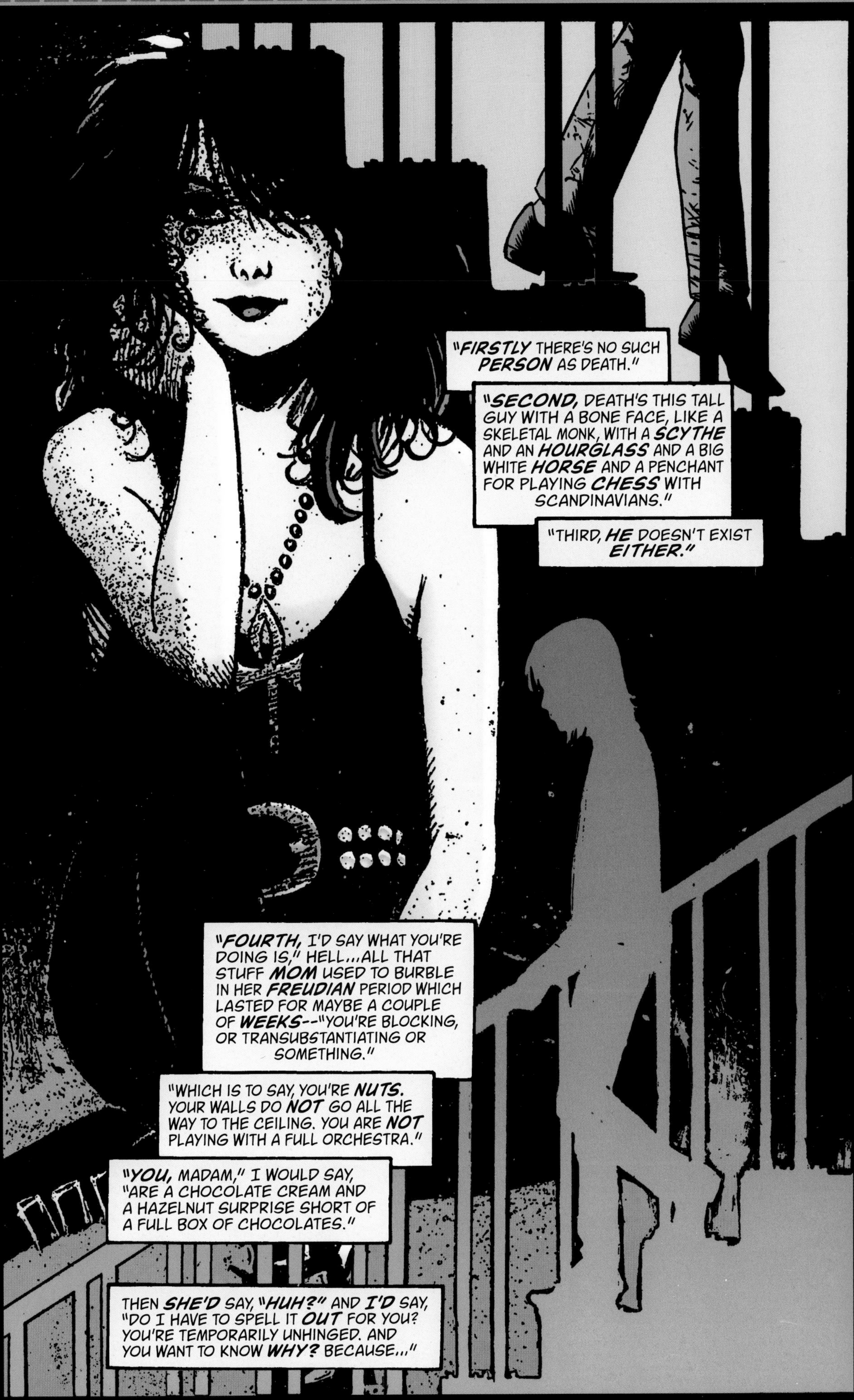
"FIRSTLY THERE'S NO SUCH PERSON AS DEATH."
"SECOND, DEATH'S THIS TALL GUY WITH A BONE FACE, LIKE A SKELETAL MONK, WITH A SCYTHE AND AN HOURGLASS AND A BIG WHITE HORSE AND A PENCHANT FOR PLAYING CHESS WITH SCANDINAVIANS."
"THIRD, HE DOESN'T EXIST EITHER."
"FOURTH, I'D SAY WHAT YOU'RE DOING IS," HELL...ALL THAT STUFF MOM USED TO BURBLE IN HER FREUDIAN PERIOD WHICH LASTED FOR MAYBE A COUPLE OF WEEKS--"YOU'RE BLOCKING, OR TRANSUBSTANTIATING OR SOMETHING."
"WHICH IS TO SAY, YOU'RE NUTS. YOUR WALLS DO NOT GO ALL THE WAY TO THE CEILING. YOU ARE NOT PLAYING WITH A FULL ORCHESTRA."
"YOU, MADAM," I WOULD SAY, "ARE A CHOCOLATE CREAM AND A HAZELNUT SURPRISE SHORT OF A FULL BOX OF CHOCOLATES."
THEN SHE'D SAY, "HUH?" AND I'D SAY, "DO I HAVE TO SPELL IT OUT FOR YOU? YOU'RE TEMPORARILY UNHINGED. AND YOU WANT TO KNOW WHY? BECAUSE..."

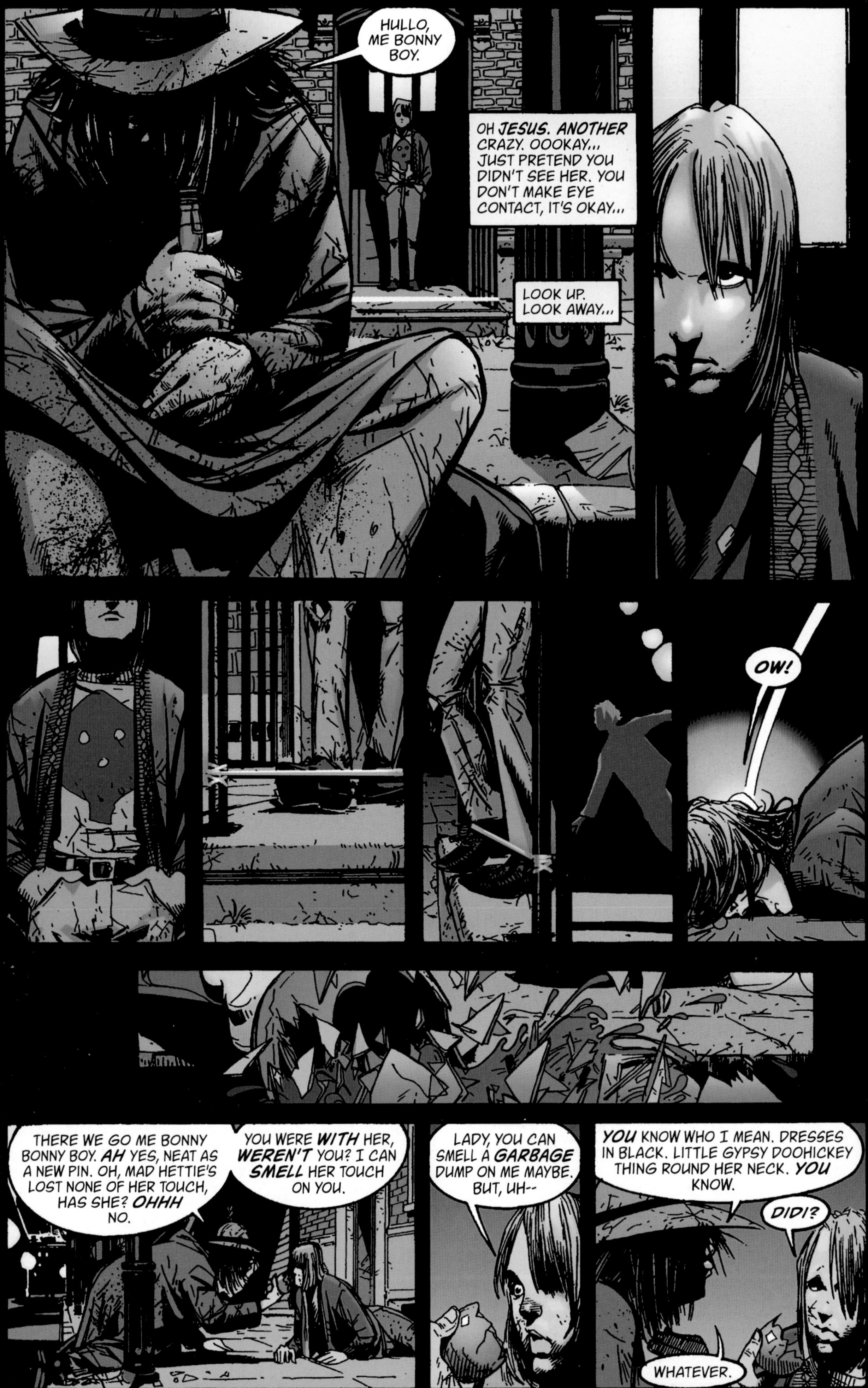
HULLO, ME BONNY BOY.
OH JESUS. ANOTHER CRAZY. OOOKAY... JUST PRETEND YOU DIDN'T SEE HER. YOU DON'T MAKE EYE CONTACT, IT'S OKAY...
LOOK UP. LOOK AWAY...
OW!
THERE WE GO ME BONNY BONNY BOY. AH YES, NEAT AS A NEW PIN. OH, MAD HETTIE'S LOST NONE OF HER TOUCH, HAS SHE? OHHH NO.
YOU WERE WITH HER, WEREN'T YOU? I CAN SMELL HER TOUCH ON YOU.
LADY, YOU CAN SMELL A GARBAGE DUMP ON ME MAYBE. BUT, UH--
YOU KNOW WHO I MEAN. DRESSES IN BLACK. LITTLE GYPSY DOOHICKEY THING ROUND HER NECK. YOU KNOW.
DIDI?
WHATEVER.

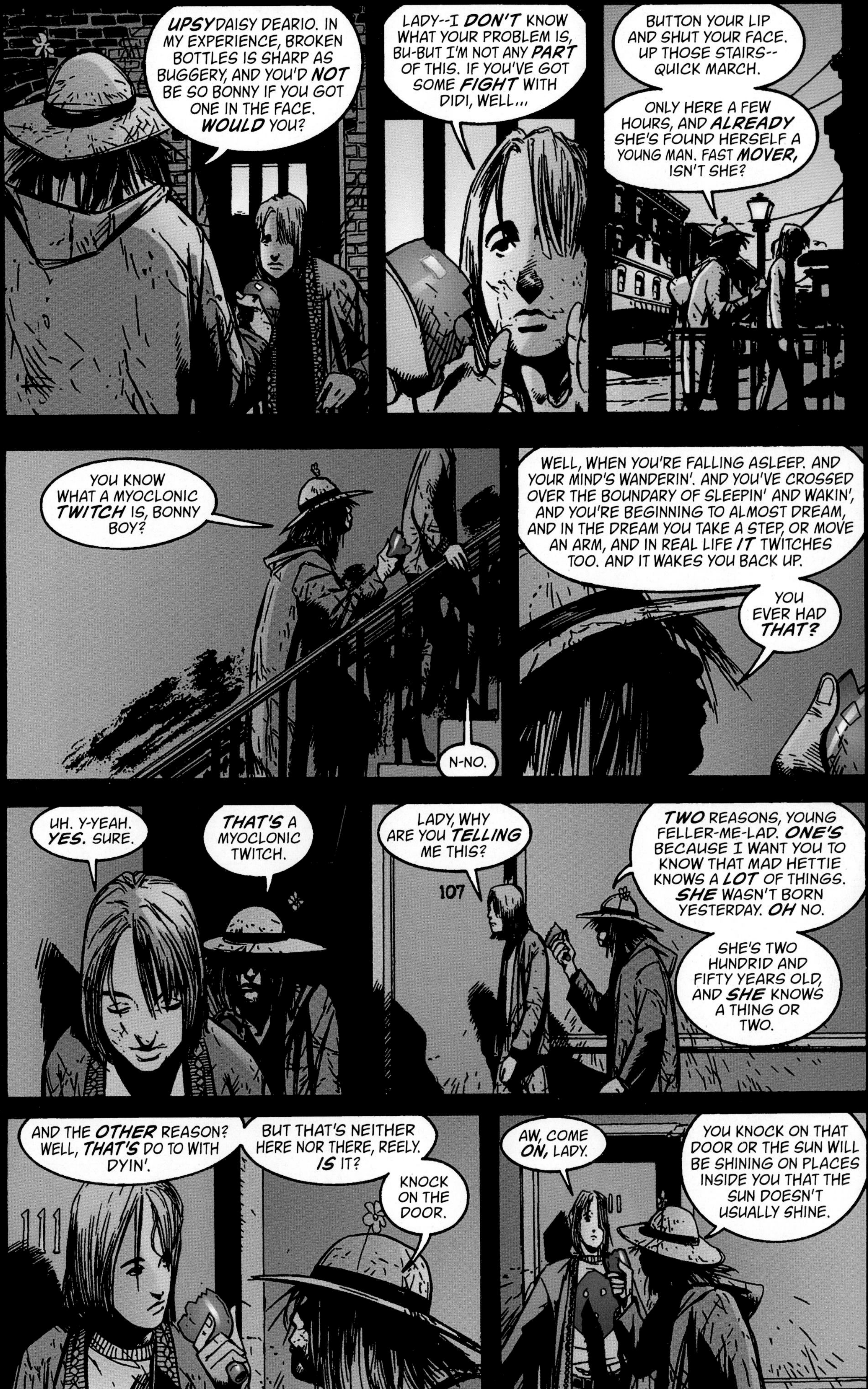
UPSY DAISY DEARIO. IN MY EXPERIENCE, BROKEN BOTTLES IS SHARP AS BUGGERY, AND YOU'D NOT BE SO BONNY IF YOU GOT ONE IN THE FACE. WOULD YOU?
LADY--I DON'T KNOW WHAT YOUR PROBLEM IS, BU-BUT I'M NOT ANY PART OF THIS. IF YOU'VE GOT SOME FIGHT WITH DIDI, WELL...
BUTTON YOUR LIP AND SHUT YOUR FACE. UP THOSE STAIRS-- QUICK MARCH.
ONLY HERE A FEW HOURS, AND ALREADY SHE'S FOUND HERSELF A YOUNG MAN. FAST MOVER, ISN'T SHE?
YOU KNOW WHAT A MYOCLONIC TWITCH IS, BONNY BOY?
N-NO.
WELL, WHEN YOU'RE FALLING ASLEEP. AND YOUR MIND'S WANDERIN'. AND YOU'VE CROSSED OVER THE BOUNDARY OF SLEEPIN' AND WAKIN', AND YOU'RE BEGINNING TO ALMOST DREAM, AND IN THE DREAM YOU TAKE A STEP, OR MOVE AN ARM, AND IN REAL LIFE IT TWITCHES TOO. AND IT WAKES YOU BACK UP.
YOU EVER HAD THAT?
UH. Y-YEAH. YES. SURE.
THAT'S A MYOCLONIC TWITCH.
LADY, WHY ARE YOU TELLING ME THIS?
107
TWO REASONS, YOUNG FELLER-ME-LAD. ONE'S BECAUSE I WANT YOU TO KNOW THAT MAD HETTIE KNOWS A LOT OF THINGS. SHE WASN'T BORN YESTERDAY. OH NO.
SHE'S TWO HUNDRID AND FIFTY YEARS OLD, AND SHE KNOWS A THING OR TWO.
AND THE OTHER REASON? WELL, THAT'S DO TO WITH DYIN'.
111
BUT THAT'S NEITHER HERE NOR THERE, REELY. IS IT?
KNOCK ON THE DOOR.
AW, COME ON, LADY.
YOU KNOCK ON THAT DOOR OR THE SUN WILL BE SHINING ON PLACES INSIDE YOU THAT THE SUN DOESN'T USUALLY SHINE.

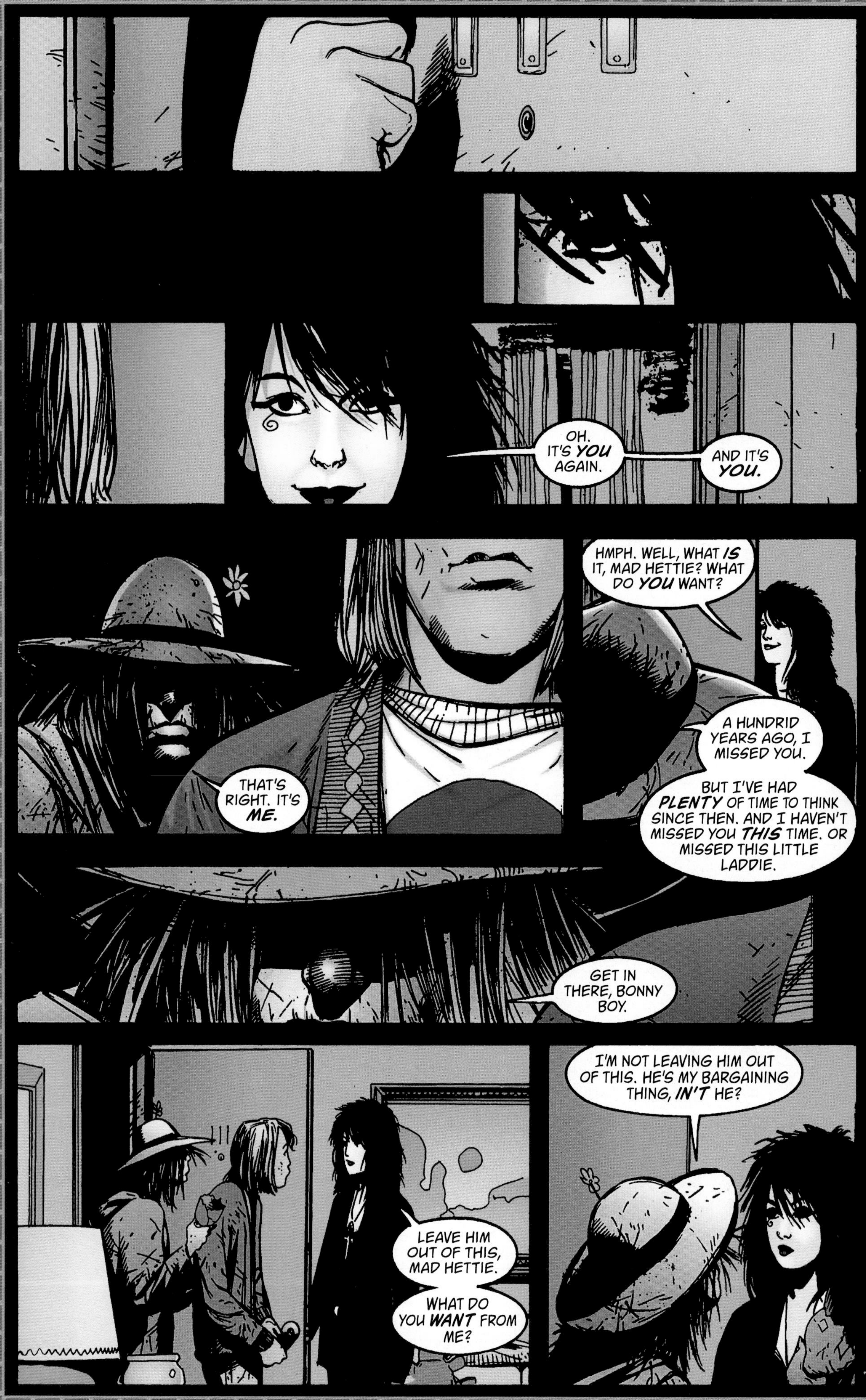
OH. IT'S YOU AGAIN.
AND IT'S YOU.
HMPH. WELL, WHAT IS IT, MAD HETTIE? WHAT DO YOU WANT?
THAT'S RIGHT. IT'S ME.
A HUNDRID YEARS AGO, I MISSED YOU.
BUT I'VE HAD PLENTY OF TIME TO THINK SINCE THEN. AND I HAVEN'T MISSED YOU THIS TIME. OR MISSED THIS LITTLE LADDIE.
GET IN THERE, BONNY BOY.
LEAVE HIM OUT OF THIS, MAD HETTIE.
WHAT DO YOU WANT FROM ME?
I'M NOT LEAVING HIM OUT OF THIS. HE'S MY BARGAINING THING, IN'T HE?

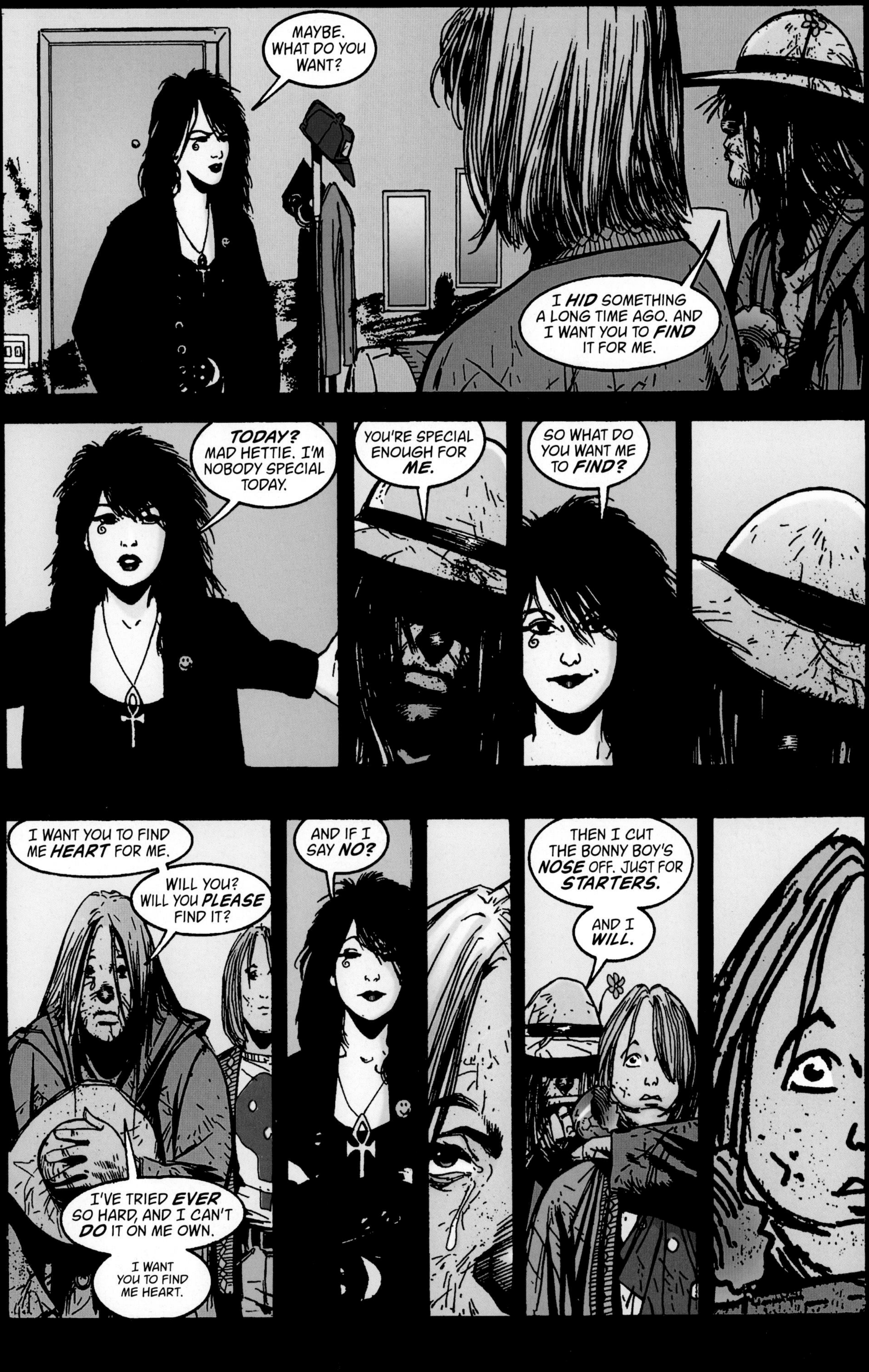
MAYBE. WHAT DO YOU WANT?
I HID SOMETHING A LONG TIME AGO. AND I WANT YOU TO FIND IT FOR ME.
TODAY? MAD HETTIE. I'M NOBODY SPECIAL TODAY.
YOU'RE SPECIAL ENOUGH FOR ME.
SO WHAT DO YOU WANT ME TO FIND?
I WANT YOU TO FIND ME HEART FOR ME.
WILL YOU? WILL YOU PLEASE FIND IT?
I'VE TRIED EVER SO HARD, AND I CAN'T DO IT ON ME OWN.
I WANT YOU TO FIND ME HEART.
AND IF I SAY NO?
THEN I CUT THE BONNY BOY'S NOSE OFF. JUST FOR STARTERS.
AND I WILL.

DC
VERTIGO
2 of 3
APR 93
$1.95 US
$2.50 CAN
£1.00 UK
SUGGESTED FOR MATURE READERS
NEIL GAIMAN
CHRIS BACHALO
MARK BUCKINGHAM
DEATH
the high cost of living

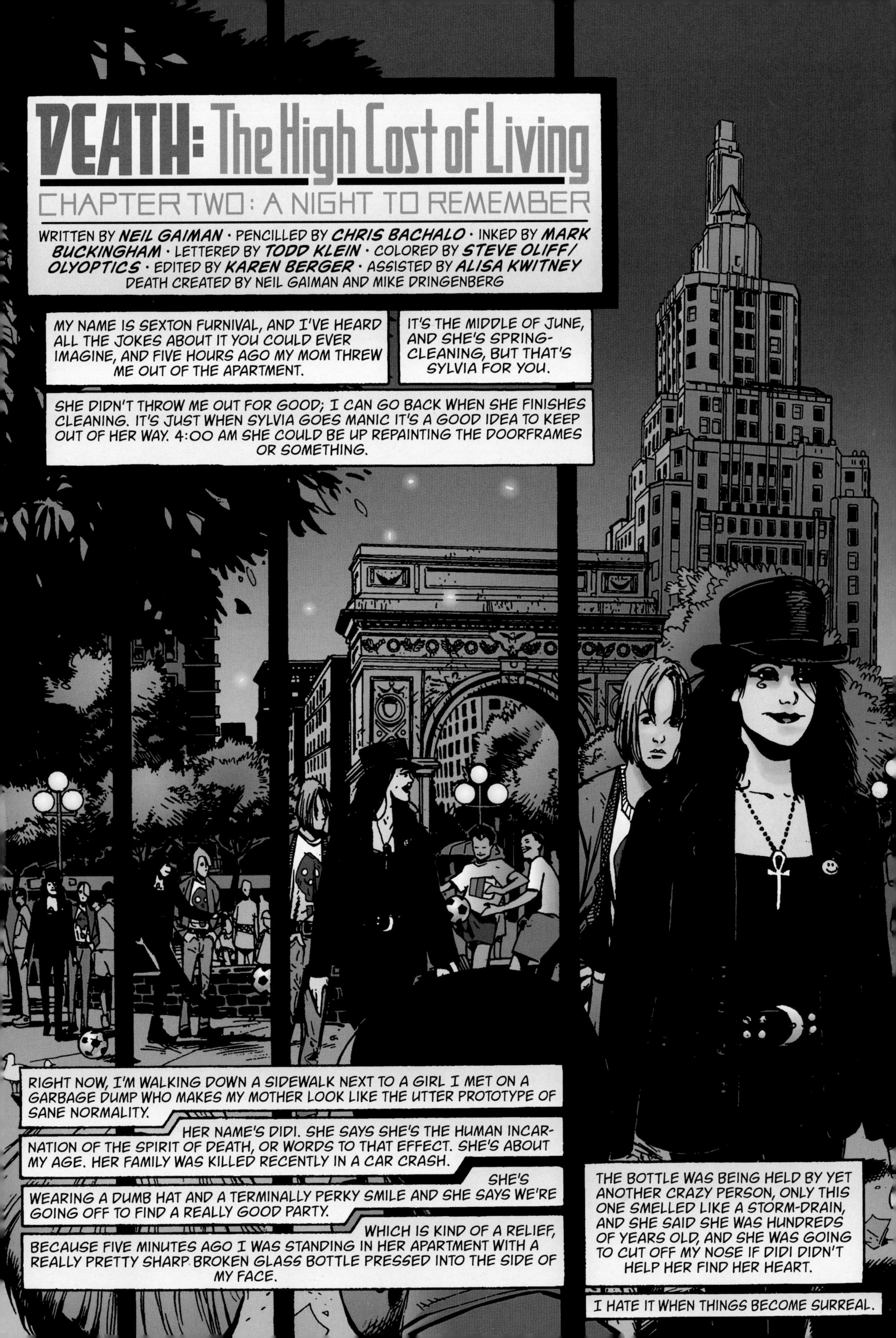

DEATH: The High Cost of Living
CHAPTER TWO: A NIGHT TO REMEMBER
WRITTEN BY NEIL GAIMAN · PENCILLED BY CHRIS BACHALO · INKED BY MARK BUCKINGHAM · LETTERED BY TODD KLEIN · COLORED BY STEVE OLIFF/ OLYOPTICS · EDITED BY KAREN BERGER · ASSISTED BY ALISA KWITNEY
DEATH CREATED BY NEIL GAIMAN AND MIKE DRINGENBERG
MY NAME IS SEXTON FURNIVAL, AND I'VE HEARD ALL THE JOKES ABOUT IT YOU COULD EVER IMAGINE, AND FIVE HOURS AGO MY MOM THREW ME OUT OF THE APARTMENT.
IT'S THE MIDDLE OF JUNE, AND SHE'S SPRING-CLEANING, BUT THAT'S SYLVIA FOR YOU.
SHE DIDN'T THROW ME OUT FOR GOOD; I CAN GO BACK WHEN SHE FINISHES CLEANING. IT'S JUST WHEN SYLVIA GOES MANIC IT'S A GOOD IDEA TO KEEP OUT OF HER WAY. 4:00 AM SHE COULD BE UP REPAINTING THE DOORFRAMES OR SOMETHING.
RIGHT NOW, I'M WALKING DOWN A SIDEWALK NEXT TO A GIRL I MET ON A GARBAGE DUMP WHO MAKES MY MOTHER LOOK LIKE THE UTTER PROTOTYPE OF SANE NORMALITY.
HER NAME'S DIDI. SHE SAYS SHE'S THE HUMAN INCARNATION OF THE SPIRIT OF DEATH, OR WORDS TO THAT EFFECT. SHE'S ABOUT MY AGE. HER FAMILY WAS KILLED RECENTLY IN A CAR CRASH.
SHE'S WEARING A DUMB HAT AND A TERMINALLY PERKY SMILE AND SHE SAYS WE'RE GOING OFF TO FIND A REALLY GOOD PARTY.
WHICH IS KIND OF A RELIEF, BECAUSE FIVE MINUTES AGO I WAS STANDING IN HER APARTMENT WITH A REALLY PRETTY SHARP BROKEN GLASS BOTTLE PRESSED INTO THE SIDE OF MY FACE.
THE BOTTLE WAS BEING HELD BY YET ANOTHER CRAZY PERSON, ONLY THIS ONE SMELLED LIKE A STORM-DRAIN, AND SHE SAID SHE WAS HUNDREDS OF YEARS OLD, AND SHE WAS GOING TO CUT OFF MY NOSE IF DIDI DIDN'T HELP HER FIND HER HEART.
I HATE IT WHEN THINGS BECOME SURREAL.

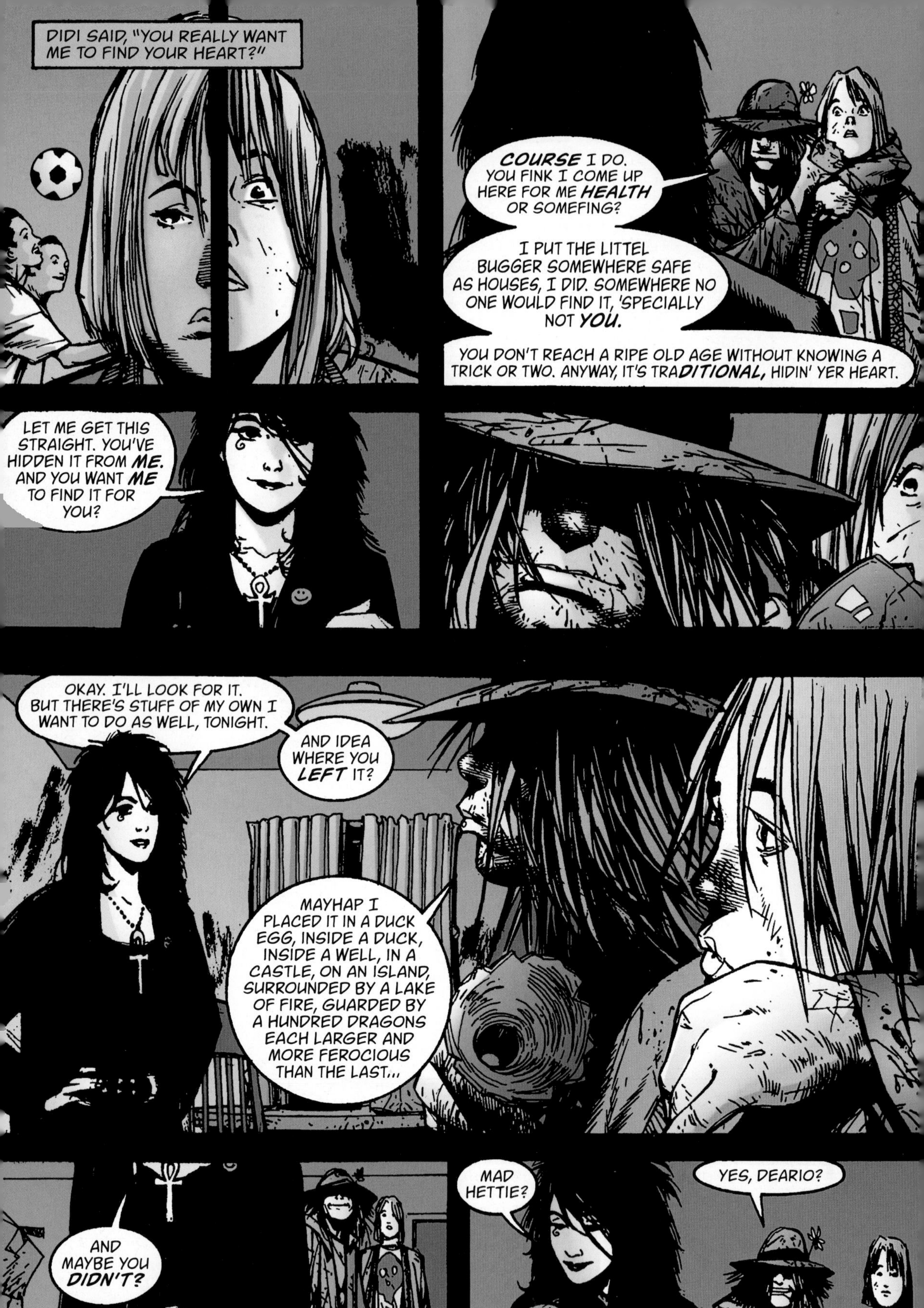
DIDI SAID, "YOU REALLY WANT ME TO FIND YOUR HEART?"
COURSE I DO. YOU FINK I COME UP HERE FOR ME HEALTH OR SOMEFING?
I PUT THE LITTEL BUGGER SOMEWHERE SAFE AS HOUSES, I DID. SOMEWHERE NO ONE WOULD FIND IT, 'SPECIALLY NOT YOU.
YOU DON'T REACH A RIPE OLD AGE WITHOUT KNOWING A TRICK OR TWO. ANYWAY, IT'S TRADITIONAL, HIDIN' YER HEART.
LET ME GET THIS STRAIGHT. YOU'VE HIDDEN IT FROM ME. AND YOU WANT ME TO FIND IT FOR YOU?
OKAY. I'LL LOOK FOR IT. BUT THERE'S STUFF OF MY OWN I WANT TO DO AS WELL, TONIGHT.
AND IDEA WHERE YOU LEFT IT?
MAYHAP I PLACED IT IN A DUCK EGG, INSIDE A DUCK, INSIDE A WELL, IN A CASTLE, ON AN ISLAND, SURROUNDED BY A LAKE OF FIRE, GUARDED BY A HUNDRED DRAGONS EACH LARGER AND MORE FEROCIOUS THAN THE LAST...
AND MAYBE YOU DIDN'T?
MAD HETTIE?
YES, DEARIO?

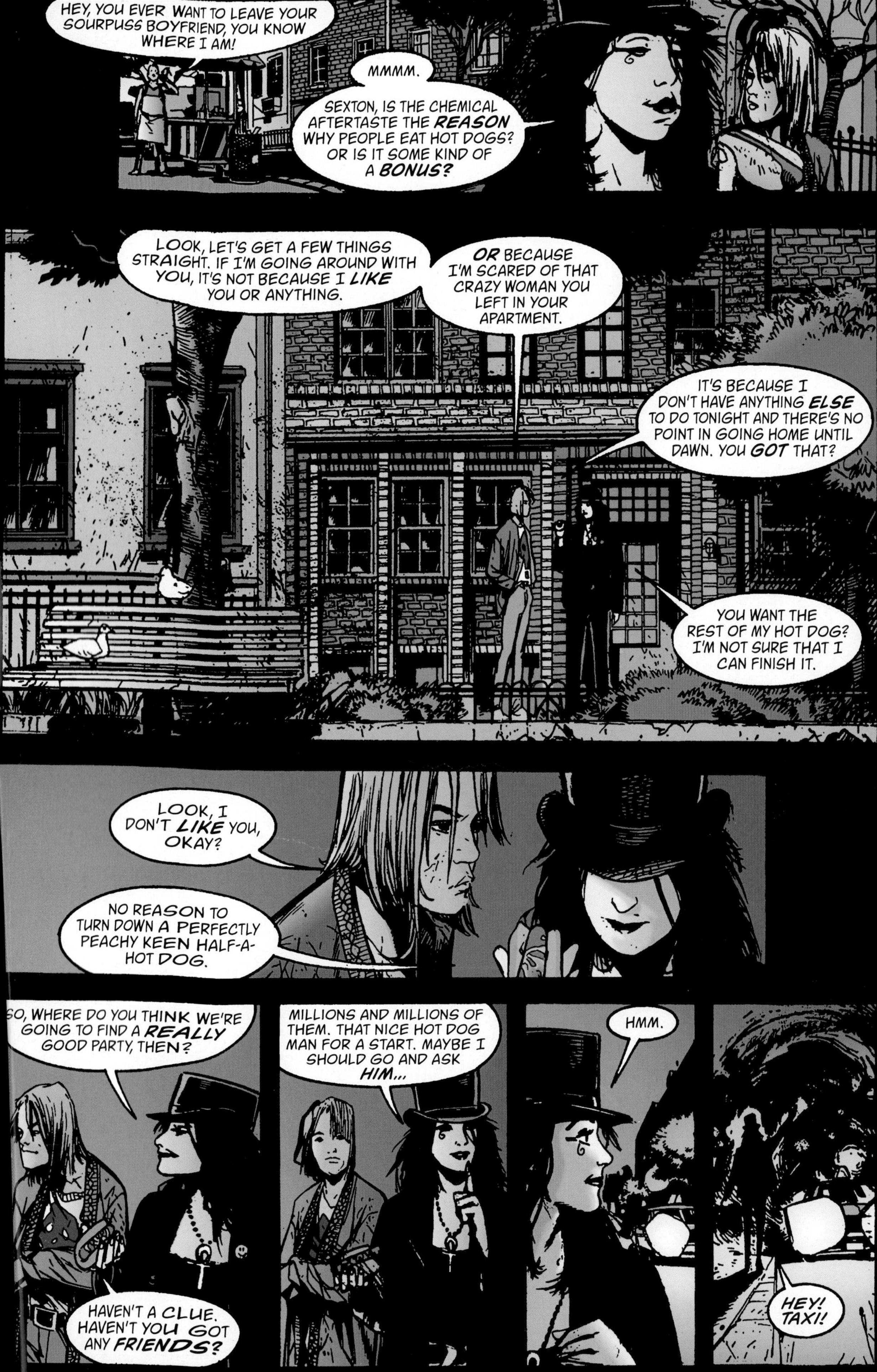
HEY, YOU EVER WANT TO LEAVE YOUR SOURPUSS BOYFRIEND, YOU KNOW WHERE I AM!
MMMM.
SEXTON, IS THE CHEMICAL AFTERTASTE THE REASON WHY PEOPLE EAT HOT DOGS? OR IS IT SOME KIND OF A BONUS?
LOOK, LET'S GET A FEW THINGS STRAIGHT. IF I'M GOING AROUND WITH YOU, IT'S NOT BECAUSE I LIKE YOU OR ANYTHING.
OR BECAUSE I'M SCARED OF THAT CRAZY WOMAN YOU LEFT IN YOUR APARTMENT.
IT'S BECAUSE I DON'T HAVE ANYTHING ELSE TO DO TONIGHT AND THERE'S NO POINT IN GOING HOME UNTIL DAWN. YOU GOT THAT?
YOU WANT THE REST OF MY HOT DOG? I'M NOT SURE THAT I CAN FINISH IT.
LOOK, I DON'T LIKE YOU, OKAY?
NO REASON TO TURN DOWN A PERFECTLY PEACHY KEEN HALF-A-HOT DOG.
SO, WHERE DO YOU THINK WE'RE GOING TO FIND A REALLY GOOD PARTY, THEN?
HAVEN'T A CLUE. HAVEN'T YOU GOT ANY FRIENDS?
MILLIONS AND MILLIONS OF THEM. THAT NICE HOT DOG MAN FOR A START. MAYBE I SHOULD GO AND ASK HIM...
HMM.
HEY! TAXI!

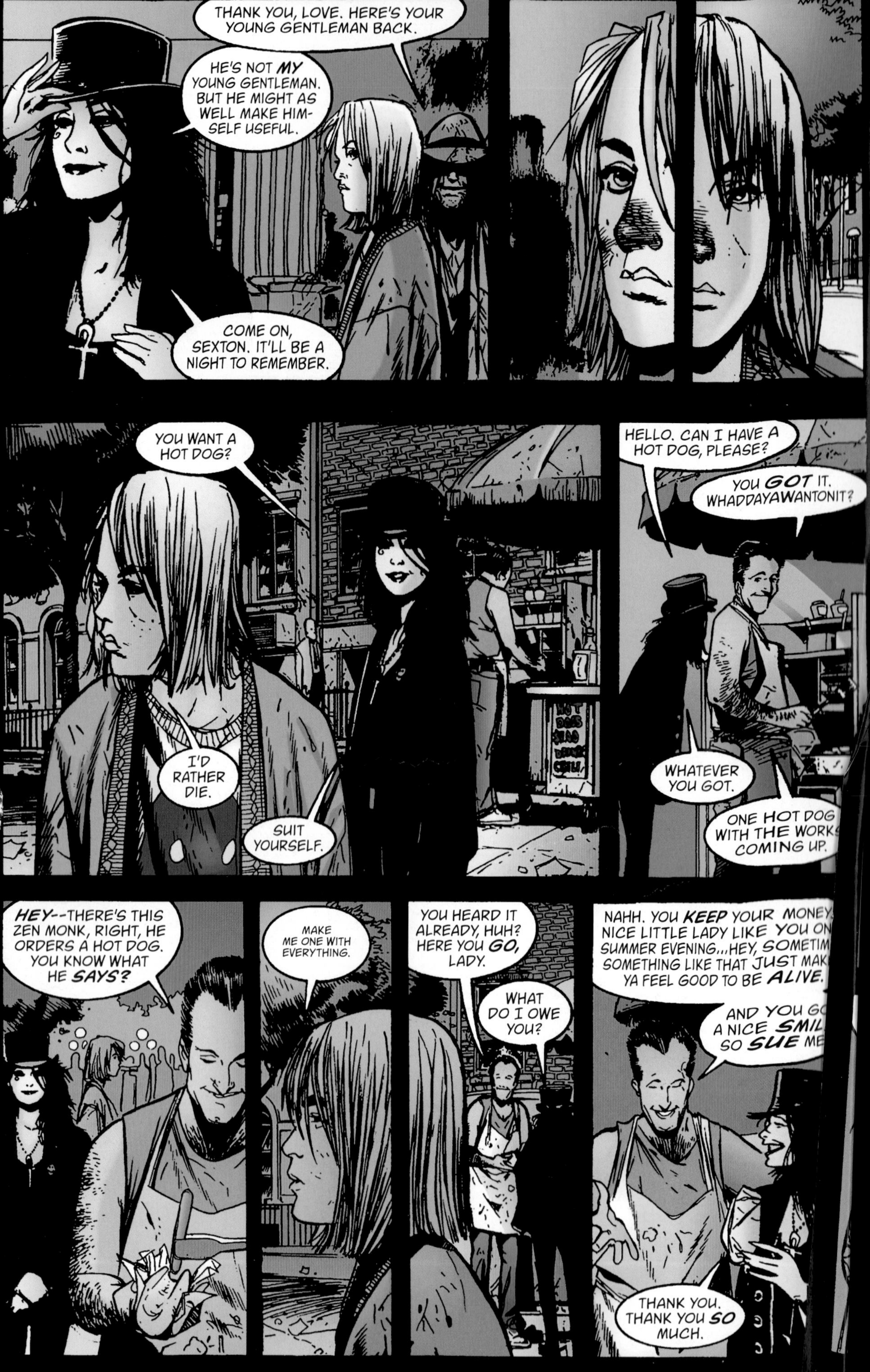
THANK YOU, LOVE. HERE'S YOUR YOUNG GENTLEMAN BACK.
HE'S NOT MY YOUNG GENTLEMAN. BUT HE MIGHT AS WELL MAKE HIMSELF USEFUL.
COME ON, SEXTON. IT'LL BE A NIGHT TO REMEMBER.
YOU WANT A HOT DOG?
I'D RATHER DIE.
SUIT YOURSELF.
HELLO. CAN I HAVE A HOT DOG, PLEASE?
YOU GOT IT. WHADDAYAWANTONIT?
WHATEVER YOU GOT.
ONE HOT DOG WITH THE WORKS COMING UP.
HEY--THERE'S THIS ZEN MONK, RIGHT, HE ORDERS A HOT DOG. YOU KNOW WHAT HE SAYS?
MAKE ME ONE WITH EVERYTHING.
YOU HEARD IT ALREADY, HUH? HERE YOU GO, LADY.
WHAT DO I OWE YOU?
NAHH. YOU KEEP YOUR MONEY. NICE LITTLE LADY LIKE YOU ON SUMMER EVENING...HEY, SOMETIM SOMETHING LIKE THAT JUST MAK YA FEEL GOOD TO BE ALIVE.
AND YOU GO A NICE SMIL SO SUE ME
THANK YOU. THANK YOU SO MUCH.

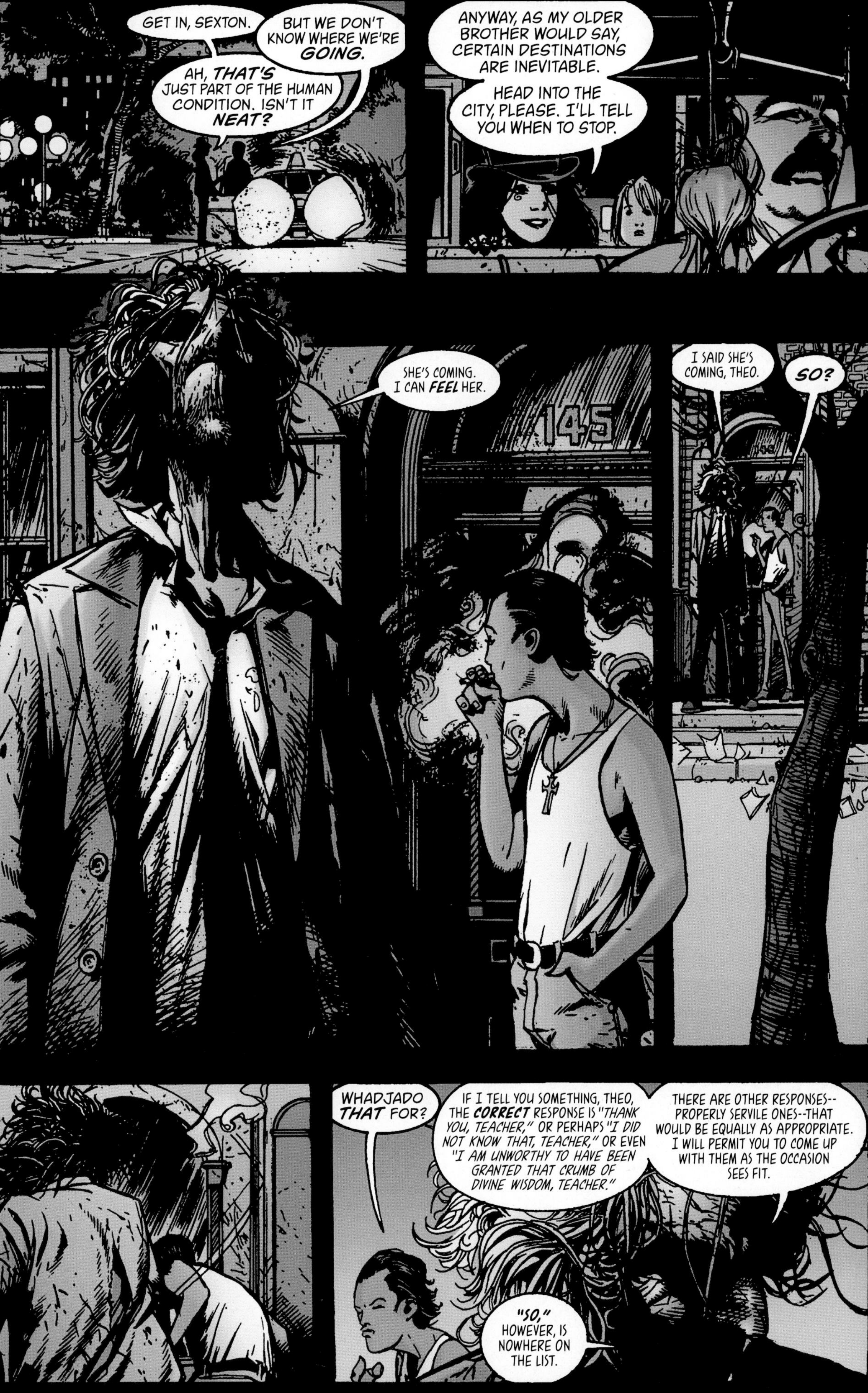
GET IN, SEXTON.
BUT WE DON'T KNOW WHERE WE'RE GOING.
AH, THAT'S JUST PART OF THE HUMAN CONDITION. ISN'T IT NEAT?
ANYWAY, AS MY OLDER BROTHER WOULD SAY, CERTAIN DESTINATIONS ARE INEVITABLE.
HEAD INTO THE CITY, PLEASE. I'LL TELL YOU WHEN TO STOP.
145
SHE'S COMING. I CAN FEEL HER.
I SAID SHE'S COMING, THEO.
SO?
WHADJADO THAT FOR?
IF I TELL YOU SOMETHING, THEO, THE CORRECT RESPONSE IS "THANK YOU, TEACHER," OR PERHAPS "I DID NOT KNOW THAT, TEACHER," OR EVEN "I AM UNWORTHY TO HAVE BEEN GRANTED THAT CRUMB OF DIVINE WISDOM, TEACHER."
THERE ARE OTHER RESPONSES--PROPERLY SERVILE ONES--THAT WOULD BE EQUALLY AS APPROPRIATE. I WILL PERMIT YOU TO COME UP WITH THEM AS THE OCCASION SEES FIT.
"SO," HOWEVER, IS NOWHERE ON THE LIST.

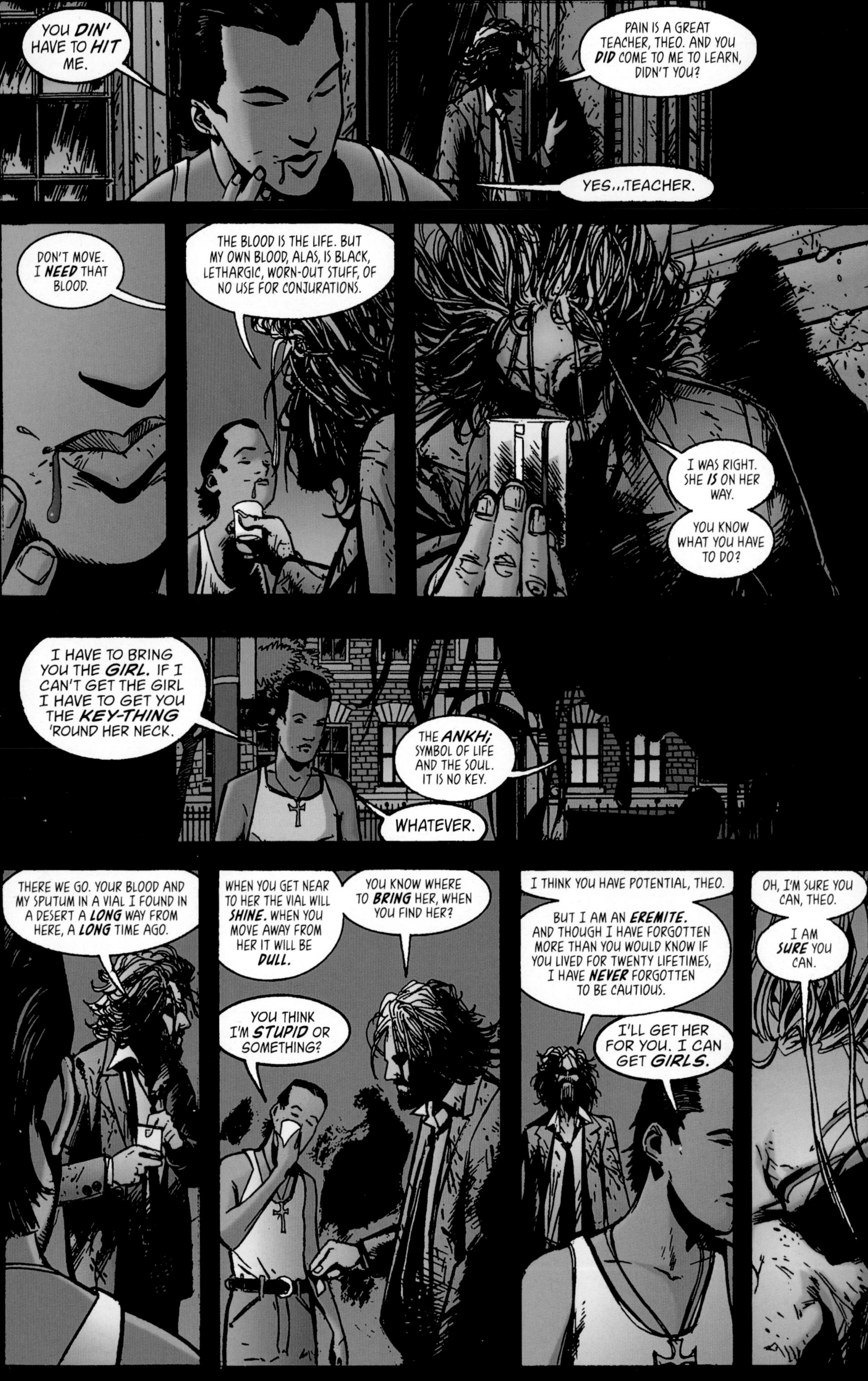
YOU DIN' HAVE TO HIT ME.
PAIN IS A GREAT TEACHER, THEO. AND YOU DID COME TO ME TO LEARN, DIDN'T YOU?
YES...TEACHER.
DON'T MOVE. I NEED THAT BLOOD.
THE BLOOD IS THE LIFE. BUT MY OWN BLOOD, ALAS, IS BLACK, LETHARGIC, WORN-OUT STUFF, OF NO USE FOR CONJURATIONS.
I WAS RIGHT. SHE IS ON HER WAY.
YOU KNOW WHAT YOU HAVE TO DO?
I HAVE TO BRING YOU THE GIRL. IF I CAN'T GET THE GIRL I HAVE TO GET YOU THE KEY-THING 'ROUND HER NECK.
THE ANKH; SYMBOL OF LIFE AND THE SOUL. IT IS NO KEY.
WHATEVER.
THERE WE GO. YOUR BLOOD AND MY SPUTUM IN A VIAL I FOUND IN A DESERT A LONG WAY FROM HERE, A LONG TIME AGO.
WHEN YOU GET NEAR TO HER THE VIAL WILL SHINE. WHEN YOU MOVE AWAY FROM HER IT WILL BE DULL.
YOU KNOW WHERE TO BRING HER, WHEN YOU FIND HER?
YOU THINK I'M STUPID OR SOMETHING?
I THINK YOU HAVE POTENTIAL, THEO.
BUT I AM AN EREMITE. AND THOUGH I HAVE FORGOTTEN MORE THAN YOU WOULD KNOW IF YOU LIVED FOR TWENTY LIFETIMES, I HAVE NEVER FORGOTTEN TO BE CAUTIOUS.
I'LL GET HER FOR YOU. I CAN GET GIRLS.
OH, I'M SURE YOU CAN, THEO.
I AM SURE YOU CAN.

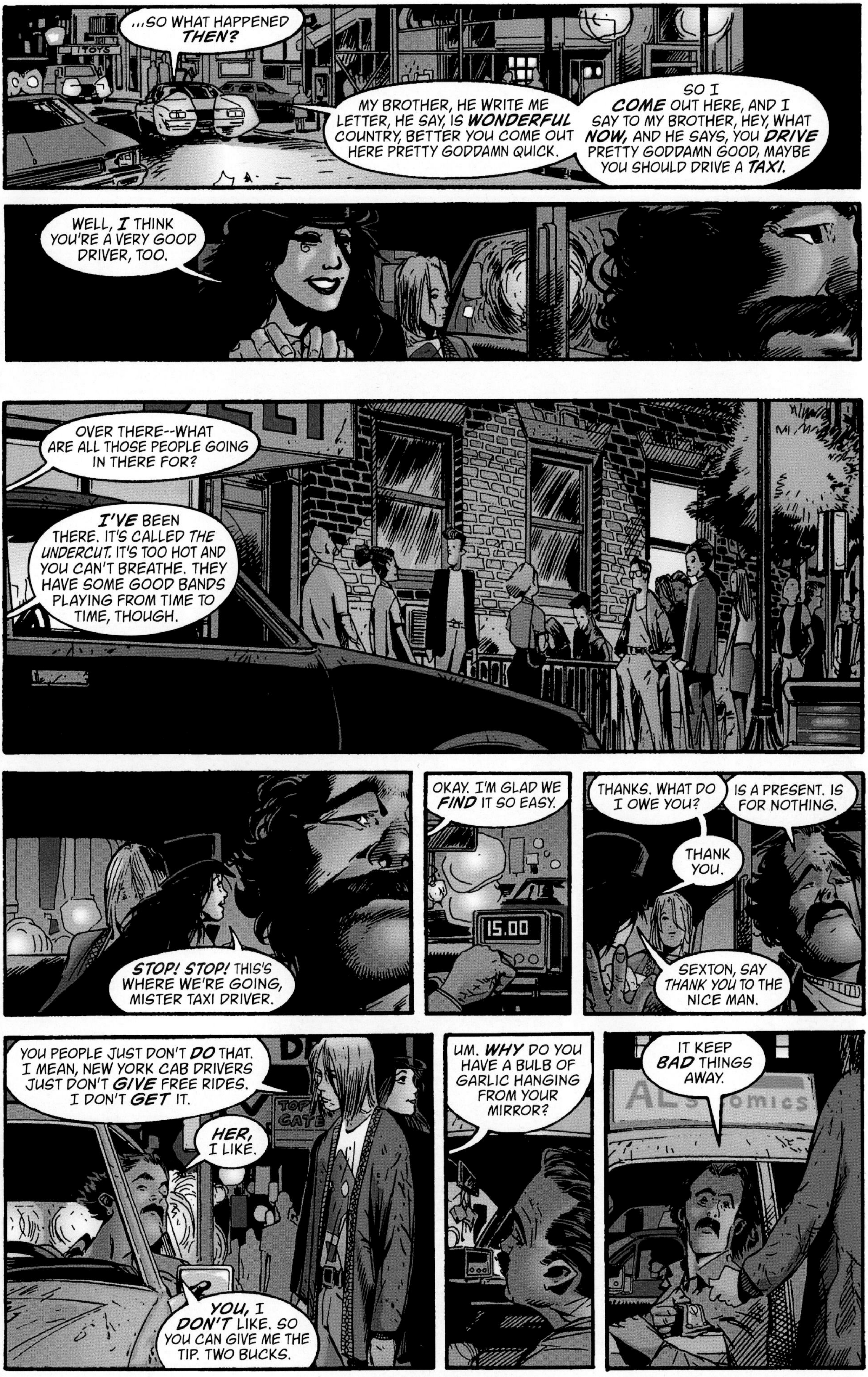
...SO WHAT HAPPENED THEN?
MY BROTHER, HE WRITE ME LETTER, HE SAY, IS WONDERFUL COUNTRY, BETTER YOU COME OUT HERE PRETTY GODDAMN QUICK.
SO I COME OUT HERE, AND I SAY TO MY BROTHER, HEY, WHAT NOW, AND HE SAYS, YOU DRIVE PRETTY GODDAMN GOOD, MAYBE YOU SHOULD DRIVE A TAXI.
TOYS
WELL, I THINK YOU'RE A VERY GOOD DRIVER, TOO.
OVER THERE--WHAT ARE ALL THOSE PEOPLE GOING IN THERE FOR?
I'VE BEEN THERE. IT'S CALLED THE UNDERCUT. IT'S TOO HOT AND YOU CAN'T BREATHE. THEY HAVE SOME GOOD BANDS PLAYING FROM TIME TO TIME, THOUGH.
STOP! STOP! THIS'S WHERE WE'RE GOING, MISTER TAXI DRIVER.
OKAY. I'M GLAD WE FIND IT SO EASY.
15.00
THANKS. WHAT DO I OWE YOU?
IS A PRESENT. IS FOR NOTHING.
THANK YOU.
SEXTON, SAY THANK YOU TO THE NICE MAN.
YOU PEOPLE JUST DON'T DO THAT. I MEAN, NEW YORK CAB DRIVERS JUST DON'T GIVE FREE RIDES. I DON'T GET IT.
HER, I LIKE.
YOU, I DON'T LIKE. SO YOU CAN GIVE ME THE TIP. TWO BUCKS.
UM. WHY DO YOU HAVE A BULB OF GARLIC HANGING FROM YOUR MIRROR?
IT KEEP BAD THINGS AWAY.

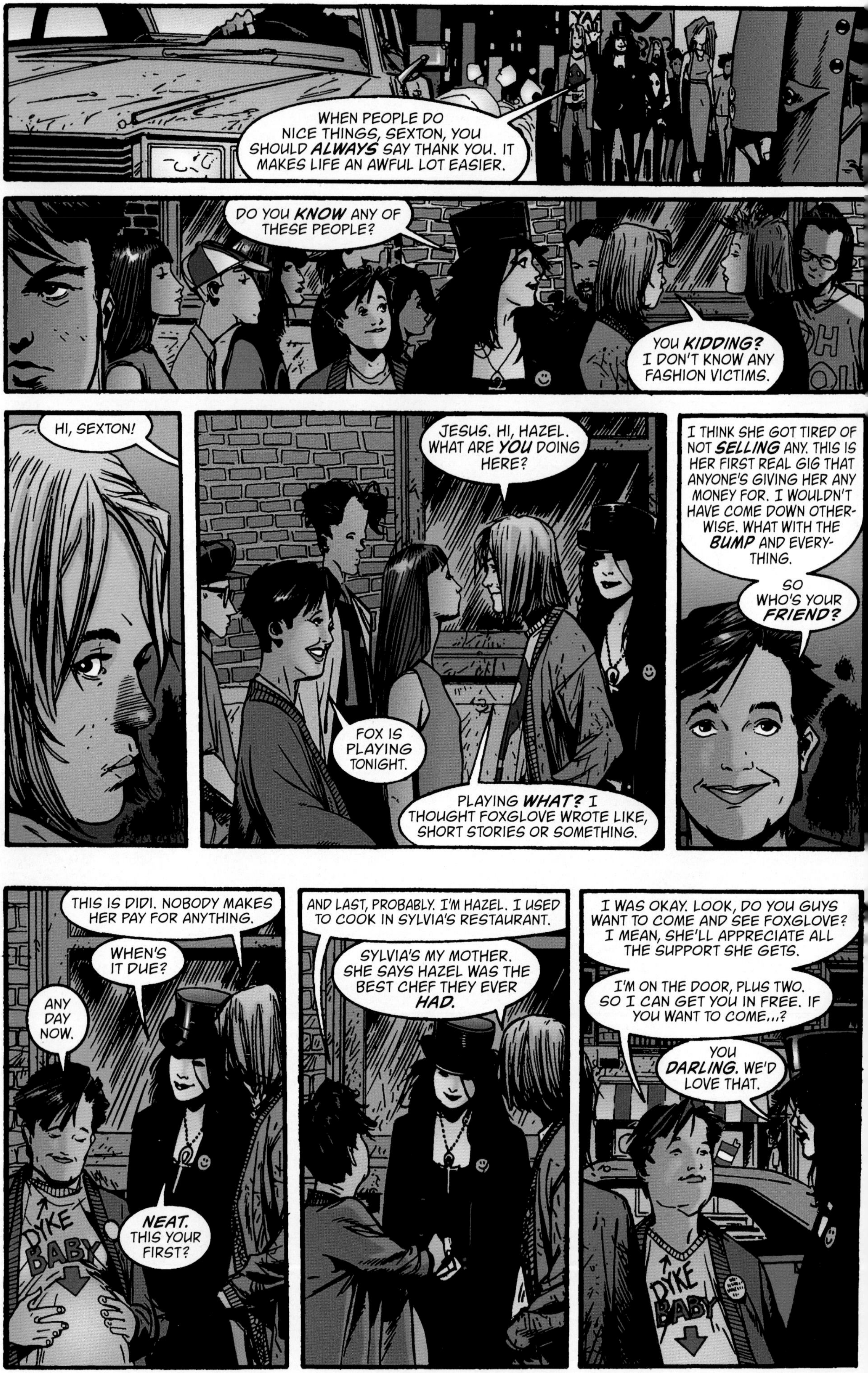
WHEN PEOPLE DO NICE THINGS, SEXTON, YOU SHOULD ALWAYS SAY THANK YOU. IT MAKES LIFE AN AWFUL LOT EASIER.
DO YOU KNOW ANY OF THESE PEOPLE?
YOU KIDDING? I DON'T KNOW ANY FASHION VICTIMS.
HI, SEXTON!
JESUS. HI, HAZEL. WHAT ARE YOU DOING HERE?
FOX IS PLAYING TONIGHT.
PLAYING WHAT? I THOUGHT FOXGLOVE WROTE LIKE, SHORT STORIES OR SOMETHING.
I THINK SHE GOT TIRED OF NOT SELLING ANY. THIS IS HER FIRST REAL GIG THAT ANYONE'S GIVING HER ANY MONEY FOR. I WOULDN'T HAVE COME DOWN OTHER-WISE. WHAT WITH THE BUMP AND EVERY-THING.
SO WHO'S YOUR FRIEND?
THIS IS DIDI. NOBODY MAKES HER PAY FOR ANYTHING.
WHEN'S IT DUE?
ANY DAY NOW.
NEAT. THIS YOUR FIRST?
DYKE BABY
AND LAST, PROBABLY. I'M HAZEL. I USED TO COOK IN SYLVIA'S RESTAURANT.
SYLVIA'S MY MOTHER. SHE SAYS HAZEL WAS THE BEST CHEF THEY EVER HAD.
I WAS OKAY. LOOK, DO YOU GUYS WANT TO COME AND SEE FOXGLOVE? I MEAN, SHE'LL APPRECIATE ALL THE SUPPORT SHE GETS.
I'M ON THE DOOR, PLUS TWO. SO I CAN GET YOU IN FREE. IF YOU WANT TO COME...?
YOU DARLING. WE'D LOVE THAT.
DYKE BABY

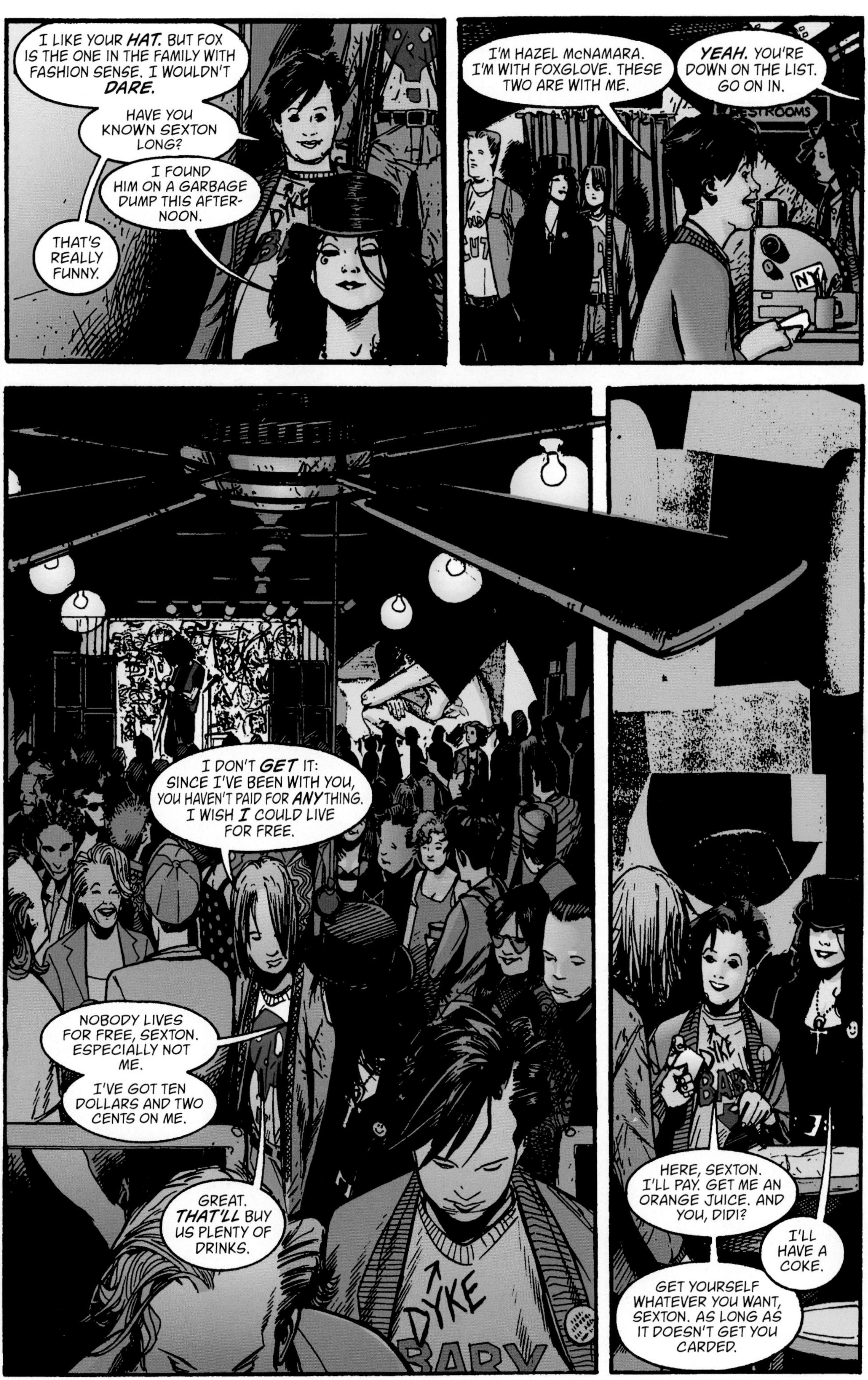
I LIKE YOUR HAT. BUT FOX IS THE ONE IN THE FAMILY WITH FASHION SENSE. I WOULDN'T DARE.
HAVE YOU KNOWN SEXTON LONG?
I FOUND HIM ON A GARBAGE DUMP THIS AFTER-NOON.
THAT'S REALLY FUNNY.
I'M HAZEL McNAMARA. I'M WITH FOXGLOVE. THESE TWO ARE WITH ME.
YEAH. YOU'RE DOWN ON THE LIST. GO ON IN.
RESTROOMS
I DON'T GET IT: SINCE I'VE BEEN WITH YOU, YOU HAVEN'T PAID FOR ANYTHING. I WISH I COULD LIVE FOR FREE.
NOBODY LIVES FOR FREE, SEXTON. ESPECIALLY NOT ME.
I'VE GOT TEN DOLLARS AND TWO CENTS ON ME.
GREAT. THAT'LL BUY US PLENTY OF DRINKS.
HERE, SEXTON. I'LL PAY. GET ME AN ORANGE JUICE. AND YOU, DIDI?
I'LL HAVE A COKE.
GET YOURSELF WHATEVER YOU WANT, SEXTON. AS LONG AS IT DOESN'T GET YOU CARDED.

I'M GLAD SEXTON'S GOT A *FRIEND*. I MEAN, I'VE KNOWN HIM SINCE HE WAS TWELVE.

HE WAS A NICE KID.

SO DO YOU STILL COOK?

NOT PROFESSIONALLY. A LOT OF STUFF WENT DOWN LAST YEAR. WHEN I GOT PREGNANT. WE *LOST* THE PLACE WE WERE STAYING, AND WE WOUND UP MOVING IN WITH MY MOTHER, AND FOX GOT REALLY SERIOUS ABOUT WRITING. AND *THEN* SHE WANTED TO START PERFORMING TOO.

OOH! HE *KICKED!* YOU WANT TO FEEL HIM *KICKING?*

SURE.

I *WON'T* TAKE YOU BACKSTAGE OR ANYTHING. FOX WILL BE THROWING UP. SHE DOESN'T LIKE PEOPLE AROUND WHILE SHE HYPERVENTILATES AND PUKES. BUT AFTER THE SHOW, IF YOU WANT...

I CHOSE TO HAVE A BABY BUT I'M GLAD I HAD A CHOICE.

OOH! HE DID IT *AGAIN.*

I GOT THE ULTRASOUND THINGIE. THAT'S HOW WE KNOW IT'S A BOY.

MY MOM LOANED US THE MONEY FOR ALL THIS BABY STUFF. IT'S SIX *THOUSAND* DOLLARS. YOU *KNOW* THAT? *SIX THOUSAND.*

ORANGE JUICE. COKE. YOUR CHANGE.

THANKS, SEXTON. WHAT ARE YOU DRINKING?

GINGER ALE.

GOOD. HEY, YOU KNOW THE *WORST* THING ABOUT BEING PREGNANT?

OH GOD. THIS ISN'T ONE OF THOSE *GROSS* THINGS, IS IT?

LIKE HAVING TO EAT THE AFTERBIRTH OR SOMETHING?

SHUT UP, BRAT. NO, IT'S NOT SMOKING. I HAVEN'T HAD A CIGARETTE FOR SEVEN *MONTHS.*

I TELL YOU, AS SOON AS BABY MCNAMARA BREATHES HIS FIRST BREATH, I'M GOING TO START INHALING SMOKE AGAIN.

LISTEN, I'M GOING BACKSTAGE TO SAY HI TO FOX. I'LL CATCH YOU TWO LATER.

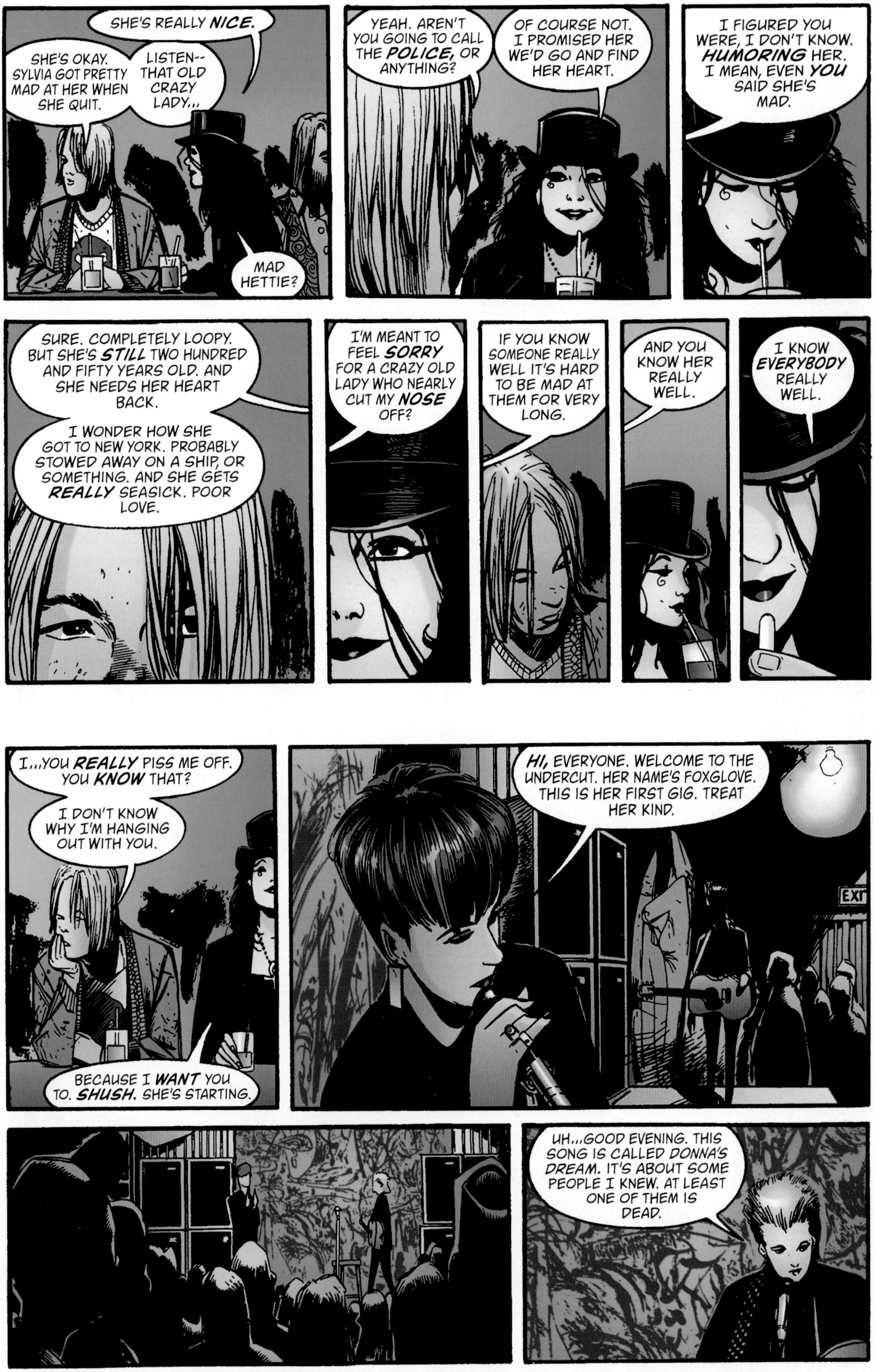
SHE'S REALLY NICE.
SHE'S OKAY. SYLVIA GOT PRETTY MAD AT HER WHEN SHE QUIT.
LISTEN-- THAT OLD CRAZY LADY...
MAD HETTIE?
YEAH. AREN'T YOU GOING TO CALL THE POLICE, OR ANYTHING?
OF COURSE NOT. I PROMISED HER WE'D GO AND FIND HER HEART.
I FIGURED YOU WERE, I DON'T KNOW. HUMORING HER. I MEAN, EVEN YOU SAID SHE'S MAD.
SURE. COMPLETELY LOOPY. BUT SHE'S STILL TWO HUNDRED AND FIFTY YEARS OLD. AND SHE NEEDS HER HEART BACK.
I WONDER HOW SHE GOT TO NEW YORK. PROBABLY STOWED AWAY ON A SHIP, OR SOMETHING. AND SHE GETS REALLY SEASICK. POOR LOVE.
I'M MEANT TO FEEL SORRY FOR A CRAZY OLD LADY WHO NEARLY CUT MY NOSE OFF?
IF YOU KNOW SOMEONE REALLY WELL IT'S HARD TO BE MAD AT THEM FOR VERY LONG.
AND YOU KNOW HER REALLY WELL.
I KNOW EVERYBODY REALLY WELL.
I...YOU REALLY PISS ME OFF. YOU KNOW THAT?
I DON'T KNOW WHY I'M HANGING OUT WITH YOU.
BECAUSE I WANT YOU TO. SHUSH. SHE'S STARTING.
HI, EVERYONE. WELCOME TO THE UNDERCUT. HER NAME'S FOXGLOVE. THIS IS HER FIRST GIG. TREAT HER KIND.
EXIT
UH...GOOD EVENING. THIS SONG IS CALLED DONNA'S DREAM. IT'S ABOUT SOME PEOPLE I KNEW. AT LEAST ONE OF THEM IS DEAD.

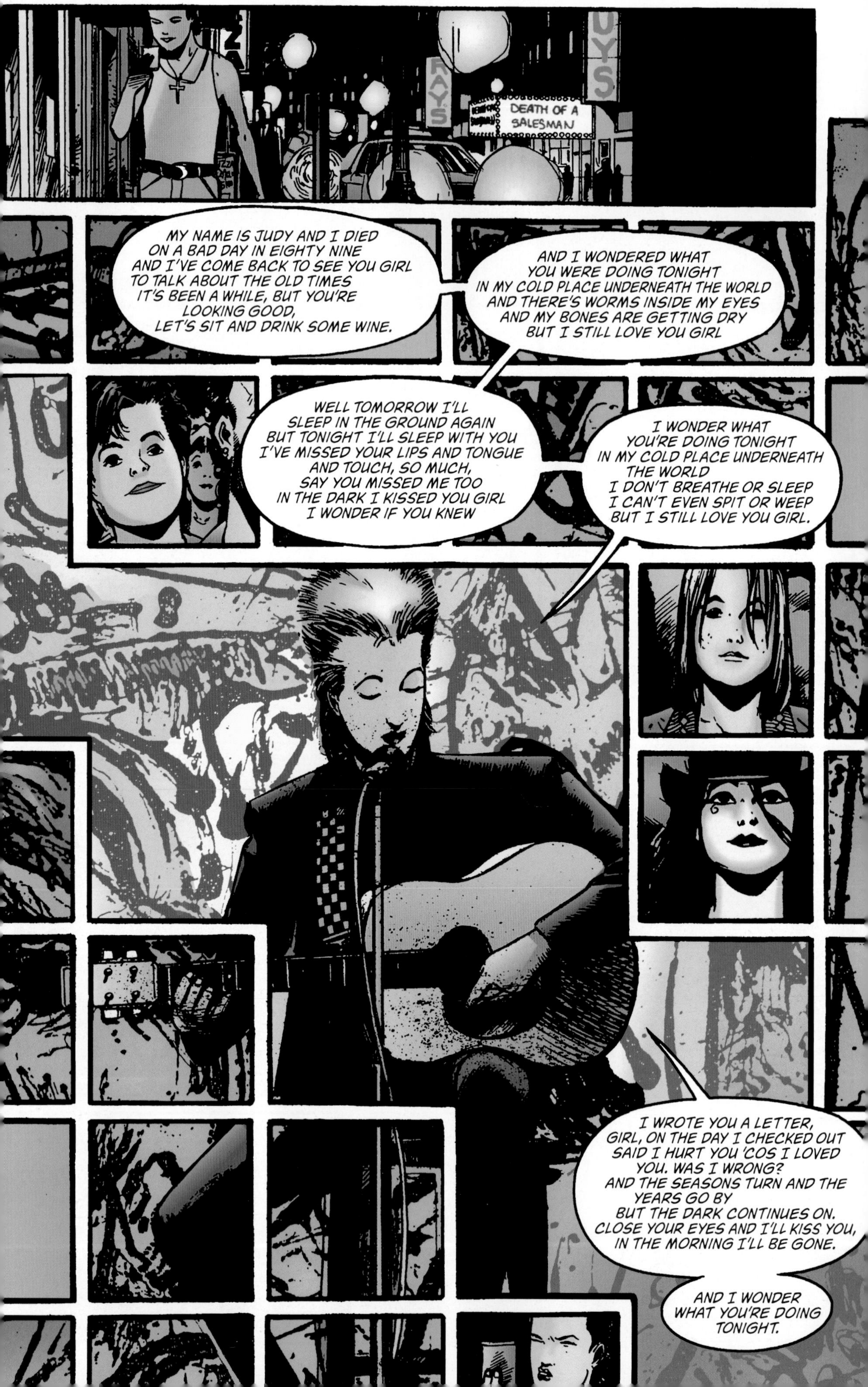
RAYS
DEATH OF A SALESMAN
MY NAME IS JUDY AND I DIED ON A BAD DAY IN EIGHTY NINE AND I'VE COME BACK TO SEE YOU GIRL TO TALK ABOUT THE OLD TIMES IT'S BEEN A WHILE, BUT YOU'RE LOOKING GOOD, LET'S SIT AND DRINK SOME WINE.
AND I WONDERED WHAT YOU WERE DOING TONIGHT IN MY COLD PLACE UNDERNEATH THE WORLD AND THERE'S WORMS INSIDE MY EYES AND MY BONES ARE GETTING DRY BUT I STILL LOVE YOU GIRL
WELL TOMORROW I'LL SLEEP IN THE GROUND AGAIN BUT TONIGHT I'LL SLEEP WITH YOU I'VE MISSED YOUR LIPS AND TONGUE AND TOUCH, SO MUCH, SAY YOU MISSED ME TOO IN THE DARK I KISSED YOU GIRL I WONDER IF YOU KNEW
I WONDER WHAT YOU'RE DOING TONIGHT IN MY COLD PLACE UNDERNEATH THE WORLD I DON'T BREATHE OR SLEEP I CAN'T EVEN SPIT OR WEEP BUT I STILL LOVE YOU GIRL.
I WROTE YOU A LETTER, GIRL, ON THE DAY I CHECKED OUT SAID I HURT YOU 'COS I LOVED YOU. WAS I WRONG? AND THE SEASONS TURN AND THE YEARS GO BY BUT THE DARK CONTINUES ON. CLOSE YOUR EYES AND I'LL KISS YOU, IN THE MORNING I'LL BE GONE.
AND I WONDER WHAT YOU'RE DOING TONIGHT.

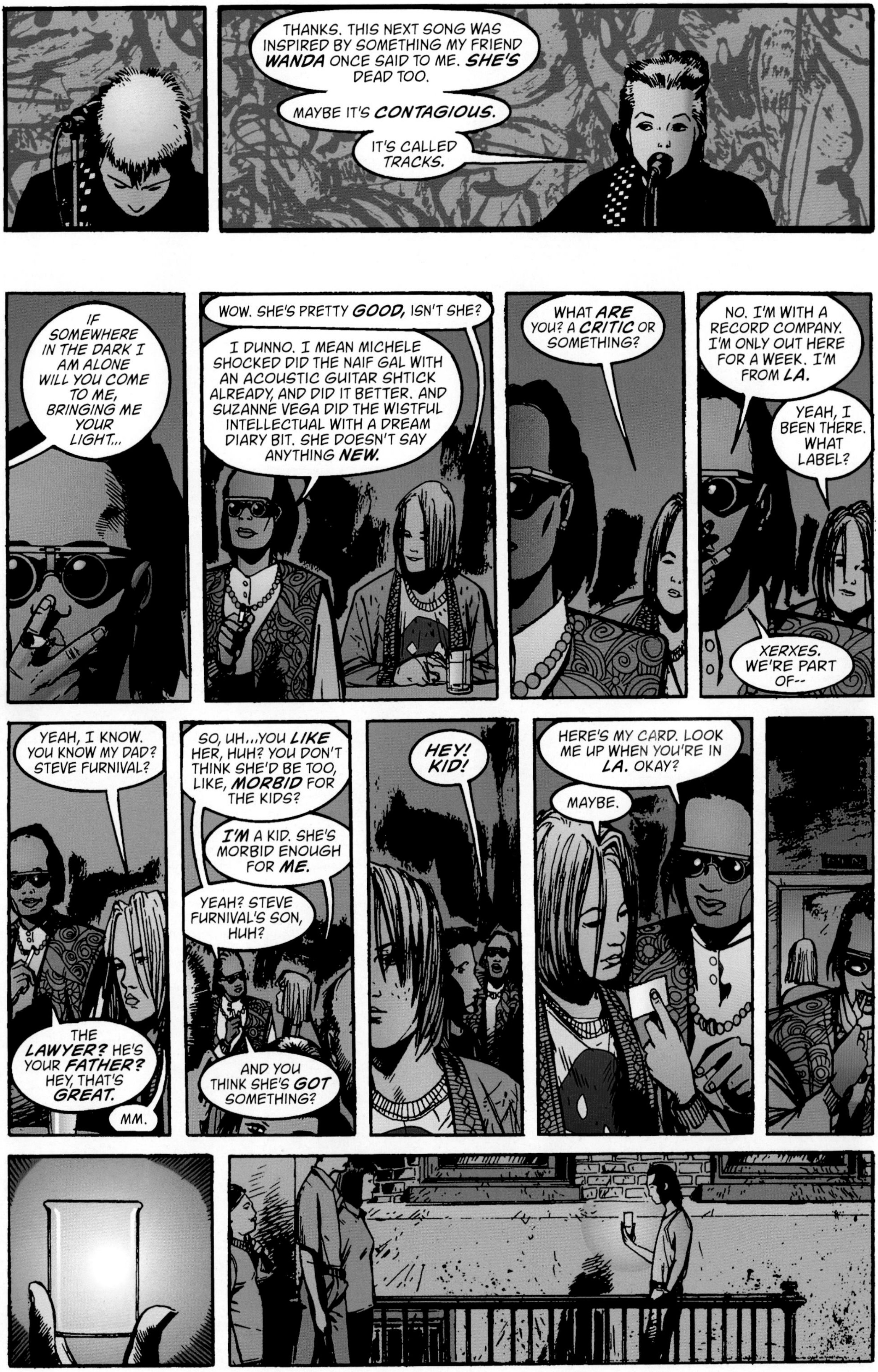
THANKS. THIS NEXT SONG WAS INSPIRED BY SOMETHING MY FRIEND WANDA ONCE SAID TO ME. SHE'S DEAD TOO.
MAYBE IT'S CONTAGIOUS.
IT'S CALLED TRACKS.
IF SOMEWHERE IN THE DARK I AM ALONE WILL YOU COME TO ME, BRINGING ME YOUR LIGHT...
WOW. SHE'S PRETTY GOOD, ISN'T SHE?
I DUNNO. I MEAN MICHELE SHOCKED DID THE NAIF GAL WITH AN ACOUSTIC GUITAR SHTICK ALREADY, AND DID IT BETTER. AND SUZANNE VEGA DID THE WISTFUL INTELLECTUAL WITH A DREAM DIARY BIT. SHE DOESN'T SAY ANYTHING NEW.
WHAT ARE YOU? A CRITIC OR SOMETHING?
NO. I'M WITH A RECORD COMPANY. I'M ONLY OUT HERE FOR A WEEK. I'M FROM LA.
YEAH, I BEEN THERE. WHAT LABEL?
XERXES. WE'RE PART OF--
YEAH, I KNOW. YOU KNOW MY DAD? STEVE FURNIVAL?
THE LAWYER? HE'S YOUR FATHER? HEY, THAT'S GREAT.
MM.
SO, UH...YOU LIKE HER, HUH? YOU DON'T THINK SHE'D BE TOO, LIKE, MORBID FOR THE KIDS?
I'M A KID. SHE'S MORBID ENOUGH FOR ME.
YEAH? STEVE FURNIVAL'S SON, HUH?
AND YOU THINK SHE'S GOT SOMETHING?
HEY! KID!
HERE'S MY CARD. LOOK ME UP WHEN YOU'RE IN LA. OKAY?
MAYBE.

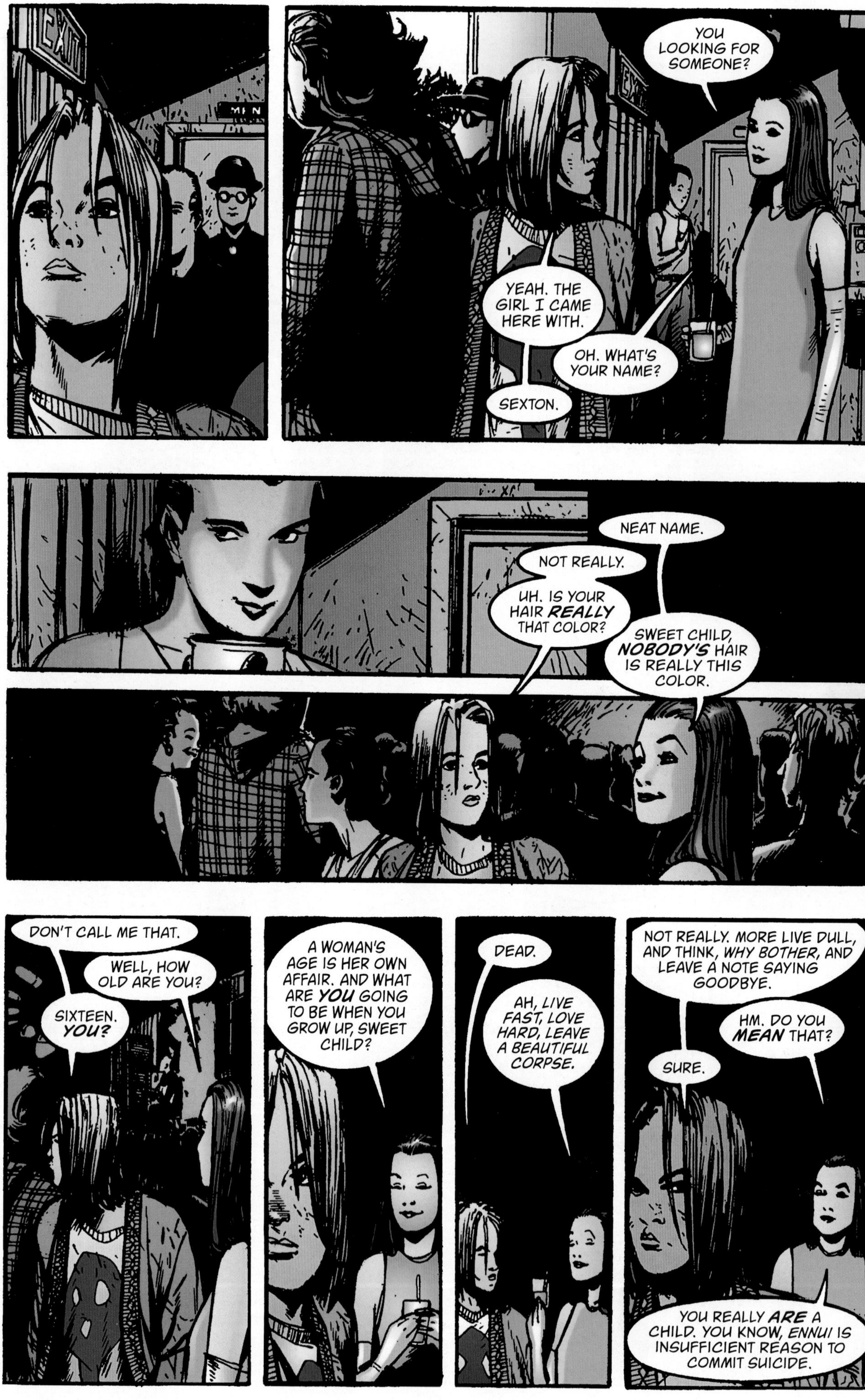
EXIT
MEN
YOU LOOKING FOR SOMEONE?
YEAH. THE GIRL I CAME HERE WITH.
OH. WHAT'S YOUR NAME?
SEXTON.
NEAT NAME.
NOT REALLY.
UH. IS YOUR HAIR *REALLY* THAT COLOR?
SWEET CHILD, *NOBODY'S* HAIR IS REALLY THIS COLOR.
DON'T CALL ME THAT.
WELL, HOW OLD ARE YOU?
SIXTEEN. *YOU?*
A WOMAN'S AGE IS HER OWN AFFAIR. AND WHAT ARE *YOU* GOING TO BE WHEN YOU GROW UP, SWEET CHILD?
DEAD.
AH, *LIVE FAST, LOVE HARD, LEAVE A BEAUTIFUL CORPSE.*
NOT REALLY. MORE LIVE DULL, AND THINK, *WHY BOTHER,* AND LEAVE A NOTE SAYING GOODBYE.
HM. DO YOU *MEAN* THAT?
SURE.
YOU REALLY *ARE* A CHILD. YOU KNOW, *ENNUI* IS INSUFFICIENT REASON TO COMMIT SUICIDE.

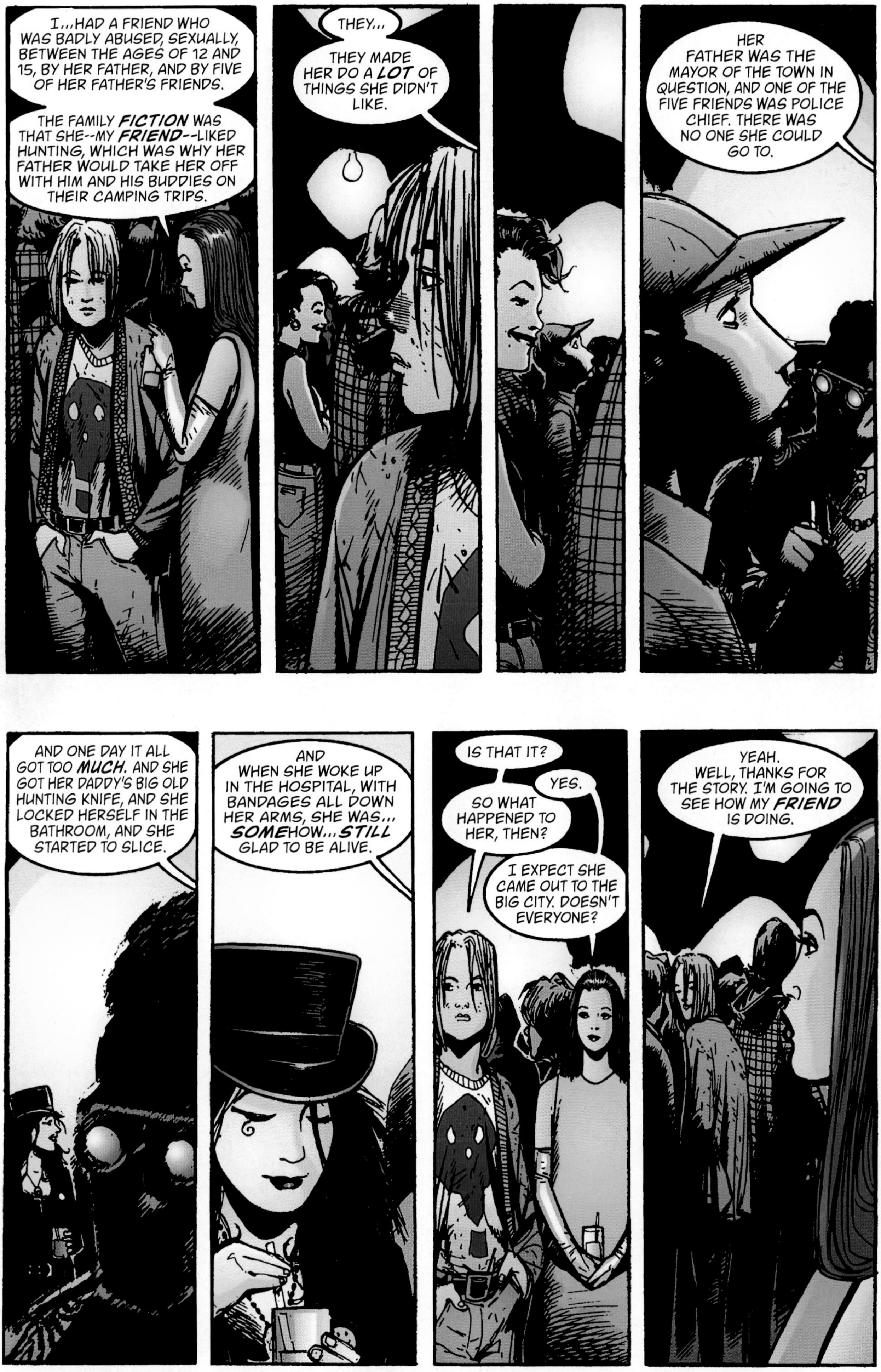
I...HAD A FRIEND WHO WAS BADLY ABUSED, SEXUALLY, BETWEEN THE AGES OF 12 AND 15, BY HER FATHER, AND BY FIVE OF HER FATHER'S FRIENDS.
THE FAMILY *FICTION* WAS THAT SHE--MY *FRIEND*--LIKED HUNTING, WHICH WAS WHY HER FATHER WOULD TAKE HER OFF WITH HIM AND HIS BUDDIES ON THEIR CAMPING TRIPS.
THEY...
THEY MADE HER DO A *LOT* OF THINGS SHE DIDN'T LIKE.
HER FATHER WAS THE MAYOR OF THE TOWN IN QUESTION, AND ONE OF THE FIVE FRIENDS WAS POLICE CHIEF. THERE WAS NO ONE SHE COULD GO TO.
AND ONE DAY IT ALL GOT TOO *MUCH*. AND SHE GOT HER DADDY'S BIG OLD HUNTING KNIFE, AND SHE LOCKED HERSELF IN THE BATHROOM, AND SHE STARTED TO SLICE.
AND WHEN SHE WOKE UP IN THE HOSPITAL, WITH BANDAGES ALL DOWN HER ARMS, SHE WAS... *SOME*HOW... *STILL* GLAD TO BE ALIVE.
IS THAT IT?
YES.
SO WHAT HAPPENED TO HER, THEN?
I EXPECT SHE CAME OUT TO THE BIG CITY. DOESN'T EVERYONE?
YEAH. WELL, THANKS FOR THE STORY. I'M GOING TO SEE HOW MY *FRIEND* IS DOING.

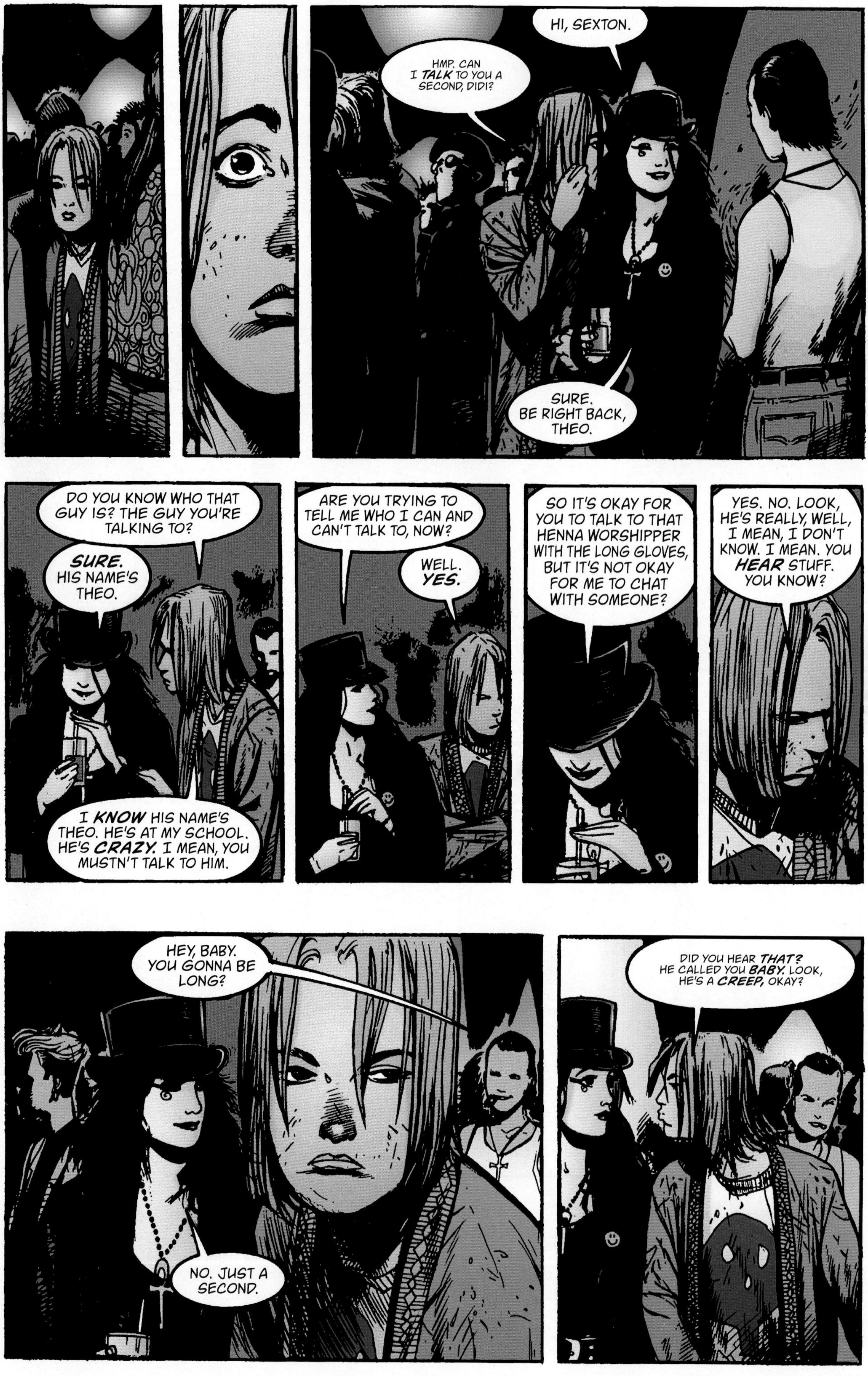
HI, SEXTON.
HMP. CAN I TALK TO YOU A SECOND, DIDI?
SURE. BE RIGHT BACK, THEO.
DO YOU KNOW WHO THAT GUY IS? THE GUY YOU'RE TALKING TO?
SURE. HIS NAME'S THEO.
I KNOW HIS NAME'S THEO. HE'S AT MY SCHOOL. HE'S CRAZY. I MEAN, YOU MUSTN'T TALK TO HIM.
ARE YOU TRYING TO TELL ME WHO I CAN AND CAN'T TALK TO, NOW?
WELL. YES.
SO IT'S OKAY FOR YOU TO TALK TO THAT HENNA WORSHIPPER WITH THE LONG GLOVES, BUT IT'S NOT OKAY FOR ME TO CHAT WITH SOMEONE?
YES. NO. LOOK, HE'S REALLY, WELL, I MEAN, I DON'T KNOW. I MEAN. YOU HEAR STUFF. YOU KNOW?
HEY, BABY. YOU GONNA BE LONG?
NO. JUST A SECOND.
DID YOU HEAR THAT? HE CALLED YOU BABY. LOOK, HE'S A CREEP, OKAY?

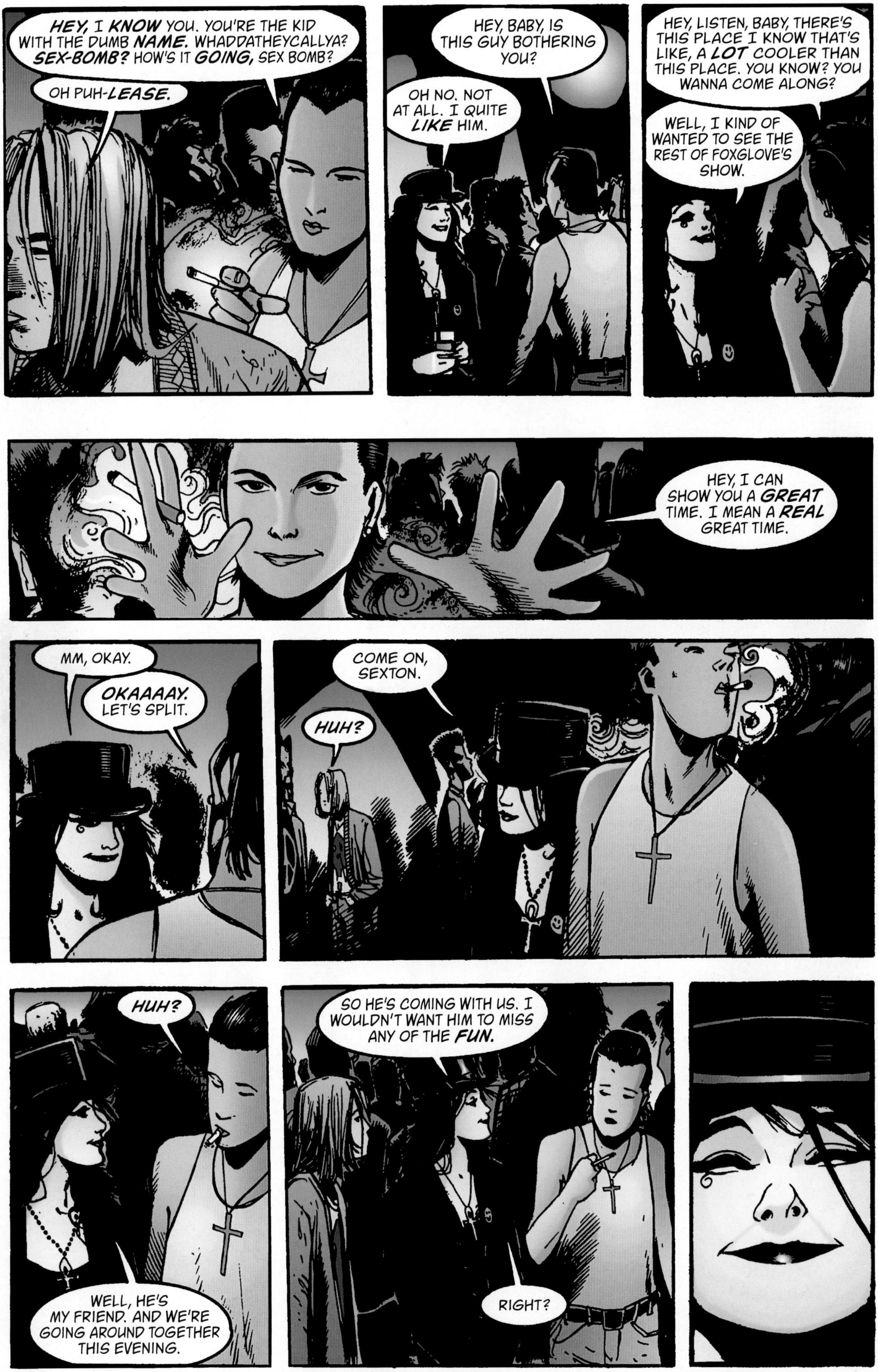
HEY, I KNOW YOU. YOU'RE THE KID WITH THE DUMB NAME. WHADDATHEYCALLYA? SEX-BOMB? HOW'S IT GOING, SEX BOMB?
OH PUH-LEASE.
HEY, BABY, IS THIS GUY BOTHERING YOU?
OH NO. NOT AT ALL. I QUITE LIKE HIM.
HEY, LISTEN, BABY, THERE'S THIS PLACE I KNOW THAT'S LIKE, A LOT COOLER THAN THIS PLACE. YOU KNOW? YOU WANNA COME ALONG?
WELL, I KIND OF WANTED TO SEE THE REST OF FOXGLOVE'S SHOW.
HEY, I CAN SHOW YOU A GREAT TIME. I MEAN A REAL GREAT TIME.
MM, OKAY.
OKAAAAY. LET'S SPLIT.
COME ON, SEXTON.
HUH?
HUH?
WELL, HE'S MY FRIEND. AND WE'RE GOING AROUND TOGETHER THIS EVENING.
SO HE'S COMING WITH US. I WOULDN'T WANT HIM TO MISS ANY OF THE FUN.
RIGHT?

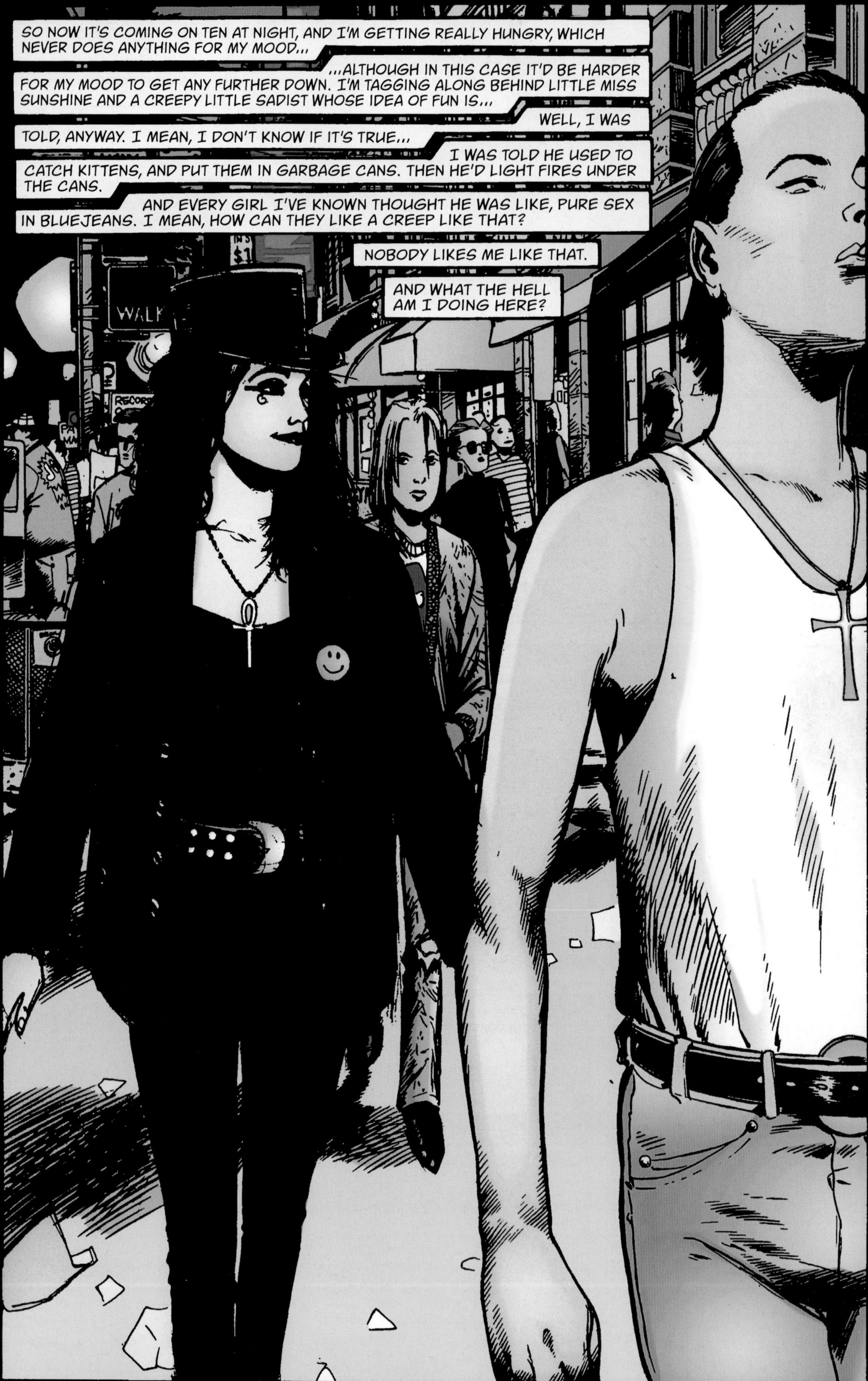
SO NOW IT'S COMING ON TEN AT NIGHT, AND I'M GETTING REALLY HUNGRY, WHICH NEVER DOES ANYTHING FOR MY MOOD...
...ALTHOUGH IN THIS CASE IT'D BE HARDER FOR MY MOOD TO GET ANY FURTHER DOWN. I'M TAGGING ALONG BEHIND LITTLE MISS SUNSHINE AND A CREEPY LITTLE SADIST WHOSE IDEA OF FUN IS...
WELL, I WAS TOLD, ANYWAY. I MEAN, I DON'T KNOW IF IT'S TRUE...
I WAS TOLD HE USED TO CATCH KITTENS, AND PUT THEM IN GARBAGE CANS. THEN HE'D LIGHT FIRES UNDER THE CANS.
AND EVERY GIRL I'VE KNOWN THOUGHT HE WAS LIKE, PURE SEX IN BLUEJEANS. I MEAN, HOW CAN THEY LIKE A CREEP LIKE THAT?
NOBODY LIKES ME LIKE THAT.
AND WHAT THE HELL AM I DOING HERE?
WALK

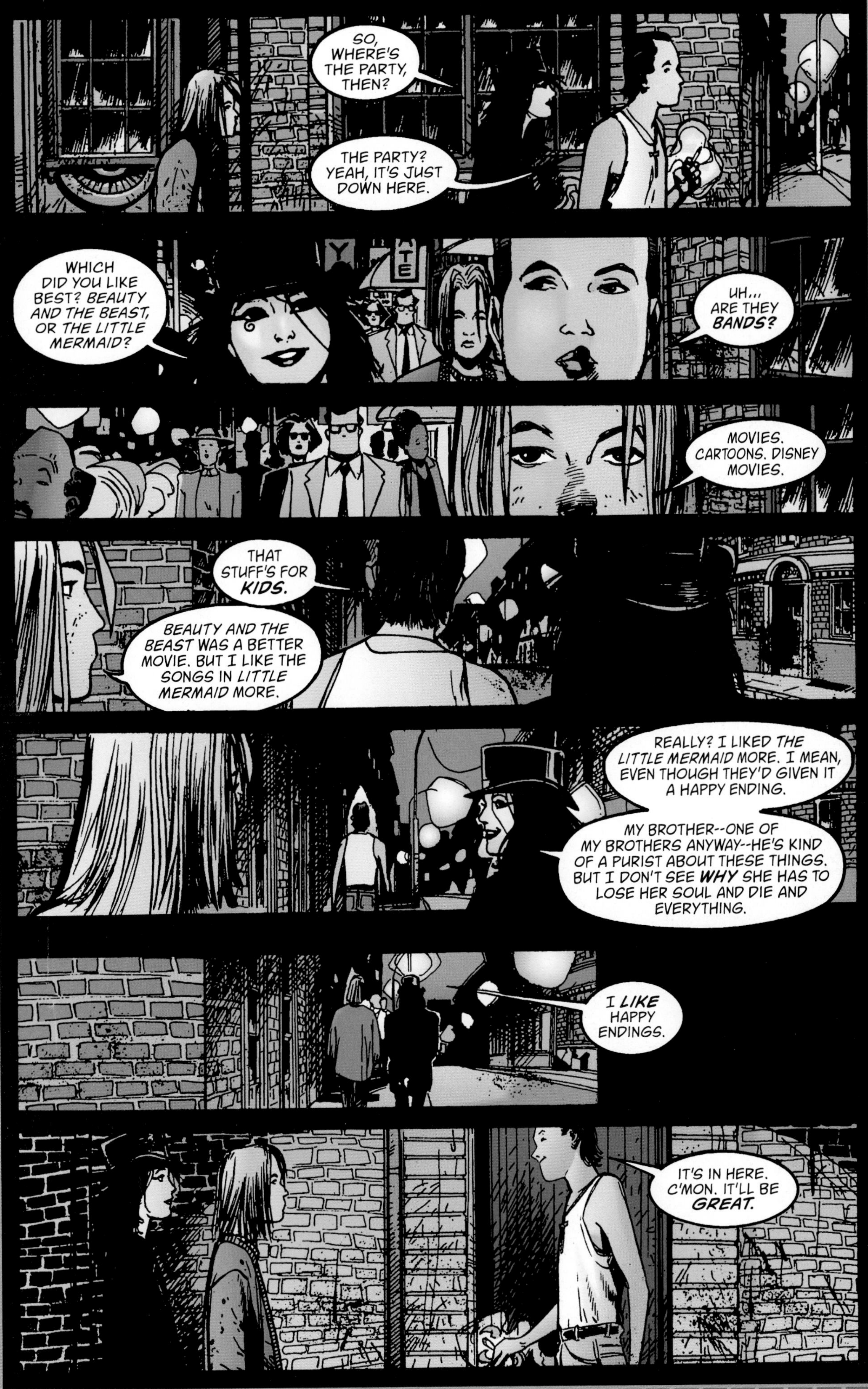
SO, WHERE'S THE PARTY, THEN?
THE PARTY? YEAH, IT'S JUST DOWN HERE.
WHICH DID YOU LIKE BEST? *BEAUTY AND THE BEAST,* OR *THE LITTLE MERMAID?*
UH... ARE THEY ***BANDS?***
MOVIES. CARTOONS. DISNEY MOVIES.
THAT STUFF'S FOR ***KIDS.***
BEAUTY AND THE BEAST WAS A BETTER MOVIE. BUT I LIKE THE SONGS IN *LITTLE MERMAID* MORE.
REALLY? I LIKED *THE LITTLE MERMAID* MORE. I MEAN, EVEN THOUGH THEY'D GIVEN IT A HAPPY ENDING.
MY BROTHER--ONE OF MY BROTHERS ANYWAY--HE'S KIND OF A PURIST ABOUT THESE THINGS. BUT I DON'T SEE ***WHY*** SHE HAS TO LOSE HER SOUL AND DIE AND EVERYTHING.
I ***LIKE*** HAPPY ENDINGS.
IT'S IN HERE. C'MON. IT'LL BE ***GREAT.***

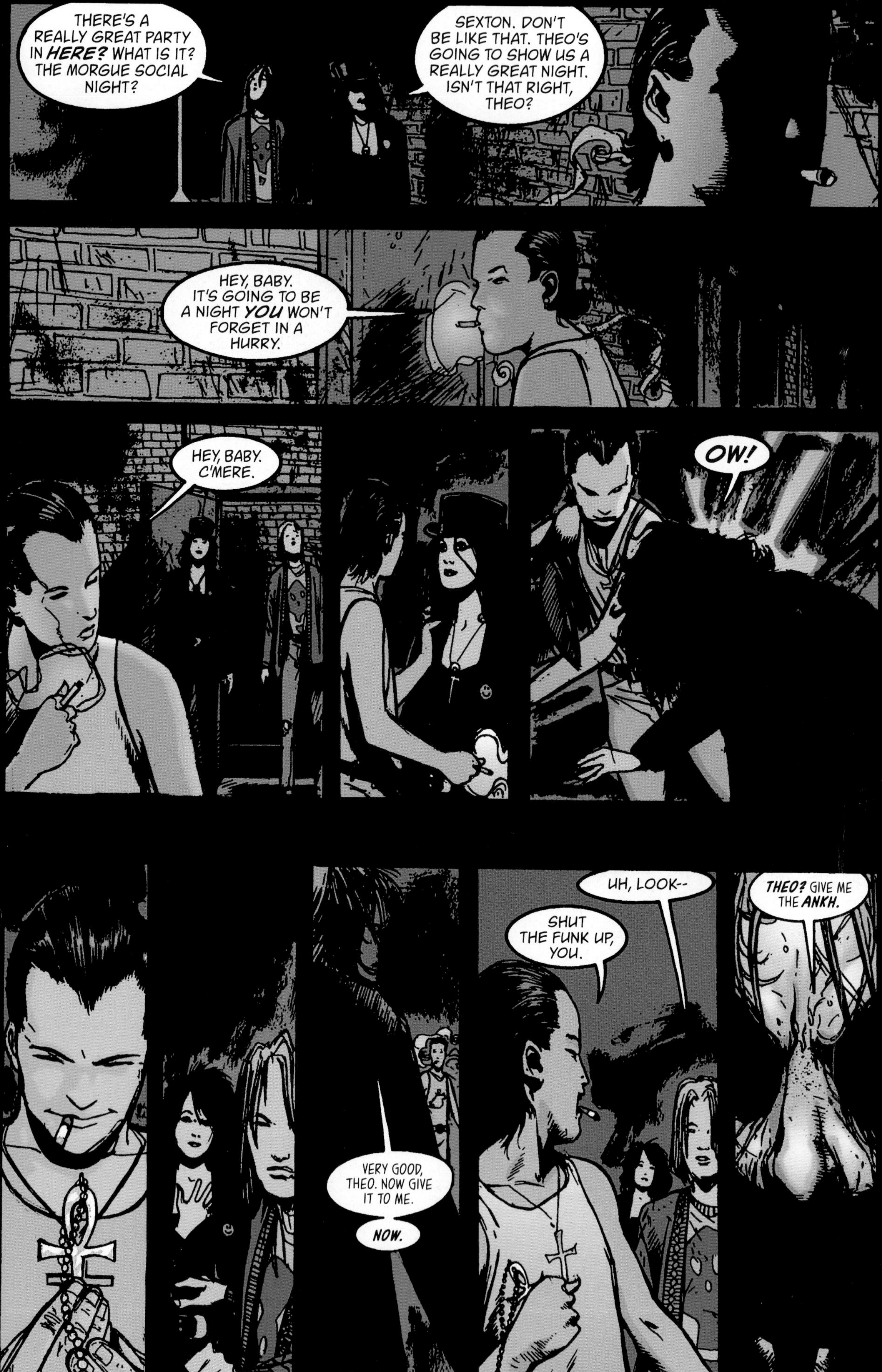
THERE'S A REALLY GREAT PARTY IN HERE? WHAT IS IT? THE MORGUE SOCIAL NIGHT?
SEXTON. DON'T BE LIKE THAT. THEO'S GOING TO SHOW US A REALLY GREAT NIGHT. ISN'T THAT RIGHT, THEO?
HEY, BABY. IT'S GOING TO BE A NIGHT YOU WON'T FORGET IN A HURRY.
HEY, BABY. C'MERE.
OW!
VERY GOOD, THEO. NOW GIVE IT TO ME.
NOW.
UH, LOOK--
SHUT THE FUNK UP, YOU.
THEO? GIVE ME THE ANKH.

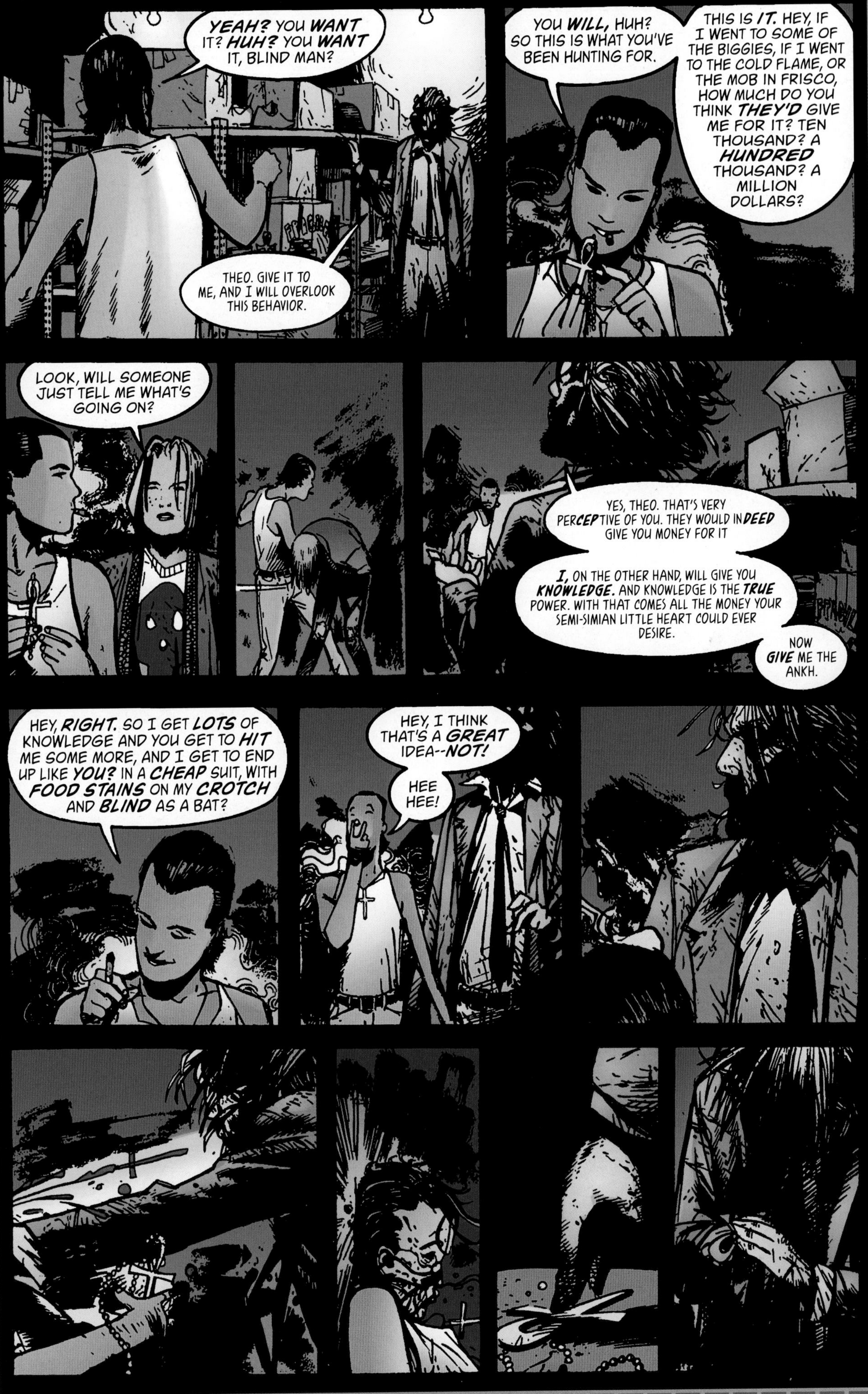

YEAH? YOU WANT IT? HUH? YOU WANT IT, BLIND MAN?
THEO. GIVE IT TO ME, AND I WILL OVERLOOK THIS BEHAVIOR.
YOU WILL, HUH? SO THIS IS WHAT YOU'VE BEEN HUNTING FOR.
THIS IS IT. HEY, IF I WENT TO SOME OF THE BIGGIES, IF I WENT TO THE COLD FLAME, OR THE MOB IN FRISCO, HOW MUCH DO YOU THINK THEY'D GIVE ME FOR IT? TEN THOUSAND? A HUNDRED THOUSAND? A MILLION DOLLARS?
LOOK, WILL SOMEONE JUST TELL ME WHAT'S GOING ON?
YES, THEO. THAT'S VERY PERCEPTIVE OF YOU. THEY WOULD INDEED GIVE YOU MONEY FOR IT
I, ON THE OTHER HAND, WILL GIVE YOU KNOWLEDGE. AND KNOWLEDGE IS THE TRUE POWER. WITH THAT COMES ALL THE MONEY YOUR SEMI-SIMIAN LITTLE HEART COULD EVER DESIRE.
NOW GIVE ME THE ANKH.
HEY, RIGHT. SO I GET LOTS OF KNOWLEDGE AND YOU GET TO HIT ME SOME MORE, AND I GET TO END UP LIKE YOU? IN A CHEAP SUIT, WITH FOOD STAINS ON MY CROTCH AND BLIND AS A BAT?
HEY, I THINK THAT'S A GREAT IDEA--NOT!
HEE HEE!

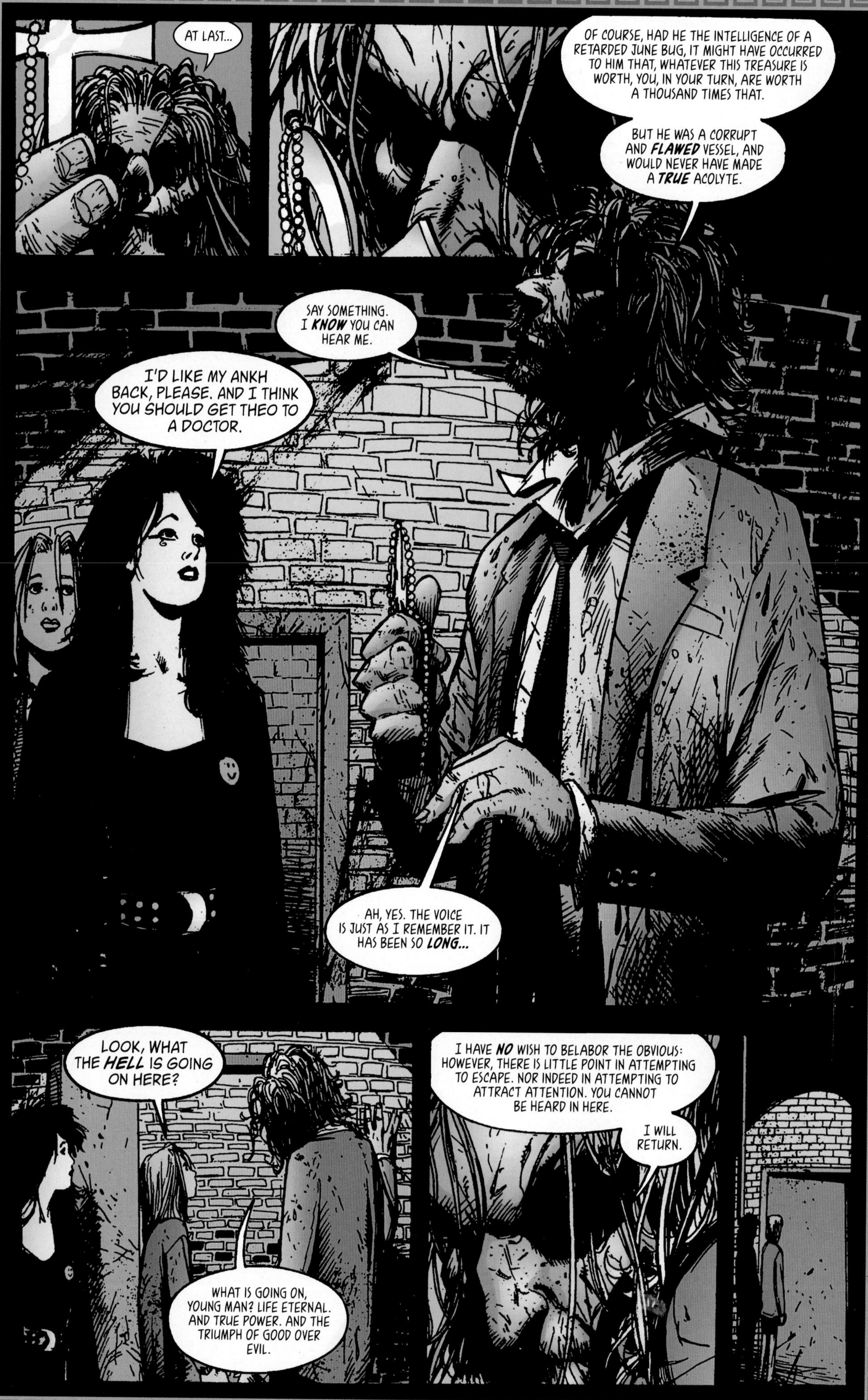
AT LAST...
OF COURSE, HAD HE THE INTELLIGENCE OF A RETARDED JUNE BUG, IT MIGHT HAVE OCCURRED TO HIM THAT, WHATEVER THIS TREASURE IS WORTH, YOU, IN YOUR TURN, ARE WORTH A THOUSAND TIMES THAT.
BUT HE WAS A CORRUPT AND *FLAWED* VESSEL, AND WOULD NEVER HAVE MADE A *TRUE* ACOLYTE.
SAY SOMETHING. I *KNOW* YOU CAN HEAR ME.
I'D LIKE MY ANKH BACK, PLEASE. AND I THINK YOU SHOULD GET THEO TO A DOCTOR.
AH, YES. THE VOICE IS JUST AS I REMEMBER IT. IT HAS BEEN SO *LONG...*
LOOK, WHAT THE *HELL* IS GOING ON HERE?
WHAT IS GOING ON, YOUNG MAN? LIFE ETERNAL. AND TRUE POWER. AND THE TRIUMPH OF GOOD OVER EVIL.
I HAVE *NO* WISH TO BELABOR THE OBVIOUS: HOWEVER, THERE IS LITTLE POINT IN ATTEMPTING TO ESCAPE. NOR INDEED IN ATTEMPTING TO ATTRACT ATTENTION. YOU CANNOT BE HEARD IN HERE.
I WILL RETURN.

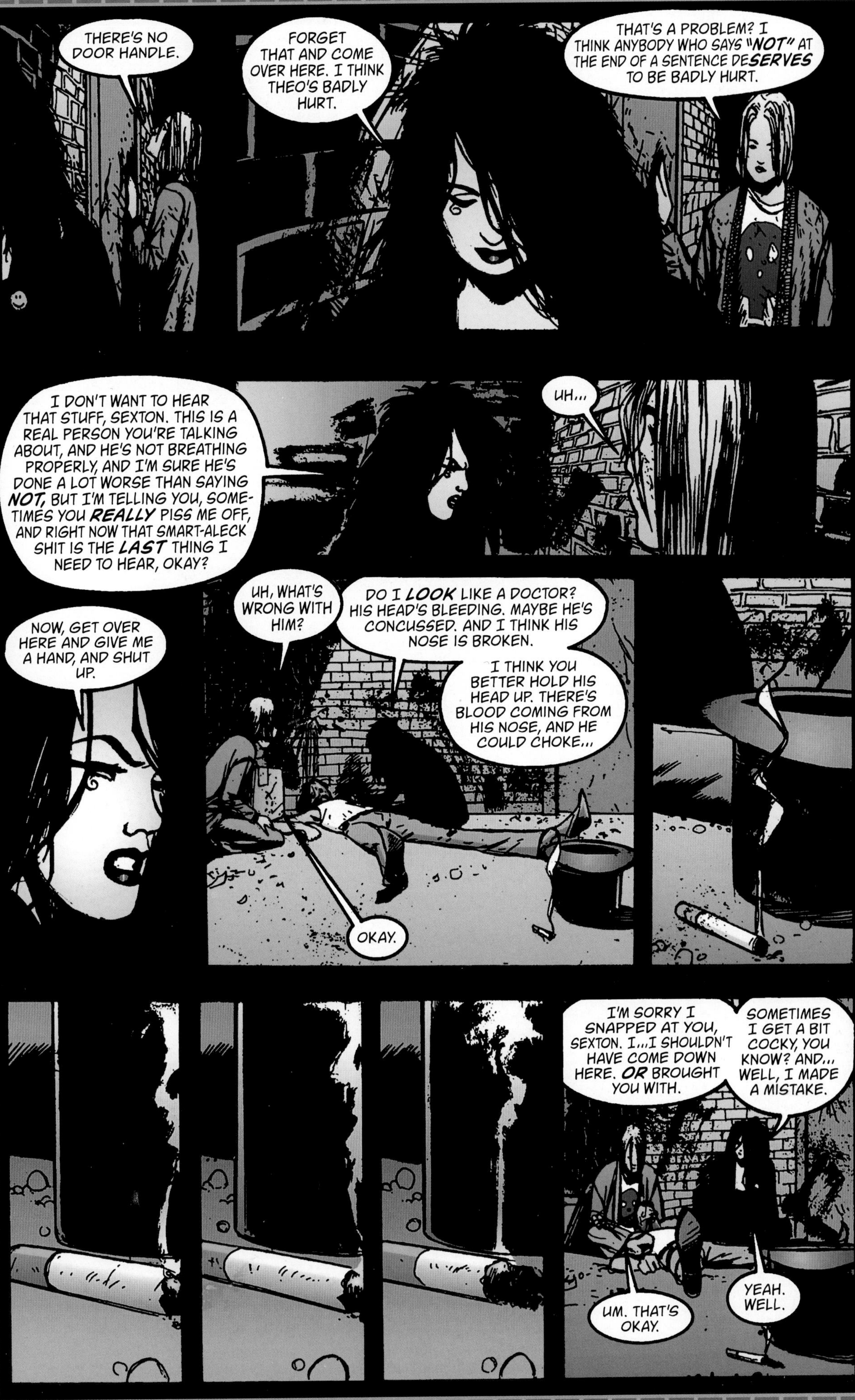
THERE'S NO DOOR HANDLE.
FORGET THAT AND COME OVER HERE. I THINK THEO'S BADLY HURT.
THAT'S A PROBLEM? I THINK ANYBODY WHO SAYS "NOT" AT THE END OF A SENTENCE DESERVES TO BE BADLY HURT.
I DON'T WANT TO HEAR THAT STUFF, SEXTON. THIS IS A REAL PERSON YOU'RE TALKING ABOUT, AND HE'S NOT BREATHING PROPERLY, AND I'M SURE HE'S DONE A LOT WORSE THAN SAYING NOT, BUT I'M TELLING YOU, SOMETIMES YOU REALLY PISS ME OFF, AND RIGHT NOW THAT SMART-ALECK SHIT IS THE LAST THING I NEED TO HEAR, OKAY?
UH...
NOW, GET OVER HERE AND GIVE ME A HAND, AND SHUT UP.
UH, WHAT'S WRONG WITH HIM?
DO I LOOK LIKE A DOCTOR? HIS HEAD'S BLEEDING. MAYBE HE'S CONCUSSED. AND I THINK HIS NOSE IS BROKEN.
I THINK YOU BETTER HOLD HIS HEAD UP. THERE'S BLOOD COMING FROM HIS NOSE, AND HE COULD CHOKE...
OKAY.
I'M SORRY I SNAPPED AT YOU, SEXTON. I...I SHOULDN'T HAVE COME DOWN HERE. OR BROUGHT YOU WITH.
SOMETIMES I GET A BIT COCKY, YOU KNOW? AND... WELL, I MADE A MISTAKE.
UM. THAT'S OKAY.
YEAH. WELL.

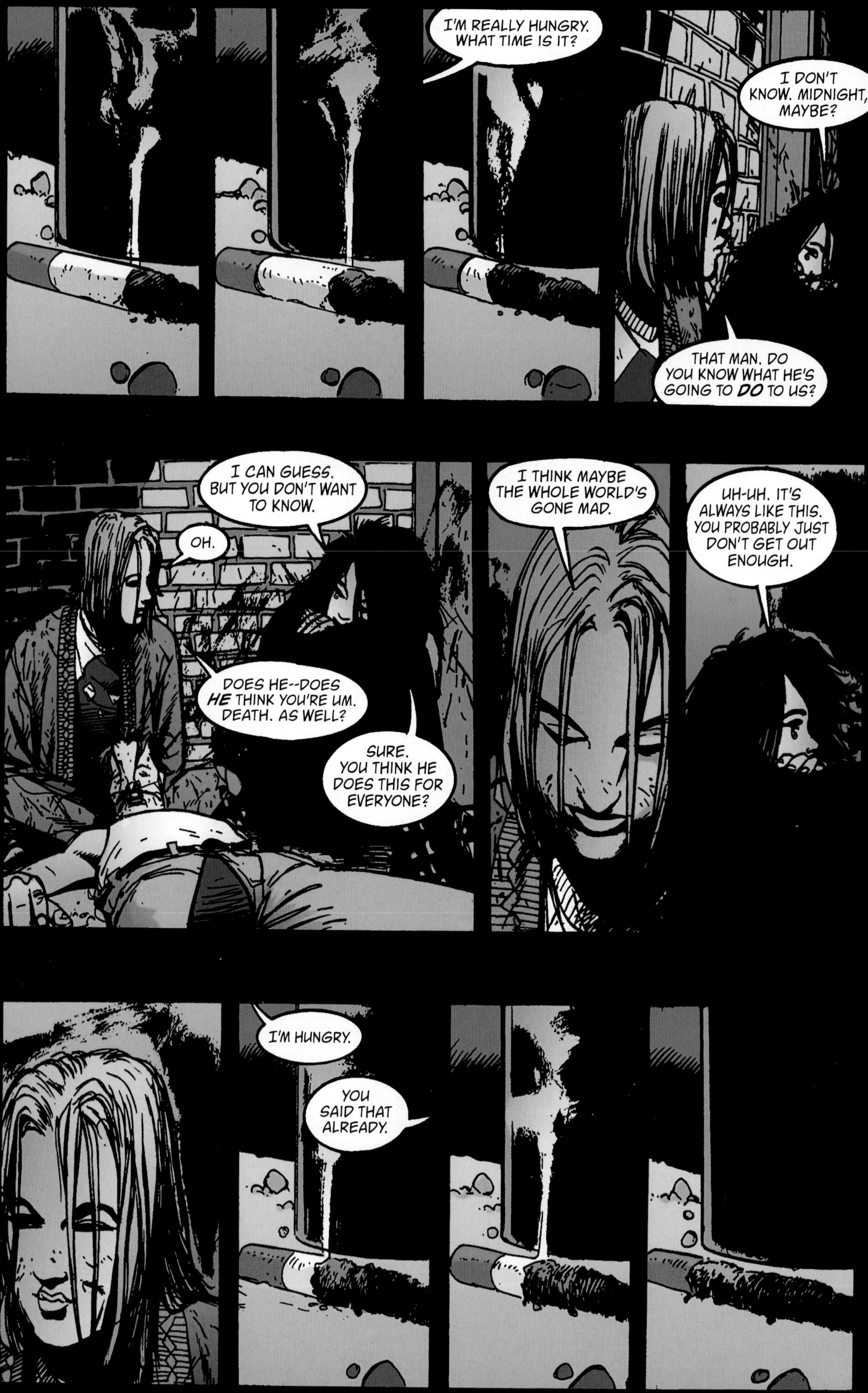
I'M REALLY HUNGRY. WHAT TIME IS IT?
I DON'T KNOW. MIDNIGHT, MAYBE?
THAT MAN. DO YOU KNOW WHAT HE'S GOING TO *DO* TO US?
I CAN GUESS. BUT YOU DON'T WANT TO KNOW.
OH.
DOES HE--DOES *HE* THINK YOU'RE UM. DEATH. AS WELL?
SURE. YOU THINK HE DOES THIS FOR EVERYONE?
I THINK MAYBE THE WHOLE WORLD'S GONE MAD.
UH-UH. IT'S ALWAYS LIKE THIS. YOU PROBABLY JUST DON'T GET OUT ENOUGH.
I'M HUNGRY.
YOU SAID THAT ALREADY.

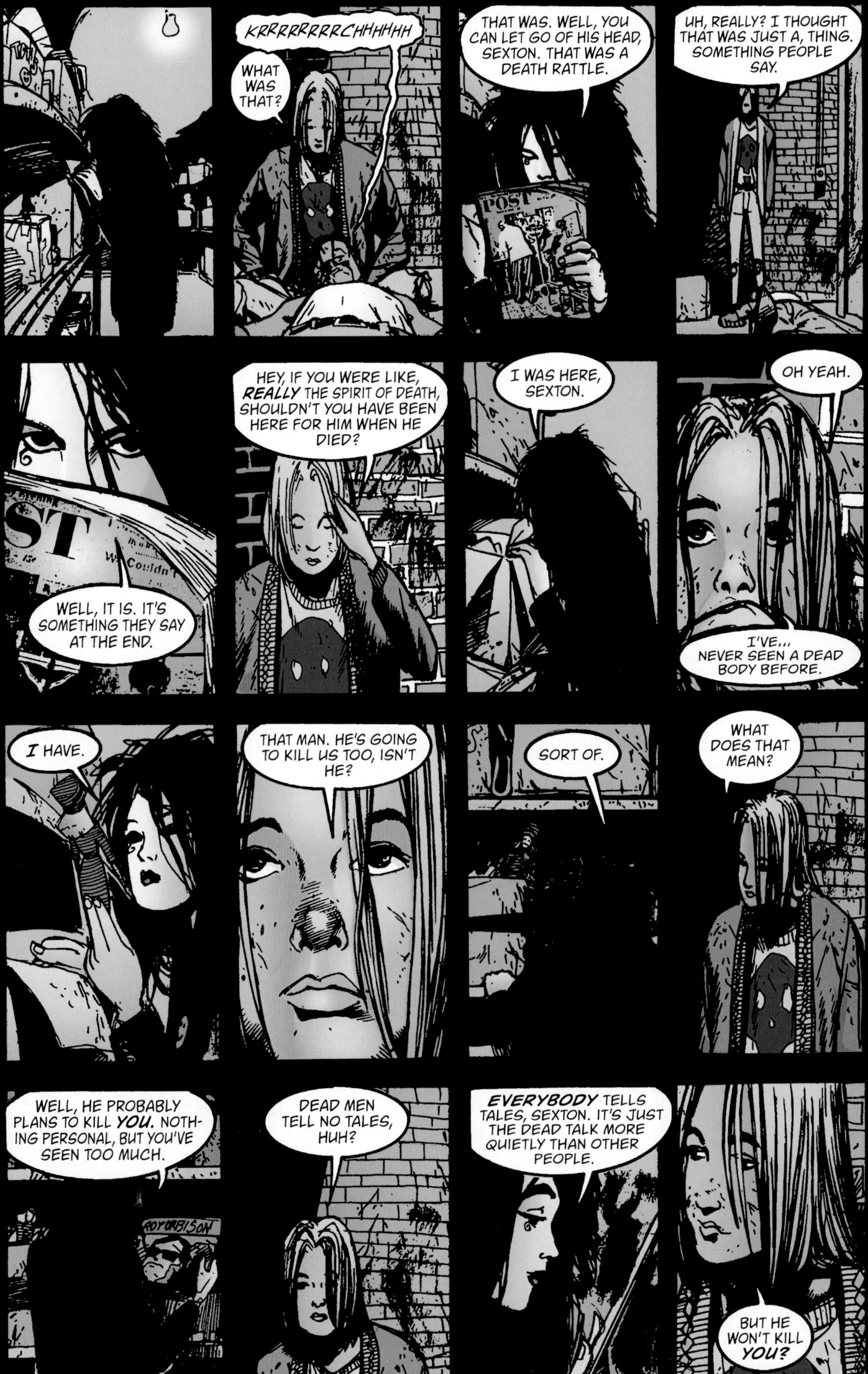
KRRRRRRRRCHHHHHH
WHAT WAS THAT?
THAT WAS. WELL, YOU CAN LET GO OF HIS HEAD, SEXTON. THAT WAS A DEATH RATTLE.
UH, REALLY? I THOUGHT THAT WAS JUST A, THING. SOMETHING PEOPLE SAY.
WELL, IT IS. IT'S SOMETHING THEY SAY AT THE END.
HEY, IF YOU WERE LIKE, REALLY THE SPIRIT OF DEATH, SHOULDN'T YOU HAVE BEEN HERE FOR HIM WHEN HE DIED?
I WAS HERE, SEXTON.
OH YEAH.
I'VE... NEVER SEEN A DEAD BODY BEFORE.
I HAVE.
THAT MAN. HE'S GOING TO KILL US TOO, ISN'T HE?
SORT OF.
WHAT DOES THAT MEAN?
WELL, HE PROBABLY PLANS TO KILL YOU. NOTHING PERSONAL, BUT YOU'VE SEEN TOO MUCH.
DEAD MEN TELL NO TALES, HUH?
EVERYBODY TELLS TALES, SEXTON. IT'S JUST THE DEAD TALK MORE QUIETLY THAN OTHER PEOPLE.
BUT HE WON'T KILL YOU?

PROBABLY NOT IMMEDIATELY. I'M TOO VALUABLE.

I'M *HUNGRY.*

POOR MAD HETTIE.

POOR MAD HETTIE? WHAT'S *THAT* SUPPOSED TO MEAN?

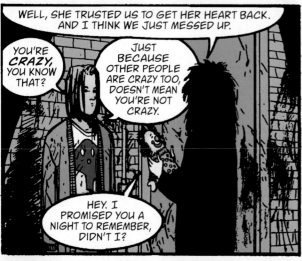

WELL, SHE TRUSTED US TO GET HER HEART BACK. AND I THINK WE JUST MESSED UP.

YOU'RE *CRAZY,* YOU KNOW THAT?

JUST BECAUSE OTHER PEOPLE ARE CRAZY TOO, DOESN'T MEAN YOU'RE NOT CRAZY.

HEY. I PROMISED YOU A NIGHT TO REMEMBER, DIDN'T I?

YOU SHOULD TAKE YOUR *MIND* OFF IT. THERE'S MORE OLD MAGAZINES HERE THAN IN A DENTIST'S WAITING ROOM. WHY DON'T YOU *READ* SOMETHING?

HUH?

OR PLAY WITH SOME OF THE *TOYS.* THEY AREN'T *ALL* BROKEN. SEE THIS CLOWN?

IF YOU KNOCK HIM *DOWN,* HE JUST *BOUNCES* RIGHT UP AGAIN.

LIKE *US.* WE'LL GET OUT OF THIS MESS. IT'LL BE FINE.

YOU'LL SEE.

WATCH *THIS!*

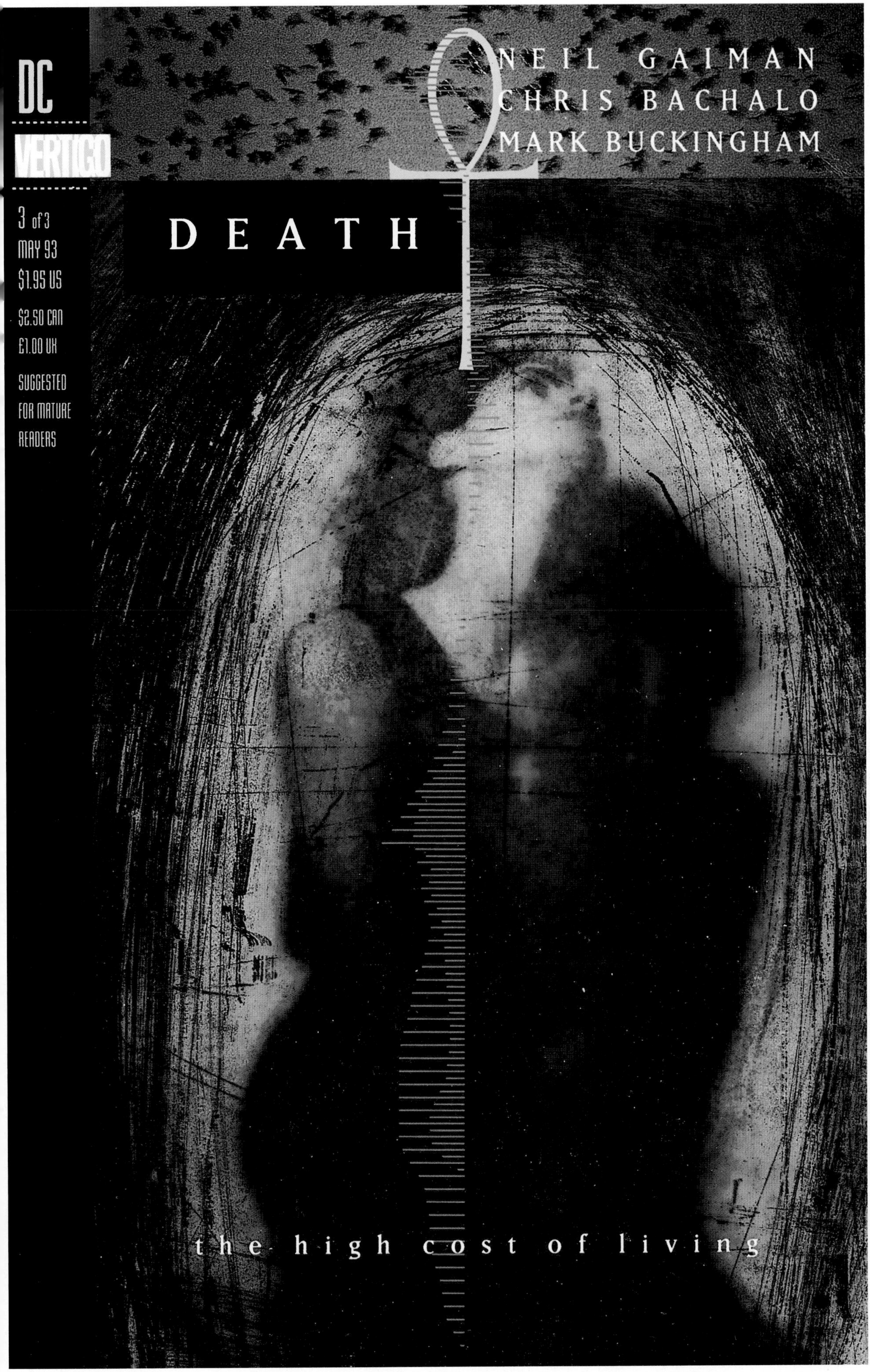
NEIL GAIMAN
CHRIS BACHALO
MARK BUCKINGHAM
3 of 3
MAY 93
$1.95 US
$2.50 CAN
£1.00 UK
SUGGESTED FOR MATURE READERS
DEATH
the high cost of living

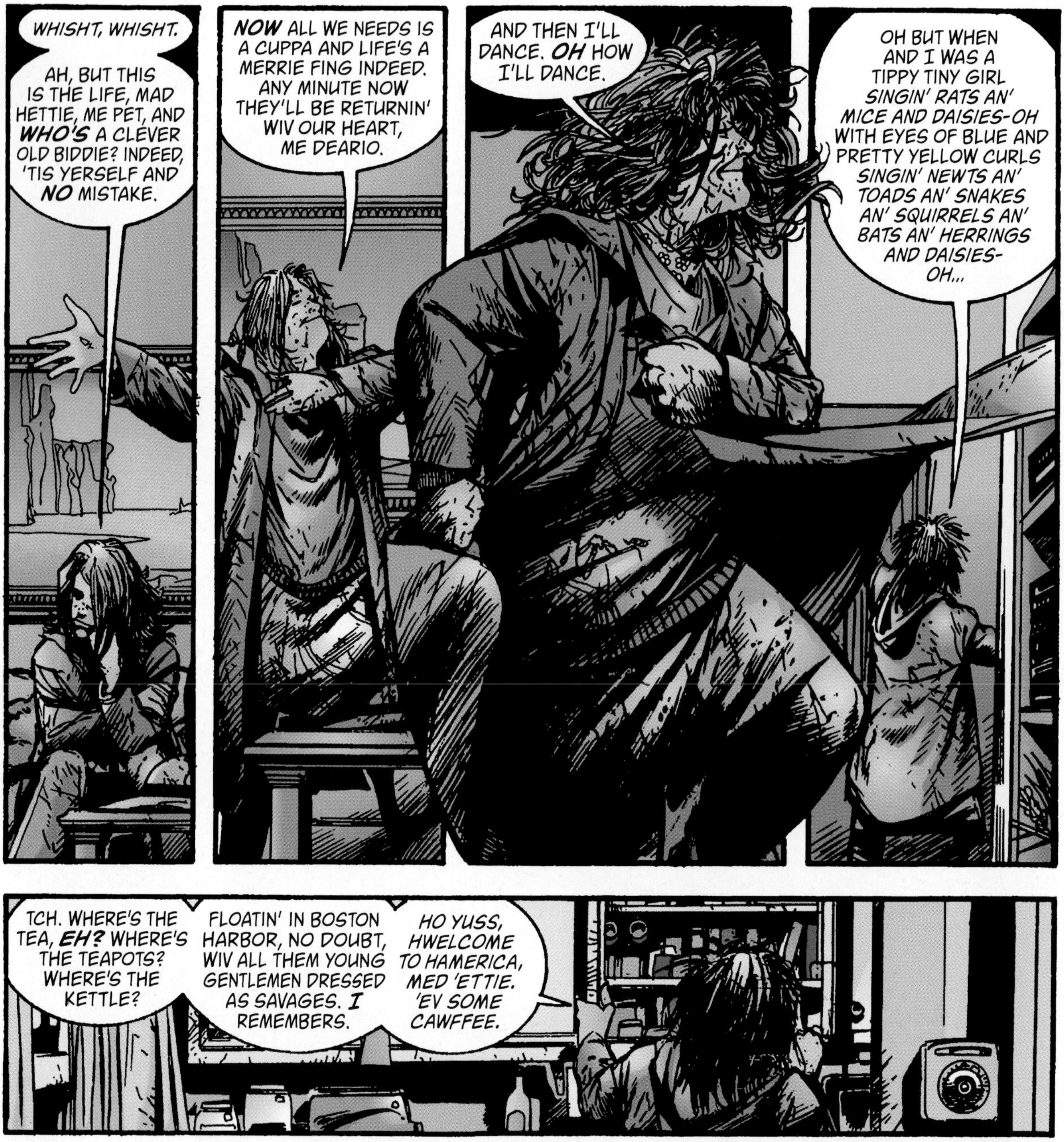
WHISHT, WHISHT.
AH, BUT THIS IS THE LIFE, MAD HETTIE, ME PET, AND WHO'S A CLEVER OLD BIDDIE? INDEED, 'TIS YERSELF AND NO MISTAKE.
NOW ALL WE NEEDS IS A CUPPA AND LIFE'S A MERRIE FING INDEED. ANY MINUTE NOW THEY'LL BE RETURNIN' WIV OUR HEART, ME DEARIO.
AND THEN I'LL DANCE. OH HOW I'LL DANCE.
OH BUT WHEN AND I WAS A TIPPY TINY GIRL SINGIN' RATS AN' MICE AND DAISIES-OH WITH EYES OF BLUE AND PRETTY YELLOW CURLS SINGIN' NEWTS AN' TOADS AN' SNAKES AN' SQUIRRELS AN' BATS AN' HERRINGS AND DAISIES-OH...
TCH. WHERE'S THE TEA, EH? WHERE'S THE TEAPOTS? WHERE'S THE KETTLE?
FLOATIN' IN BOSTON HARBOR, NO DOUBT, WIV ALL THEM YOUNG GENTLEMEN DRESSED AS SAVAGES. I REMEMBERS.
HO YUSS, HWELCOME TO HAMERICA, MED 'ETTIE. 'EV SOME CAWFFEE.

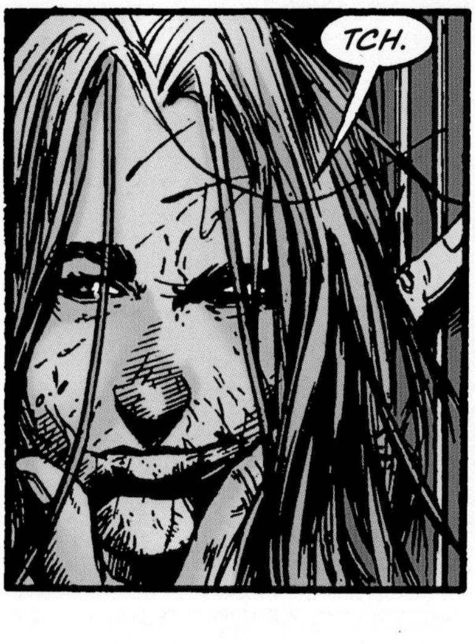
TCH.

DEATH: The High Cost of Living

CHAPTER THREE: THE HIGH COST OF LIVING

WRITTEN BY **NEIL GAIMAN** · PENCILLED BY **CHRIS BACHALO**
INKED BY **MARK BUCKINGHAM** · LETTERED BY **TODD KLEIN**
COLORED BY **STEVE OLIFF/OLYOPTICS**
EDITED BY **KAREN BERGER** · ASSISTED BY **ALISA KWITNEY**
DEATH CREATED BY NEIL GAIMAN AND MIKE DRINGENBERG

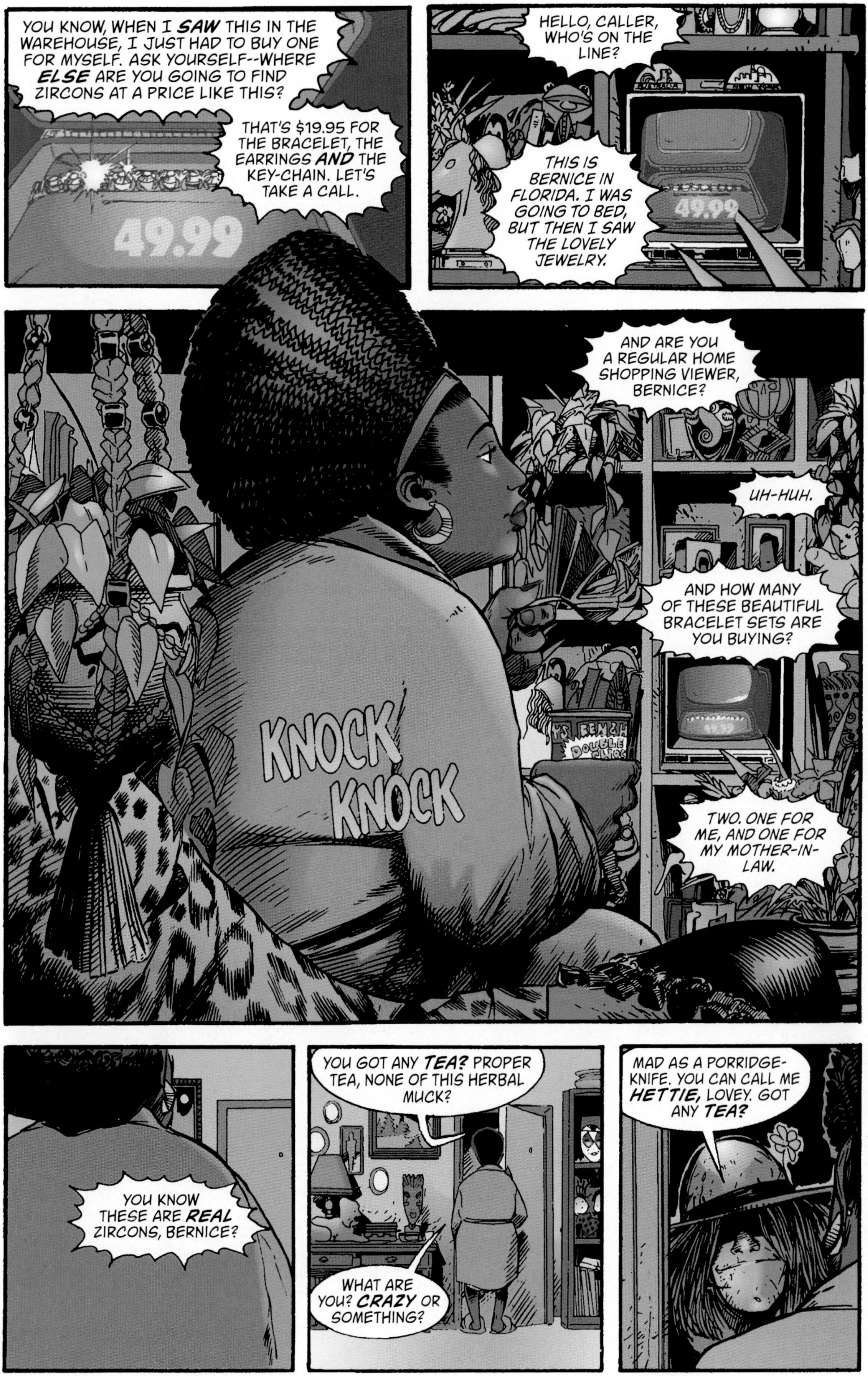
YOU KNOW, WHEN I SAW THIS IN THE WAREHOUSE, I JUST HAD TO BUY ONE FOR MYSELF. ASK YOURSELF--WHERE ELSE ARE YOU GOING TO FIND ZIRCONS AT A PRICE LIKE THIS?
THAT'S $19.95 FOR THE BRACELET, THE EARRINGS AND THE KEY-CHAIN. LET'S TAKE A CALL.
49.99
HELLO, CALLER, WHO'S ON THE LINE?
THIS IS BERNICE IN FLORIDA. I WAS GOING TO BED, BUT THEN I SAW THE LOVELY JEWELRY.
49.99
AND ARE YOU A REGULAR HOME SHOPPING VIEWER, BERNICE?
UH-HUH.
AND HOW MANY OF THESE BEAUTIFUL BRACELET SETS ARE YOU BUYING?
KNOCK
KNOCK
TWO. ONE FOR ME, AND ONE FOR MY MOTHER-IN-LAW.
YOU KNOW THESE ARE REAL ZIRCONS, BERNICE?
YOU GOT ANY TEA? PROPER TEA, NONE OF THIS HERBAL MUCK?
WHAT ARE YOU? CRAZY OR SOMETHING?
MAD AS A PORRIDGE-KNIFE. YOU CAN CALL ME HETTIE, LOVEY. GOT ANY TEA?

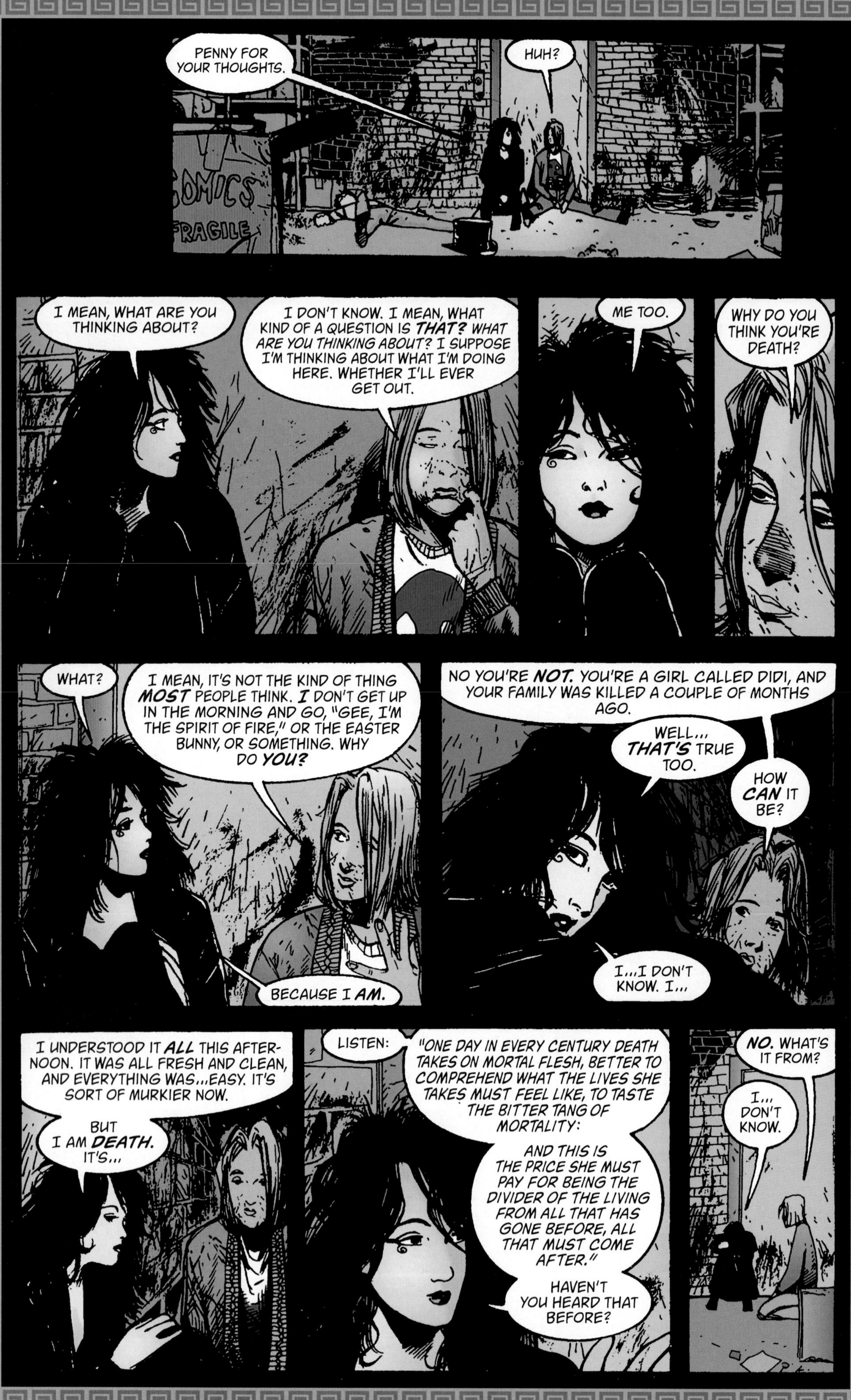

PENNY FOR YOUR THOUGHTS.
HUH?
COMICS
FRAGILE
I MEAN, WHAT ARE YOU THINKING ABOUT?
I DON'T KNOW. I MEAN, WHAT KIND OF A QUESTION IS *THAT?* WHAT ARE YOU THINKING ABOUT? I SUPPOSE I'M THINKING ABOUT WHAT I'M DOING HERE. WHETHER I'LL EVER GET OUT.
ME TOO.
WHY DO YOU THINK YOU'RE DEATH?
WHAT?
I MEAN, IT'S NOT THE KIND OF THING *MOST* PEOPLE THINK. *I* DON'T GET UP IN THE MORNING AND GO, "GEE, I'M THE SPIRIT OF FIRE," OR THE EASTER BUNNY, OR SOMETHING. WHY DO *YOU?*
BECAUSE I *AM.*
NO YOU'RE *NOT.* YOU'RE A GIRL CALLED DIDI, AND YOUR FAMILY WAS KILLED A COUPLE OF MONTHS AGO.
WELL... *THAT'S* TRUE TOO.
HOW *CAN* IT BE?
I...I DON'T KNOW. I...
I UNDERSTOOD IT *ALL* THIS AFTER-NOON. IT WAS ALL FRESH AND CLEAN, AND EVERYTHING WAS...EASY. IT'S SORT OF MURKIER NOW.
BUT I AM *DEATH.* IT'S...
LISTEN:
"ONE DAY IN EVERY CENTURY DEATH TAKES ON MORTAL FLESH, BETTER TO COMPREHEND WHAT THE LIVES SHE TAKES MUST FEEL LIKE, TO TASTE THE BITTER TANG OF MORTALITY:
AND THIS IS THE PRICE SHE MUST PAY FOR BEING THE DIVIDER OF THE LIVING FROM ALL THAT HAS GONE BEFORE, ALL THAT MUST COME AFTER."
HAVEN'T YOU HEARD THAT BEFORE?
NO. WHAT'S IT FROM?
I... DON'T KNOW.

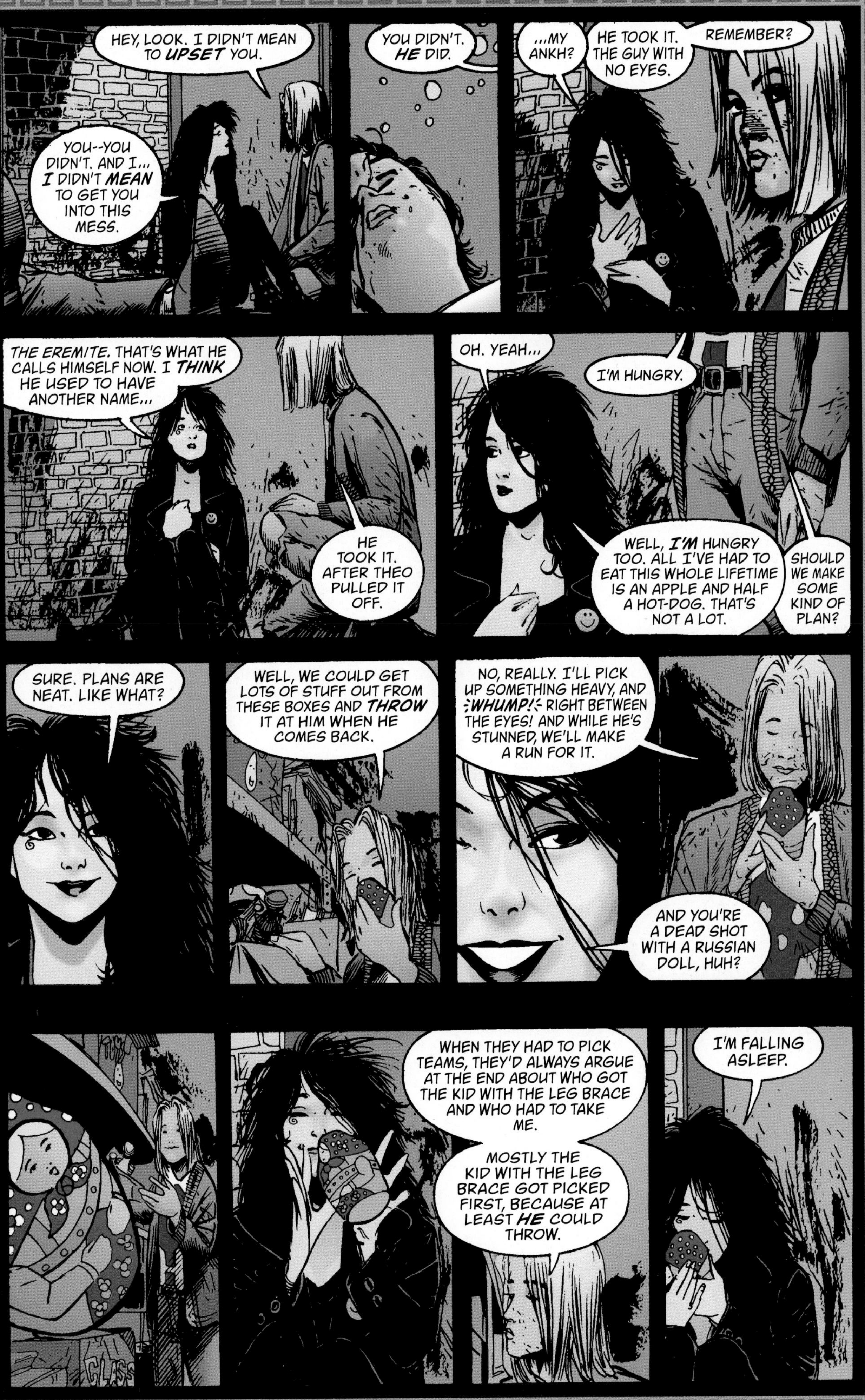
HEY, LOOK. I DIDN'T MEAN TO UPSET YOU.
YOU--YOU DIDN'T. AND I... I DIDN'T MEAN TO GET YOU INTO THIS MESS.
YOU DIDN'T. HE DID.
...MY ANKH?
HE TOOK IT. THE GUY WITH NO EYES.
REMEMBER?
THE EREMITE. THAT'S WHAT HE CALLS HIMSELF NOW. I THINK HE USED TO HAVE ANOTHER NAME...
HE TOOK IT. AFTER THEO PULLED IT OFF.
OH. YEAH...
I'M HUNGRY.
WELL, I'M HUNGRY TOO. ALL I'VE HAD TO EAT THIS WHOLE LIFETIME IS AN APPLE AND HALF A HOT-DOG. THAT'S NOT A LOT.
SHOULD WE MAKE SOME KIND OF PLAN?
SURE. PLANS ARE NEAT. LIKE WHAT?
WELL, WE COULD GET LOTS OF STUFF OUT FROM THESE BOXES AND THROW IT AT HIM WHEN HE COMES BACK.
NO, REALLY. I'LL PICK UP SOMETHING HEAVY, AND WHUMP! RIGHT BETWEEN THE EYES! AND WHILE HE'S STUNNED, WE'LL MAKE A RUN FOR IT.
AND YOU'RE A DEAD SHOT WITH A RUSSIAN DOLL, HUH?
WHEN THEY HAD TO PICK TEAMS, THEY'D ALWAYS ARGUE AT THE END ABOUT WHO GOT THE KID WITH THE LEG BRACE AND WHO HAD TO TAKE ME.
MOSTLY THE KID WITH THE LEG BRACE GOT PICKED FIRST, BECAUSE AT LEAST HE COULD THROW.
I'M FALLING ASLEEP.

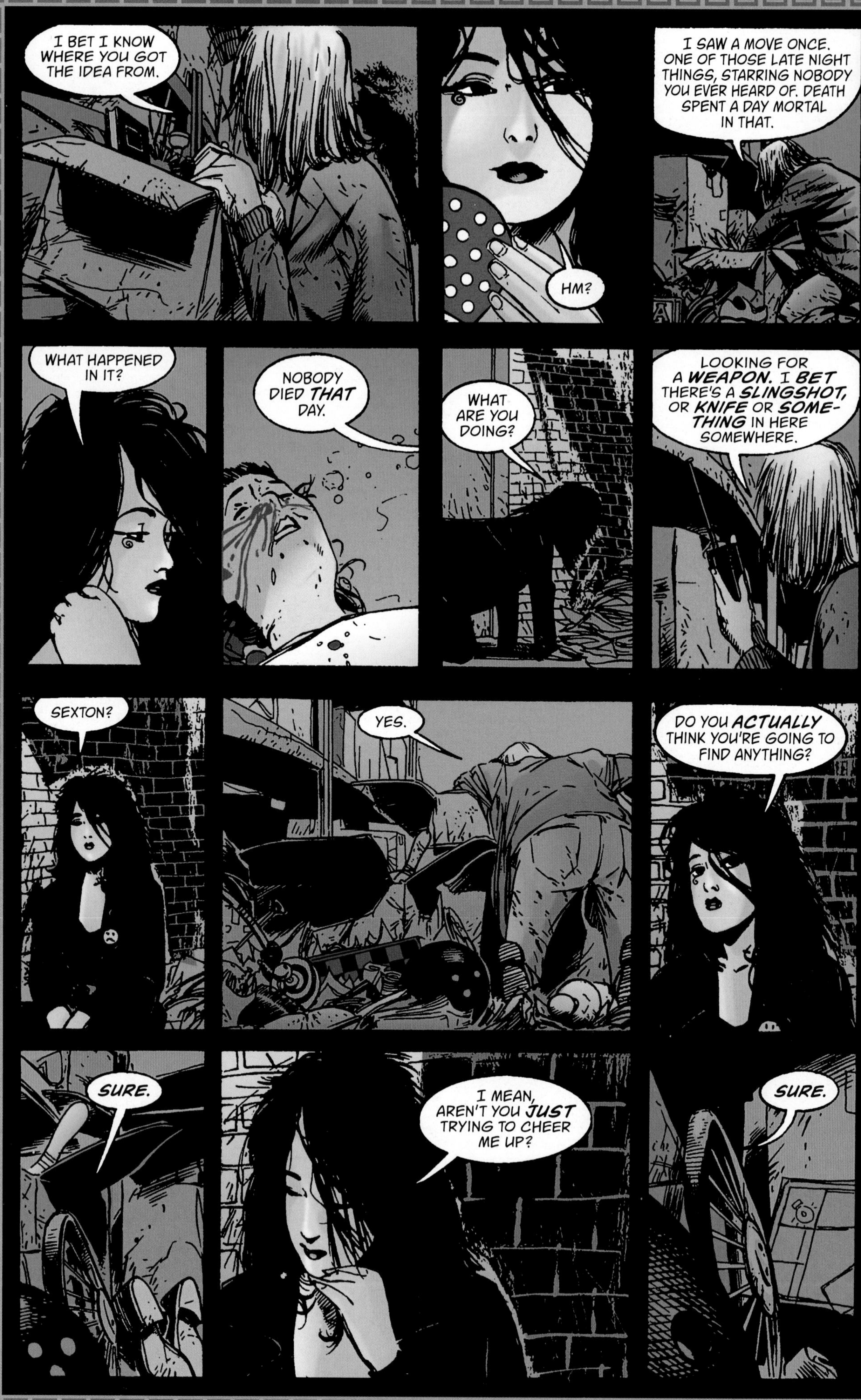
I BET I KNOW WHERE YOU GOT THE IDEA FROM.
HM?
I SAW A MOVE ONCE. ONE OF THOSE LATE NIGHT THINGS, STARRING NOBODY YOU EVER HEARD OF. DEATH SPENT A DAY MORTAL IN THAT.
WHAT HAPPENED IN IT?
NOBODY DIED **THAT** DAY.
WHAT ARE YOU DOING?
LOOKING FOR A **WEAPON.** I **BET** THERE'S A **SLINGSHOT,** OR **KNIFE** OR **SOMETHING** IN HERE SOMEWHERE.
SEXTON?
YES.
DO YOU **ACTUALLY** THINK YOU'RE GOING TO FIND ANYTHING?
SURE.
I MEAN, AREN'T YOU **JUST** TRYING TO CHEER ME UP?
SURE.

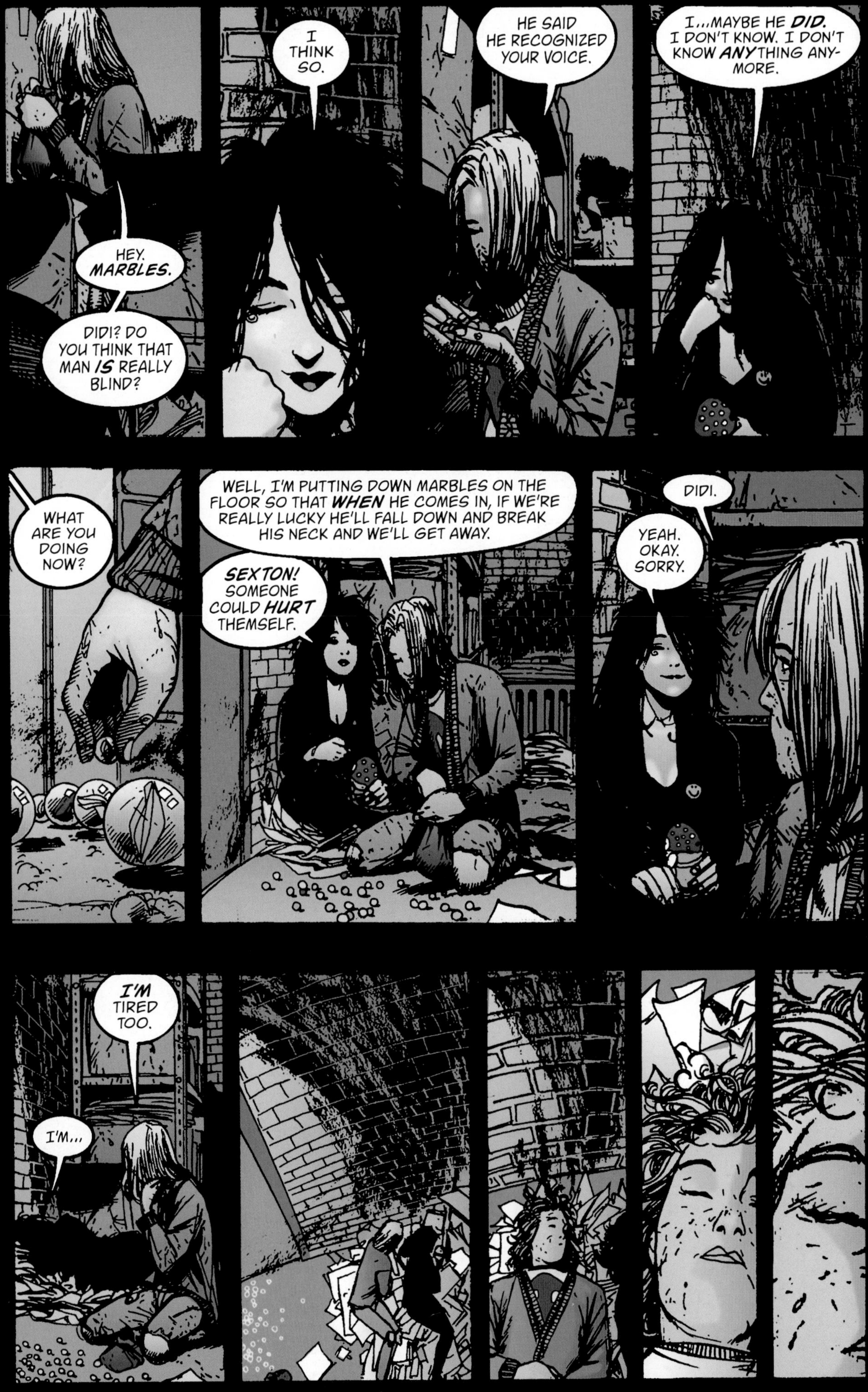
HEY. MARBLES.
DIDI? DO YOU THINK THAT MAN IS REALLY BLIND?
I THINK SO.
HE SAID HE RECOGNIZED YOUR VOICE.
I...MAYBE HE DID. I DON'T KNOW. I DON'T KNOW ANYTHING ANY-MORE.
WHAT ARE YOU DOING NOW?
WELL, I'M PUTTING DOWN MARBLES ON THE FLOOR SO THAT WHEN HE COMES IN, IF WE'RE REALLY LUCKY HE'LL FALL DOWN AND BREAK HIS NECK AND WE'LL GET AWAY.
SEXTON! SOMEONE COULD HURT THEMSELF.
DIDI.
YEAH. OKAY. SORRY.
I'M TIRED TOO.
I'M...

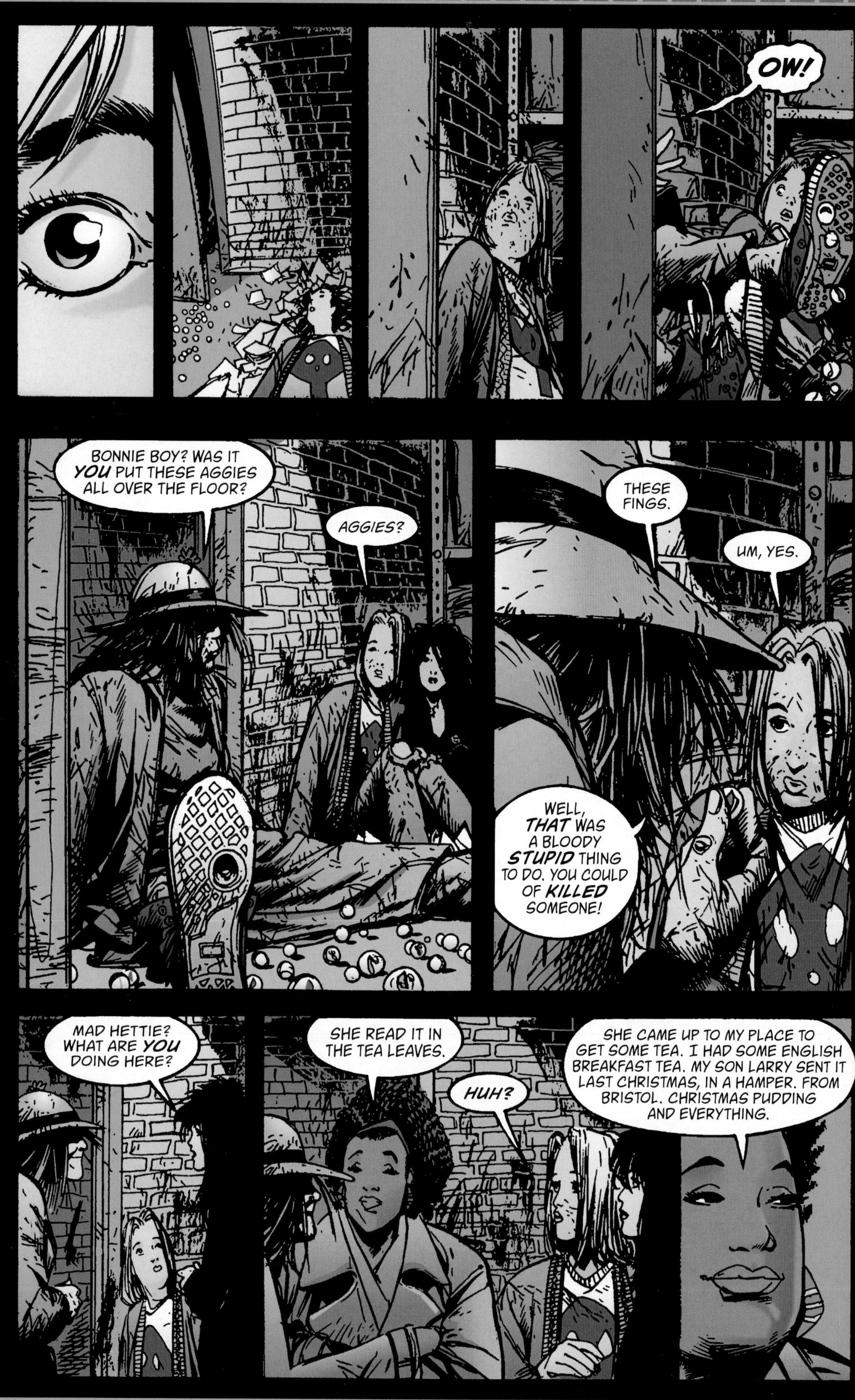
OW!
BONNIE BOY? WAS IT YOU PUT THESE AGGIES ALL OVER THE FLOOR?
AGGIES?
THESE FINGS.
UM, YES.
WELL, THAT WAS A BLOODY STUPID THING TO DO. YOU COULD OF KILLED SOMEONE!
MAD HETTIE? WHAT ARE YOU DOING HERE?
SHE READ IT IN THE TEA LEAVES.
HUH?
SHE CAME UP TO MY PLACE TO GET SOME TEA. I HAD SOME ENGLISH BREAKFAST TEA. MY SON LARRY SENT IT LAST CHRISTMAS, IN A HAMPER. FROM BRISTOL. CHRISTMAS PUDDING AND EVERYTHING.

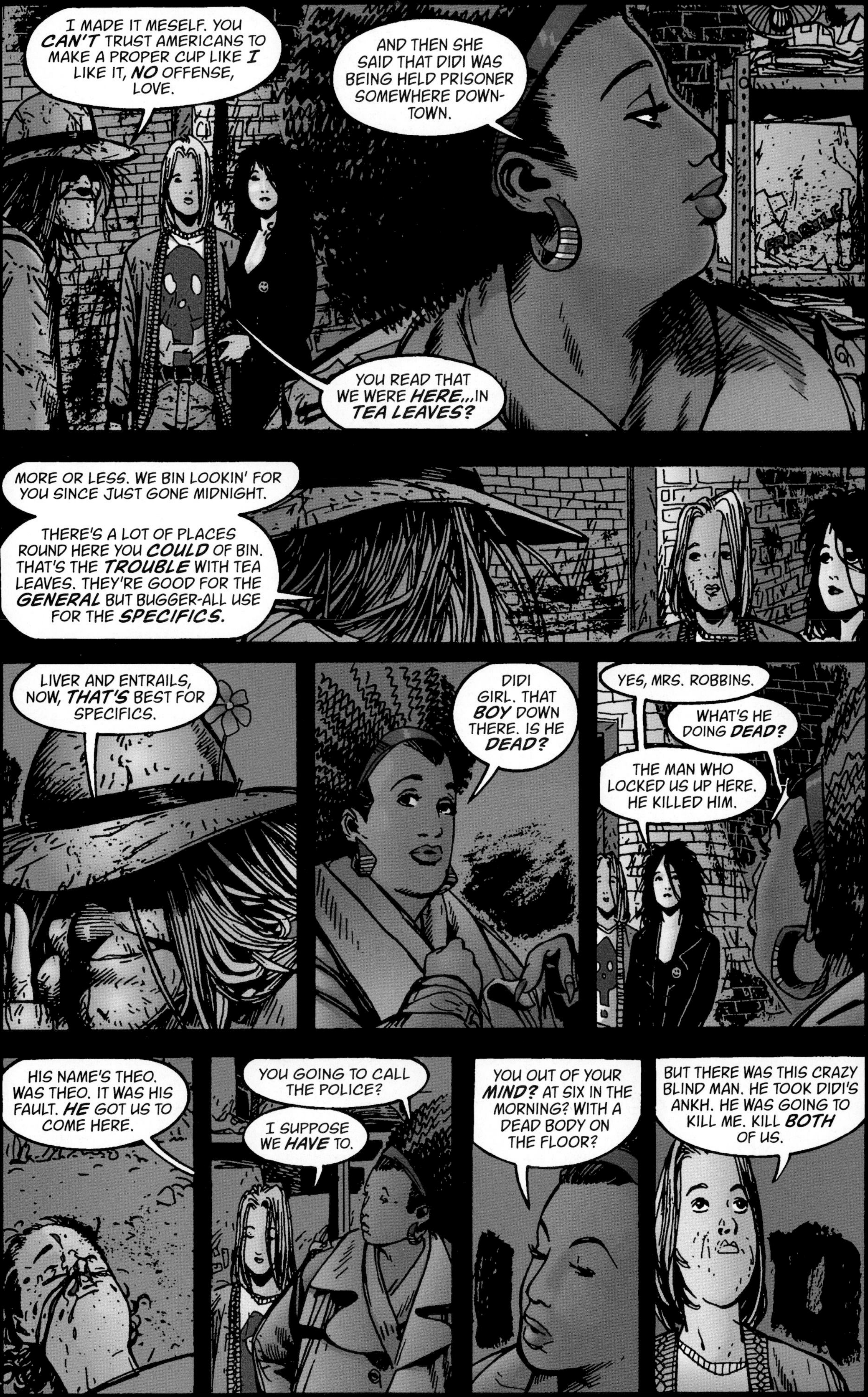
I MADE IT MESELF. YOU CAN'T TRUST AMERICANS TO MAKE A PROPER CUP LIKE I LIKE IT, NO OFFENSE, LOVE.
AND THEN SHE SAID THAT DIDI WAS BEING HELD PRISONER SOMEWHERE DOWN-TOWN.
YOU READ THAT WE WERE HERE...IN TEA LEAVES?
MORE OR LESS. WE BIN LOOKIN' FOR YOU SINCE JUST GONE MIDNIGHT.
THERE'S A LOT OF PLACES ROUND HERE YOU COULD OF BIN. THAT'S THE TROUBLE WITH TEA LEAVES. THEY'RE GOOD FOR THE GENERAL BUT BUGGER-ALL USE FOR THE SPECIFICS.
LIVER AND ENTRAILS, NOW, THAT'S BEST FOR SPECIFICS.
DIDI GIRL. THAT BOY DOWN THERE. IS HE DEAD?
YES, MRS. ROBBINS.
WHAT'S HE DOING DEAD?
THE MAN WHO LOCKED US UP HERE. HE KILLED HIM.
HIS NAME'S THEO. WAS THEO. IT WAS HIS FAULT. HE GOT US TO COME HERE.
YOU GOING TO CALL THE POLICE?
I SUPPOSE WE HAVE TO.
YOU OUT OF YOUR MIND? AT SIX IN THE MORNING? WITH A DEAD BODY ON THE FLOOR?
BUT THERE WAS THIS CRAZY BLIND MAN. HE TOOK DIDI'S ANKH. HE WAS GOING TO KILL ME. KILL BOTH OF US.

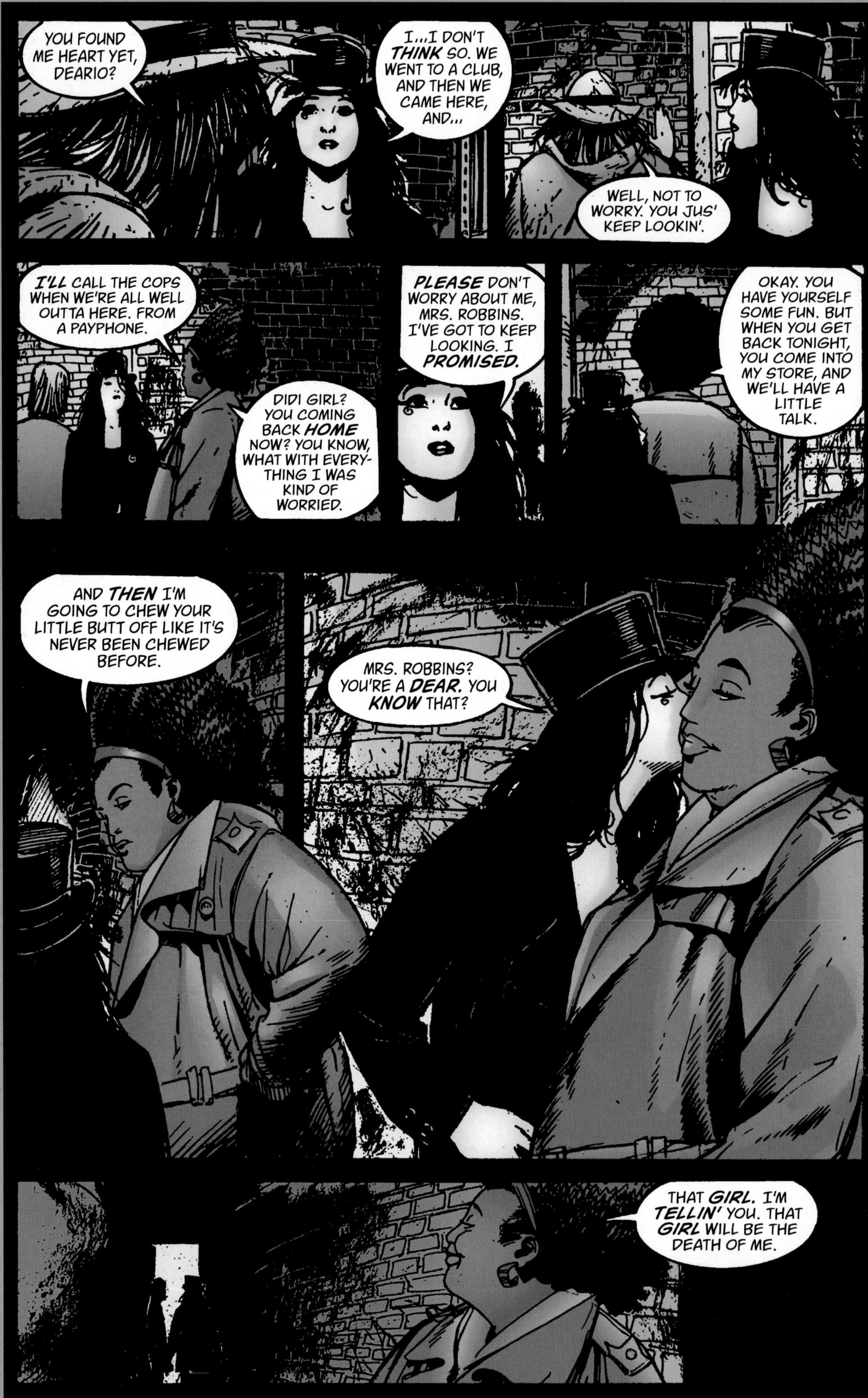
YOU FOUND ME HEART YET, DEARIO?
I...I DON'T THINK SO. WE WENT TO A CLUB, AND THEN WE CAME HERE, AND...
WELL, NOT TO WORRY. YOU JUS' KEEP LOOKIN'.
I'LL CALL THE COPS WHEN WE'RE ALL WELL OUTTA HERE. FROM A PAYPHONE.
DIDI GIRL? YOU COMING BACK HOME NOW? YOU KNOW, WHAT WITH EVERY-THING I WAS KIND OF WORRIED.
PLEASE DON'T WORRY ABOUT ME, MRS. ROBBINS. I'VE GOT TO KEEP LOOKING. I PROMISED.
OKAY. YOU HAVE YOURSELF SOME FUN. BUT WHEN YOU GET BACK TONIGHT, YOU COME INTO MY STORE, AND WE'LL HAVE A LITTLE TALK.
AND THEN I'M GOING TO CHEW YOUR LITTLE BUTT OFF LIKE IT'S NEVER BEEN CHEWED BEFORE.
MRS. ROBBINS? YOU'RE A DEAR. YOU KNOW THAT?
THAT GIRL. I'M TELLIN' YOU. THAT GIRL WILL BE THE DEATH OF ME.

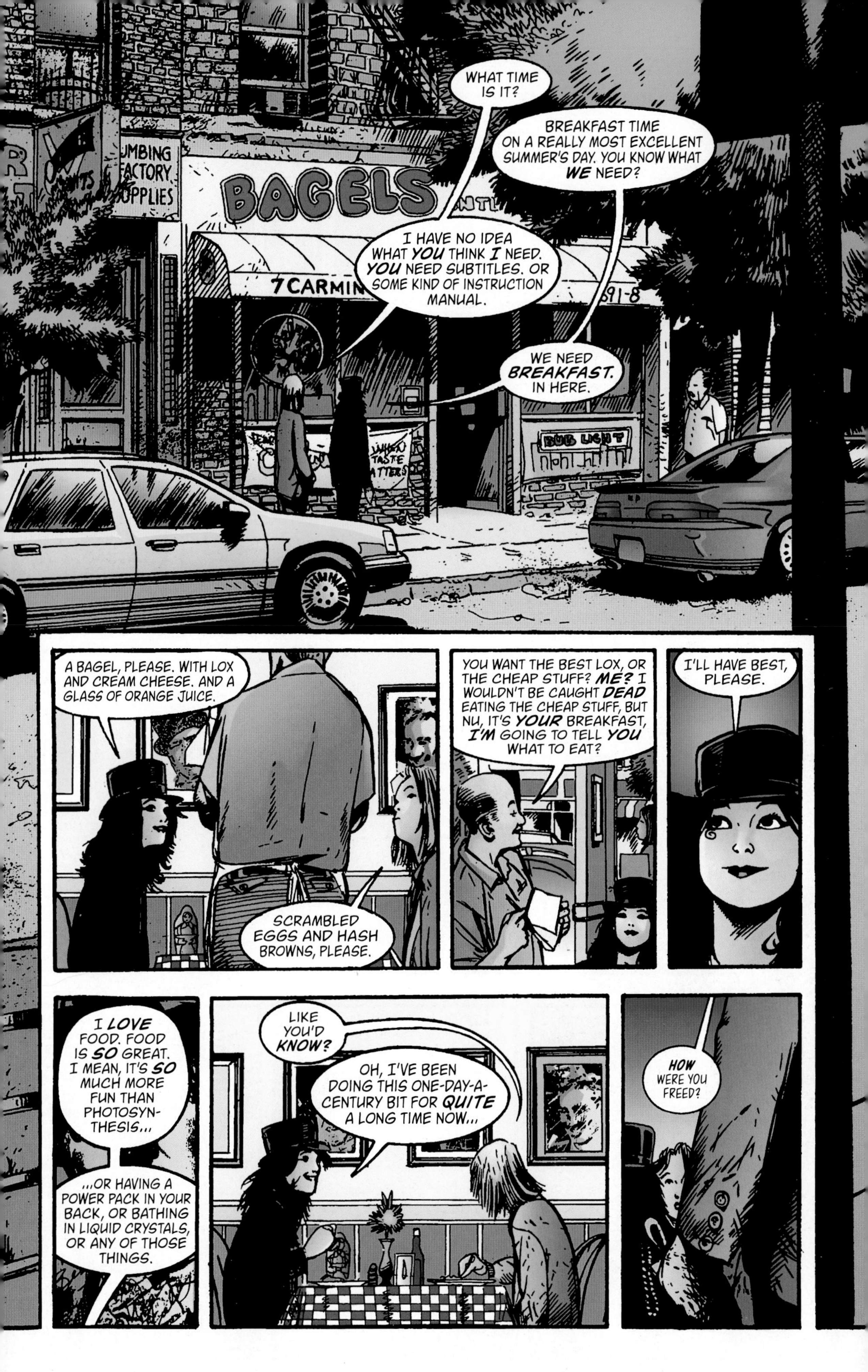
WHAT TIME IS IT?
BREAKFAST TIME ON A REALLY MOST EXCELLENT SUMMER'S DAY. YOU KNOW WHAT WE NEED?
I HAVE NO IDEA WHAT YOU THINK I NEED. YOU NEED SUBTITLES. OR SOME KIND OF INSTRUCTION MANUAL.
WE NEED BREAKFAST. IN HERE.
BAGELS
7 CARMIN
A BAGEL, PLEASE. WITH LOX AND CREAM CHEESE. AND A GLASS OF ORANGE JUICE.
SCRAMBLED EGGS AND HASH BROWNS, PLEASE.
YOU WANT THE BEST LOX, OR THE CHEAP STUFF? ME? I WOULDN'T BE CAUGHT DEAD EATING THE CHEAP STUFF, BUT NU, IT'S YOUR BREAKFAST, I'M GOING TO TELL YOU WHAT TO EAT?
I'LL HAVE BEST, PLEASE.
I LOVE FOOD. FOOD IS SO GREAT. I MEAN, IT'S SO MUCH MORE FUN THAN PHOTOSYN-THESIS...
...OR HAVING A POWER PACK IN YOUR BACK, OR BATHING IN LIQUID CRYSTALS, OR ANY OF THOSE THINGS.
LIKE YOU'D KNOW?
OH, I'VE BEEN DOING THIS ONE-DAY-A-CENTURY BIT FOR QUITE A LONG TIME NOW...
HOW WERE YOU FREED?

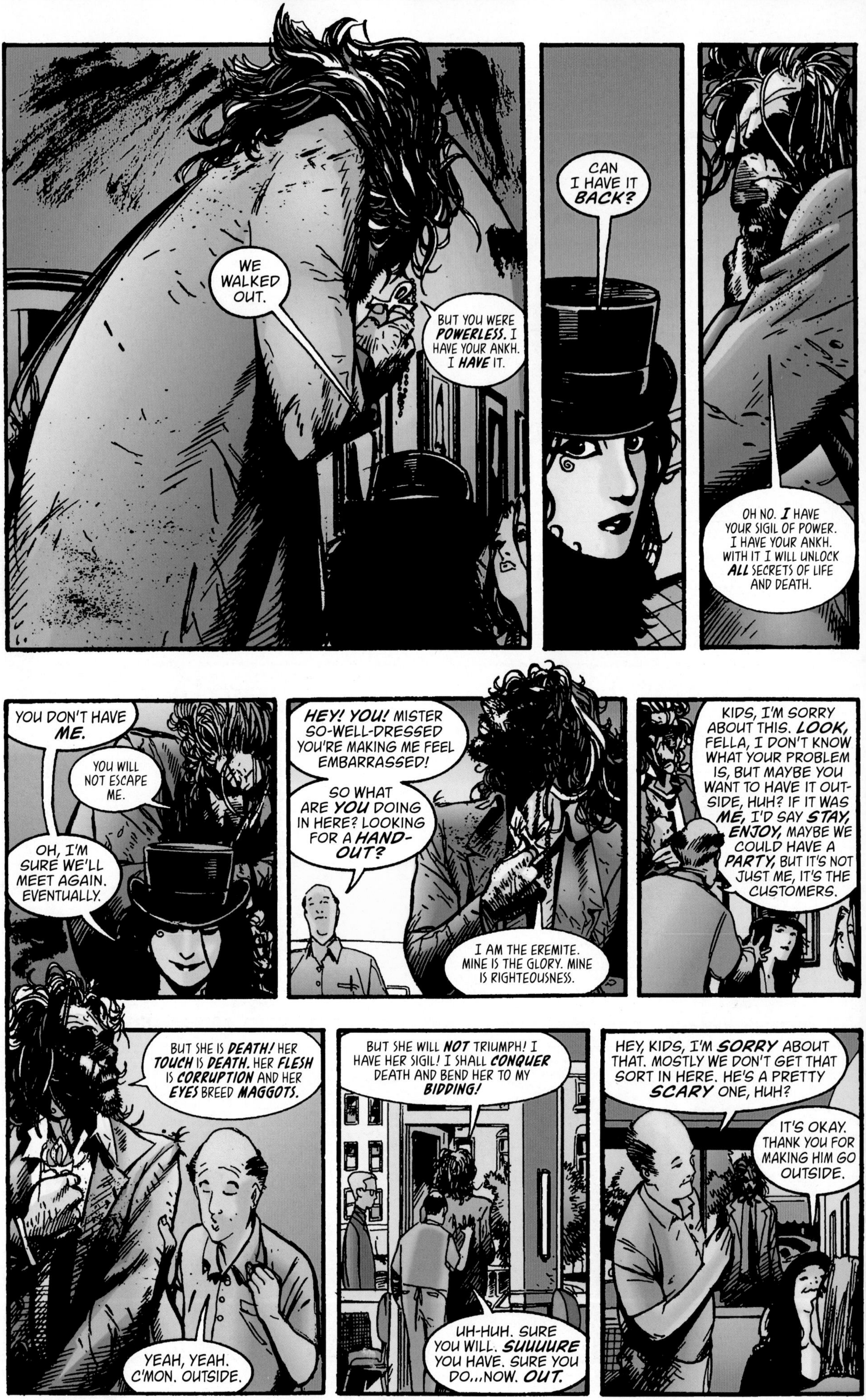

WE WALKED OUT.
BUT YOU WERE POWERLESS. I HAVE YOUR ANKH. I HAVE IT.
CAN I HAVE IT BACK?
OH NO. I HAVE YOUR SIGIL OF POWER. I HAVE YOUR ANKH. WITH IT I WILL UNLOCK ALL SECRETS OF LIFE AND DEATH.
YOU DON'T HAVE ME.
YOU WILL NOT ESCAPE ME.
OH, I'M SURE WE'LL MEET AGAIN. EVENTUALLY.
HEY! YOU! MISTER SO-WELL-DRESSED YOU'RE MAKING ME FEEL EMBARRASSED!
SO WHAT ARE YOU DOING IN HERE? LOOKING FOR A HAND-OUT?
I AM THE EREMITE. MINE IS THE GLORY. MINE IS RIGHTEOUSNESS.
KIDS, I'M SORRY ABOUT THIS. LOOK, FELLA, I DON'T KNOW WHAT YOUR PROBLEM IS, BUT MAYBE YOU WANT TO HAVE IT OUT-SIDE, HUH? IF IT WAS ME, I'D SAY STAY, ENJOY, MAYBE WE COULD HAVE A PARTY, BUT IT'S NOT JUST ME, IT'S THE CUSTOMERS.
BUT SHE IS DEATH! HER TOUCH IS DEATH. HER FLESH IS CORRUPTION AND HER EYES BREED MAGGOTS.
YEAH, YEAH. C'MON. OUTSIDE.
BUT SHE WILL NOT TRIUMPH! I HAVE HER SIGIL! I SHALL CONQUER DEATH AND BEND HER TO MY BIDDING!
UH-HUH. SURE YOU WILL. SUUUURE YOU HAVE. SURE YOU DO...NOW. OUT.
HEY, KIDS, I'M SORRY ABOUT THAT. MOSTLY WE DON'T GET THAT SORT IN HERE. HE'S A PRETTY SCARY ONE, HUH?
IT'S OKAY. THANK YOU FOR MAKING HIM GO OUTSIDE.

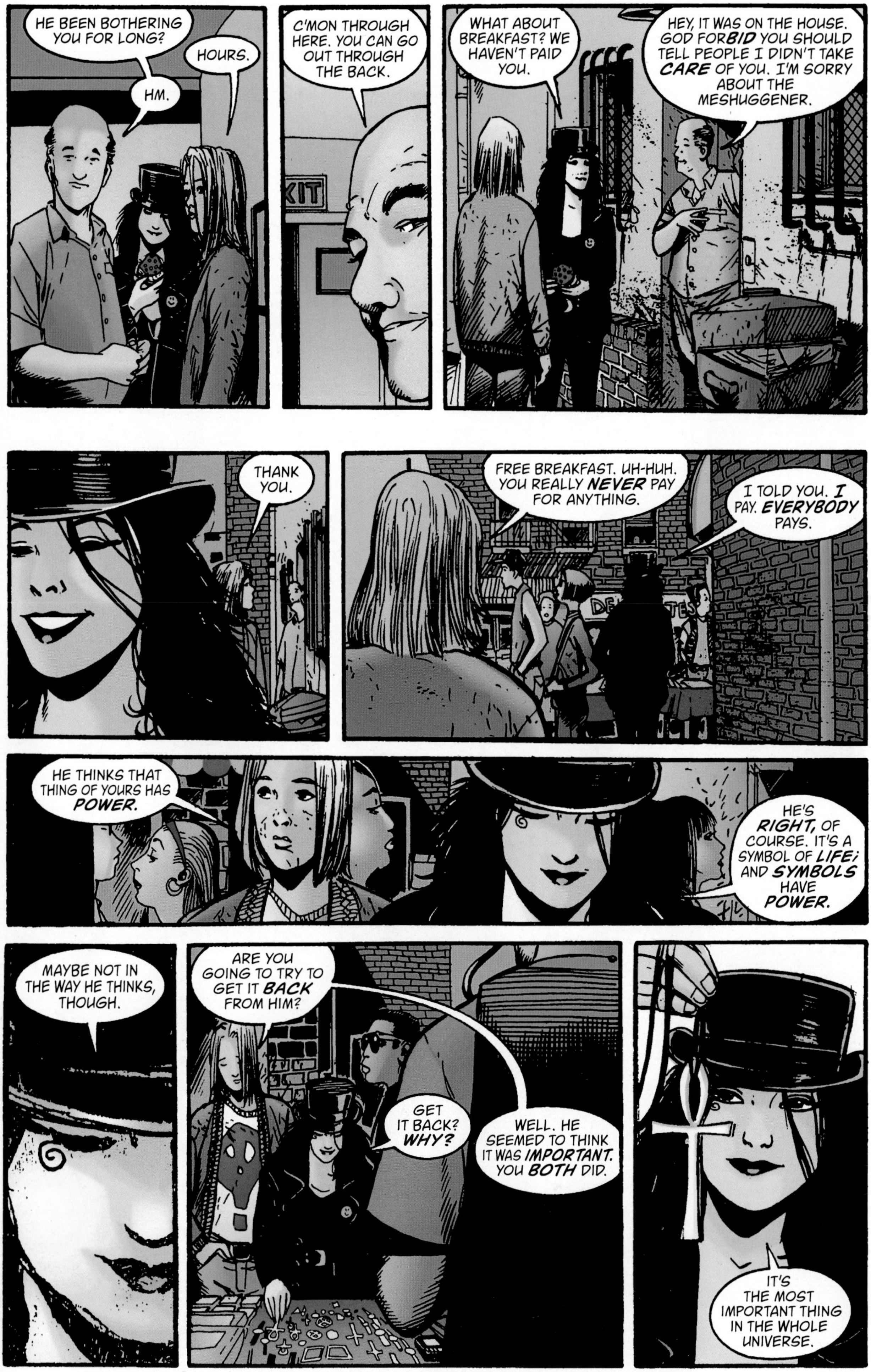
HE BEEN BOTHERING YOU FOR LONG?
HOURS.
HM.
C'MON THROUGH HERE. YOU CAN GO OUT THROUGH THE BACK.
KIT
WHAT ABOUT BREAKFAST? WE HAVEN'T PAID YOU.
HEY, IT WAS ON THE HOUSE. GOD FOR**BID** YOU SHOULD TELL PEOPLE I DIDN'T TAKE ***CARE*** OF YOU. I'M SORRY ABOUT THE MESHUGGENER.
THANK YOU.
FREE BREAKFAST. UH-HUH. YOU REALLY ***NEVER*** PAY FOR ANYTHING.
I TOLD YOU. ***I*** PAY. ***EVERYBODY*** PAYS.
HE THINKS THAT THING OF YOURS HAS ***POWER.***
HE'S ***RIGHT,*** OF COURSE. IT'S A SYMBOL OF ***LIFE;*** AND ***SYMBOLS*** HAVE ***POWER.***
MAYBE NOT IN THE WAY HE THINKS, THOUGH.
ARE YOU GOING TO TRY TO GET IT ***BACK*** FROM HIM?
GET IT BACK? ***WHY?***
WELL. HE SEEMED TO THINK IT WAS ***IMPORTANT.*** YOU ***BOTH*** DID.
IT'S THE MOST IMPORTANT THING IN THE WHOLE UNIVERSE.

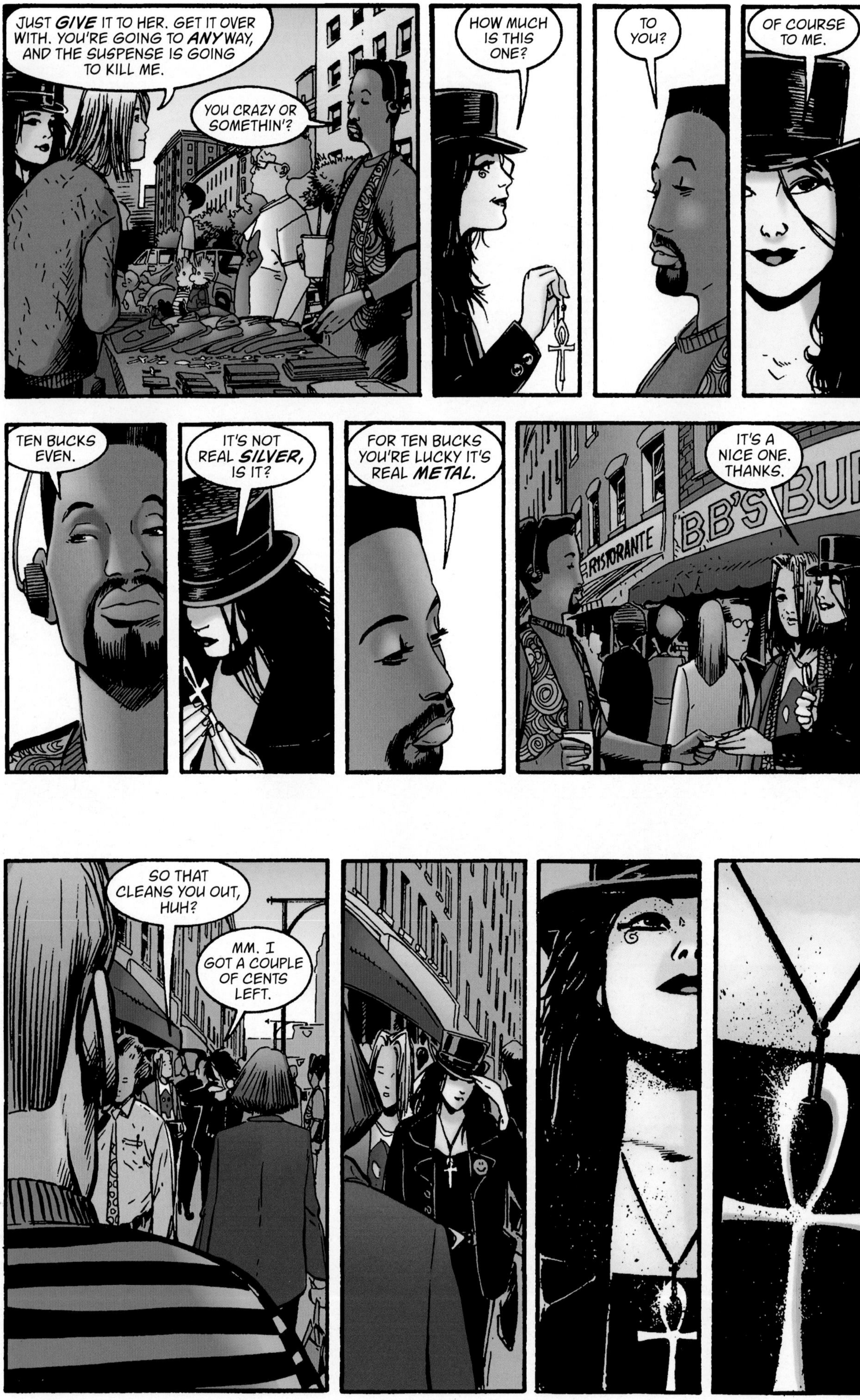
JUST GIVE IT TO HER. GET IT OVER WITH. YOU'RE GOING TO ANYWAY, AND THE SUSPENSE IS GOING TO KILL ME.
YOU CRAZY OR SOMETHIN'?
HOW MUCH IS THIS ONE?
TO YOU?
OF COURSE TO ME.
TEN BUCKS EVEN.
IT'S NOT REAL SILVER, IS IT?
FOR TEN BUCKS YOU'RE LUCKY IT'S REAL METAL.
IT'S A NICE ONE. THANKS.
BB'S BUR
RISTORANTE
SO THAT CLEANS YOU OUT, HUH?
MM. I GOT A COUPLE OF CENTS LEFT.

SEXTON? ISN'T YOUR MOTHER GOING TO BE WORRIED ABOUT YOU BY NOW?

SYLVIA? SHE WOULDN'T NOTICE IF I WENT TO THE MOON.

SHE PROBABLY WOULD. MOTHERS *NOTICE* THAT KIND OF THING.

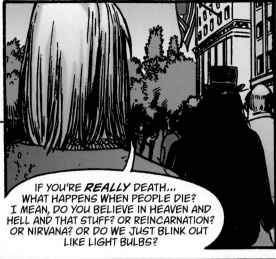

IF YOU'RE *REALLY* DEATH... WHAT HAPPENS WHEN PEOPLE DIE? I MEAN, DO YOU BELIEVE IN HEAVEN AND HELL AND THAT STUFF? OR REINCARNATION? OR NIRVANA? OR DO WE JUST BLINK OUT LIKE LIGHT BULBS?

IF I *WAS* REALLY DEATH, DO YOU THINK I'D TELL *YOU?*

I DON'T KNOW *WHAT* YOU'RE GOING TO DO ANY MORE. IF A HUNDRED PENGUINS CAME DOWN BROADWAY AND DID A LITTLE DANCE WITH YOU I DON'T THINK I'D EVEN *BLINK.*

SEXTON? YOU KNOW, *UNDER-NEATH,* YOU'RE PRETTY OKAY.

YEAH? WELL, UNDERNEATH, YOU'RE...

YES?

HAVE YOU EVER NOTICED HOW MUCH *BETTER* EVERYTHING SEEMS AFTER A GOOD BREAKFAST?

SURE.

I'M GOING UP TO CENTRAL PARK. YOU WANT TO GO HOME NOW?

IT'S NOT THAT I EN*JOY* HANGING AROUND WITH YOU OR ANYTHING. BUT IF I WENT HOME. WELL, HOW WOULD I KNOW HOW ALL THIS IS GOING TO *END?*

ANYWAY, HOW ARE YOU GOING TO CONVINCE MAD HETTIE YOU'VE FOUND HER HEART?

OH, SHE'LL KNOW.

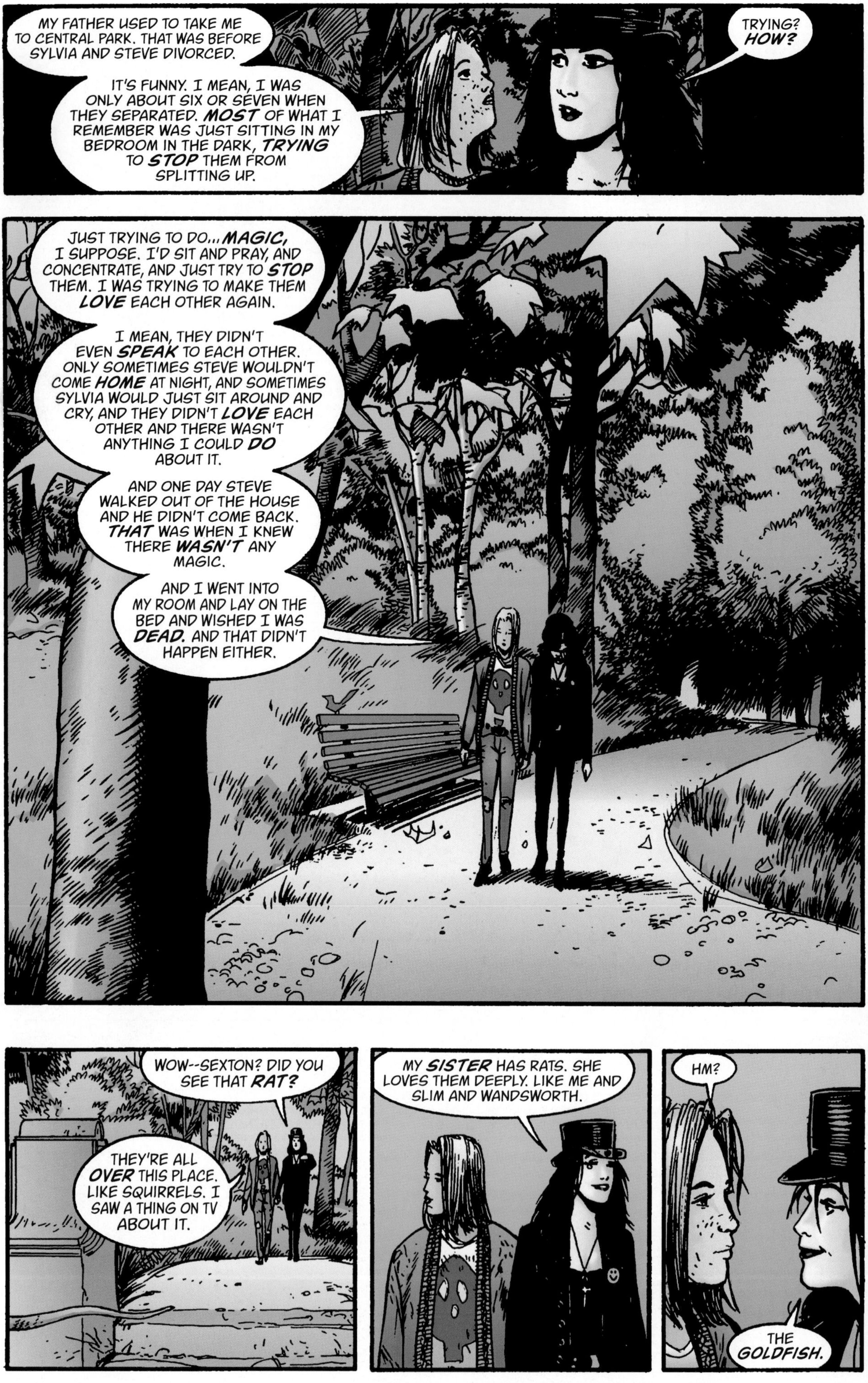
MY FATHER USED TO TAKE ME TO CENTRAL PARK. THAT WAS BEFORE SYLVIA AND STEVE DIVORCED.
IT'S FUNNY. I MEAN, I WAS ONLY ABOUT SIX OR SEVEN WHEN THEY SEPARATED. MOST OF WHAT I REMEMBER WAS JUST SITTING IN MY BEDROOM IN THE DARK, TRYING TO STOP THEM FROM SPLITTING UP.
TRYING? HOW?
JUST TRYING TO DO... MAGIC, I SUPPOSE. I'D SIT AND PRAY, AND CONCENTRATE, AND JUST TRY TO STOP THEM. I WAS TRYING TO MAKE THEM LOVE EACH OTHER AGAIN.
I MEAN, THEY DIDN'T EVEN SPEAK TO EACH OTHER. ONLY SOMETIMES STEVE WOULDN'T COME HOME AT NIGHT, AND SOMETIMES SYLVIA WOULD JUST SIT AROUND AND CRY, AND THEY DIDN'T LOVE EACH OTHER AND THERE WASN'T ANYTHING I COULD DO ABOUT IT.
AND ONE DAY STEVE WALKED OUT OF THE HOUSE AND HE DIDN'T COME BACK. THAT WAS WHEN I KNEW THERE WASN'T ANY MAGIC.
AND I WENT INTO MY ROOM AND LAY ON THE BED AND WISHED I WAS DEAD. AND THAT DIDN'T HAPPEN EITHER.
WOW--SEXTON? DID YOU SEE THAT RAT?
THEY'RE ALL OVER THIS PLACE. LIKE SQUIRRELS. I SAW A THING ON TV ABOUT IT.
MY SISTER HAS RATS. SHE LOVES THEM DEEPLY. LIKE ME AND SLIM AND WANDSWORTH.
HM?
THE GOLDFISH.

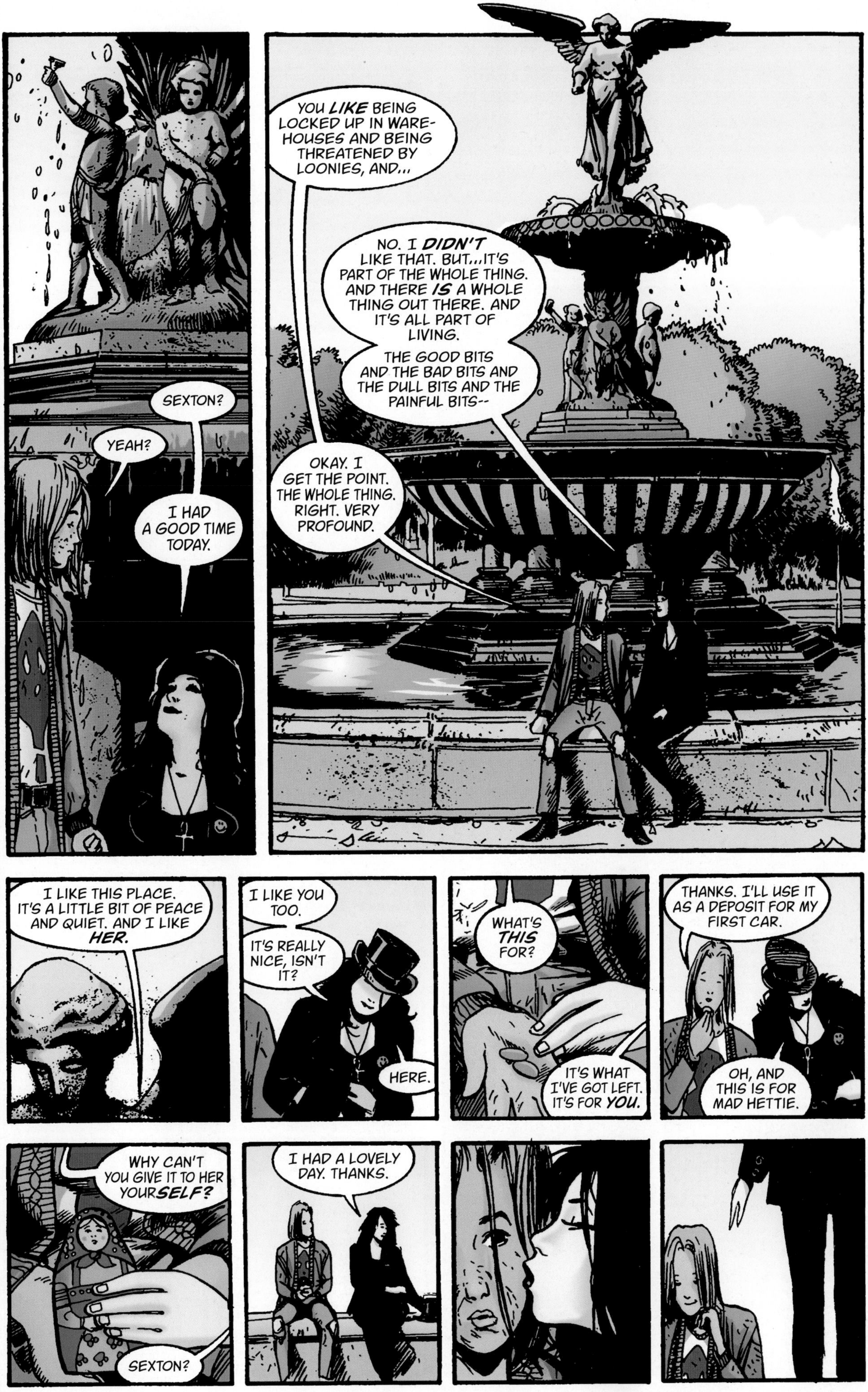
SEXTON?
YEAH?
I HAD A GOOD TIME TODAY.
YOU LIKE BEING LOCKED UP IN WARE-HOUSES AND BEING THREATENED BY LOONIES, AND...
NO. I DIDN'T LIKE THAT. BUT...IT'S PART OF THE WHOLE THING. AND THERE IS A WHOLE THING OUT THERE. AND IT'S ALL PART OF LIVING.
THE GOOD BITS AND THE BAD BITS AND THE DULL BITS AND THE PAINFUL BITS--
OKAY. I GET THE POINT. THE WHOLE THING. RIGHT. VERY PROFOUND.
I LIKE THIS PLACE. IT'S A LITTLE BIT OF PEACE AND QUIET. AND I LIKE HER.
I LIKE YOU TOO.
IT'S REALLY NICE, ISN'T IT?
HERE.
WHAT'S THIS FOR?
IT'S WHAT I'VE GOT LEFT. IT'S FOR YOU.
THANKS. I'LL USE IT AS A DEPOSIT FOR MY FIRST CAR.
OH, AND THIS IS FOR MAD HETTIE.
WHY CAN'T YOU GIVE IT TO HER YOURSELF?
SEXTON?
I HAD A LOVELY DAY. THANKS.

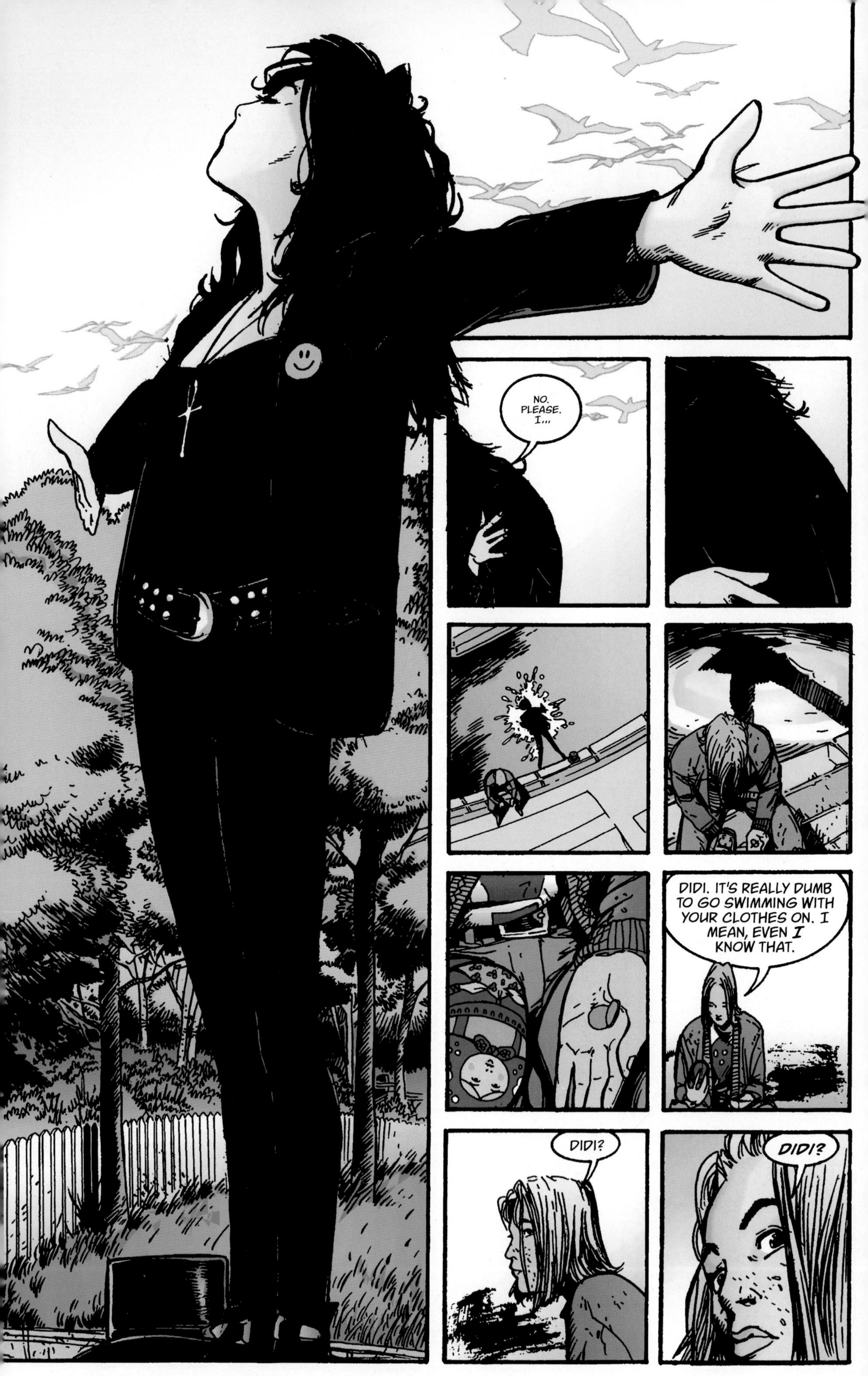
NO. PLEASE. I...
DIDI. IT'S REALLY DUMB TO GO SWIMMING WITH YOUR CLOTHES ON. I MEAN, EVEN I KNOW THAT.
DIDI?
DIDI?

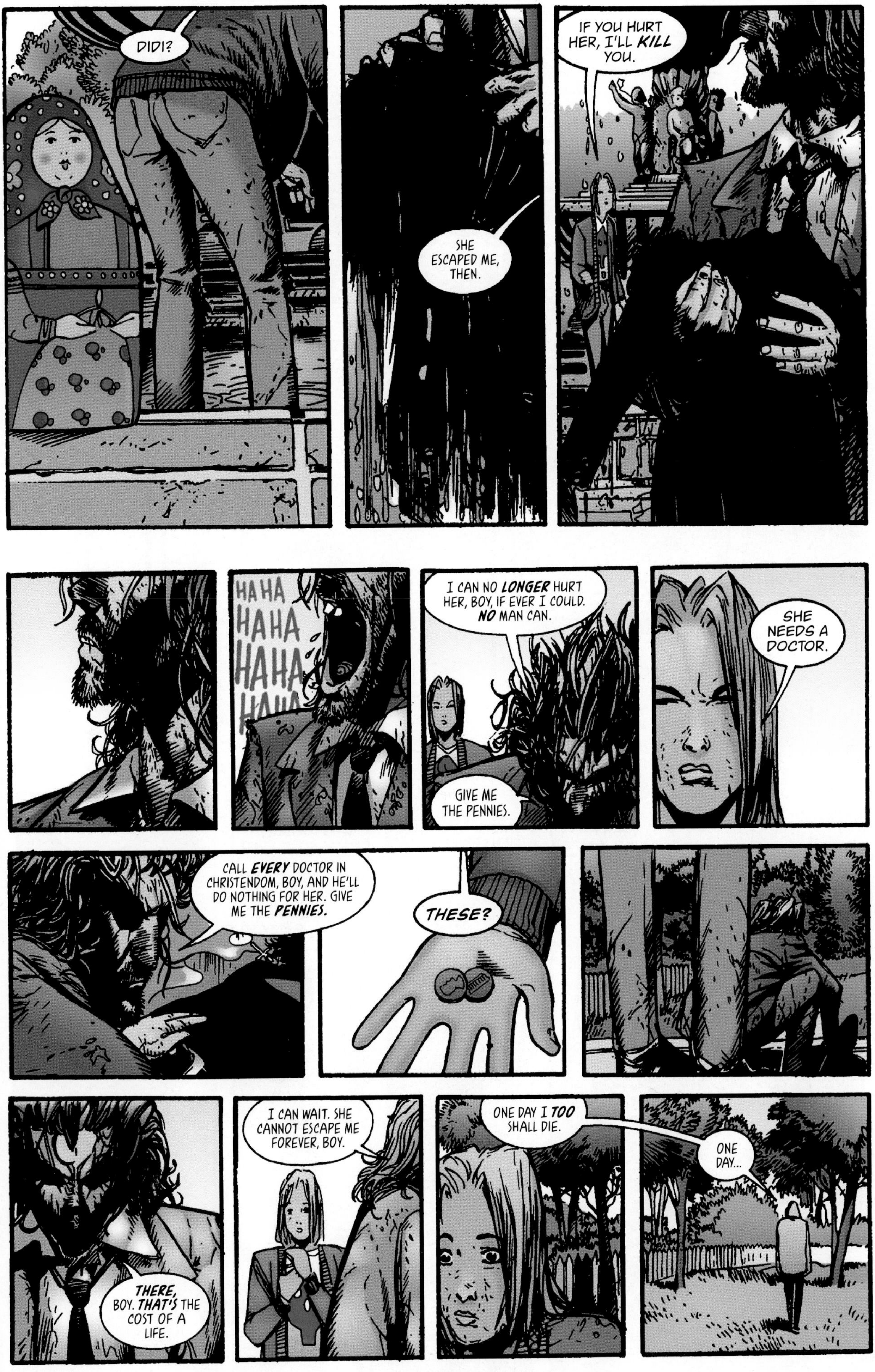
DIDI?
SHE ESCAPED ME, THEN.
IF YOU HURT HER, I'LL KILL YOU.
HA HA HA HA HA HA
I CAN NO LONGER HURT HER, BOY, IF EVER I COULD. NO MAN CAN.
GIVE ME THE PENNIES.
SHE NEEDS A DOCTOR.
CALL EVERY DOCTOR IN CHRISTENDOM, BOY, AND HE'LL DO NOTHING FOR HER. GIVE ME THE PENNIES.
THESE?
THERE, BOY. THAT'S THE COST OF A LIFE.
I CAN WAIT. SHE CANNOT ESCAPE ME FOREVER, BOY.
ONE DAY I TOO SHALL DIE.
ONE DAY...

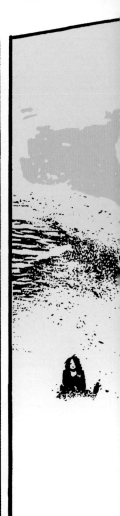

OH, IT WAS **WONDERFUL.** IT WAS FILLED WITH **PEOPLE.** I GOT TO BREATHE AND EAT AND...ALL **SORTS** OF STUFF.

I WISH IT COULD HAVE GONE ON FOR-**EVER. I WISH** IT DIDN'T HAVE TO END LIKE THAT...

IT ALWAYS ENDS. THAT'S WHAT GIVES IT VALUE.

WHEN YOU GET TO BE ALIVE, EVEN FOR A DAY...

WELL, THERE'S ONLY ONE WAY TO STOP LIVING.

I SUPPOSE SO.

WAS IT WORTH IT?

I....I DON'T KNOW. I **THINK** SO. I HOPE SO. I MET SUCH NEAT PEOPLE.

AND I HEARD A SONG AND I WENT IN A TAXI, AND I HAD A HOT DOG AND A BAGEL AND....

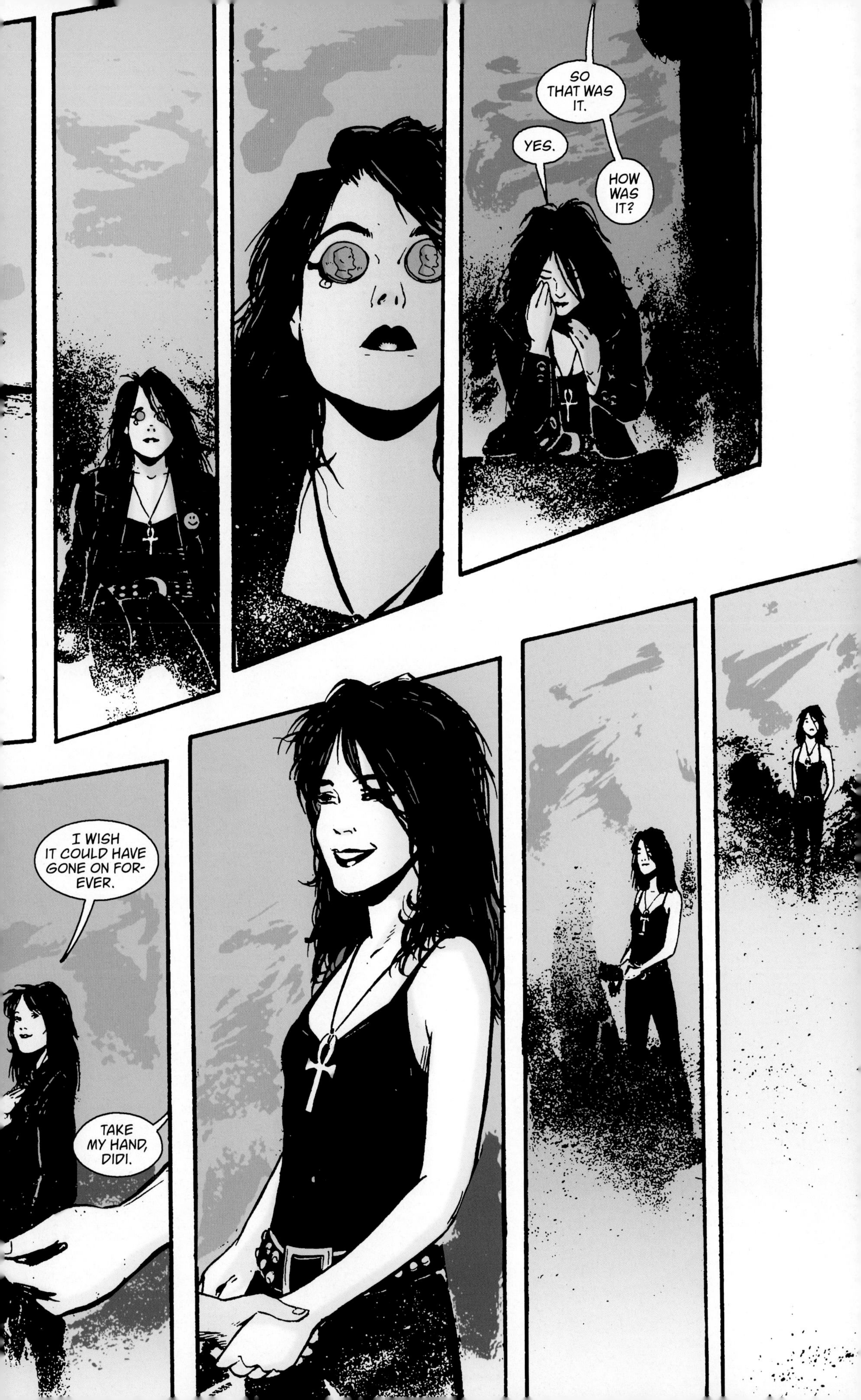
SO THAT WAS IT.
YES.
HOW WAS IT?
I WISH IT COULD HAVE GONE ON FOR-EVER.
TAKE MY HAND, DIDI.

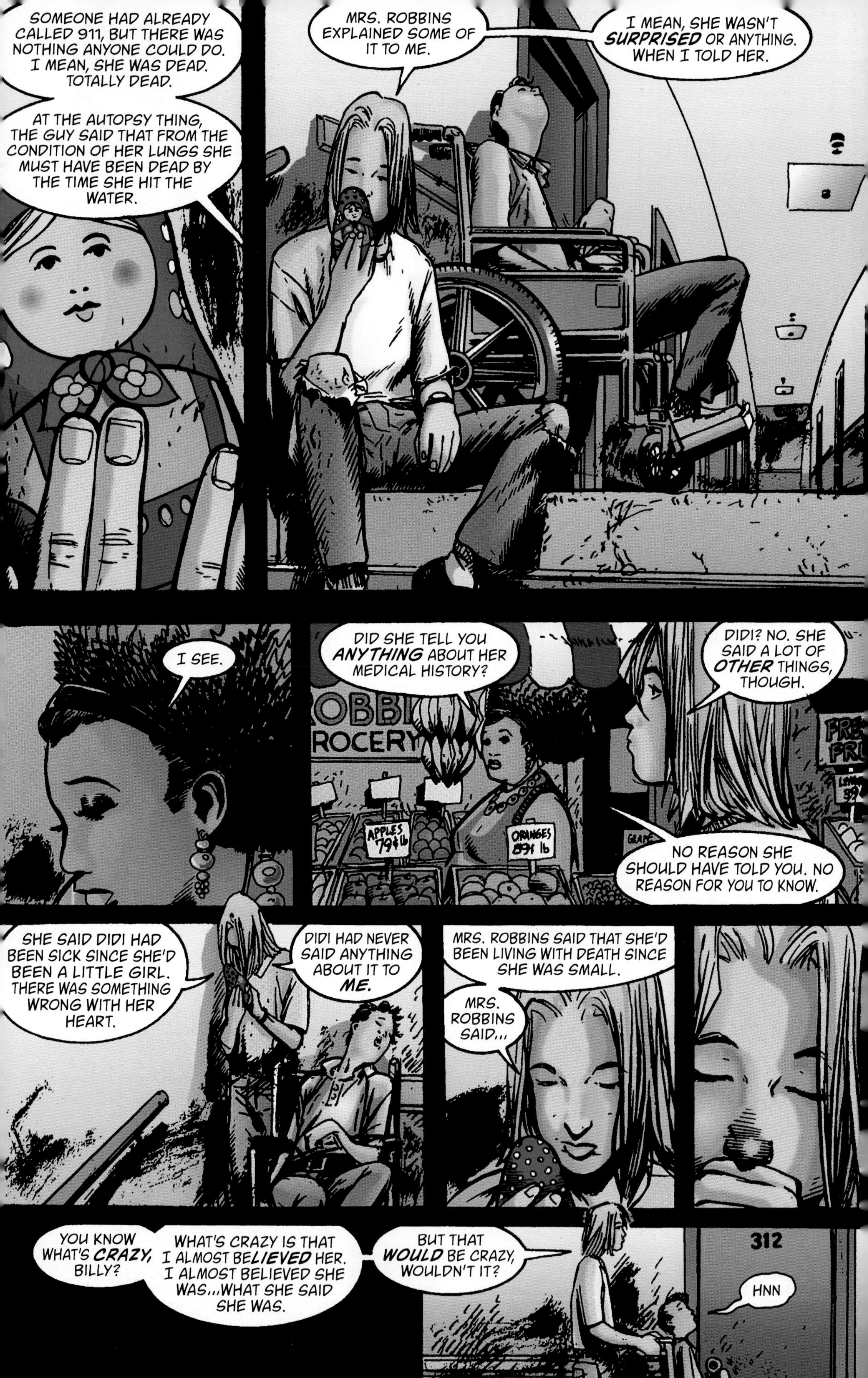
SOMEONE HAD ALREADY CALLED 911, BUT THERE WAS NOTHING ANYONE COULD DO. I MEAN, SHE WAS DEAD. TOTALLY DEAD.
AT THE AUTOPSY THING, THE GUY SAID THAT FROM THE CONDITION OF HER LUNGS SHE MUST HAVE BEEN DEAD BY THE TIME SHE HIT THE WATER.
MRS. ROBBINS EXPLAINED SOME OF IT TO ME.
I MEAN, SHE WASN'T SURPRISED OR ANYTHING. WHEN I TOLD HER.
I SEE.
DID SHE TELL YOU ANYTHING ABOUT HER MEDICAL HISTORY?
ROBBI
ROCERY
APPLES 79¢ lb
ORANGES 89¢ lb
DIDI? NO. SHE SAID A LOT OF OTHER THINGS, THOUGH.
NO REASON SHE SHOULD HAVE TOLD YOU. NO REASON FOR YOU TO KNOW.
SHE SAID DIDI HAD BEEN SICK SINCE SHE'D BEEN A LITTLE GIRL. THERE WAS SOMETHING WRONG WITH HER HEART.
DIDI HAD NEVER SAID ANYTHING ABOUT IT TO ME.
MRS. ROBBINS SAID THAT SHE'D BEEN LIVING WITH DEATH SINCE SHE WAS SMALL.
MRS. ROBBINS SAID...
YOU KNOW WHAT'S CRAZY, BILLY?
WHAT'S CRAZY IS THAT I ALMOST BELIEVED HER. I ALMOST BELIEVED SHE WAS...WHAT SHE SAID SHE WAS.
BUT THAT WOULD BE CRAZY, WOULDN'T IT?
312
HNN

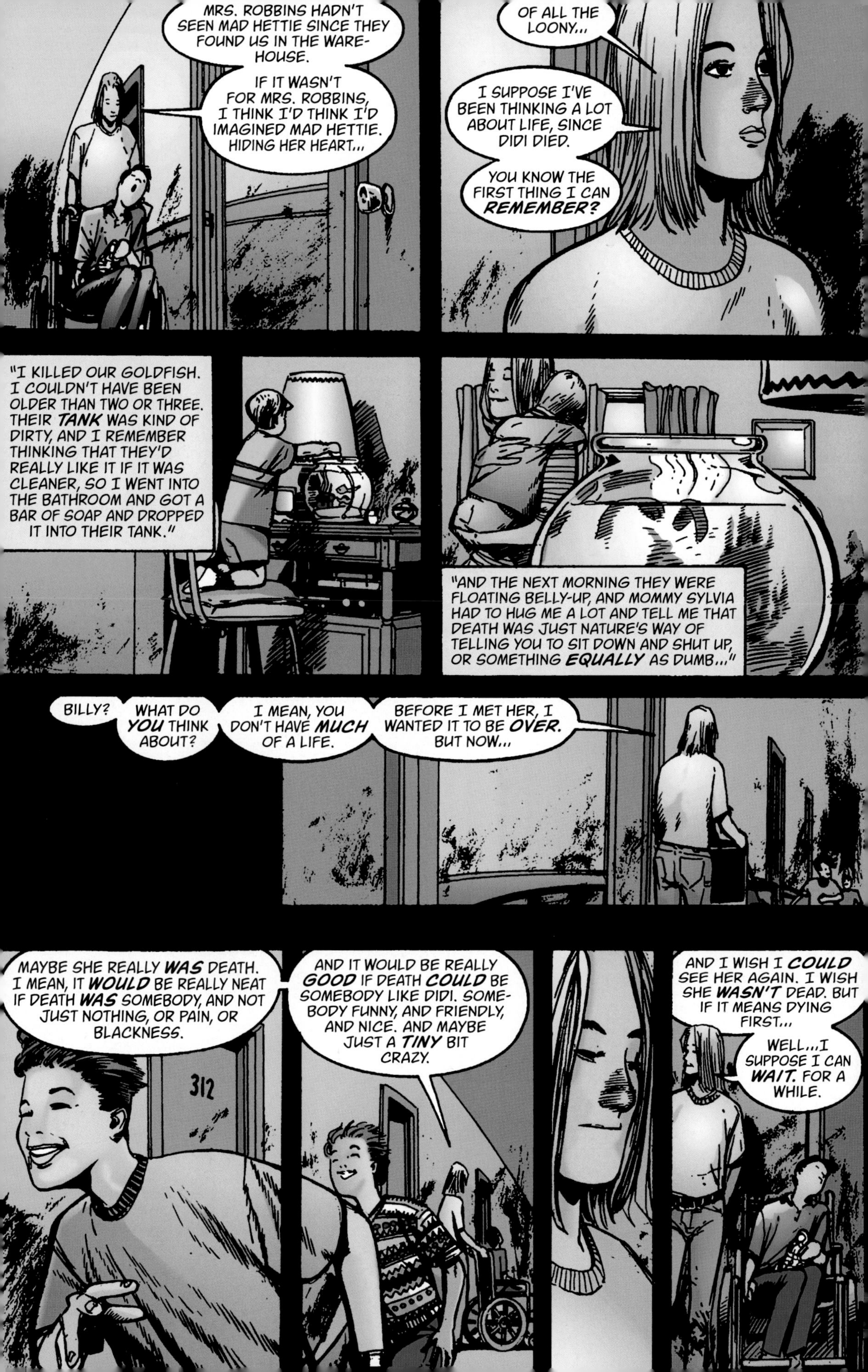
MRS. ROBBINS HADN'T SEEN MAD HETTIE SINCE THEY FOUND US IN THE WARE-HOUSE.
IF IT WASN'T FOR MRS. ROBBINS, I THINK I'D THINK I'D IMAGINED MAD HETTIE. HIDING HER HEART...
OF ALL THE LOONY...
I SUPPOSE I'VE BEEN THINKING A LOT ABOUT LIFE, SINCE DIDI DIED.
YOU KNOW THE FIRST THING I CAN REMEMBER?
"I KILLED OUR GOLDFISH. I COULDN'T HAVE BEEN OLDER THAN TWO OR THREE. THEIR TANK WAS KIND OF DIRTY, AND I REMEMBER THINKING THAT THEY'D REALLY LIKE IT IF IT WAS CLEANER, SO I WENT INTO THE BATHROOM AND GOT A BAR OF SOAP AND DROPPED IT INTO THEIR TANK."
"AND THE NEXT MORNING THEY WERE FLOATING BELLY-UP, AND MOMMY SYLVIA HAD TO HUG ME A LOT AND TELL ME THAT DEATH WAS JUST NATURE'S WAY OF TELLING YOU TO SIT DOWN AND SHUT UP, OR SOMETHING EQUALLY AS DUMB..."
BILLY?
WHAT DO YOU THINK ABOUT?
I MEAN, YOU DON'T HAVE MUCH OF A LIFE.
BEFORE I MET HER, I WANTED IT TO BE OVER. BUT NOW...
MAYBE SHE REALLY WAS DEATH. I MEAN, IT WOULD BE REALLY NEAT IF DEATH WAS SOMEBODY, AND NOT JUST NOTHING, OR PAIN, OR BLACKNESS.
312
AND IT WOULD BE REALLY GOOD IF DEATH COULD BE SOMEBODY LIKE DIDI. SOME-BODY FUNNY, AND FRIENDLY, AND NICE. AND MAYBE JUST A TINY BIT CRAZY.
AND I WISH I COULD SEE HER AGAIN. I WISH SHE WASN'T DEAD. BUT IF IT MEANS DYING FIRST...
WELL...I SUPPOSE I CAN WAIT. FOR A WHILE.

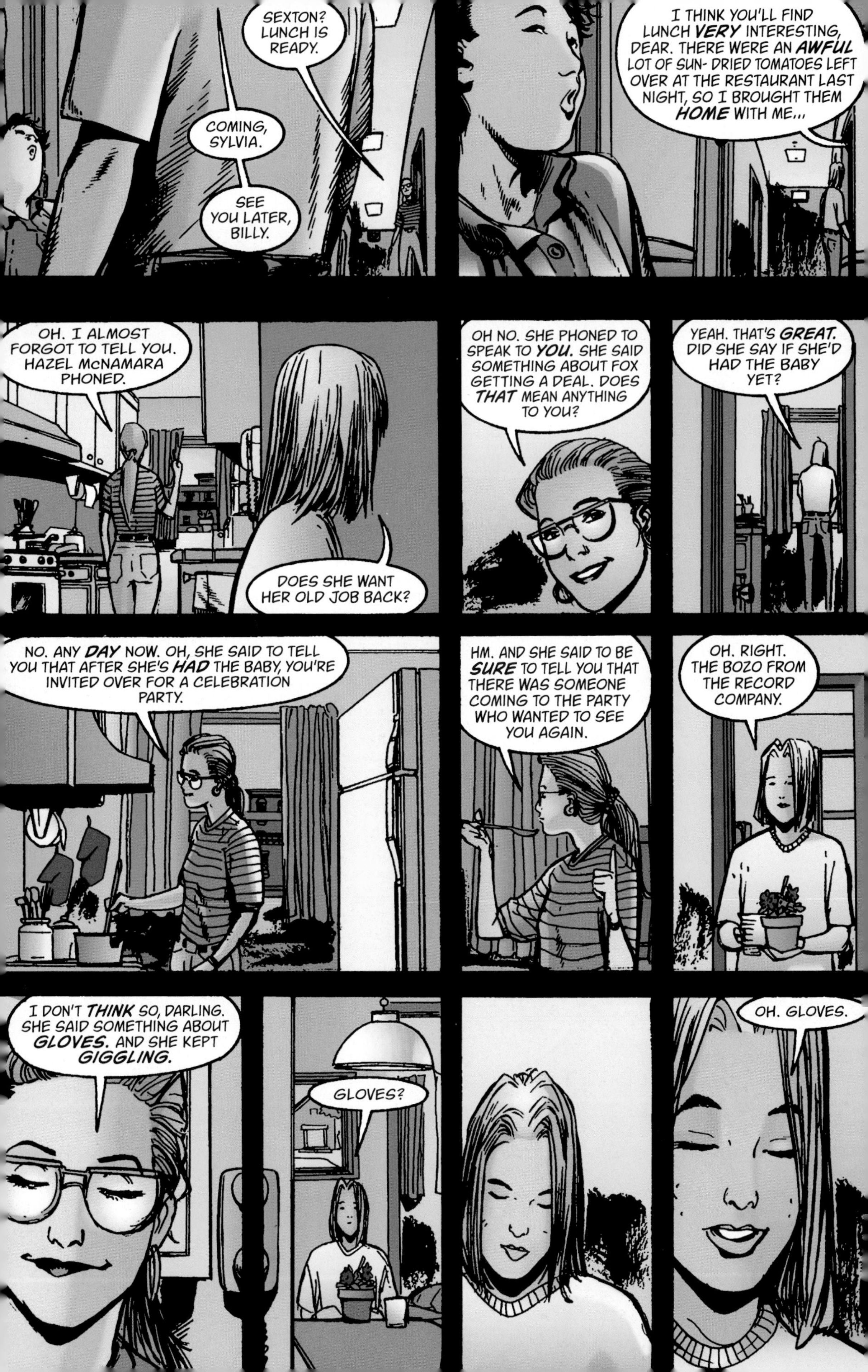
SEXTON? LUNCH IS READY.
COMING, SYLVIA.
SEE YOU LATER, BILLY.
I THINK YOU'LL FIND LUNCH VERY INTERESTING, DEAR. THERE WERE AN AWFUL LOT OF SUN- DRIED TOMATOES LEFT OVER AT THE RESTAURANT LAST NIGHT, SO I BROUGHT THEM HOME WITH ME...
OH. I ALMOST FORGOT TO TELL YOU. HAZEL McNAMARA PHONED.
DOES SHE WANT HER OLD JOB BACK?
OH NO. SHE PHONED TO SPEAK TO YOU. SHE SAID SOMETHING ABOUT FOX GETTING A DEAL. DOES THAT MEAN ANYTHING TO YOU?
YEAH. THAT'S GREAT. DID SHE SAY IF SHE'D HAD THE BABY YET?
NO. ANY DAY NOW. OH, SHE SAID TO TELL YOU THAT AFTER SHE'S HAD THE BABY, YOU'RE INVITED OVER FOR A CELEBRATION PARTY.
HM. AND SHE SAID TO BE SURE TO TELL YOU THAT THERE WAS SOMEONE COMING TO THE PARTY WHO WANTED TO SEE YOU AGAIN.
OH. RIGHT. THE BOZO FROM THE RECORD COMPANY.
I DON'T THINK SO, DARLING. SHE SAID SOMETHING ABOUT GLOVES. AND SHE KEPT GIGGLING.
GLOVES?
OH. GLOVES.

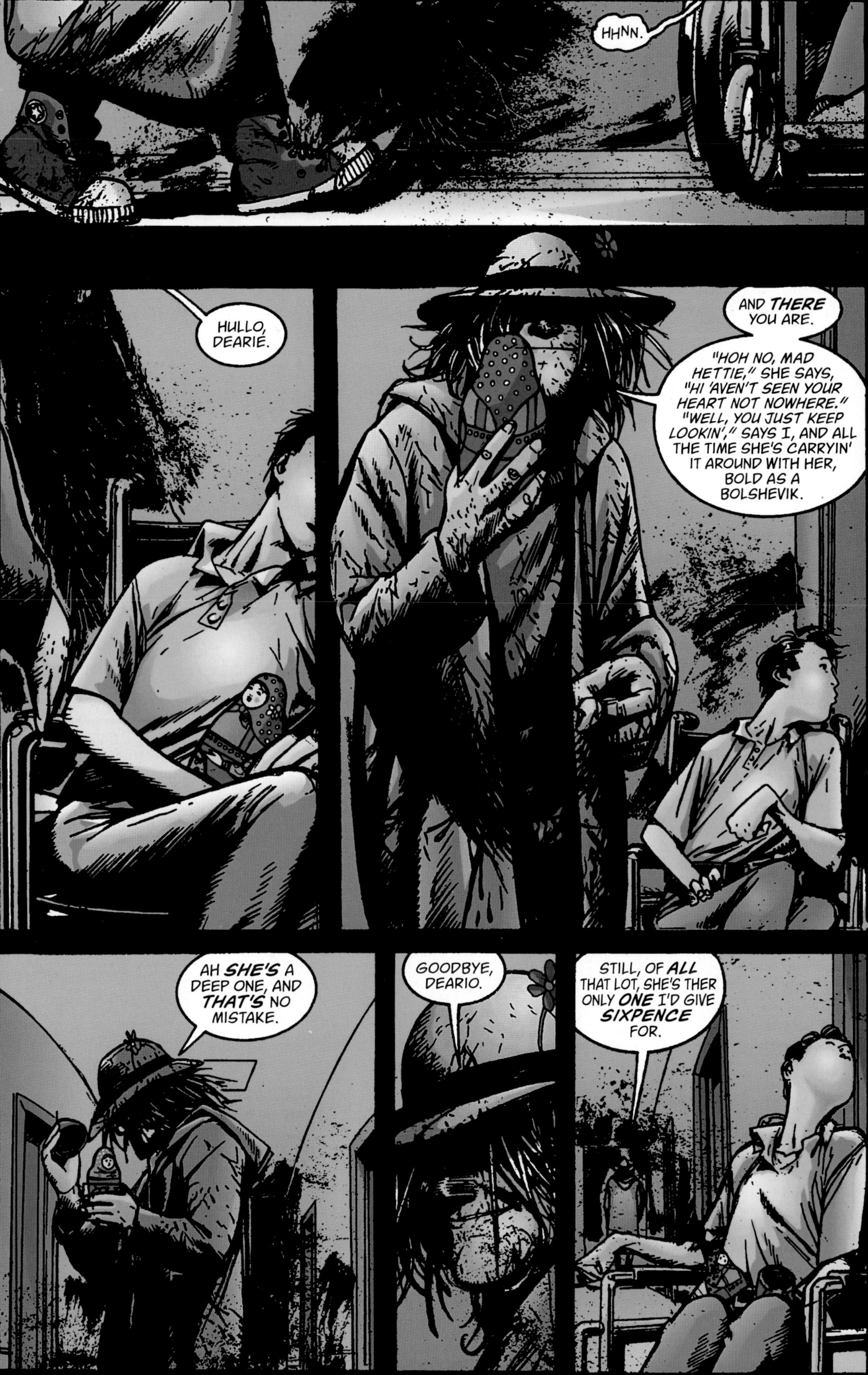
HHNN.
HULLO, DEARIE.
AND THERE YOU ARE.
"HOH NO, MAD HETTIE," SHE SAYS, "HI 'AVEN'T SEEN YOUR HEART NOT NOWHERE." "WELL, YOU JUST KEEP LOOKIN'," SAYS I, AND ALL THE TIME SHE'S CARRYIN' IT AROUND WITH HER, BOLD AS A BOLSHEVIK.
AH SHE'S A DEEP ONE, AND THAT'S NO MISTAKE.
GOODBYE, DEARIO.
STILL, OF ALL THAT LOT, SHE'S THER ONLY ONE I'D GIVE SIXPENCE FOR.

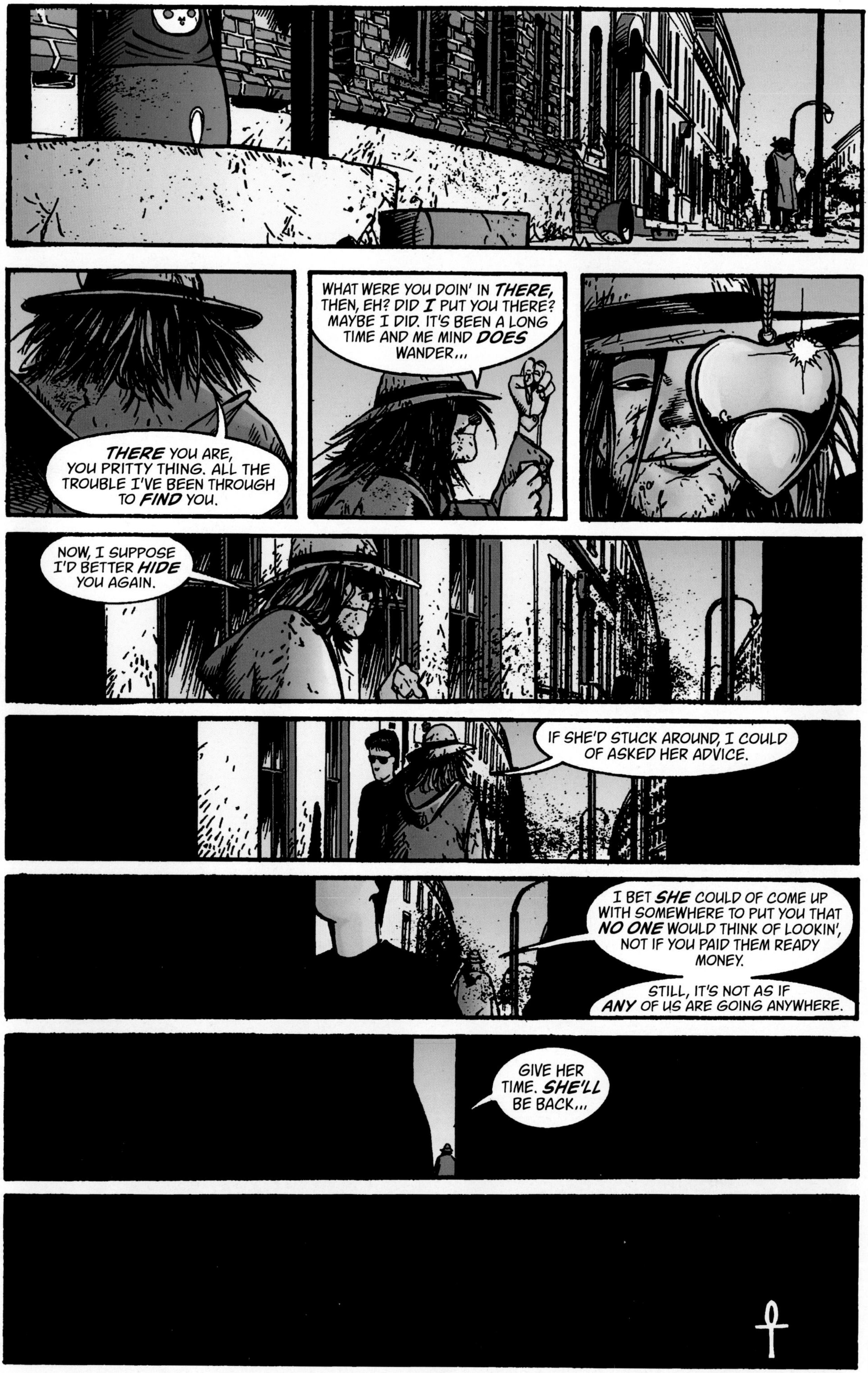
THERE YOU ARE, YOU PRITTY THING. ALL THE TROUBLE I'VE BEEN THROUGH TO FIND YOU.
WHAT WERE YOU DOIN' IN THERE, THEN, EH? DID I PUT YOU THERE? MAYBE I DID. IT'S BEEN A LONG TIME AND ME MIND DOES WANDER...
NOW, I SUPPOSE I'D BETTER HIDE YOU AGAIN.
IF SHE'D STUCK AROUND, I COULD OF ASKED HER ADVICE.
I BET SHE COULD OF COME UP WITH SOMEWHERE TO PUT YOU THAT NO ONE WOULD THINK OF LOOKIN', NOT IF YOU PAID THEM READY MONEY.
STILL, IT'S NOT AS IF ANY OF US ARE GOING ANYWHERE.
GIVE HER TIME. SHE'LL BE BACK...

THE WHEEL

STORY NEIL GAIMAN
ART CHRIS BACHALO
LETTERS TODD KLEIN
COLOR ROB RO AND ALEX BLEYAERT

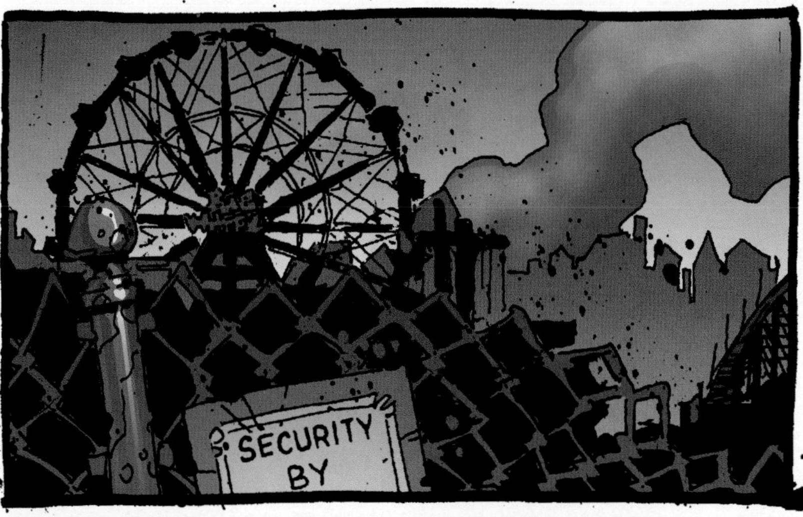
SECURITY
BY

I made this story up to make me feel better.
Now I'm writing it down. It's not true.

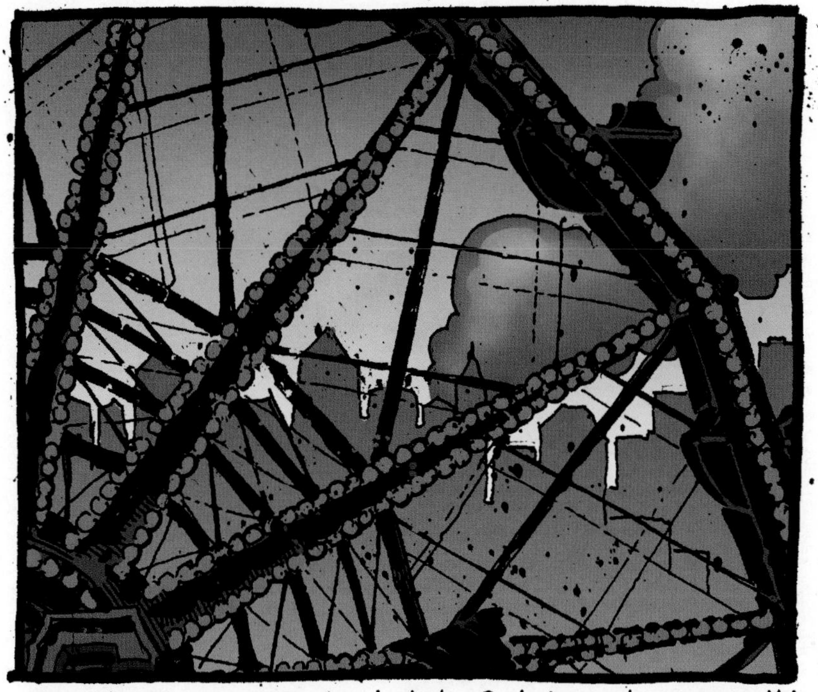

It's about how, one day in late October when everything was gray and there was nobody about, I climbed over a wire fence, and then I climbed over another wire fence.

There were signs on the fences, saying the place was patrolled by security and by dogs, but I didn't see anyone. Just an empty fairground, and the wheel.

When I got to the big wheel I started to climb. I'm a good climber. At school I can climb better than anybody.

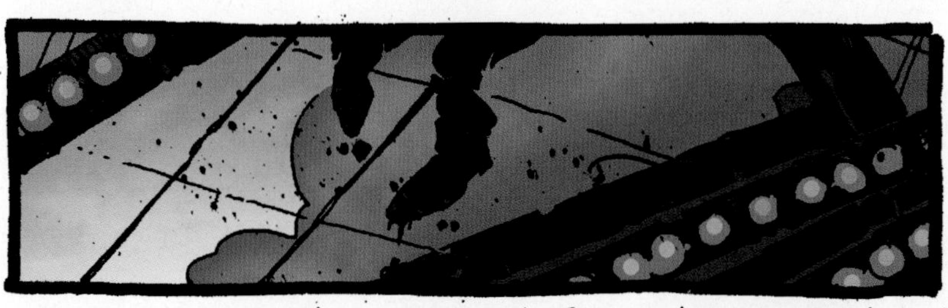

One time I slipped, and I nearly fell, but I grabbed a strut and I caught myself. My heart was thumping in my chest.

Now, the crazy thing is this: I was only climbing the wheel to jump off. So you'd think that falling off would be something I'd want.

But I wanted to do this right. I had to do everything right. I kept climbing. And eventually, I got to the top of the wheel.

So I'm at the top. I tore a finger when I fell, and it's bleeding, and I suck it.

Apart from that, it's all pretty much as I expected. The light is fading fast, but I can see everything from here.

When I was a kid, about six months ago, I came here in the summer and I could see the towers, and I'd wave at my mom. I knew she couldn't see me, but I'd still wave.

It's strange how some things just vanish.

HEY! YOU! UP THERE!

And I freeze, and I think it's security, with dogs, now I'm really in trouble and I figure I'll duck down low and keep real still and maybe he'll move on.

But I can hear a clambering, and then a huge thud as somebody drops into the car I'm in, and this big guy with a beard is saying --

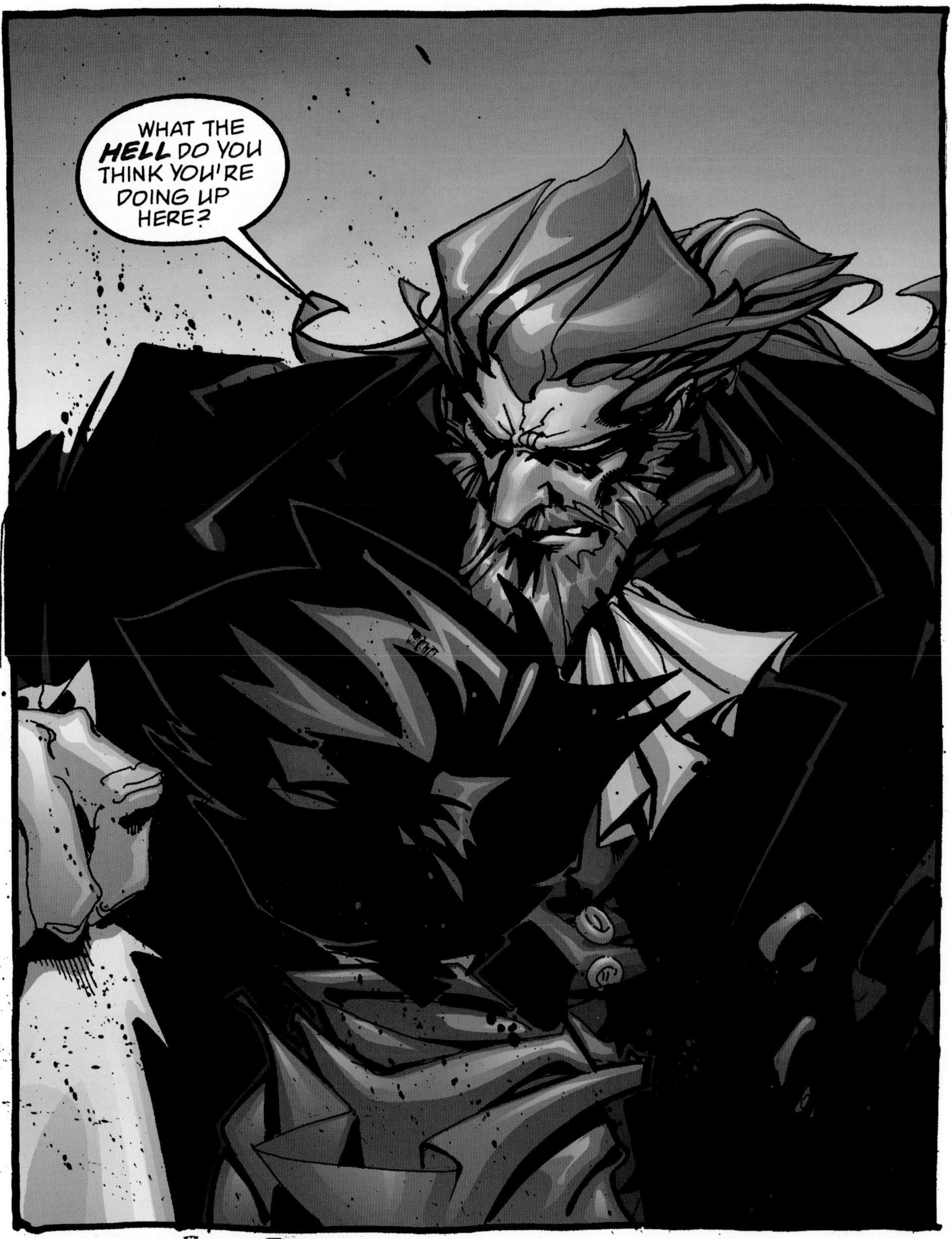
WHAT THE HELL DO YOU THINK YOU'RE DOING UP HERE?

And I go blank. Utterly, completely blank.
I'm trying to think of a story--
maybe I saw something moving back here,
I thought it was terrorists, so I came to investigate...

...and then I realize that I'm crying. Like a little kid. And I can't stop.

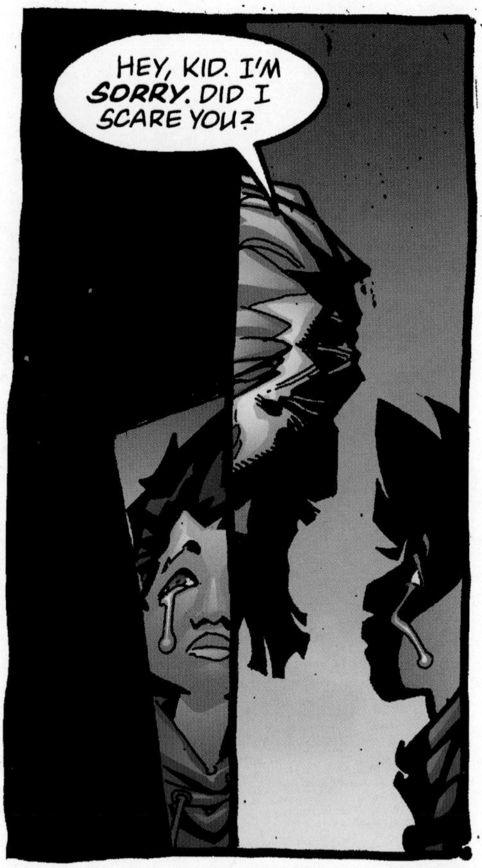
HEY, KID. I'M SORRY. DID I SCARE YOU?

And I'm trying to find a way to say no, you didn't scare me, it's just all been inside, I've been holding it together so well, and now it's all coming out of me, Mom and everything...

And then the big guy picks me up like I don't weigh anything at all, and he holds me gently, and it makes me think of being held by a bear, and I can feel our car swaying in the wind at the top of the wheel.

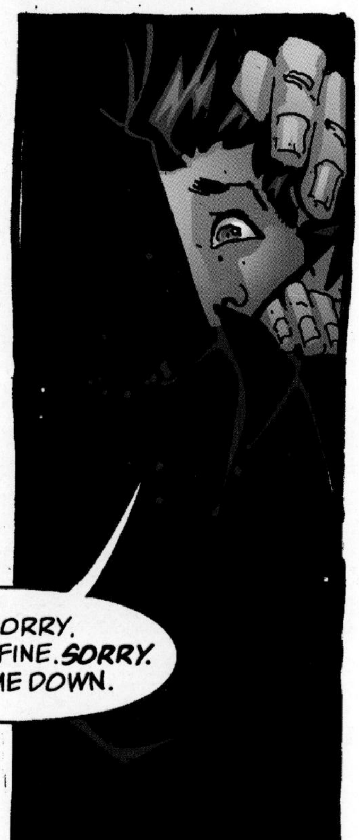
I'M SORRY. I'LL BE FINE. SORRY. PUT ME DOWN.

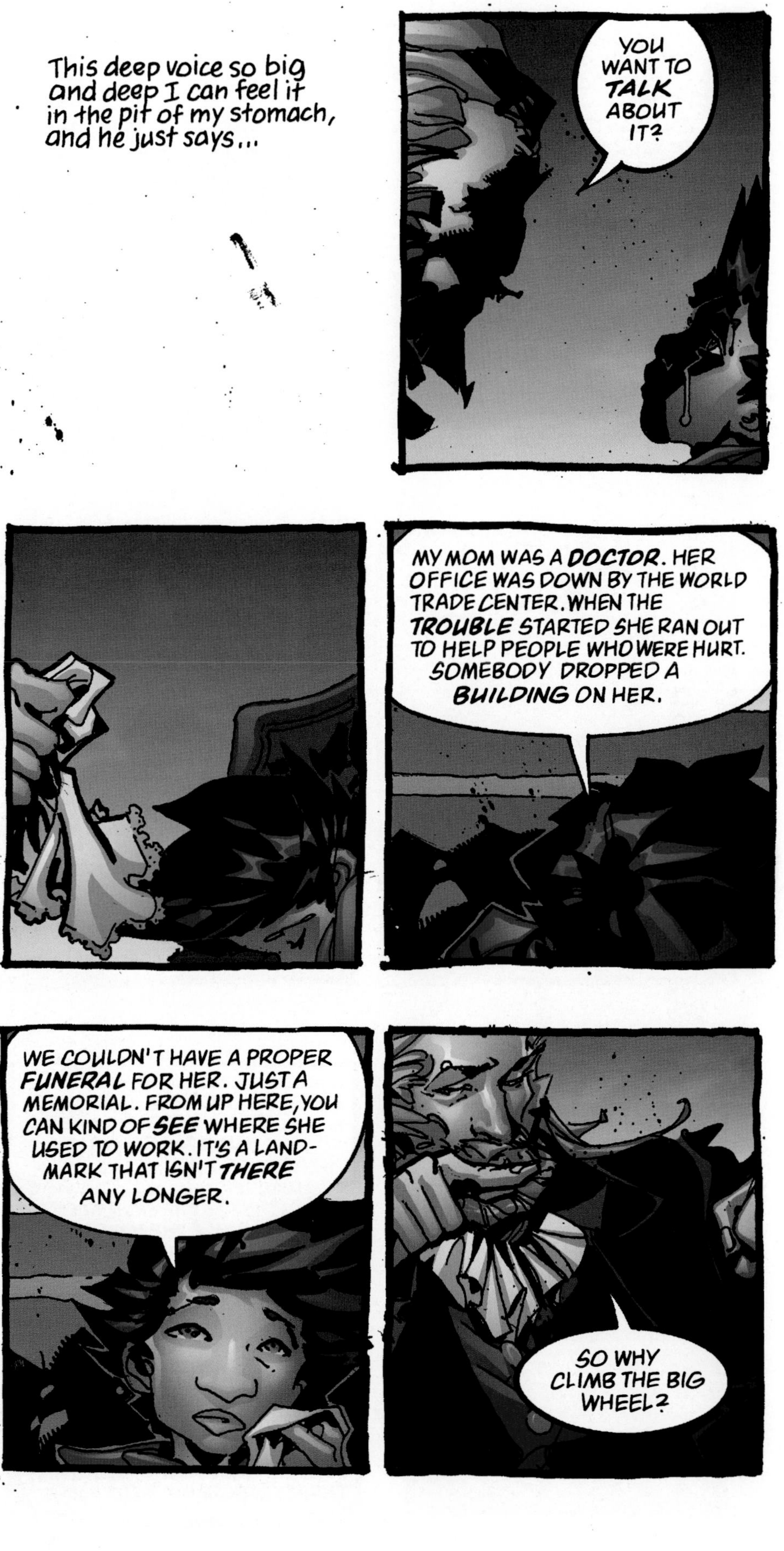
This deep voice so big and deep I can feel it in the pit of my stomach, and he just says...
YOU WANT TO TALK ABOUT IT?
MY MOM WAS A DOCTOR. HER OFFICE WAS DOWN BY THE WORLD TRADE CENTER. WHEN THE TROUBLE STARTED SHE RAN OUT TO HELP PEOPLE WHO WERE HURT. SOMEBODY DROPPED A BUILDING ON HER.
WE COULDN'T HAVE A PROPER FUNERAL FOR HER. JUST A MEMORIAL. FROM UP HERE, YOU CAN KIND OF SEE WHERE SHE USED TO WORK. IT'S A LANDMARK THAT ISN'T THERE ANY LONGER.
SO WHY CLIMB THE BIG WHEEL?

I'M GOING TO *JUMP*. AND I'M GOING TO DIE. I'M GOING TO GO TO GOD.

YOU WANT TO SEE YOUR MOTHER AGAIN? BECAUSE IT DOESN'T WORK LIKE--

NO, DUMMY. YOU DON'T GET IT. MOM'S *DEAD*.

I WANT AN *EXPLANATION*.

YOU'RE *SERIOUS*?

DAMN RIGHT. I'M GOING TO TALK TO GOD. I WANT AN EXPLANATION.

COULD BE A PROBLEM. GOD DOESN'T *DO* EXPLANATIONS.

HE'D LET SOMETHING LIKE *THAT* HAPPEN, AND NOT BE ABLE TO *EXPLAIN*? WELL, THE LEAST I WANT IS TO HEAR HIM SAY SORRY.

GOD DOESN'T *APOLOGIZE*, EITHER.

SO TELL ME, WHAT HAPPENS IF YOU HIT THE GROUND AND DIE AND THERE'S *NOTHING* AFTER?

THEN I *WON'T* BE AROUND TO *CARE*, WILL I?

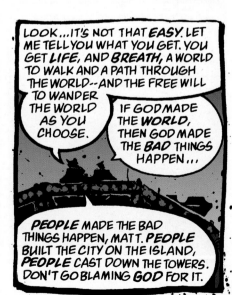

LOOK...IT'S NOT THAT *EASY*. LET ME TELL YOU WHAT YOU GET. YOU GET *LIFE*, AND *BREATH*, A WORLD TO WALK AND A PATH THROUGH THE WORLD--AND THE FREE WILL TO WANDER THE WORLD AS YOU CHOOSE.

IF GOD MADE THE *WORLD*, THEN GOD MADE THE *BAD* THINGS HAPPEN...

PEOPLE MADE THE BAD THINGS HAPPEN, MATT. *PEOPLE* BUILT THE CITY ON THE ISLAND, *PEOPLE* CAST DOWN THE TOWERS. DON'T GO BLAMING *GOD* FOR IT.

This is how you know I'm making this up.
I'm not telling you it's true.
I wouldn't try to convince anybody.
Because now there were three of us in the car, at the top of the dark wheel.

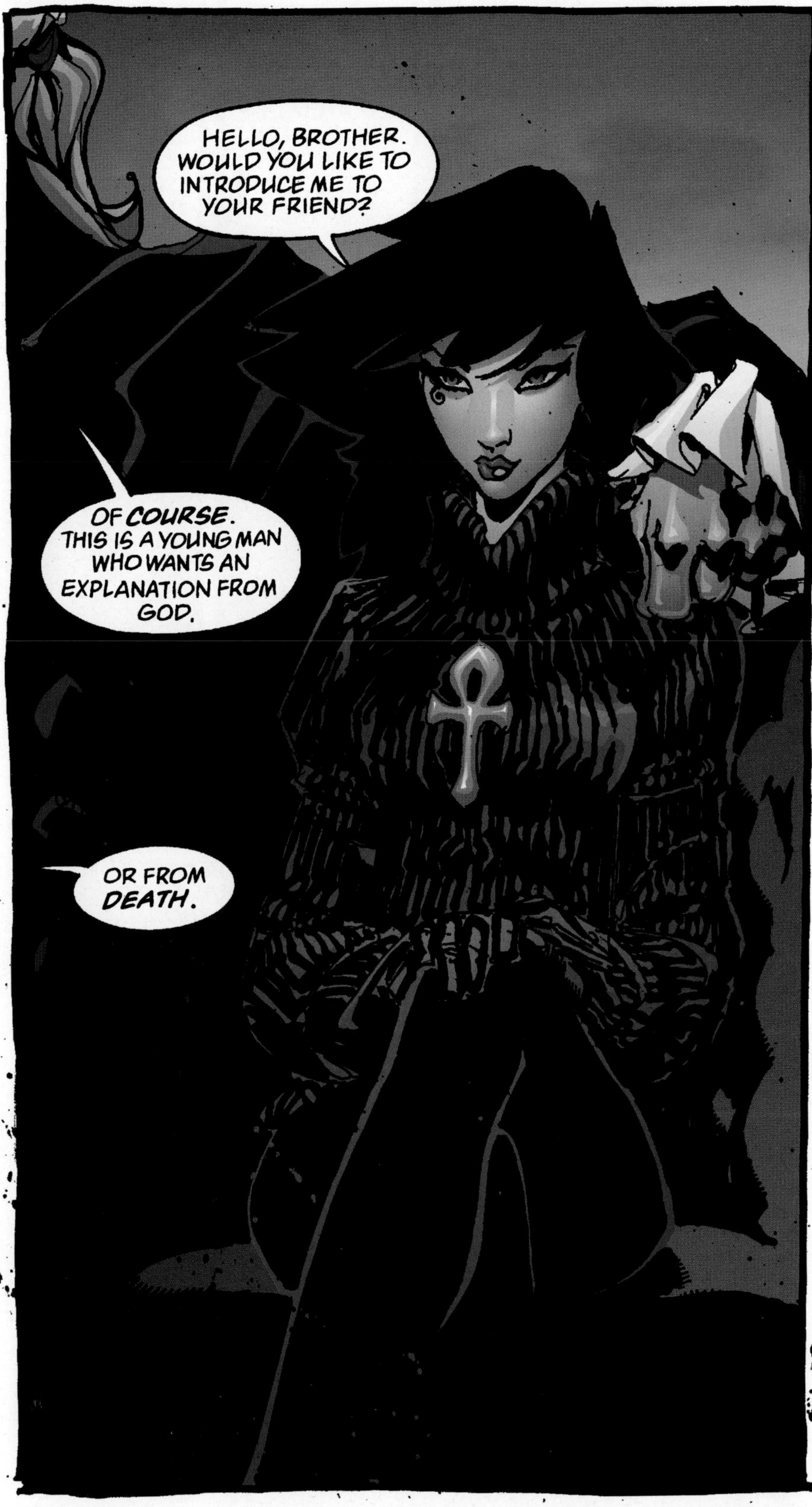
HELLO, BROTHER. WOULD YOU LIKE TO INTRODUCE ME TO YOUR FRIEND?
OF COURSE. THIS IS A YOUNG MAN WHO WANTS AN EXPLANATION FROM GOD.
OR FROM DEATH.

I don't know what made me say that.
But she just nodded, as if I had said something sensible after all.

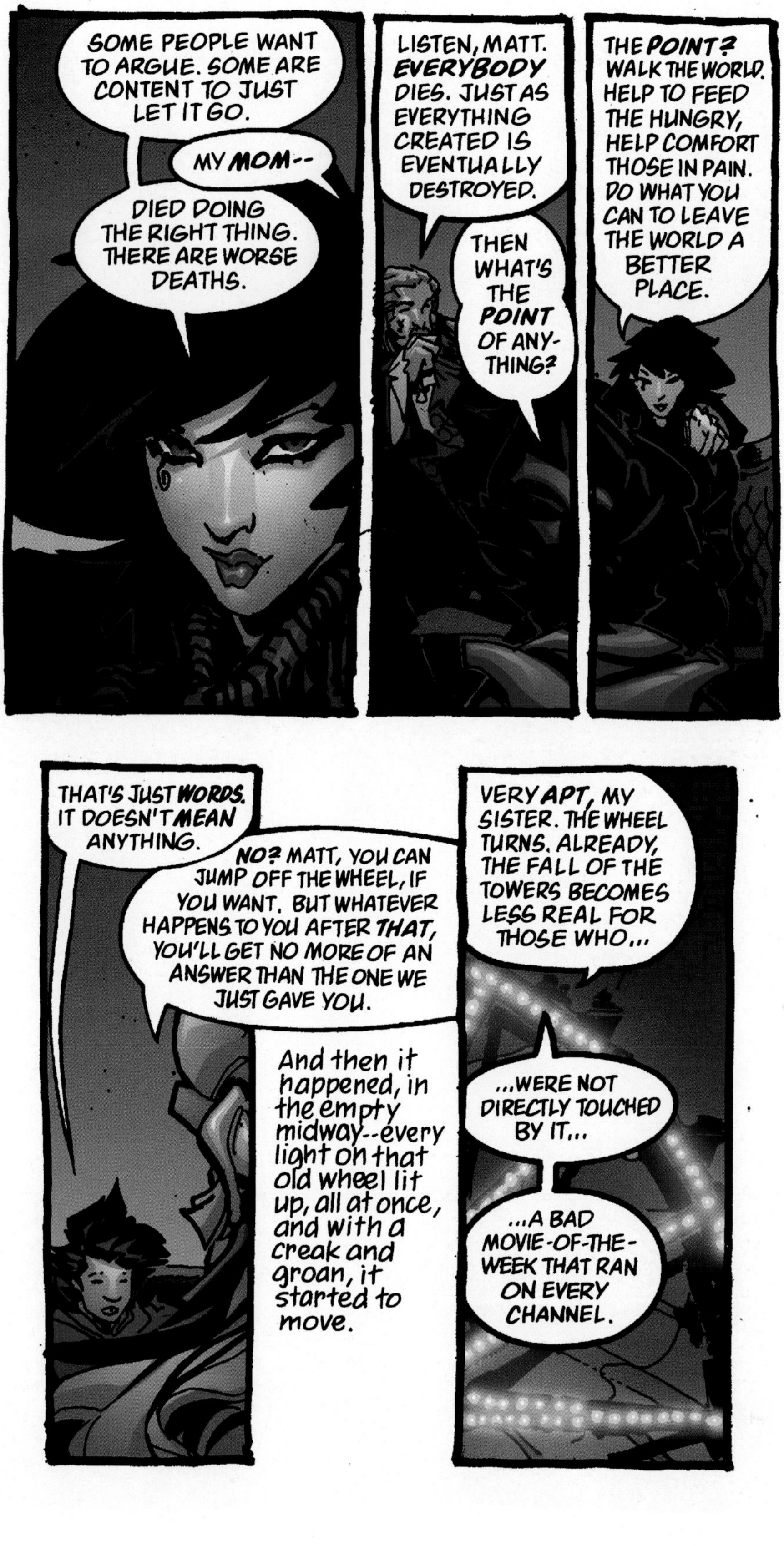
SOME PEOPLE WANT TO ARGUE. SOME ARE CONTENT TO JUST LET IT GO.
MY MOM--
DIED DOING THE RIGHT THING. THERE ARE WORSE DEATHS.
LISTEN, MATT. EVERYBODY DIES. JUST AS EVERYTHING CREATED IS EVENTUALLY DESTROYED.
THEN WHAT'S THE POINT OF ANYTHING?
THE POINT? WALK THE WORLD. HELP TO FEED THE HUNGRY, HELP COMFORT THOSE IN PAIN. DO WHAT YOU CAN TO LEAVE THE WORLD A BETTER PLACE.
THAT'S JUST WORDS. IT DOESN'T MEAN ANYTHING.
NO? MATT, YOU CAN JUMP OFF THE WHEEL, IF YOU WANT. BUT WHATEVER HAPPENS TO YOU AFTER THAT, YOU'LL GET NO MORE OF AN ANSWER THAN THE ONE WE JUST GAVE YOU.
And then it happened, in the empty midway--every light on that old wheel lit up, all at once, and with a creak and groan, it started to move.
VERY APT, MY SISTER. THE WHEEL TURNS. ALREADY, THE FALL OF THE TOWERS BECOMES LESS REAL FOR THOSE WHO...
...WERE NOT DIRECTLY TOUCHED BY IT...
...A BAD MOVIE-OF-THE-WEEK THAT RAN ON EVERY CHANNEL.

IT'S JUST SO HARD.

IT'S ALWAYS HARD. RIDE THE WHEEL, MATT.

And she squeezed my hand.

When I grow up, I thought,
I'll have a girlfriend like you.

Which meant, I guessed, that
I wasn't going to be jumping
off the top of the wheel.

So, no, I don't know who
turned on the wheel, who
turned on the lights. I guess I
must have made up the people
in the car, because if they *had*
ever been there, they weren't
anymore.

So I was all alone in the car,
riding the wonder wheel, and
then the music began to play.
Corny carnival music. Mom
said it always made her
remember what it was to be
a kid again, and just for a
moment, I knew what she
meant.

And the music was playing,
and the lights were burning,
and when I got to the top of
the wheel it felt like I could
see forever.

156

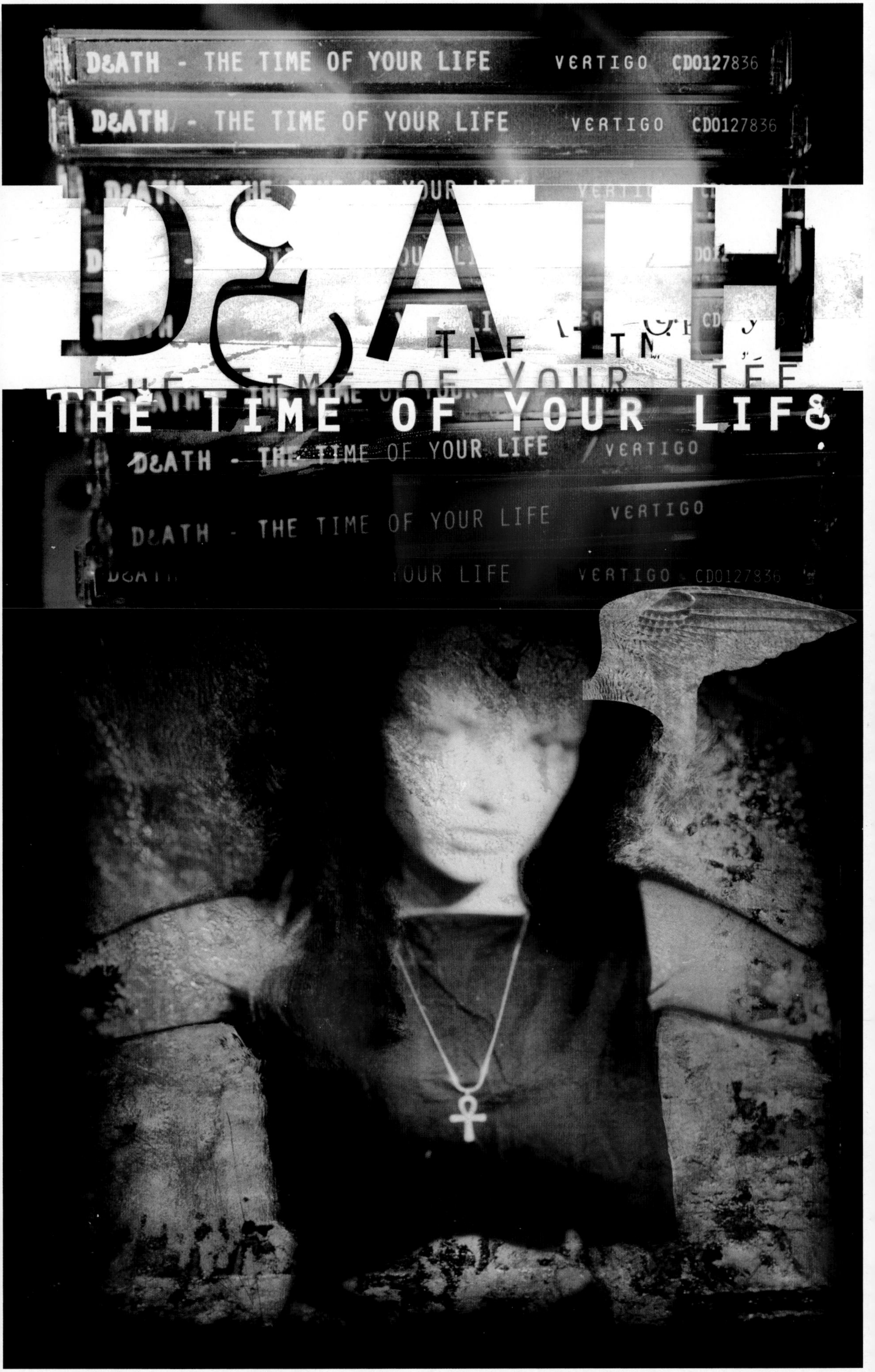
DEATH - THE TIME OF YOUR LIFE VERTIGO CD0127836
DEATH
THE TIME OF YOUR LIFE

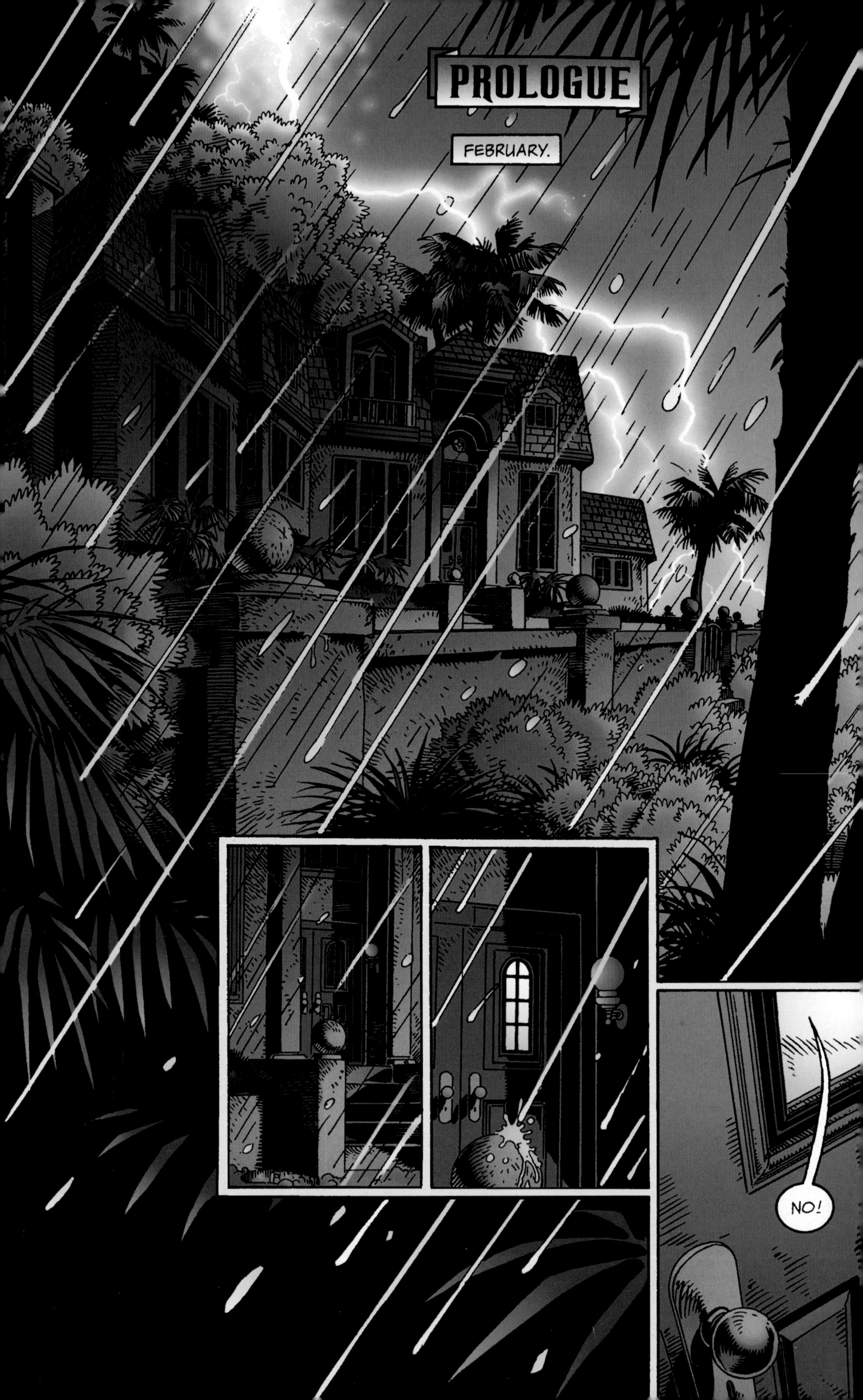
PROLOGUE
FEBRUARY.
NO!

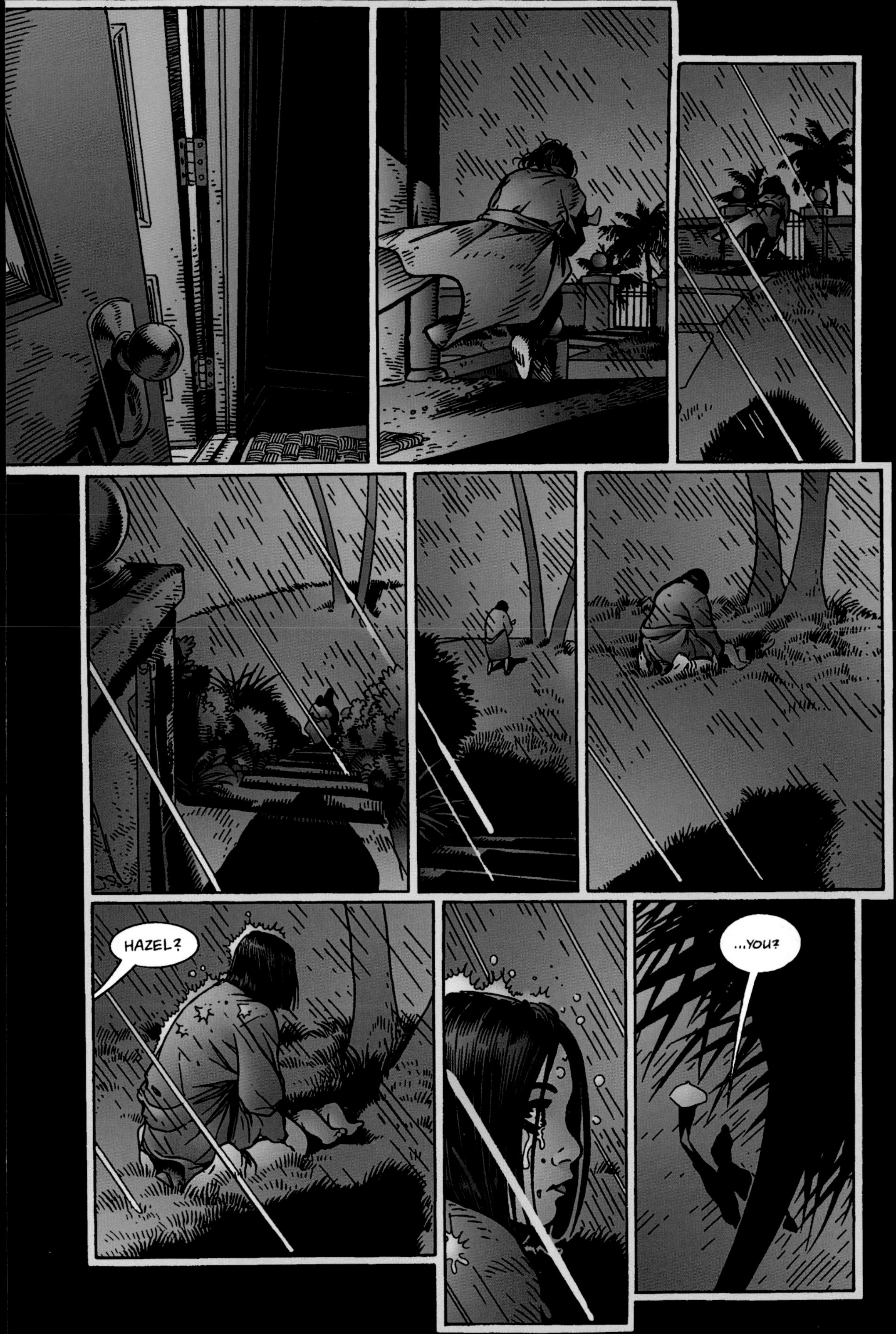
HAZEL?
...YOU?

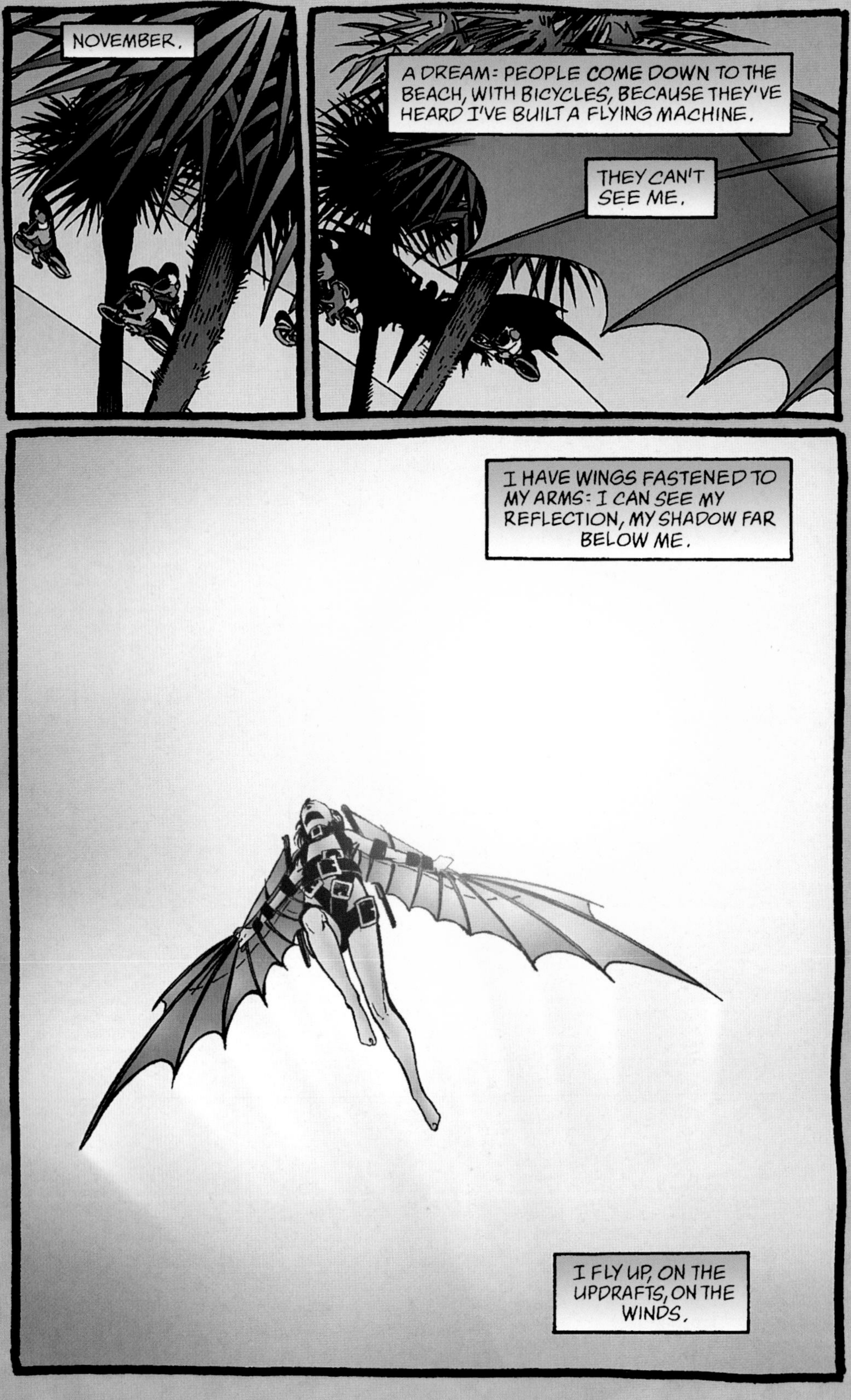
NOVEMBER.
A DREAM: PEOPLE COME DOWN TO THE BEACH, WITH BICYCLES, BECAUSE THEY'VE HEARD I'VE BUILT A FLYING MACHINE.
THEY CAN'T SEE ME.
I HAVE WINGS FASTENED TO MY ARMS: I CAN SEE MY REFLECTION, MY SHADOW FAR BELOW ME.
I FLY UP, ON THE UPDRAFTS, ON THE WINDS.

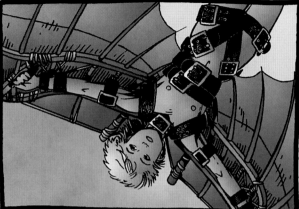

TUMBLING THROUGH CLOUDS, I CANNOT TELL WHICH WAY IS UP ANY MORE, WHICH WAY IS DOWN: UTTERLY DISORIENTED, ALL I KNOW IS THAT I'M FALLING, WITH NO SENSE OF WHERE.

MAYBE I'M FALLING INTO THE SKY.

MAYBE I'M FALLING DOWN, THROUGH THE STORM CLOUDS (HUGE DARK CUMULUS CLOUDS, HOW DO YOU TELL IF A CLOUD IS UPSIDE-DOWN?)

MAYBE I'M GOING TO DIE.

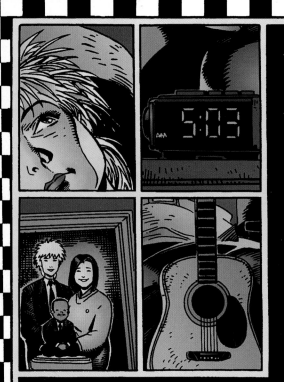

DEATH: THE TIME of your LIFE

NEIL GAIMAN writer • **CHRIS BACHALO** penciller • **MARK BUCKINGHAM** inker

MATT HOLLINGSWORTH colorist-separations • **TODD KLEIN** letterer

SHELLY ROEBERG associate editor • **KAREN BERGER** editor

DEATH created by Neil Gaiman & Mike Dringenberg • HAZEL & FOXGLOVE created by Neil Gaiman & Shawn McManus

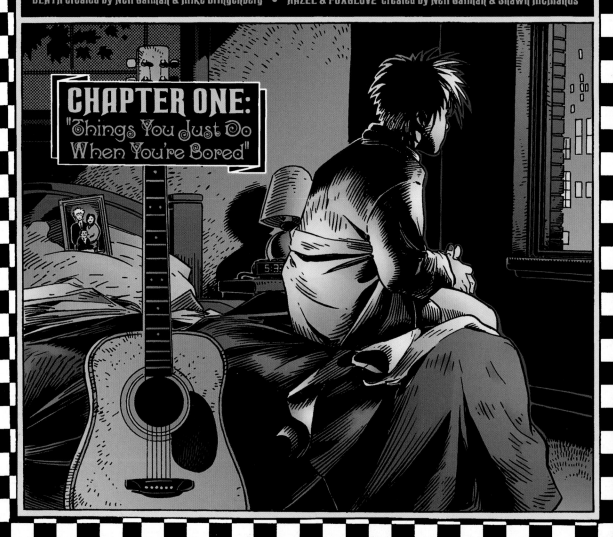

CHAPTER ONE:
"Things You Just Do When You're Bored"

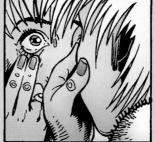

HOTEL ROOMS ARE LONELY.

ALL THE CRAZINESSES THAT YOU AVOID IN THE DAY-TO-DAY BUSINESS OF LIFE COME TO YOU IN HOTEL ROOMS AND EAT YOUR MIND. THE PEOPLE THEY FIND DEAD IN HOTEL ROOMS WOULDN'T HAVE KILLED THEM-SELVES AT HOME.

HOTEL ROOMS DON'T CARE IF YOU LIVE OR DIE.

SOMEONE WILL COME AND CLEAN THE ROOM IN THE MORN-ING WHATEVER YOU DO, AND THEY'LL RE-STOCK THE MINIBAR AND MAKE THE BED AND TAKE THE SCRUNCHED-UP TISSUES AND THE DEAD BODIES AWAY...

KNOCK KNOCK

ROOM SERVICE!

YOU ORDERED COFFEE AND AN ORANGE JUICE?

YEAH. COME ON IN.

UH. LOOK, THEY DON'T LIKE IT IF WE, UM. BUT I *GOT* TO ASK, ARE YOU *FOXGLOVE*? THE *SINGER*?

MM-HMM.

OH *GOD.* I CAN'T BE*LIEVE* THIS, I'M MEETING YOU. PLEASE DON'T TELL ANYONE THAT I ASKED YOU IF YOU WERE YOU, I MEAN THEY'D FIRE ME OR SOMETHING.

I HAD TO ASK.

"THE POETRY INSPECTOR" WAS LIKE MY FAVORITE *CD* OF THE WHOLE YEAR.

I JUST *PLAYED* IT AND *PLAYED* IT.

IT GAVE ME THE STRENGTH TO WALK OUT ON THIS GUY.

WHAT ARE YOU DOING IN NEW YORK? ARE YOU *PLAYING* ANYWHERE?

LETTERMAN TONIGHT.

I'LL WATCH. I'LL STAY *UP* AND WATCH. LISTEN, WILL YOU *SIGN* SOMETHING FOR ME?

WHAT'S YOUR NAME?

JUDE. LIKE 'HEY JUDE,' Y' KNOW?

AND THEN I SIGN A SECOND TIME, FOR THE ROOM SERVICE, AND SHE LEAVES.

AND NOW I THINK ABOUT WORKING ON A SONG, BUT I DON'T FEEL LIKE IT, AND I THINK ABOUT PHONING HAZEL AND SAYING HI TO ALVIE...

BUT IT'S 4:00 AM THERE, AND SHE WOULDN'T APPRECIATE IT, AND I CAN'T FACE ANOTHER ARGUMENT.

SO I DRINK MY ORANGE JUICE, AND I DRINK MY COFFEE. AND I PUT ON MY FACE, AND MY BOTTLE-GREEN LEATHER JACKET, AND A SKIRT WHICH IS, BETWEEN OURSELVES, IN SLIGHTLY QUESTIONABLE TASTE...

...AND I READ MY COMPLIMENTARY COPY OF USA TODAY, WHICH MENTIONS THAT ADVANCE ORDERS FOR "SLITS OF LOVE" HAVE TOPPED 650,000, ONLY THEY'VE GOT THE TITLE AS "SLICES OF LOVE," WHICH KIND OF PISSES ME OFF...

USA
BLUE M+M
HITS THE MARK

...AND AT PRECISELY 9:30 THE TELEPHONE RINGS.

FOX? IT'S LARRY. I'M IN THE LOBBY. YOU WANT ME TO COME UP?

I'LL COME DOWN.

ELEVATOR →

LARRY IS A MANAGER OF THE OLD SCHOOL, WHICH, HE TELLS ME, IS THE CRAWLEY GRAMMAR SCHOOL FOR BOYS, SOMEWHERE SOUTH OF LONDON.

RUMOR HAS IT HE BEGAN LIFE AS A DEALER TO HERMAN'S HERMITS. OR THE KINKS. I FORGET. ONE OF THOSE BANDS. CAME OUT TO THE STATES IN '67. I THINK HE WAS JANIS JOPLIN'S DEALER TOO. OR SOMETHING.

THEN HE DID SECURITY FOR A WHILE-- HE STILL COMPLAINS THAT THE STONES SHOULD'VE HIRED HIS SQUAD FOR ALTAMONT. AFTER THAT HE MOVED INTO ARTIST MANAGEMENT AND TURNED OUT TO BE FRIGHTENINGLY GOOD AT IT.

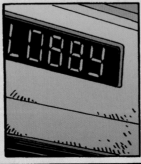

LOBBY

WE'VE BEEN TOGETHER NOW FOR A COUPLE OF YEARS. IT'S KIND OF LIKE A MARRIAGE. EXCEPT THERE'S NEVER ANY NOT-TALKING. AND NO FIGHTS ABOUT SEX. AND NO EATING ICE-CREAM TOGETHER AT TWO IN THE MORNING. NOT THAT THERE'S BEEN MUCH OF THAT RECENTLY...

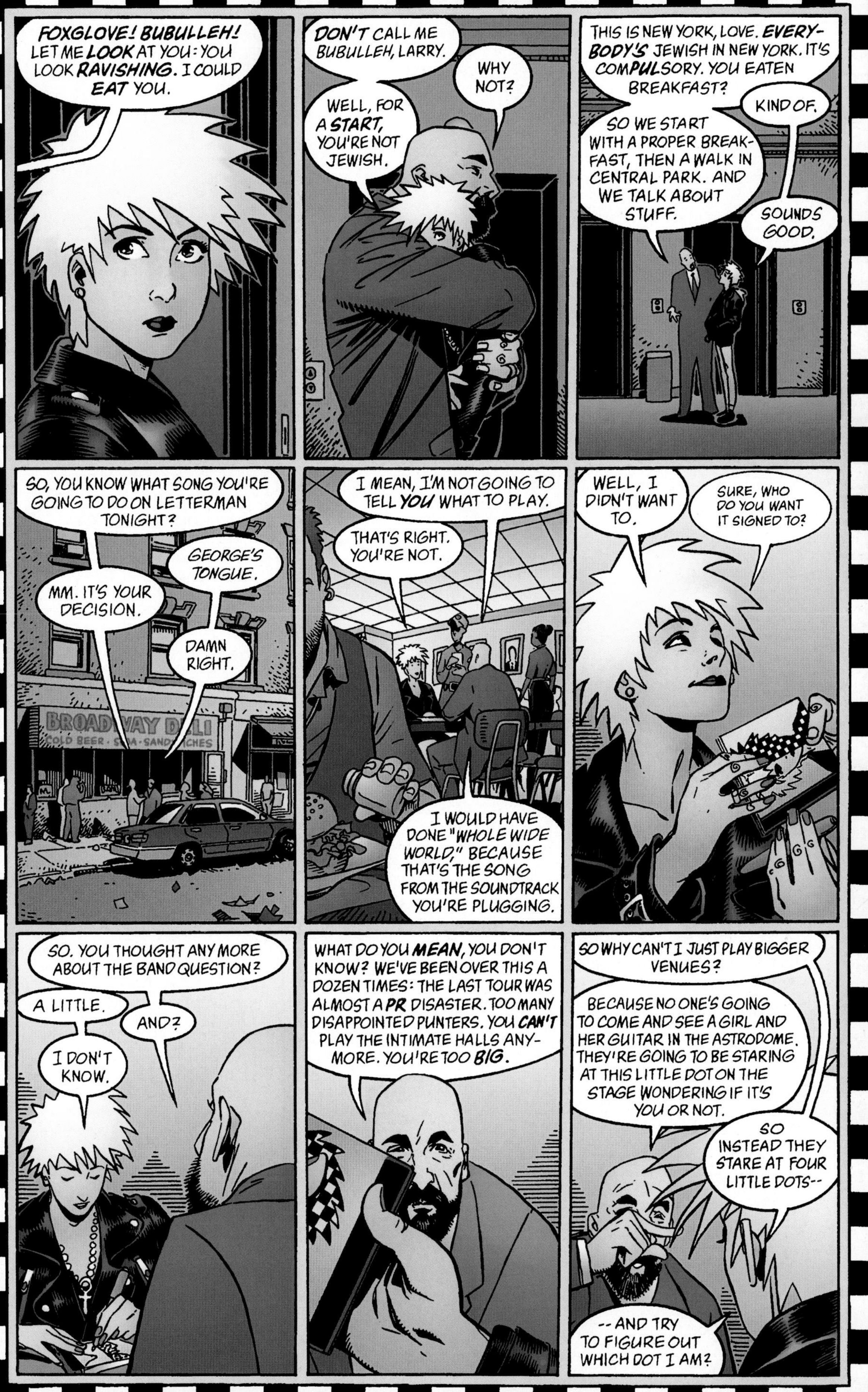
FOXGLOVE! BUBULLEH! LET ME LOOK AT YOU: YOU LOOK RAVISHING. I COULD EAT YOU.
DON'T CALL ME BUBULLEH, LARRY.
WHY NOT?
WELL, FOR A START, YOU'RE NOT JEWISH.
THIS IS NEW YORK, LOVE. EVERYBODY'S JEWISH IN NEW YORK. IT'S COMPULSORY. YOU EATEN BREAKFAST?
KIND OF.
SO WE START WITH A PROPER BREAKFAST, THEN A WALK IN CENTRAL PARK. AND WE TALK ABOUT STUFF.
SOUNDS GOOD.
SO, YOU KNOW WHAT SONG YOU'RE GOING TO DO ON LETTERMAN TONIGHT?
GEORGE'S TONGUE.
MM. IT'S YOUR DECISION.
DAMN RIGHT.
BROADWAY DELI
COLD BEER · SODA · SANDWICHES
I MEAN, I'M NOT GOING TO TELL YOU WHAT TO PLAY.
THAT'S RIGHT. YOU'RE NOT.
I WOULD HAVE DONE "WHOLE WIDE WORLD," BECAUSE THAT'S THE SONG FROM THE SOUNDTRACK YOU'RE PLUGGING.
WELL, I DIDN'T WANT TO.
SURE, WHO DO YOU WANT IT SIGNED TO?
SO. YOU THOUGHT ANY MORE ABOUT THE BAND QUESTION?
A LITTLE.
AND?
I DON'T KNOW.
WHAT DO YOU MEAN, YOU DON'T KNOW? WE'VE BEEN OVER THIS A DOZEN TIMES: THE LAST TOUR WAS ALMOST A PR DISASTER. TOO MANY DISAPPOINTED PUNTERS. YOU CAN'T PLAY THE INTIMATE HALLS ANYMORE. YOU'RE TOO BIG.
SO WHY CAN'T I JUST PLAY BIGGER VENUES?
BECAUSE NO ONE'S GOING TO COME AND SEE A GIRL AND HER GUITAR IN THE ASTRODOME. THEY'RE GOING TO BE STARING AT THIS LITTLE DOT ON THE STAGE WONDERING IF IT'S YOU OR NOT.
SO INSTEAD THEY STARE AT FOUR LITTLE DOTS--
--AND TRY TO FIGURE OUT WHICH DOT I AM?

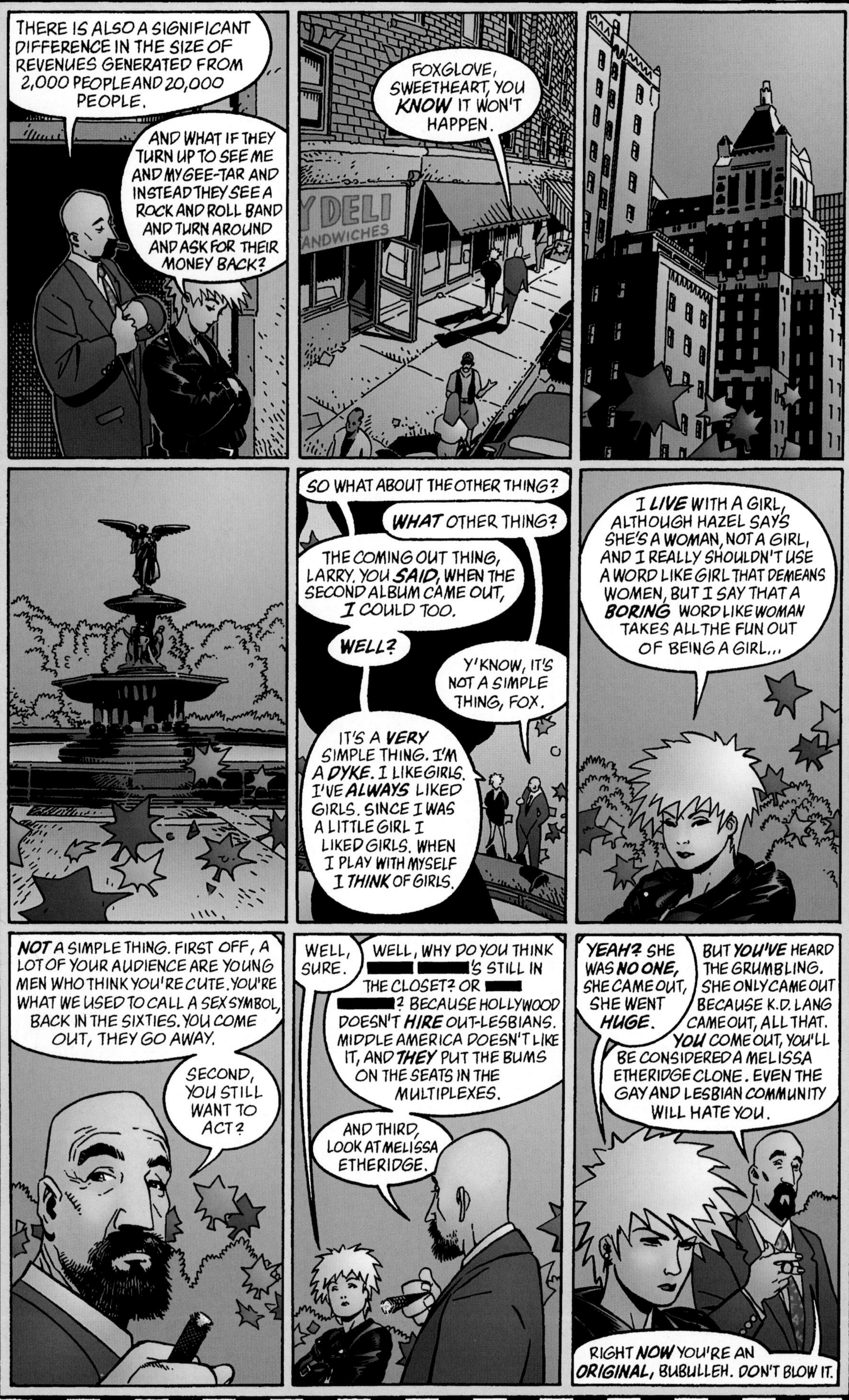
THERE IS ALSO A SIGNIFICANT DIFFERENCE IN THE SIZE OF REVENUES GENERATED FROM 2,000 PEOPLE AND 20,000 PEOPLE.
AND WHAT IF THEY TURN UP TO SEE ME AND MY GEE-TAR AND INSTEAD THEY SEE A ROCK AND ROLL BAND AND TURN AROUND AND ASK FOR THEIR MONEY BACK?
FOXGLOVE, SWEETHEART, YOU KNOW IT WON'T HAPPEN.
DELI
SANDWICHES
SO WHAT ABOUT THE OTHER THING?
WHAT OTHER THING?
THE COMING OUT THING, LARRY. YOU SAID, WHEN THE SECOND ALBUM CAME OUT, I COULD TOO.
WELL?
Y'KNOW, IT'S NOT A SIMPLE THING, FOX.
IT'S A VERY SIMPLE THING. I'M A DYKE. I LIKE GIRLS. I'VE ALWAYS LIKED GIRLS. SINCE I WAS A LITTLE GIRL I LIKED GIRLS. WHEN I PLAY WITH MYSELF I THINK OF GIRLS.
I LIVE WITH A GIRL, ALTHOUGH HAZEL SAYS SHE'S A WOMAN, NOT A GIRL, AND I REALLY SHOULDN'T USE A WORD LIKE GIRL THAT DEMEANS WOMEN, BUT I SAY THAT A BORING WORD LIKE WOMAN TAKES ALL THE FUN OUT OF BEING A GIRL...
NOT A SIMPLE THING. FIRST OFF, A LOT OF YOUR AUDIENCE ARE YOUNG MEN WHO THINK YOU'RE CUTE. YOU'RE WHAT WE USED TO CALL A SEX SYMBOL, BACK IN THE SIXTIES. YOU COME OUT, THEY GO AWAY.
SECOND, YOU STILL WANT TO ACT?
WELL, SURE.
WELL, WHY DO YOU THINK [redacted]'S STILL IN THE CLOSET? OR [redacted]? BECAUSE HOLLYWOOD DOESN'T HIRE OUT-LESBIANS. MIDDLE AMERICA DOESN'T LIKE IT, AND THEY PUT THE BUMS ON THE SEATS IN THE MULTIPLEXES.
AND THIRD, LOOK AT MELISSA ETHERIDGE.
YEAH? SHE WAS NO ONE, SHE CAME OUT, SHE WENT HUGE.
BUT YOU'VE HEARD THE GRUMBLING. SHE ONLY CAME OUT BECAUSE K.D. LANG CAME OUT, ALL THAT. YOU COME OUT, YOU'LL BE CONSIDERED A MELISSA ETHERIDGE CLONE. EVEN THE GAY AND LESBIAN COMMUNITY WILL HATE YOU.
RIGHT NOW YOU'RE AN ORIGINAL, BUBULLEH. DON'T BLOW IT.

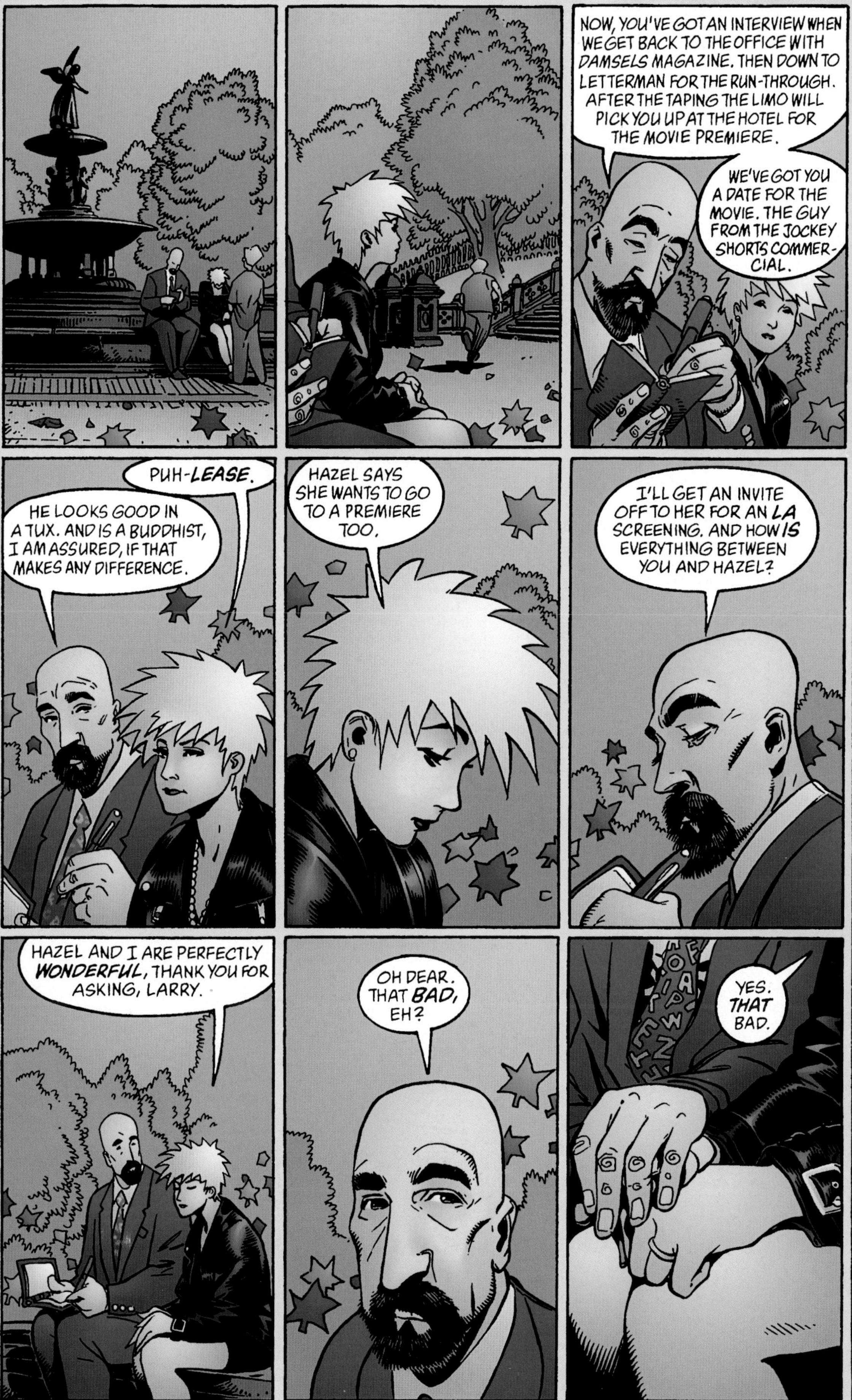
NOW, YOU'VE GOT AN INTERVIEW WHEN WE GET BACK TO THE OFFICE WITH DAMSELS MAGAZINE. THEN DOWN TO LETTERMAN FOR THE RUN-THROUGH. AFTER THE TAPING THE LIMO WILL PICK YOU UP AT THE HOTEL FOR THE MOVIE PREMIERE.
WE'VE GOT YOU A DATE FOR THE MOVIE. THE GUY FROM THE JOCKEY SHORTS COMMERCIAL.
PUH-LEASE.
HE LOOKS GOOD IN A TUX. AND IS A BUDDHIST, I AM ASSURED, IF THAT MAKES ANY DIFFERENCE.
HAZEL SAYS SHE WANTS TO GO TO A PREMIERE TOO.
I'LL GET AN INVITE OFF TO HER FOR AN LA SCREENING. AND HOW IS EVERYTHING BETWEEN YOU AND HAZEL?
HAZEL AND I ARE PERFECTLY WONDERFUL, THANK YOU FOR ASKING, LARRY.
OH DEAR. THAT BAD, EH?
YES. THAT BAD.

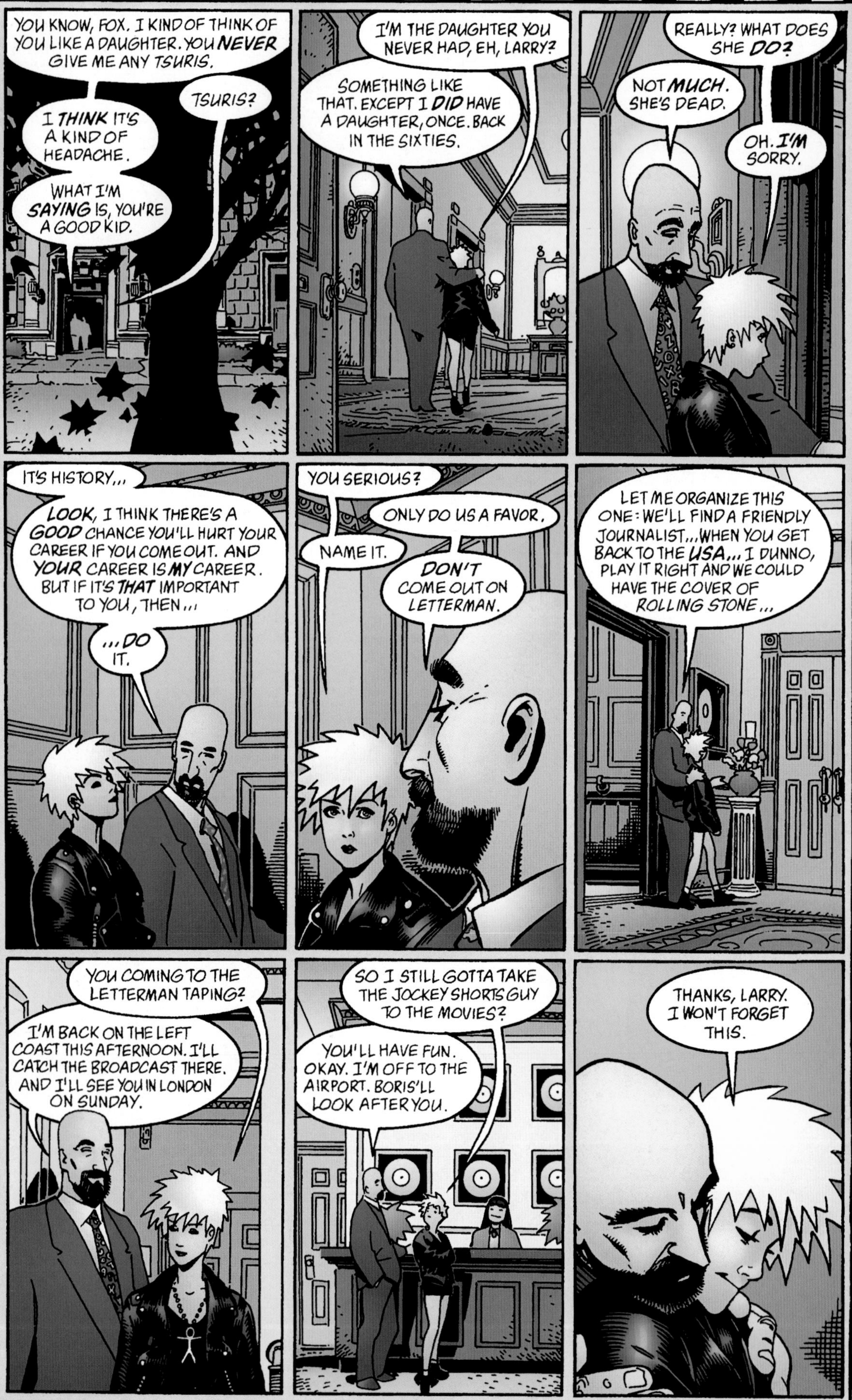
YOU KNOW, FOX. I KIND OF THINK OF YOU LIKE A DAUGHTER. YOU NEVER GIVE ME ANY TSURIS.
TSURIS?
I THINK IT'S A KIND OF HEADACHE.
WHAT I'M SAYING IS, YOU'RE A GOOD KID.
I'M THE DAUGHTER YOU NEVER HAD, EH, LARRY?
SOMETHING LIKE THAT. EXCEPT I DID HAVE A DAUGHTER, ONCE. BACK IN THE SIXTIES.
REALLY? WHAT DOES SHE DO?
NOT MUCH. SHE'S DEAD.
OH. I'M SORRY.
IT'S HISTORY...
LOOK, I THINK THERE'S A GOOD CHANCE YOU'LL HURT YOUR CAREER IF YOU COME OUT. AND YOUR CAREER IS MY CAREER. BUT IF IT'S THAT IMPORTANT TO YOU, THEN...
...DO IT.
YOU SERIOUS?
NAME IT.
ONLY DO US A FAVOR.
DON'T COME OUT ON LETTERMAN.
LET ME ORGANIZE THIS ONE: WE'LL FIND A FRIENDLY JOURNALIST...WHEN YOU GET BACK TO THE USA... I DUNNO, PLAY IT RIGHT AND WE COULD HAVE THE COVER OF ROLLING STONE...
YOU COMING TO THE LETTERMAN TAPING?
I'M BACK ON THE LEFT COAST THIS AFTERNOON. I'LL CATCH THE BROADCAST THERE. AND I'LL SEE YOU IN LONDON ON SUNDAY.
SO I STILL GOTTA TAKE THE JOCKEY SHORTS GUY TO THE MOVIES?
YOU'LL HAVE FUN. OKAY. I'M OFF TO THE AIRPORT. BORIS'LL LOOK AFTER YOU.
THANKS, LARRY. I WON'T FORGET THIS.

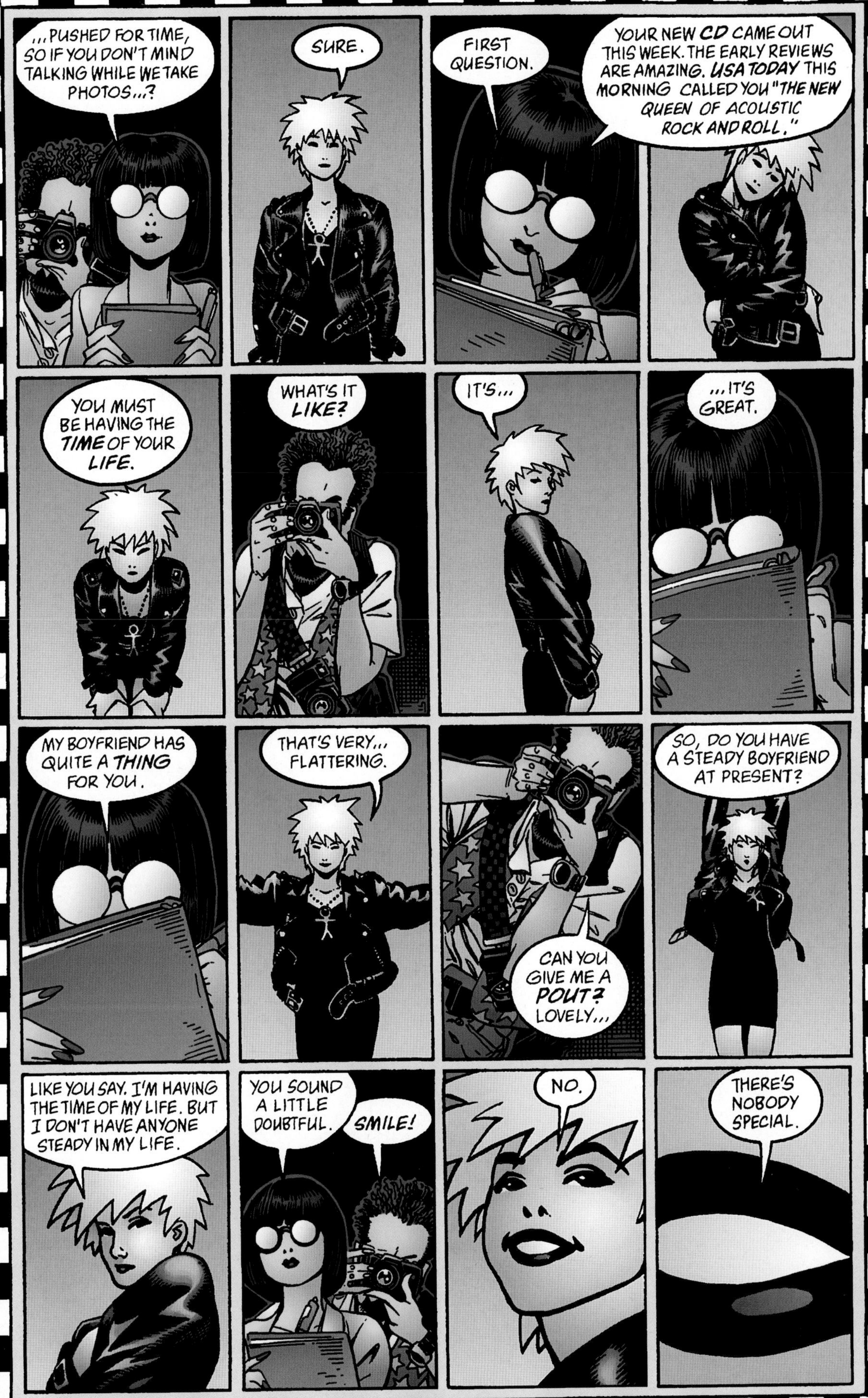
...PUSHED FOR TIME, SO IF YOU DON'T MIND TALKING WHILE WE TAKE PHOTOS...?
SURE.
FIRST QUESTION.
YOUR NEW CD CAME OUT THIS WEEK. THE EARLY REVIEWS ARE AMAZING. USA TODAY THIS MORNING CALLED YOU "THE NEW QUEEN OF ACOUSTIC ROCK AND ROLL."
YOU MUST BE HAVING THE TIME OF YOUR LIFE.
WHAT'S IT LIKE?
IT'S...
...IT'S GREAT.
MY BOYFRIEND HAS QUITE A THING FOR YOU.
THAT'S VERY... FLATTERING.
CAN YOU GIVE ME A POUT? LOVELY...
SO, DO YOU HAVE A STEADY BOYFRIEND AT PRESENT?
LIKE YOU SAY. I'M HAVING THE TIME OF MY LIFE. BUT I DON'T HAVE ANYONE STEADY IN MY LIFE.
YOU SOUND A LITTLE DOUBTFUL.
SMILE!
NO.
THERE'S NOBODY SPECIAL.

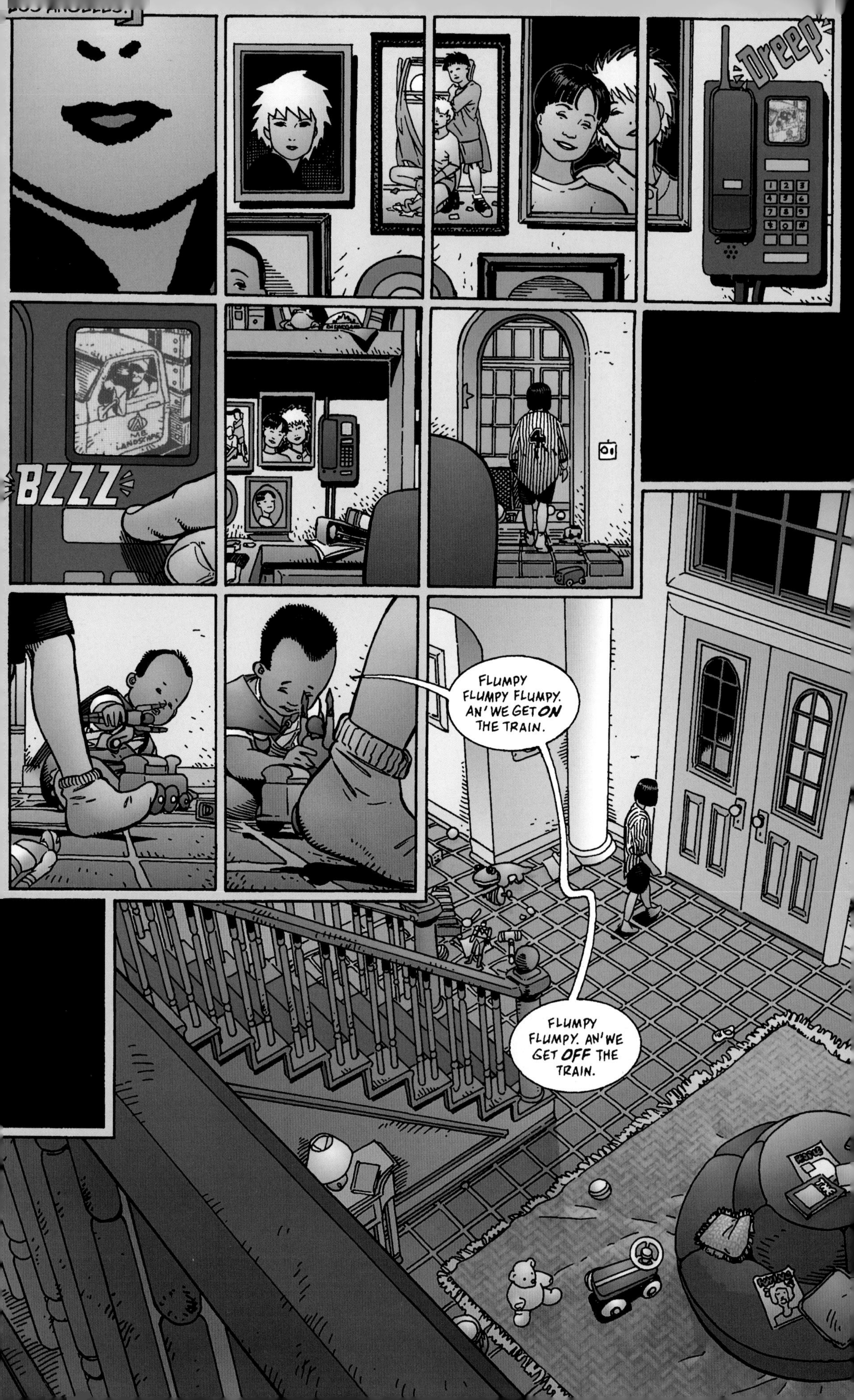
DREEP
BZZZ
FLUMPY FLUMPY FLUMPY. AN' WE GET ON THE TRAIN.
FLUMPY FLUMPY. AN' WE GET OFF THE TRAIN.

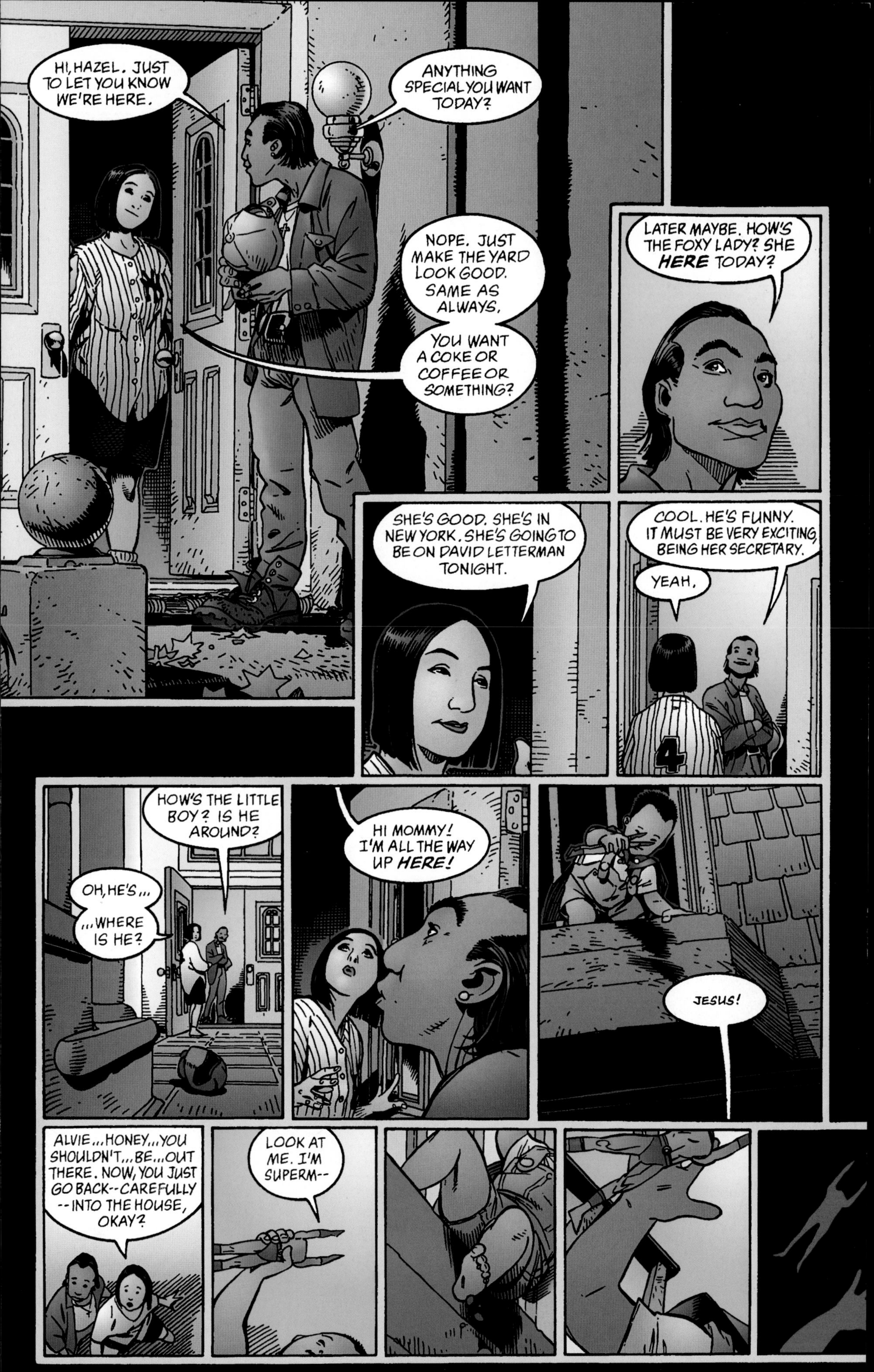
HI, HAZEL. JUST TO LET YOU KNOW WE'RE HERE.
ANYTHING SPECIAL YOU WANT TODAY?
NOPE. JUST MAKE THE YARD LOOK GOOD. SAME AS ALWAYS.
YOU WANT A COKE OR COFFEE OR SOMETHING?
LATER MAYBE. HOW'S THE FOXY LADY? SHE **HERE** TODAY?
SHE'S GOOD. SHE'S IN NEW YORK. SHE'S GOING TO BE ON DAVID LETTERMAN TONIGHT.
COOL. HE'S FUNNY. IT MUST BE VERY EXCITING, BEING HER SECRETARY.
YEAH.
HOW'S THE LITTLE BOY? IS HE AROUND?
OH, HE'S...
...WHERE IS HE?
HI MOMMY! I'M ALL THE WAY UP **HERE!**
JESUS!
ALVIE... HONEY... YOU SHOULDN'T... BE... OUT THERE. NOW, YOU JUST GO BACK--CAREFULLY --INTO THE HOUSE, OKAY?
LOOK AT ME. I'M SUPERM--

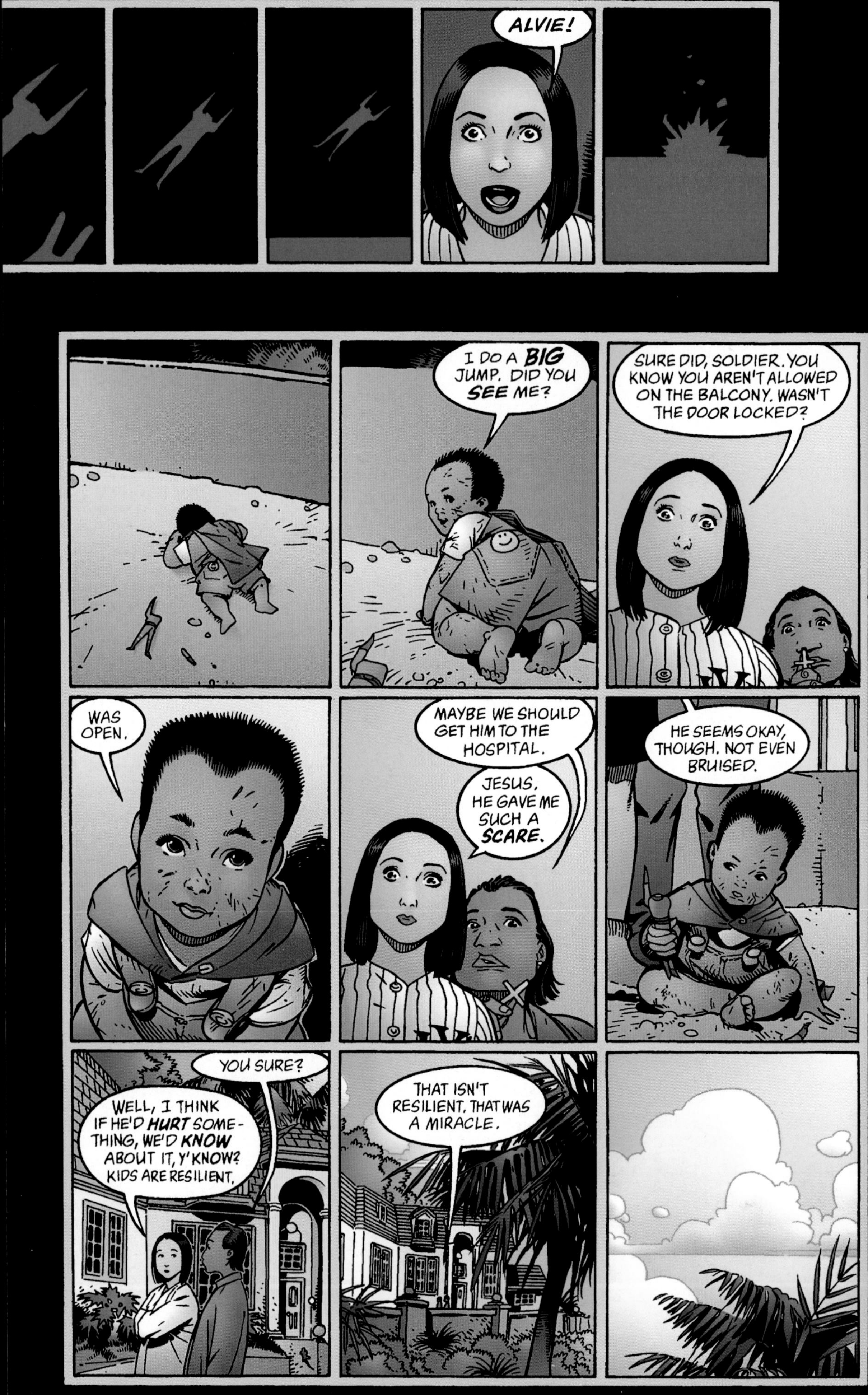
ALVIE!
I DO A BIG JUMP. DID YOU SEE ME?
SURE DID, SOLDIER. YOU KNOW YOU AREN'T ALLOWED ON THE BALCONY. WASN'T THE DOOR LOCKED?
WAS OPEN.
MAYBE WE SHOULD GET HIM TO THE HOSPITAL.
JESUS, HE GAVE ME SUCH A SCARE.
HE SEEMS OKAY, THOUGH. NOT EVEN BRUISED.
YOU SURE?
WELL, I THINK IF HE'D HURT SOME-THING, WE'D KNOW ABOUT IT, Y'KNOW? KIDS ARE RESILIENT.
THAT ISN'T RESILIENT. THAT WAS A MIRACLE.

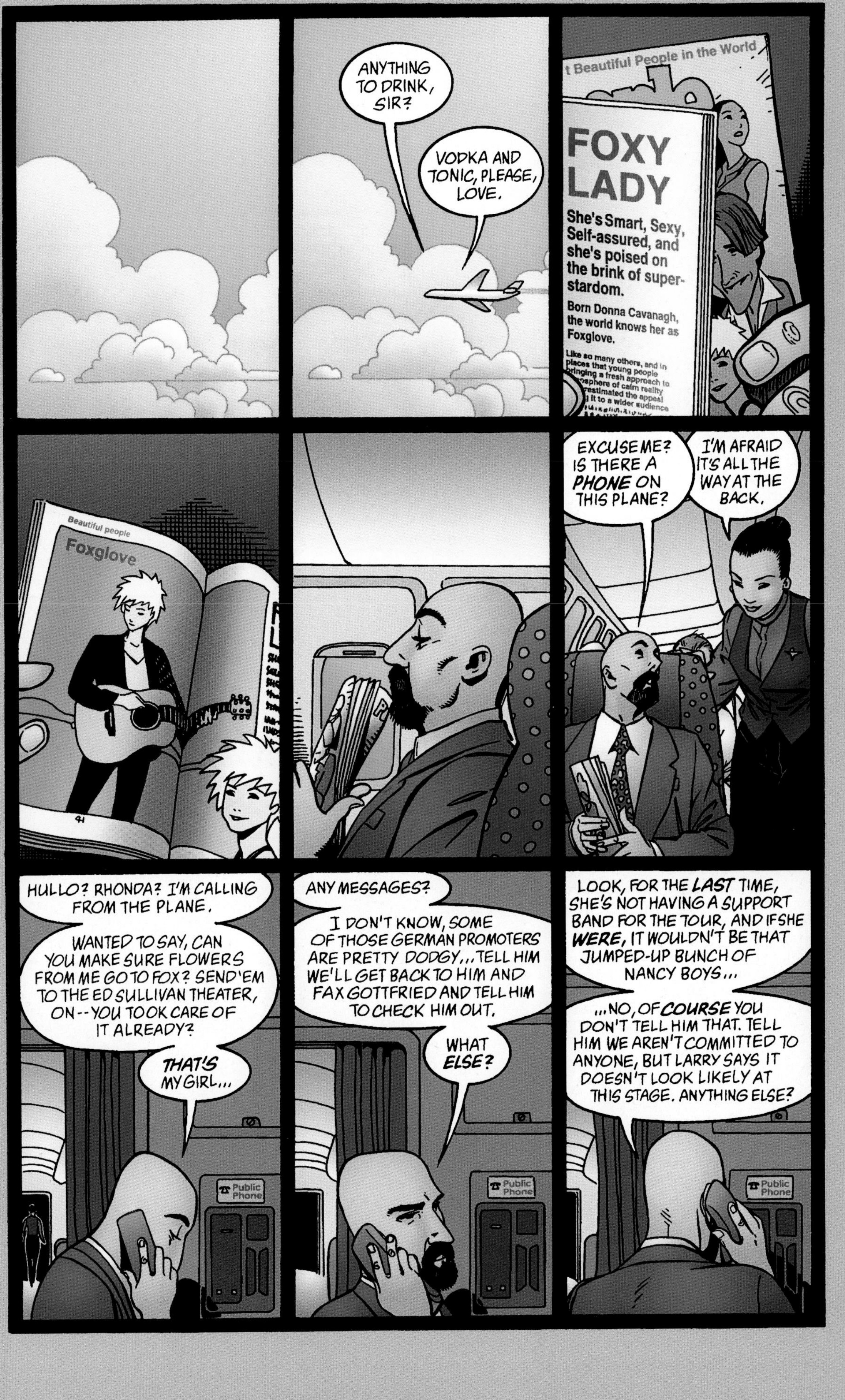
ANYTHING TO DRINK, SIR?
VODKA AND TONIC, PLEASE, LOVE.
t Beautiful People in the World
FOXY LADY
She's Smart, Sexy, Self-assured, and she's poised on the brink of super-stardom.
Born Donna Cavanagh, the world knows her as Foxglove.
Beautiful people
Foxglove
41
EXCUSE ME? IS THERE A PHONE ON THIS PLANE?
I'M AFRAID IT'S ALL THE WAY AT THE BACK.
HULLO? RHONDA? I'M CALLING FROM THE PLANE.
WANTED TO SAY, CAN YOU MAKE SURE FLOWERS FROM ME GO TO FOX? SEND'EM TO THE ED SULLIVAN THEATER, ON-- YOU TOOK CARE OF IT ALREADY?
THAT'S MY GIRL...
Public Phone
ANY MESSAGES?
I DON'T KNOW, SOME OF THOSE GERMAN PROMOTERS ARE PRETTY DODGY... TELL HIM WE'LL GET BACK TO HIM AND FAX GOTTFRIED AND TELL HIM TO CHECK HIM OUT.
WHAT ELSE?
Public Phone
LOOK, FOR THE LAST TIME, SHE'S NOT HAVING A SUPPORT BAND FOR THE TOUR, AND IF SHE WERE, IT WOULDN'T BE THAT JUMPED-UP BUNCH OF NANCY BOYS...
...NO, OF COURSE YOU DON'T TELL HIM THAT. TELL HIM WE AREN'T COMMITTED TO ANYONE, BUT LARRY SAYS IT DOESN'T LOOK LIKELY AT THIS STAGE. ANYTHING ELSE?
Public Phone

NO, I'M....

ow.

AND HE TRIED TO SAY: CHRIST, RHONDA! IT FELT LIKE SOME-THING JUST HIT ME IN THE FUCKING CHEST. AND HE THOUGHT MAYBE HE HAD, BUT HE COULD HEAR RHONDA SAYING, "I DIDN'T GET THAT, MISTER MORTH. COULD YOU SAY THAT AGAIN?"

AND THEN HE LET GO OF THE TELEPHONE AND SAT ON THE FLOOR, BECAUSE THAT WAS SUDDENLY THE ONLY SENSIBLE THING TO DO.

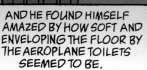

AND HE FOUND HIMSELF AMAZED BY HOW SOFT AND ENVELOPING THE FLOOR BY THE AEROPLANE TOILETS SEEMED TO BE.

THEY MUST KEEP IT A SECRET, THOUGHT LARRY MORTH, TO STOP PEOPLE COMING BACK HERE AND LYING DOWN ON THIS SOFT FLOOR. AND MY CHEST STILL HURTS.

AND HE COULD HEAR A WOMAN SAYING, "IF THERE IS A MEDICAL DOCTOR ON BOARD THE PLANE, OR ANYONE WITH MEDICAL OR PARAMEDICAL EXPERIENCE, COULD THEY IDENTIFY THEMSELVES TO A MEMBER OF THE CABIN CREW?"

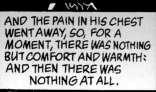

AND THE PAIN IN HIS CHEST WENT AWAY, SO, FOR A MOMENT, THERE WAS NOTHING BUT COMFORT AND WARMTH: AND THEN THERE WAS NOTHING AT ALL.

JUST A VOICE THAT SAID:

"LARRY?"

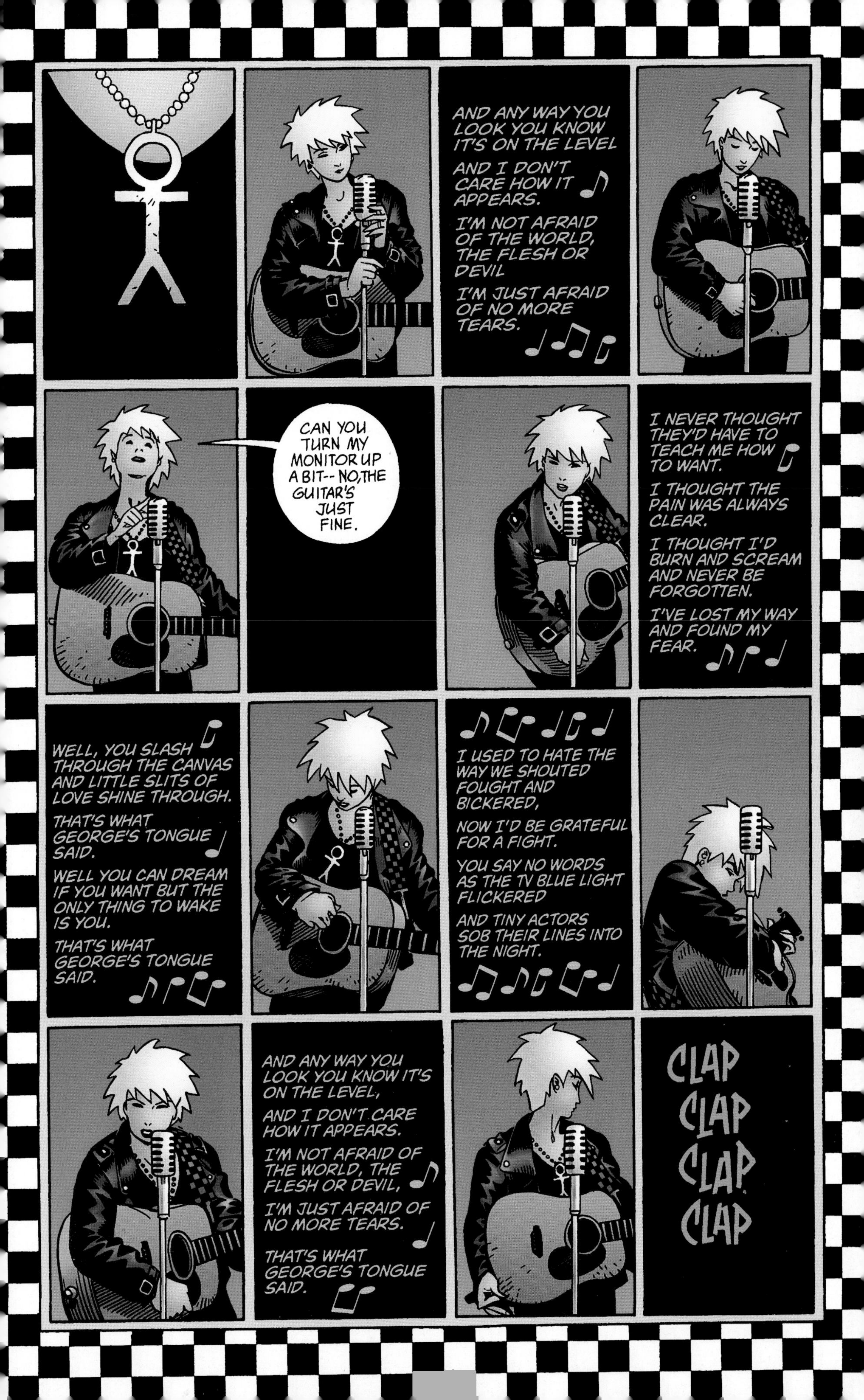
AND ANY WAY YOU LOOK YOU KNOW IT'S ON THE LEVEL
AND I DON'T CARE HOW IT APPEARS.
I'M NOT AFRAID OF THE WORLD, THE FLESH OR DEVIL
I'M JUST AFRAID OF NO MORE TEARS.
CAN YOU TURN MY MONITOR UP A BIT-- NO, THE GUITAR'S JUST FINE.
I NEVER THOUGHT THEY'D HAVE TO TEACH ME HOW TO WANT.
I THOUGHT THE PAIN WAS ALWAYS CLEAR.
I THOUGHT I'D BURN AND SCREAM AND NEVER BE FORGOTTEN.
I'VE LOST MY WAY AND FOUND MY FEAR.
WELL, YOU SLASH THROUGH THE CANVAS AND LITTLE SLITS OF LOVE SHINE THROUGH.
THAT'S WHAT GEORGE'S TONGUE SAID.
WELL YOU CAN DREAM IF YOU WANT BUT THE ONLY THING TO WAKE IS YOU.
THAT'S WHAT GEORGE'S TONGUE SAID.
I USED TO HATE THE WAY WE SHOUTED FOUGHT AND BICKERED,
NOW I'D BE GRATEFUL FOR A FIGHT.
YOU SAY NO WORDS AS THE TV BLUE LIGHT FLICKERED
AND TINY ACTORS SOB THEIR LINES INTO THE NIGHT.
AND ANY WAY YOU LOOK YOU KNOW IT'S ON THE LEVEL,
AND I DON'T CARE HOW IT APPEARS.
I'M NOT AFRAID OF THE WORLD, THE FLESH OR DEVIL,
I'M JUST AFRAID OF NO MORE TEARS.
THAT'S WHAT GEORGE'S TONGUE SAID.
CLAP
CLAP
CLAP
CLAP

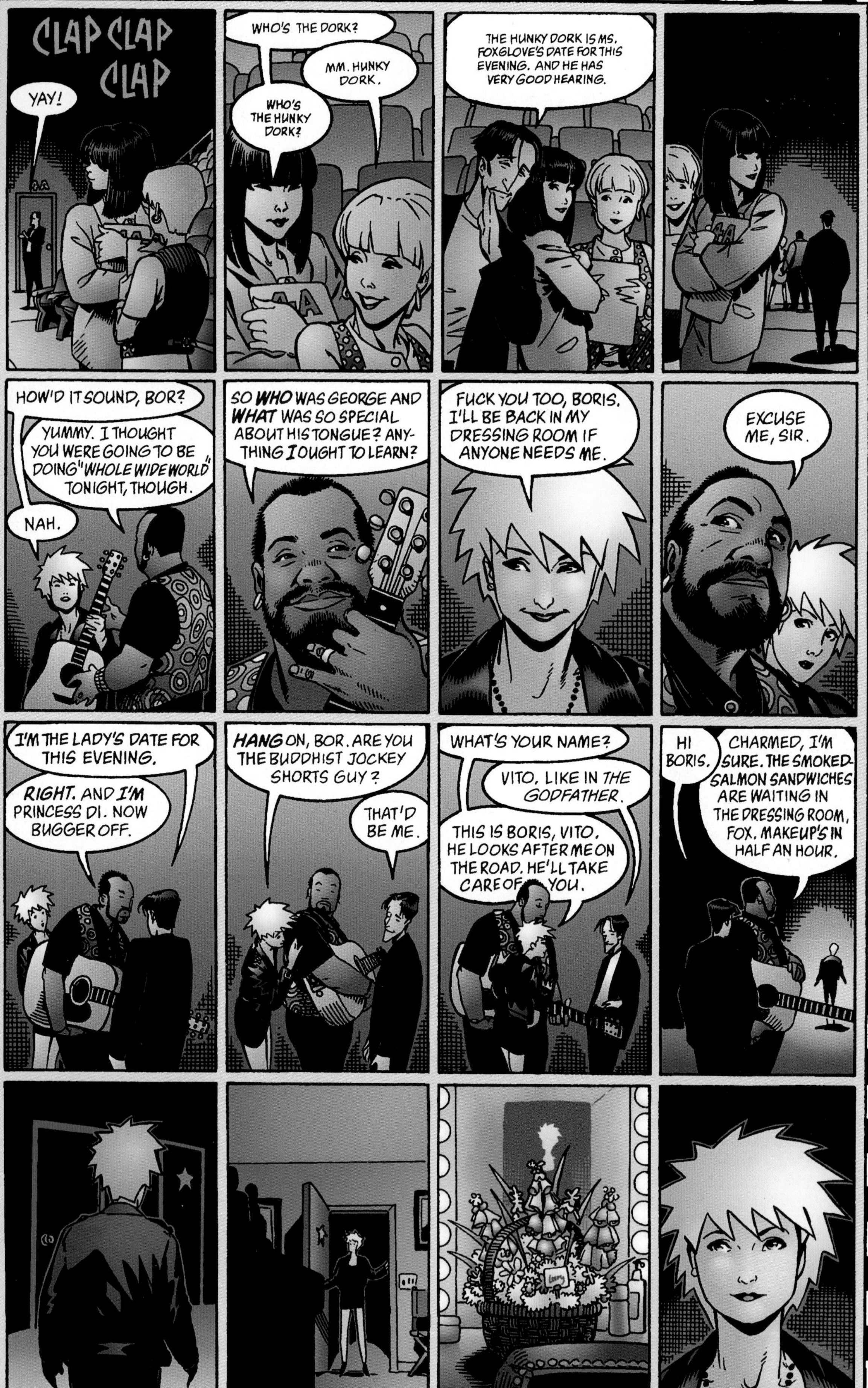
CLAP CLAP CLAP
YAY!
WHO'S THE DORK?
MM. HUNKY DORK.
WHO'S THE HUNKY DORK?
THE HUNKY DORK IS MS. FOXGLOVE'S DATE FOR THIS EVENING. AND HE HAS VERY GOOD HEARING.
HOW'D IT SOUND, BOR?
YUMMY. I THOUGHT YOU WERE GOING TO BE DOING "WHOLE WIDE WORLD" TONIGHT, THOUGH.
NAH.
SO WHO WAS GEORGE AND WHAT WAS SO SPECIAL ABOUT HIS TONGUE? ANY-THING I OUGHT TO LEARN?
FUCK YOU TOO, BORIS. I'LL BE BACK IN MY DRESSING ROOM IF ANYONE NEEDS ME.
EXCUSE ME, SIR.
I'M THE LADY'S DATE FOR THIS EVENING.
RIGHT. AND I'M PRINCESS DI. NOW BUGGER OFF.
HANG ON, BOR. ARE YOU THE BUDDHIST JOCKEY SHORTS GUY?
THAT'D BE ME.
WHAT'S YOUR NAME?
VITO. LIKE IN THE GODFATHER.
THIS IS BORIS, VITO. HE LOOKS AFTER ME ON THE ROAD. HE'LL TAKE CARE OF YOU.
HI BORIS.
CHARMED, I'M SURE. THE SMOKED-SALMON SANDWICHES ARE WAITING IN THE DRESSING ROOM, FOX. MAKEUP'S IN HALF AN HOUR.

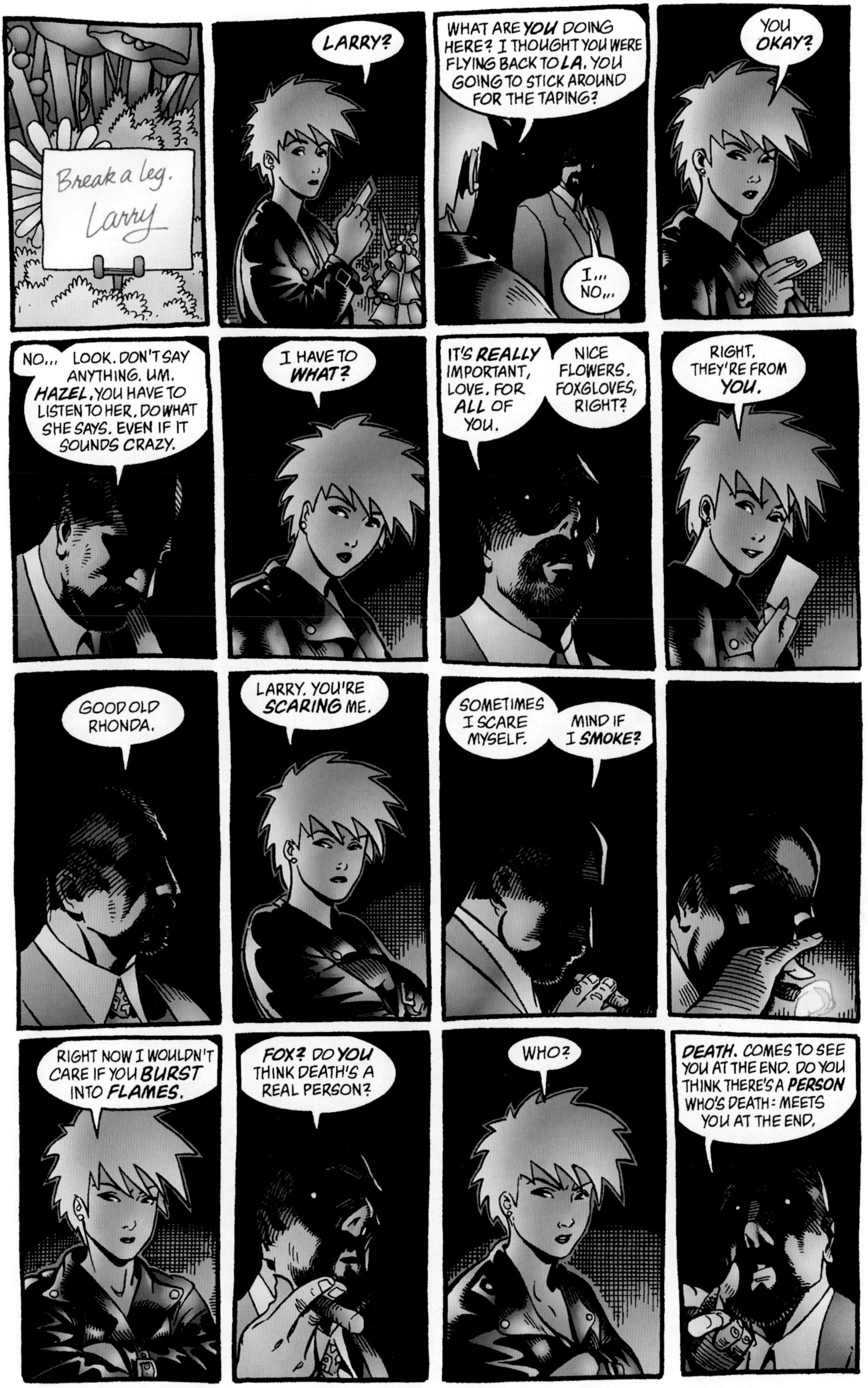
Break a leg.
Larry
LARRY?
WHAT ARE YOU DOING HERE? I THOUGHT YOU WERE FLYING BACK TO LA. YOU GOING TO STICK AROUND FOR THE TAPING?
I... NO...
YOU OKAY?
NO... LOOK. DON'T SAY ANYTHING. UM. HAZEL. YOU HAVE TO LISTEN TO HER. DO WHAT SHE SAYS. EVEN IF IT SOUNDS CRAZY.
I HAVE TO WHAT?
IT'S REALLY IMPORTANT, LOVE. FOR ALL OF YOU.
NICE FLOWERS. FOXGLOVES, RIGHT?
RIGHT. THEY'RE FROM YOU.
GOOD OLD RHONDA.
LARRY. YOU'RE SCARING ME.
SOMETIMES I SCARE MYSELF.
MIND IF I SMOKE?
RIGHT NOW I WOULDN'T CARE IF YOU BURST INTO FLAMES.
FOX? DO YOU THINK DEATH'S A REAL PERSON?
WHO?
DEATH. COMES TO SEE YOU AT THE END. DO YOU THINK THERE'S A PERSON WHO'S DEATH: MEETS YOU AT THE END.

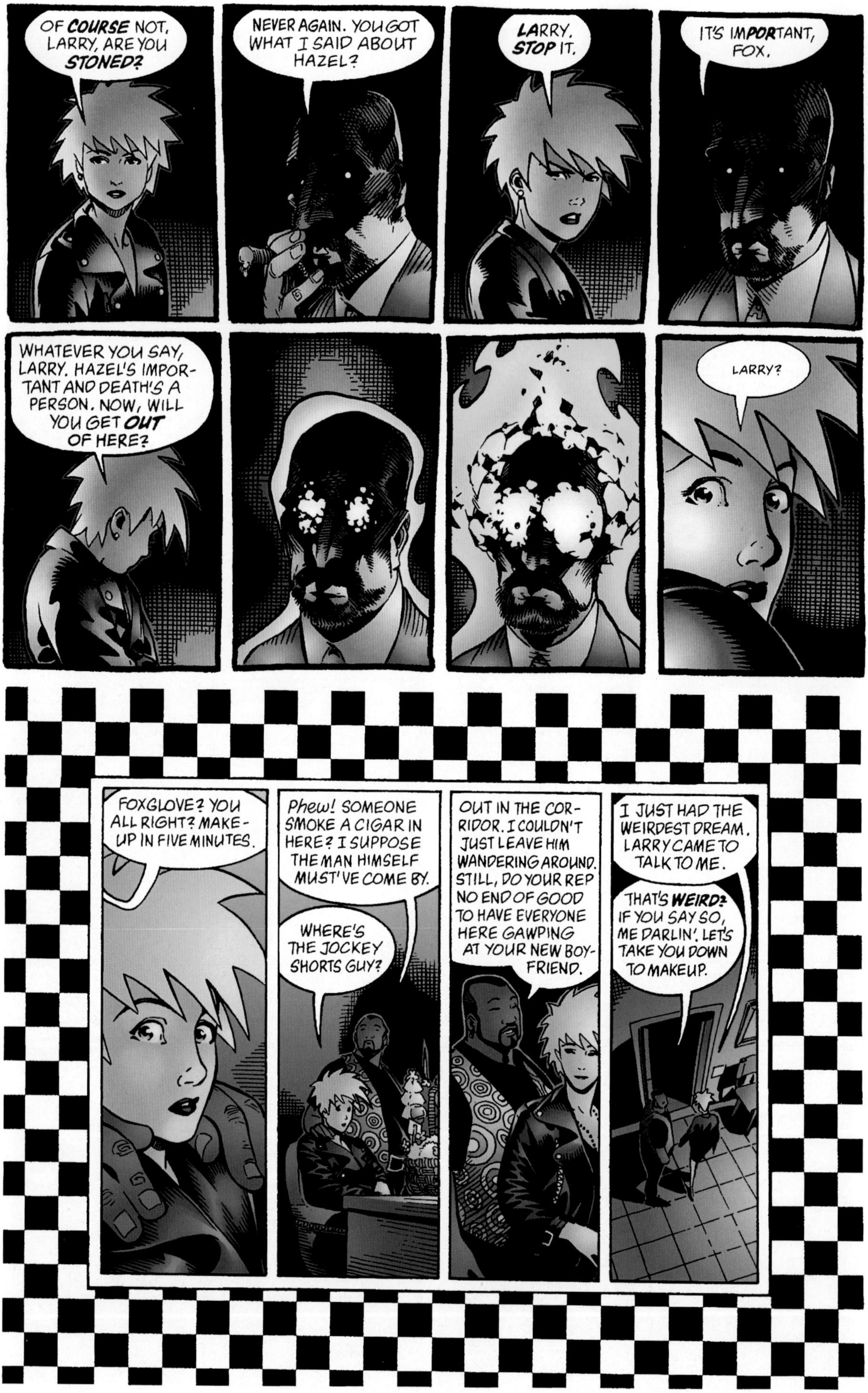
OF COURSE NOT, LARRY, ARE YOU STONED?
NEVER AGAIN. YOU GOT WHAT I SAID ABOUT HAZEL?
LARRY, STOP IT.
IT'S IMPORTANT, FOX.
WHATEVER YOU SAY, LARRY. HAZEL'S IMPORTANT AND DEATH'S A PERSON. NOW, WILL YOU GET OUT OF HERE?
LARRY?
FOXGLOVE? YOU ALL RIGHT? MAKE-UP IN FIVE MINUTES.
Phew! SOMEONE SMOKE A CIGAR IN HERE? I SUPPOSE THE MAN HIMSELF MUST'VE COME BY.
WHERE'S THE JOCKEY SHORTS GUY?
OUT IN THE CORRIDOR. I COULDN'T JUST LEAVE HIM WANDERING AROUND. STILL, DO YOUR REP NO END OF GOOD TO HAVE EVERYONE HERE GAWPING AT YOUR NEW BOYFRIEND.
I JUST HAD THE WEIRDEST DREAM. LARRY CAME TO TALK TO ME.
THAT'S WEIRD? IF YOU SAY SO, ME DARLIN'. LET'S TAKE YOU DOWN TO MAKEUP.

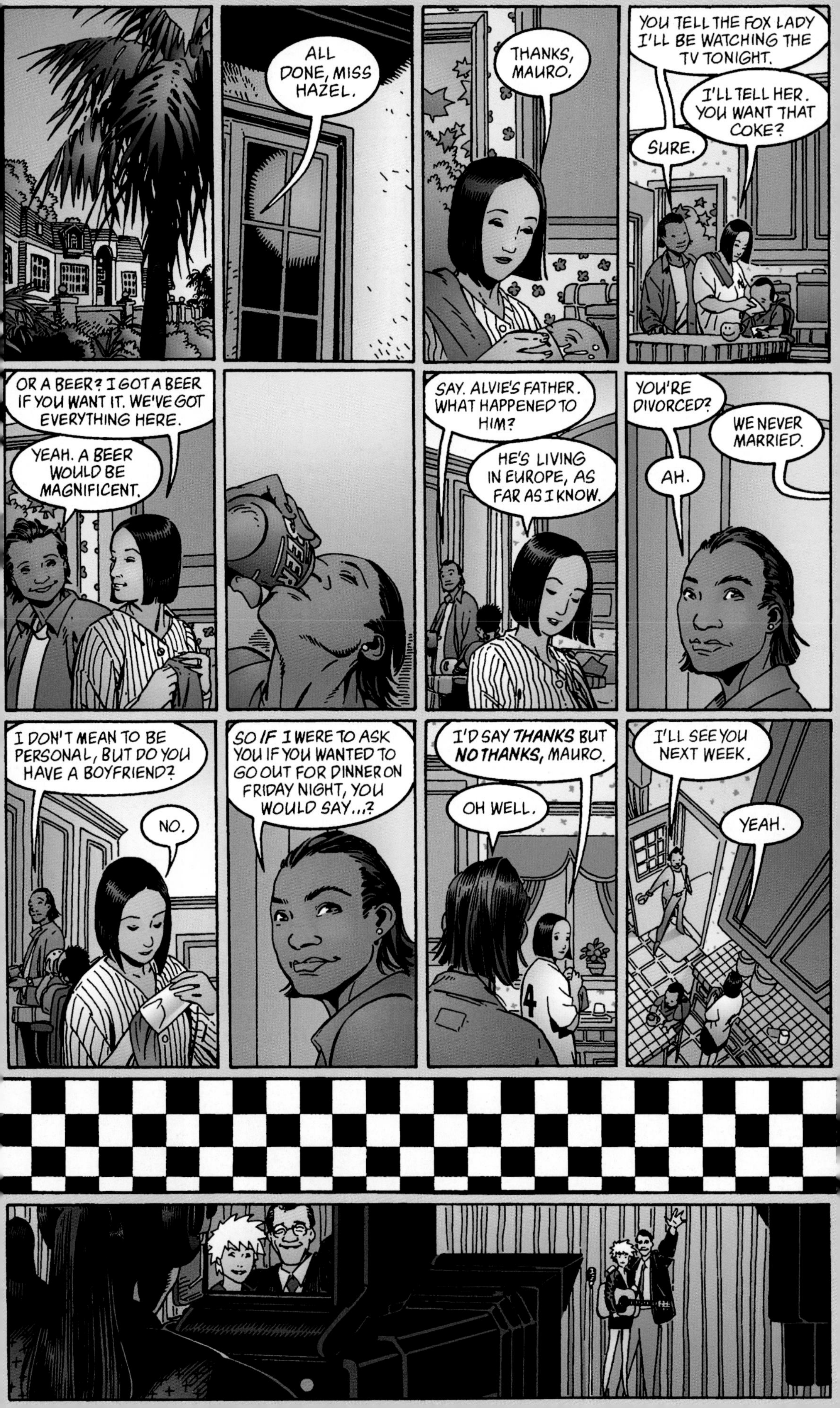

ALL DONE, MISS HAZEL.
THANKS, MAURO.
YOU TELL THE FOX LADY I'LL BE WATCHING THE TV TONIGHT.
I'LL TELL HER. YOU WANT THAT COKE?
SURE.
OR A BEER? I GOT A BEER IF YOU WANT IT. WE'VE GOT EVERYTHING HERE.
YEAH. A BEER WOULD BE MAGNIFICENT.
BEER
SAY. ALVIE'S FATHER. WHAT HAPPENED TO HIM?
HE'S LIVING IN EUROPE, AS FAR AS I KNOW.
YOU'RE DIVORCED?
WE NEVER MARRIED.
AH.
I DON'T MEAN TO BE PERSONAL, BUT DO YOU HAVE A BOYFRIEND?
NO.
SO IF I WERE TO ASK YOU IF YOU WANTED TO GO OUT FOR DINNER ON FRIDAY NIGHT, YOU WOULD SAY...?
I'D SAY THANKS BUT NO THANKS, MAURO.
OH WELL.
I'LL SEE YOU NEXT WEEK.
YEAH.

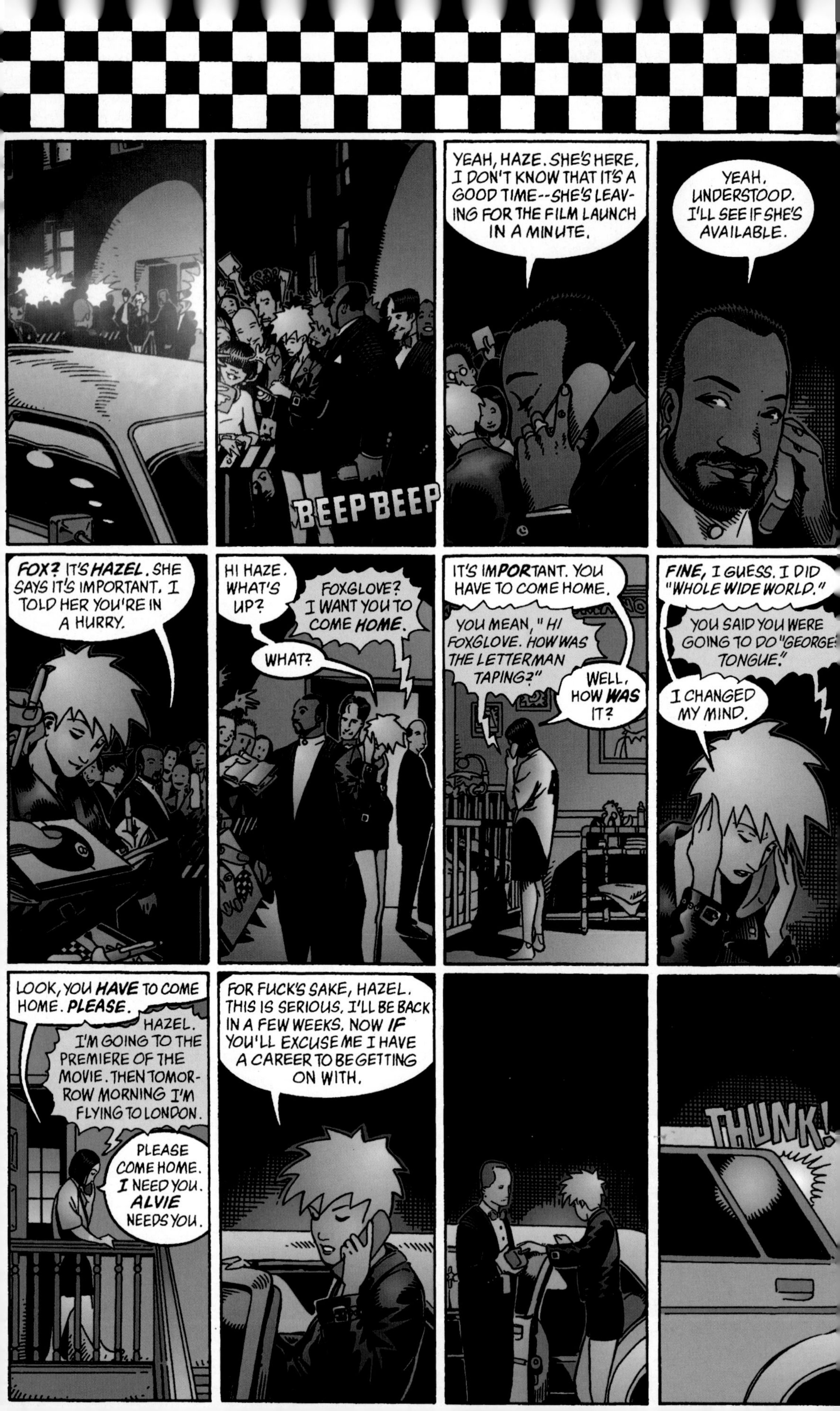
BEEP BEEP
YEAH, HAZE. SHE'S HERE. I DON'T KNOW THAT IT'S A GOOD TIME--SHE'S LEAVING FOR THE FILM LAUNCH IN A MINUTE.
YEAH. UNDERSTOOD. I'LL SEE IF SHE'S AVAILABLE.
FOX? IT'S HAZEL. SHE SAYS IT'S IMPORTANT. I TOLD HER YOU'RE IN A HURRY.
HI HAZE. WHAT'S UP?
FOXGLOVE? I WANT YOU TO COME HOME.
WHAT?
IT'S IMPORTANT. YOU HAVE TO COME HOME.
YOU MEAN, "HI FOXGLOVE. HOW WAS THE LETTERMAN TAPING?"
WELL, HOW WAS IT?
FINE, I GUESS. I DID "WHOLE WIDE WORLD."
YOU SAID YOU WERE GOING TO DO "GEORGE TONGUE."
I CHANGED MY MIND.
LOOK, YOU HAVE TO COME HOME. PLEASE.
HAZEL. I'M GOING TO THE PREMIERE OF THE MOVIE. THEN TOMORROW MORNING I'M FLYING TO LONDON.
PLEASE COME HOME. I NEED YOU. ALVIE NEEDS YOU.
FOR FUCK'S SAKE, HAZEL. THIS IS SERIOUS. I'LL BE BACK IN A FEW WEEKS. NOW IF YOU'LL EXCUSE ME I HAVE A CAREER TO BE GETTING ON WITH.
THUNK!

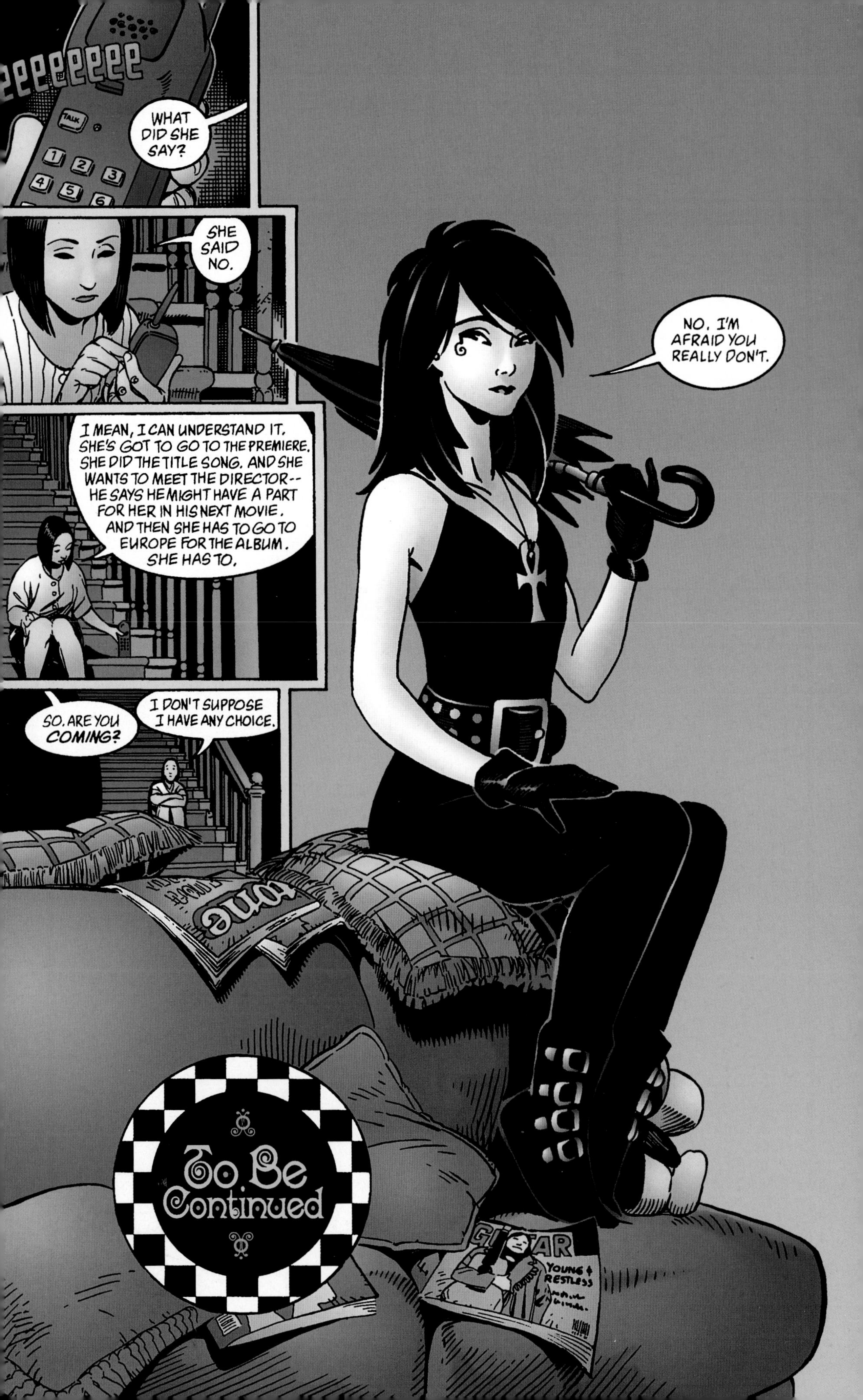
eeeeeeee
WHAT DID SHE SAY?
SHE SAID NO.
NO. I'M AFRAID YOU REALLY DON'T.
I MEAN, I CAN UNDERSTAND IT. SHE'S GOT TO GO TO THE PREMIERE. SHE DID THE TITLE SONG. AND SHE WANTS TO MEET THE DIRECTOR-- HE SAYS HE MIGHT HAVE A PART FOR HER IN HIS NEXT MOVIE. AND THEN SHE HAS TO GO TO EUROPE FOR THE ALBUM. SHE HAS TO.
SO. ARE YOU COMING?
I DON'T SUPPOSE I HAVE ANY CHOICE.
GUITAR
YOUNG & RESTLESS
To Be Continued

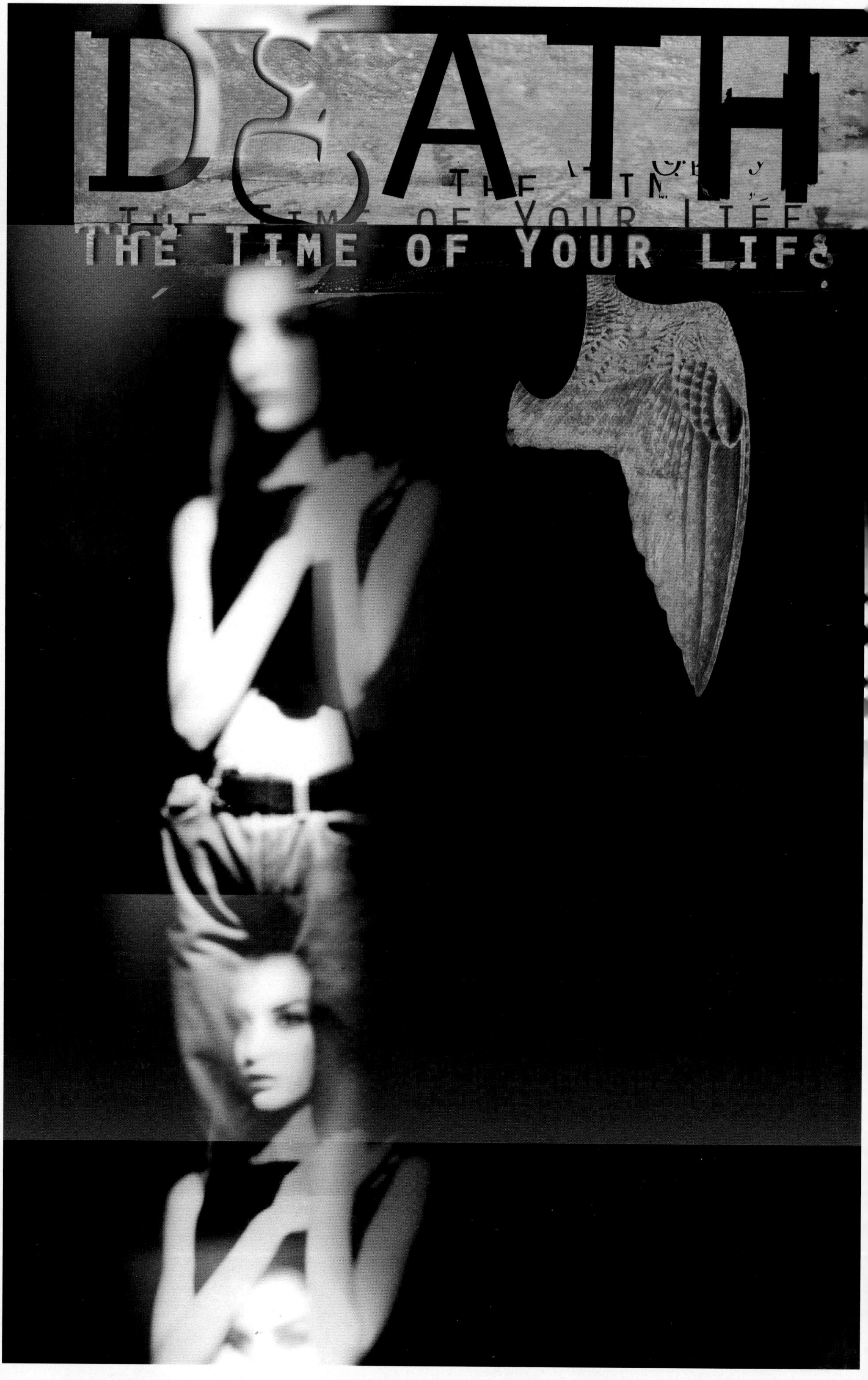
DEATH
THE TIME OF YOUR LIFE

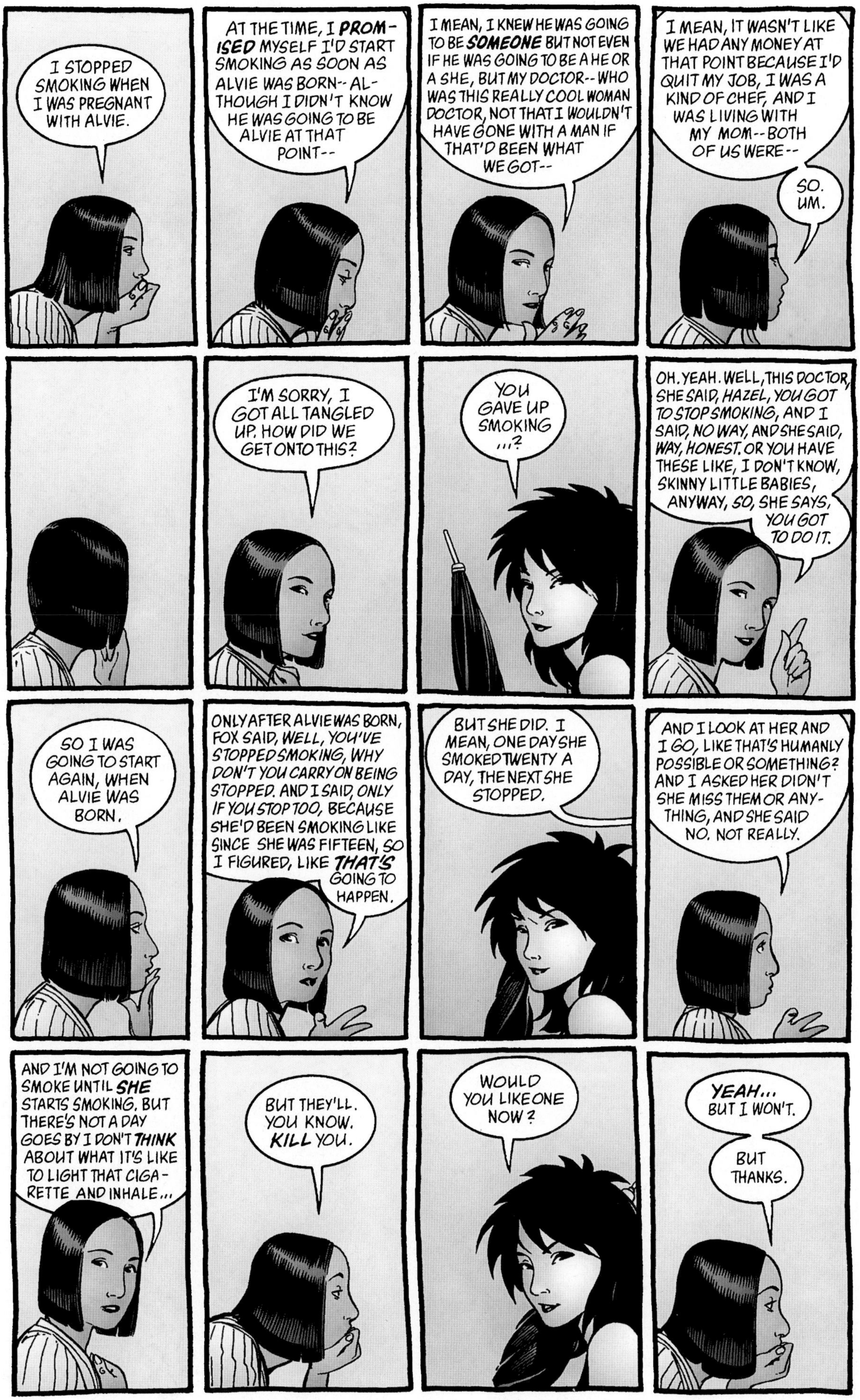
I STOPPED SMOKING WHEN I WAS PREGNANT WITH ALVIE.
AT THE TIME, I **PROMISED** MYSELF I'D START SMOKING AS SOON AS ALVIE WAS BORN-- ALTHOUGH I DIDN'T KNOW HE WAS GOING TO BE ALVIE AT THAT POINT--
I MEAN, I KNEW HE WAS GOING TO BE **SOMEONE** BUT NOT EVEN IF HE WAS GOING TO BE A HE OR A SHE, BUT MY DOCTOR-- WHO WAS THIS REALLY COOL WOMAN DOCTOR, NOT THAT I WOULDN'T HAVE GONE WITH A MAN IF THAT'D BEEN WHAT WE GOT--
I MEAN, IT WASN'T LIKE WE HAD ANY MONEY AT THAT POINT BECAUSE I'D QUIT MY JOB, I WAS A KIND OF CHEF, AND I WAS LIVING WITH MY MOM-- BOTH OF US WERE--
SO. UM.
I'M SORRY, I GOT ALL TANGLED UP. HOW DID WE GET ONTO THIS?
YOU GAVE UP SMOKING ...?
OH. YEAH. WELL, THIS DOCTOR, SHE SAID, HAZEL, YOU GOT TO STOP SMOKING, AND I SAID, NO WAY, AND SHE SAID, WAY, HONEST. OR YOU HAVE THESE LIKE, I DON'T KNOW, SKINNY LITTLE BABIES, ANYWAY, SO, SHE SAYS, YOU GOT TO DO IT.
SO I WAS GOING TO START AGAIN, WHEN ALVIE WAS BORN.
ONLY AFTER ALVIE WAS BORN, FOX SAID, WELL, YOU'VE STOPPED SMOKING, WHY DON'T YOU CARRY ON BEING STOPPED. AND I SAID, ONLY IF YOU STOP TOO, BECAUSE SHE'D BEEN SMOKING LIKE SINCE SHE WAS FIFTEEN, SO I FIGURED, LIKE **THAT'S** GOING TO HAPPEN.
BUT SHE DID. I MEAN, ONE DAY SHE SMOKED TWENTY A DAY, THE NEXT SHE STOPPED.
AND I LOOK AT HER AND I GO, LIKE THAT'S HUMANLY POSSIBLE OR SOMETHING? AND I ASKED HER DIDN'T SHE MISS THEM OR ANYTHING, AND SHE SAID NO. NOT REALLY.
AND I'M NOT GOING TO SMOKE UNTIL **SHE** STARTS SMOKING. BUT THERE'S NOT A DAY GOES BY I DON'T **THINK** ABOUT WHAT IT'S LIKE TO LIGHT THAT CIGARETTE AND INHALE...
BUT THEY'LL. YOU KNOW. **KILL** YOU.
WOULD YOU LIKE ONE NOW?
YEAH... BUT I WON'T.
BUT THANKS.

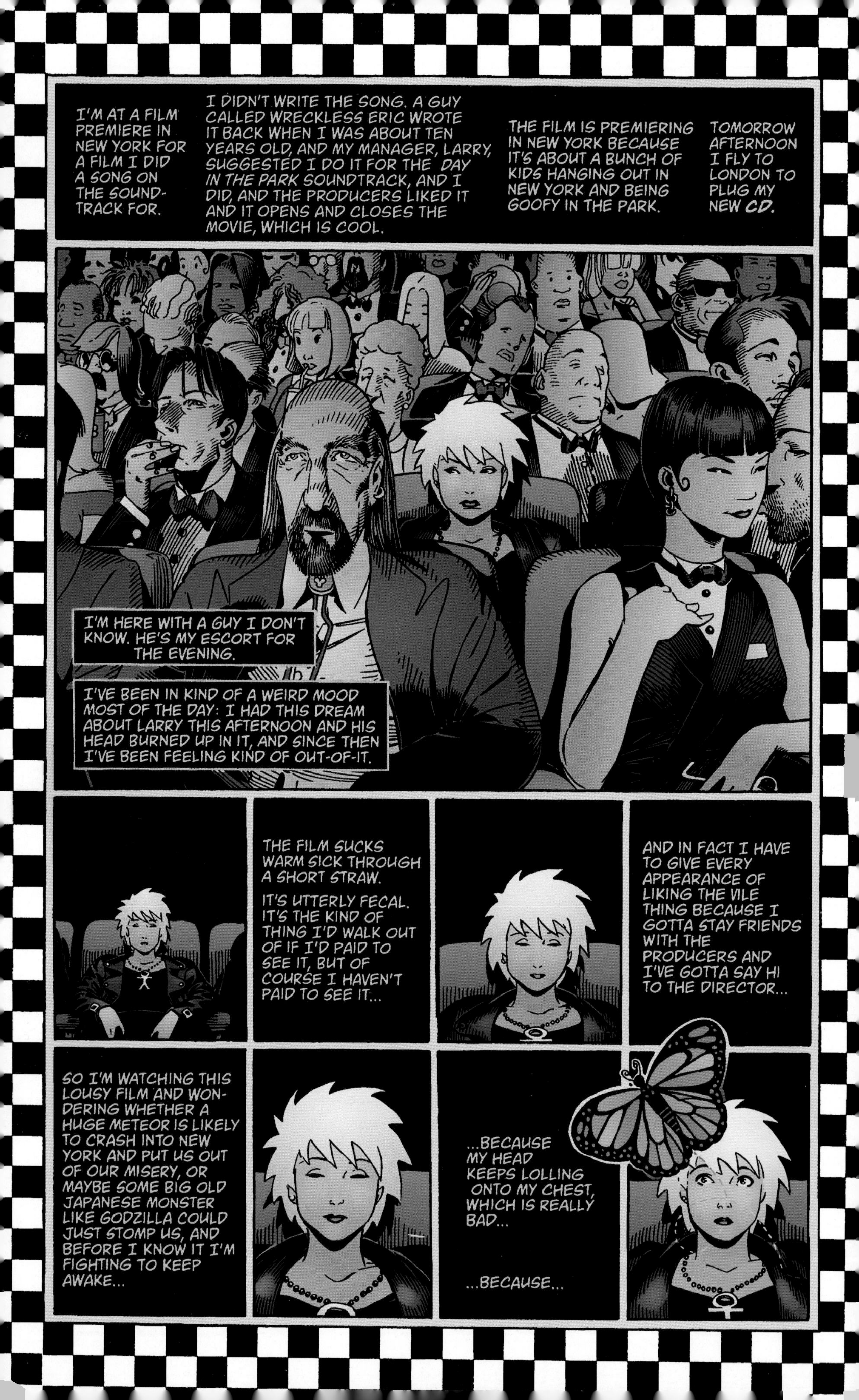

I'M AT A FILM PREMIERE IN NEW YORK FOR A FILM I DID A SONG ON THE SOUND-TRACK FOR.
I DIDN'T WRITE THE SONG. A GUY CALLED WRECKLESS ERIC WROTE IT BACK WHEN I WAS ABOUT TEN YEARS OLD, AND MY MANAGER, LARRY, SUGGESTED I DO IT FOR THE *DAY IN THE PARK* SOUNDTRACK, AND I DID, AND THE PRODUCERS LIKED IT AND IT OPENS AND CLOSES THE MOVIE, WHICH IS COOL.
THE FILM IS PREMIERING IN NEW YORK BECAUSE IT'S ABOUT A BUNCH OF KIDS HANGING OUT IN NEW YORK AND BEING GOOFY IN THE PARK.
TOMORROW AFTERNOON I FLY TO LONDON TO PLUG MY NEW **CD.**
I'M HERE WITH A GUY I DON'T KNOW. HE'S MY ESCORT FOR THE EVENING.
I'VE BEEN IN KIND OF A WEIRD MOOD MOST OF THE DAY: I HAD THIS DREAM ABOUT LARRY THIS AFTERNOON AND HIS HEAD BURNED UP IN IT, AND SINCE THEN I'VE BEEN FEELING KIND OF OUT-OF-IT.
THE FILM SUCKS WARM SICK THROUGH A SHORT STRAW.
IT'S UTTERLY FECAL. IT'S THE KIND OF THING I'D WALK OUT OF IF I'D PAID TO SEE IT, BUT OF COURSE I HAVEN'T PAID TO SEE IT...
AND IN FACT I HAVE TO GIVE EVERY APPEARANCE OF LIKING THE VILE THING BECAUSE I GOTTA STAY FRIENDS WITH THE PRODUCERS AND I'VE GOTTA SAY HI TO THE DIRECTOR...
SO I'M WATCHING THIS LOUSY FILM AND WON-DERING WHETHER A HUGE METEOR IS LIKELY TO CRASH INTO NEW YORK AND PUT US OUT OF OUR MISERY, OR MAYBE SOME BIG OLD JAPANESE MONSTER LIKE GODZILLA COULD JUST STOMP US, AND BEFORE I KNOW IT I'M FIGHTING TO KEEP AWAKE...
...BECAUSE MY HEAD KEEPS LOLLING ONTO MY CHEST, WHICH IS REALLY BAD...
...BECAUSE...

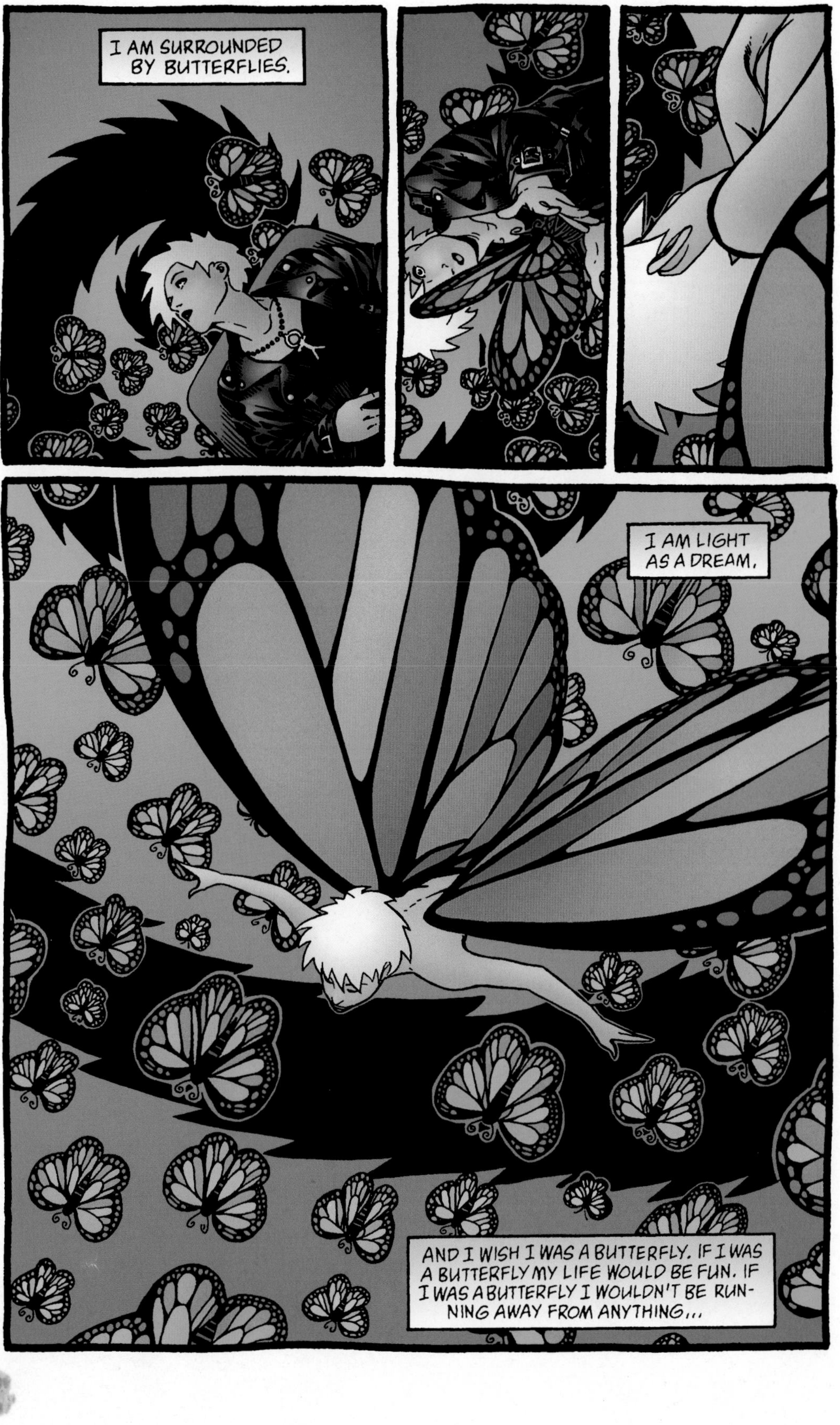
I AM SURROUNDED BY BUTTERFLIES.
I AM LIGHT AS A DREAM.
AND I WISH I WAS A BUTTERFLY. IF I WAS A BUTTERFLY MY LIFE WOULD BE FUN. IF I WAS A BUTTERFLY I WOULDN'T BE RUNNING AWAY FROM ANYTHING...

I WISH I WAS A BUTTERFLY.

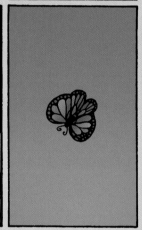

FOX? SOMETHING'S COME UP, LUV. IT'S A BIT URGENT.

WHUH--?

DEATH created by Neil Gaiman & Mike Dringenberg

DEATH: THE TIME of your LIFE
CHAPTER TWO: Imaginary Solutions

NEIL GAIMAN
writer

CHRIS BACHALO
penciller 1-13

MARK BUCKINGHAM
inker 1-13 penciller 14-24

MARK PENNINGTON
inker 14-24

MATT HOLLINGSWORTH
colorist-separations

TODD KLEIN
letters

SHELLY ROEBERG
associate editor

KAREN BERGER
editor

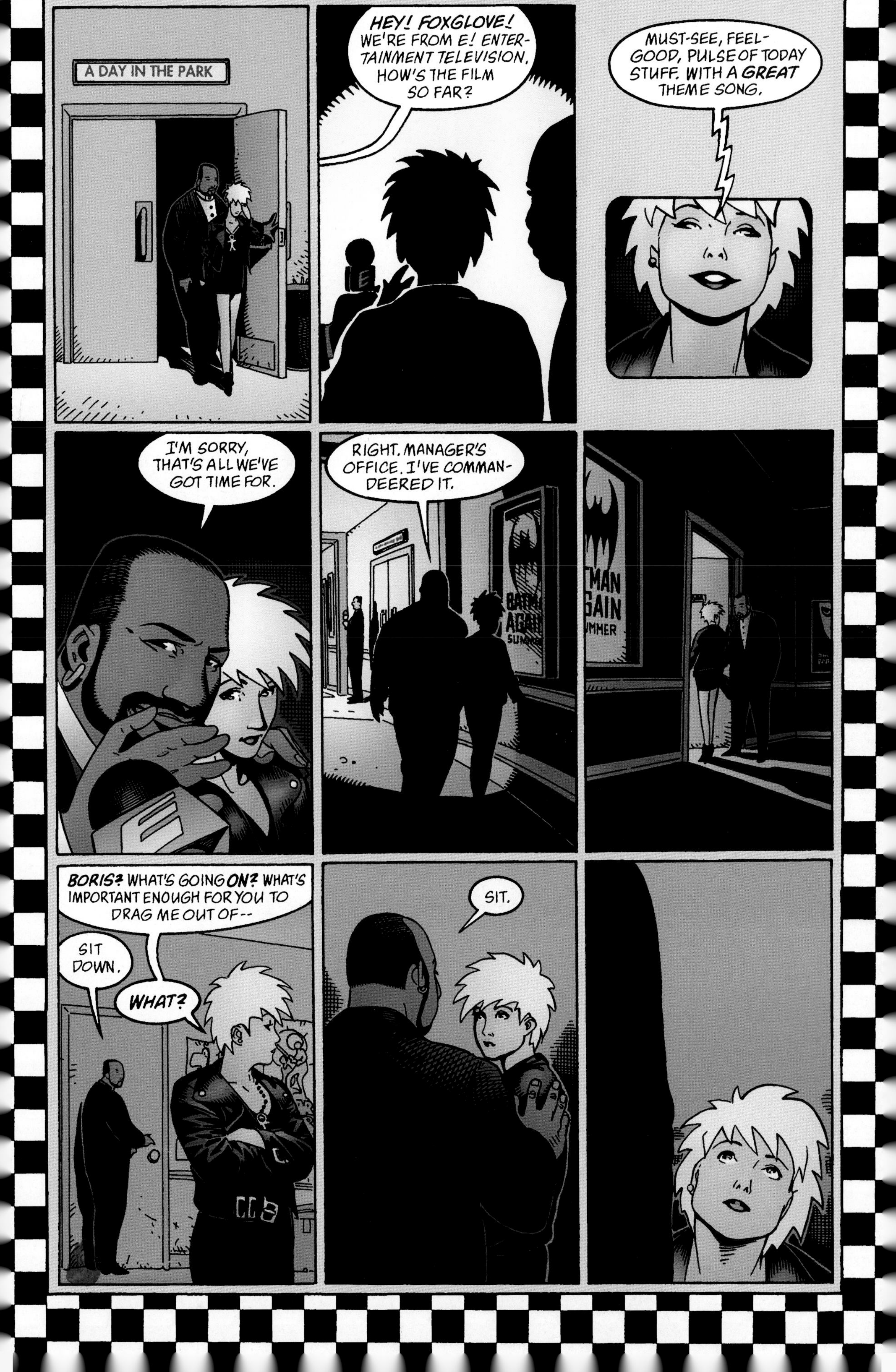
A DAY IN THE PARK
HEY! FOXGLOVE! WE'RE FROM E! ENTERTAINMENT TELEVISION. HOW'S THE FILM SO FAR?
MUST-SEE, FEEL-GOOD, PULSE OF TODAY STUFF. WITH A GREAT THEME SONG.
I'M SORRY, THAT'S ALL WE'VE GOT TIME FOR.
RIGHT. MANAGER'S OFFICE. I'VE COMMANDEERED IT.
BORIS? WHAT'S GOING ON? WHAT'S IMPORTANT ENOUGH FOR YOU TO DRAG ME OUT OF--
SIT DOWN.
WHAT?
SIT.

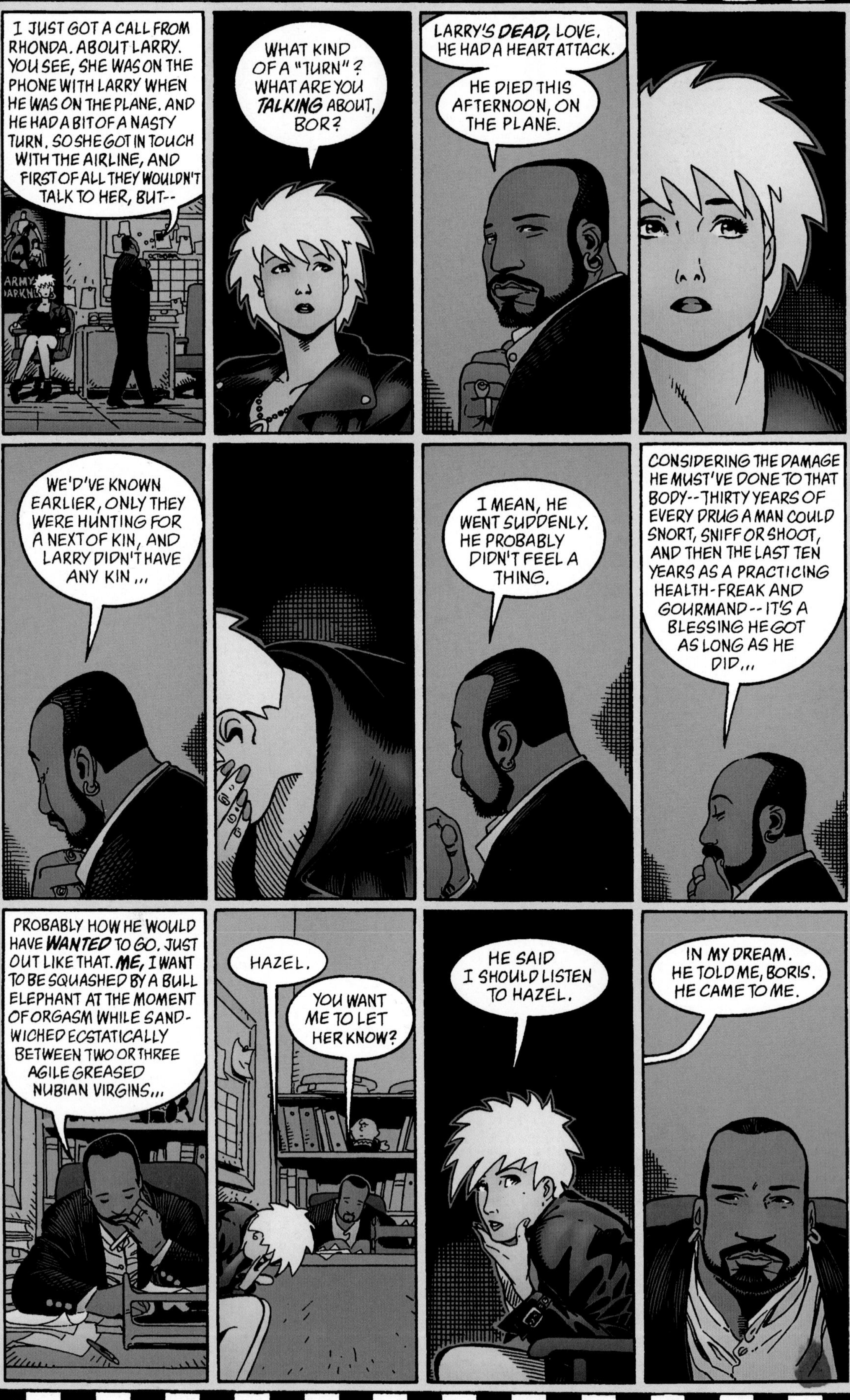
I JUST GOT A CALL FROM RHONDA. ABOUT LARRY. YOU SEE, SHE WAS ON THE PHONE WITH LARRY WHEN HE WAS ON THE PLANE. AND HE HAD A BIT OF A NASTY TURN. SO SHE GOT IN TOUCH WITH THE AIRLINE, AND FIRST OF ALL THEY WOULDN'T TALK TO HER, BUT--
WHAT KIND OF A "TURN"? WHAT ARE YOU TALKING ABOUT, BOR?
LARRY'S DEAD, LOVE. HE HAD A HEART ATTACK.
HE DIED THIS AFTERNOON, ON THE PLANE.
WE'D'VE KNOWN EARLIER, ONLY THEY WERE HUNTING FOR A NEXT OF KIN, AND LARRY DIDN'T HAVE ANY KIN...
I MEAN, HE WENT SUDDENLY. HE PROBABLY DIDN'T FEEL A THING.
CONSIDERING THE DAMAGE HE MUST'VE DONE TO THAT BODY--THIRTY YEARS OF EVERY DRUG A MAN COULD SNORT, SNIFF OR SHOOT, AND THEN THE LAST TEN YEARS AS A PRACTICING HEALTH-FREAK AND GOURMAND--IT'S A BLESSING HE GOT AS LONG AS HE DID...
PROBABLY HOW HE WOULD HAVE WANTED TO GO. JUST OUT LIKE THAT. ME, I WANT TO BE SQUASHED BY A BULL ELEPHANT AT THE MOMENT OF ORGASM WHILE SAND-WICHED ECSTATICALLY BETWEEN TWO OR THREE AGILE GREASED NUBIAN VIRGINS...
HAZEL.
YOU WANT ME TO LET HER KNOW?
HE SAID I SHOULD LISTEN TO HAZEL.
IN MY DREAM. HE TOLD ME, BORIS. HE CAME TO ME.

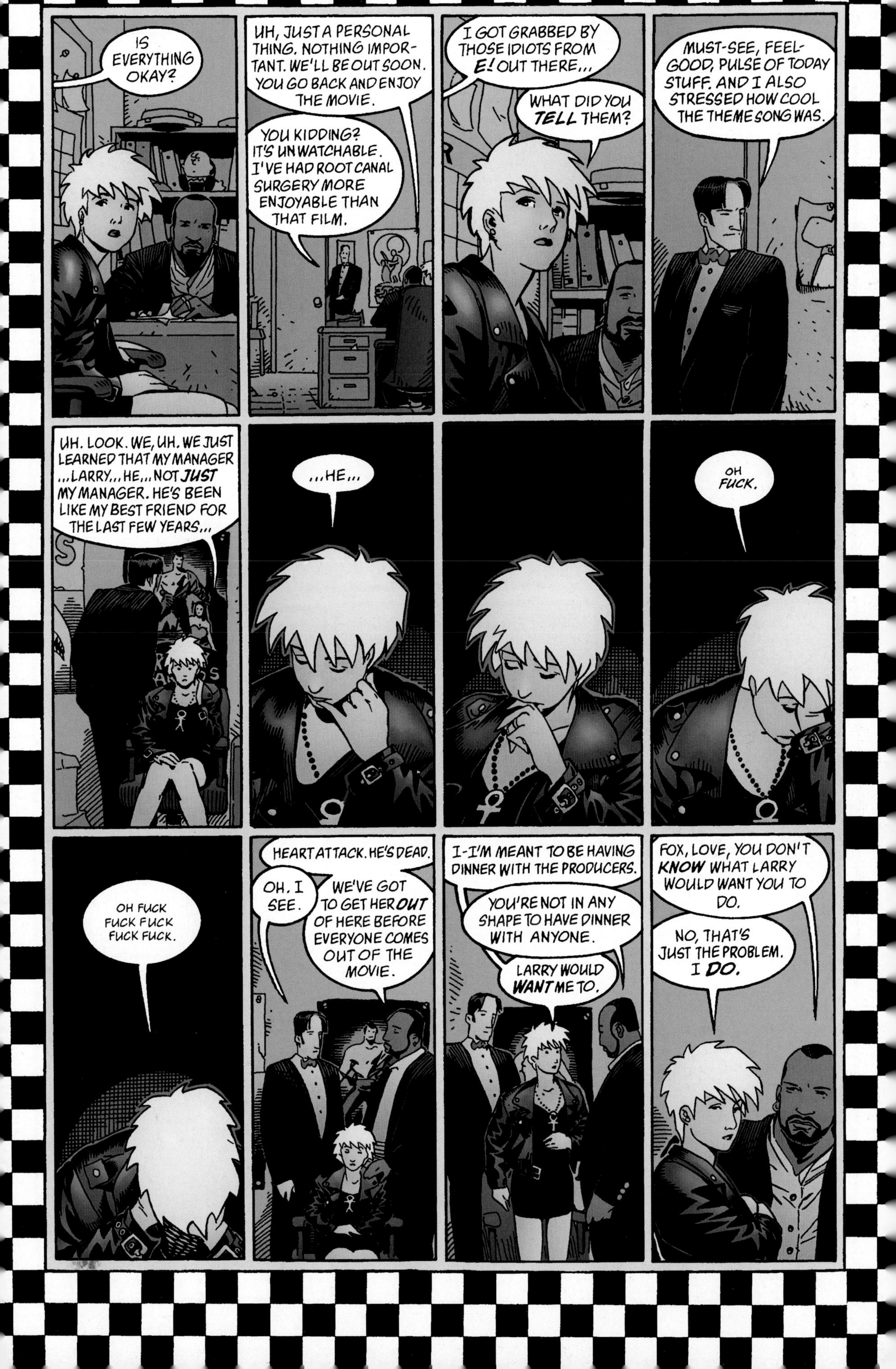
IS EVERYTHING OKAY?
UH, JUST A PERSONAL THING. NOTHING IMPORTANT. WE'LL BE OUT SOON. YOU GO BACK AND ENJOY THE MOVIE.
YOU KIDDING? IT'S UNWATCHABLE. I'VE HAD ROOT CANAL SURGERY MORE ENJOYABLE THAN THAT FILM.
I GOT GRABBED BY THOSE IDIOTS FROM E! OUT THERE...
WHAT DID YOU TELL THEM?
MUST-SEE, FEEL-GOOD, PULSE OF TODAY STUFF. AND I ALSO STRESSED HOW COOL THE THEME SONG WAS.
UH. LOOK. WE, UH. WE JUST LEARNED THAT MY MANAGER ...LARRY... HE... NOT JUST MY MANAGER. HE'S BEEN LIKE MY BEST FRIEND FOR THE LAST FEW YEARS...
...HE...
OH FUCK.
OH FUCK FUCK FUCK FUCK FUCK.
HEART ATTACK. HE'S DEAD.
OH. I SEE.
WE'VE GOT TO GET HER OUT OF HERE BEFORE EVERYONE COMES OUT OF THE MOVIE.
I-I'M MEANT TO BE HAVING DINNER WITH THE PRODUCERS.
YOU'RE NOT IN ANY SHAPE TO HAVE DINNER WITH ANYONE.
LARRY WOULD WANT ME TO.
FOX, LOVE, YOU DON'T KNOW WHAT LARRY WOULD WANT YOU TO DO.
NO, THAT'S JUST THE PROBLEM. I DO.

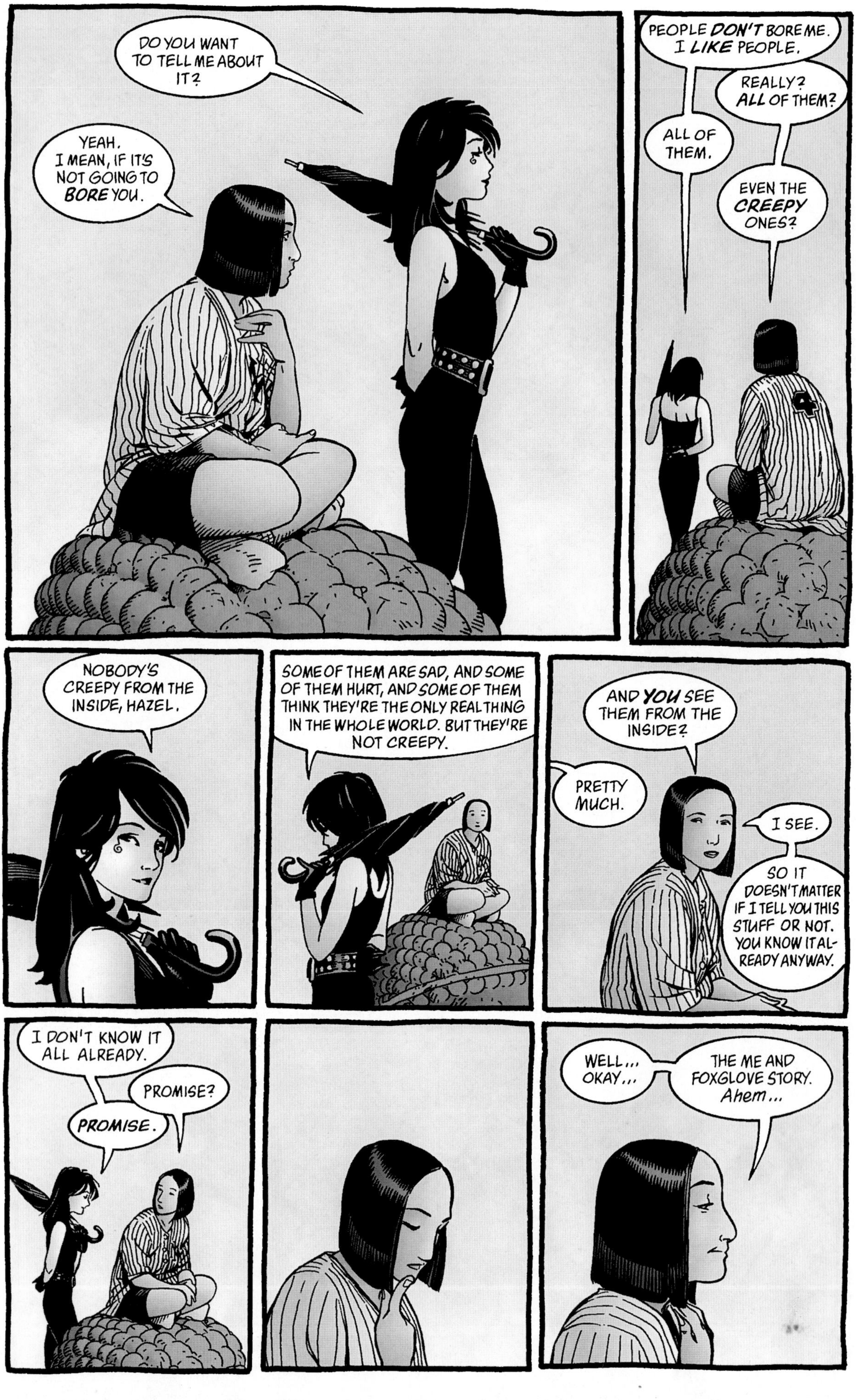
DO YOU WANT TO TELL ME ABOUT IT?
YEAH. I MEAN, IF IT'S NOT GOING TO BORE YOU.
PEOPLE DON'T BORE ME. I LIKE PEOPLE.
REALLY? ALL OF THEM?
ALL OF THEM.
EVEN THE CREEPY ONES?
NOBODY'S CREEPY FROM THE INSIDE, HAZEL.
SOME OF THEM ARE SAD, AND SOME OF THEM HURT, AND SOME OF THEM THINK THEY'RE THE ONLY REAL THING IN THE WHOLE WORLD. BUT THEY'RE NOT CREEPY.
AND YOU SEE THEM FROM THE INSIDE?
PRETTY MUCH.
I SEE.
SO IT DOESN'T MATTER IF I TELL YOU THIS STUFF OR NOT. YOU KNOW IT ALREADY ANYWAY.
I DON'T KNOW IT ALL ALREADY.
PROMISE?
PROMISE.
WELL... OKAY...
THE ME AND FOXGLOVE STORY. Ahem...

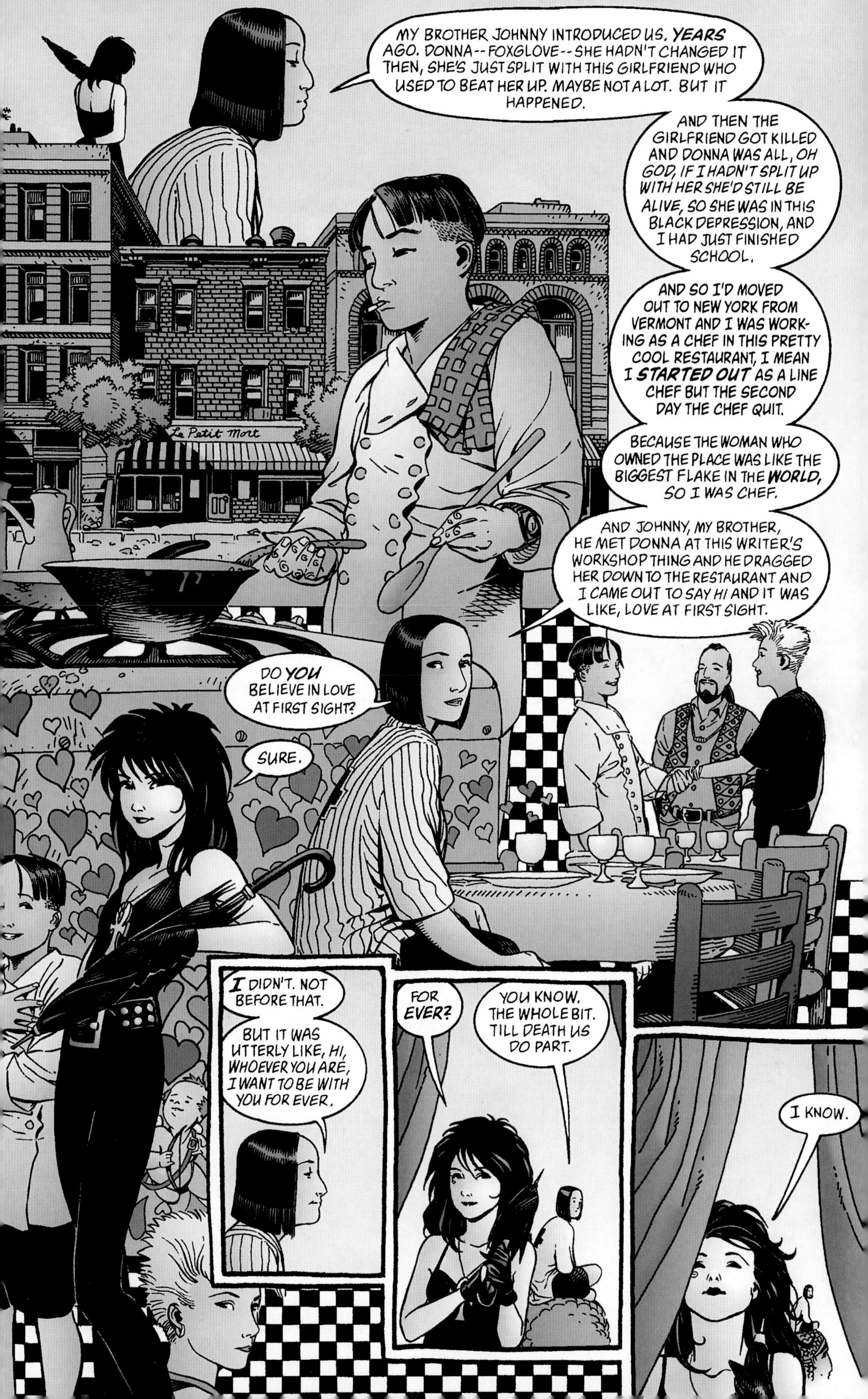
MY BROTHER JOHNNY INTRODUCED US, YEARS AGO. DONNA--FOXGLOVE--SHE HADN'T CHANGED IT THEN, SHE'S JUST SPLIT WITH THIS GIRLFRIEND WHO USED TO BEAT HER UP. MAYBE NOT A LOT. BUT IT HAPPENED.
AND THEN THE GIRLFRIEND GOT KILLED AND DONNA WAS ALL, OH GOD, IF I HADN'T SPLIT UP WITH HER SHE'D STILL BE ALIVE, SO SHE WAS IN THIS BLACK DEPRESSION, AND I HAD JUST FINISHED SCHOOL.
AND SO I'D MOVED OUT TO NEW YORK FROM VERMONT AND I WAS WORKING AS A CHEF IN THIS PRETTY COOL RESTAURANT, I MEAN I STARTED OUT AS A LINE CHEF BUT THE SECOND DAY THE CHEF QUIT.
BECAUSE THE WOMAN WHO OWNED THE PLACE WAS LIKE THE BIGGEST FLAKE IN THE WORLD, SO I WAS CHEF.
Le Petit Mort
AND JOHNNY, MY BROTHER, HE MET DONNA AT THIS WRITER'S WORKSHOP THING AND HE DRAGGED HER DOWN TO THE RESTAURANT AND I CAME OUT TO SAY HI AND IT WAS LIKE, LOVE AT FIRST SIGHT.
DO YOU BELIEVE IN LOVE AT FIRST SIGHT?
SURE.
I DIDN'T. NOT BEFORE THAT.
BUT IT WAS UTTERLY LIKE, HI, WHOEVER YOU ARE, I WANT TO BE WITH YOU FOR EVER.
FOR EVER?
YOU KNOW. THE WHOLE BIT. TILL DEATH US DO PART.
I KNOW.

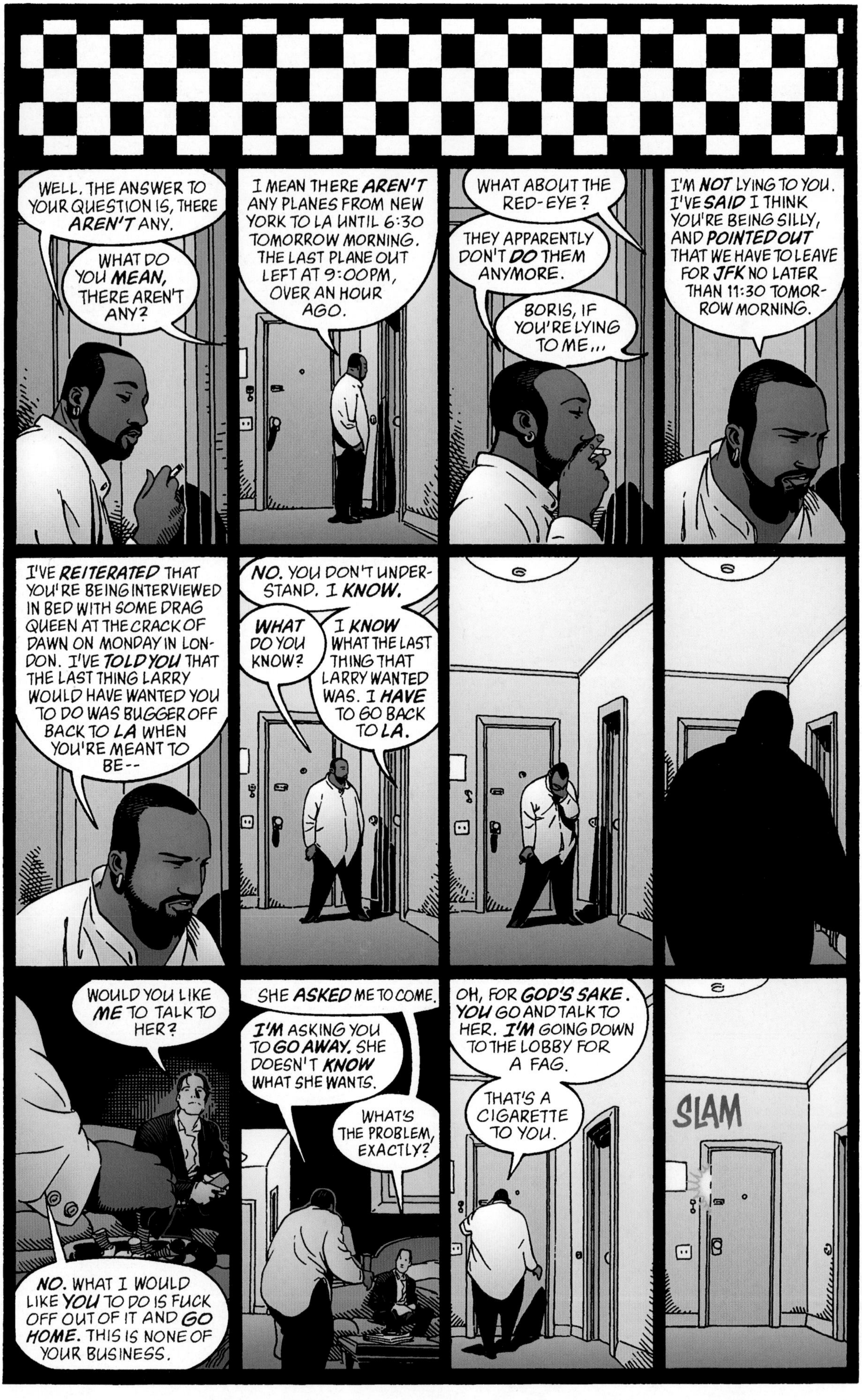
WELL, THE ANSWER TO YOUR QUESTION IS, THERE AREN'T ANY.
WHAT DO YOU MEAN, THERE AREN'T ANY?
I MEAN THERE AREN'T ANY PLANES FROM NEW YORK TO LA UNTIL 6:30 TOMORROW MORNING. THE LAST PLANE OUT LEFT AT 9:00PM, OVER AN HOUR AGO.
WHAT ABOUT THE RED-EYE?
THEY APPARENTLY DON'T DO THEM ANYMORE.
BORIS, IF YOU'RE LYING TO ME...
I'M NOT LYING TO YOU. I'VE SAID I THINK YOU'RE BEING SILLY, AND POINTED OUT THAT WE HAVE TO LEAVE FOR JFK NO LATER THAN 11:30 TOMORROW MORNING.
I'VE REITERATED THAT YOU'RE BEING INTERVIEWED IN BED WITH SOME DRAG QUEEN AT THE CRACK OF DAWN ON MONDAY IN LONDON. I'VE TOLD YOU THAT THE LAST THING LARRY WOULD HAVE WANTED YOU TO DO WAS BUGGER OFF BACK TO LA WHEN YOU'RE MEANT TO BE--
NO. YOU DON'T UNDERSTAND. I KNOW.
WHAT DO YOU KNOW?
I KNOW WHAT THE LAST THING THAT LARRY WANTED WAS. I HAVE TO GO BACK TO LA.
WOULD YOU LIKE ME TO TALK TO HER?
NO. WHAT I WOULD LIKE YOU TO DO IS FUCK OFF OUT OF IT AND GO HOME. THIS IS NONE OF YOUR BUSINESS.
SHE ASKED ME TO COME.
I'M ASKING YOU TO GO AWAY. SHE DOESN'T KNOW WHAT SHE WANTS.
WHAT'S THE PROBLEM, EXACTLY?
OH, FOR GOD'S SAKE. YOU GO AND TALK TO HER. I'M GOING DOWN TO THE LOBBY FOR A FAG.
THAT'S A CIGARETTE TO YOU.
SLAM

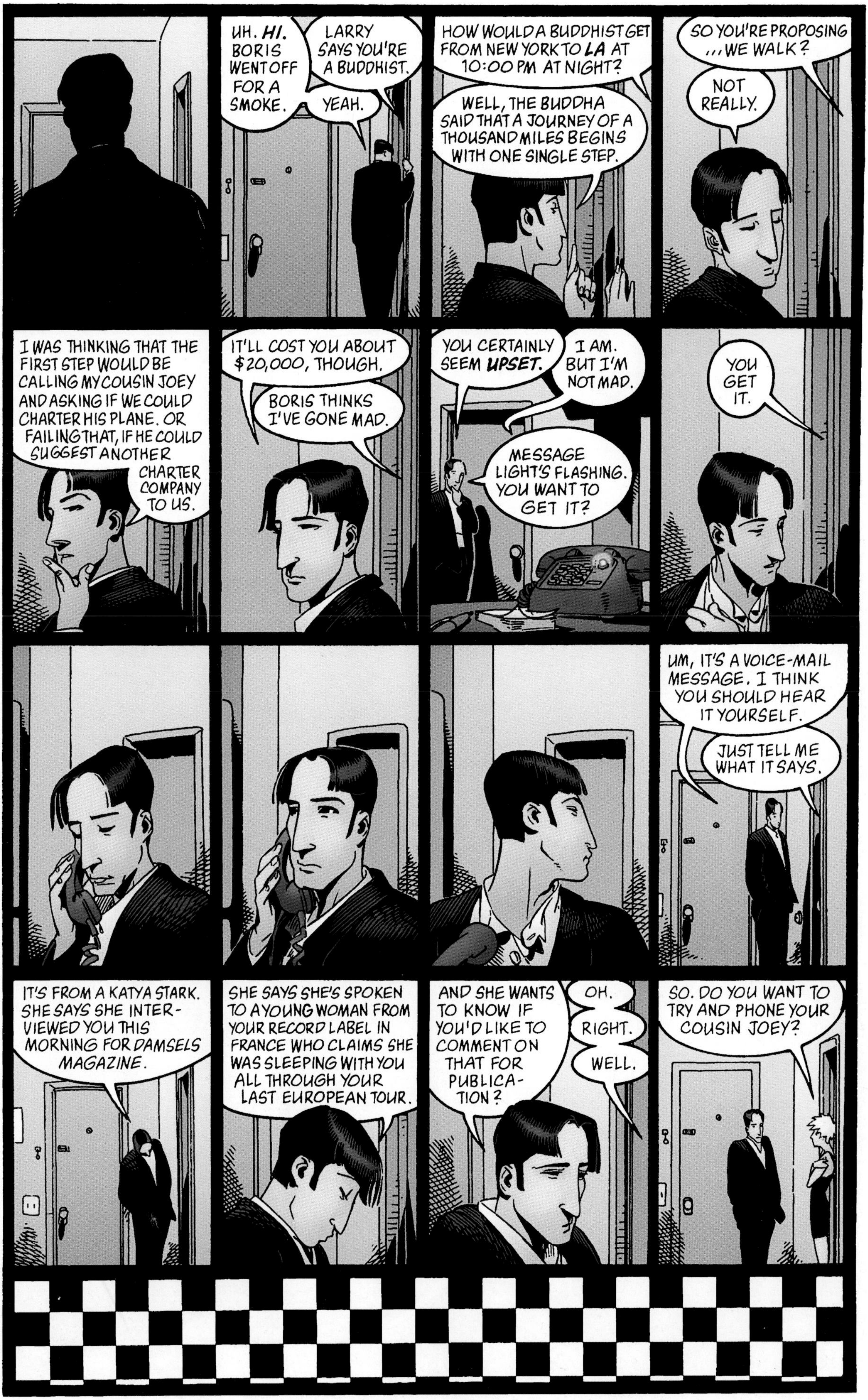
UH. HI. BORIS WENT OFF FOR A SMOKE.
LARRY SAYS YOU'RE A BUDDHIST.
YEAH.
HOW WOULD A BUDDHIST GET FROM NEW YORK TO LA AT 10:00 PM AT NIGHT?
WELL, THE BUDDHA SAID THAT A JOURNEY OF A THOUSAND MILES BEGINS WITH ONE SINGLE STEP.
SO YOU'RE PROPOSING ... WE WALK?
NOT REALLY.
I WAS THINKING THAT THE FIRST STEP WOULD BE CALLING MY COUSIN JOEY AND ASKING IF WE COULD CHARTER HIS PLANE. OR FAILING THAT, IF HE COULD SUGGEST ANOTHER CHARTER COMPANY TO US.
IT'LL COST YOU ABOUT $20,000, THOUGH.
BORIS THINKS I'VE GONE MAD.
YOU CERTAINLY SEEM UPSET.
I AM. BUT I'M NOT MAD.
MESSAGE LIGHT'S FLASHING. YOU WANT TO GET IT?
YOU GET IT.
UM, IT'S A VOICE-MAIL MESSAGE. I THINK YOU SHOULD HEAR IT YOURSELF.
JUST TELL ME WHAT IT SAYS.
IT'S FROM A KATYA STARK. SHE SAYS SHE INTERVIEWED YOU THIS MORNING FOR DAMSELS MAGAZINE.
SHE SAYS SHE'S SPOKEN TO A YOUNG WOMAN FROM YOUR RECORD LABEL IN FRANCE WHO CLAIMS SHE WAS SLEEPING WITH YOU ALL THROUGH YOUR LAST EUROPEAN TOUR.
AND SHE WANTS TO KNOW IF YOU'D LIKE TO COMMENT ON THAT FOR PUBLICATION?
OH.
RIGHT.
WELL.
SO. DO YOU WANT TO TRY AND PHONE YOUR COUSIN JOEY?

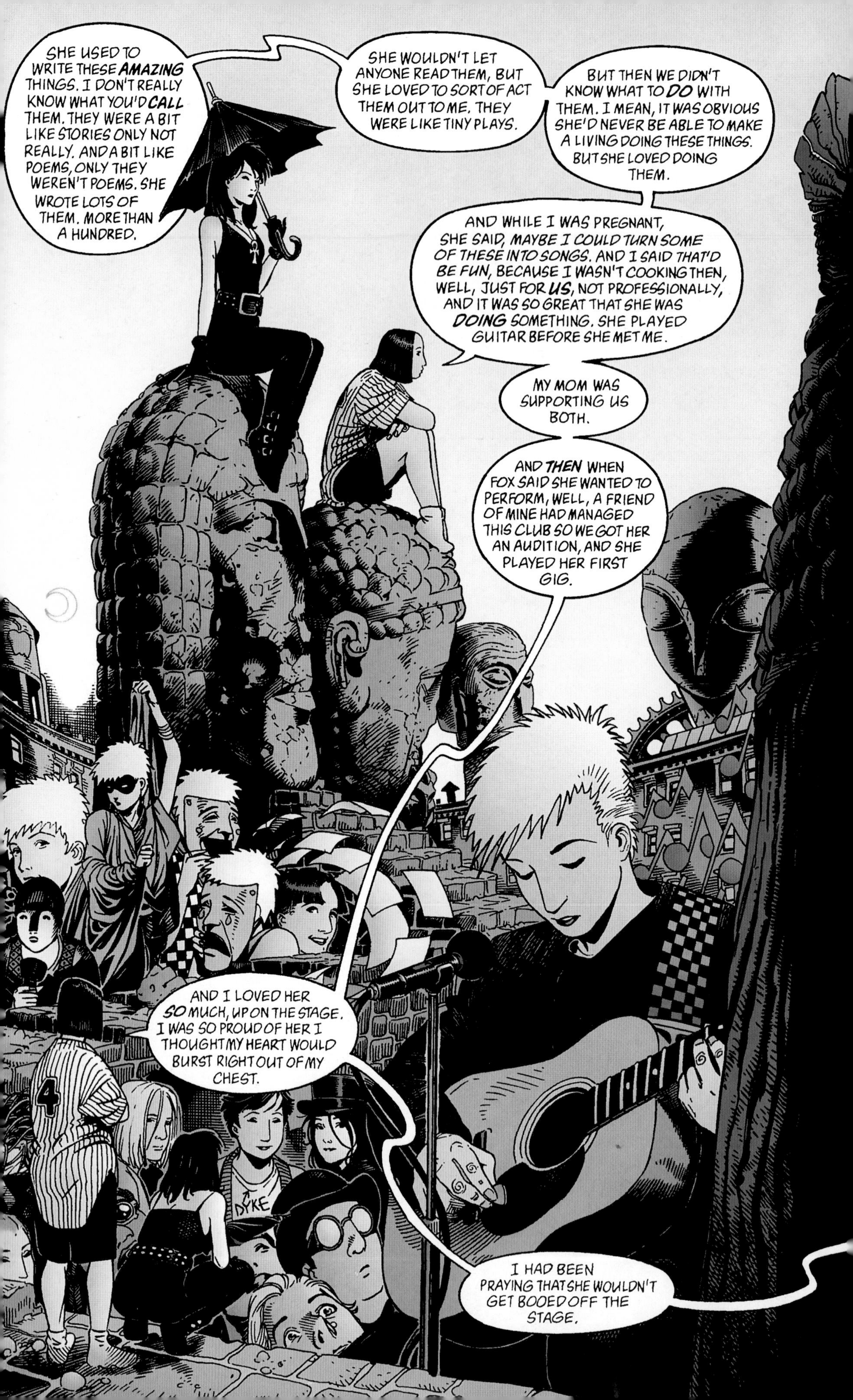
SHE USED TO WRITE THESE AMAZING THINGS. I DON'T REALLY KNOW WHAT YOU'D CALL THEM. THEY WERE A BIT LIKE STORIES ONLY NOT REALLY. AND A BIT LIKE POEMS, ONLY THEY WEREN'T POEMS. SHE WROTE LOTS OF THEM. MORE THAN A HUNDRED.
SHE WOULDN'T LET ANYONE READ THEM, BUT SHE LOVED TO SORT OF ACT THEM OUT TO ME. THEY WERE LIKE TINY PLAYS.
BUT THEN WE DIDN'T KNOW WHAT TO DO WITH THEM. I MEAN, IT WAS OBVIOUS SHE'D NEVER BE ABLE TO MAKE A LIVING DOING THESE THINGS. BUT SHE LOVED DOING THEM.
AND WHILE I WAS PREGNANT, SHE SAID, MAYBE I COULD TURN SOME OF THESE INTO SONGS. AND I SAID THAT'D BE FUN, BECAUSE I WASN'T COOKING THEN, WELL, JUST FOR US, NOT PROFESSIONALLY, AND IT WAS SO GREAT THAT SHE WAS DOING SOMETHING. SHE PLAYED GUITAR BEFORE SHE MET ME.
MY MOM WAS SUPPORTING US BOTH.
AND THEN WHEN FOX SAID SHE WANTED TO PERFORM, WELL, A FRIEND OF MINE HAD MANAGED THIS CLUB SO WE GOT HER AN AUDITION, AND SHE PLAYED HER FIRST GIG.
AND I LOVED HER SO MUCH, UP ON THE STAGE. I WAS SO PROUD OF HER I THOUGHT MY HEART WOULD BURST RIGHT OUT OF MY CHEST.
I HAD BEEN PRAYING THAT SHE WOULDN'T GET BOOED OFF THE STAGE.
DYKE

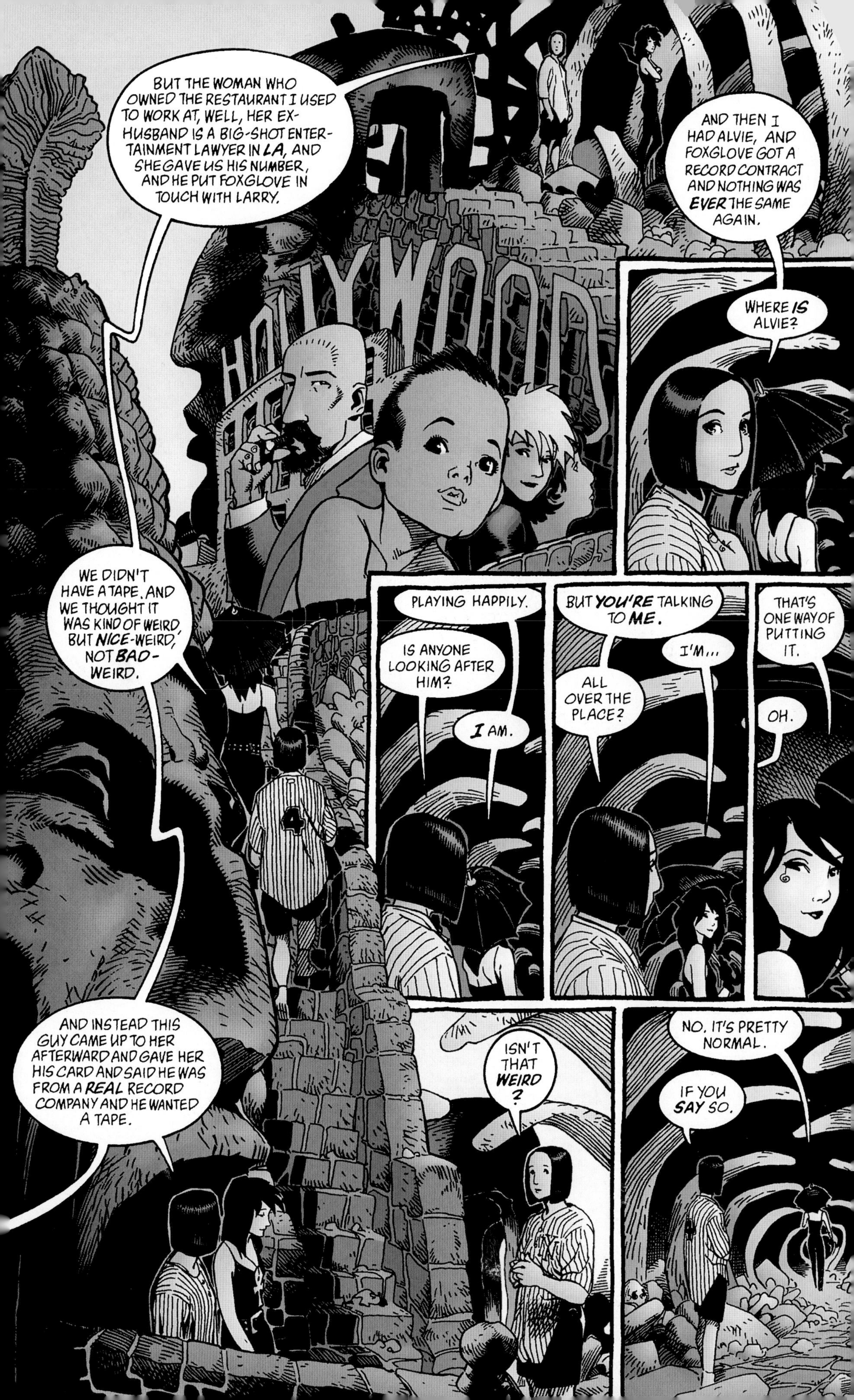

BUT THE WOMAN WHO OWNED THE RESTAURANT I USED TO WORK AT, WELL, HER EX-HUSBAND IS A BIG-SHOT ENTERTAINMENT LAWYER IN **LA**, AND SHE GAVE US HIS NUMBER, AND HE PUT FOXGLOVE IN TOUCH WITH LARRY.
AND THEN I HAD ALVIE, AND FOXGLOVE GOT A RECORD CONTRACT AND NOTHING WAS **EVER** THE SAME AGAIN.
WHERE **IS** ALVIE?
WE DIDN'T HAVE A TAPE, AND WE THOUGHT IT WAS KIND OF WEIRD, BUT **NICE**-WEIRD, NOT **BAD**-WEIRD.
PLAYING HAPPILY.
IS ANYONE LOOKING AFTER HIM?
I AM.
BUT **YOU'RE** TALKING TO **ME**.
I'M...
ALL OVER THE PLACE?
THAT'S ONE WAY OF PUTTING IT.
OH.
AND INSTEAD THIS GUY CAME UP TO HER AFTERWARD AND GAVE HER HIS CARD AND SAID HE WAS FROM A **REAL** RECORD COMPANY AND HE WANTED A TAPE.
ISN'T THAT **WEIRD**?
NO, IT'S PRETTY NORMAL.
IF YOU **SAY** SO.

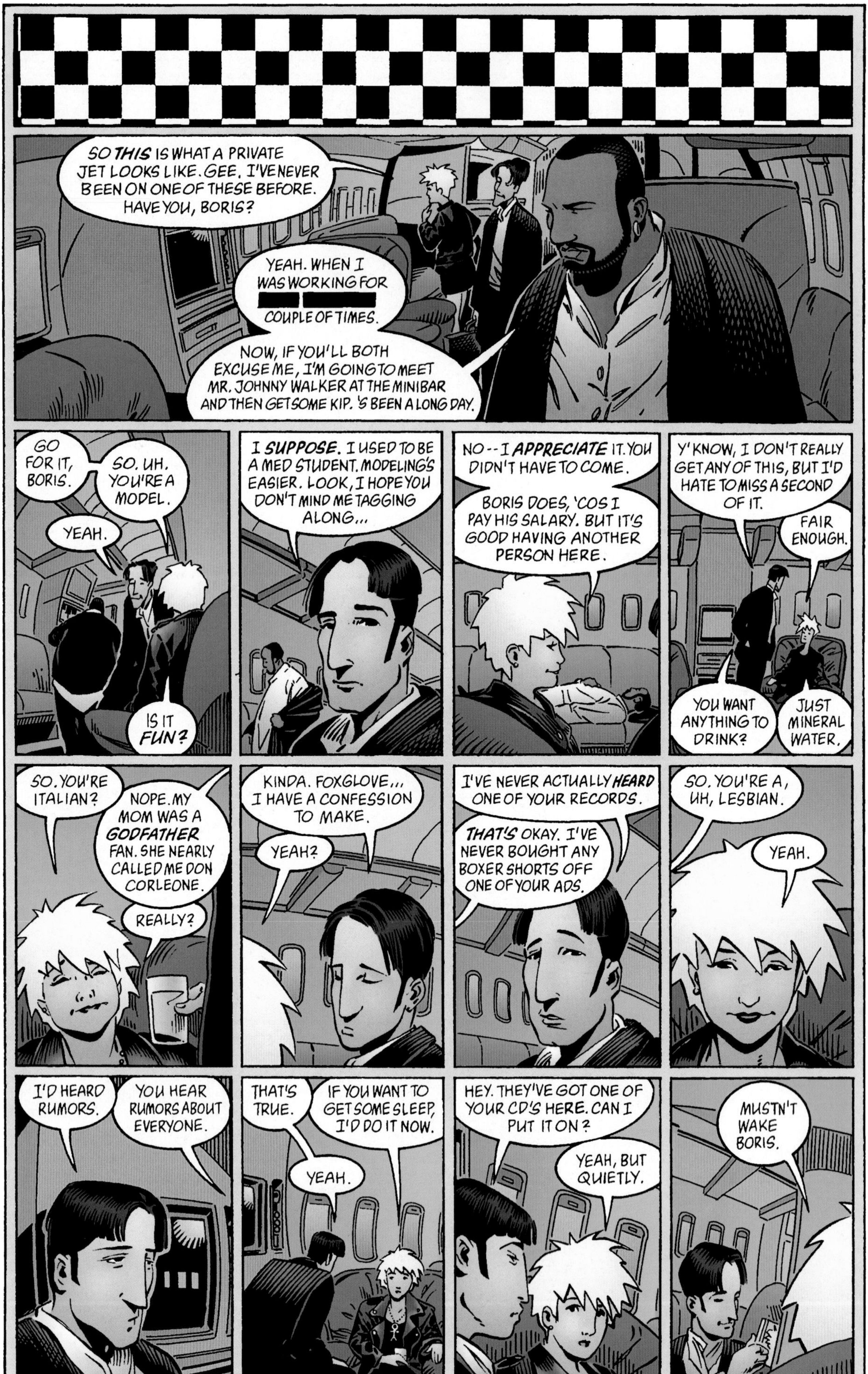
SO THIS IS WHAT A PRIVATE JET LOOKS LIKE. GEE. I'VE NEVER BEEN ON ONE OF THESE BEFORE. HAVE YOU, BORIS?
YEAH. WHEN I WAS WORKING FOR [redacted] COUPLE OF TIMES.
NOW, IF YOU'LL BOTH EXCUSE ME, I'M GOING TO MEET MR. JOHNNY WALKER AT THE MINIBAR AND THEN GET SOME KIP. 'S BEEN A LONG DAY.
GO FOR IT, BORIS.
SO. UH. YOU'RE A MODEL.
YEAH.
IS IT FUN?
I SUPPOSE. I USED TO BE A MED STUDENT. MODELING'S EASIER. LOOK, I HOPE YOU DON'T MIND ME TAGGING ALONG...
NO--I APPRECIATE IT. YOU DIDN'T HAVE TO COME.
BORIS DOES, 'COS I PAY HIS SALARY. BUT IT'S GOOD HAVING ANOTHER PERSON HERE.
Y'KNOW, I DON'T REALLY GET ANY OF THIS, BUT I'D HATE TO MISS A SECOND OF IT.
FAIR ENOUGH.
YOU WANT ANYTHING TO DRINK?
JUST MINERAL WATER.
SO. YOU'RE ITALIAN?
NOPE. MY MOM WAS A GODFATHER FAN. SHE NEARLY CALLED ME DON CORLEONE.
REALLY?
KINDA. FOXGLOVE... I HAVE A CONFESSION TO MAKE.
YEAH?
I'VE NEVER ACTUALLY HEARD ONE OF YOUR RECORDS.
THAT'S OKAY. I'VE NEVER BOUGHT ANY BOXER SHORTS OFF ONE OF YOUR ADS.
SO. YOU'RE A, UH, LESBIAN.
YEAH.
I'D HEARD RUMORS.
YOU HEAR RUMORS ABOUT EVERYONE.
THAT'S TRUE.
IF YOU WANT TO GET SOME SLEEP, I'D DO IT NOW.
YEAH.
HEY. THEY'VE GOT ONE OF YOUR CD'S HERE. CAN I PUT IT ON?
YEAH, BUT QUIETLY.
MUSTN'T WAKE BORIS.

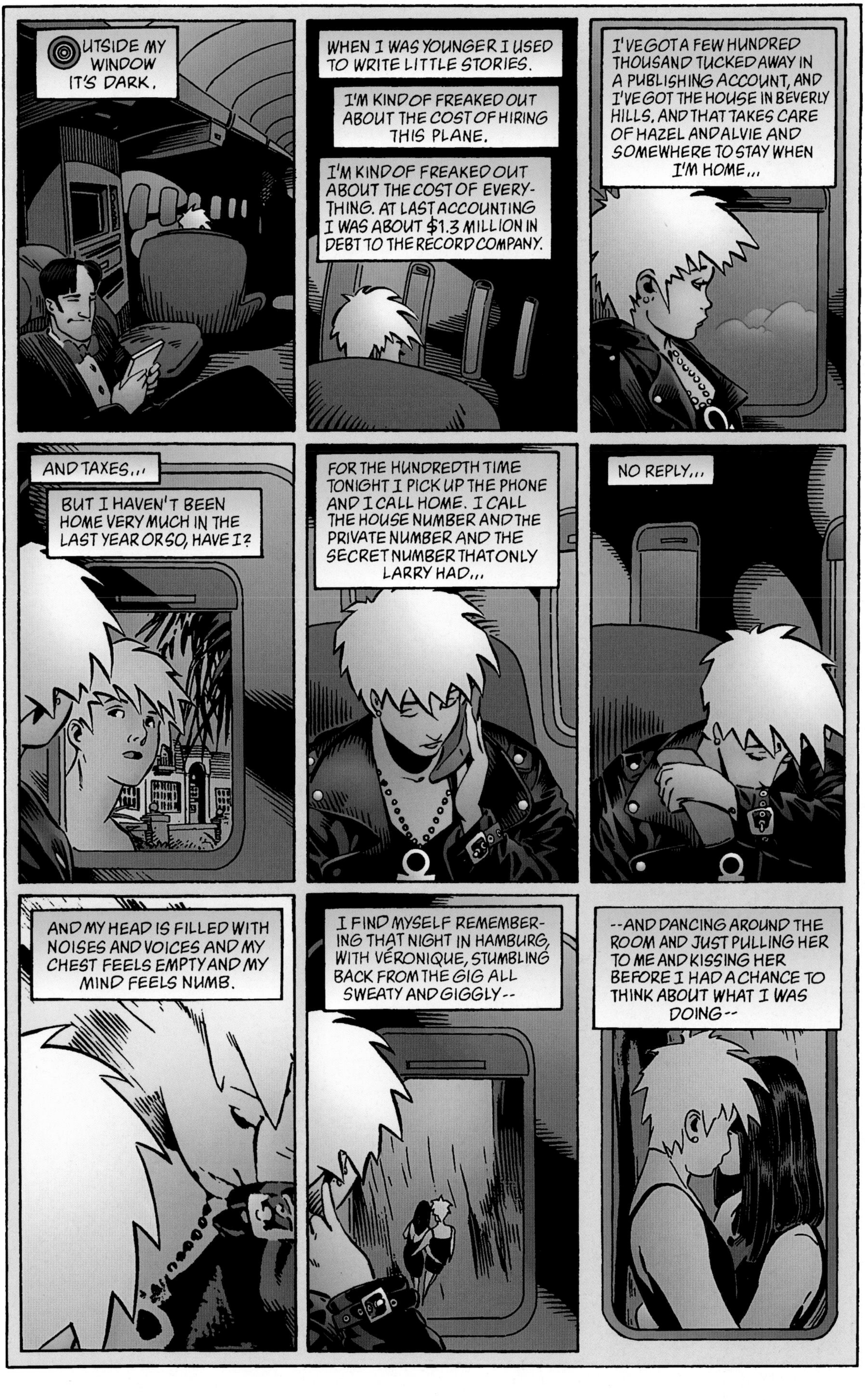
OUTSIDE MY WINDOW IT'S DARK.
WHEN I WAS YOUNGER I USED TO WRITE LITTLE STORIES.
I'M KIND OF FREAKED OUT ABOUT THE COST OF HIRING THIS PLANE.
I'M KIND OF FREAKED OUT ABOUT THE COST OF EVERYTHING. AT LAST ACCOUNTING I WAS ABOUT $1.3 MILLION IN DEBT TO THE RECORD COMPANY.
I'VE GOT A FEW HUNDRED THOUSAND TUCKED AWAY IN A PUBLISHING ACCOUNT, AND I'VE GOT THE HOUSE IN BEVERLY HILLS, AND THAT TAKES CARE OF HAZEL AND ALVIE AND SOMEWHERE TO STAY WHEN I'M HOME...
AND TAXES...
BUT I HAVEN'T BEEN HOME VERY MUCH IN THE LAST YEAR OR SO, HAVE I?
FOR THE HUNDREDTH TIME TONIGHT I PICK UP THE PHONE AND I CALL HOME. I CALL THE HOUSE NUMBER AND THE PRIVATE NUMBER AND THE SECRET NUMBER THAT ONLY LARRY HAD...
NO REPLY...
AND MY HEAD IS FILLED WITH NOISES AND VOICES AND MY CHEST FEELS EMPTY AND MY MIND FEELS NUMB.
I FIND MYSELF REMEMBERING THAT NIGHT IN HAMBURG, WITH VÉRONIQUE, STUMBLING BACK FROM THE GIG ALL SWEATY AND GIGGLY--
--AND DANCING AROUND THE ROOM AND JUST PULLING HER TO ME AND KISSING HER BEFORE I HAD A CHANCE TO THINK ABOUT WHAT I WAS DOING--

--BECAUSE I WAS SO FAR FROM HOME--

--HER HEAD BETWEEN MY LEGS--

--STUTTERING MY LUST INTO THE NIGHT--

--KNOWING SOMEWHERE DOWN DEEP THAT I COULD TAKE WHATEVER I WANTED, BUT THAT ONE DAY IT WOULD ALL HAVE TO BE PAID FOR--

--WAVING GOODBYE TO VÉRONIQUE IN AMSTERDAM AIRPORT AT THE END OF THE TOUR, AND PROMISING TO KEEP IN TOUCH, AND KNOWING I NEVER WOULD--

-- SHIVERING NOW, MY FINGERS AND MY BODY ARE CHILLED. I WISH I WAS ASLEEP. BORIS SNUFFLES AND GRUNTS IN HIS SLEEP LIKE AN OLD BEAR HIBERNATING. WONDERING WHERE HAZEL COULD BE, IF ALVIE'S OKAY...

AND AN AIRPLANE IS SUCH A PERFECT MACHINE, IF IT CRASHES IT'S NOT YOUR FAULT. A FAST FIREBALL TRIP INTO NOTHING...

THAT ISN'T SUICIDE. IS IT?

THE THOUGHT COMFORTS ME. OUTSIDE MY WINDOW THE SKY IS TURNING A COLD PRE-DAWN GRAY. THE DESERT BENEATH US LOOKS LIKE A SLICE OF NOWHERE.

AND I REALIZE I'VE FORGOTTEN THE NAME OF THE BUDDHIST JOCKEY SHORTS GUY ALREADY

AND

WE'LL BE LANDING IN

UNDER AN HOUR

SO THERE'S NO

POINT

IN

FALLING

ASLEEP...

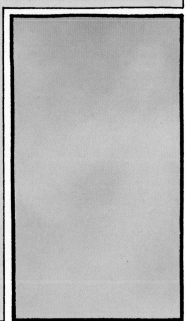

I'M STANDING ON THE ROOF OF A SKYSCRAPER WITH LARRY. AND HE POINTS TO THE CLOUDS, AND WARNS ME.

STORMY WEATHER.

AND I'M WORRIED. THIS IS THE KIND OF WEATHER THAT SPAWNS HURRICANES, MONSOONS AND CYCLONES.

MY LIFE WAS BLOWN APART ONCE BY A HURRICANE.

I SURVIVED.

OTHER PEOPLE DIED, BUT NOT ME.

I LOOK FOR SOMEWHERE TO RUN, CERTAIN I'M ABOUT TO BE BLOWN AWAY TO MY DEATH, WHEN ABOVE ME I SEE THE SMALLEST, SWEETEST TORNADO: IT LOOKS LIKE IT'S MADE OF CRYSTAL, SPINNING IN THE SKY.

IT'S ONLY THERE FOR A MOMENT, AND THEN IT'S GONE.

AND I WANT TO ASK LARRY IF HE SAW THE TORNADO TOO, BUT HE'S GONE. AND UP WHERE THE TORNADO WAS, BUTTERFLIES ARE APPEARING, OUT OF THE NOWHERE AND INTO THE HERE.

"THAT," I TELL MYSELF, "IS A FORTEAN PHENOMENON."

AND IT MAKES ME SO HAPPY. SO UTTERLY AND COMPLETELY HAPPY.

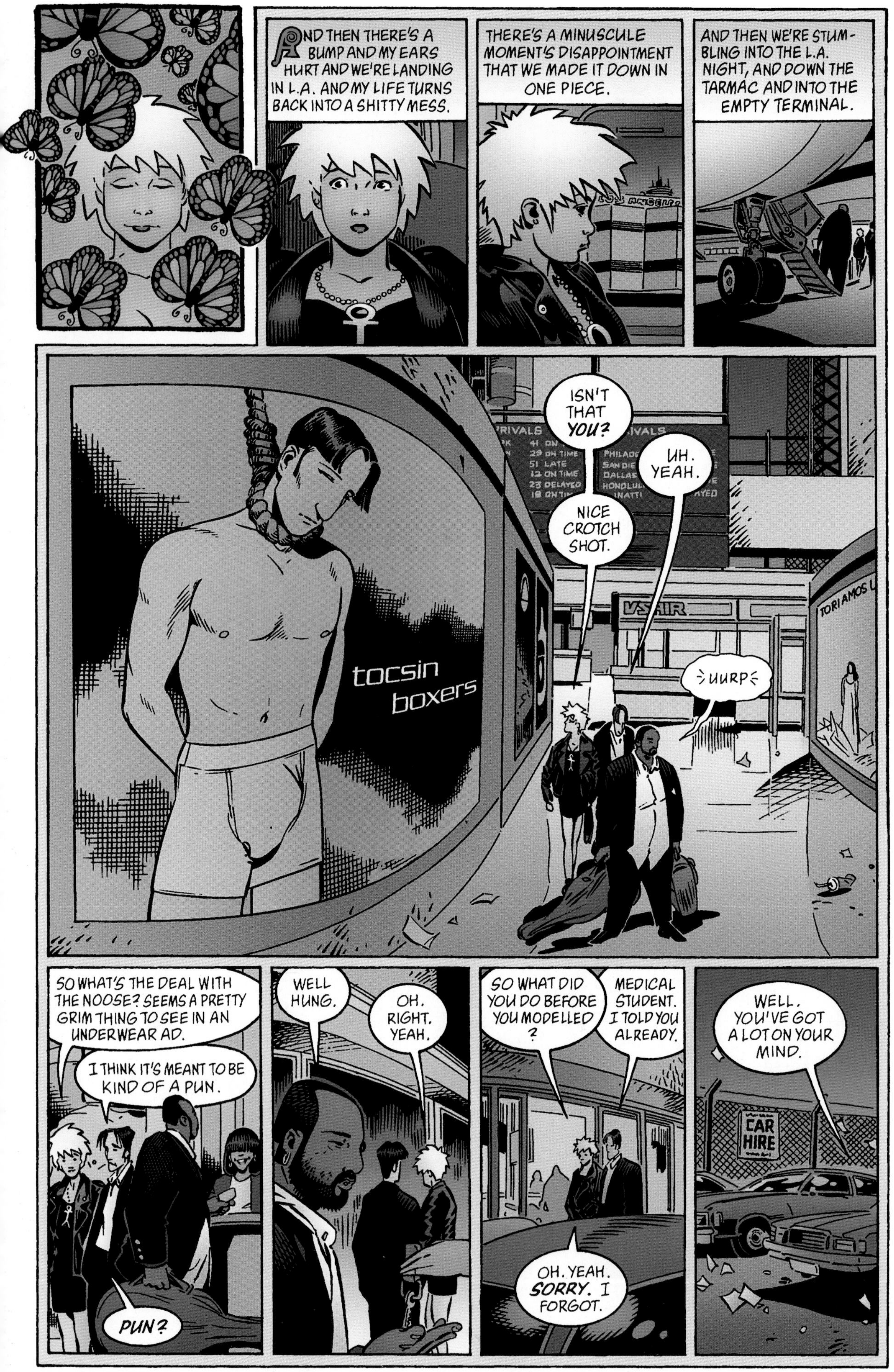
AND THEN THERE'S A BUMP AND MY EARS HURT AND WE'RE LANDING IN L.A. AND MY LIFE TURNS BACK INTO A SHITTY MESS.
THERE'S A MINUSCULE MOMENT'S DISAPPOINTMENT THAT WE MADE IT DOWN IN ONE PIECE.
AND THEN WE'RE STUMBLING INTO THE L.A. NIGHT, AND DOWN THE TARMAC AND INTO THE EMPTY TERMINAL.
tocsin boxers
ISN'T THAT YOU?
NICE CROTCH SHOT.
UH. YEAH.
UURP
SO WHAT'S THE DEAL WITH THE NOOSE? SEEMS A PRETTY GRIM THING TO SEE IN AN UNDERWEAR AD.
I THINK IT'S MEANT TO BE KIND OF A PUN.
PUN?
WELL HUNG.
OH. RIGHT. YEAH.
SO WHAT DID YOU DO BEFORE YOU MODELLED?
MEDICAL STUDENT. I TOLD YOU ALREADY.
OH. YEAH. SORRY. I FORGOT.
CAR HIRE
WELL. YOU'VE GOT A LOT ON YOUR MIND.

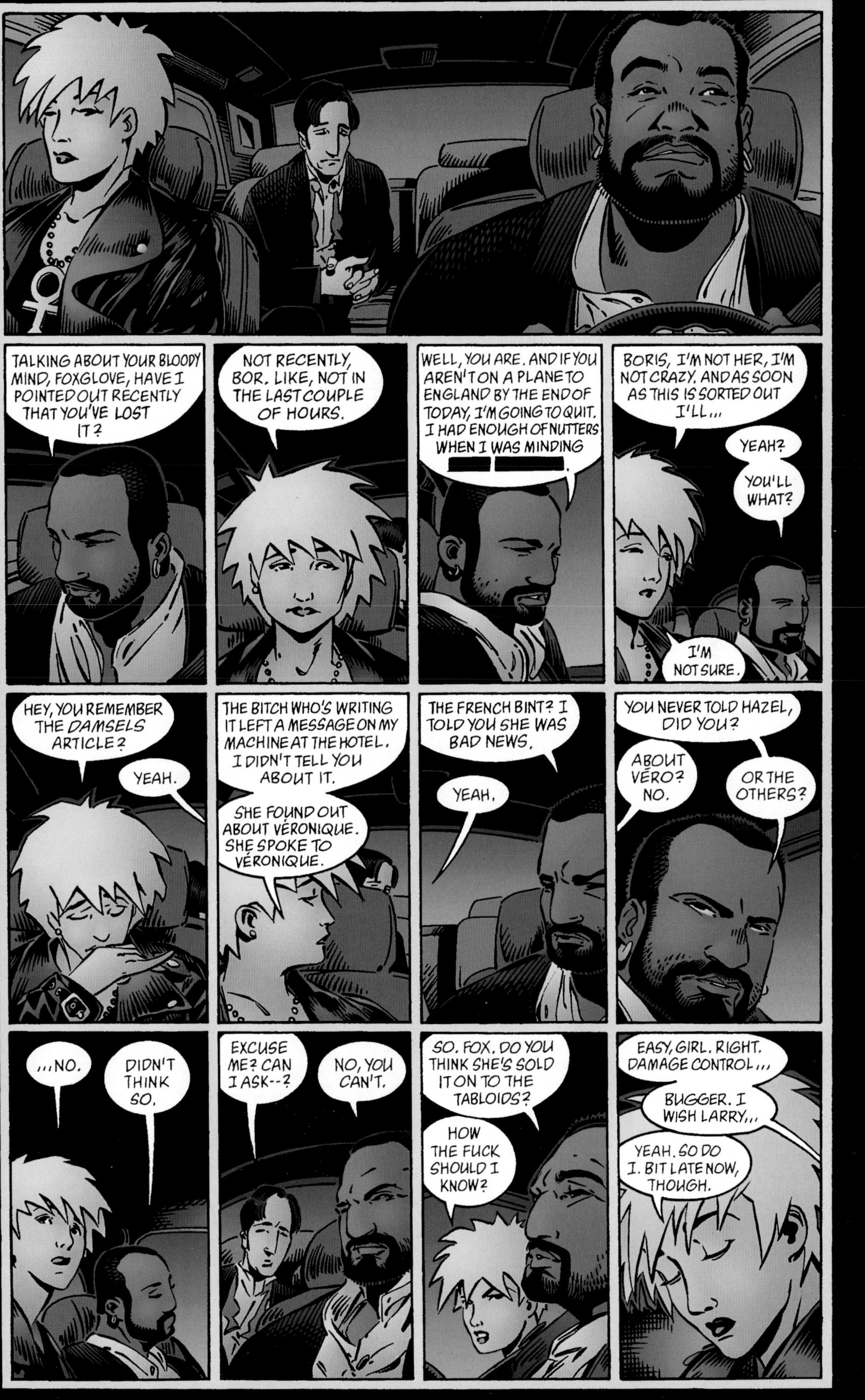
TALKING ABOUT YOUR BLOODY MIND, FOXGLOVE, HAVE I POINTED OUT RECENTLY THAT YOU'VE LOST IT?
NOT RECENTLY, BOR. LIKE, NOT IN THE LAST COUPLE OF HOURS.
WELL, YOU ARE. AND IF YOU AREN'T ON A PLANE TO ENGLAND BY THE END OF TODAY, I'M GOING TO QUIT. I HAD ENOUGH OF NUTTERS WHEN I WAS MINDING [redacted].
BORIS, I'M NOT HER, I'M NOT CRAZY. AND AS SOON AS THIS IS SORTED OUT I'LL...
YEAH?
YOU'LL WHAT?
I'M NOT SURE.
HEY, YOU REMEMBER THE *DAMSELS* ARTICLE?
YEAH.
THE BITCH WHO'S WRITING IT LEFT A MESSAGE ON MY MACHINE AT THE HOTEL. I DIDN'T TELL YOU ABOUT IT.
SHE FOUND OUT ABOUT VÉRONIQUE. SHE SPOKE TO VÉRONIQUE.
THE FRENCH BINT? I TOLD YOU SHE WAS BAD NEWS.
YEAH.
YOU NEVER TOLD HAZEL, DID YOU?
ABOUT VÉRO? NO.
OR THE OTHERS?
...NO.
DIDN'T THINK SO.
EXCUSE ME? CAN I ASK--?
NO, YOU CAN'T.
SO. FOX. DO YOU THINK SHE'S SOLD IT ON TO THE TABLOIDS?
HOW THE FUCK SHOULD I KNOW?
EASY, GIRL. RIGHT. DAMAGE CONTROL...
BUGGER. I WISH LARRY...
YEAH. SO DO I. BIT LATE NOW, THOUGH.

BORIS, WHAT'S THE BURGLAR ALARM CODE AGAIN?

1812. THINK OF THE OVERTURE.

UH-HUH.

THIS IS YOUR PLACE?

KIND-OF, YEAH...

OKAY. YOU TWO, SIT THERE. I HAVE TO LOOK AROUND.

LOOK, IF SHE'S NOT HERE, SHE'S PROBABLY JUST GONE TO STAY WITH A FRIEND OR SOMETHING...

SIT. OR MAKE COFFEE OR TEA, WHATEVER. BEER IN THE FRIDGE.

CAN I SMOKE IN HERE?

NO. OUTSIDE.

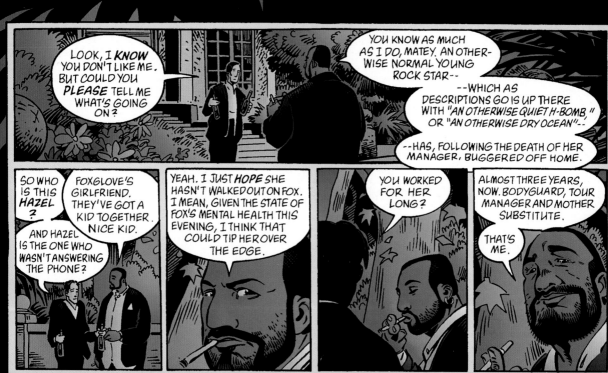

LOOK, I KNOW YOU DON'T LIKE ME. BUT COULD YOU PLEASE TELL ME WHAT'S GOING ON?

YOU KNOW AS MUCH AS I DO, MATEY. AN OTHERWISE NORMAL YOUNG ROCK STAR--

--WHICH AS DESCRIPTIONS GO IS UP THERE WITH "AN OTHERWISE QUIET H-BOMB," OR "AN OTHERWISE DRY OCEAN"--

--HAS, FOLLOWING THE DEATH OF HER MANAGER, BUGGERED OFF HOME.

SO WHO IS THIS HAZEL?

FOXGLOVE'S GIRLFRIEND. THEY'VE GOT A KID TOGETHER. NICE KID.

AND HAZEL IS THE ONE WHO WASN'T ANSWERING THE PHONE?

YEAH. I JUST HOPE SHE HASN'T WALKED OUT ON FOX. I MEAN, GIVEN THE STATE OF FOX'S MENTAL HEALTH THIS EVENING, I THINK THAT COULD TIP HER OVER THE EDGE.

YOU WORKED FOR HER LONG?

ALMOST THREE YEARS, NOW. BODYGUARD, TOUR MANAGER AND MOTHER SUBSTITUTE.

THAT'S ME.

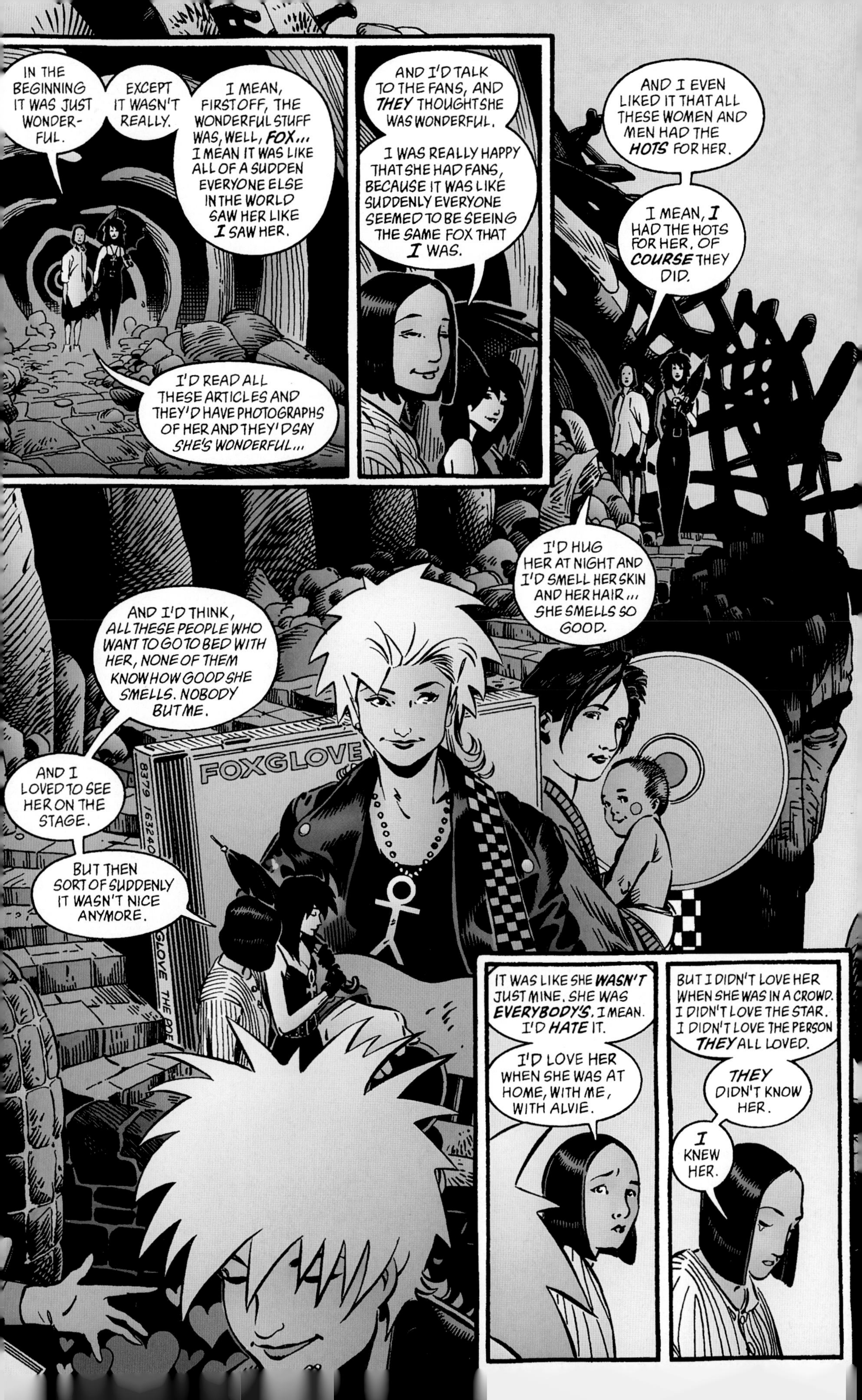
IN THE BEGINNING IT WAS JUST WONDER-FUL.
EXCEPT IT WASN'T REALLY.
I MEAN, FIRST OFF, THE WONDERFUL STUFF WAS, WELL, FOX... I MEAN IT WAS LIKE ALL OF A SUDDEN EVERYONE ELSE IN THE WORLD SAW HER LIKE I SAW HER.
I'D READ ALL THESE ARTICLES AND THEY'D HAVE PHOTOGRAPHS OF HER AND THEY'D SAY SHE'S WONDERFUL...
AND I'D TALK TO THE FANS, AND THEY THOUGHT SHE WAS WONDERFUL.
I WAS REALLY HAPPY THAT SHE HAD FANS, BECAUSE IT WAS LIKE SUDDENLY EVERYONE SEEMED TO BE SEEING THE SAME FOX THAT I WAS.
AND I EVEN LIKED IT THAT ALL THESE WOMEN AND MEN HAD THE HOTS FOR HER.
I MEAN, I HAD THE HOTS FOR HER, OF COURSE THEY DID.
I'D HUG HER AT NIGHT AND I'D SMELL HER SKIN AND HER HAIR... SHE SMELLS SO GOOD.
AND I'D THINK, ALL THESE PEOPLE WHO WANT TO GO TO BED WITH HER, NONE OF THEM KNOW HOW GOOD SHE SMELLS. NOBODY BUT ME.
FOXGLOVE
8379 16324
AND I LOVED TO SEE HER ON THE STAGE.
BUT THEN SORT OF SUDDENLY IT WASN'T NICE ANYMORE.
IT WAS LIKE SHE WASN'T JUST MINE. SHE WAS EVERYBODY'S. I MEAN. I'D HATE IT.
I'D LOVE HER WHEN SHE WAS AT HOME, WITH ME, WITH ALVIE.
BUT I DIDN'T LOVE HER WHEN SHE WAS IN A CROWD. I DIDN'T LOVE THE STAR. I DIDN'T LOVE THE PERSON THEY ALL LOVED.
THEY DIDN'T KNOW HER.
I KNEW HER.

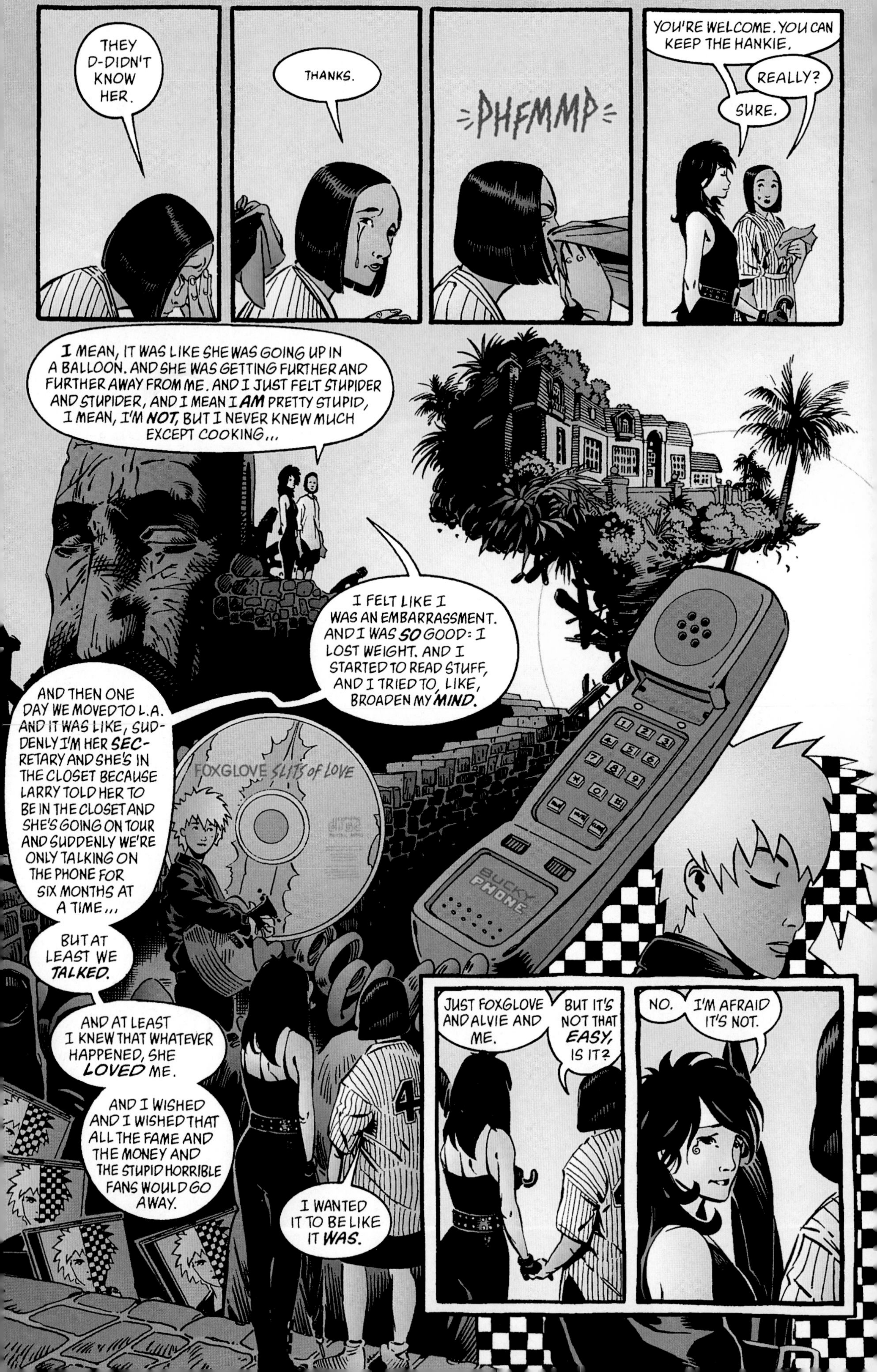

THEY D-DIDN'T KNOW HER.
THANKS.
PHFMMP
YOU'RE WELCOME. YOU CAN KEEP THE HANKIE.
REALLY?
SURE.
I MEAN, IT WAS LIKE SHE WAS GOING UP IN A BALLOON. AND SHE WAS GETTING FURTHER AND FURTHER AWAY FROM ME. AND I JUST FELT STUPIDER AND STUPIDER, AND I MEAN I AM PRETTY STUPID, I MEAN, I'M NOT, BUT I NEVER KNEW MUCH EXCEPT COOKING...
I FELT LIKE I WAS AN EMBARRASSMENT. AND I WAS SO GOOD: I LOST WEIGHT. AND I STARTED TO READ STUFF, AND I TRIED TO, LIKE, BROADEN MY MIND.
AND THEN ONE DAY WE MOVED TO L.A. AND IT WAS LIKE, SUDDENLY I'M HER SECRETARY AND SHE'S IN THE CLOSET BECAUSE LARRY TOLD HER TO BE IN THE CLOSET AND SHE'S GOING ON TOUR AND SUDDENLY WE'RE ONLY TALKING ON THE PHONE FOR SIX MONTHS AT A TIME...
FOXGLOVE SLITS of LOVE
BUCKY PHONE
BUT AT LEAST WE TALKED.
AND AT LEAST I KNEW THAT WHATEVER HAPPENED, SHE LOVED ME.
AND I WISHED AND I WISHED THAT ALL THE FAME AND THE MONEY AND THE STUPID HORRIBLE FANS WOULD GO AWAY.
I WANTED IT TO BE LIKE IT WAS.
JUST FOXGLOVE AND ALVIE AND ME.
BUT IT'S NOT THAT EASY, IS IT?
NO.
I'M AFRAID IT'S NOT.

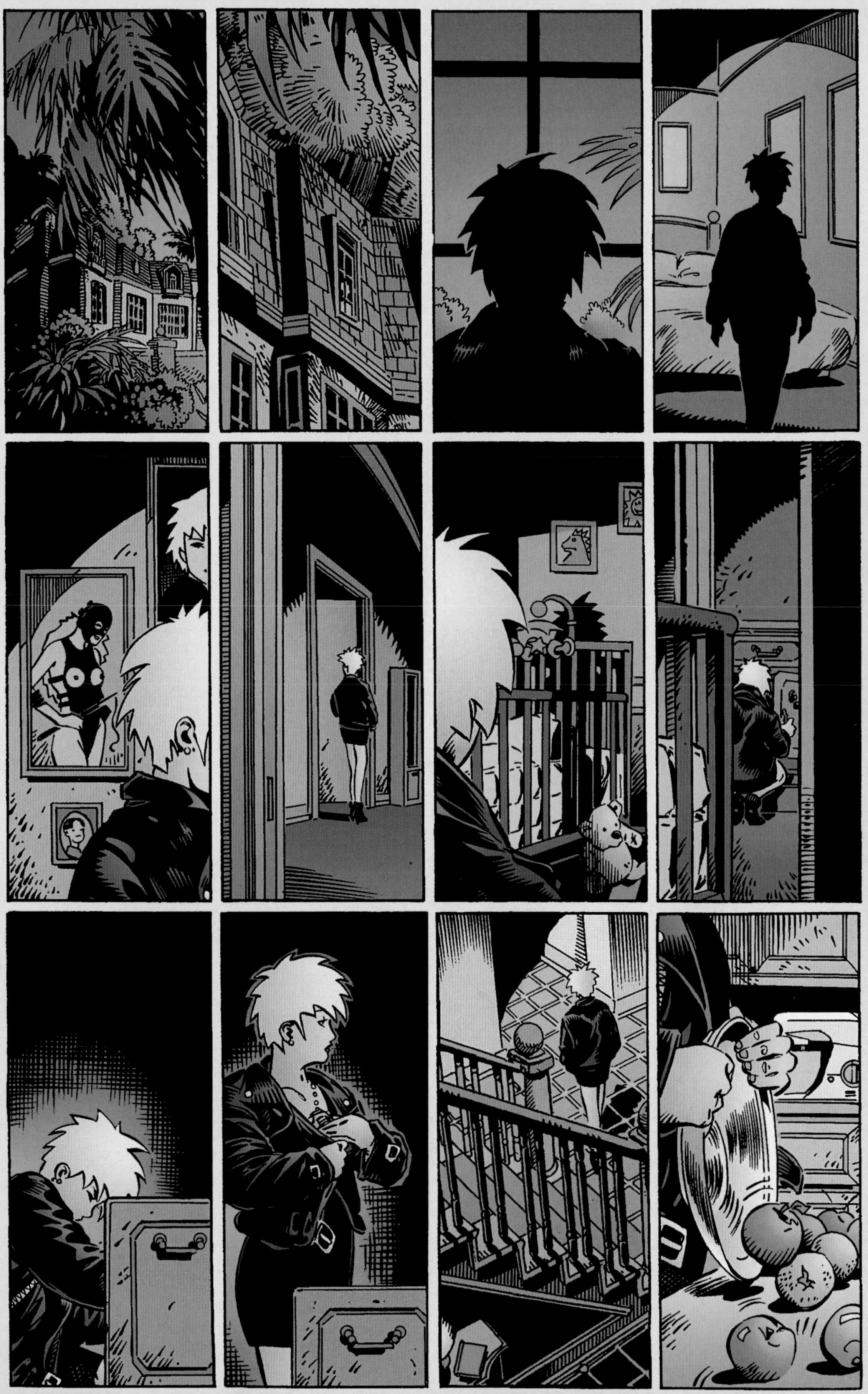

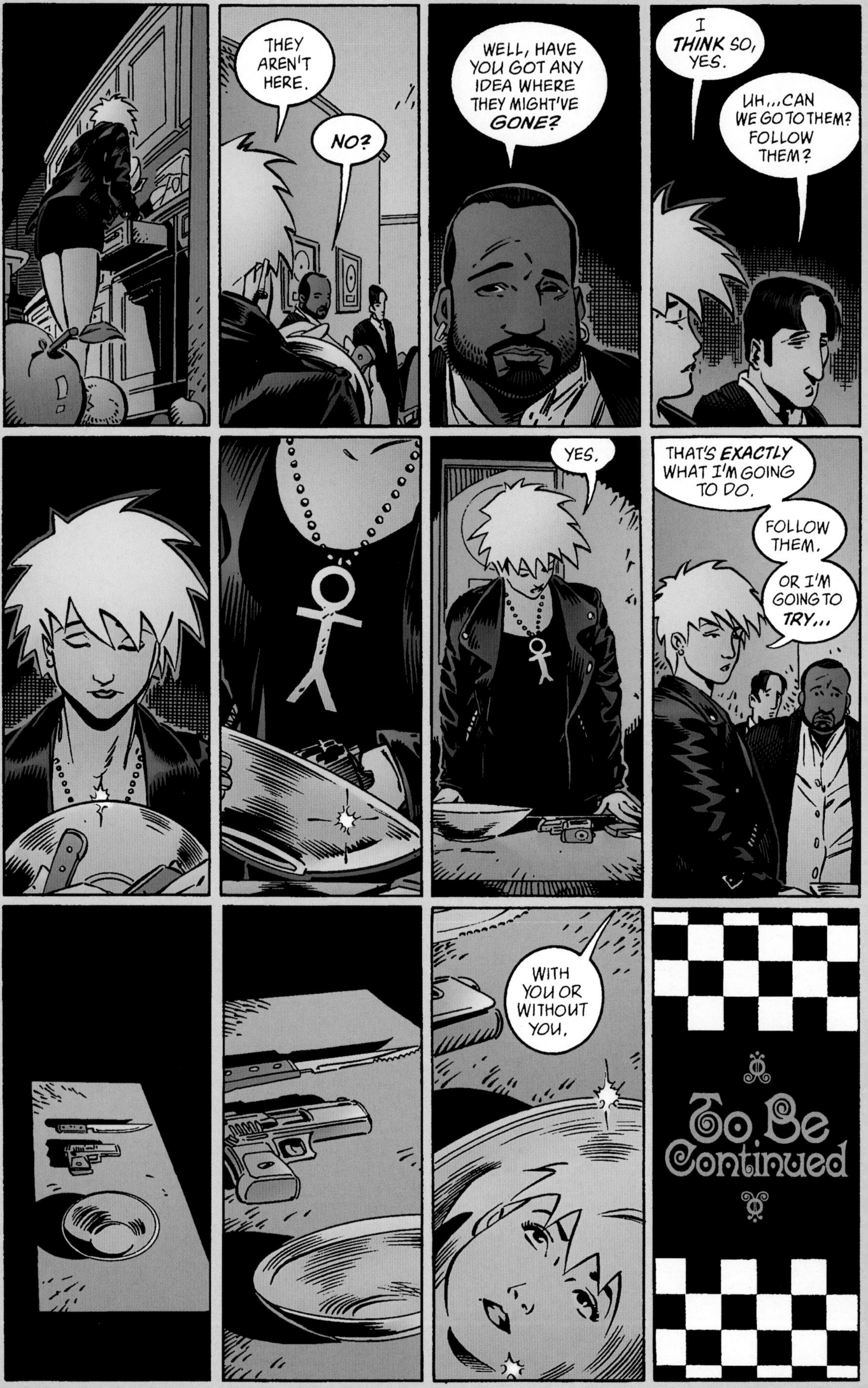
THEY AREN'T HERE.
NO?
WELL, HAVE YOU GOT ANY IDEA WHERE THEY MIGHT'VE GONE?
I THINK SO, YES.
UH... CAN WE GO TO THEM? FOLLOW THEM?
YES.
THAT'S EXACTLY WHAT I'M GOING TO DO.
FOLLOW THEM.
OR I'M GOING TO TRY...
WITH YOU OR WITHOUT YOU.
To Be Continued

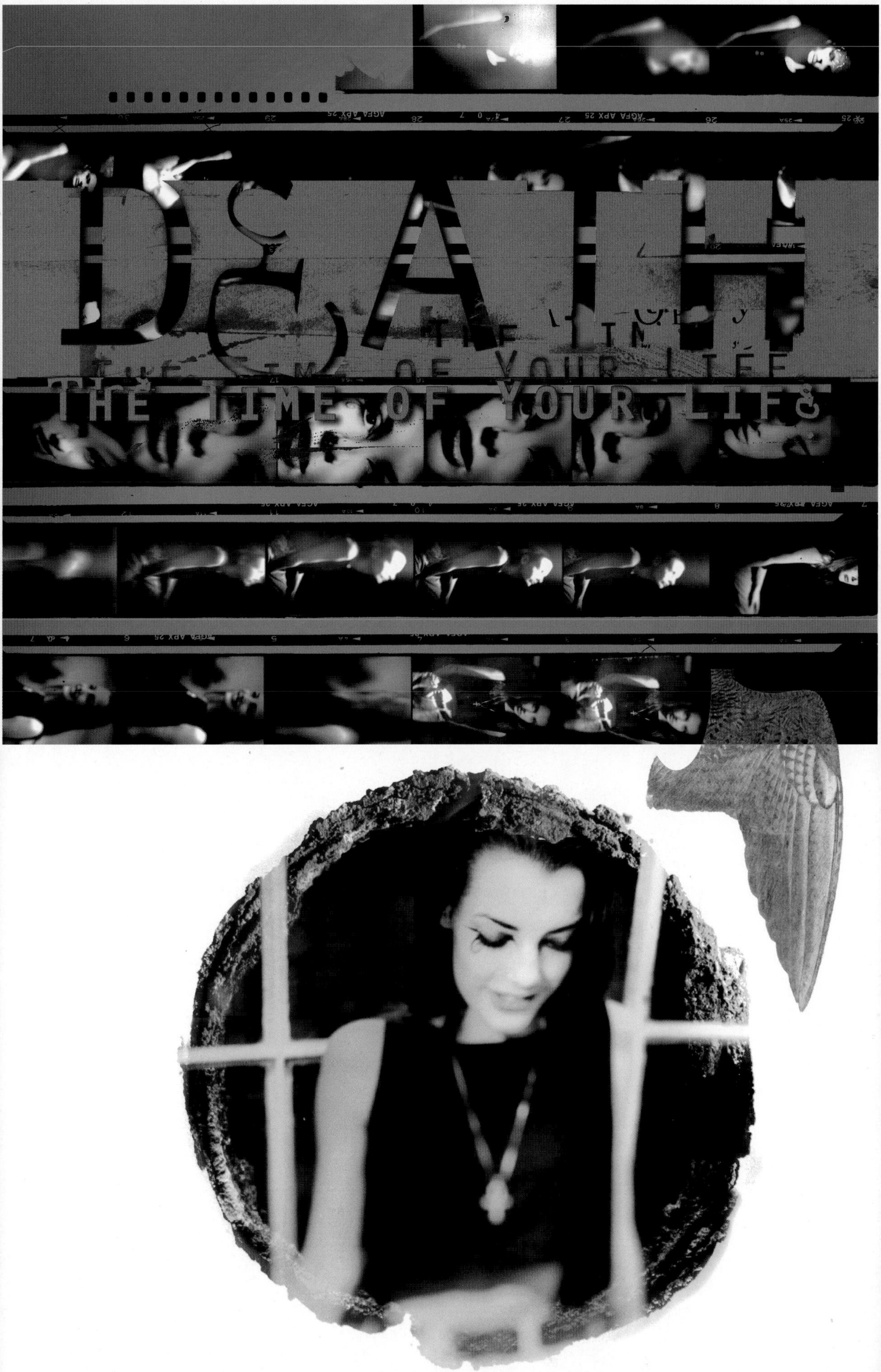
DEATH
THE TIME OF YOUR LIFE

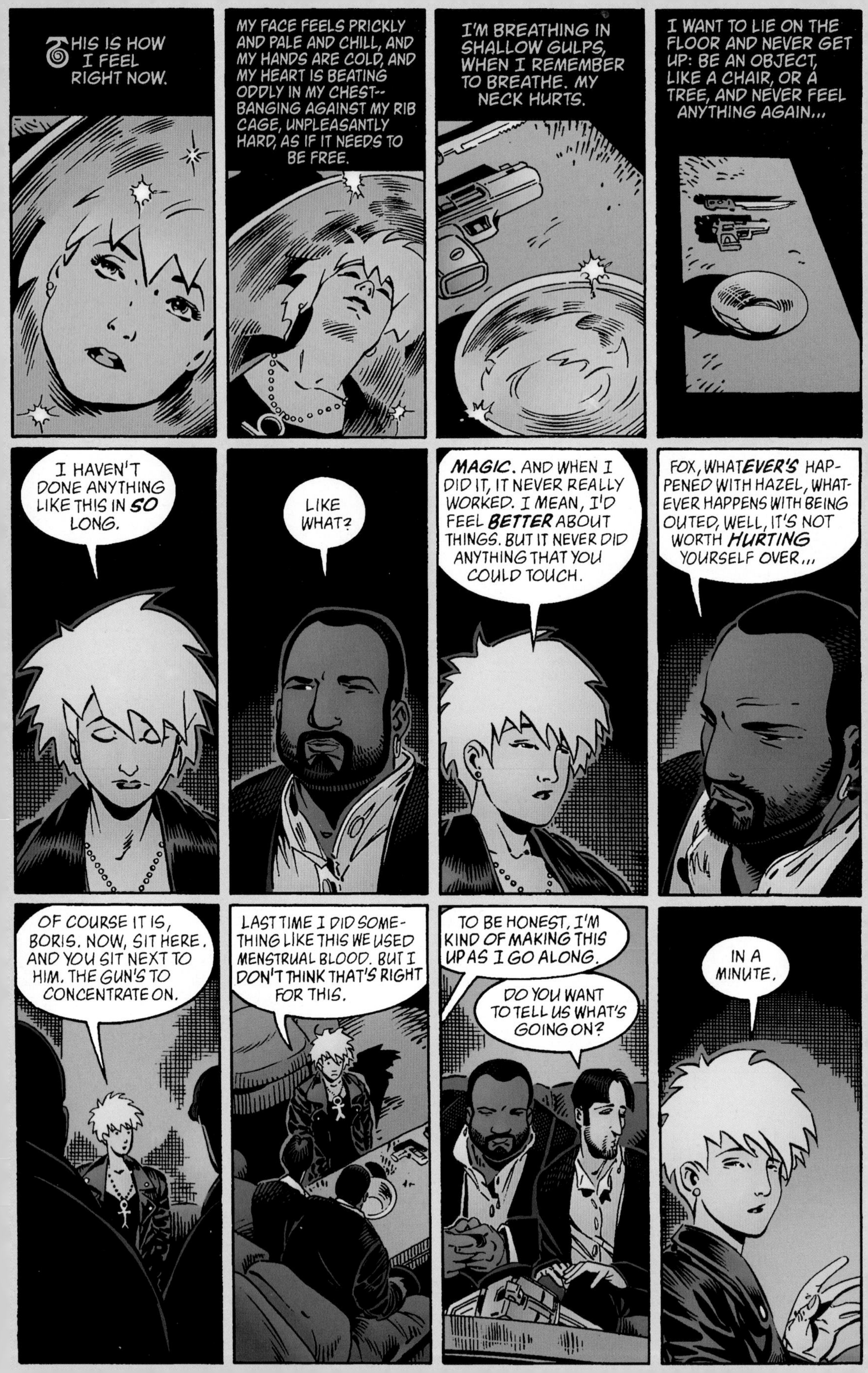
THIS IS HOW I FEEL RIGHT NOW.
MY FACE FEELS PRICKLY AND PALE AND CHILL, AND MY HANDS ARE COLD, AND MY HEART IS BEATING ODDLY IN MY CHEST-- BANGING AGAINST MY RIB CAGE, UNPLEASANTLY HARD, AS IF IT NEEDS TO BE FREE.
I'M BREATHING IN SHALLOW GULPS, WHEN I REMEMBER TO BREATHE. MY NECK HURTS.
I WANT TO LIE ON THE FLOOR AND NEVER GET UP: BE AN OBJECT, LIKE A CHAIR, OR A TREE, AND NEVER FEEL ANYTHING AGAIN...
I HAVEN'T DONE ANYTHING LIKE THIS IN SO LONG.
LIKE WHAT?
MAGIC. AND WHEN I DID IT, IT NEVER REALLY WORKED. I MEAN, I'D FEEL BETTER ABOUT THINGS. BUT IT NEVER DID ANYTHING THAT YOU COULD TOUCH.
FOX, WHATEVER'S HAPPENED WITH HAZEL, WHATEVER HAPPENS WITH BEING OUTED, WELL, IT'S NOT WORTH HURTING YOURSELF OVER...
OF COURSE IT IS, BORIS. NOW, SIT HERE. AND YOU SIT NEXT TO HIM. THE GUN'S TO CONCENTRATE ON.
LAST TIME I DID SOMETHING LIKE THIS WE USED MENSTRUAL BLOOD. BUT I DON'T THINK THAT'S RIGHT FOR THIS.
TO BE HONEST, I'M KIND OF MAKING THIS UP AS I GO ALONG.
DO YOU WANT TO TELL US WHAT'S GOING ON?
IN A MINUTE.

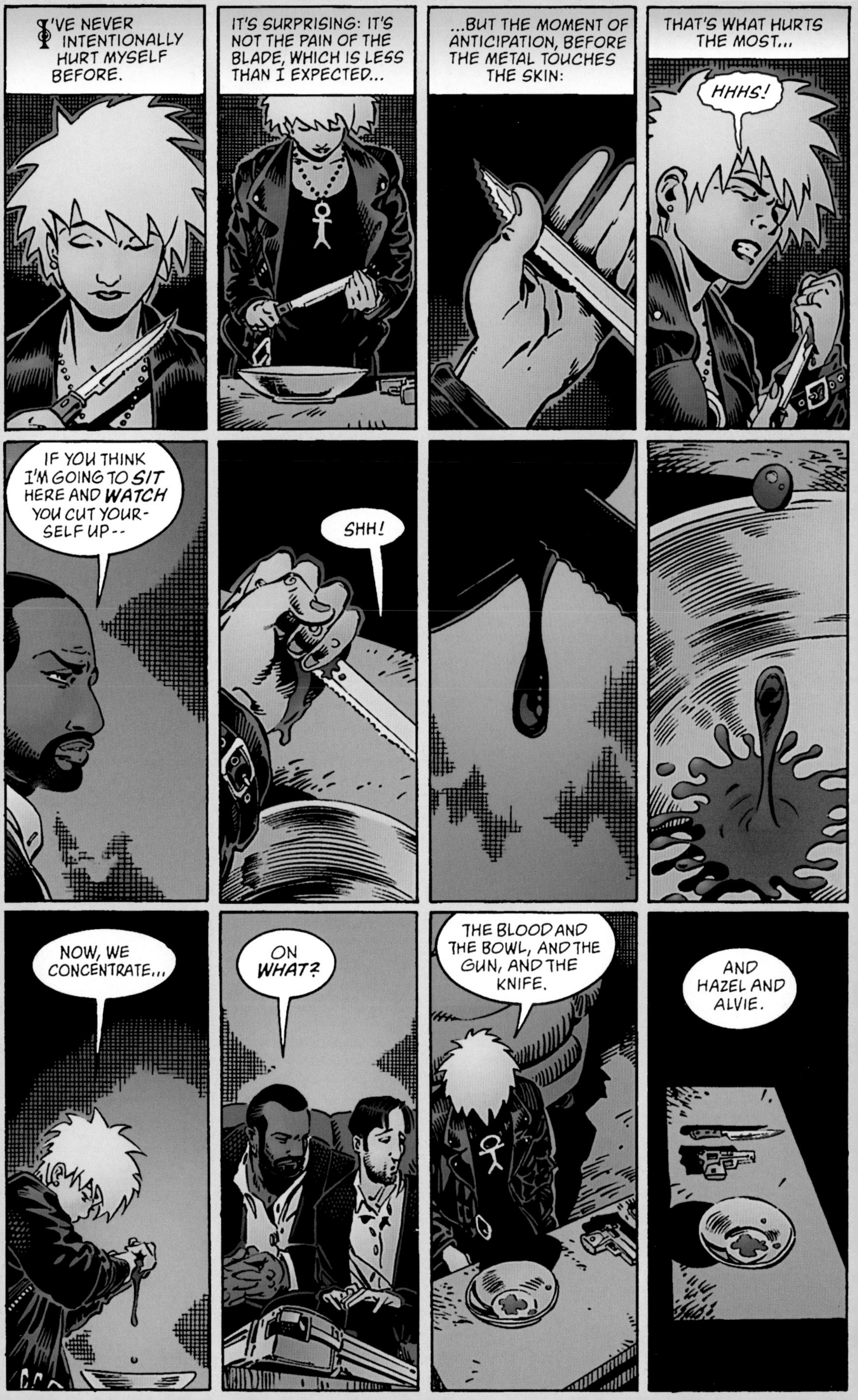
I'VE NEVER INTENTIONALLY HURT MYSELF BEFORE.
IT'S SURPRISING: IT'S NOT THE PAIN OF THE BLADE, WHICH IS LESS THAN I EXPECTED...
...BUT THE MOMENT OF ANTICIPATION, BEFORE THE METAL TOUCHES THE SKIN:
THAT'S WHAT HURTS THE MOST...
HHHS!
IF YOU THINK I'M GOING TO SIT HERE AND WATCH YOU CUT YOURSELF UP--
SHH!
NOW, WE CONCENTRATE...
ON WHAT?
THE BLOOD AND THE BOWL, AND THE GUN, AND THE KNIFE.
AND HAZEL AND ALVIE.

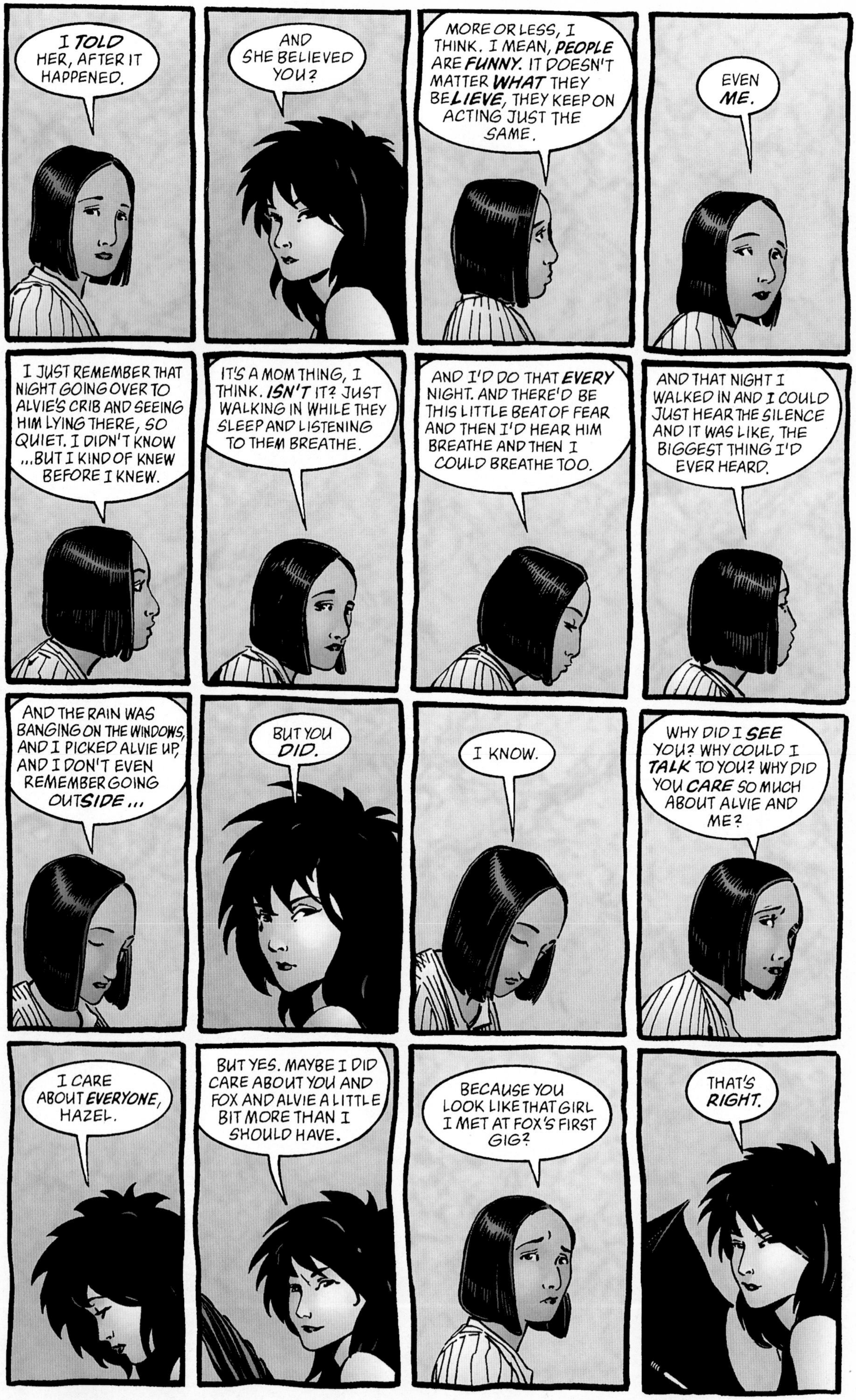
I TOLD HER, AFTER IT HAPPENED.
AND SHE BELIEVED YOU?
MORE OR LESS, I THINK. I MEAN, PEOPLE ARE FUNNY. IT DOESN'T MATTER WHAT THEY BELIEVE, THEY KEEP ON ACTING JUST THE SAME.
EVEN ME.
I JUST REMEMBER THAT NIGHT GOING OVER TO ALVIE'S CRIB AND SEEING HIM LYING THERE, SO QUIET. I DIDN'T KNOW ...BUT I KIND OF KNEW BEFORE I KNEW.
IT'S A MOM THING, I THINK. ISN'T IT? JUST WALKING IN WHILE THEY SLEEP AND LISTENING TO THEM BREATHE.
AND I'D DO THAT EVERY NIGHT. AND THERE'D BE THIS LITTLE BEAT OF FEAR AND THEN I'D HEAR HIM BREATHE AND THEN I COULD BREATHE TOO.
AND THAT NIGHT I WALKED IN AND I COULD JUST HEAR THE SILENCE AND IT WAS LIKE, THE BIGGEST THING I'D EVER HEARD.
AND THE RAIN WAS BANGING ON THE WINDOWS, AND I PICKED ALVIE UP, AND I DON'T EVEN REMEMBER GOING OUTSIDE...
BUT YOU DID.
I KNOW.
WHY DID I SEE YOU? WHY COULD I TALK TO YOU? WHY DID YOU CARE SO MUCH ABOUT ALVIE AND ME?
I CARE ABOUT EVERYONE, HAZEL.
BUT YES. MAYBE I DID CARE ABOUT YOU AND FOX AND ALVIE A LITTLE BIT MORE THAN I SHOULD HAVE.
BECAUSE YOU LOOK LIKE THAT GIRL I MET AT FOX'S FIRST GIG?
THAT'S RIGHT.

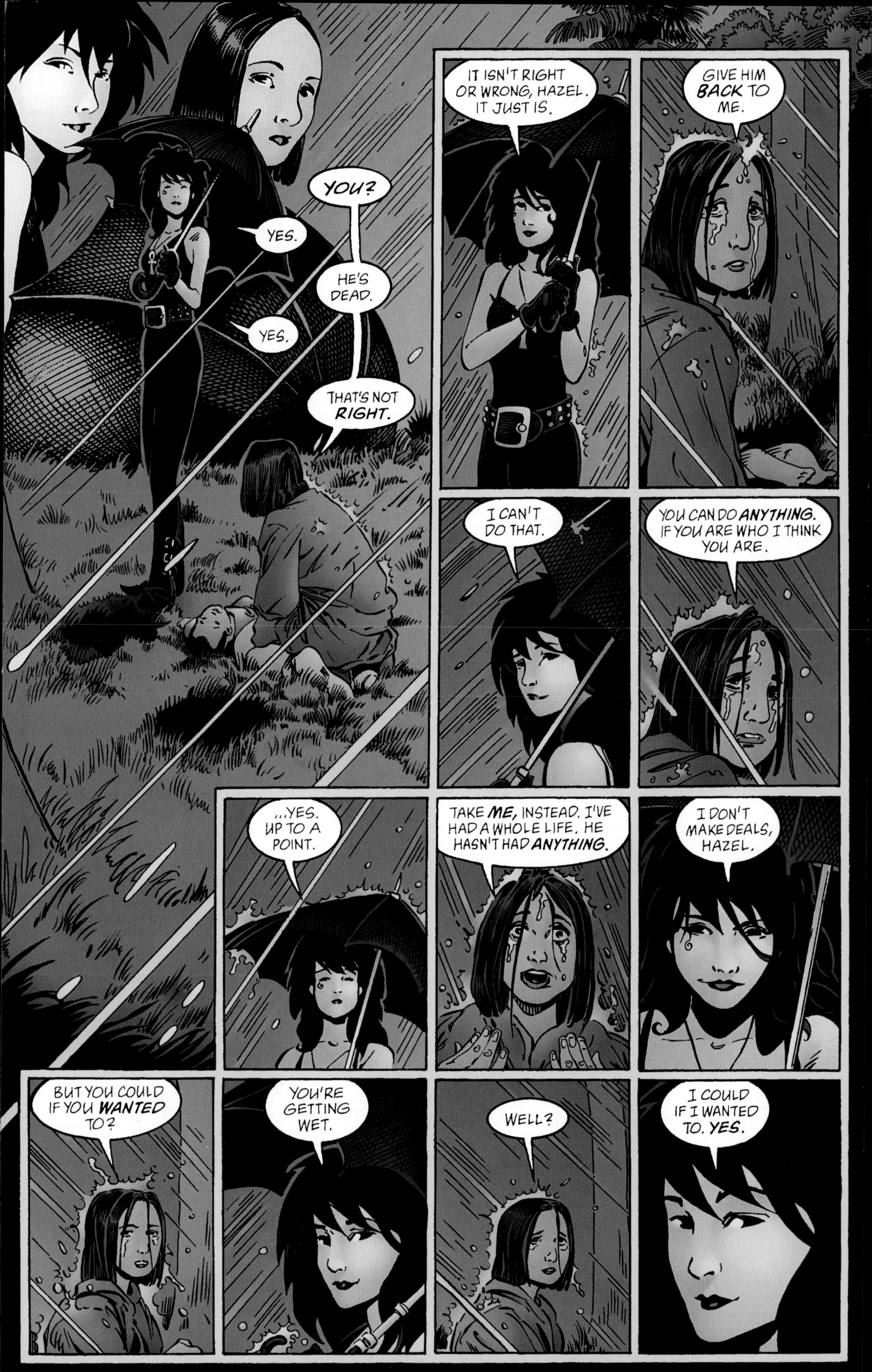
YOU?
YES.
HE'S DEAD.
YES.
THAT'S NOT RIGHT.
IT ISN'T RIGHT OR WRONG, HAZEL. IT JUST IS.
GIVE HIM BACK TO ME.
I CAN'T DO THAT.
YOU CAN DO ANYTHING. IF YOU ARE WHO I THINK YOU ARE.
...YES. UP TO A POINT.
TAKE ME, INSTEAD. I'VE HAD A WHOLE LIFE. HE HASN'T HAD ANYTHING.
I DON'T MAKE DEALS, HAZEL.
BUT YOU COULD IF YOU WANTED TO?
YOU'RE GETTING WET.
WELL?
I COULD IF I WANTED TO. YES.

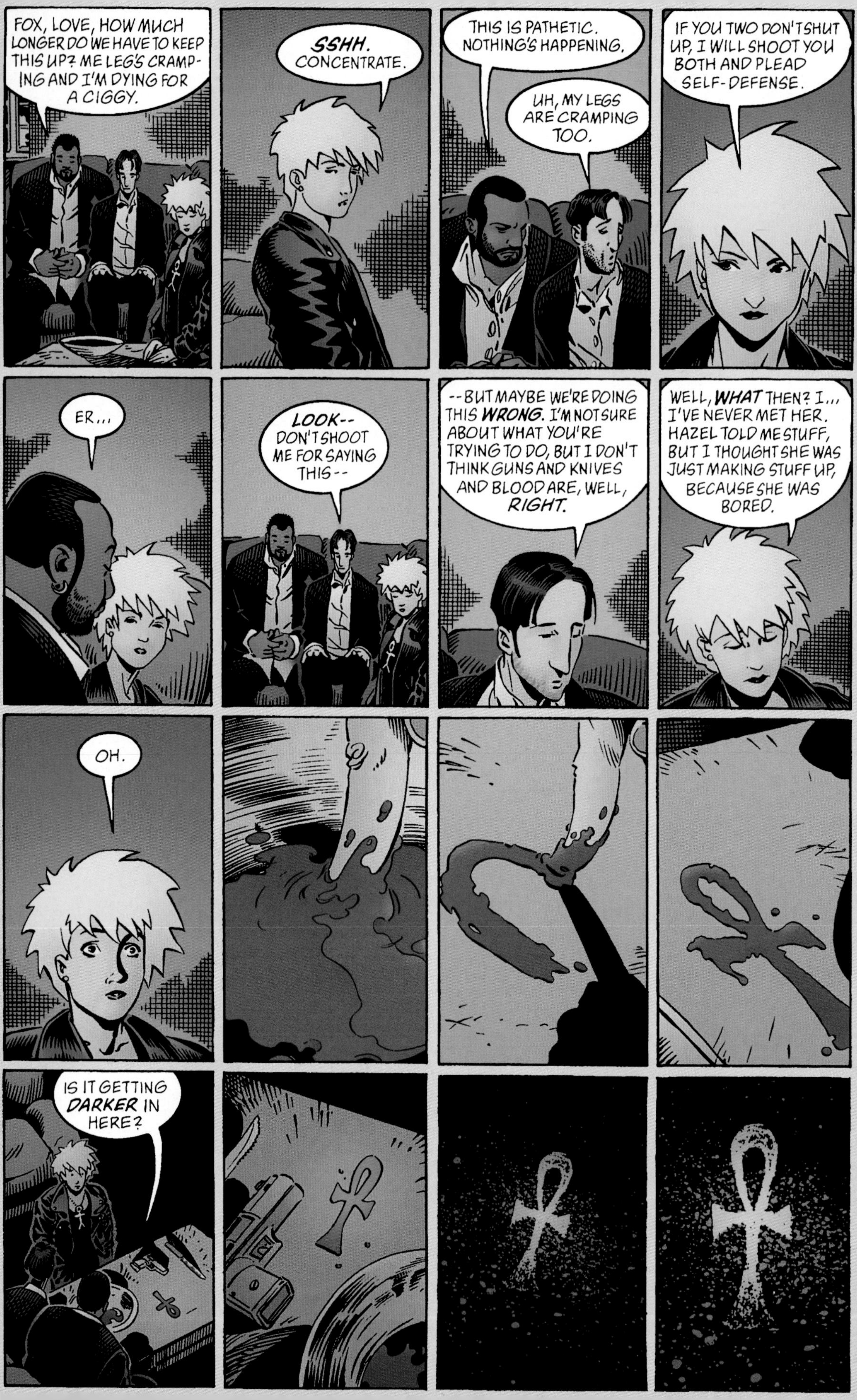
FOX, LOVE, HOW MUCH LONGER DO WE HAVE TO KEEP THIS UP? ME LEG'S CRAMPING AND I'M DYING FOR A CIGGY.
SSHH. CONCENTRATE.
THIS IS PATHETIC. NOTHING'S HAPPENING.
UH, MY LEGS ARE CRAMPING TOO.
IF YOU TWO DON'T SHUT UP, I WILL SHOOT YOU BOTH AND PLEAD SELF-DEFENSE.
ER...
LOOK-- DON'T SHOOT ME FOR SAYING THIS--
--BUT MAYBE WE'RE DOING THIS WRONG. I'M NOT SURE ABOUT WHAT YOU'RE TRYING TO DO, BUT I DON'T THINK GUNS AND KNIVES AND BLOOD ARE, WELL, RIGHT.
WELL, WHAT THEN? I... I'VE NEVER MET HER. HAZEL TOLD ME STUFF, BUT I THOUGHT SHE WAS JUST MAKING STUFF UP, BECAUSE SHE WAS BORED.
OH.
IS IT GETTING DARKER IN HERE?

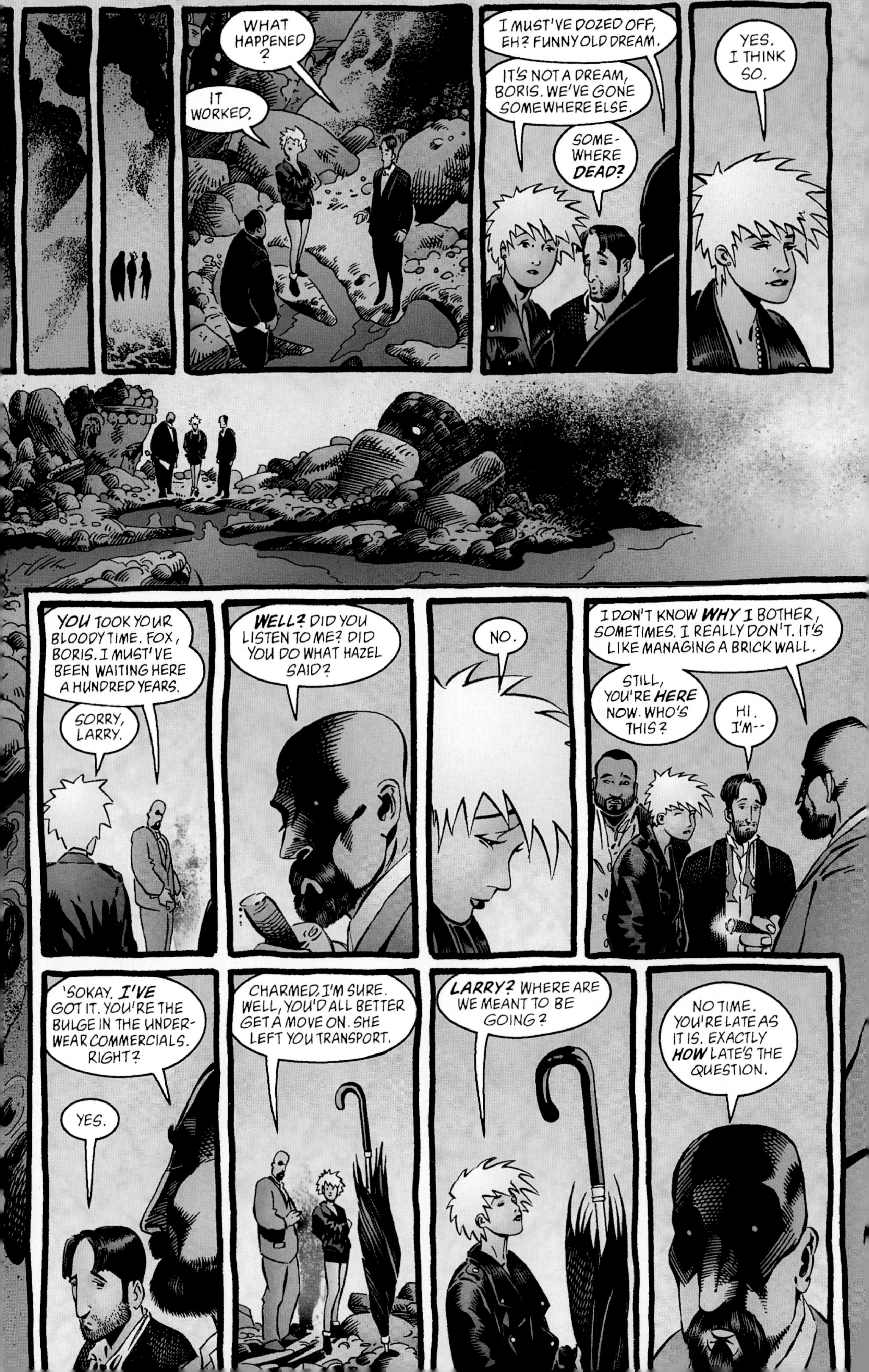
WHAT HAPPENED ?
IT WORKED.
I MUST'VE DOZED OFF, EH? FUNNY OLD DREAM.
IT'S NOT A DREAM, BORIS. WE'VE GONE SOMEWHERE ELSE.
SOME-WHERE DEAD?
YES. I THINK SO.
YOU TOOK YOUR BLOODY TIME. FOX, BORIS. I MUST'VE BEEN WAITING HERE A HUNDRED YEARS.
SORRY, LARRY.
WELL? DID YOU LISTEN TO ME? DID YOU DO WHAT HAZEL SAID?
NO.
I DON'T KNOW WHY I BOTHER, SOMETIMES. I REALLY DON'T. IT'S LIKE MANAGING A BRICK WALL.
STILL, YOU'RE HERE NOW. WHO'S THIS?
HI. I'M--
'SOKAY. I'VE GOT IT. YOU'RE THE BULGE IN THE UNDER-WEAR COMMERCIALS. RIGHT?
YES.
CHARMED, I'M SURE. WELL, YOU'D ALL BETTER GET A MOVE ON. SHE LEFT YOU TRANSPORT.
LARRY? WHERE ARE WE MEANT TO BE GOING?
NO TIME. YOU'RE LATE AS IT IS. EXACTLY HOW LATE'S THE QUESTION.

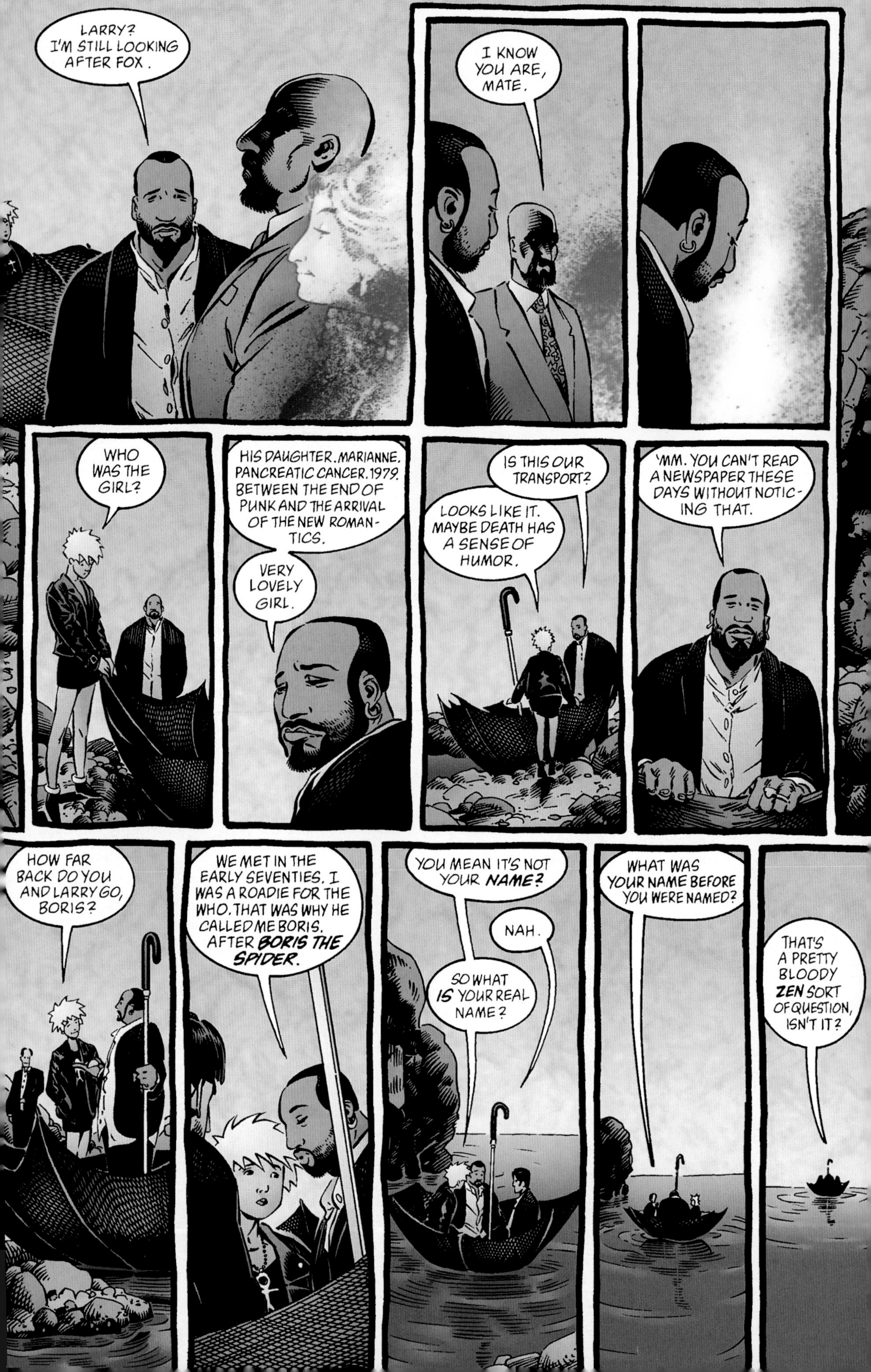
LARRY? I'M STILL LOOKING AFTER FOX.
I KNOW YOU ARE, MATE.
WHO WAS THE GIRL?
HIS DAUGHTER. MARIANNE. PANCREATIC CANCER. 1979. BETWEEN THE END OF PUNK AND THE ARRIVAL OF THE NEW ROMAN-TICS.
VERY LOVELY GIRL.
IS THIS OUR TRANSPORT?
LOOKS LIKE IT. MAYBE DEATH HAS A SENSE OF HUMOR.
'MM. YOU CAN'T READ A NEWSPAPER THESE DAYS WITHOUT NOTIC-ING THAT.
HOW FAR BACK DO YOU AND LARRY GO, BORIS?
WE MET IN THE EARLY SEVENTIES. I WAS A ROADIE FOR THE WHO. THAT WAS WHY HE CALLED ME BORIS. AFTER **BORIS THE SPIDER**.
YOU MEAN IT'S NOT YOUR **NAME?**
NAH.
SO WHAT **IS** YOUR REAL NAME?
WHAT WAS YOUR NAME BEFORE YOU WERE NAMED?
THAT'S A PRETTY BLOODY **ZEN** SORT OF QUESTION, ISN'T IT?

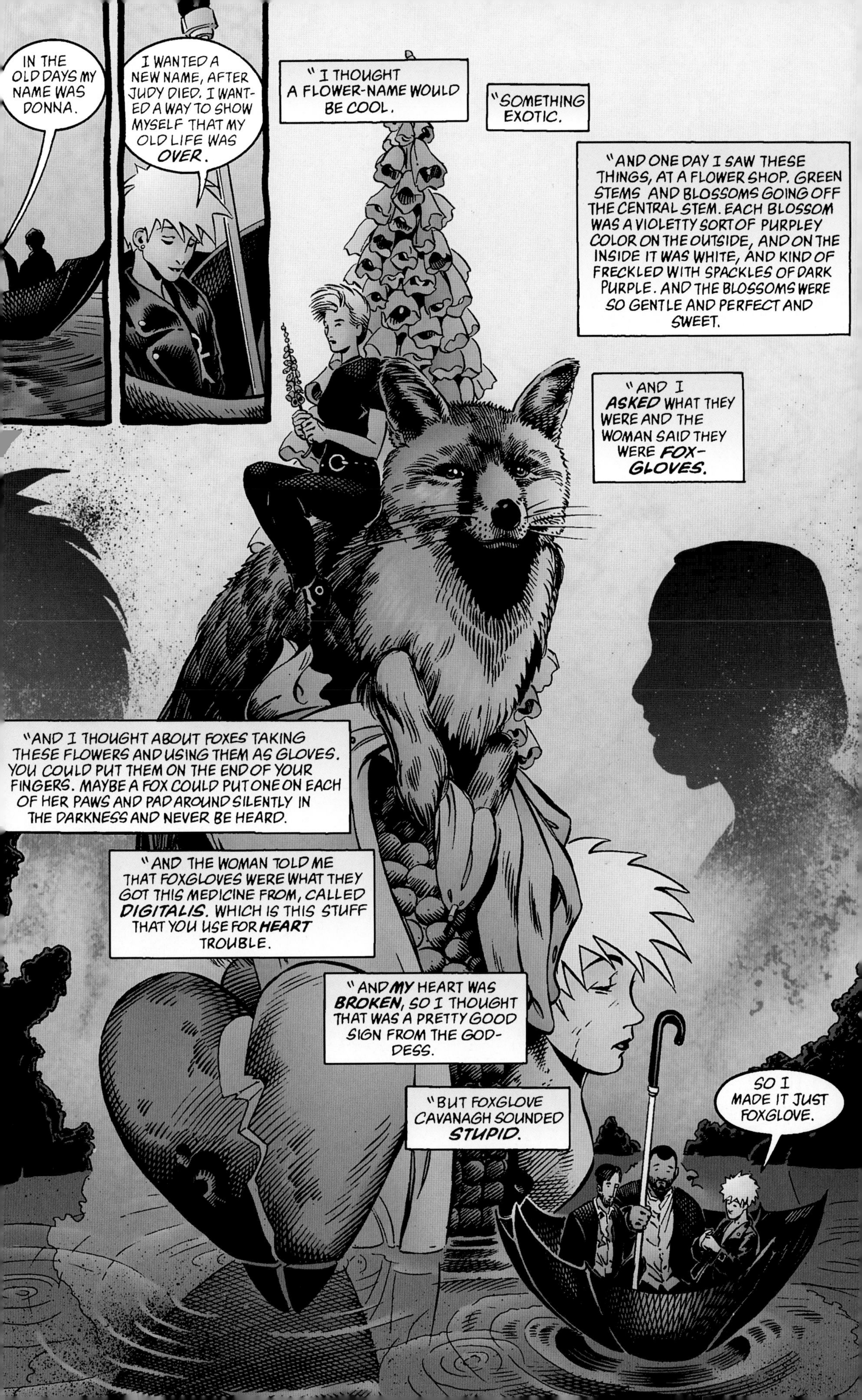

IN THE OLD DAYS MY NAME WAS DONNA.
I WANTED A NEW NAME, AFTER JUDY DIED. I WANTED A WAY TO SHOW MYSELF THAT MY OLD LIFE WAS OVER.
"I THOUGHT A FLOWER-NAME WOULD BE COOL.
"SOMETHING EXOTIC.
"AND ONE DAY I SAW THESE THINGS, AT A FLOWER SHOP. GREEN STEMS AND BLOSSOMS GOING OFF THE CENTRAL STEM. EACH BLOSSOM WAS A VIOLETTY SORT OF PURPLEY COLOR ON THE OUTSIDE, AND ON THE INSIDE IT WAS WHITE, AND KIND OF FRECKLED WITH SPACKLES OF DARK PURPLE. AND THE BLOSSOMS WERE SO GENTLE AND PERFECT AND SWEET.
"AND I ASKED WHAT THEY WERE AND THE WOMAN SAID THEY WERE FOX-GLOVES.
"AND I THOUGHT ABOUT FOXES TAKING THESE FLOWERS AND USING THEM AS GLOVES. YOU COULD PUT THEM ON THE END OF YOUR FINGERS. MAYBE A FOX COULD PUT ONE ON EACH OF HER PAWS AND PAD AROUND SILENTLY IN THE DARKNESS AND NEVER BE HEARD.
"AND THE WOMAN TOLD ME THAT FOXGLOVES WERE WHAT THEY GOT THIS MEDICINE FROM, CALLED DIGITALIS. WHICH IS THIS STUFF THAT YOU USE FOR HEART TROUBLE.
"AND MY HEART WAS BROKEN, SO I THOUGHT THAT WAS A PRETTY GOOD SIGN FROM THE GOD-DESS.
"BUT FOXGLOVE CAVANAGH SOUNDED STUPID.
SO I MADE IT JUST FOXGLOVE.

SHE'S COMING.

REALLY?

SURE.

I HOPED SHE WOULD. I MEAN, I KNEW SHE WOULD.

SO, LISTEN, WAS SHE YOU, THEN, THE GIRL IN THE TOP HAT AT FOX'S FIRST GIG?

KIND OF.

I GOT THIS AWFUL CRUSH ON HER. I KEPT THINKING ABOUT HER. WHEN YOU TURNED UP FIRST I THOUGHT THAT WAS WHO IT WAS-- HER.

NO. NOT REALLY.

AM I DEAD?

IS ALVIE?

NO.

NOT YET.

CAN I ASK A STUPID QUESTION?

SURE. ASK AWAY.

IT'S SORT OF MORE THAN ONE QUESTION. BUT, LOOK, UM, WHY DO WE HURT? WHY DO WE DIE? WHY ISN'T LIFE GOOD ALL THE TIME? WHY ISN'T IT FAIR?

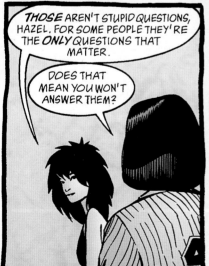

THOSE AREN'T STUPID QUESTIONS, HAZEL. FOR SOME PEOPLE THEY'RE THE ONLY QUESTIONS THAT MATTER.

DOES THAT MEAN YOU WON'T ANSWER THEM?

SURE, I'LL ANSWER. BUT IT'S KIND OF A BIG SUBJECT, AND IT'S GOT LOTS OF ANSWERS. AND THE ANSWERS DON'T REALLY MEAN ANYTHING-- THEY AREN'T STUPID QUESTIONS BUT THEY COULD JUST AS WELL BE "WHEN IS PURPLE?" OR "WHY DOES THURSDAY?", IF YOU SEE WHAT I MEAN...

NOT REALLY.

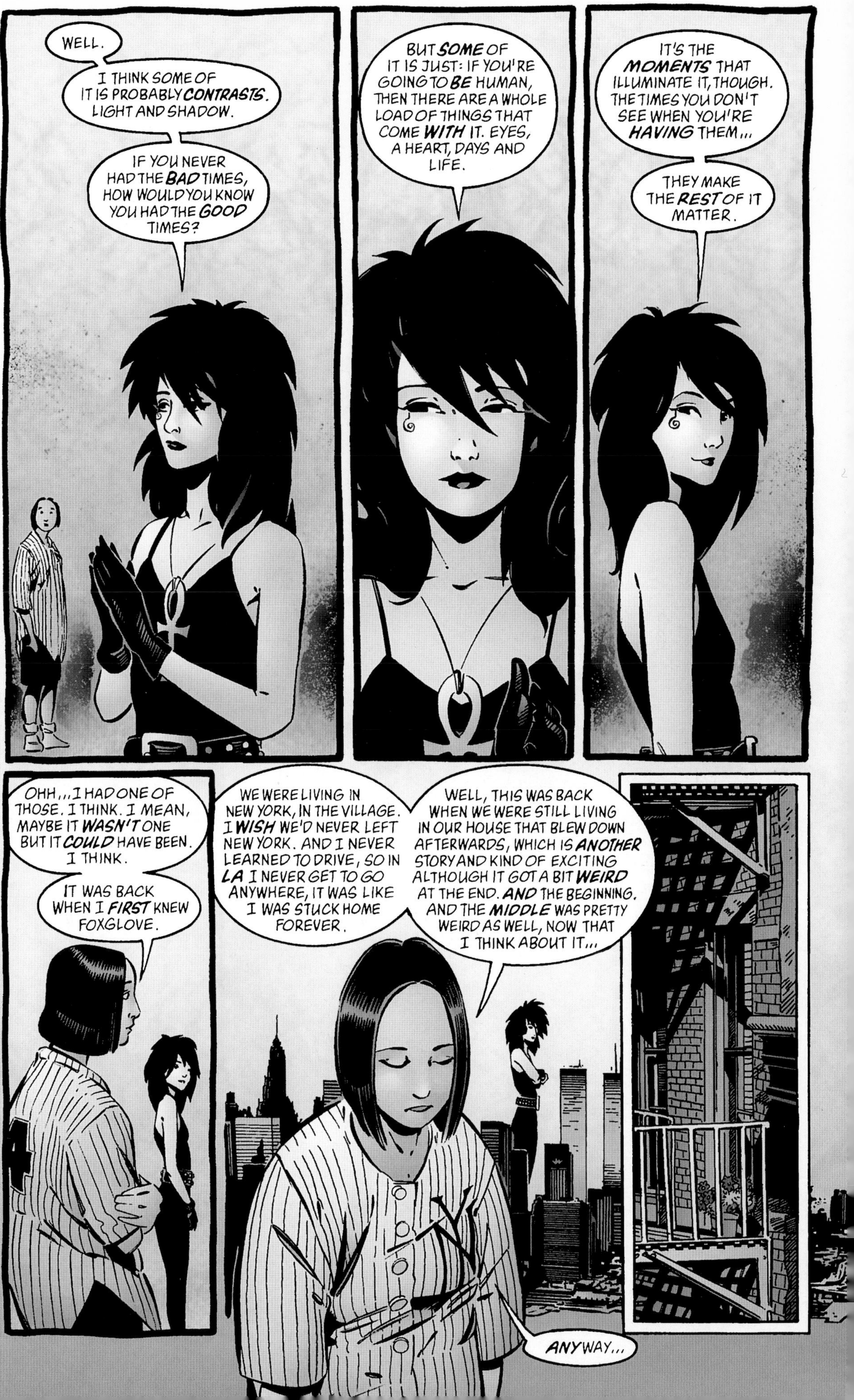
WELL.
I THINK SOME OF IT IS PROBABLY CONTRASTS. LIGHT AND SHADOW.
IF YOU NEVER HAD THE BAD TIMES, HOW WOULD YOU KNOW YOU HAD THE GOOD TIMES?
BUT SOME OF IT IS JUST: IF YOU'RE GOING TO BE HUMAN, THEN THERE ARE A WHOLE LOAD OF THINGS THAT COME WITH IT. EYES, A HEART, DAYS AND LIFE.
IT'S THE MOMENTS THAT ILLUMINATE IT, THOUGH. THE TIMES YOU DON'T SEE WHEN YOU'RE HAVING THEM...
THEY MAKE THE REST OF IT MATTER.
OHH...I HAD ONE OF THOSE. I THINK. I MEAN, MAYBE IT WASN'T ONE BUT IT COULD HAVE BEEN. I THINK.
IT WAS BACK WHEN I FIRST KNEW FOXGLOVE.
WE WERE LIVING IN NEW YORK, IN THE VILLAGE. I WISH WE'D NEVER LEFT NEW YORK. AND I NEVER LEARNED TO DRIVE, SO IN LA I NEVER GET TO GO ANYWHERE, IT WAS LIKE I WAS STUCK HOME FOREVER.
WELL, THIS WAS BACK WHEN WE WERE STILL LIVING IN OUR HOUSE THAT BLEW DOWN AFTERWARDS, WHICH IS ANOTHER STORY AND KIND OF EXCITING ALTHOUGH IT GOT A BIT WEIRD AT THE END. AND THE BEGINNING. AND THE MIDDLE WAS PRETTY WEIRD AS WELL, NOW THAT I THINK ABOUT IT...
ANYWAY...

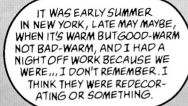

IT WAS EARLY SUMMER IN NEW YORK, LATE MAY MAYBE, WHEN IT'S WARM BUT GOOD-WARM NOT BAD-WARM, AND I HAD A NIGHT OFF WORK BECAUSE WE WERE... I DON'T REMEMBER. I THINK THEY WERE REDECORATING OR SOMETHING.

AND FOX HAD A LIBRARY BOOK.

"AND SHE WAS SITTING IN THE PARK WITH HER BOOK WHEN I GOT THERE, AND I BOUGHT AN ICE CREAM FOR ME AND AN ICE CREAM FOR HER.

"AND I SAT WHILE SHE FINISHED HER BOOK, AND THEN WE WENT FOR A WALK, ONLY IT WASN'T A WALK, IT WAS KIND OF A *WANDER*.

WE HELD HANDS.

"AND WE WALKED THROUGH LITTLE STREETS I DIDN'T EVER REMEMBER GOING DOWN BEFORE, AND WE ATE OUR ICE CREAMS, AND TALKED ABOUT LIFE...

"...SILLY THINGS. *I* TALKED ABOUT HOW I WANTED TO OPEN MY OWN RESTAURANT, AND *SHE* TALKED ABOUT WRITING HER STORY-THINGS AND HOW SHE WAS GOING TO PHOTOCOPY THEM AND LEAVE THEM ON PEOPLE'S WINDSHIELDS AND IN THEIR MAIL AS A SURPRISE.

AND THEN I STARTED HUMMING THIS SONG BY ELVIS COSTELLO, CALLED *HOOVER FACTORY*, AND I THOUGHT I WAS THE ONLY PERSON IN THE WORLD WHO KNEW IT. BUT FOX STARTED SINGING ALONG. "

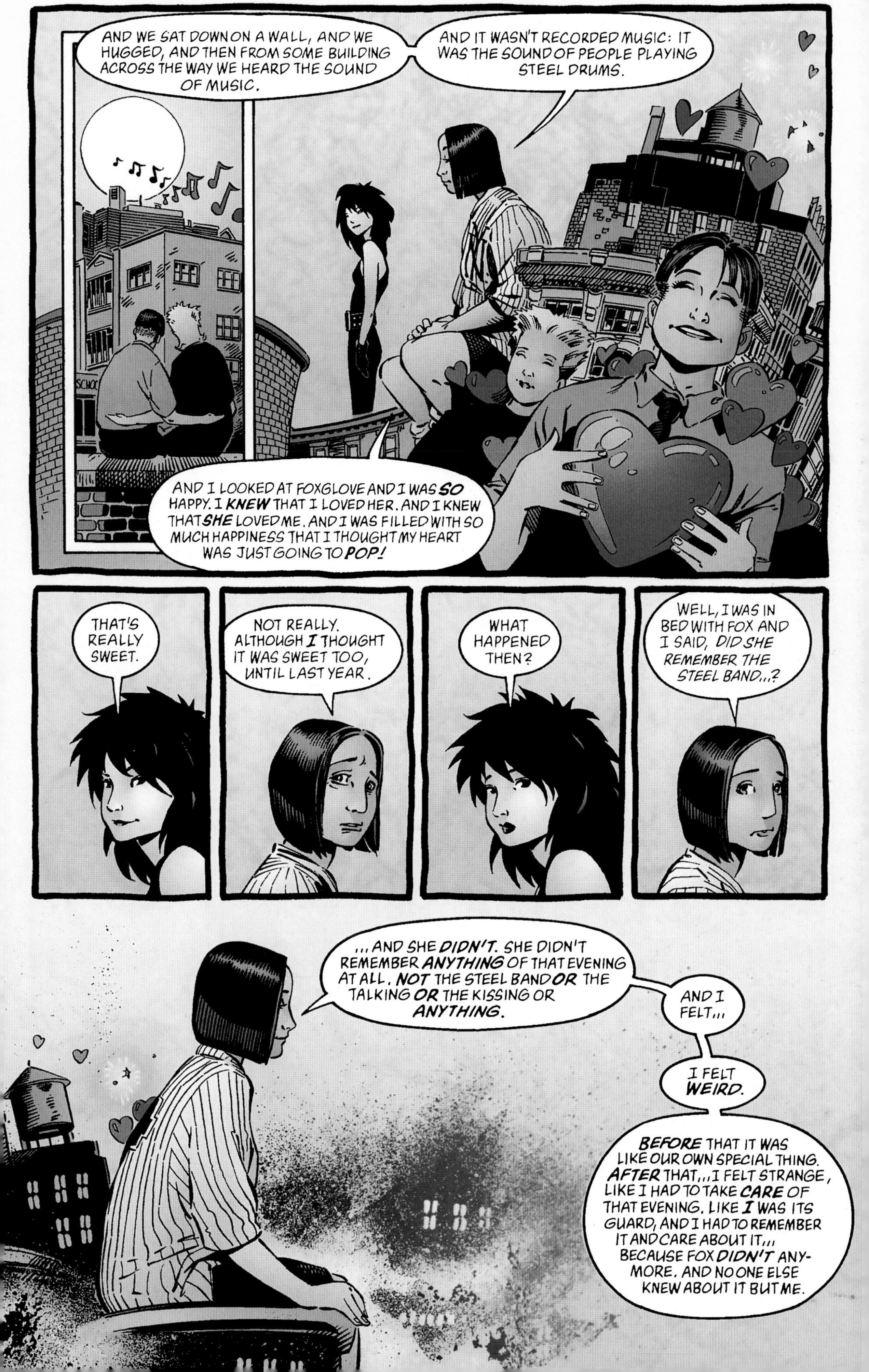
AND WE SAT DOWN ON A WALL, AND WE HUGGED, AND THEN FROM SOME BUILDING ACROSS THE WAY WE HEARD THE SOUND OF MUSIC.
AND IT WASN'T RECORDED MUSIC: IT WAS THE SOUND OF PEOPLE PLAYING STEEL DRUMS.
AND I LOOKED AT FOXGLOVE AND I WAS **SO** HAPPY. I **KNEW** THAT I LOVED HER. AND I KNEW THAT **SHE** LOVED ME. AND I WAS FILLED WITH SO MUCH HAPPINESS THAT I THOUGHT MY HEART WAS JUST GOING TO **POP!**
THAT'S REALLY SWEET.
NOT REALLY. ALTHOUGH **I** THOUGHT IT WAS SWEET TOO, UNTIL LAST YEAR.
WHAT HAPPENED THEN?
WELL, I WAS IN BED WITH FOX AND I SAID, *DID SHE REMEMBER THE STEEL BAND...?*
...AND SHE **DIDN'T**. SHE DIDN'T REMEMBER **ANYTHING** OF THAT EVENING AT ALL. **NOT** THE STEEL BAND **OR** THE TALKING **OR** THE KISSING OR **ANYTHING**.
AND I FELT...
I FELT **WEIRD**.
BEFORE THAT IT WAS LIKE OUR OWN SPECIAL THING. **AFTER** THAT... I FELT STRANGE, LIKE I HAD TO TAKE **CARE** OF THAT EVENING. LIKE **I** WAS ITS GUARD, AND I HAD TO REMEMBER IT AND CARE ABOUT IT... BECAUSE FOX **DIDN'T** ANYMORE. AND NO ONE ELSE KNEW ABOUT IT BUT ME.

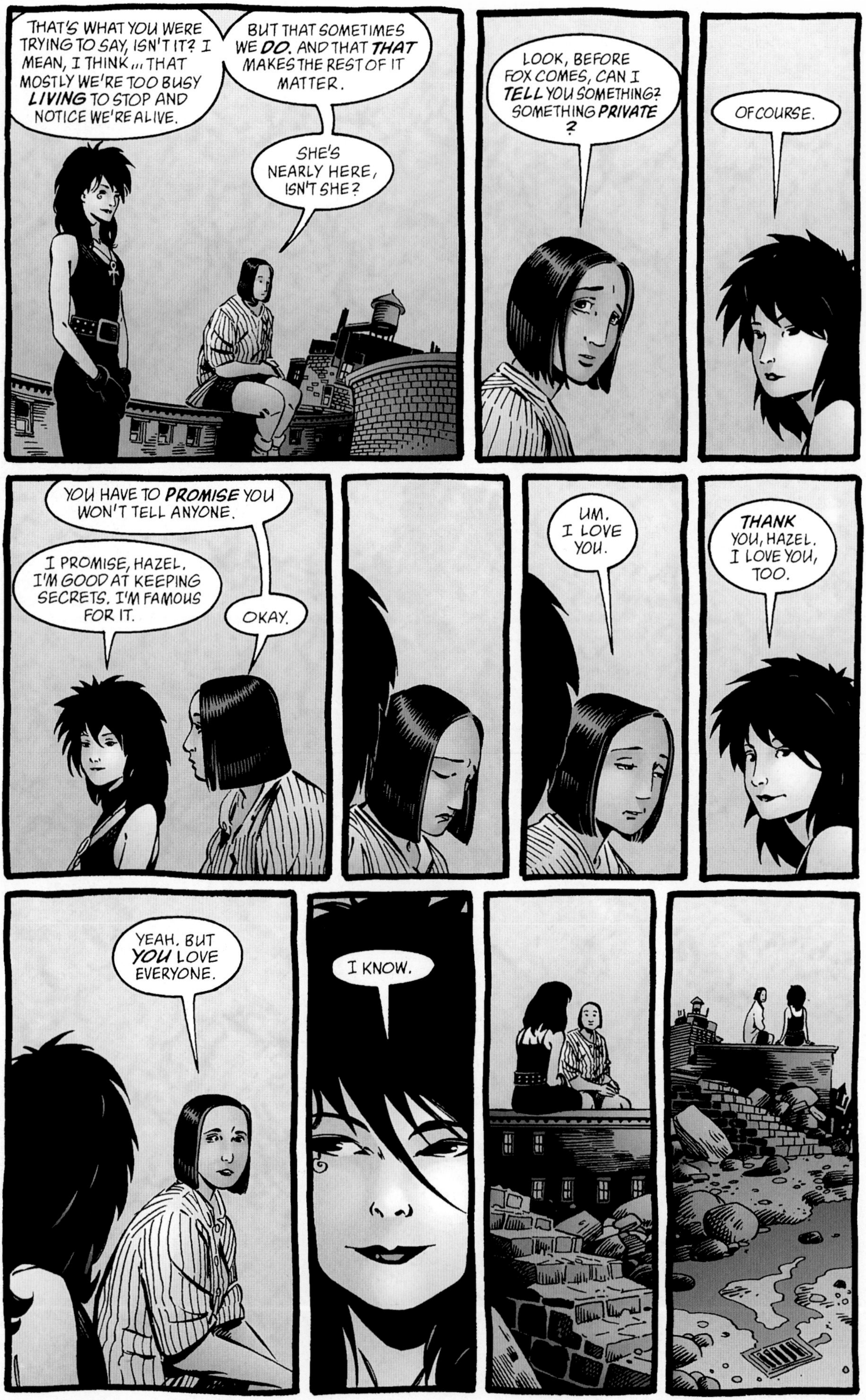
THAT'S WHAT YOU WERE TRYING TO SAY, ISN'T IT? I MEAN, I THINK... THAT MOSTLY WE'RE TOO BUSY LIVING TO STOP AND NOTICE WE'RE ALIVE.
BUT THAT SOMETIMES WE DO. AND THAT THAT MAKES THE REST OF IT MATTER.
SHE'S NEARLY HERE, ISN'T SHE?
LOOK, BEFORE FOX COMES, CAN I TELL YOU SOMETHING? SOMETHING PRIVATE?
OF COURSE.
YOU HAVE TO PROMISE YOU WON'T TELL ANYONE.
I PROMISE, HAZEL. I'M GOOD AT KEEPING SECRETS. I'M FAMOUS FOR IT.
OKAY.
UM. I LOVE YOU.
THANK YOU, HAZEL. I LOVE YOU, TOO.
YEAH. BUT YOU LOVE EVERYONE.
I KNOW.

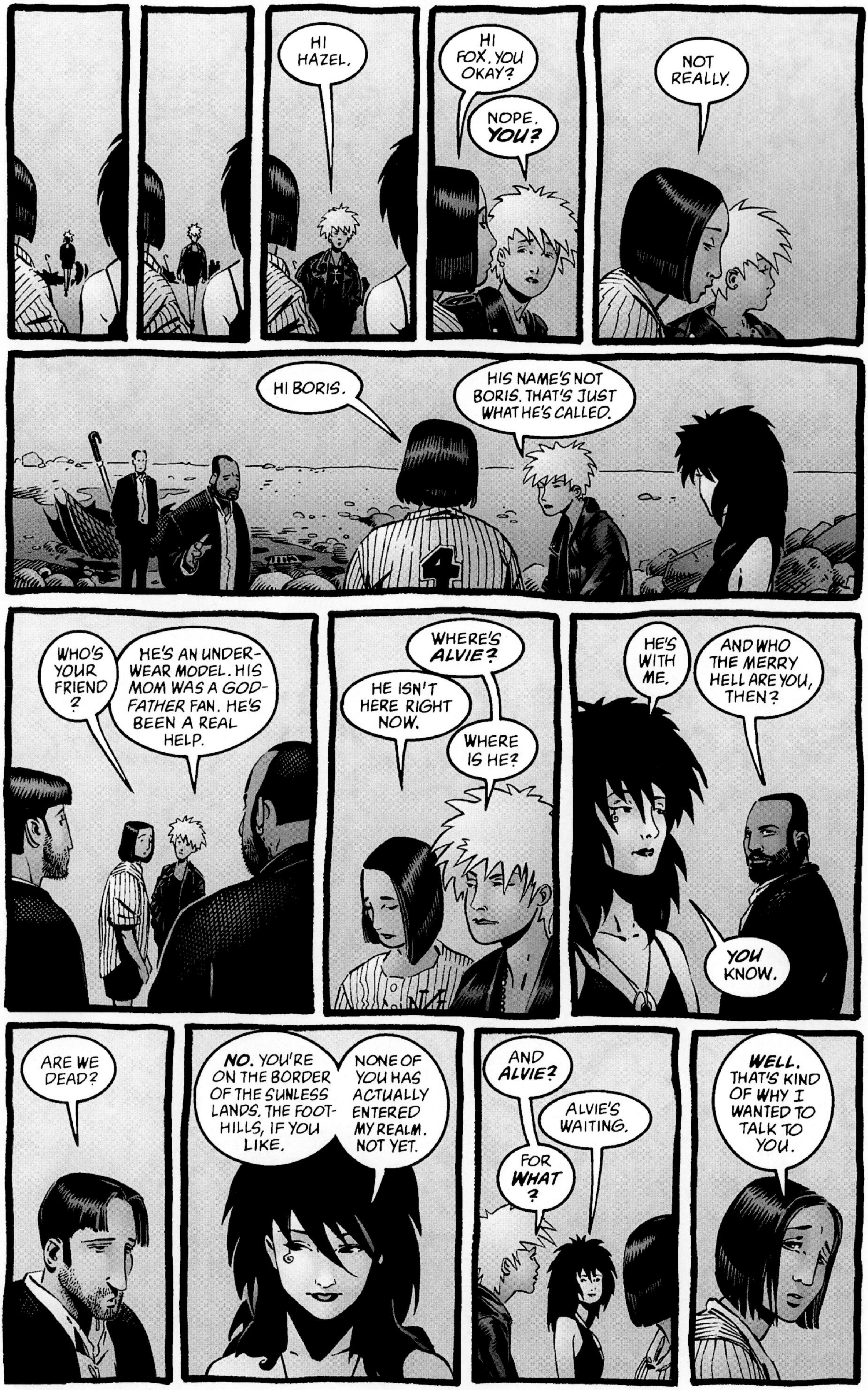
HI HAZEL.
HI FOX. YOU OKAY?
NOPE. YOU?
NOT REALLY.
HI BORIS.
HIS NAME'S NOT BORIS. THAT'S JUST WHAT HE'S CALLED.
WHO'S YOUR FRIEND?
HE'S AN UNDERWEAR MODEL. HIS MOM WAS A GODFATHER FAN. HE'S BEEN A REAL HELP.
WHERE'S ALVIE?
HE ISN'T HERE RIGHT NOW.
WHERE IS HE?
HE'S WITH ME.
AND WHO THE MERRY HELL ARE YOU, THEN?
YOU KNOW.
ARE WE DEAD?
NO. YOU'RE ON THE BORDER OF THE SUNLESS LANDS. THE FOOTHILLS, IF YOU LIKE.
NONE OF YOU HAS ACTUALLY ENTERED MY REALM. NOT YET.
AND ALVIE?
ALVIE'S WAITING.
FOR WHAT?
WELL. THAT'S KIND OF WHY I WANTED TO TALK TO YOU.

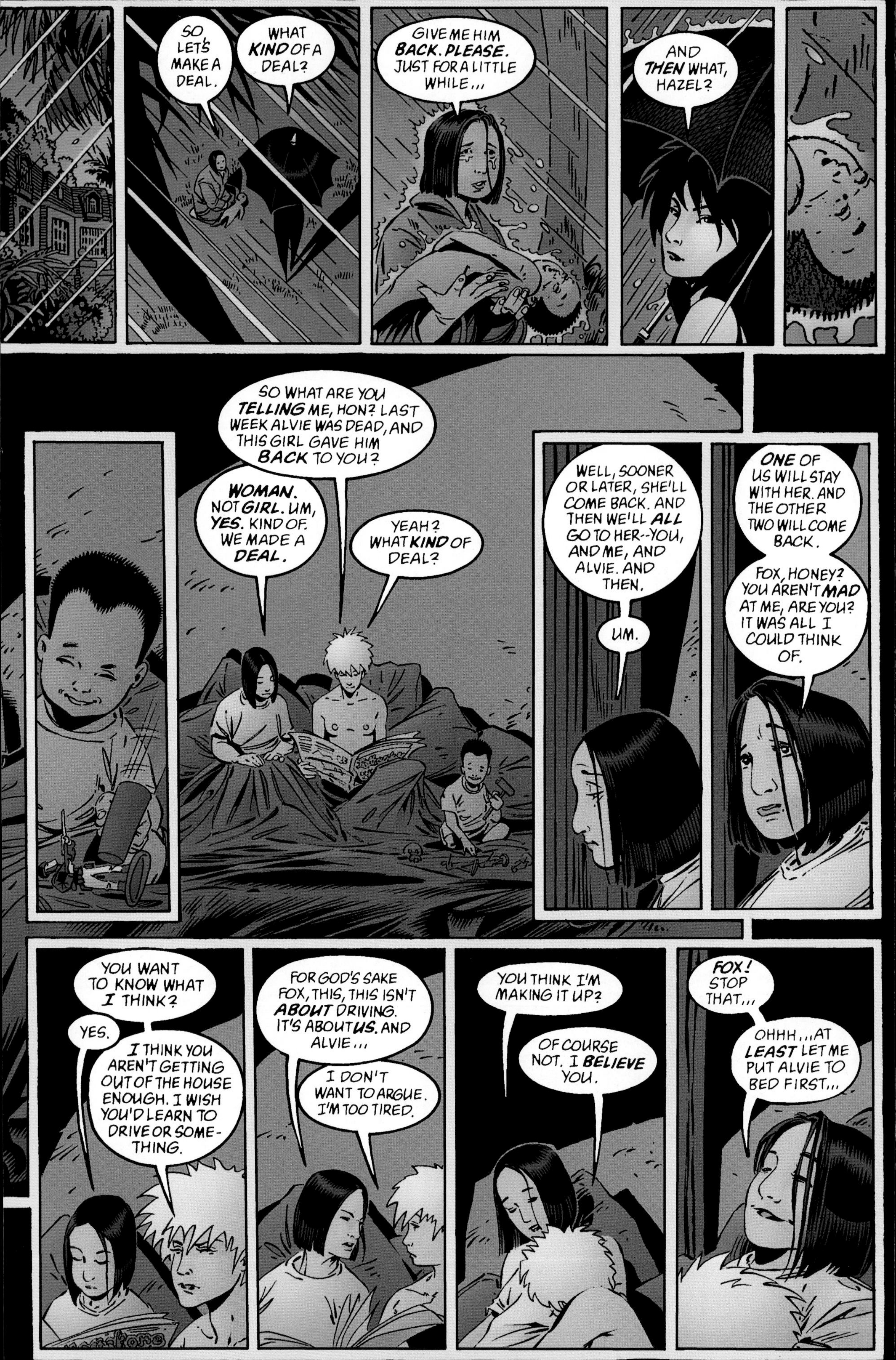
SO LET'S MAKE A DEAL.
WHAT KIND OF A DEAL?
GIVE ME HIM BACK. PLEASE. JUST FOR A LITTLE WHILE...
AND THEN WHAT, HAZEL?
SO WHAT ARE YOU TELLING ME, HON? LAST WEEK ALVIE WAS DEAD, AND THIS GIRL GAVE HIM BACK TO YOU?
WOMAN. NOT GIRL. UM, YES. KIND OF. WE MADE A DEAL.
YEAH? WHAT KIND OF DEAL?
WELL, SOONER OR LATER, SHE'LL COME BACK. AND THEN WE'LL ALL GO TO HER--YOU, AND ME, AND ALVIE. AND THEN.
UM.
ONE OF US WILL STAY WITH HER. AND THE OTHER TWO WILL COME BACK.
FOX, HONEY? YOU AREN'T MAD AT ME, ARE YOU? IT WAS ALL I COULD THINK OF.
YOU WANT TO KNOW WHAT I THINK?
YES.
I THINK YOU AREN'T GETTING OUT OF THE HOUSE ENOUGH. I WISH YOU'D LEARN TO DRIVE OR SOME-THING.
FOR GOD'S SAKE FOX, THIS, THIS ISN'T ABOUT DRIVING. IT'S ABOUT US. AND ALVIE...
I DON'T WANT TO ARGUE. I'M TOO TIRED.
YOU THINK I'M MAKING IT UP?
OF COURSE NOT. I BELIEVE YOU.
FOX! STOP THAT...
OHHH...AT LEAST LET ME PUT ALVIE TO BED FIRST...

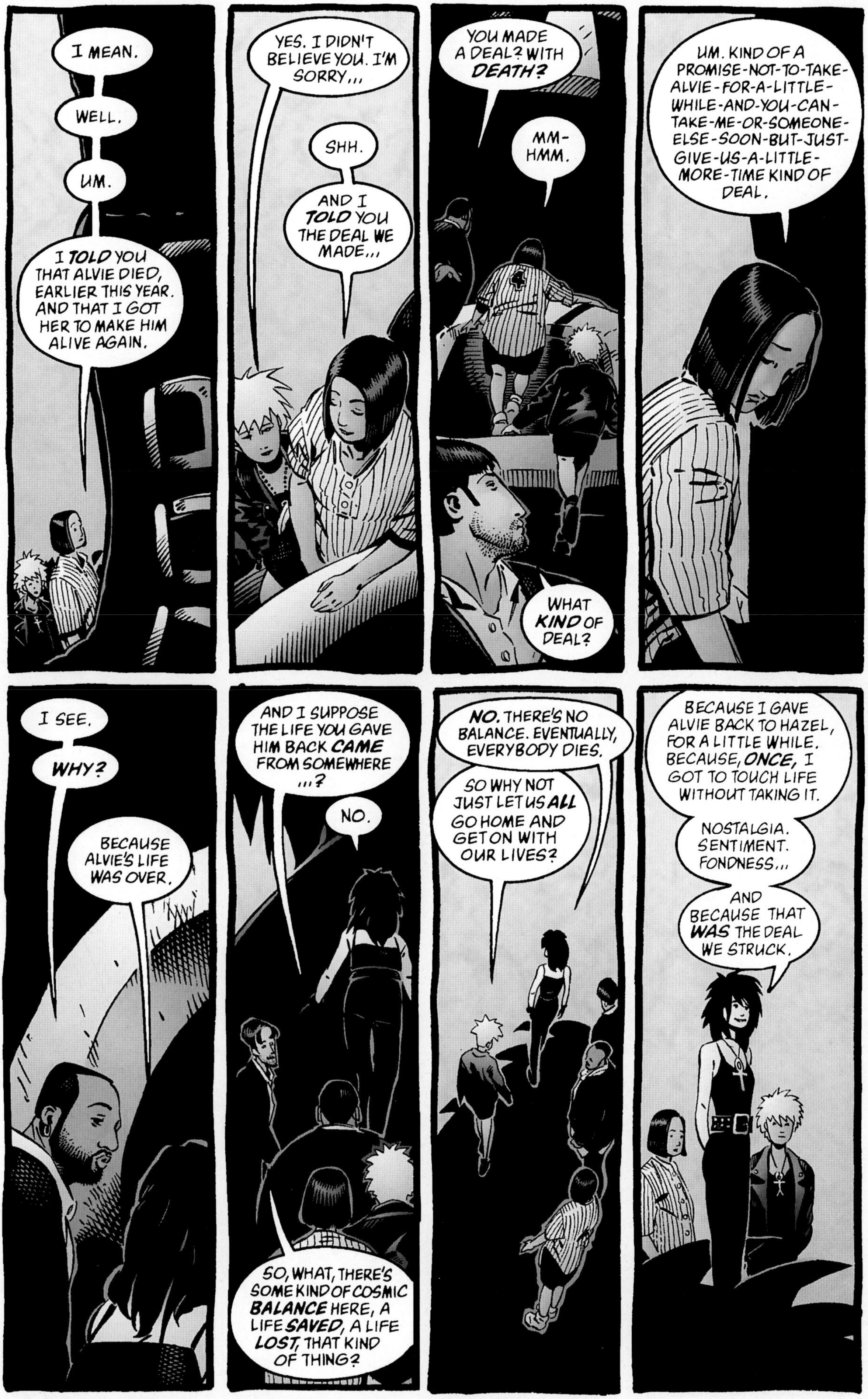
I MEAN.
WELL.
UM.
I TOLD YOU THAT ALVIE DIED, EARLIER THIS YEAR. AND THAT I GOT HER TO MAKE HIM ALIVE AGAIN.
YES. I DIDN'T BELIEVE YOU. I'M SORRY...
SHH.
AND I TOLD YOU THE DEAL WE MADE...
YOU MADE A DEAL? WITH DEATH?
MM-HMM.
WHAT KIND OF DEAL?
UM. KIND OF A PROMISE-NOT-TO-TAKE-ALVIE-FOR-A-LITTLE-WHILE-AND-YOU-CAN-TAKE-ME-OR-SOMEONE-ELSE-SOON-BUT-JUST-GIVE-US-A-LITTLE-MORE-TIME KIND OF DEAL.
I SEE.
WHY?
BECAUSE ALVIE'S LIFE WAS OVER.
AND I SUPPOSE THE LIFE YOU GAVE HIM BACK CAME FROM SOMEWHERE ...?
NO.
SO, WHAT, THERE'S SOME KIND OF COSMIC BALANCE HERE, A LIFE SAVED, A LIFE LOST, THAT KIND OF THING?
NO. THERE'S NO BALANCE. EVENTUALLY, EVERYBODY DIES.
SO WHY NOT JUST LET US ALL GO HOME AND GET ON WITH OUR LIVES?
BECAUSE I GAVE ALVIE BACK TO HAZEL, FOR A LITTLE WHILE. BECAUSE, ONCE, I GOT TO TOUCH LIFE WITHOUT TAKING IT.
NOSTALGIA. SENTIMENT. FONDNESS...
AND BECAUSE THAT WAS THE DEAL WE STRUCK.

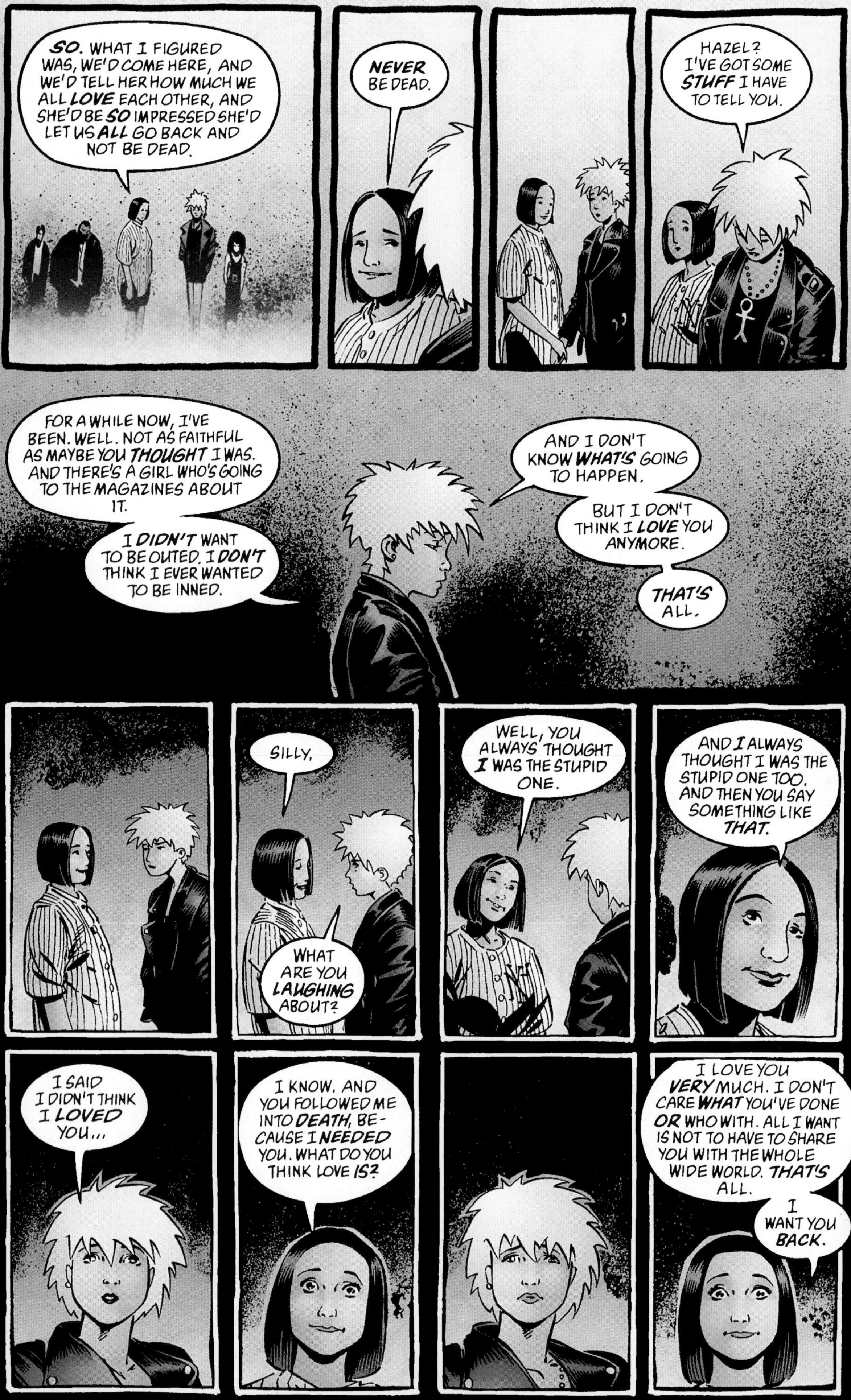
SO. WHAT I FIGURED WAS, WE'D COME HERE, AND WE'D TELL HER HOW MUCH WE ALL LOVE EACH OTHER, AND SHE'D BE SO IMPRESSED SHE'D LET US ALL GO BACK AND NOT BE DEAD.
NEVER BE DEAD.
HAZEL? I'VE GOT SOME STUFF I HAVE TO TELL YOU.
FOR A WHILE NOW, I'VE BEEN. WELL. NOT AS FAITHFUL AS MAYBE YOU THOUGHT I WAS. AND THERE'S A GIRL WHO'S GOING TO THE MAGAZINES ABOUT IT.
I DIDN'T WANT TO BE OUTED. I DON'T THINK I EVER WANTED TO BE INNED.
AND I DON'T KNOW WHAT'S GOING TO HAPPEN.
BUT I DON'T THINK I LOVE YOU ANYMORE.
THAT'S ALL.
SILLY.
WHAT ARE YOU LAUGHING ABOUT?
WELL, YOU ALWAYS THOUGHT I WAS THE STUPID ONE.
AND I ALWAYS THOUGHT I WAS THE STUPID ONE TOO. AND THEN YOU SAY SOMETHING LIKE THAT.
I SAID I DIDN'T THINK I LOVED YOU...
I KNOW. AND YOU FOLLOWED ME INTO DEATH, BECAUSE I NEEDED YOU. WHAT DO YOU THINK LOVE IS?
I LOVE YOU VERY MUCH. I DON'T CARE WHAT YOU'VE DONE OR WHO WITH. ALL I WANT IS NOT TO HAVE TO SHARE YOU WITH THE WHOLE WIDE WORLD. THAT'S ALL.
I WANT YOU BACK.

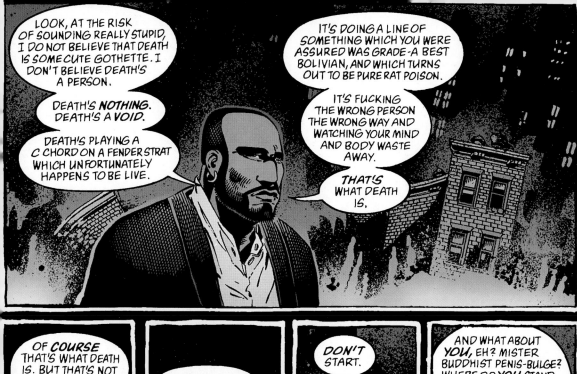

LOOK, AT THE RISK OF SOUNDING REALLY STUPID, I DO NOT BELIEVE THAT DEATH IS SOME CUTE GOTHETTE. I DON'T BELIEVE DEATH'S A PERSON.

DEATH'S *NOTHING*. DEATH'S A *VOID*.

DEATH'S PLAYING A C CHORD ON A FENDER STRAT WHICH UNFORTUNATELY HAPPENS TO BE LIVE.

IT'S DOING A LINE OF SOMETHING WHICH YOU WERE ASSURED WAS GRADE-A BEST BOLIVIAN, AND WHICH TURNS OUT TO BE PURE RAT POISON.

IT'S FUCKING THE WRONG PERSON THE WRONG WAY AND WATCHING YOUR MIND AND BODY WASTE AWAY.

THAT'S WHAT DEATH IS.

OF *COURSE* THAT'S WHAT DEATH IS. BUT THAT'S NOT *ALL* DEATH IS, ENDYMION.

ENDYMION?

DON'T START.

AND I PREFER BORIS, HONESTLY.

SORRY.

AND WHAT ABOUT *YOU*, EH? MISTER BUDDHIST PENIS-BULGE? WHERE *DO* YOU STAND ON ALL THIS? SHOULDN'T YOU BE SAYING SOMETHING ABOUT KARMIC REBIRTH HERE? BIT OF KARMIC RELIEF?

I DON'T REALLY KNOW *WHAT* TO SAY.

I SUPPOSE... I SUPPOSE THAT, YES, I *DO* BELIEVE THAT I'LL BE BACK AGAIN. THAT I WON'T DIE --THE WHATEVER-MAKES-ME-*ME*, *THAT* WON'T DIE.

BUT THAT'S WHAT I BELIEVE IN MY *HEAD*.

IN MY *HEART*... I DON'T WANT TO DIE.

...I DON'T KNOW.

tocsin boxers

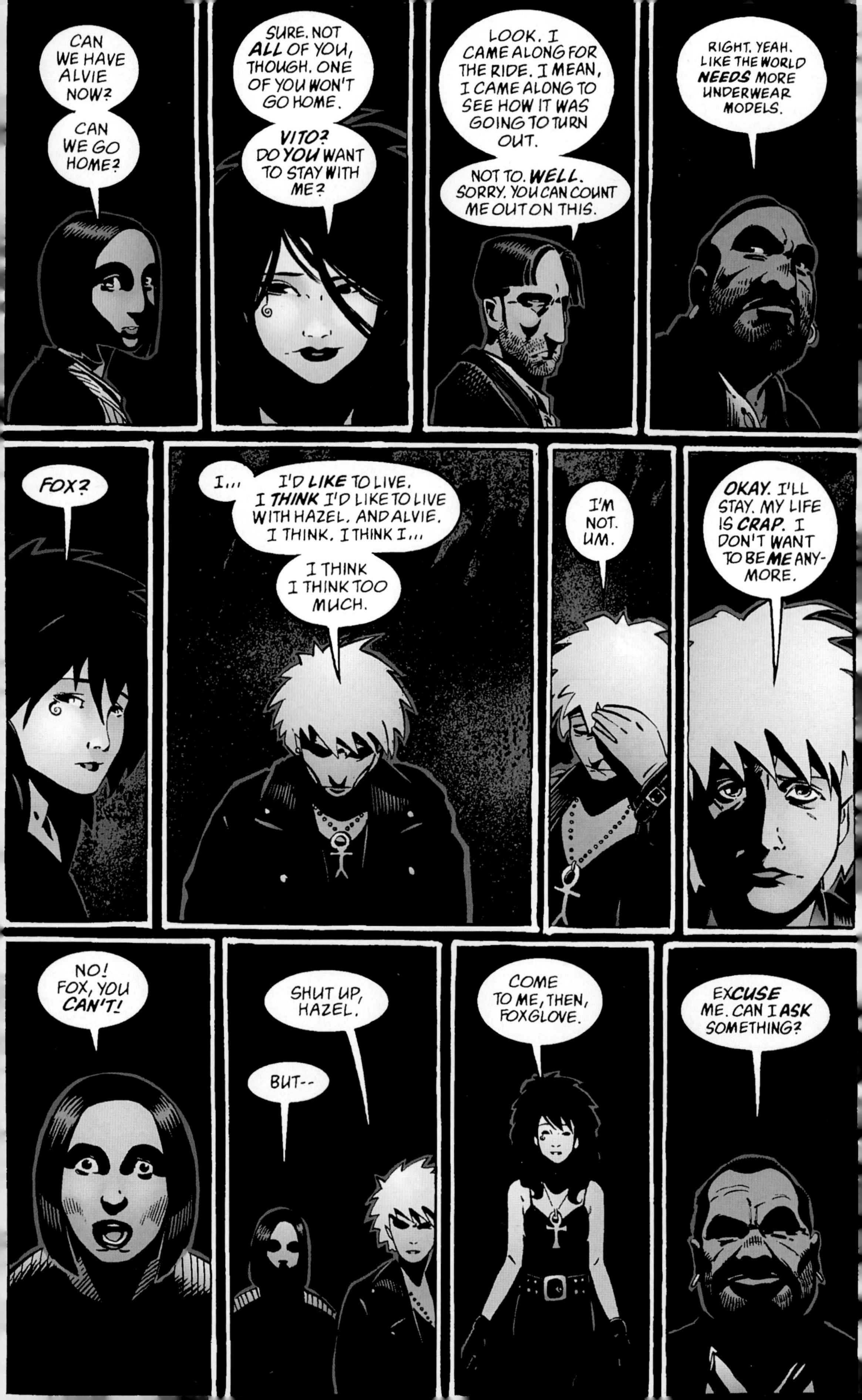
CAN WE HAVE ALVIE NOW?
CAN WE GO HOME?
SURE. NOT ALL OF YOU, THOUGH. ONE OF YOU WON'T GO HOME.
VITO? DO YOU WANT TO STAY WITH ME?
LOOK. I CAME ALONG FOR THE RIDE. I MEAN, I CAME ALONG TO SEE HOW IT WAS GOING TO TURN OUT.
NOT TO. WELL. SORRY. YOU CAN COUNT ME OUT ON THIS.
RIGHT. YEAH. LIKE THE WORLD NEEDS MORE UNDERWEAR MODELS.
FOX?
I...
I'D LIKE TO LIVE. I THINK I'D LIKE TO LIVE WITH HAZEL. AND ALVIE. I THINK. I THINK I...
I THINK I THINK TOO MUCH.
I'M NOT. UM.
OKAY. I'LL STAY. MY LIFE IS CRAP. I DON'T WANT TO BE ME ANYMORE.
NO! FOX, YOU CAN'T!
SHUT UP, HAZEL.
BUT--
COME TO ME, THEN, FOXGLOVE.
EXCUSE ME. CAN I ASK SOMETHING?

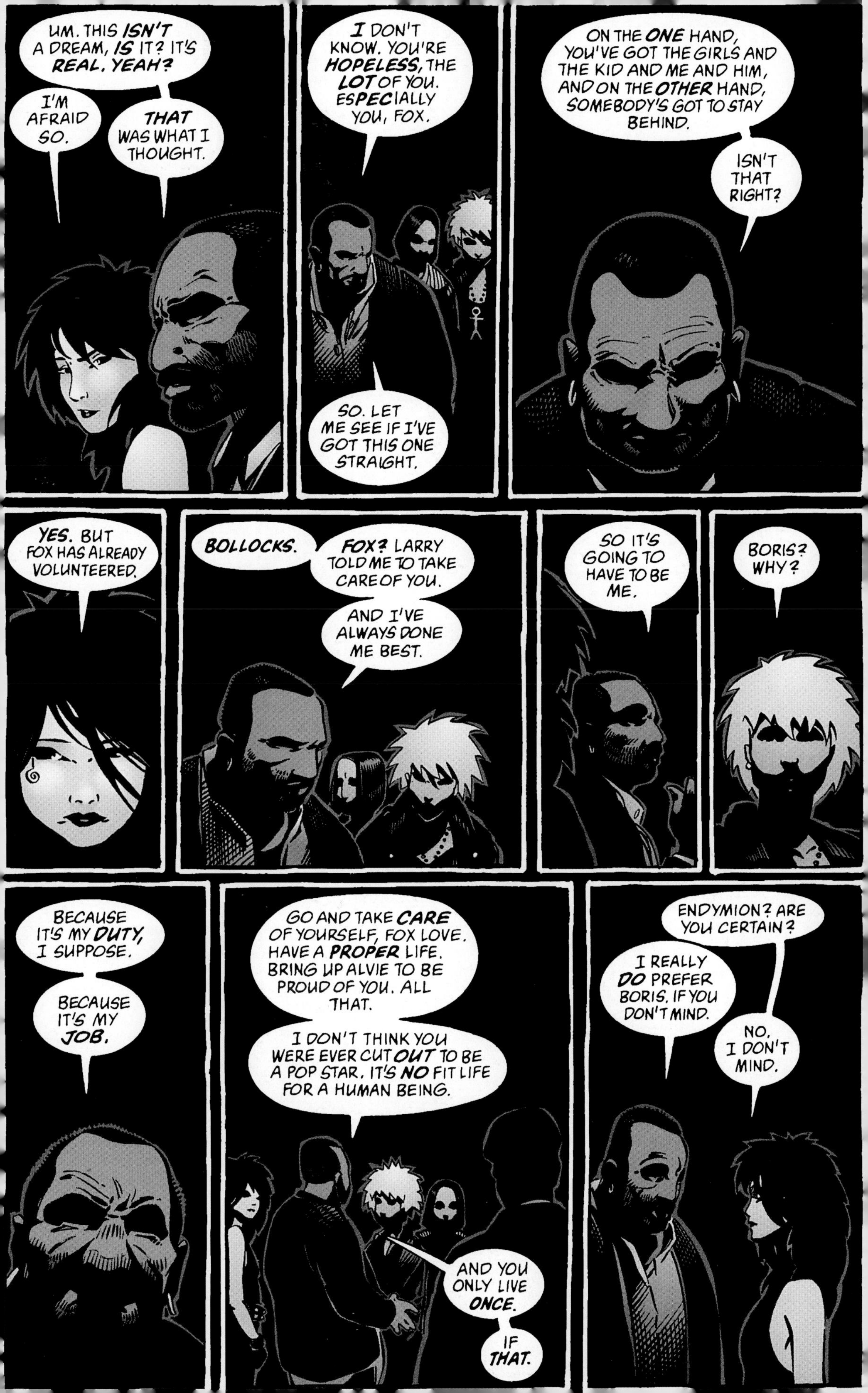
UM. THIS ISN'T A DREAM, IS IT? IT'S REAL. YEAH?
I'M AFRAID SO.
THAT WAS WHAT I THOUGHT.
I DON'T KNOW. YOU'RE HOPELESS, THE LOT OF YOU. ESPECIALLY YOU, FOX.
SO. LET ME SEE IF I'VE GOT THIS ONE STRAIGHT.
ON THE ONE HAND, YOU'VE GOT THE GIRLS AND THE KID AND ME AND HIM, AND ON THE OTHER HAND, SOMEBODY'S GOT TO STAY BEHIND.
ISN'T THAT RIGHT?
YES. BUT FOX HAS ALREADY VOLUNTEERED.
BOLLOCKS.
FOX? LARRY TOLD ME TO TAKE CARE OF YOU.
AND I'VE ALWAYS DONE ME BEST.
SO IT'S GOING TO HAVE TO BE ME.
BORIS? WHY?
BECAUSE IT'S MY DUTY, I SUPPOSE.
BECAUSE IT'S MY JOB.
GO AND TAKE CARE OF YOURSELF, FOX LOVE. HAVE A PROPER LIFE. BRING UP ALVIE TO BE PROUD OF YOU. ALL THAT.
I DON'T THINK YOU WERE EVER CUT OUT TO BE A POP STAR. IT'S NO FIT LIFE FOR A HUMAN BEING.
AND YOU ONLY LIVE ONCE.
IF THAT.
ENDYMION? ARE YOU CERTAIN?
I REALLY DO PREFER BORIS, IF YOU DON'T MIND.
NO, I DON'T MIND.

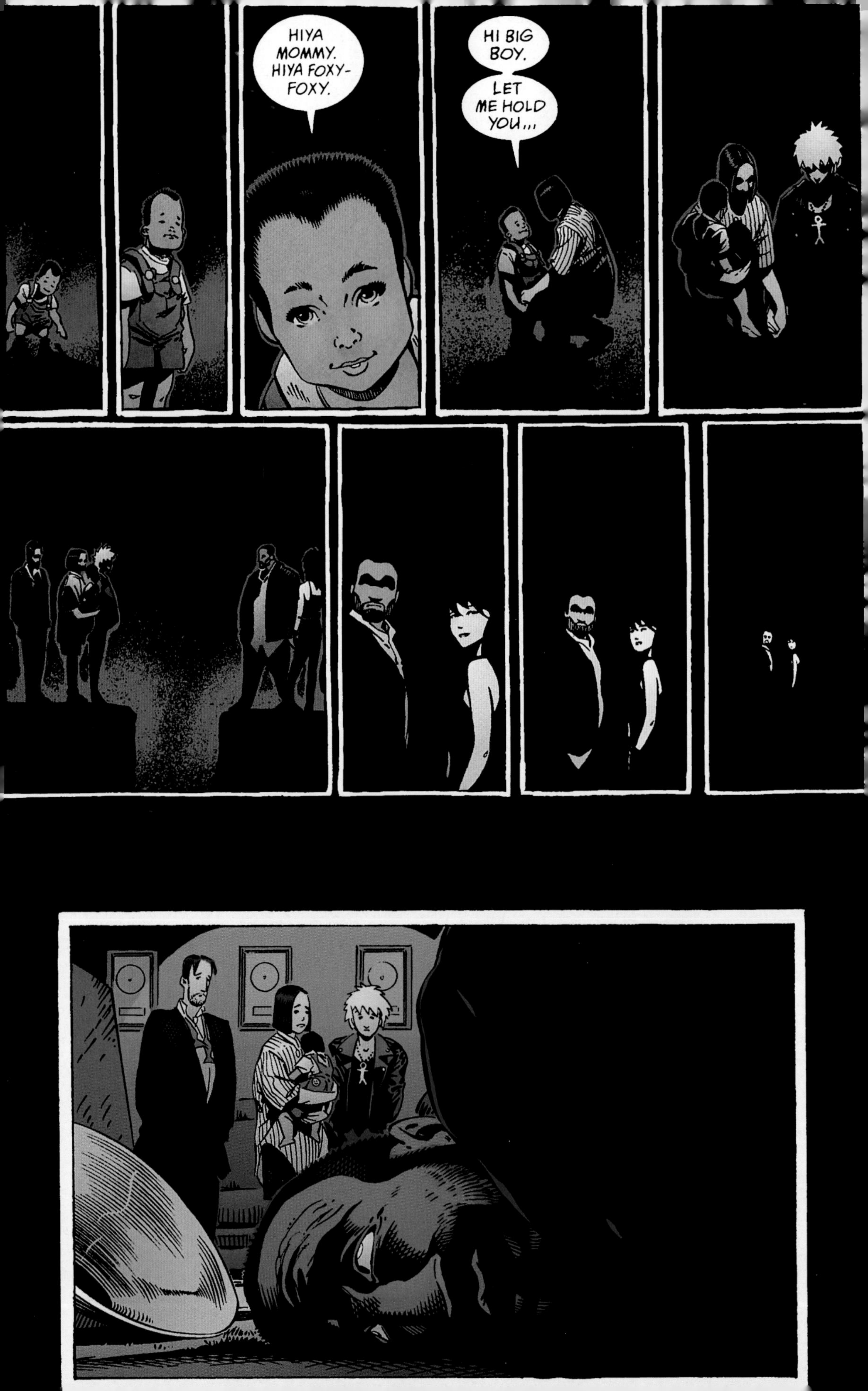
HIYA MOMMY. HIYA FOXY-FOXY.
HI BIG BOY.
LET ME HOLD YOU...

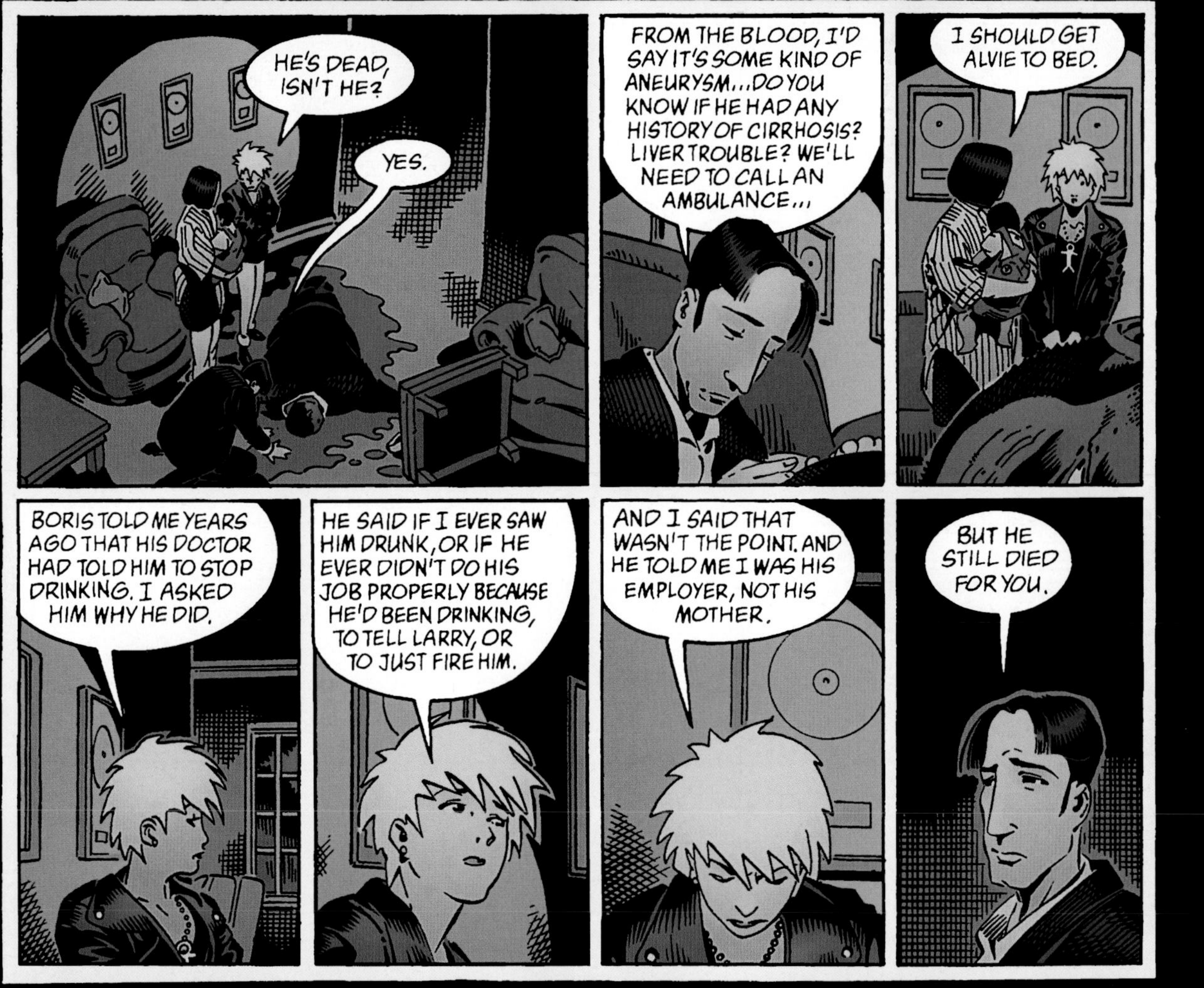
HE'S DEAD, ISN'T HE?
YES.
FROM THE BLOOD, I'D SAY IT'S SOME KIND OF ANEURYSM... DO YOU KNOW IF HE HAD ANY HISTORY OF CIRRHOSIS? LIVER TROUBLE? WE'LL NEED TO CALL AN AMBULANCE...
I SHOULD GET ALVIE TO BED.
BORIS TOLD ME YEARS AGO THAT HIS DOCTOR HAD TOLD HIM TO STOP DRINKING. I ASKED HIM WHY HE DID.
HE SAID IF I EVER SAW HIM DRUNK, OR IF HE EVER DIDN'T DO HIS JOB PROPERLY BECAUSE HE'D BEEN DRINKING, TO TELL LARRY, OR TO JUST FIRE HIM.
AND I SAID THAT WASN'T THE POINT. AND HE TOLD ME I WAS HIS EMPLOYER, NOT HIS MOTHER.
BUT HE STILL DIED FOR YOU.

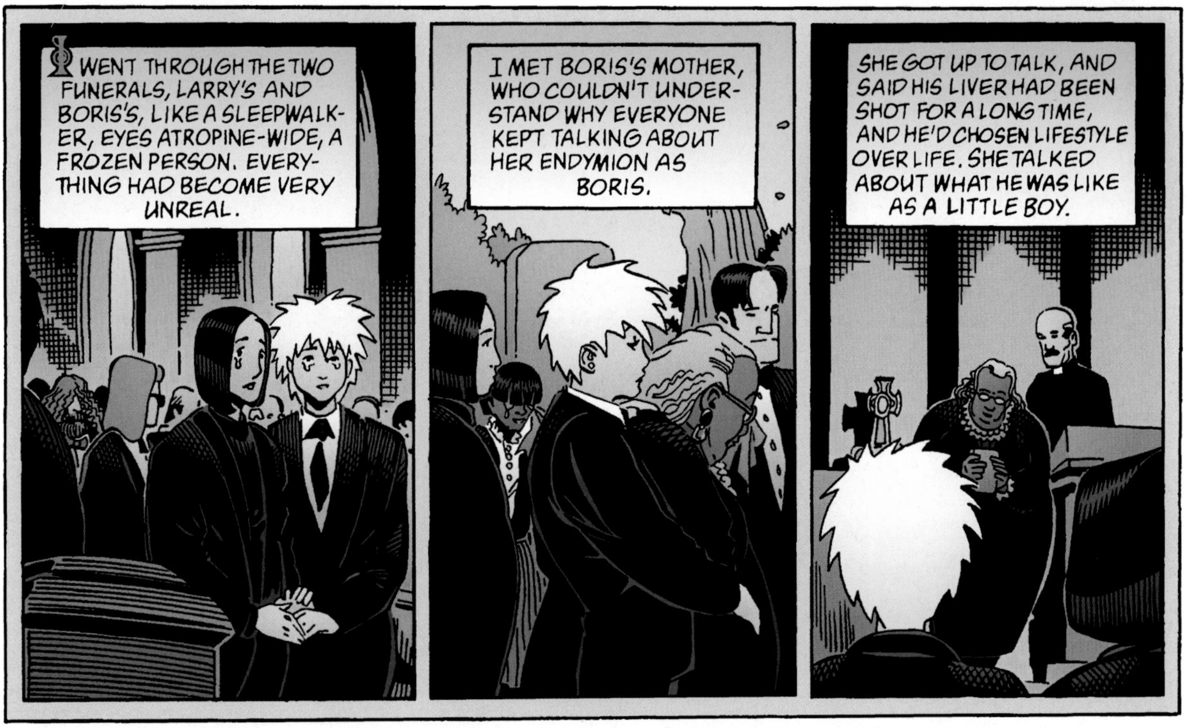
I WENT THROUGH THE TWO FUNERALS, LARRY'S AND BORIS'S, LIKE A SLEEPWALKER, EYES ATROPINE-WIDE, A FROZEN PERSON. EVERYTHING HAD BECOME VERY UNREAL.
I MET BORIS'S MOTHER, WHO COULDN'T UNDERSTAND WHY EVERYONE KEPT TALKING ABOUT HER ENDYMION AS BORIS.
SHE GOT UP TO TALK, AND SAID HIS LIVER HAD BEEN SHOT FOR A LONG TIME, AND HE'D CHOSEN LIFESTYLE OVER LIFE. SHE TALKED ABOUT WHAT HE WAS LIKE AS A LITTLE BOY.

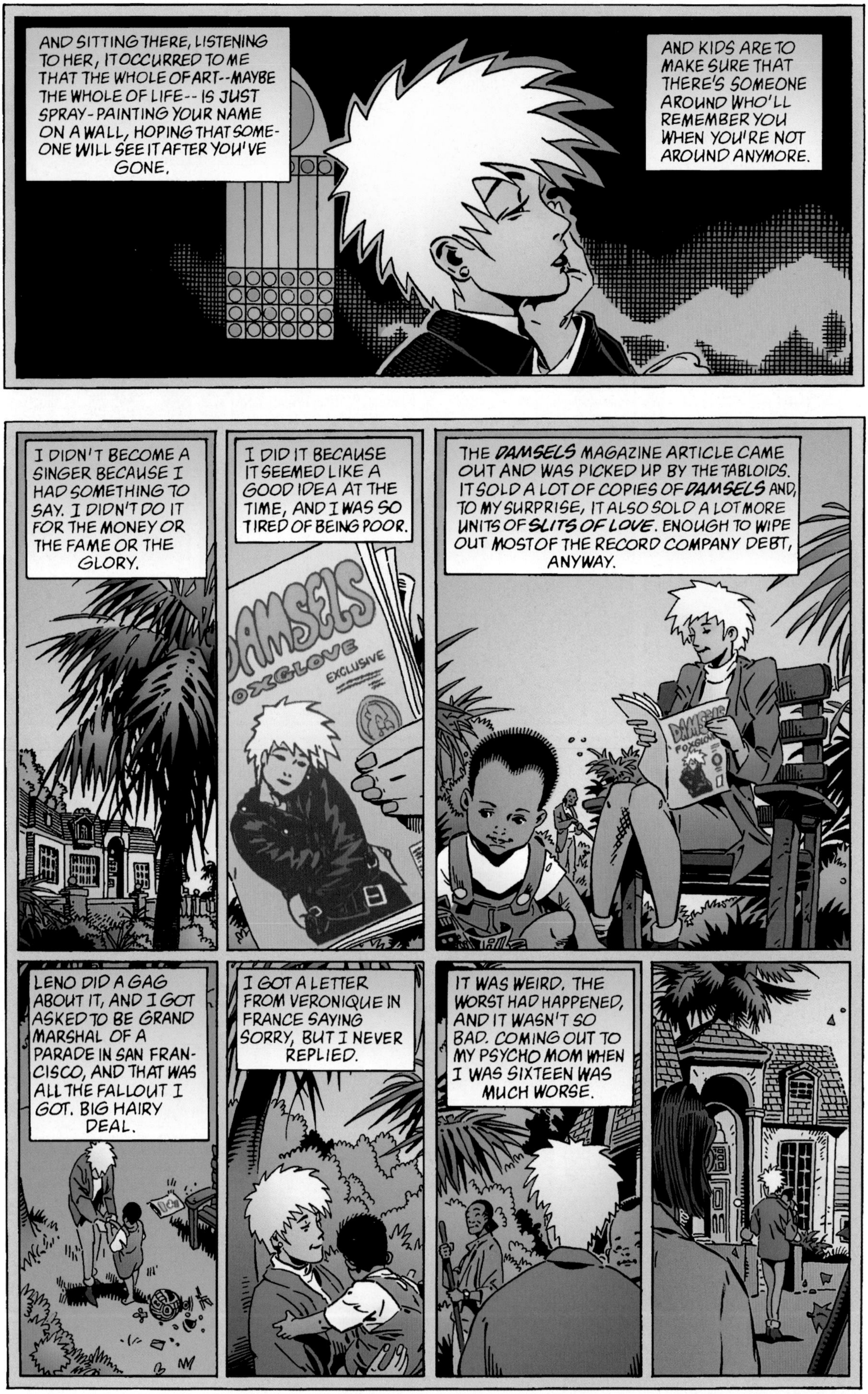
AND SITTING THERE, LISTENING TO HER, IT OCCURRED TO ME THAT THE WHOLE OF ART--MAYBE THE WHOLE OF LIFE-- IS JUST SPRAY-PAINTING YOUR NAME ON A WALL, HOPING THAT SOMEONE WILL SEE IT AFTER YOU'VE GONE.
AND KIDS ARE TO MAKE SURE THAT THERE'S SOMEONE AROUND WHO'LL REMEMBER YOU WHEN YOU'RE NOT AROUND ANYMORE.
I DIDN'T BECOME A SINGER BECAUSE I HAD SOMETHING TO SAY. I DIDN'T DO IT FOR THE MONEY OR THE FAME OR THE GLORY.
I DID IT BECAUSE IT SEEMED LIKE A GOOD IDEA AT THE TIME, AND I WAS SO TIRED OF BEING POOR.
DAMSELS
FOXGLOVE
EXCLUSIVE
THE DAMSELS MAGAZINE ARTICLE CAME OUT AND WAS PICKED UP BY THE TABLOIDS. IT SOLD A LOT OF COPIES OF DAMSELS AND, TO MY SURPRISE, IT ALSO SOLD A LOT MORE UNITS OF SLITS OF LOVE. ENOUGH TO WIPE OUT MOST OF THE RECORD COMPANY DEBT, ANYWAY.
LENO DID A GAG ABOUT IT, AND I GOT ASKED TO BE GRAND MARSHAL OF A PARADE IN SAN FRANCISCO, AND THAT WAS ALL THE FALLOUT I GOT. BIG HAIRY DEAL.
I GOT A LETTER FROM VERONIQUE IN FRANCE SAYING SORRY, BUT I NEVER REPLIED.
IT WAS WEIRD. THE WORST HAD HAPPENED, AND IT WASN'T SO BAD. COMING OUT TO MY PSYCHO MOM WHEN I WAS SIXTEEN WAS MUCH WORSE.

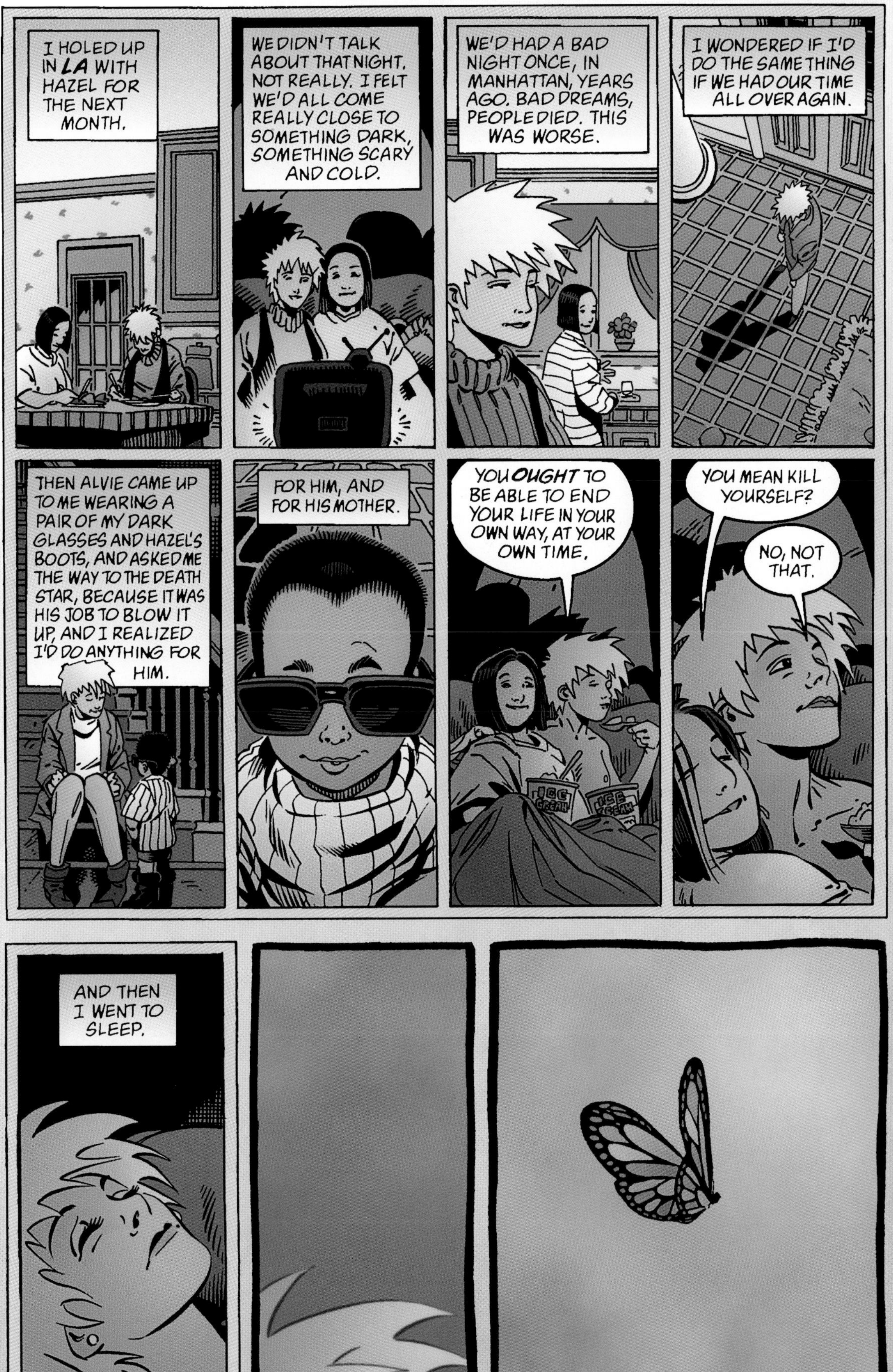
I HOLED UP IN LA WITH HAZEL FOR THE NEXT MONTH.
WE DIDN'T TALK ABOUT THAT NIGHT. NOT REALLY. I FELT WE'D ALL COME REALLY CLOSE TO SOMETHING DARK, SOMETHING SCARY AND COLD.
WE'D HAD A BAD NIGHT ONCE, IN MANHATTAN, YEARS AGO. BAD DREAMS, PEOPLE DIED. THIS WAS WORSE.
I WONDERED IF I'D DO THE SAME THING IF WE HAD OUR TIME ALL OVER AGAIN.
THEN ALVIE CAME UP TO ME WEARING A PAIR OF MY DARK GLASSES AND HAZEL'S BOOTS, AND ASKED ME THE WAY TO THE DEATH STAR, BECAUSE IT WAS HIS JOB TO BLOW IT UP, AND I REALIZED I'D DO ANYTHING FOR HIM.
FOR HIM, AND FOR HIS MOTHER.
YOU OUGHT TO BE ABLE TO END YOUR LIFE IN YOUR OWN WAY, AT YOUR OWN TIME.
ICE CREAM
ICE CREAM
YOU MEAN KILL YOURSELF?
NO, NOT THAT.
AND THEN I WENT TO SLEEP.

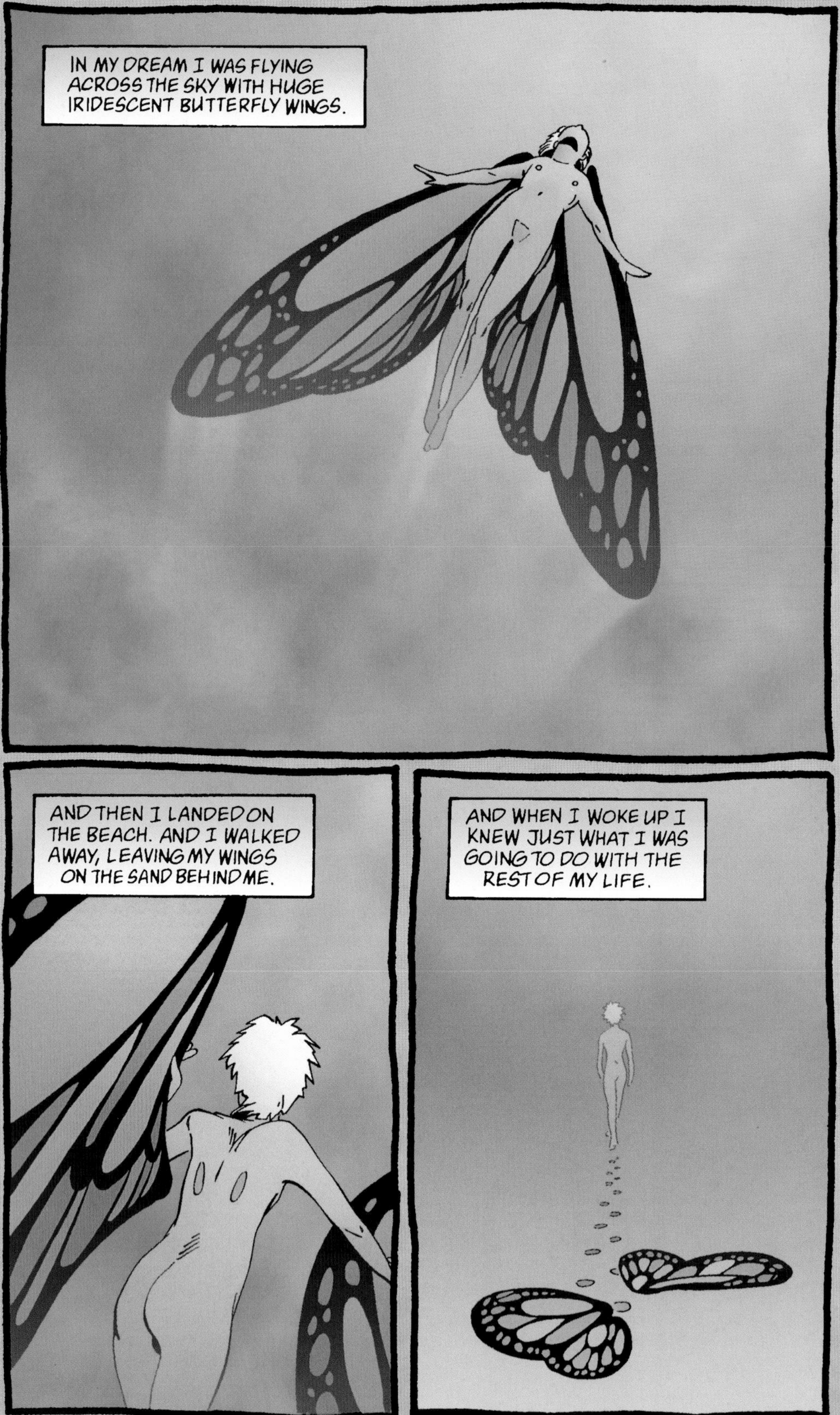
IN MY DREAM I WAS FLYING ACROSS THE SKY WITH HUGE IRIDESCENT BUTTERFLY WINGS.
AND THEN I LANDED ON THE BEACH. AND I WALKED AWAY, LEAVING MY WINGS ON THE SAND BEHIND ME.
AND WHEN I WOKE UP I KNEW JUST WHAT I WAS GOING TO DO WITH THE REST OF MY LIFE.

EPILOGUE

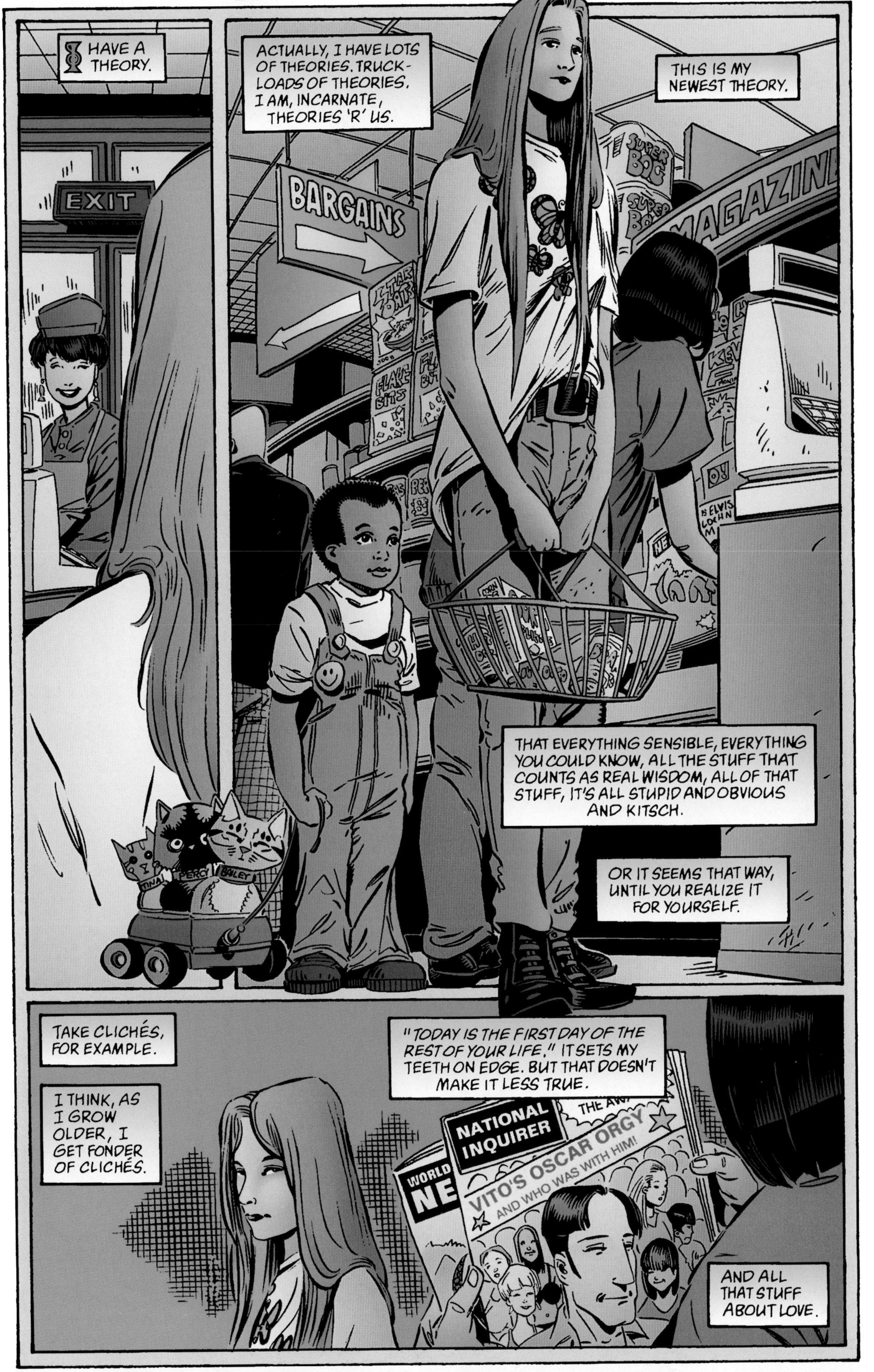

I HAVE A THEORY.
ACTUALLY, I HAVE LOTS OF THEORIES. TRUCK-LOADS OF THEORIES. I AM, INCARNATE, THEORIES 'R' US.
THIS IS MY NEWEST THEORY.
EXIT
BARGAINS
THAT EVERYTHING SENSIBLE, EVERYTHING YOU COULD KNOW, ALL THE STUFF THAT COUNTS AS REAL WISDOM, ALL OF THAT STUFF, IT'S ALL STUPID AND OBVIOUS AND KITSCH.
OR IT SEEMS THAT WAY, UNTIL YOU REALIZE IT FOR YOURSELF.
TAKE CLICHÉS, FOR EXAMPLE.
I THINK, AS I GROW OLDER, I GET FONDER OF CLICHÉS.
"TODAY IS THE FIRST DAY OF THE REST OF YOUR LIFE." IT SETS MY TEETH ON EDGE. BUT THAT DOESN'T MAKE IT LESS TRUE.
NATIONAL INQUIRER
VITO'S OSCAR ORGY
AND WHO WAS WITH HIM!
AND ALL THAT STUFF ABOUT LOVE.

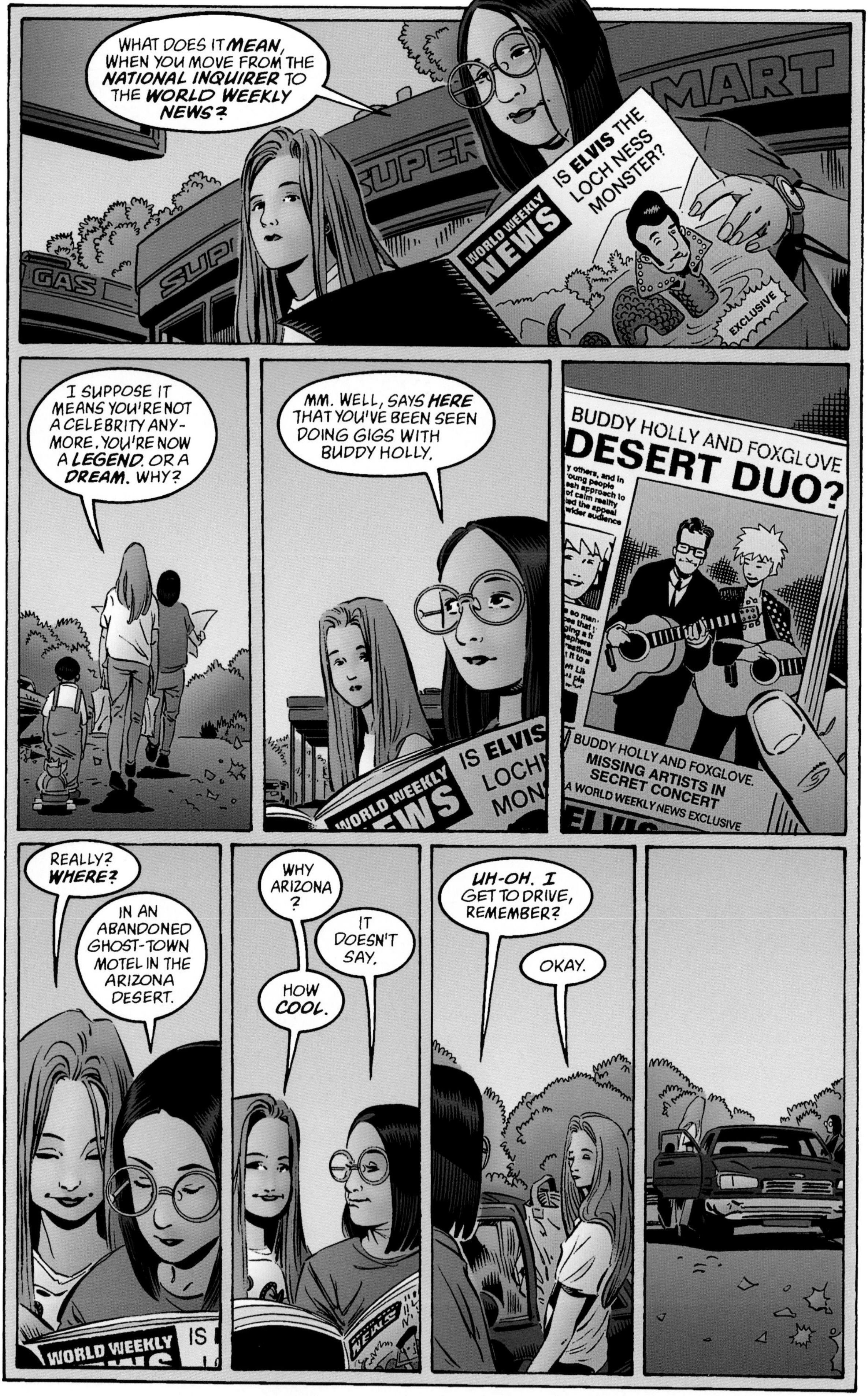
WHAT DOES IT MEAN, WHEN YOU MOVE FROM THE NATIONAL INQUIRER TO THE WORLD WEEKLY NEWS?
SUPER
MART
GAS
WORLD WEEKLY NEWS
IS ELVIS THE LOCH NESS MONSTER?
EXCLUSIVE
I SUPPOSE IT MEANS YOU'RE NOT A CELEBRITY ANY-MORE. YOU'RE NOW A LEGEND. OR A DREAM. WHY?
MM. WELL, SAYS HERE THAT YOU'VE BEEN SEEN DOING GIGS WITH BUDDY HOLLY.
BUDDY HOLLY AND FOXGLOVE
DESERT DUO?
BUDDY HOLLY AND FOXGLOVE. MISSING ARTISTS IN SECRET CONCERT
A WORLD WEEKLY NEWS EXCLUSIVE
REALLY? WHERE?
IN AN ABANDONED GHOST-TOWN MOTEL IN THE ARIZONA DESERT.
WHY ARIZONA?
IT DOESN'T SAY.
HOW COOL.
UH-OH. I GET TO DRIVE, REMEMBER?
OKAY.

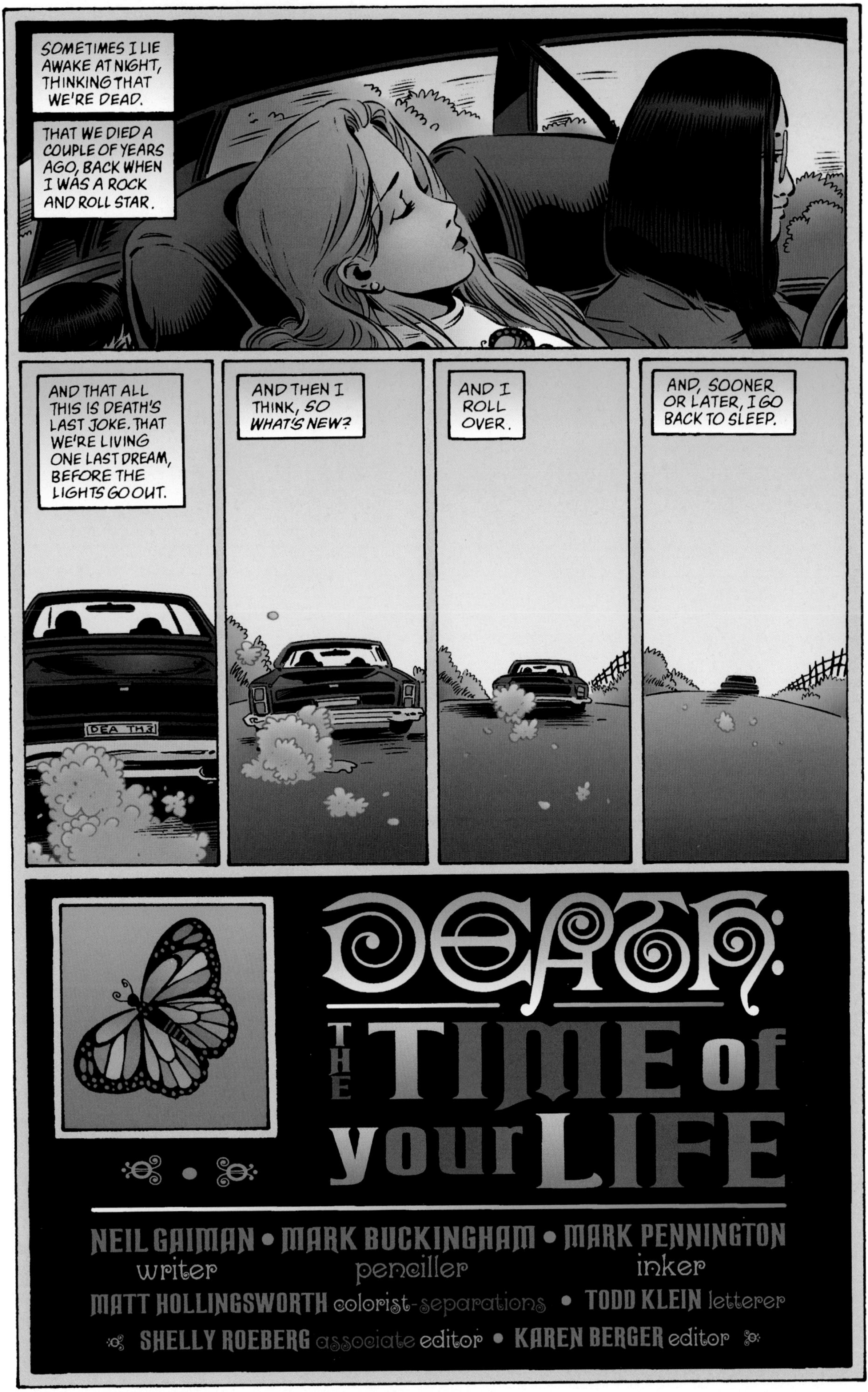
SOMETIMES I LIE AWAKE AT NIGHT, THINKING THAT WE'RE DEAD.
THAT WE DIED A COUPLE OF YEARS AGO, BACK WHEN I WAS A ROCK AND ROLL STAR.
AND THAT ALL THIS IS DEATH'S LAST JOKE. THAT WE'RE LIVING ONE LAST DREAM, BEFORE THE LIGHTS GO OUT.
DEA TH3
AND THEN I THINK, SO WHAT'S NEW?
AND I ROLL OVER.
AND, SOONER OR LATER, I GO BACK TO SLEEP.
DEATH: THE TIME of your LIFE
NEIL GAIMAN • MARK BUCKINGHAM • MARK PENNINGTON
writer penciller inker
MATT HOLLINGSWORTH colorist-separations • TODD KLEIN letterer
SHELLY ROEBERG associate editor • KAREN BERGER editor

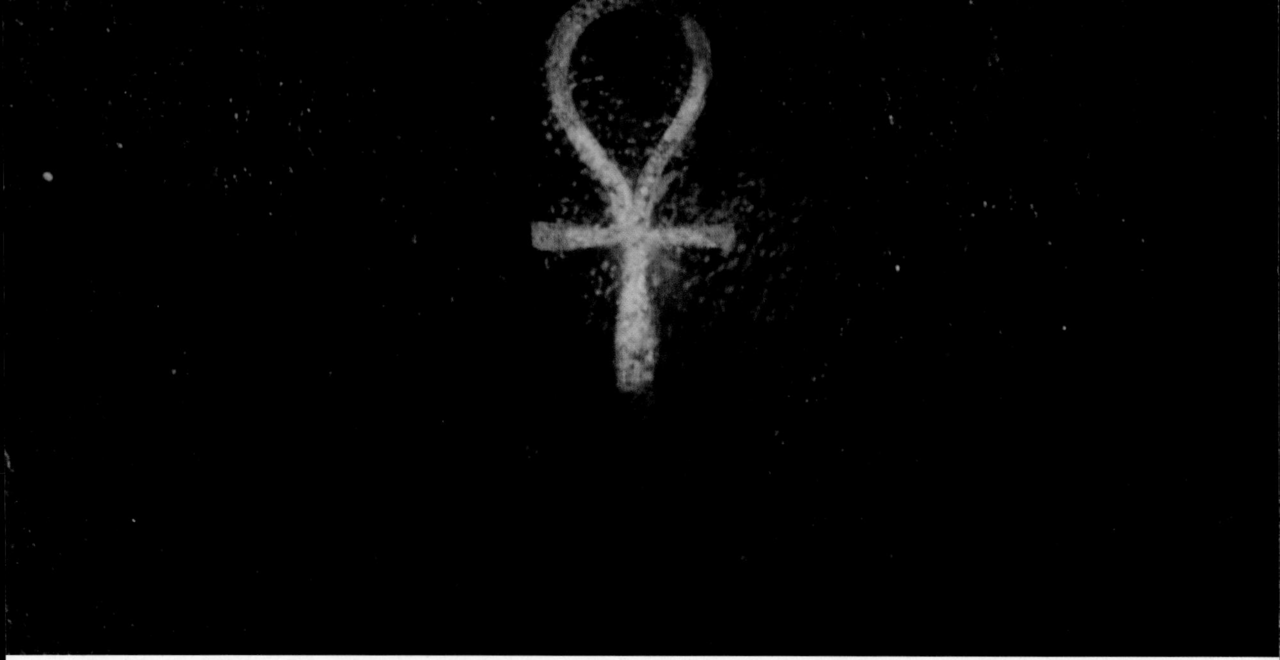

Death and Venice

Art by P. Craig Russell   Colors by Lovern Kindzierski   Letters by Todd Klein

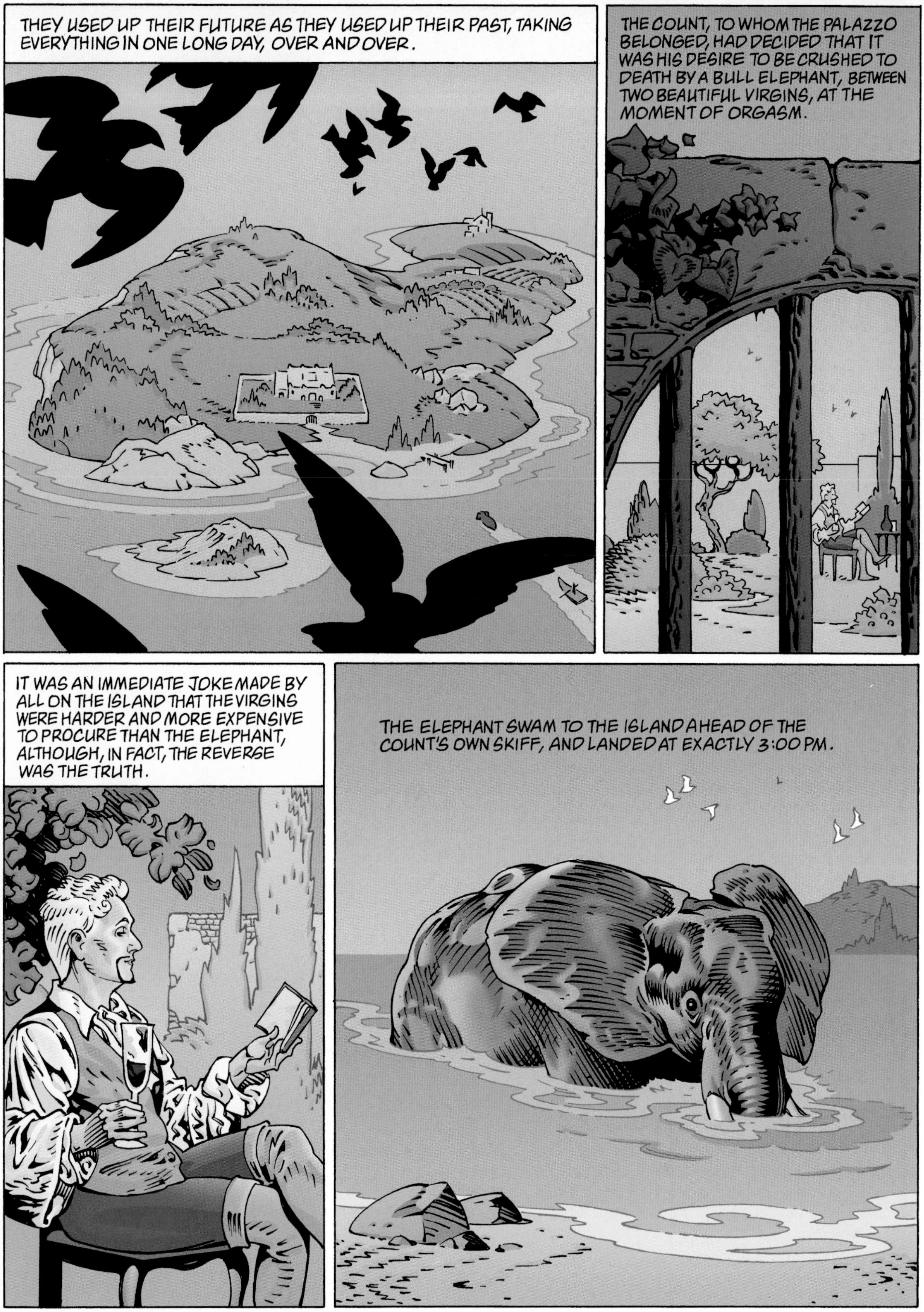
THEY USED UP THEIR FUTURE AS THEY USED UP THEIR PAST, TAKING EVERYTHING IN ONE LONG DAY, OVER AND OVER.
THE COUNT, TO WHOM THE PALAZZO BELONGED, HAD DECIDED THAT IT WAS HIS DESIRE TO BE CRUSHED TO DEATH BY A BULL ELEPHANT, BETWEEN TWO BEAUTIFUL VIRGINS, AT THE MOMENT OF ORGASM.
IT WAS AN IMMEDIATE JOKE MADE BY ALL ON THE ISLAND THAT THE VIRGINS WERE HARDER AND MORE EXPENSIVE TO PROCURE THAN THE ELEPHANT, ALTHOUGH, IN FACT, THE REVERSE WAS THE TRUTH.
THE ELEPHANT SWAM TO THE ISLAND AHEAD OF THE COUNT'S OWN SKIFF, AND LANDED AT EXACTLY 3:00 PM.

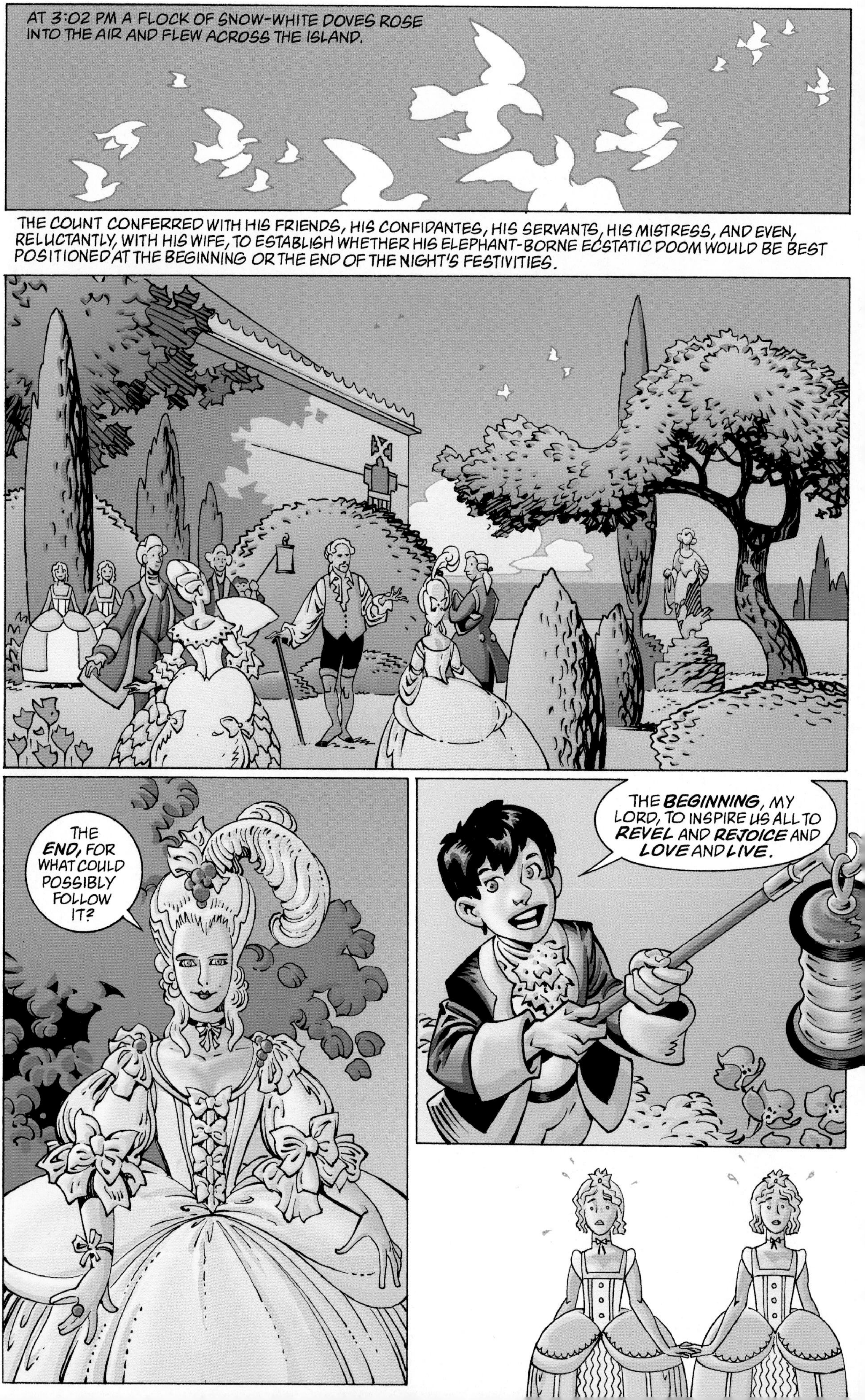
AT 3:02 PM A FLOCK OF SNOW-WHITE DOVES ROSE INTO THE AIR AND FLEW ACROSS THE ISLAND.
THE COUNT CONFERRED WITH HIS FRIENDS, HIS CONFIDANTES, HIS SERVANTS, HIS MISTRESS, AND EVEN, RELUCTANTLY, WITH HIS WIFE, TO ESTABLISH WHETHER HIS ELEPHANT-BORNE ECSTATIC DOOM WOULD BE BEST POSITIONED AT THE BEGINNING OR THE END OF THE NIGHT'S FESTIVITIES.
THE END, FOR WHAT COULD POSSIBLY FOLLOW IT?
THE BEGINNING, MY LORD, TO INSPIRE US ALL TO REVEL AND REJOICE AND LOVE AND LIVE.

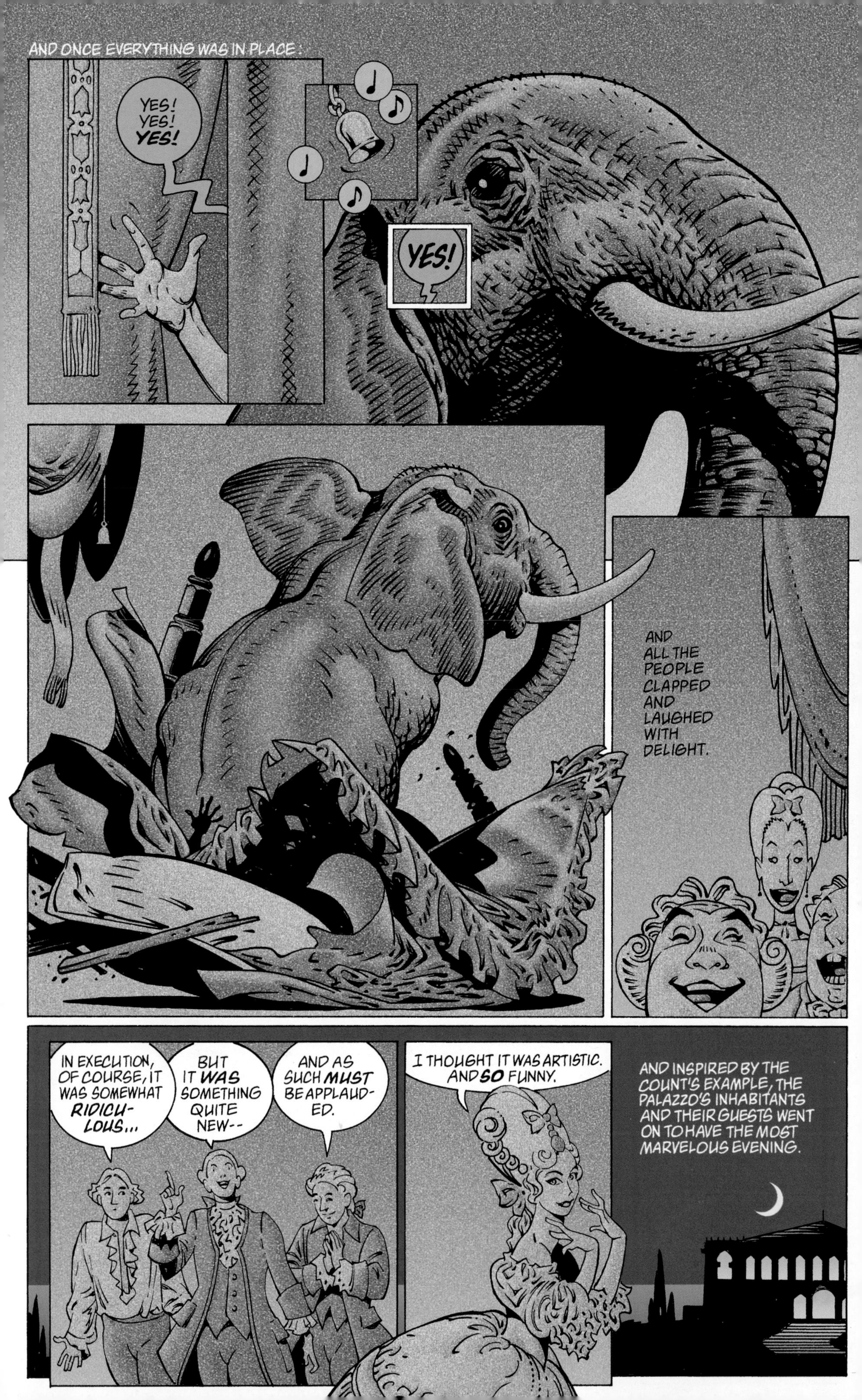
AND ONCE EVERYTHING WAS IN PLACE:
YES! YES! YES!
YES!
AND ALL THE PEOPLE CLAPPED AND LAUGHED WITH DELIGHT.
IN EXECUTION, OF COURSE, IT WAS SOMEWHAT RIDICULOUS...
BUT IT WAS SOMETHING QUITE NEW--
AND AS SUCH MUST BE APPLAUDED.
I THOUGHT IT WAS ARTISTIC. AND SO FUNNY.
AND INSPIRED BY THE COUNT'S EXAMPLE, THE PALAZZO'S INHABITANTS AND THEIR GUESTS WENT ON TO HAVE THE MOST MARVELOUS EVENING.

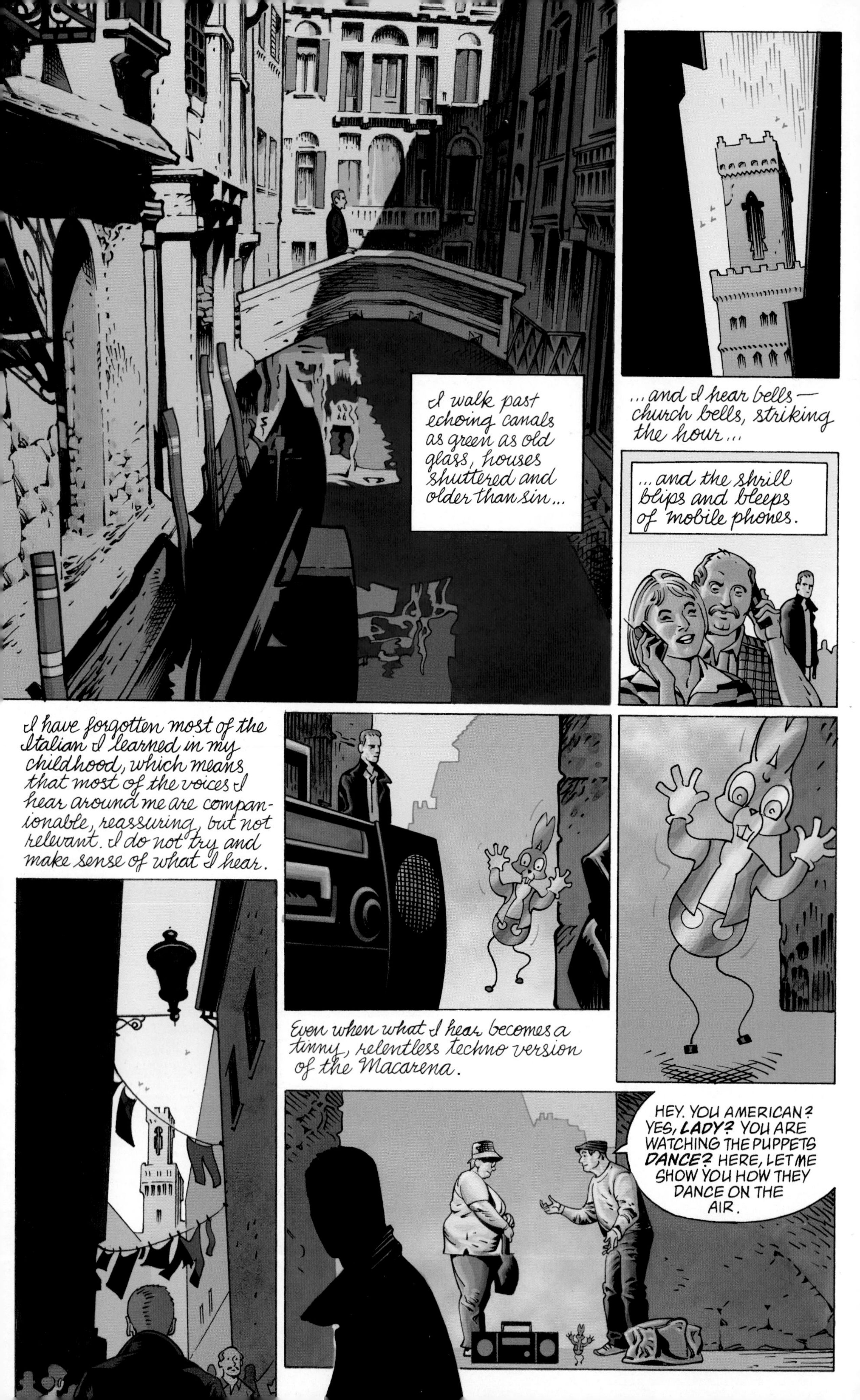
I walk past echoing canals as green as old glass, houses shuttered and older than sin...
...and I hear bells— church bells, striking the hour...
...and the shrill blips and bleeps of mobile phones.
I have forgotten most of the Italian I learned in my childhood, which means that most of the voices I hear around me are companionable, reassuring, but not relevant. I do not try and make sense of what I hear.
Even when what I hear becomes a tinny, relentless techno version of the Macarena.
HEY. YOU AMERICAN? YES, LADY? YOU ARE WATCHING THE PUPPETS DANCE? HERE, LET ME SHOW YOU HOW THEY DANCE ON THE AIR.

YOU SEE THE MAGNETS ON *FEET?* AND MAGNET ON HEAD? THEY FEEL THE MUSIC, THEY *DANCE.* LIKE DANCING COKE CAN.

YES?

ONLY FIVE DOLLAR EACH.

OH! THESE ARE JUST SO *CUTE.* AND WHAT DO I *DO* TO MAKE THEM DANCE?

JUST PUT THEM CLOSE TO SPEAKERS, PLAY MUSIC, THEY WILL DANCE. *ONLY* FIVE DOLLAR.

FOR *YOU,* TEN FOR FORTY DOLLAR.

THEY ARE THE *CUTEST* THINGS. MY GRANDCHILDREN WILL *LOVE* THEM...

EXCUSE ME. SORRY TO BUTT IN, BUT IF YOU TAKE THEM HOME FOR YOUR KIDS, THEY WON'T DANCE. IT'S JUST AN ILLUSION.

HE IS *MAD.*

GO *AWAY* MAD MAN.

THERE'S A *MOTOR* IN THE DUFFEL BAG. A *MONOFILAMENT LINE* RUNNING FROM THE BAG TO THE BOOMBOX. THE PUPPETS HANG ON THE LINE AND ARE JERKING UP AND DOWN.

IS *MAGNETS!*

NO *MAGNETS.* NO *MAGIC.* JUST STRING SO FINE YOU CAN'T SEE IT WHEN IT'S MOVING. BUT IF YOU *WANT* TO PAY FIVE DOLLARS EACH FOR PAPER DOLLS, YOU GO AHEAD.

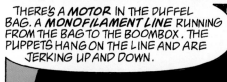

I SEE. THANK YOU, YOUNG MAN.

EH. *THIS* IS HOW I EARN MY *LIVING.* PLEASE. LEAVE ME *ALONE.*

He has a point. There are worse ways to earn a living. I leave him be.

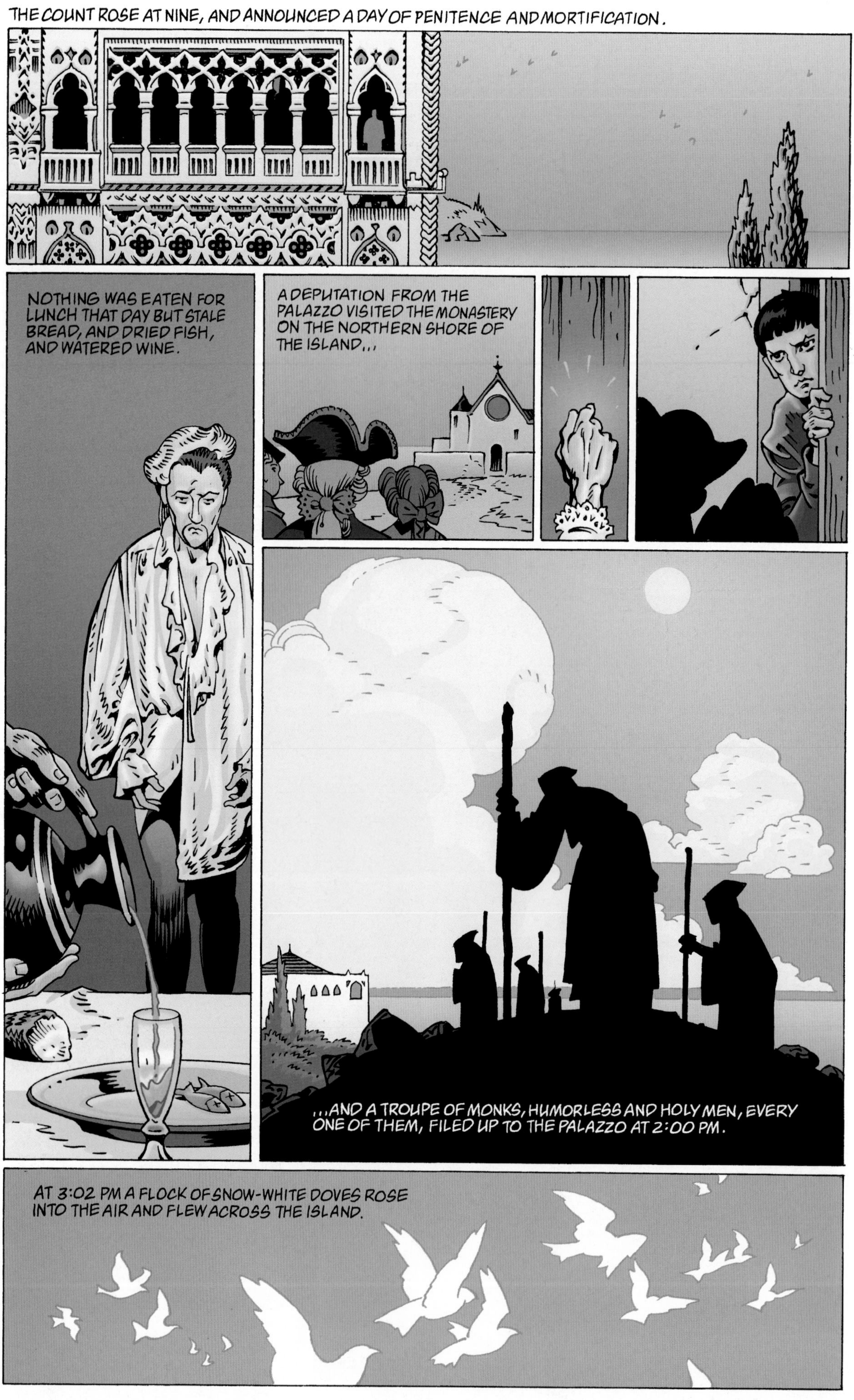
THE COUNT ROSE AT NINE, AND ANNOUNCED A DAY OF PENITENCE AND MORTIFICATION.
NOTHING WAS EATEN FOR LUNCH THAT DAY BUT STALE BREAD, AND DRIED FISH, AND WATERED WINE.
A DEPUTATION FROM THE PALAZZO VISITED THE MONASTERY ON THE NORTHERN SHORE OF THE ISLAND...
...AND A TROUPE OF MONKS, HUMORLESS AND HOLY MEN, EVERY ONE OF THEM, FILED UP TO THE PALAZZO AT 2:00 PM.
AT 3:02 PM A FLOCK OF SNOW-WHITE DOVES ROSE INTO THE AIR AND FLEW ACROSS THE ISLAND.

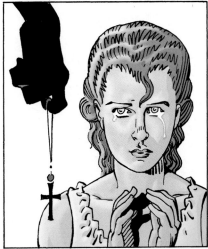

THE CONFESSIONS WERE HEARTFELT, AND ACCOMPANIED BY TEARS.

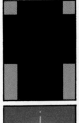

AND ONCE CONFESSED, THE PENITENTS KNELT, TO BE SCOURGED UPON THEIR NAKED BACKS, FLOGGED UNTIL THEIR SKIN WAS LACERATED AND BLOOD RAN ACROSS THE PALAZZO'S MOSAIC FLOOR.

AND NO MAN THERE, AND NO WOMAN WAS MORE PENITENT...

...MORE HONEST, SHED SO MANY TEARS...

...OR SO MUCH BLOOD,...

...AS THE COUNT HIMSELF.

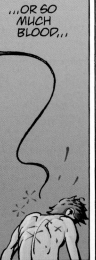

THEY PRAYED...

...AND THEY WAILED,...

...AND THEY REPENTED,...

...AND THEY BLED UNTIL MIDNIGHT.

A MARVELOUS END TO A PERFECT DAY.

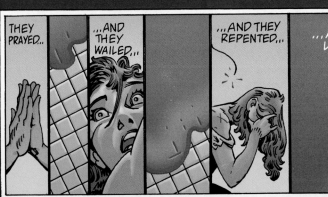

They've been parting visitors from their money for so long here in Venice that they can't help but be good at it. Normally, they give value for money. That last encounter left a sour taste in my mouth. They didn't cheat the tourists when I came here as a boy.

And that starts me remembering once again.

I have remembered this too much; so now I can no longer be sure whether it is the event that I am remembering, or my memory of the event.

A hot, still day. Lizards, on the side of a brick wall, watch me warily.

You could catch them, if you were fast enough. But if you grabbed them by the tail it would break off, wriggling, in your hand, while the lizard ran away.

I had been staying with my aunt and uncle, with my cousins. My Italian was not good, but I could make myself understood, and we all spoke some English.

We loaded the picnic food and the bottles of fruit-juice and the wine into my Uncle's vaporetto, the water-taxi he drove, and we travelled out into the lagoon until we reached the island.

There are many islands in the Venice Lagoon. Over the years they have all been inhabited, my Uncle told me, as I proudly steered the boat. But times change. He pointed out the islands that hold factories, barracks, munitions, convents, as we passed.

I remember the slosh, slosh, slosh of the water against the side of the motorboat.

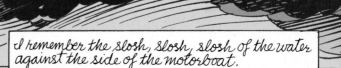

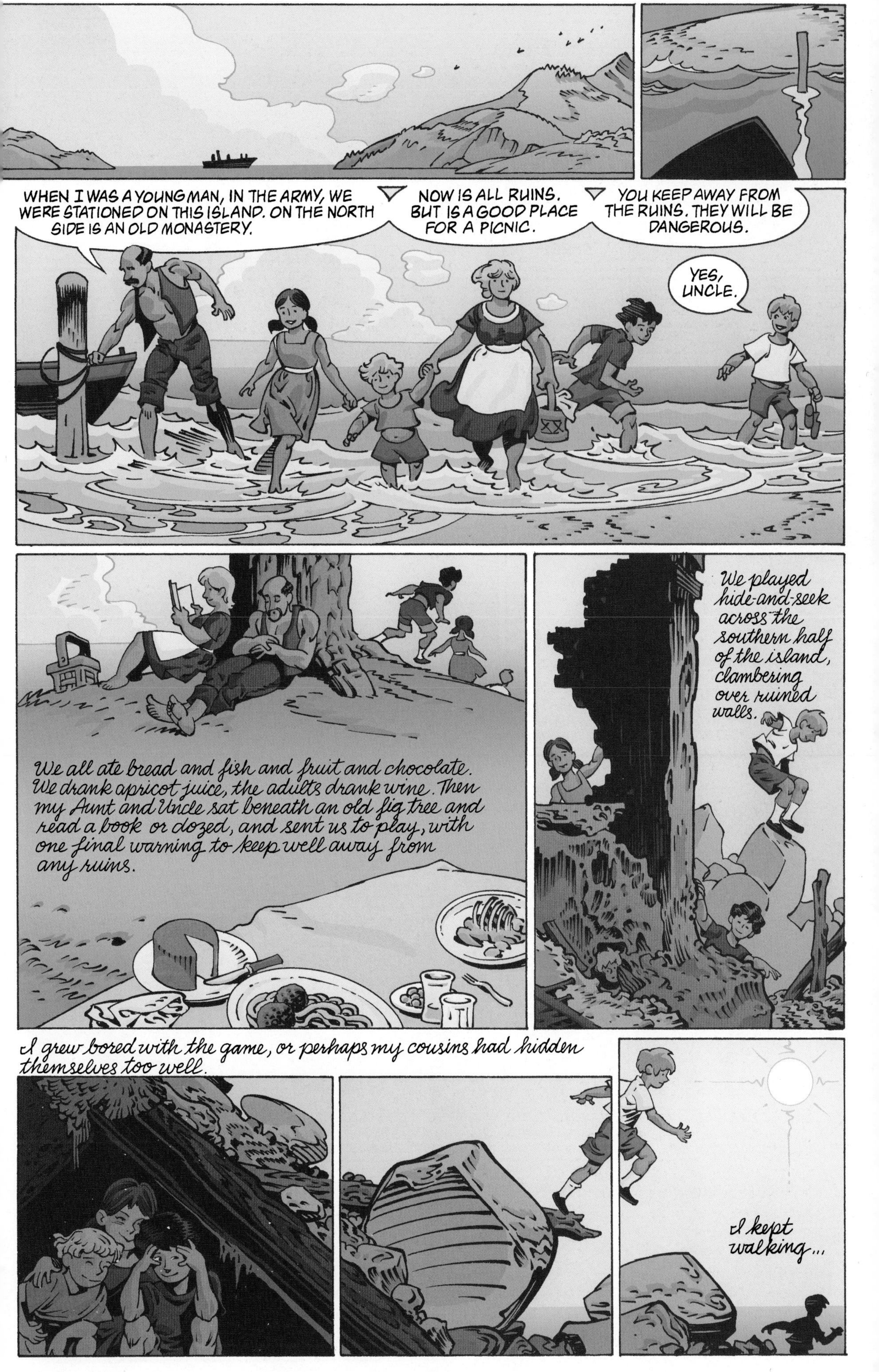
WHEN I WAS A YOUNG MAN, IN THE ARMY, WE WERE STATIONED ON THIS ISLAND. ON THE NORTH SIDE IS AN OLD MONASTERY.
NOW IS ALL RUINS. BUT IS A GOOD PLACE FOR A PICNIC.
YOU KEEP AWAY FROM THE RUINS. THEY WILL BE DANGEROUS.
YES, UNCLE.
We all ate bread and fish and fruit and chocolate. We drank apricot juice, the adults drank wine. Then my Aunt and Uncle sat beneath an old fig tree and read a book or dozed, and sent us to play, with one final warning to keep well away from any ruins.
We played hide-and-seek across the southern half of the island, clambering over ruined walls.
I grew bored with the game, or perhaps my cousins had hidden themselves too well.
I kept walking...

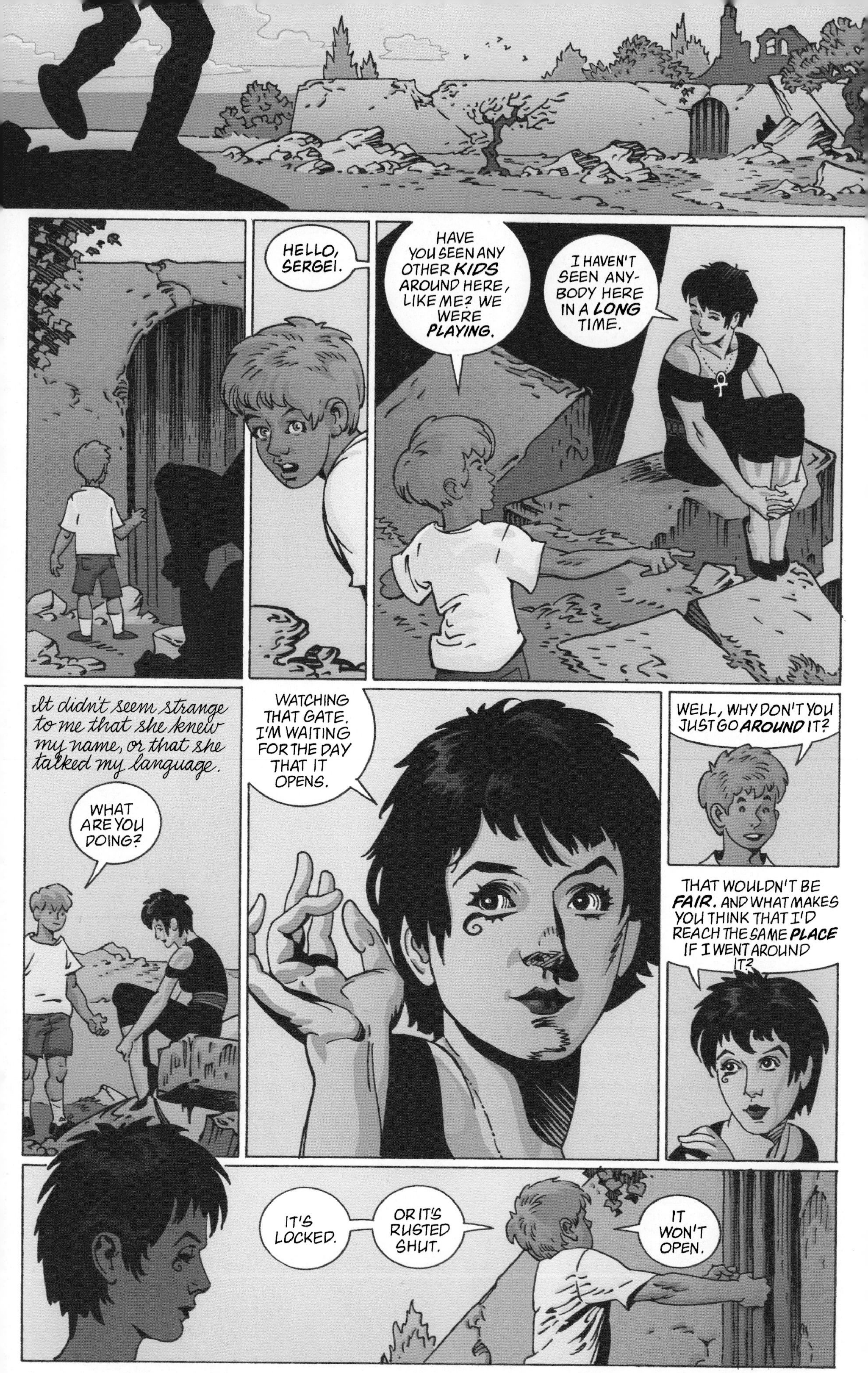
HELLO, SERGEI.
HAVE YOU SEEN ANY OTHER KIDS AROUND HERE, LIKE ME? WE WERE PLAYING.
I HAVEN'T SEEN ANYBODY HERE IN A LONG TIME.
It didn't seem strange to me that she knew my name, or that she talked my language.
WHAT ARE YOU DOING?
WATCHING THAT GATE. I'M WAITING FOR THE DAY THAT IT OPENS.
WELL, WHY DON'T YOU JUST GO AROUND IT?
THAT WOULDN'T BE FAIR. AND WHAT MAKES YOU THINK THAT I'D REACH THE SAME PLACE IF I WENT AROUND IT?
IT WON'T OPEN.
IT'S LOCKED.
OR IT'S RUSTED SHUT.

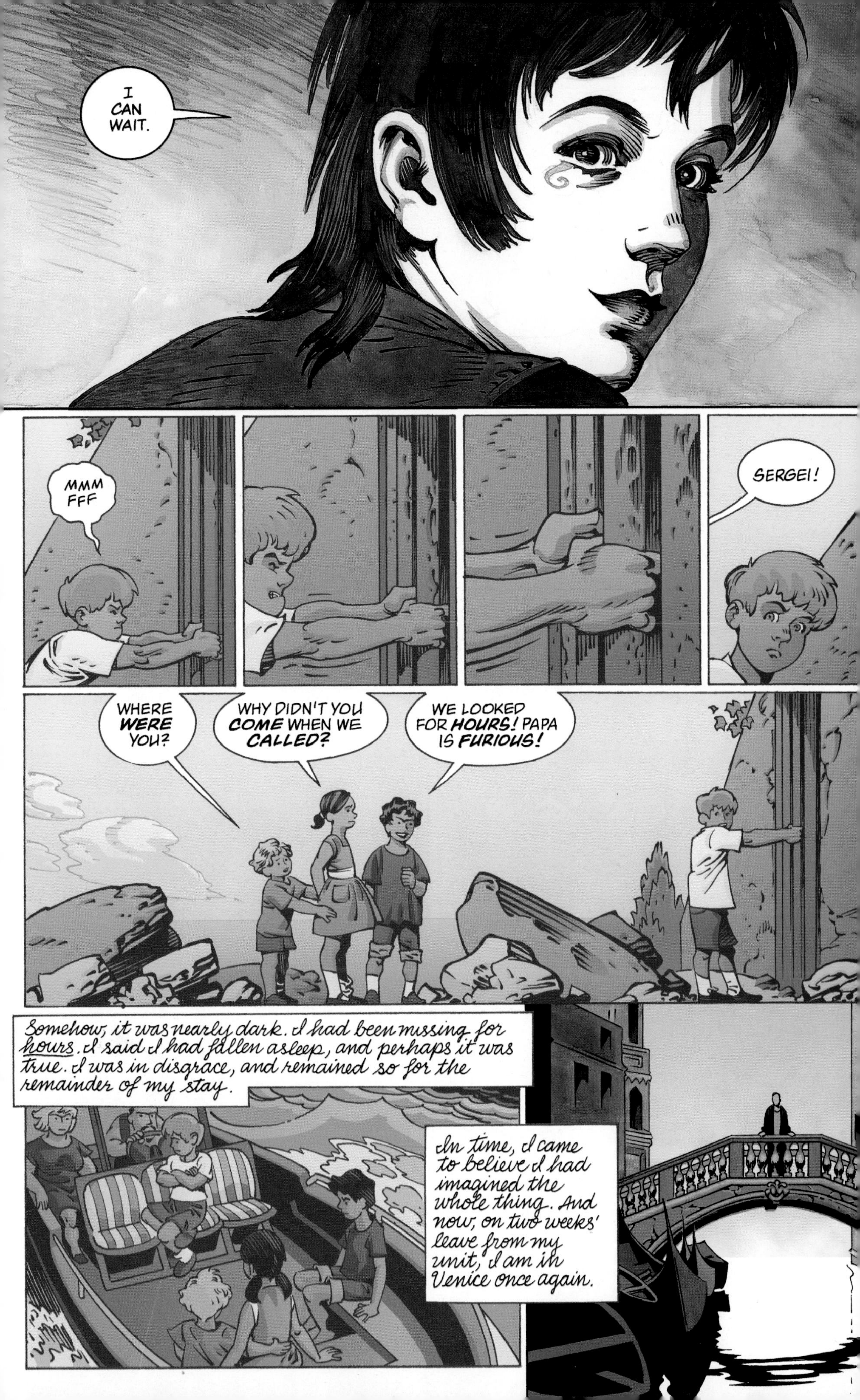
I CAN WAIT.
MMM FFF
SERGEI!
WHERE **WERE** YOU?
WHY DIDN'T YOU **COME** WHEN WE **CALLED?**
WE LOOKED FOR **HOURS!** PAPA IS **FURIOUS!**
Somehow, it was nearly dark. I had been missing for hours. I said I had fallen asleep, and perhaps it was true. I was in disgrace, and remained so for the remainder of my stay.
In time, I came to believe I had imagined the whole thing. And now, on two weeks' leave from my unit, I am in Venice once again.

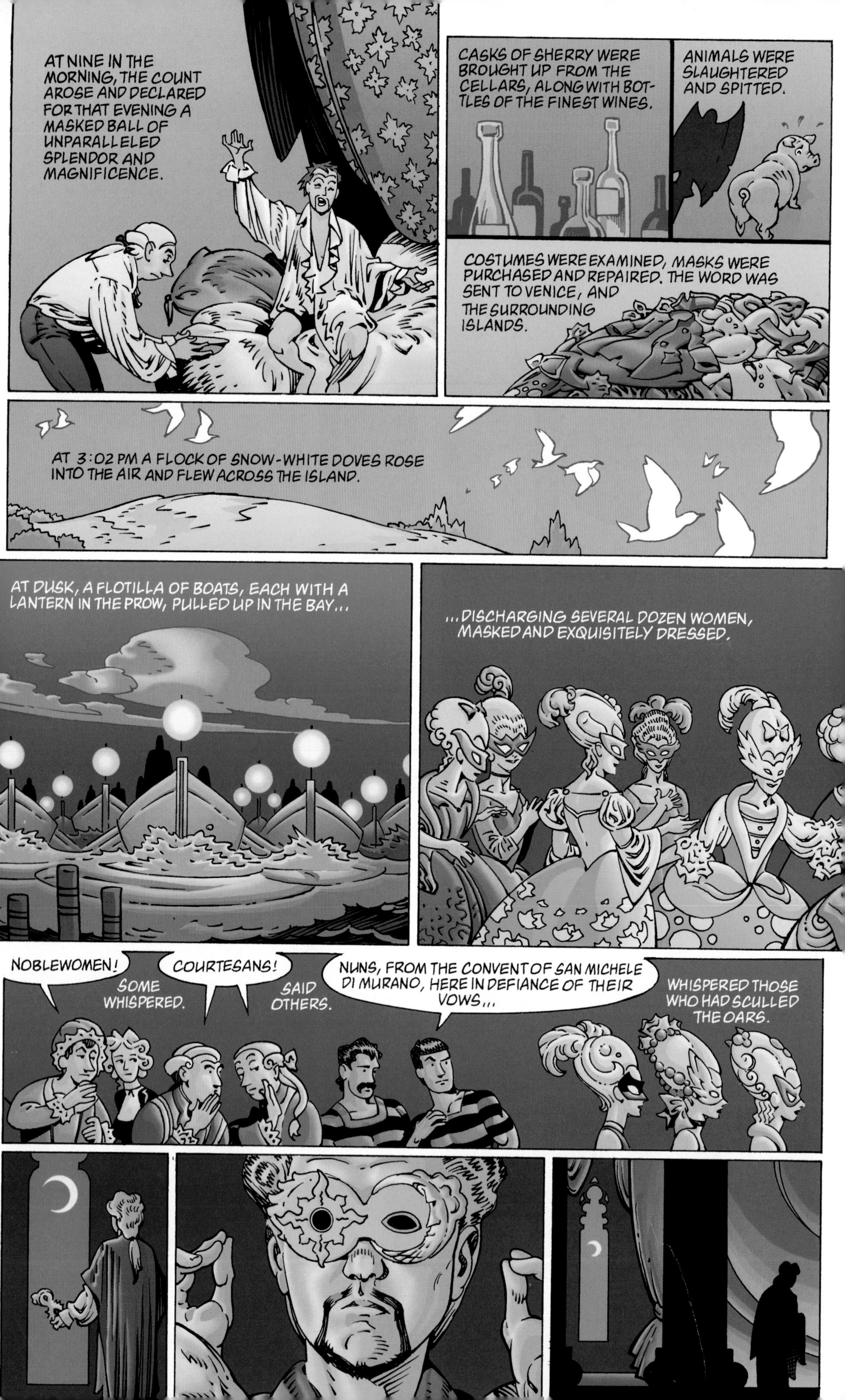
AT NINE IN THE MORNING, THE COUNT AROSE AND DECLARED FOR THAT EVENING A MASKED BALL OF UNPARALLELED SPLENDOR AND MAGNIFICENCE.
CASKS OF SHERRY WERE BROUGHT UP FROM THE CELLARS, ALONG WITH BOTTLES OF THE FINEST WINES.
ANIMALS WERE SLAUGHTERED AND SPITTED.
COSTUMES WERE EXAMINED, MASKS WERE PURCHASED AND REPAIRED. THE WORD WAS SENT TO VENICE, AND THE SURROUNDING ISLANDS.
AT 3:02 PM A FLOCK OF SNOW-WHITE DOVES ROSE INTO THE AIR AND FLEW ACROSS THE ISLAND.
AT DUSK, A FLOTILLA OF BOATS, EACH WITH A LANTERN IN THE PROW, PULLED UP IN THE BAY...
...DISCHARGING SEVERAL DOZEN WOMEN, MASKED AND EXQUISITELY DRESSED.
NOBLEWOMEN!
SOME WHISPERED.
COURTESANS!
SAID OTHERS.
NUNS, FROM THE CONVENT OF SAN MICHELE DI MURANO, HERE IN DEFIANCE OF THEIR VOWS...
WHISPERED THOSE WHO HAD SCULLED THE OARS.

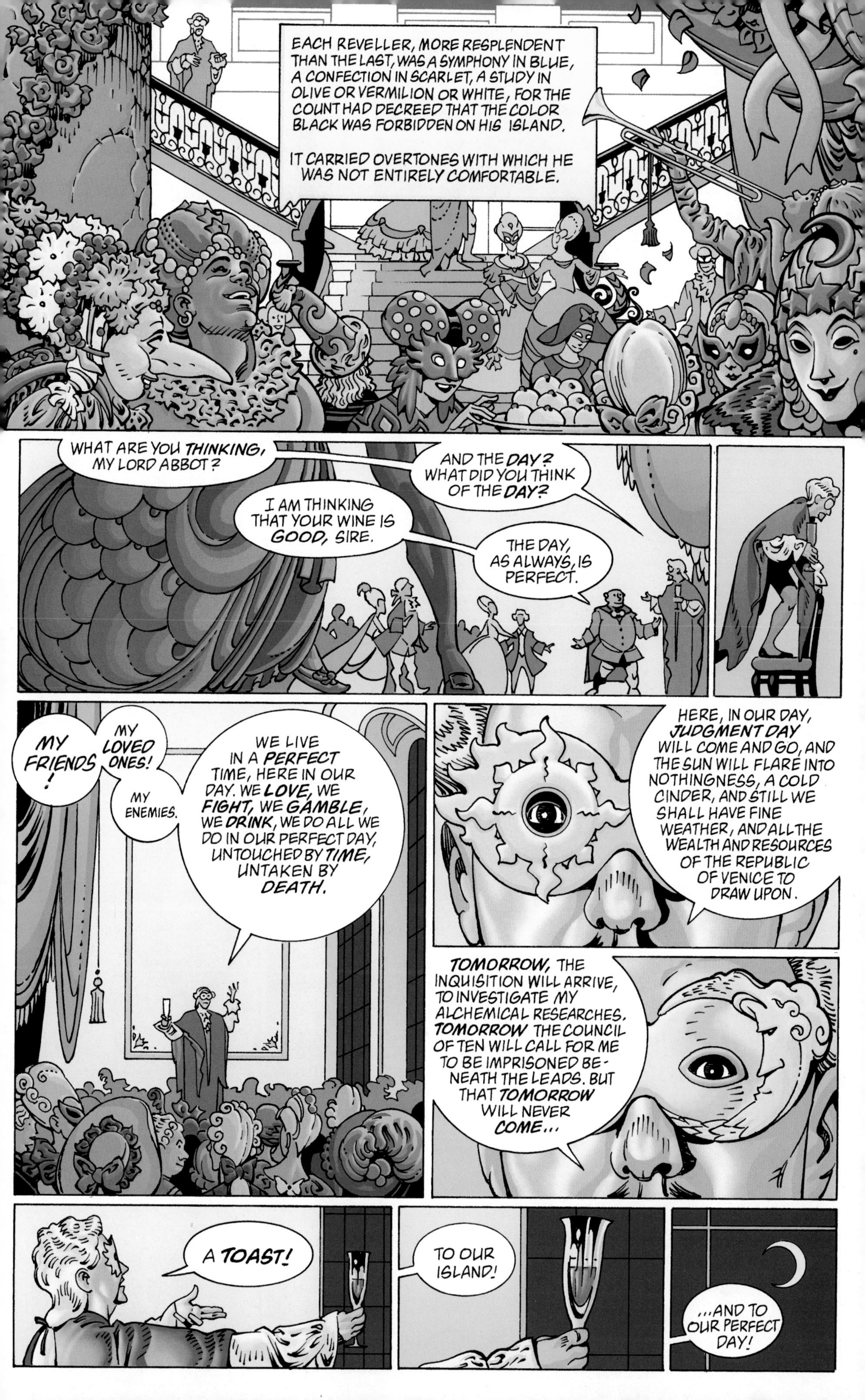
EACH REVELLER, MORE RESPLENDENT THAN THE LAST, WAS A SYMPHONY IN BLUE, A CONFECTION IN SCARLET, A STUDY IN OLIVE OR VERMILION OR WHITE, FOR THE COUNT HAD DECREED THAT THE COLOR BLACK WAS FORBIDDEN ON HIS ISLAND.
IT CARRIED OVERTONES WITH WHICH HE WAS NOT ENTIRELY COMFORTABLE.
WHAT ARE YOU THINKING, MY LORD ABBOT?
I AM THINKING THAT YOUR WINE IS GOOD, SIRE.
AND THE DAY? WHAT DID YOU THINK OF THE DAY?
THE DAY, AS ALWAYS, IS PERFECT.
MY FRIENDS!
MY LOVED ONES!
MY ENEMIES.
WE LIVE IN A PERFECT TIME, HERE IN OUR DAY. WE LOVE, WE FIGHT, WE GAMBLE, WE DRINK, WE DO ALL WE DO IN OUR PERFECT DAY, UNTOUCHED BY TIME, UNTAKEN BY DEATH.
HERE, IN OUR DAY, JUDGMENT DAY WILL COME AND GO, AND THE SUN WILL FLARE INTO NOTHINGNESS, A COLD CINDER, AND STILL WE SHALL HAVE FINE WEATHER, AND ALL THE WEALTH AND RESOURCES OF THE REPUBLIC OF VENICE TO DRAW UPON.
TOMORROW, THE INQUISITION WILL ARRIVE, TO INVESTIGATE MY ALCHEMICAL RESEARCHES. TOMORROW THE COUNCIL OF TEN WILL CALL FOR ME TO BE IMPRISONED BENEATH THE LEADS. BUT THAT TOMORROW WILL NEVER COME...
A TOAST!
TO OUR ISLAND!
...AND TO OUR PERFECT DAY!

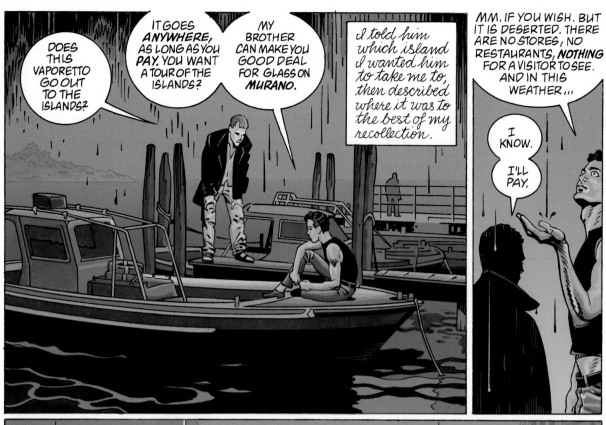

DOES THIS VAPORETTO GO OUT TO THE ISLANDS?

IT GOES *ANYWHERE*, AS LONG AS YOU *PAY*. YOU WANT A TOUR OF THE ISLANDS?

MY BROTHER CAN MAKE YOU GOOD DEAL FOR GLASS ON *MURANO*.

I told him which island I wanted him to take me to, then described where it was to the best of my recollection.

MM. IF YOU WISH. BUT IT IS DESERTED. THERE ARE NO STORES, NO RESTAURANTS, *NOTHING* FOR A VISITOR TO SEE. AND IN THIS WEATHER...

I KNOW.

I'LL PAY.

So he took my money, and the vaporetto, the water taxi, sped through the canals of Venice on its way to the lagoon.

From the canals, you can see the damage the rising water levels is doing to the city.

History, I thought, accretes in Venice like silt in a canal...

...and it laps against the bricks and rocks and the deep wooden piles.

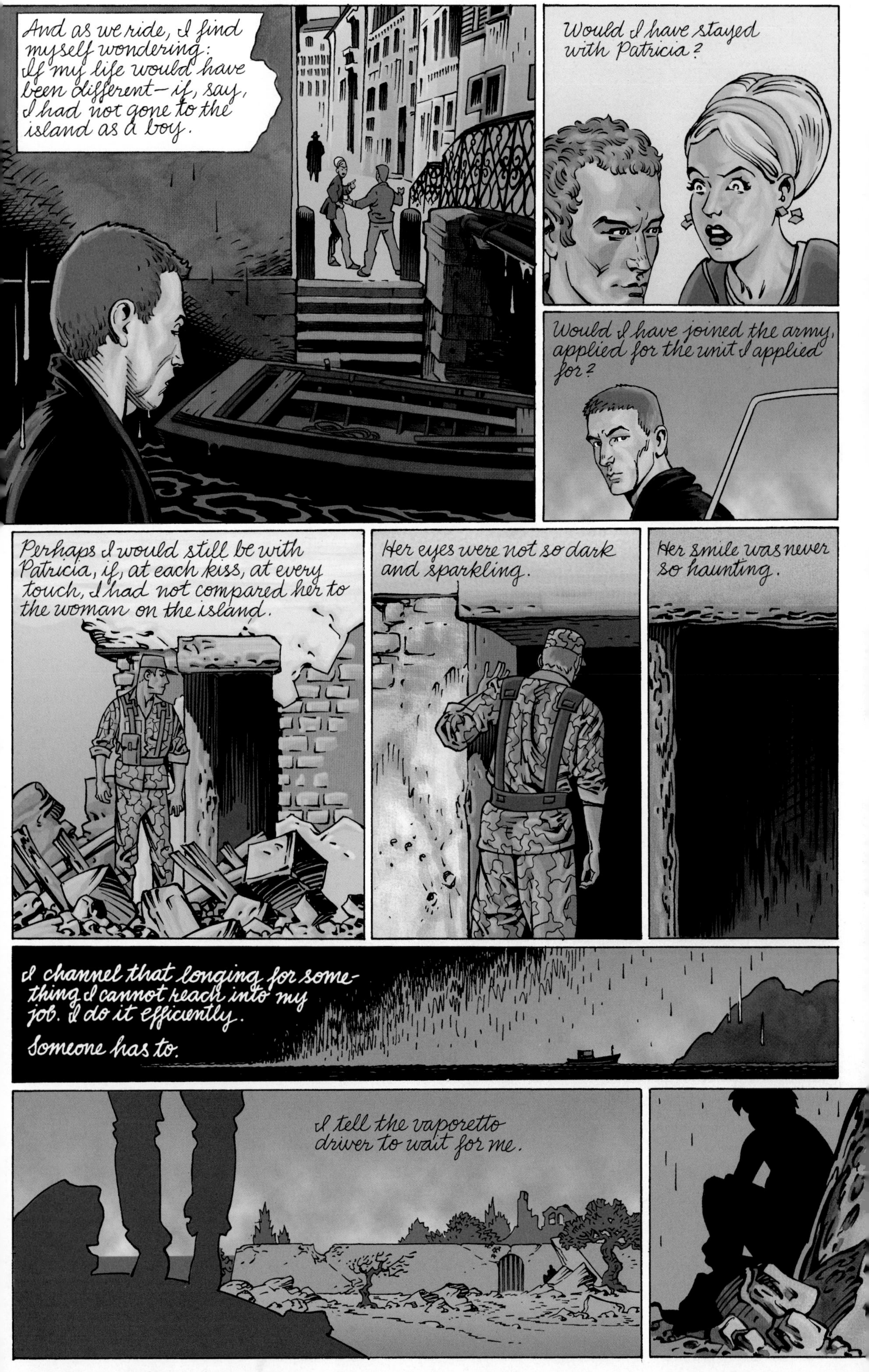

And as we ride, I find myself wondering: If my life would have been different—if, say, I had not gone to the island as a boy.
Would I have stayed with Patricia?
Would I have joined the army, applied for the unit I applied for?
Perhaps I would still be with Patricia, if, at each kiss, at every touch, I had not compared her to the woman on the island.
Her eyes were not so dark and sparkling.
Her smile was never so haunting.
I channel that longing for something I cannot reach into my job. I do it efficiently.
Someone has to.
I tell the vaporetto driver to wait for me.

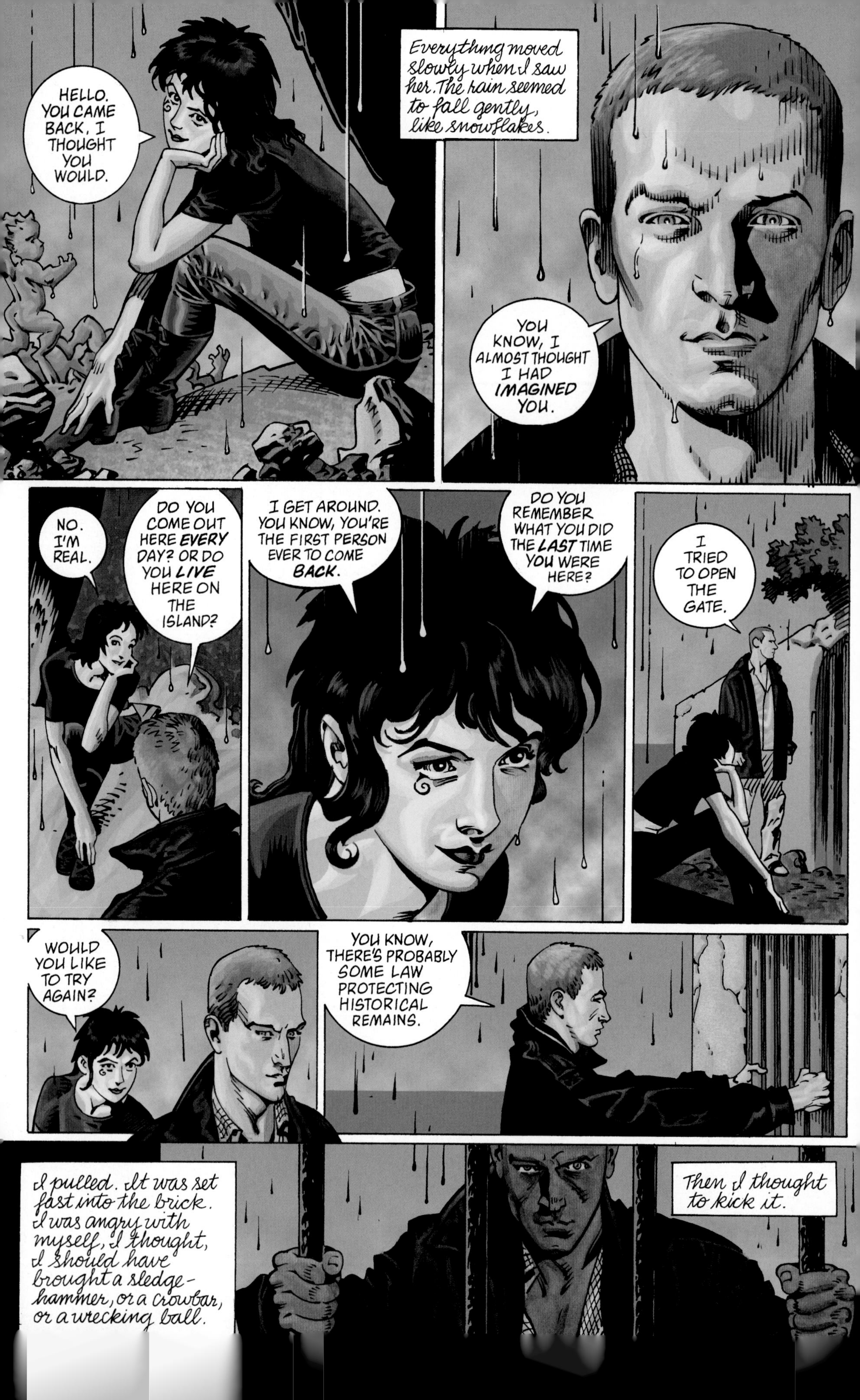
HELLO. YOU CAME BACK, I THOUGHT YOU WOULD.
Everything moved slowly when I saw her. The rain seemed to fall gently, like snowflakes.
YOU KNOW, I ALMOST THOUGHT I HAD IMAGINED YOU.
NO. I'M REAL.
DO YOU COME OUT HERE EVERY DAY? OR DO YOU LIVE HERE ON THE ISLAND?
I GET AROUND. YOU KNOW, YOU'RE THE FIRST PERSON EVER TO COME BACK.
DO YOU REMEMBER WHAT YOU DID THE LAST TIME YOU WERE HERE?
I TRIED TO OPEN THE GATE.
WOULD YOU LIKE TO TRY AGAIN?
YOU KNOW, THERE'S PROBABLY SOME LAW PROTECTING HISTORICAL REMAINS.
I pulled. It was set fast into the brick. I was angry with myself, I thought, I should have brought a sledge-hammer, or a crowbar, or a wrecking ball.
Then I thought to kick it.

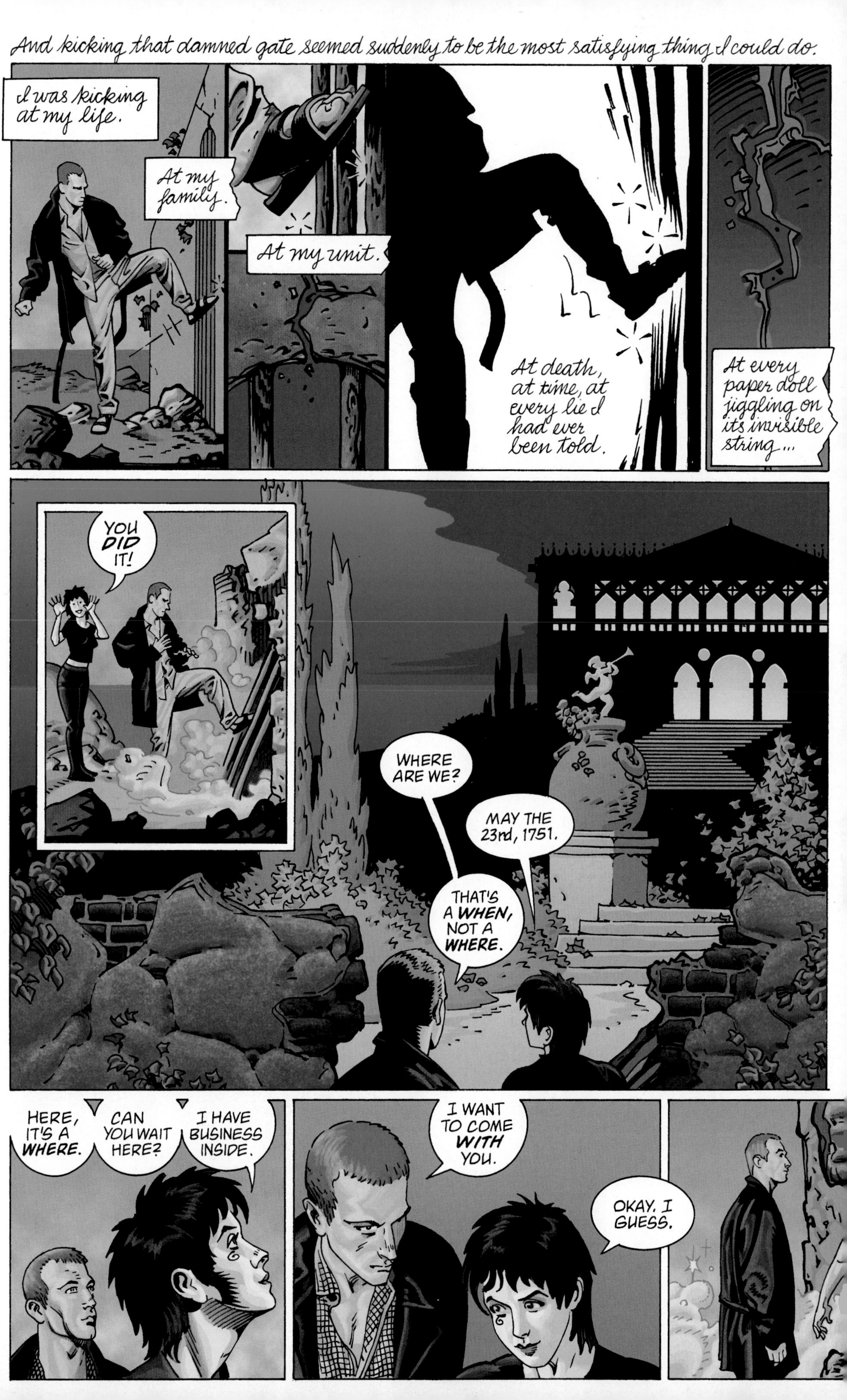

And kicking that damned gate seemed suddenly to be the most satisfying thing I could do.
I was kicking at my life.
At my family.
At my unit.
At death, at time, at every lie I had ever been told.
At every paper doll jiggling on its invisible string...
YOU DID IT!
WHERE ARE WE?
MAY THE 23rd, 1751.
THAT'S A WHEN, NOT A WHERE.
HERE, IT'S A WHERE.
CAN YOU WAIT HERE?
I HAVE BUSINESS INSIDE.
I WANT TO COME WITH YOU.
OKAY. I GUESS.

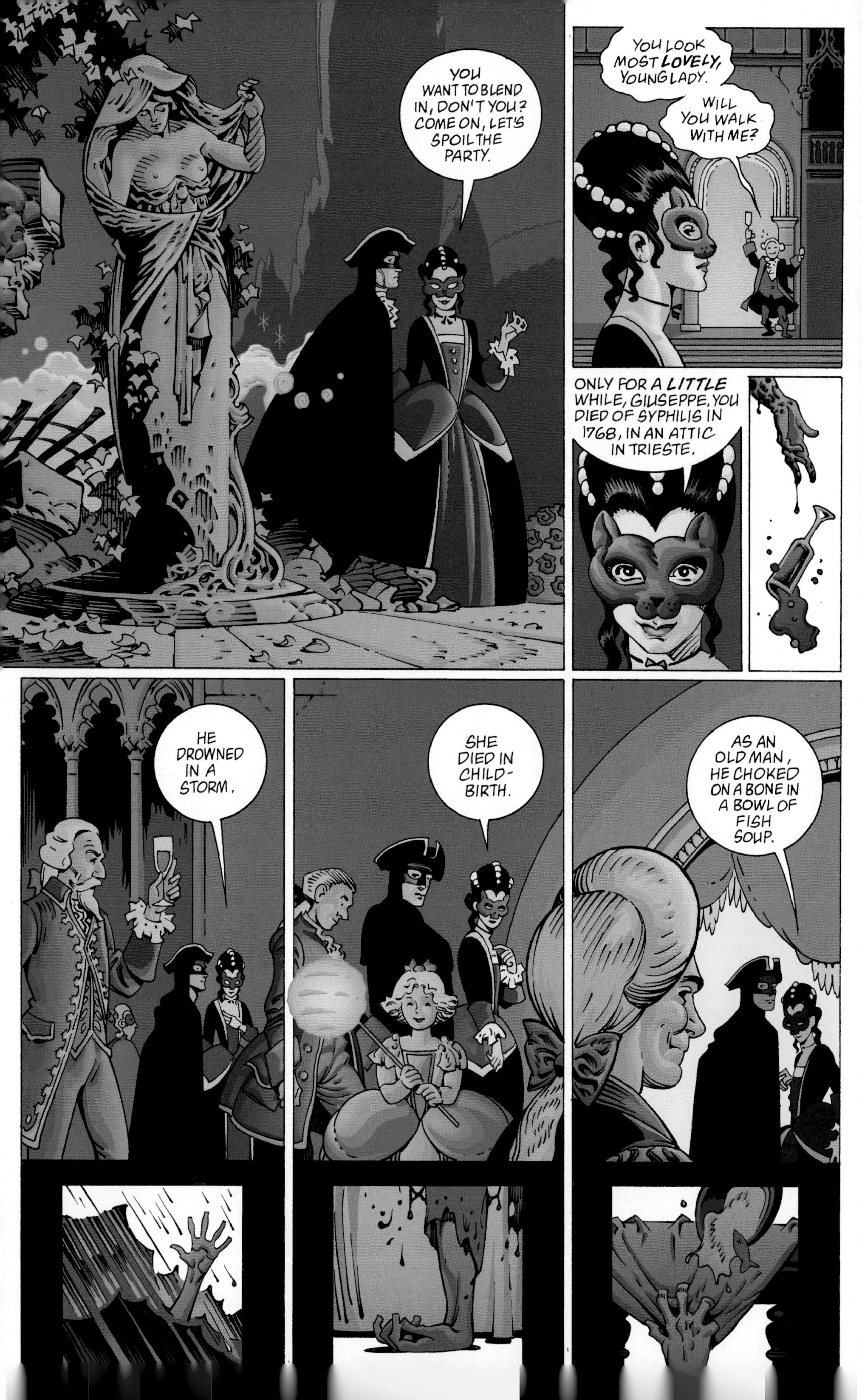
YOU WANT TO BLEND IN, DON'T YOU? COME ON, LET'S SPOIL THE PARTY.
YOU LOOK MOST LOVELY, YOUNG LADY.
WILL YOU WALK WITH ME?
ONLY FOR A LITTLE WHILE, GIUSEPPE. YOU DIED OF SYPHILIS IN 1768, IN AN ATTIC IN TRIESTE.
HE DROWNED IN A STORM.
SHE DIED IN CHILD-BIRTH.
AS AN OLD MAN, HE CHOKED ON A BONE IN A BOWL OF FISH SOUP.

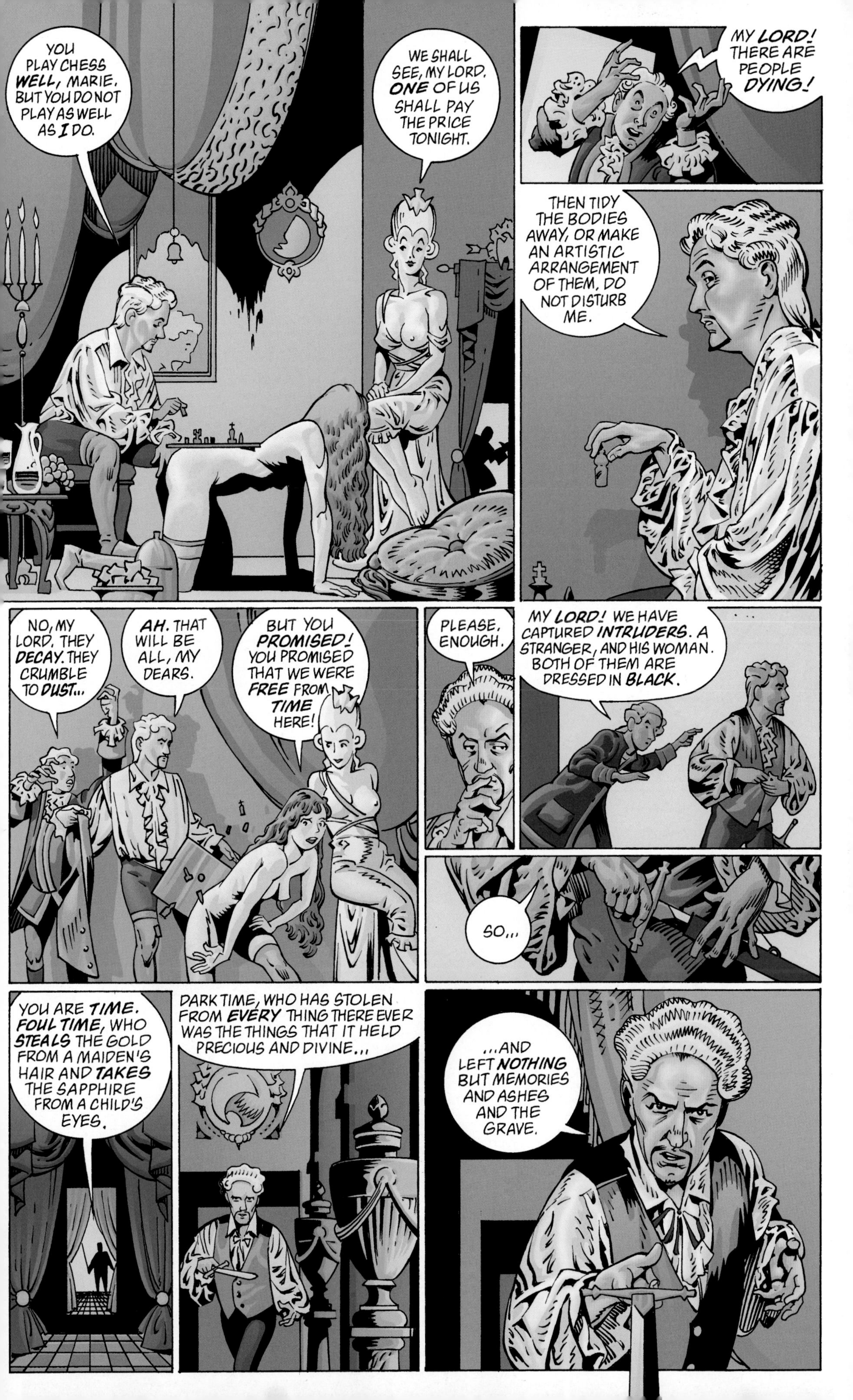
YOU PLAY CHESS WELL, MARIE. BUT YOU DO NOT PLAY AS WELL AS I DO.
WE SHALL SEE, MY LORD. ONE OF US SHALL PAY THE PRICE TONIGHT.
MY LORD! THERE ARE PEOPLE DYING!
THEN TIDY THE BODIES AWAY, OR MAKE AN ARTISTIC ARRANGEMENT OF THEM. DO NOT DISTURB ME.
NO, MY LORD. THEY DECAY. THEY CRUMBLE TO DUST...
AH. THAT WILL BE ALL, MY DEARS.
BUT YOU PROMISED! YOU PROMISED THAT WE WERE FREE FROM TIME HERE!
PLEASE. ENOUGH.
MY LORD! WE HAVE CAPTURED INTRUDERS. A STRANGER, AND HIS WOMAN. BOTH OF THEM ARE DRESSED IN BLACK.
...
SO...
YOU ARE TIME. FOUL TIME, WHO STEALS THE GOLD FROM A MAIDEN'S HAIR AND TAKES THE SAPPHIRE FROM A CHILD'S EYES.
DARK TIME, WHO HAS STOLEN FROM EVERY THING THERE EVER WAS THE THINGS THAT IT HELD PRECIOUS AND DIVINE...
...AND LEFT NOTHING BUT MEMORIES AND ASHES AND THE GRAVE.

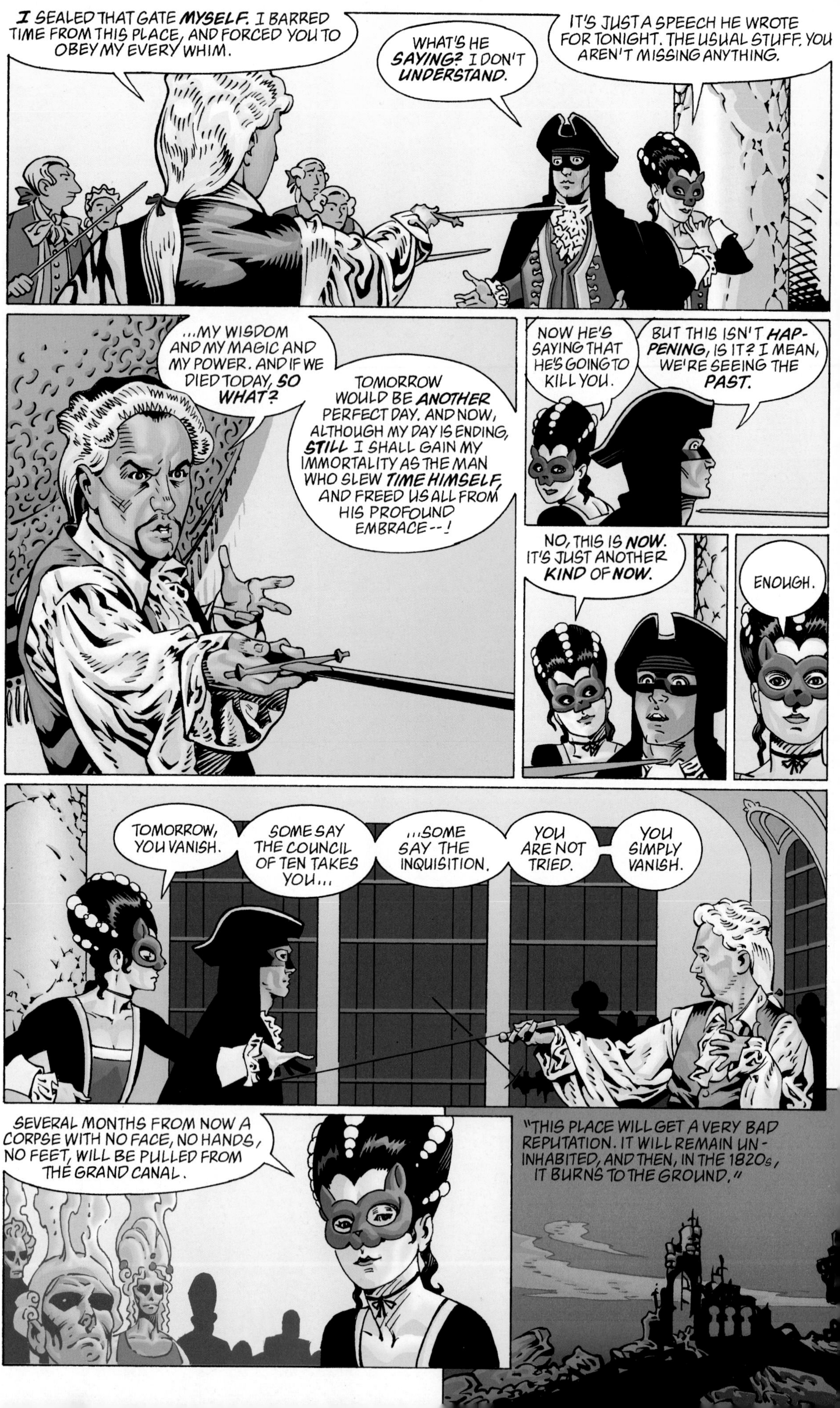
I SEALED THAT GATE MYSELF. I BARRED TIME FROM THIS PLACE, AND FORCED YOU TO OBEY MY EVERY WHIM.
WHAT'S HE SAYING? I DON'T UNDERSTAND.
IT'S JUST A SPEECH HE WROTE FOR TONIGHT. THE USUAL STUFF. YOU AREN'T MISSING ANYTHING.
...MY WISDOM AND MY MAGIC AND MY POWER. AND IF WE DIED TODAY, SO WHAT?
TOMORROW WOULD BE ANOTHER PERFECT DAY. AND NOW, ALTHOUGH MY DAY IS ENDING, STILL I SHALL GAIN MY IMMORTALITY AS THE MAN WHO SLEW TIME HIMSELF, AND FREED US ALL FROM HIS PROFOUND EMBRACE--!
NOW HE'S SAYING THAT HE'S GOING TO KILL YOU.
BUT THIS ISN'T HAPPENING, IS IT? I MEAN, WE'RE SEEING THE PAST.
NO, THIS IS NOW. IT'S JUST ANOTHER KIND OF NOW.
ENOUGH.
TOMORROW, YOU VANISH.
SOME SAY THE COUNCIL OF TEN TAKES YOU...
...SOME SAY THE INQUISITION.
YOU ARE NOT TRIED.
YOU SIMPLY VANISH.
SEVERAL MONTHS FROM NOW A CORPSE WITH NO FACE, NO HANDS, NO FEET, WILL BE PULLED FROM THE GRAND CANAL.
"THIS PLACE WILL GET A VERY BAD REPUTATION. IT WILL REMAIN UNINHABITED, AND THEN, IN THE 1820s, IT BURNS TO THE GROUND."

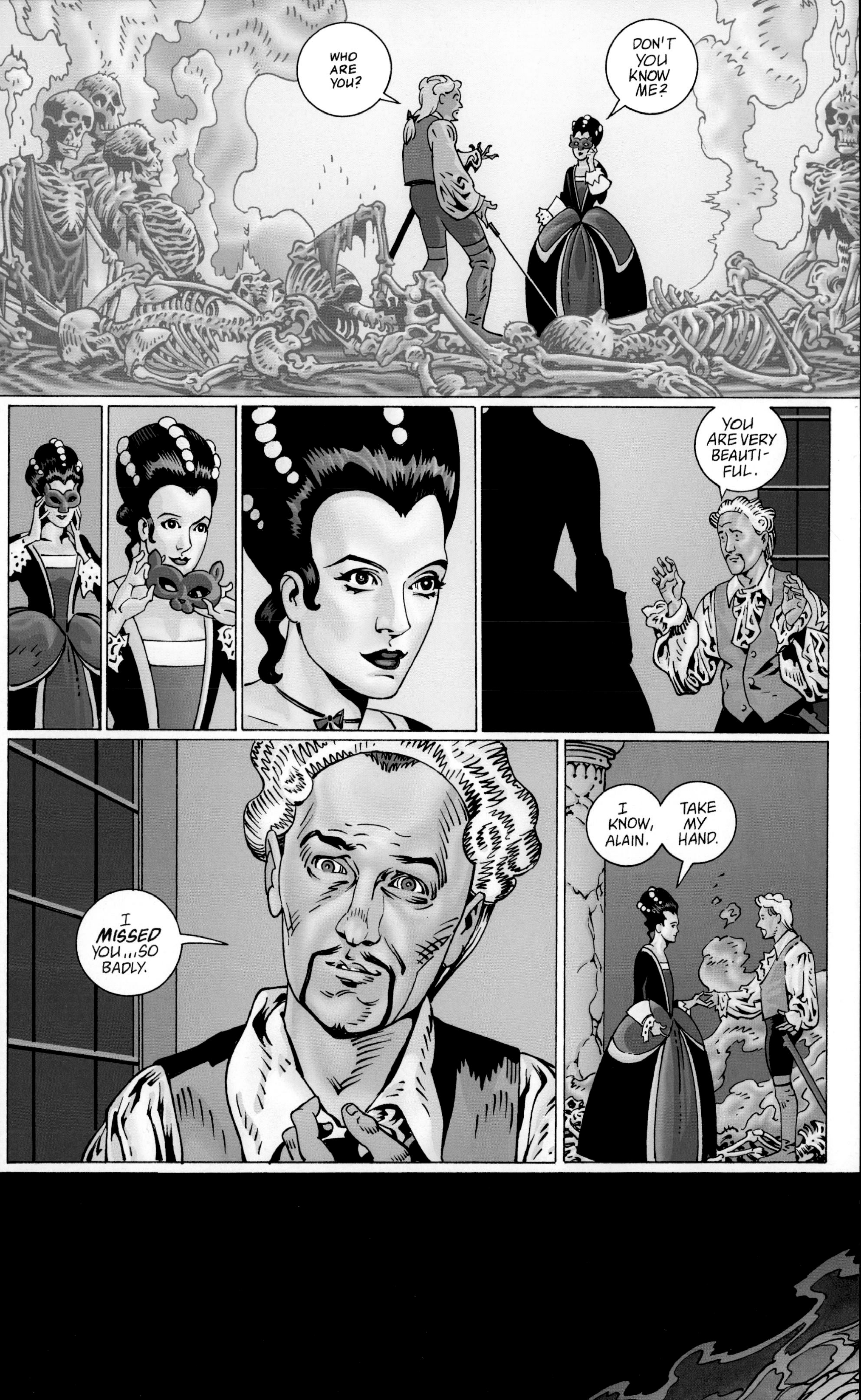
WHO ARE YOU?
DON'T YOU KNOW ME?
YOU ARE VERY BEAUTI- FUL.
I MISSED YOU...SO BADLY.
I KNOW, ALAIN.
TAKE MY HAND.

SIGNOR? YOU ARE SLEEPING?

ARE YOU **UNWELL?** SHALL I TAKE YOU BACK NOW?

I cannot speak. I nod.

He takes my arm, and leads me across the rubble, as if he is leading a very old man.

A flock of white doves flies above us, through the mist, like the souls of the dead...

...and then they, too, leave the island.

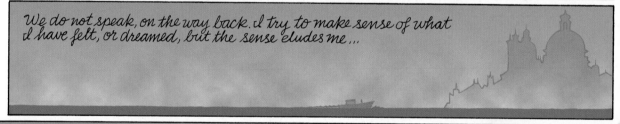

We do not speak, on the way back. I try to make sense of what I have felt, or dreamed, but the sense eludes me...

When I get back to the city everything seems thin and unreal. I stare at the tourists, and I wonder what goes on behind the eyes, inside their heads, inside their worlds.

I shall see her again.

I know that in my heart.

One last time.

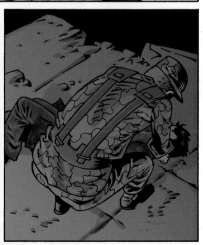

Until then, I shall continue to send people to her.

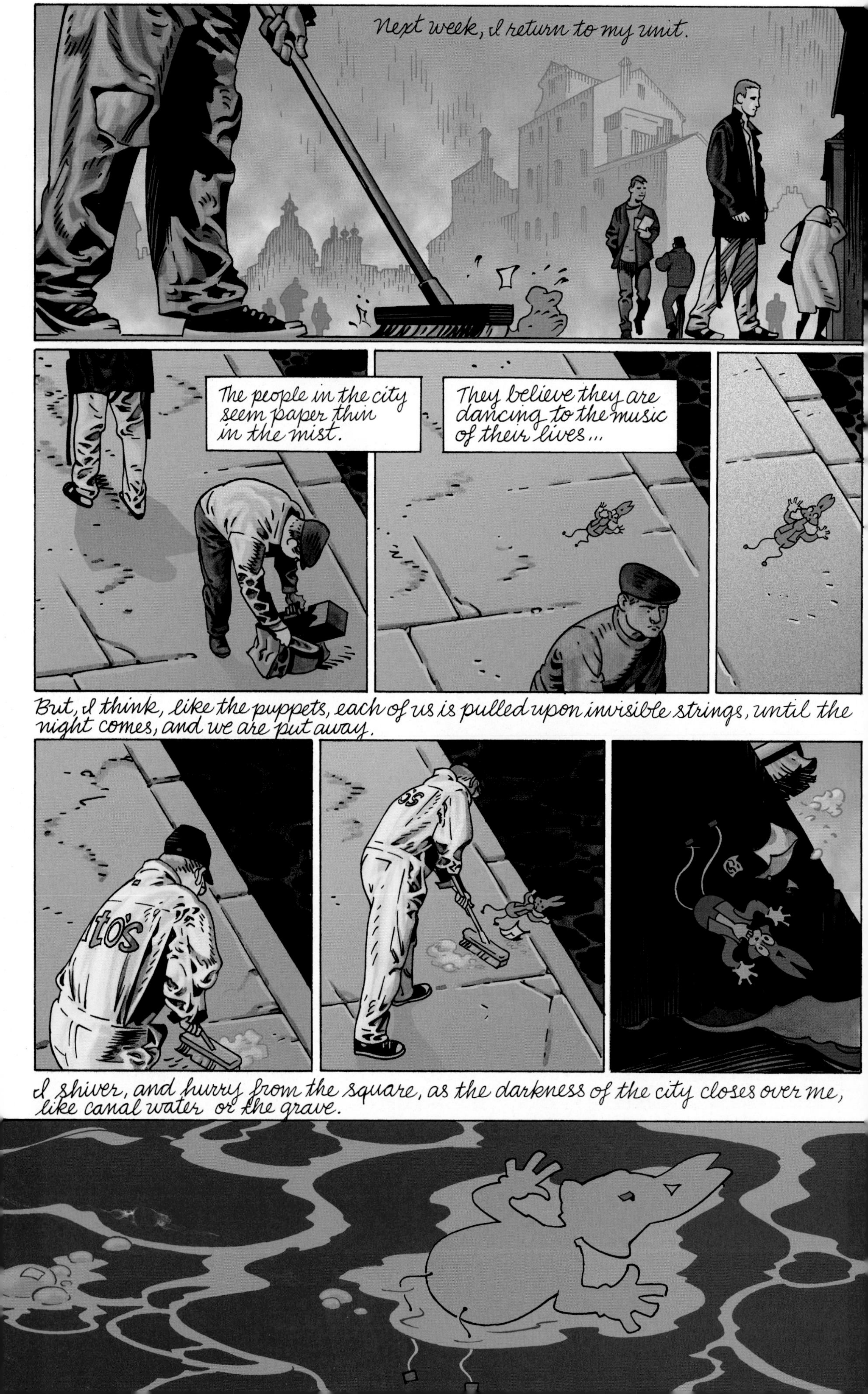
Next week, I return to my unit.
The people in the city seem paper thin in the mist.
They believe they are dancing to the music of their lives...
But, I think, like the puppets, each of us is pulled upon invisible strings, until the night comes, and we are put away.
I shiver, and hurry from the square, as the darkness of the city closes over me, like canal water or the grave.

A DEATH GALLERY

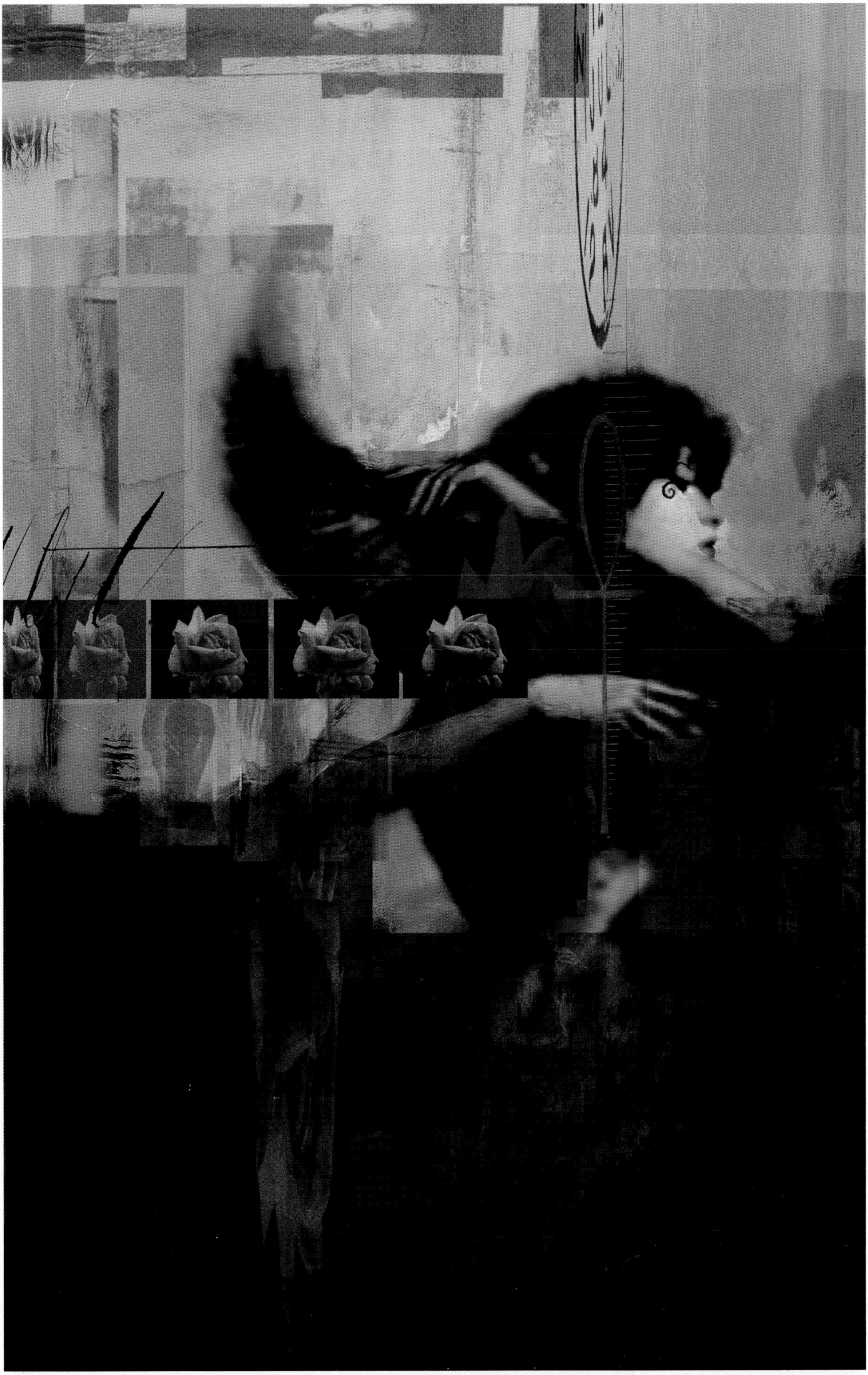

Dave McKean

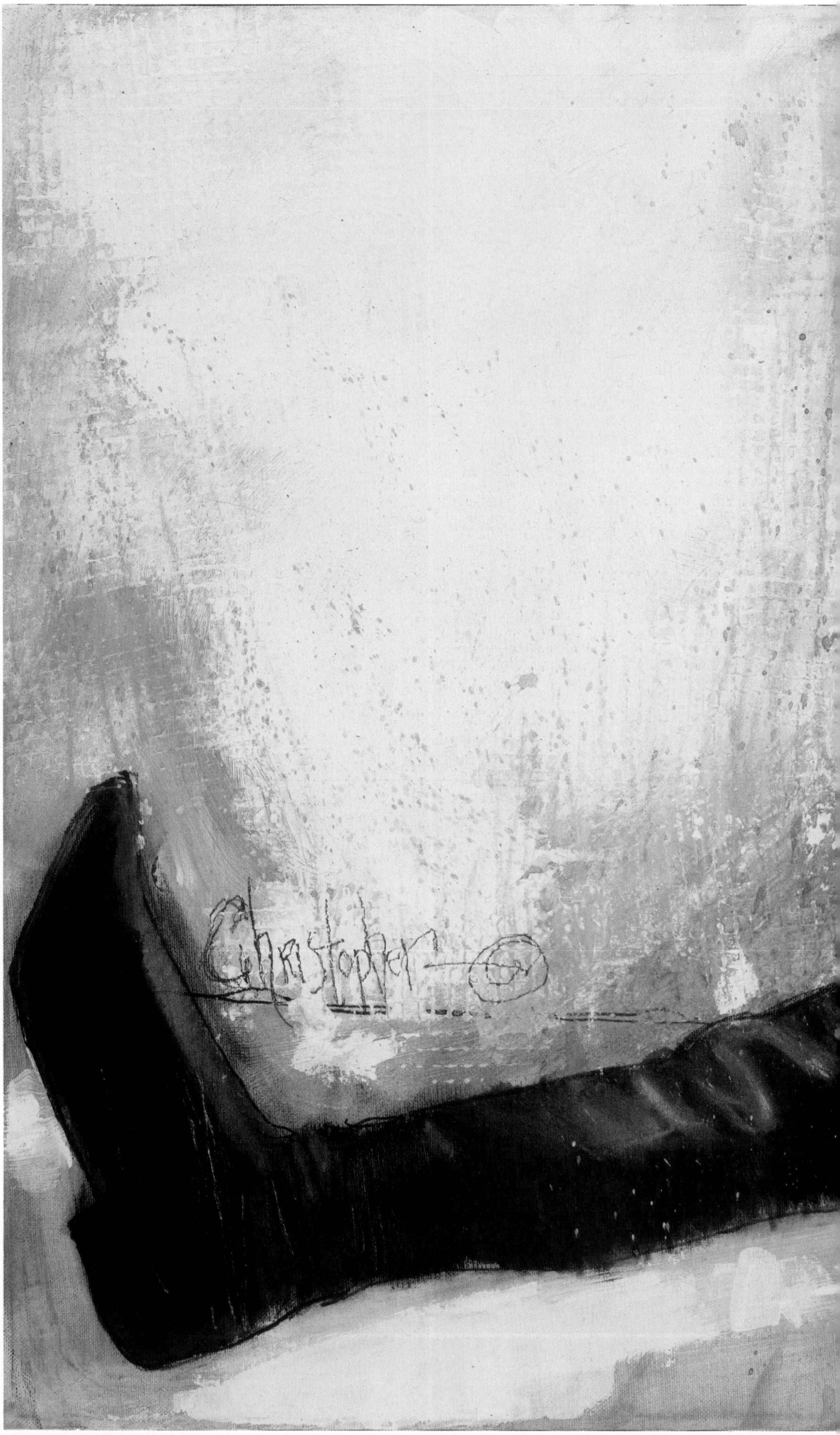
Christopher

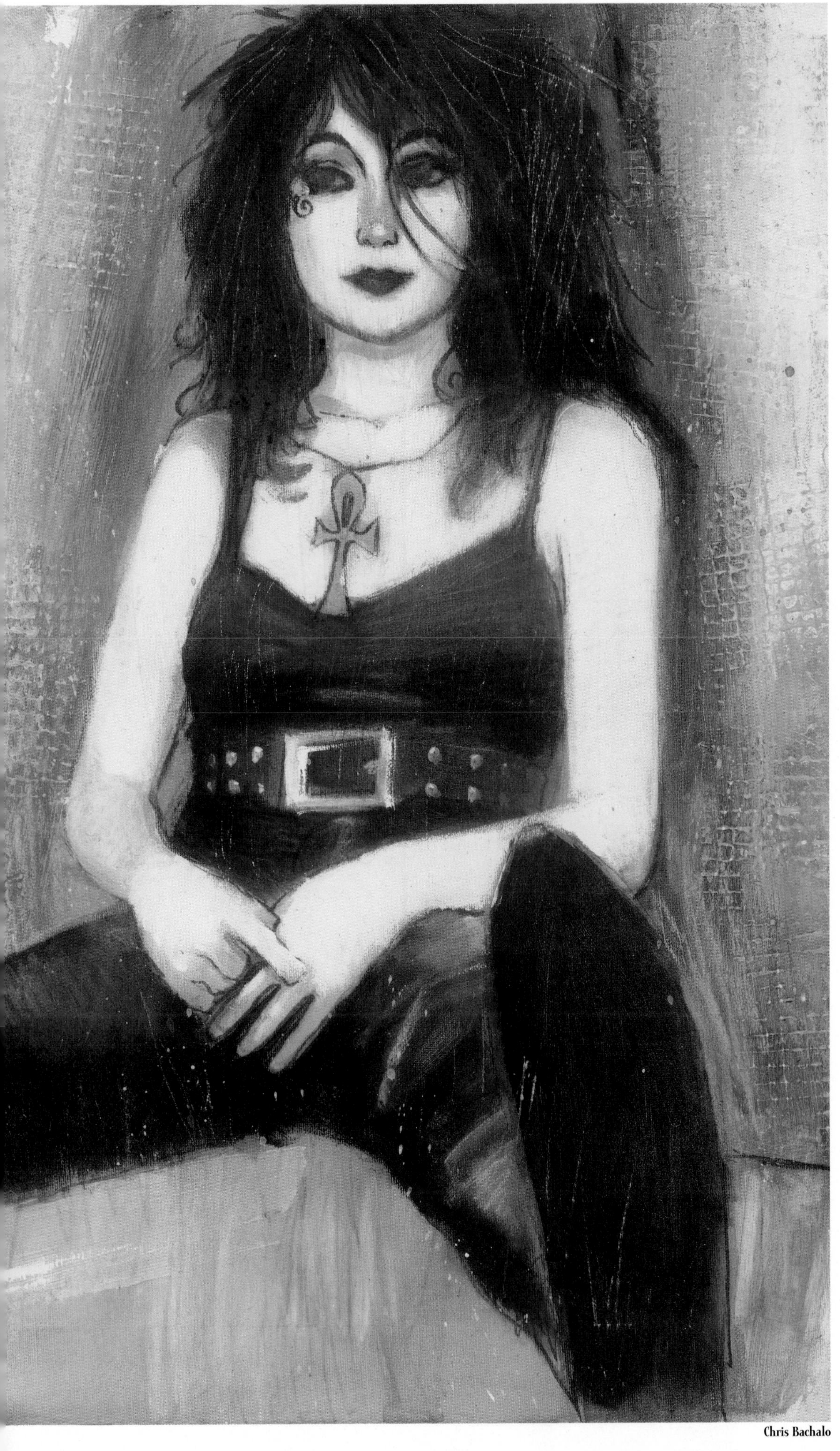

Chris Bachalo

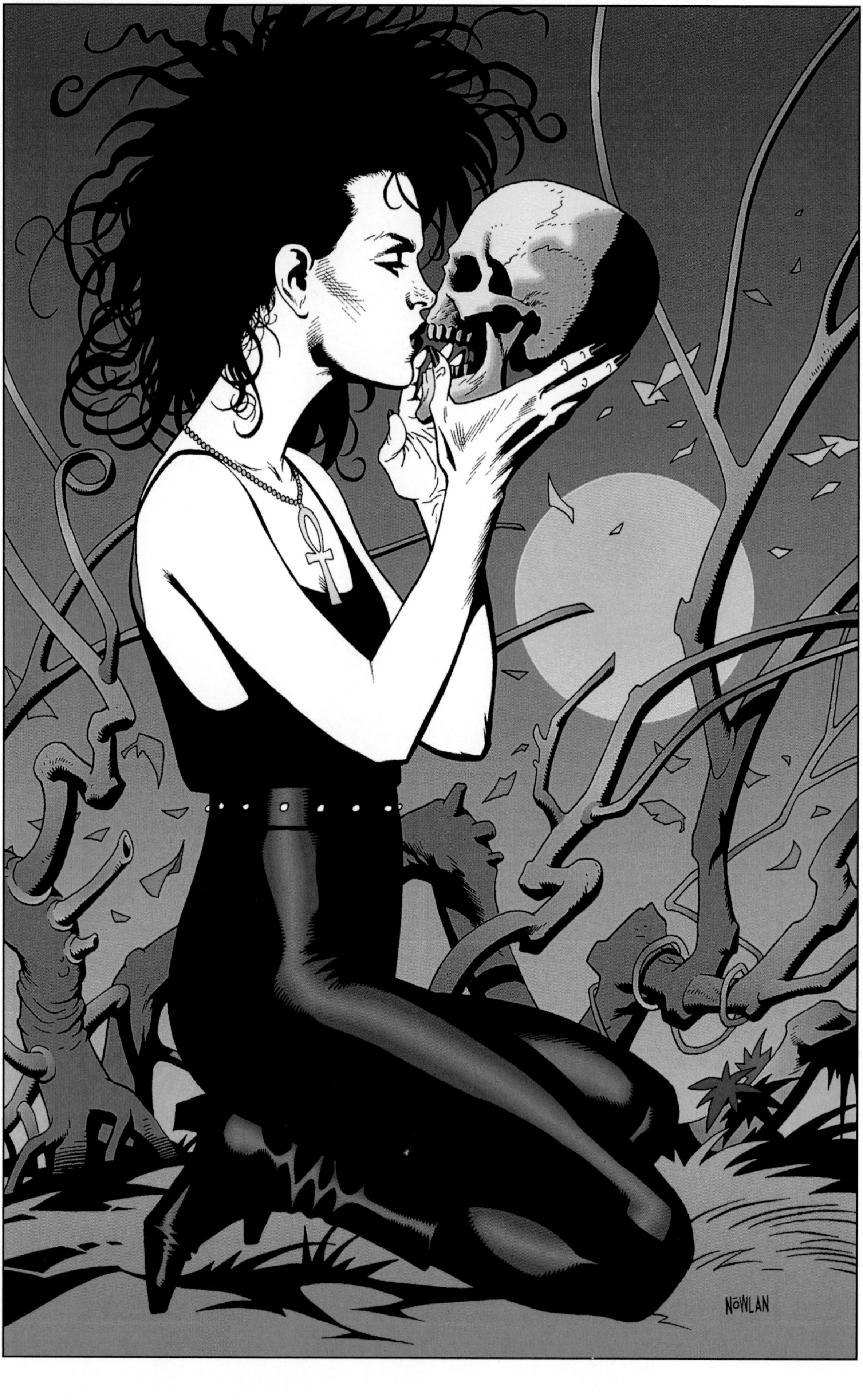
NOWLAN

Kevin Nowlan

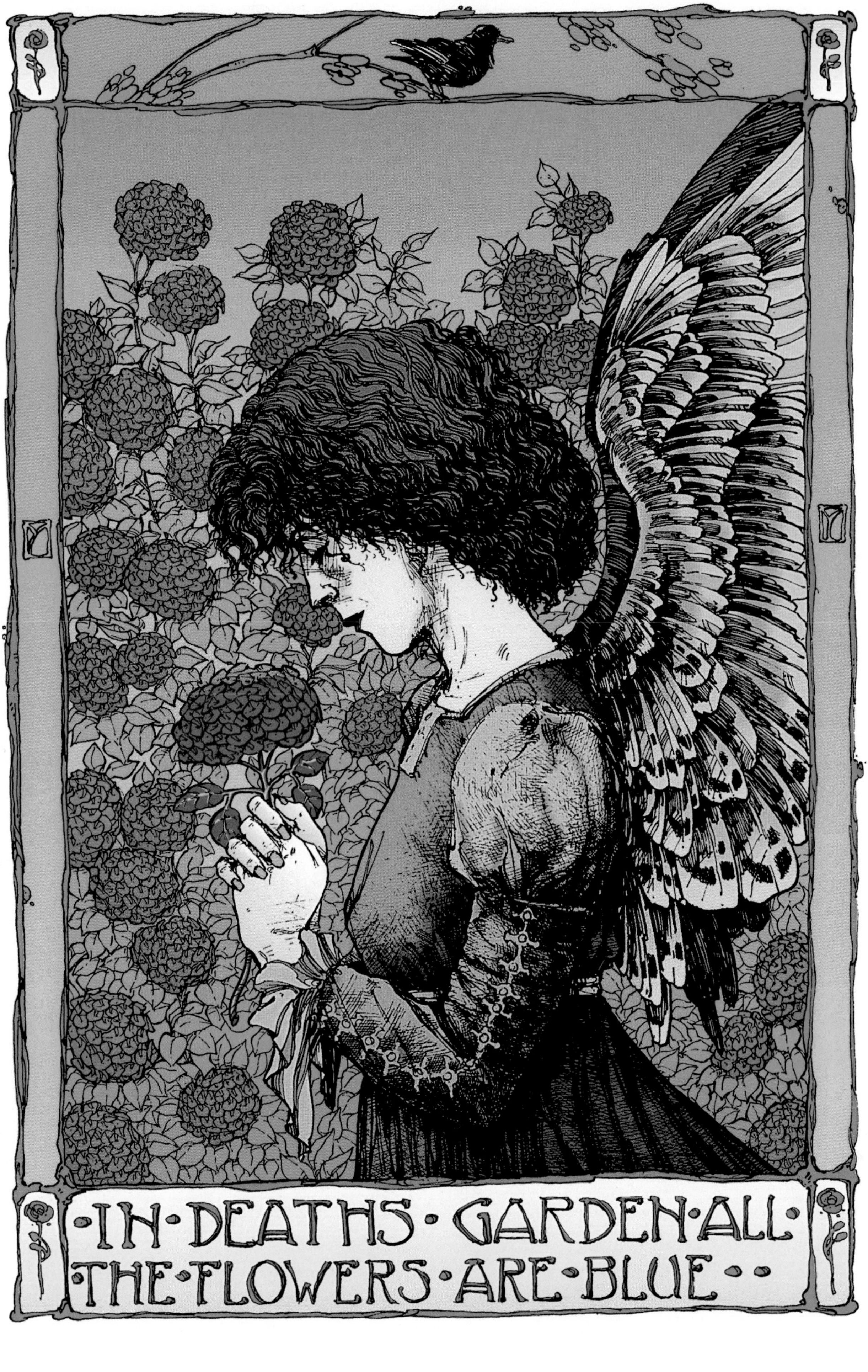
·IN·DEATHS·GARDEN·ALL·
·THE·FLOWERS·ARE·BLUE··

Michael Zulli (color by Daniel Vozzo)

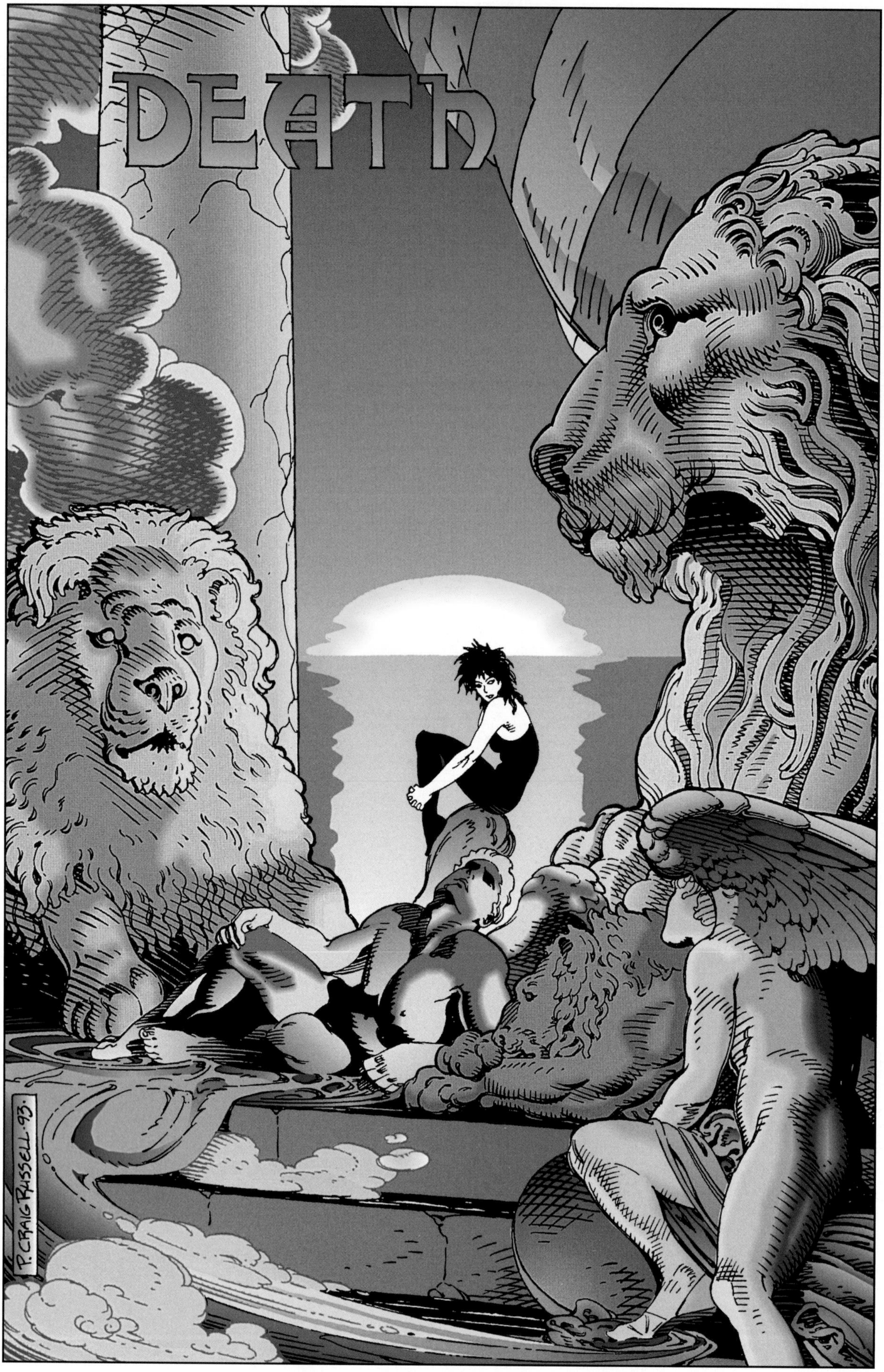
DEATH
P. CRAIG RUSSELL '93

P. Craig Russell (color by Lovern Kindzierski)

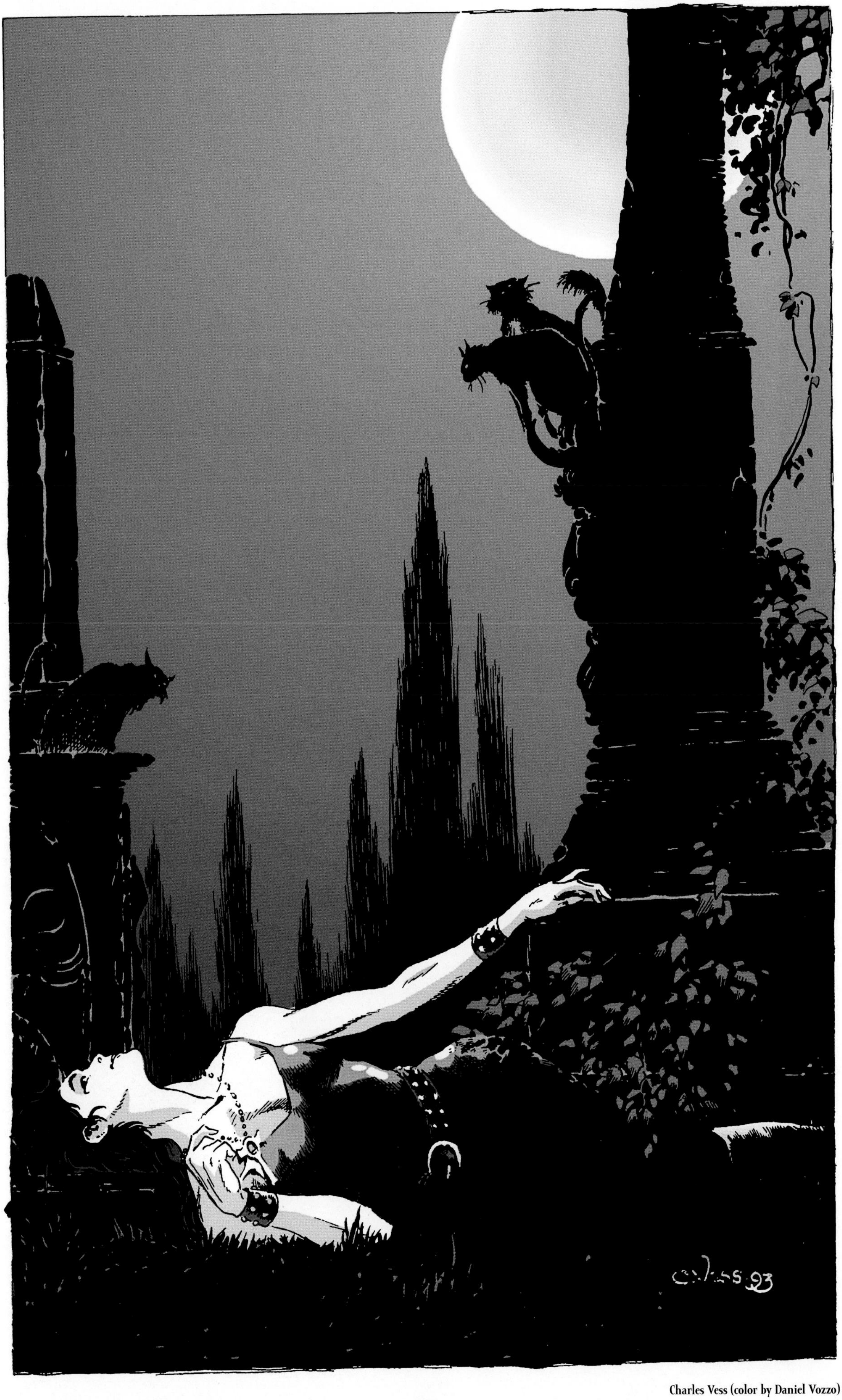

Charles Vess (color by Daniel Vozzo)

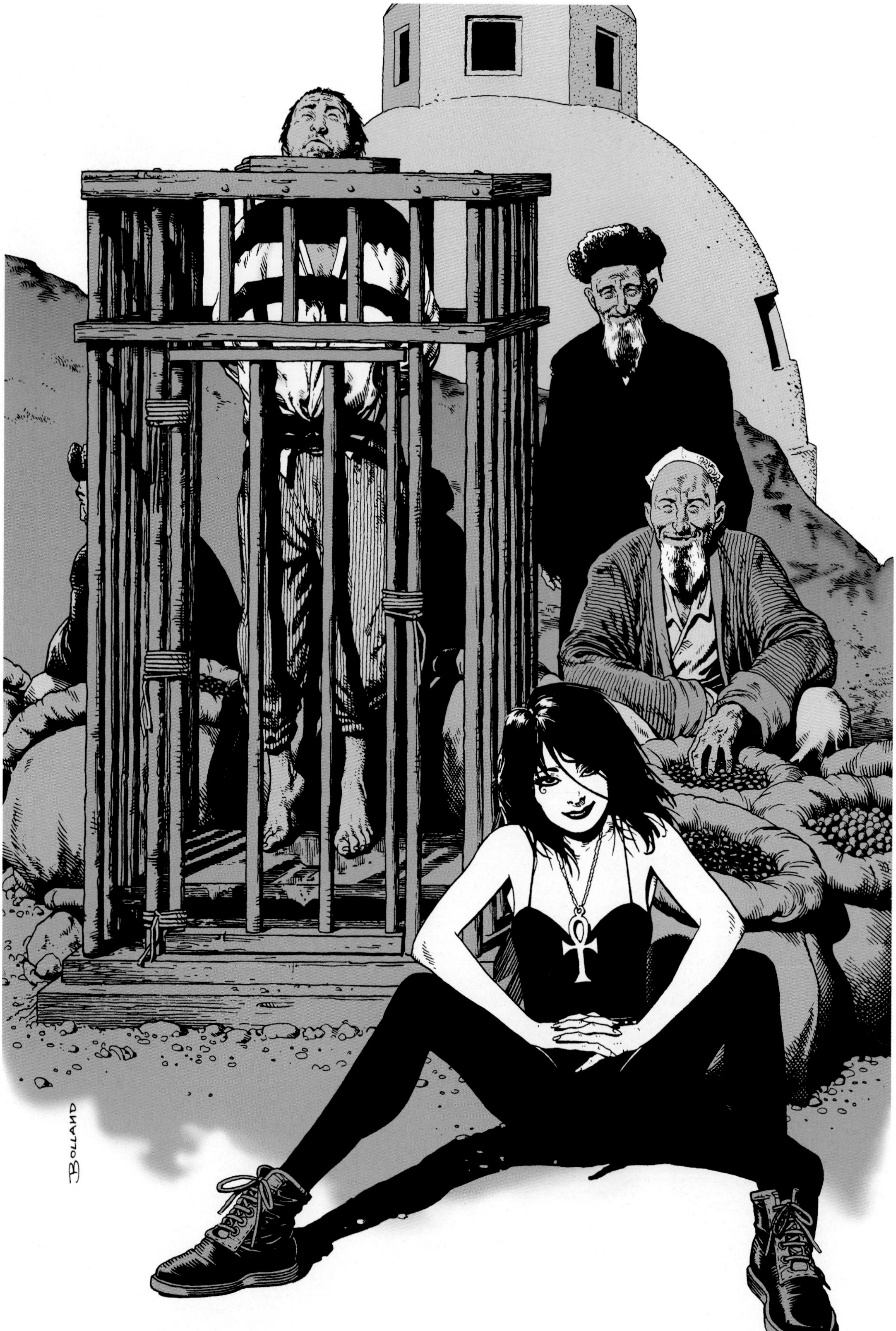
BOLLAND

Brian Bolland

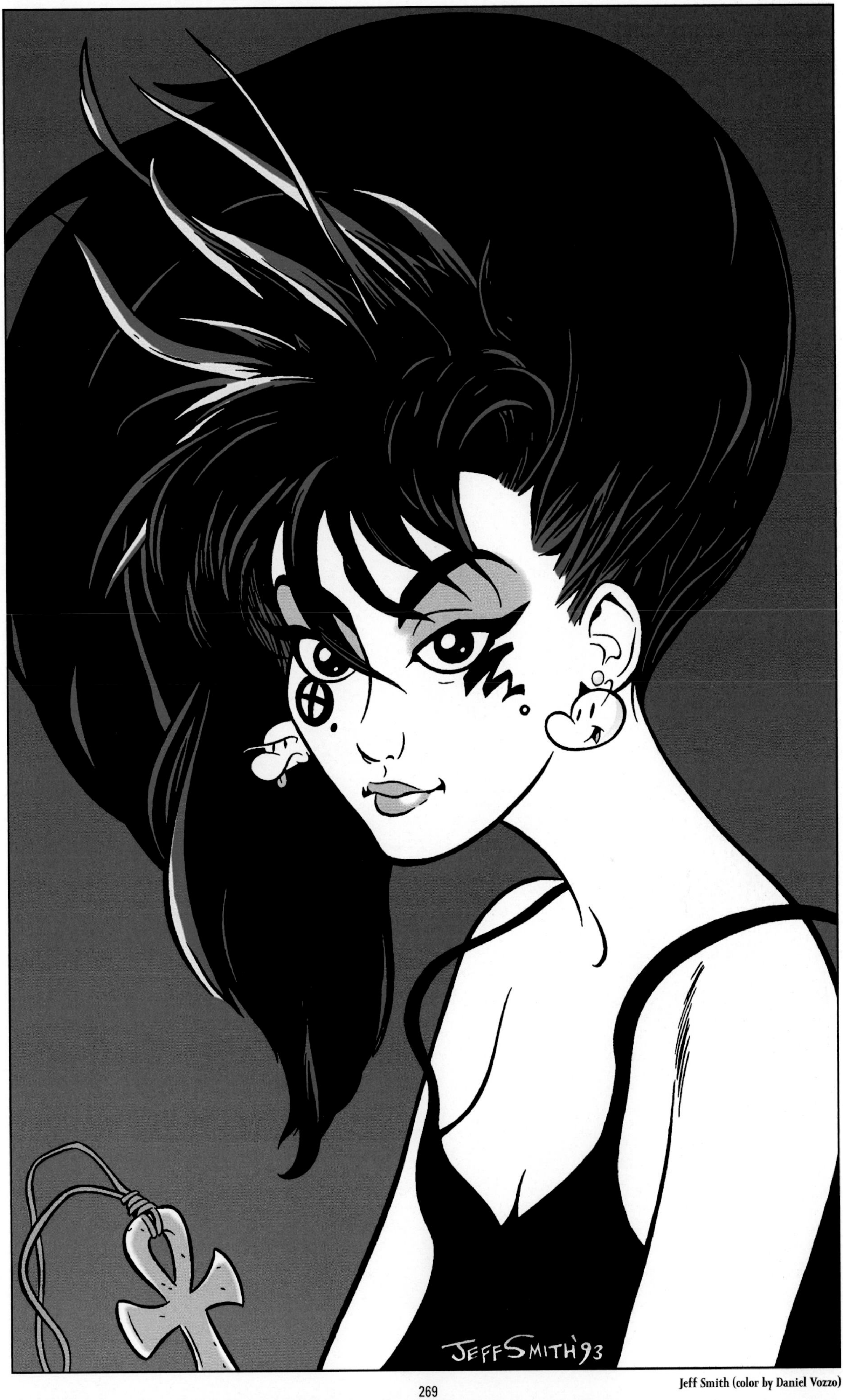
JEFF SMITH '93

Jeff Smith (color by Daniel Vozzo)

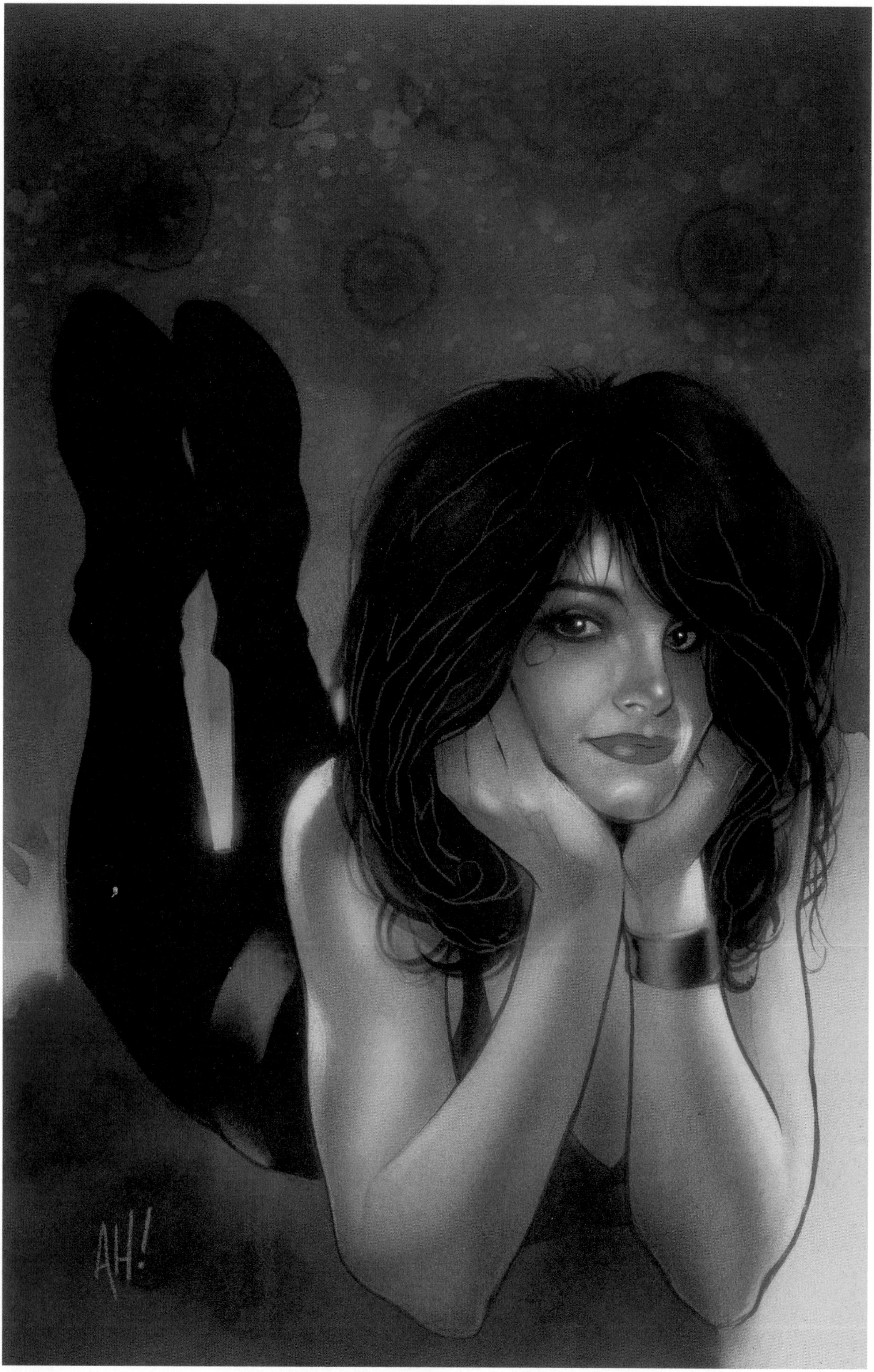
AH!

Adam Hughes

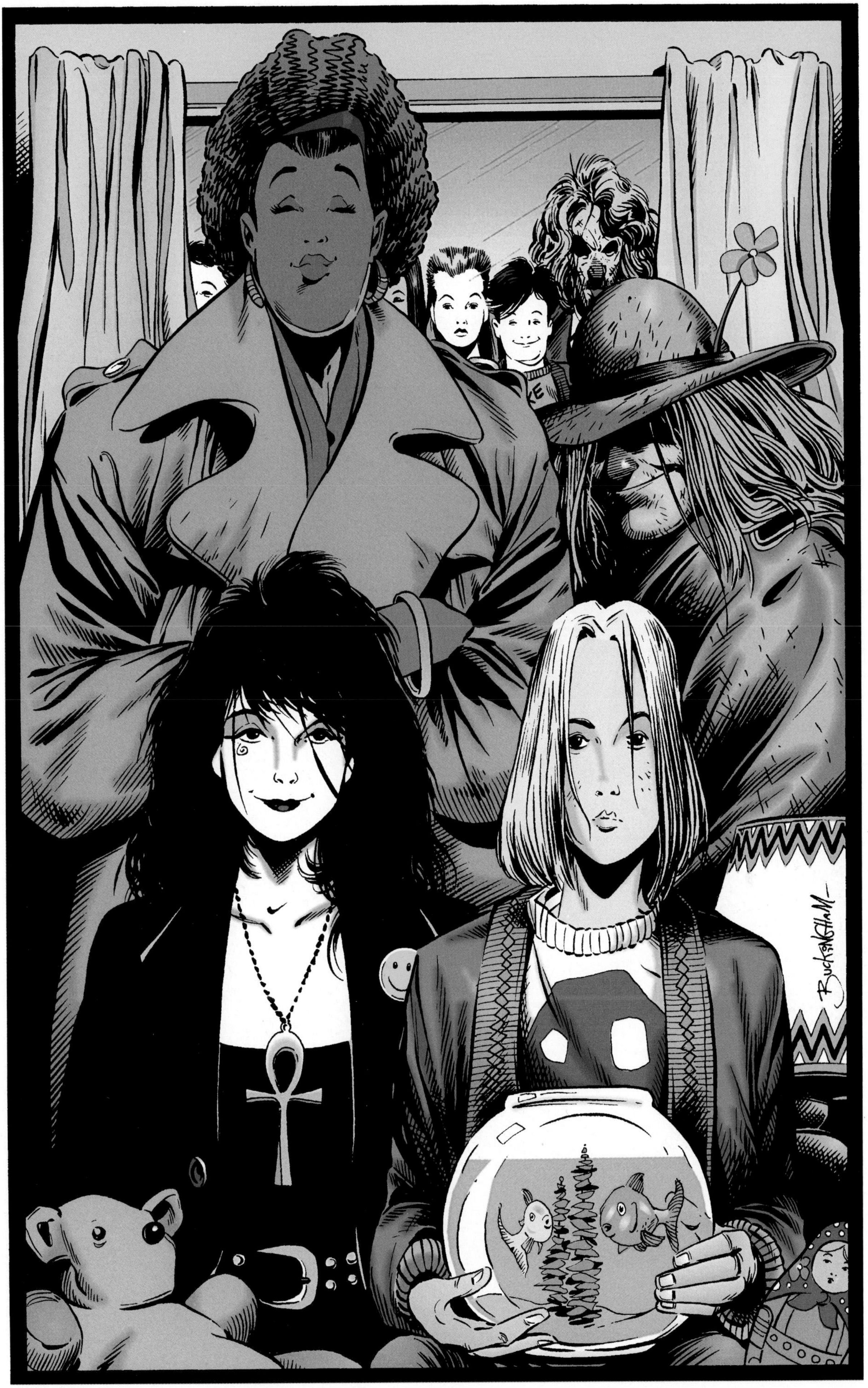
BUCKINGHAM

Mark Buckingham (color by Daniel Vozzo)

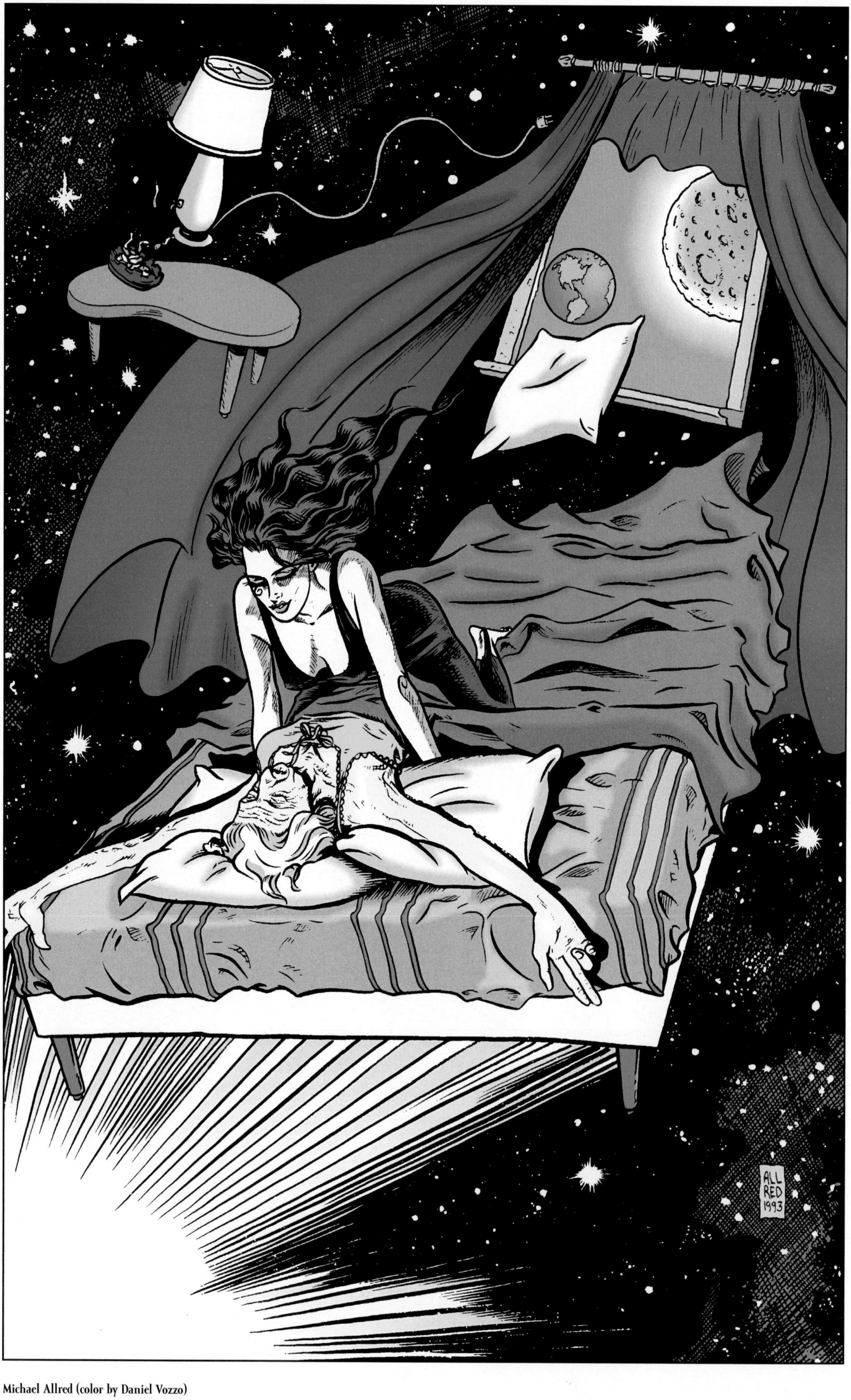
ALL
RED
1993

Michael Allred (color by Daniel Vozzo)

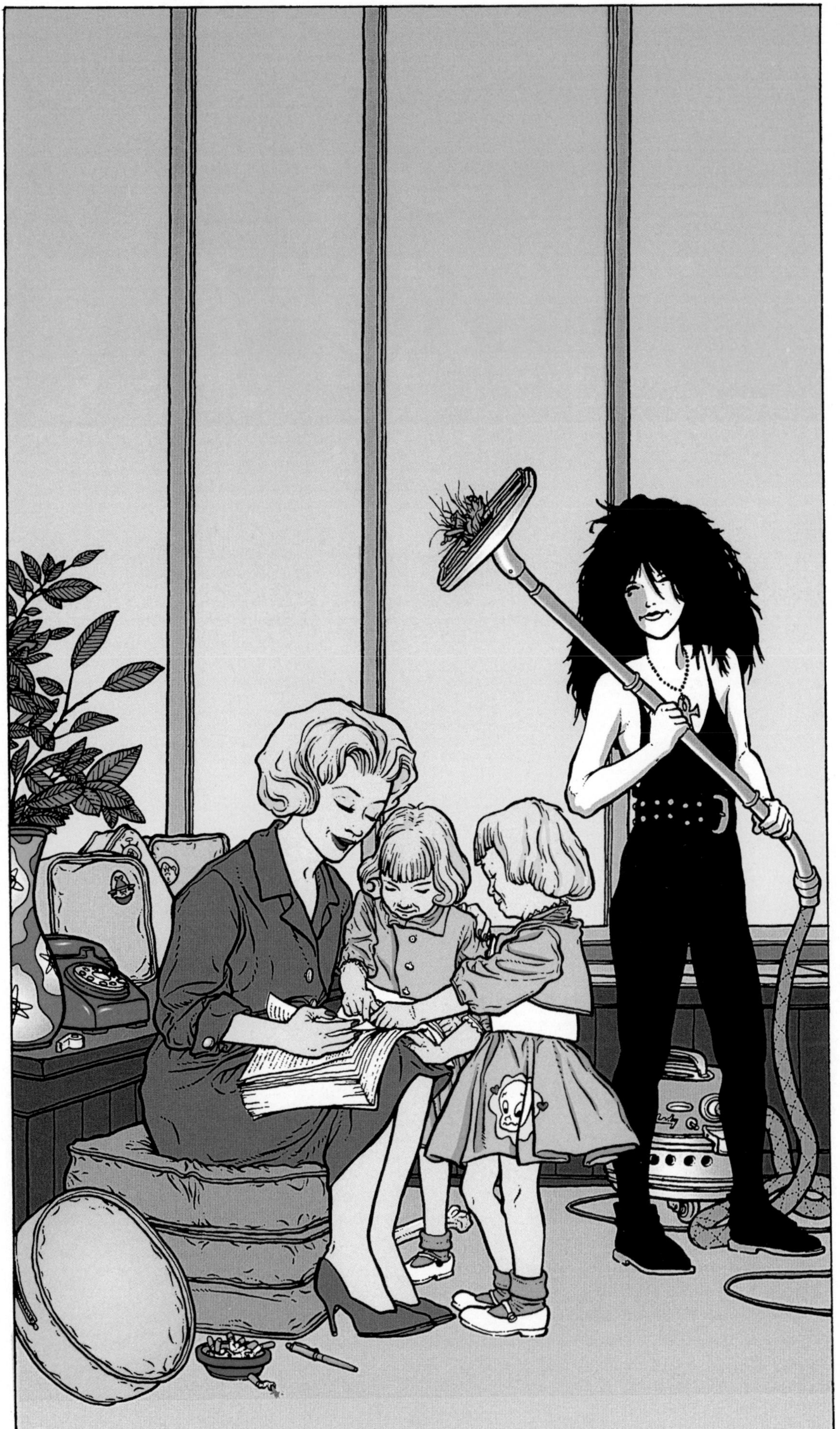

Geof Darrow (color by Daniel Vozzo)

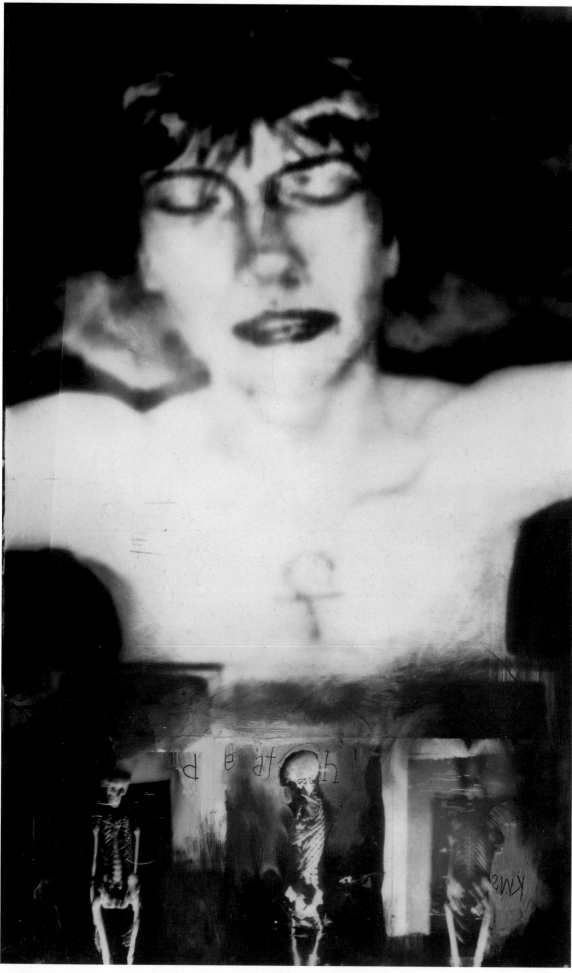

Kent Williams

274

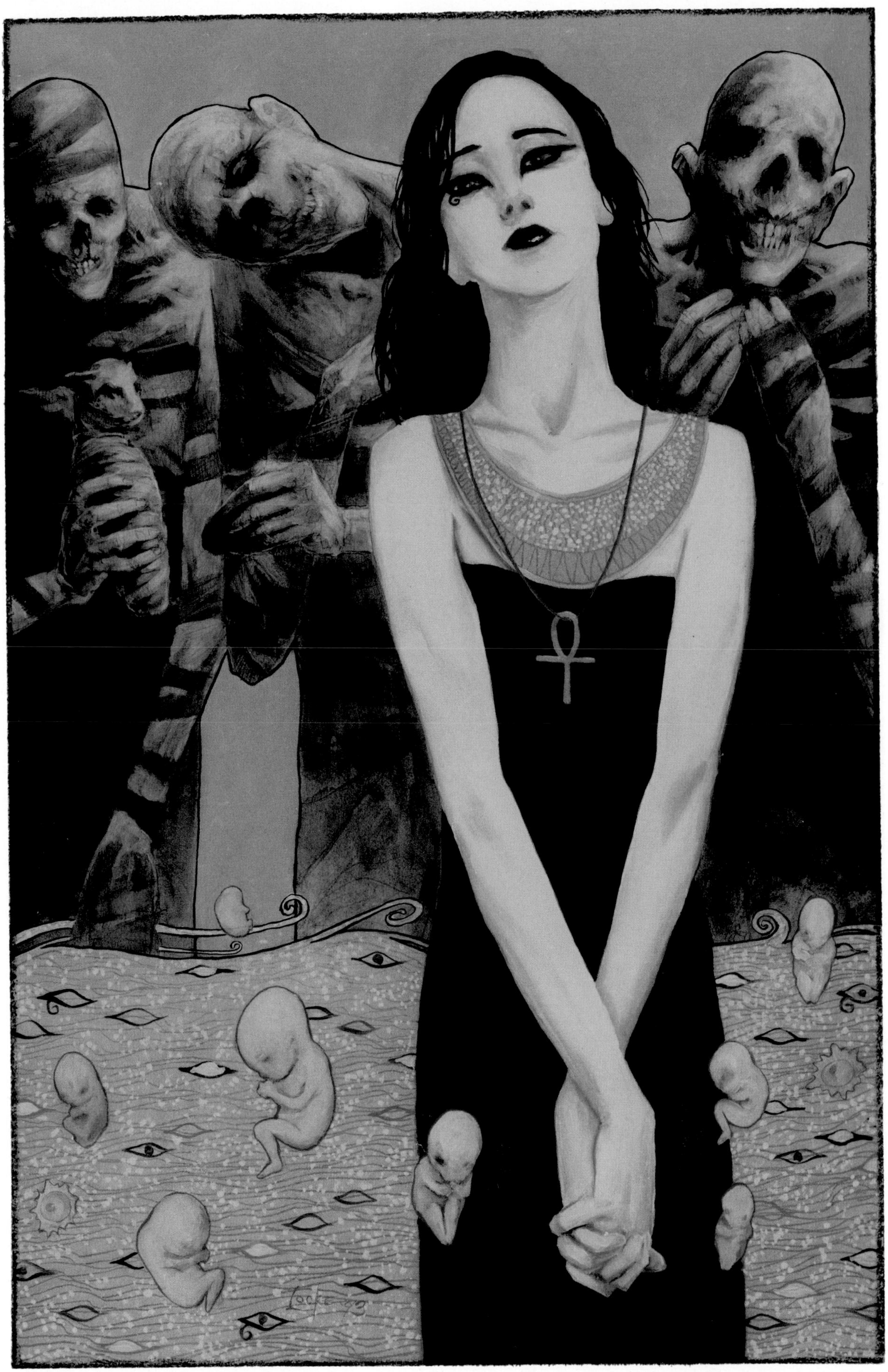

Vince Locke

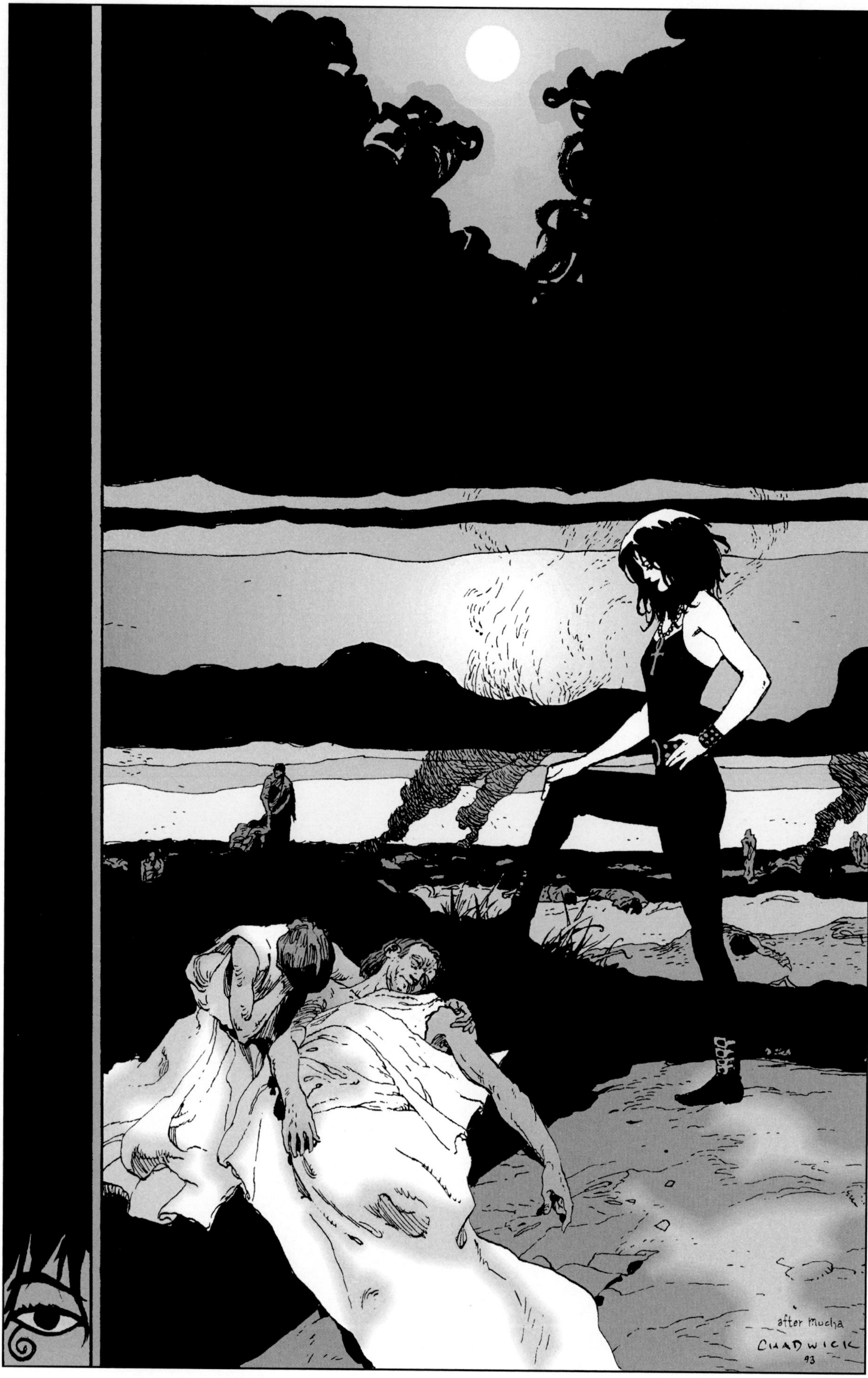
after Mucha
CHADWICK
93

Paul Chadwick

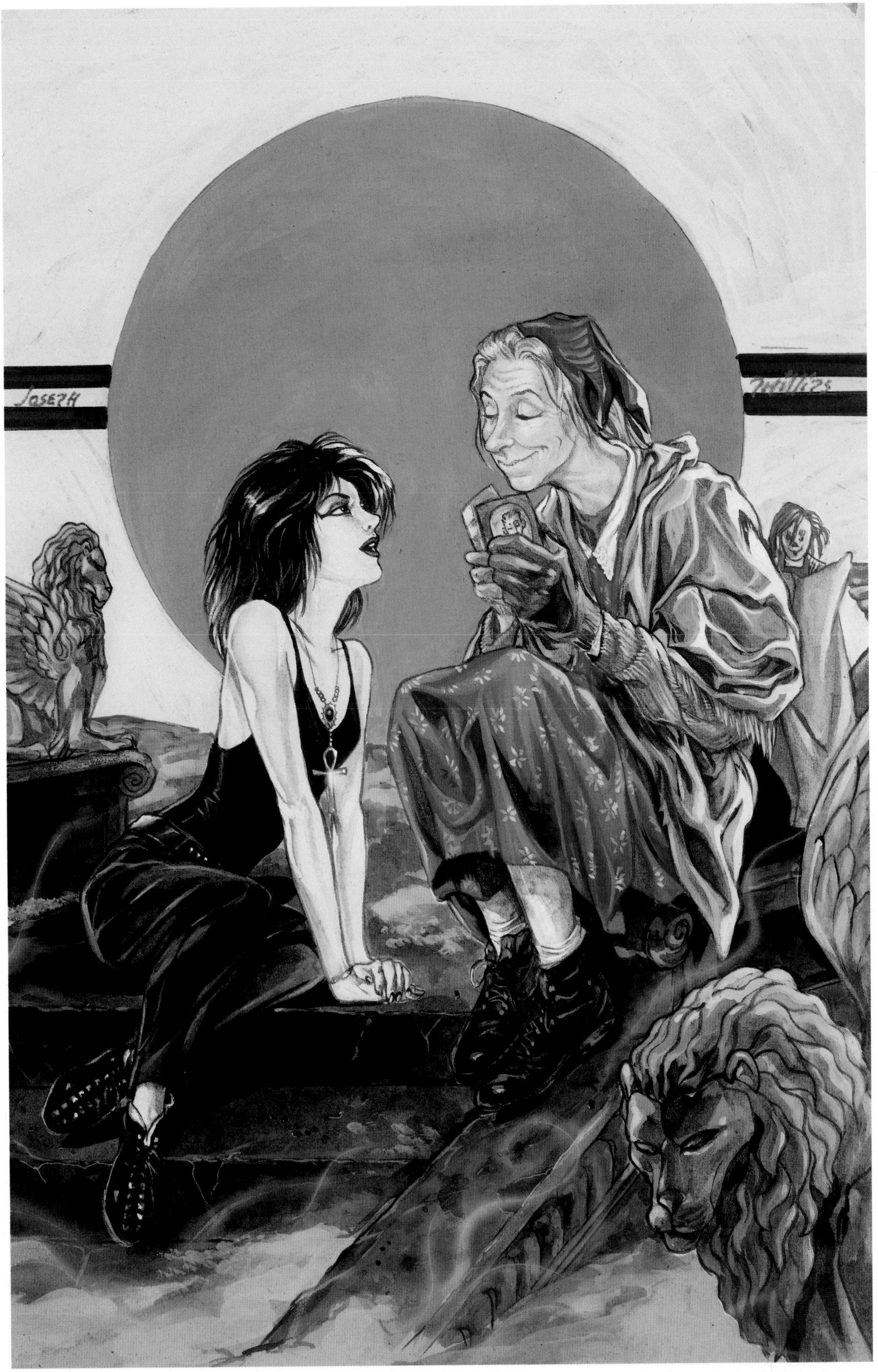

Joe Phillips

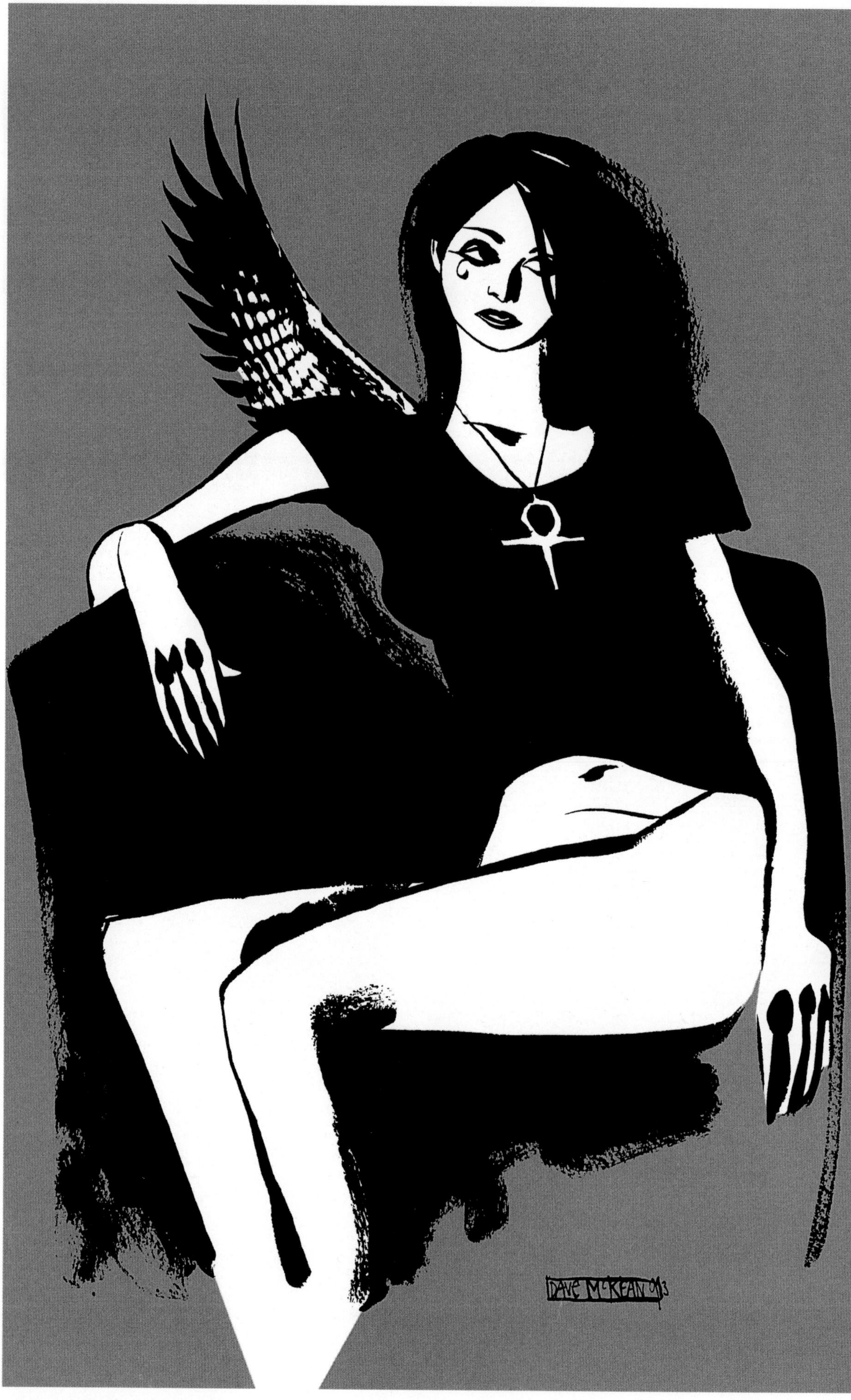
DAVE McKEAN 93

Dave McKean (color by Daniel Vozzo)

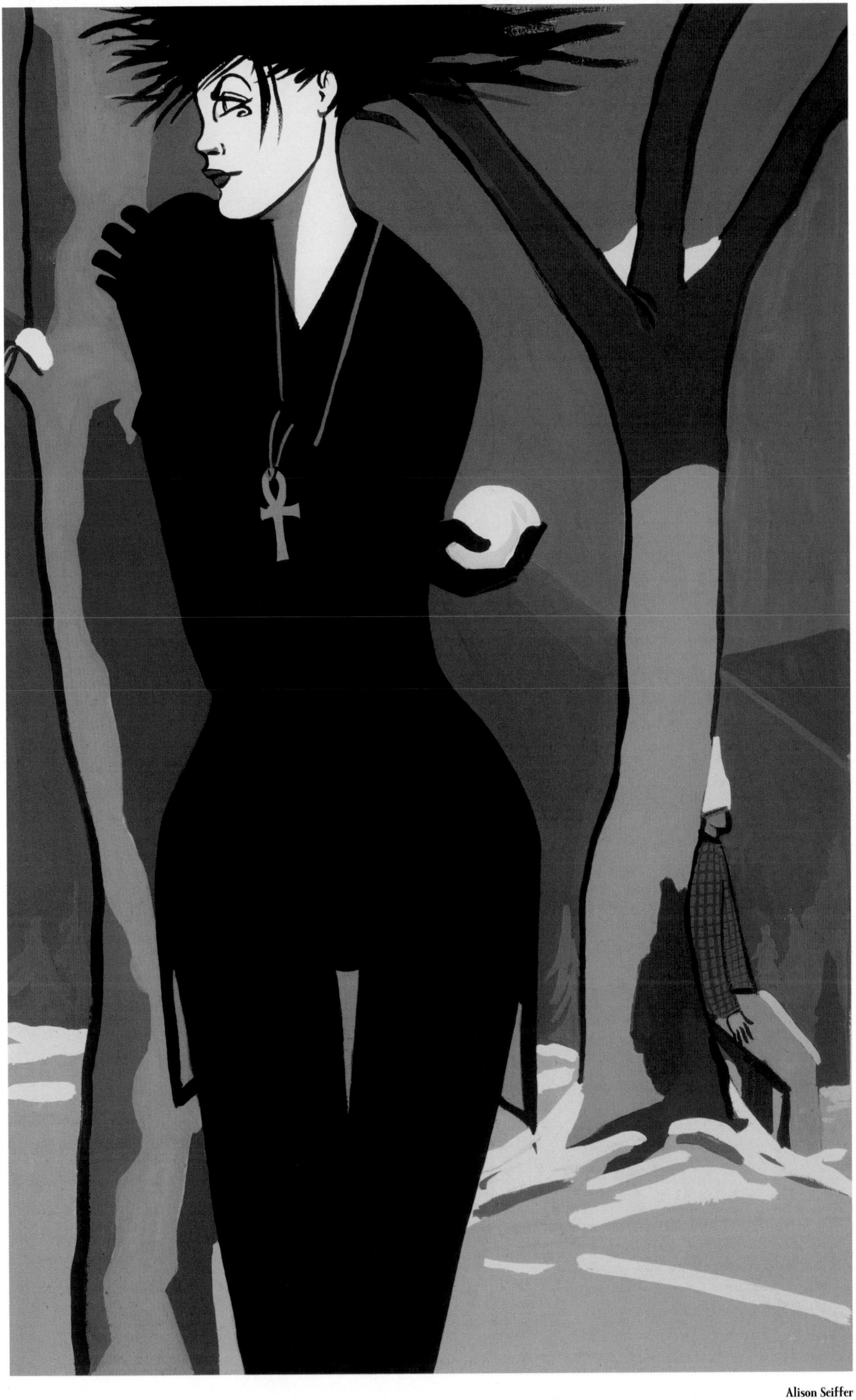

Alison Seiffer

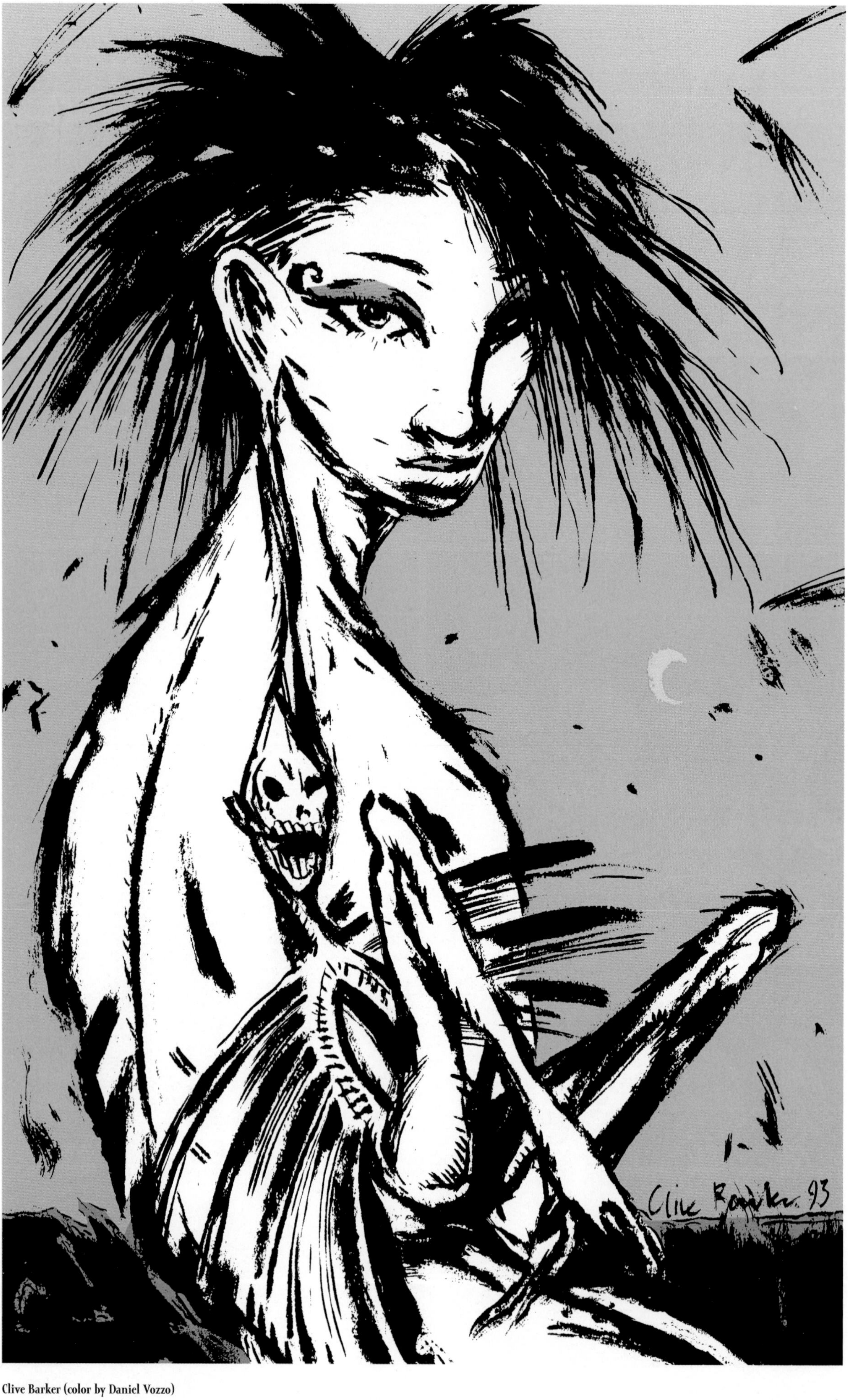
Clive Barker 93

Clive Barker (color by Daniel Vozzo)

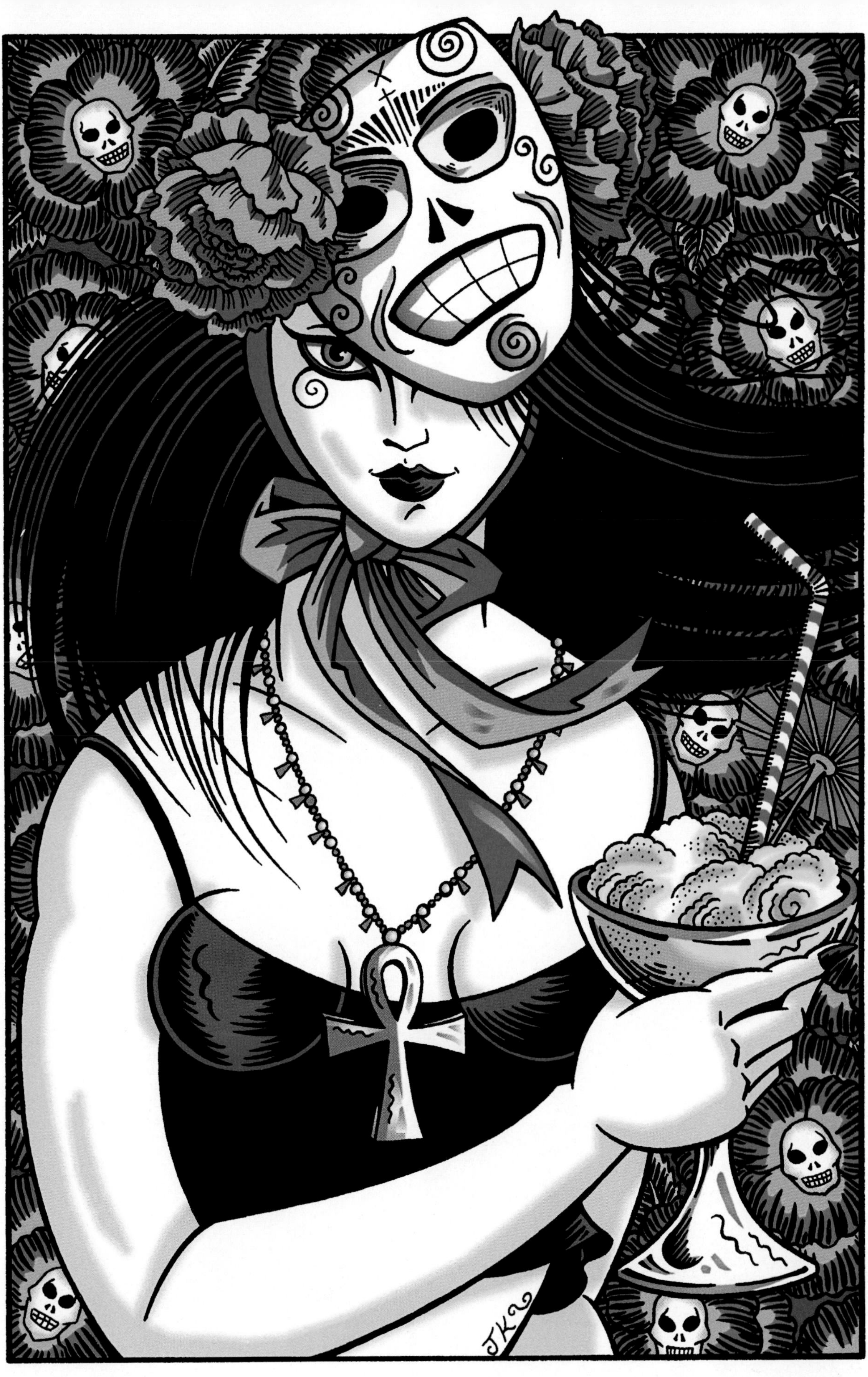

Jill Karla Schwarz

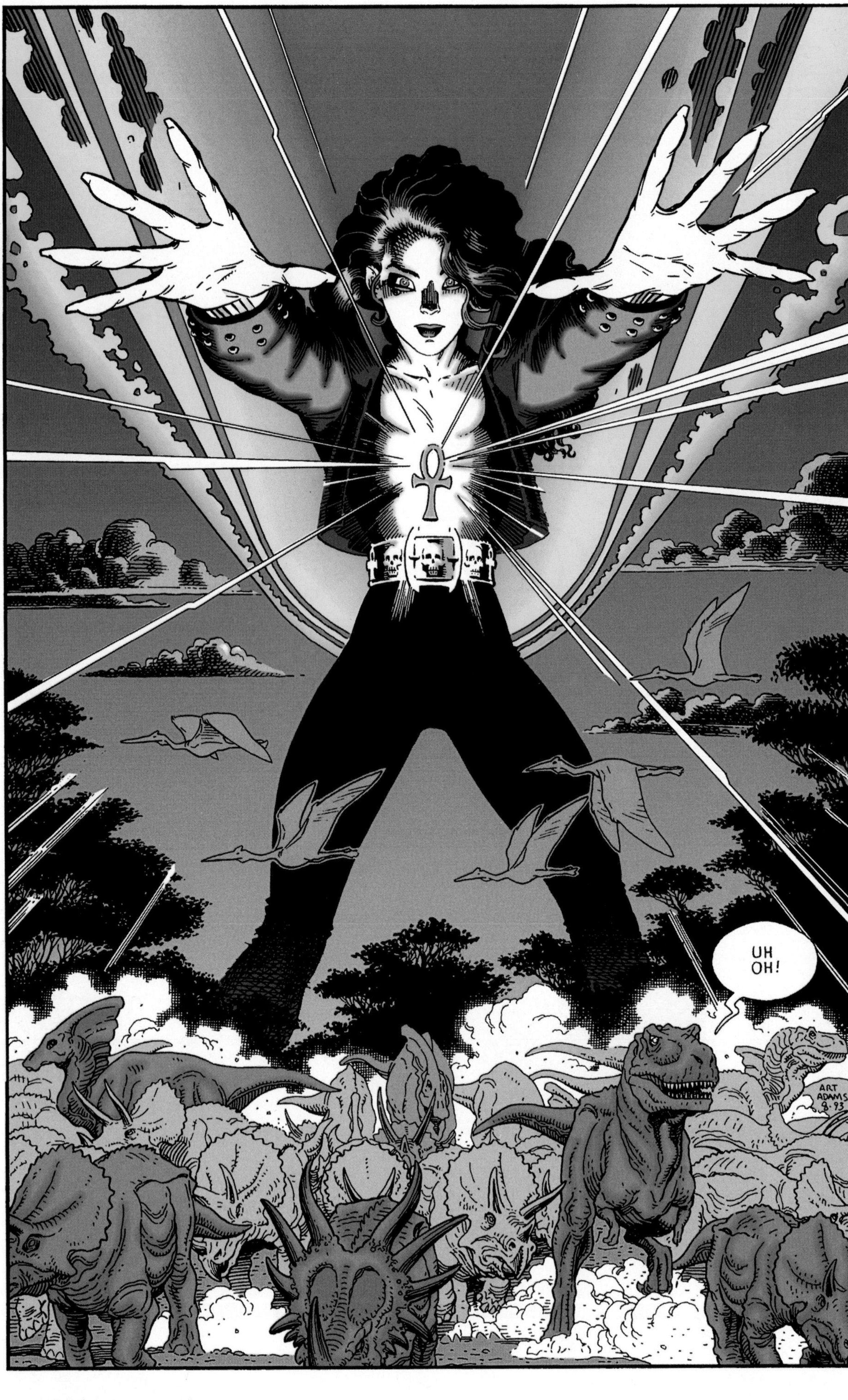
UH
OH!
ART
ADAMS
8-93

Arthur Adams (color by Daniel Vozzo)

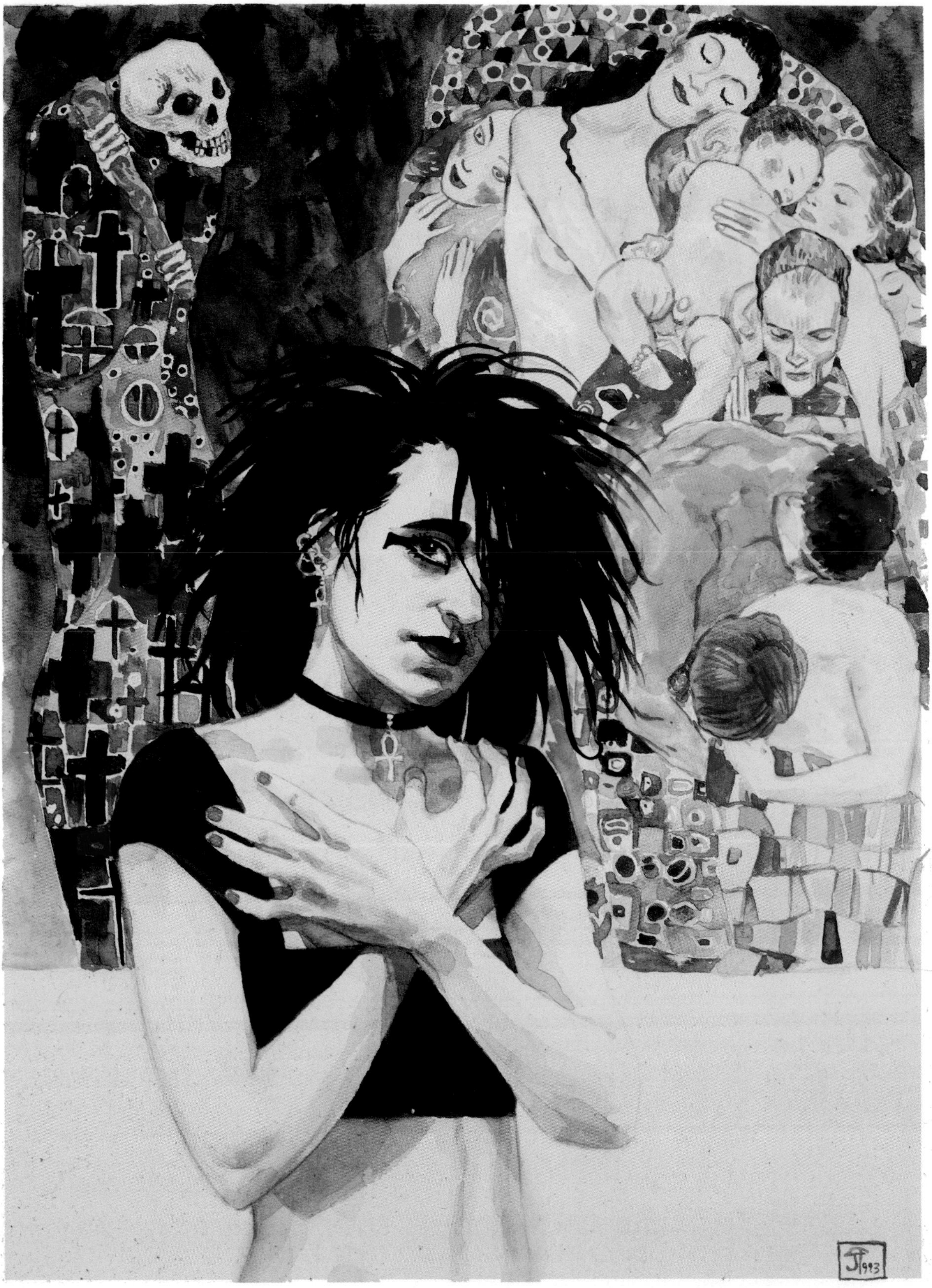
JT 1993

Jill Thompson

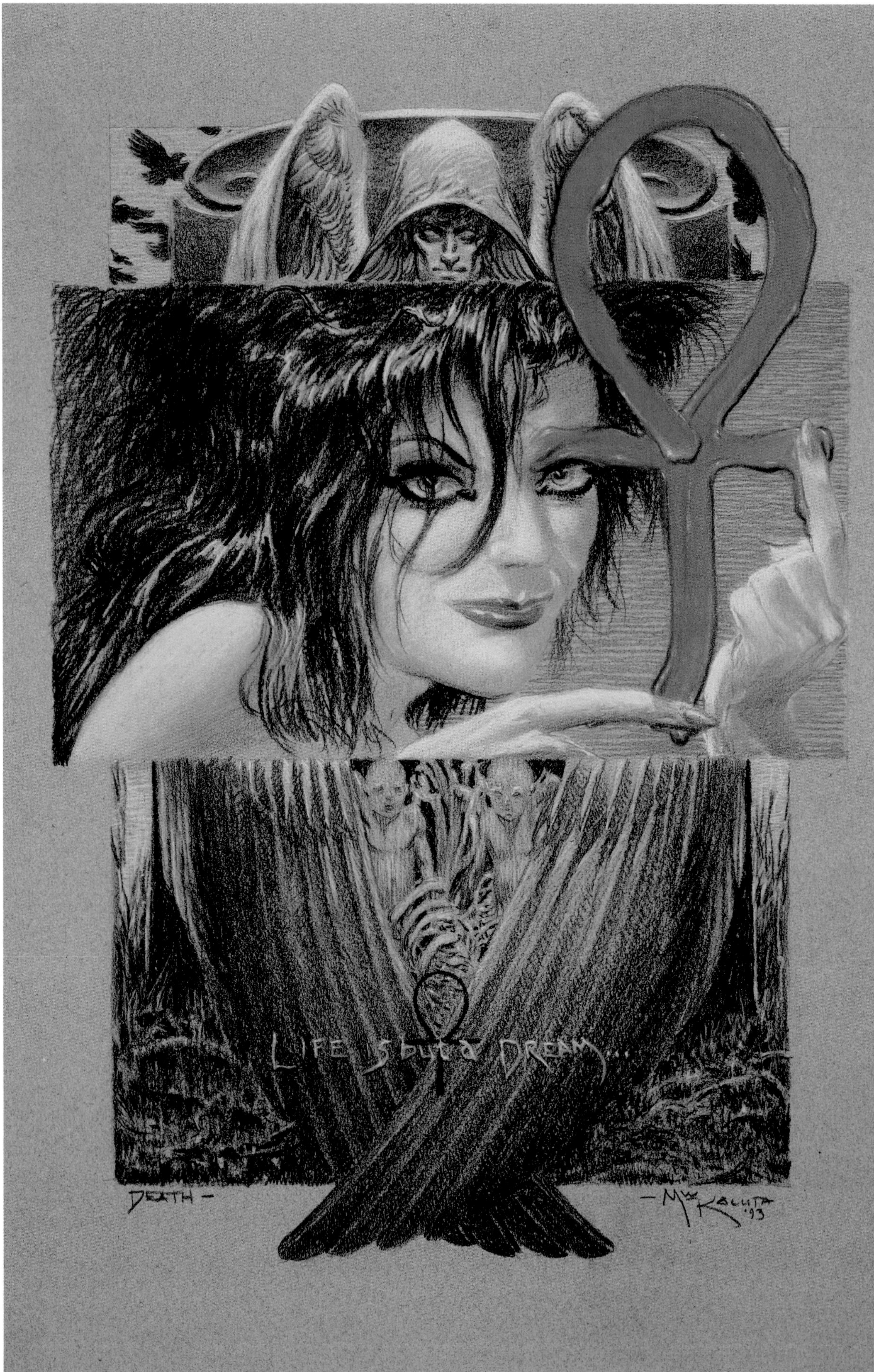
LIFE is but a DREAM...
DEATH -

Michael Wm. Kaluta

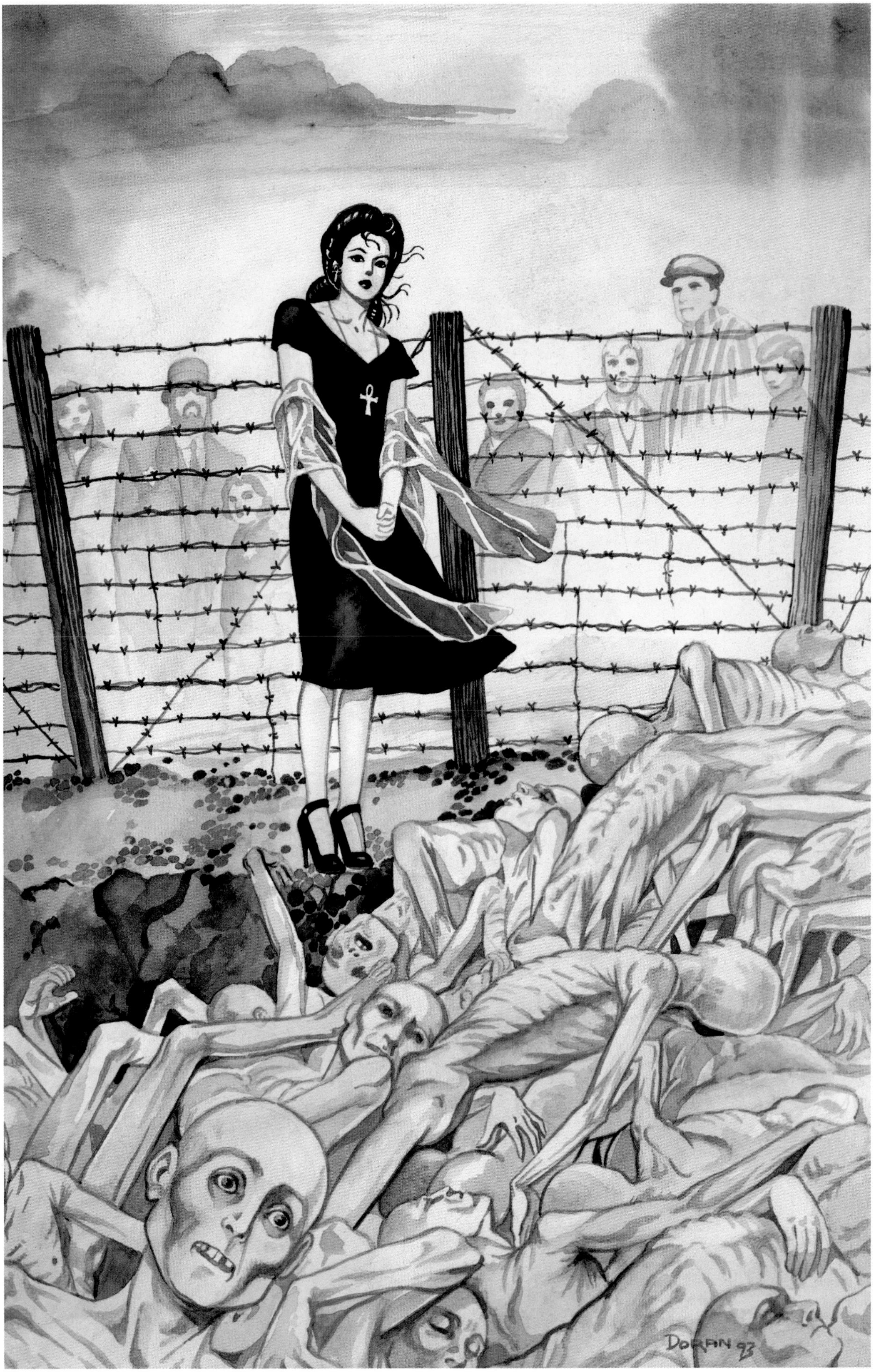
DORAN 93

Colleen Doran

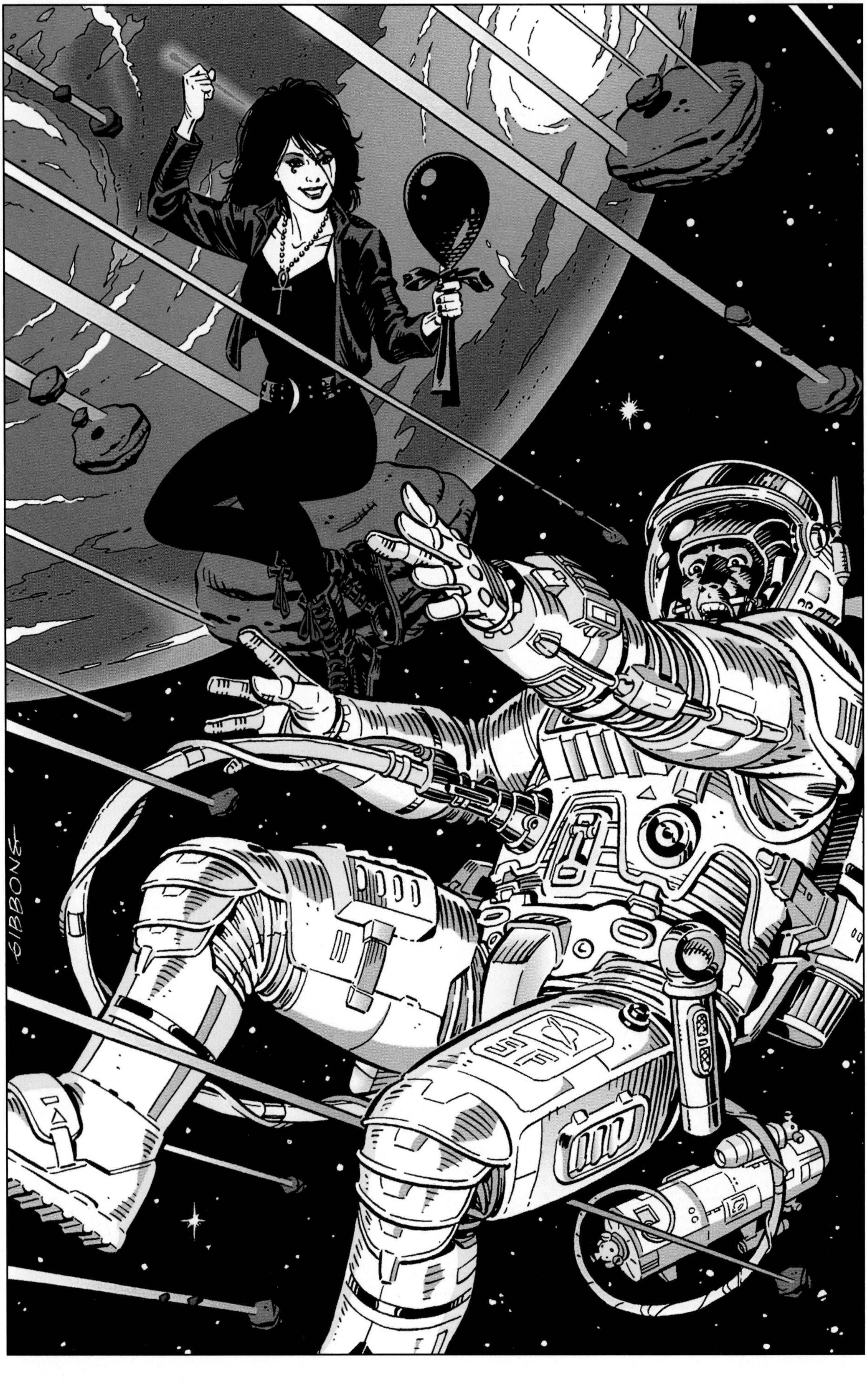
GIBBONS
SF

Dave Gibbons (color by Daniel Vozzo)

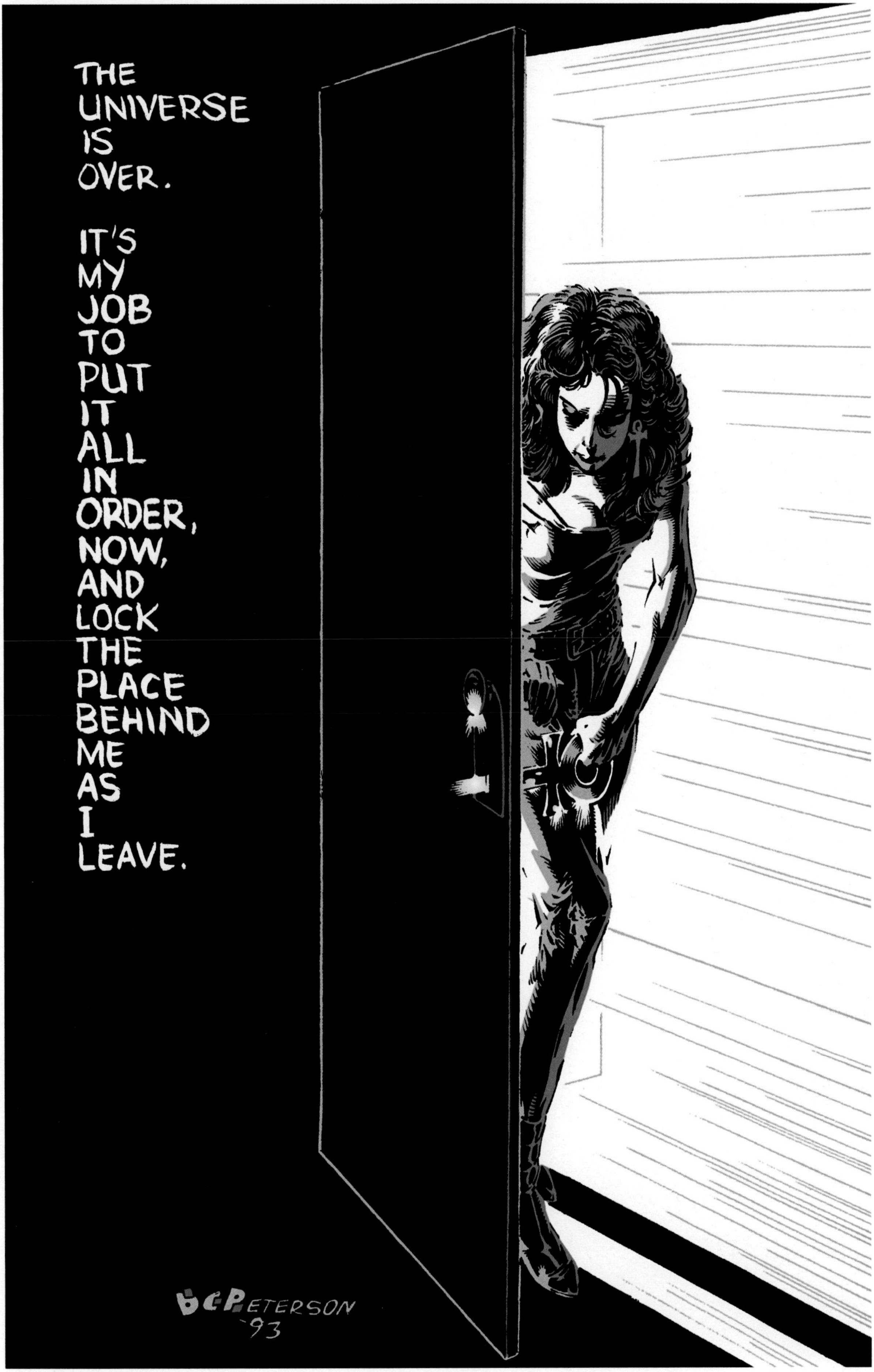
THE UNIVERSE IS OVER.

IT'S MY JOB TO PUT IT ALL IN ORDER, NOW, AND LOCK THE PLACE BEHIND ME AS I LEAVE.
BGPETERSON '93

Brandon Peterson (color by Daniel Vozzo)

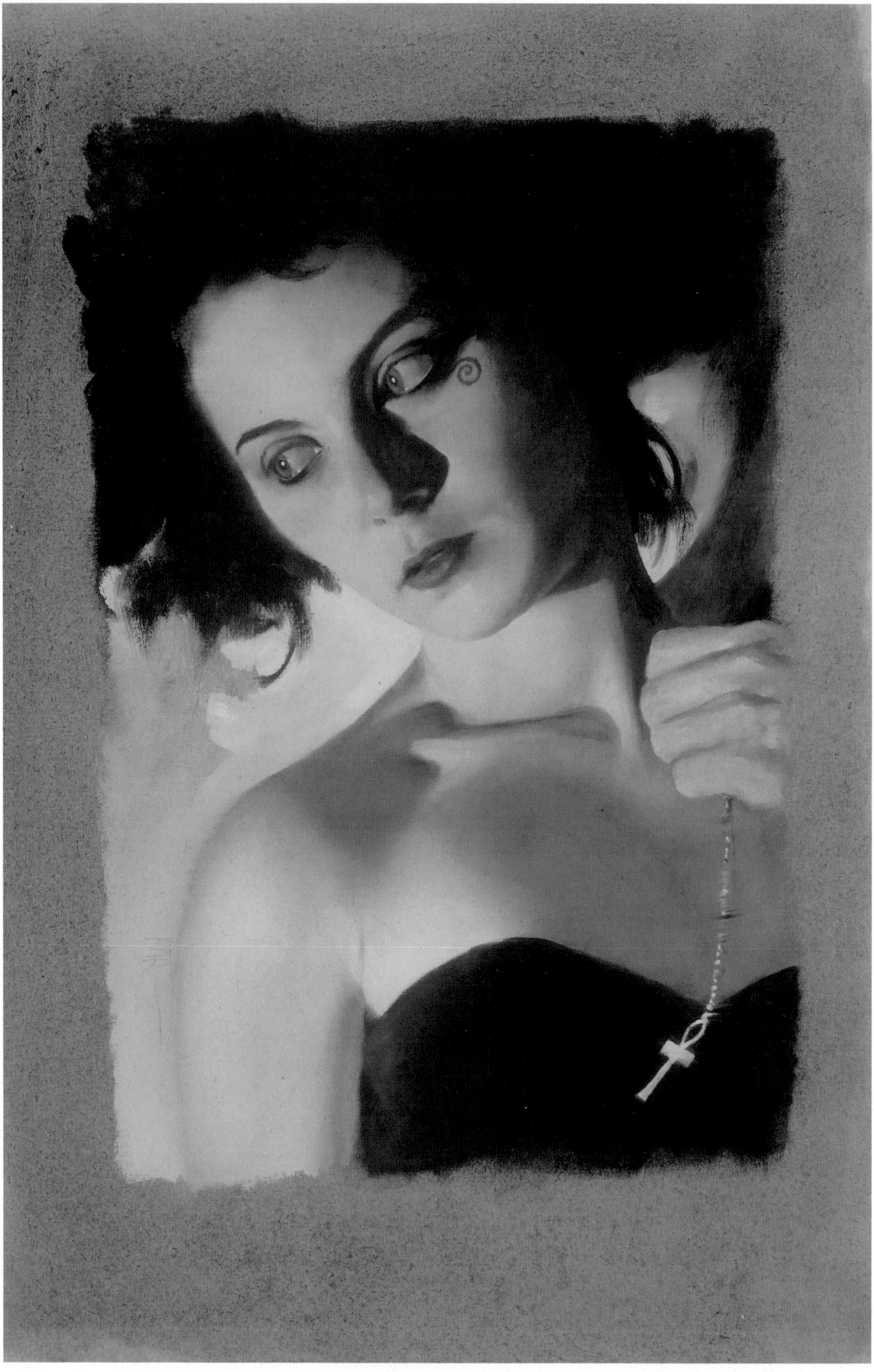

Jon J Muth

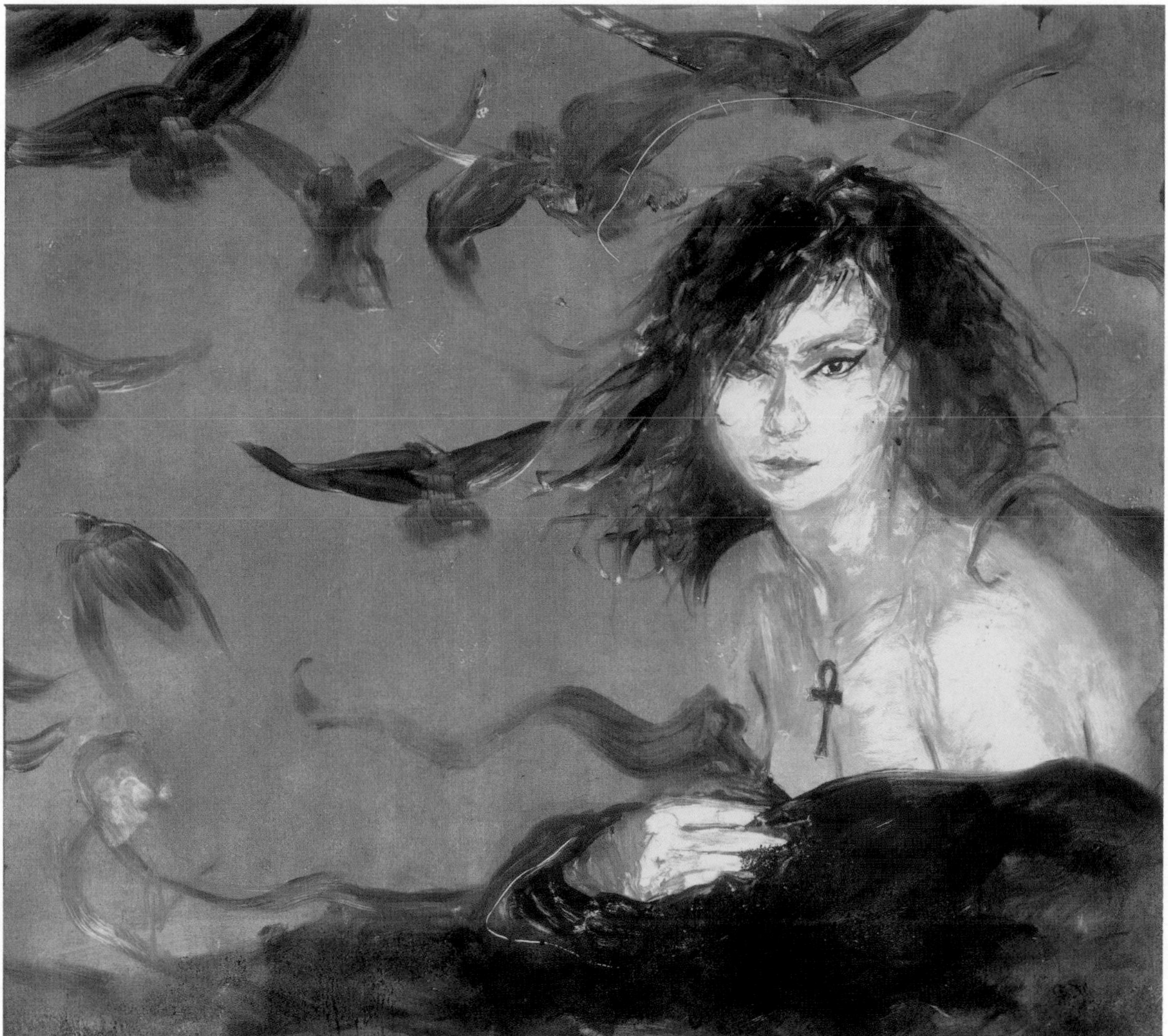

George Pratt

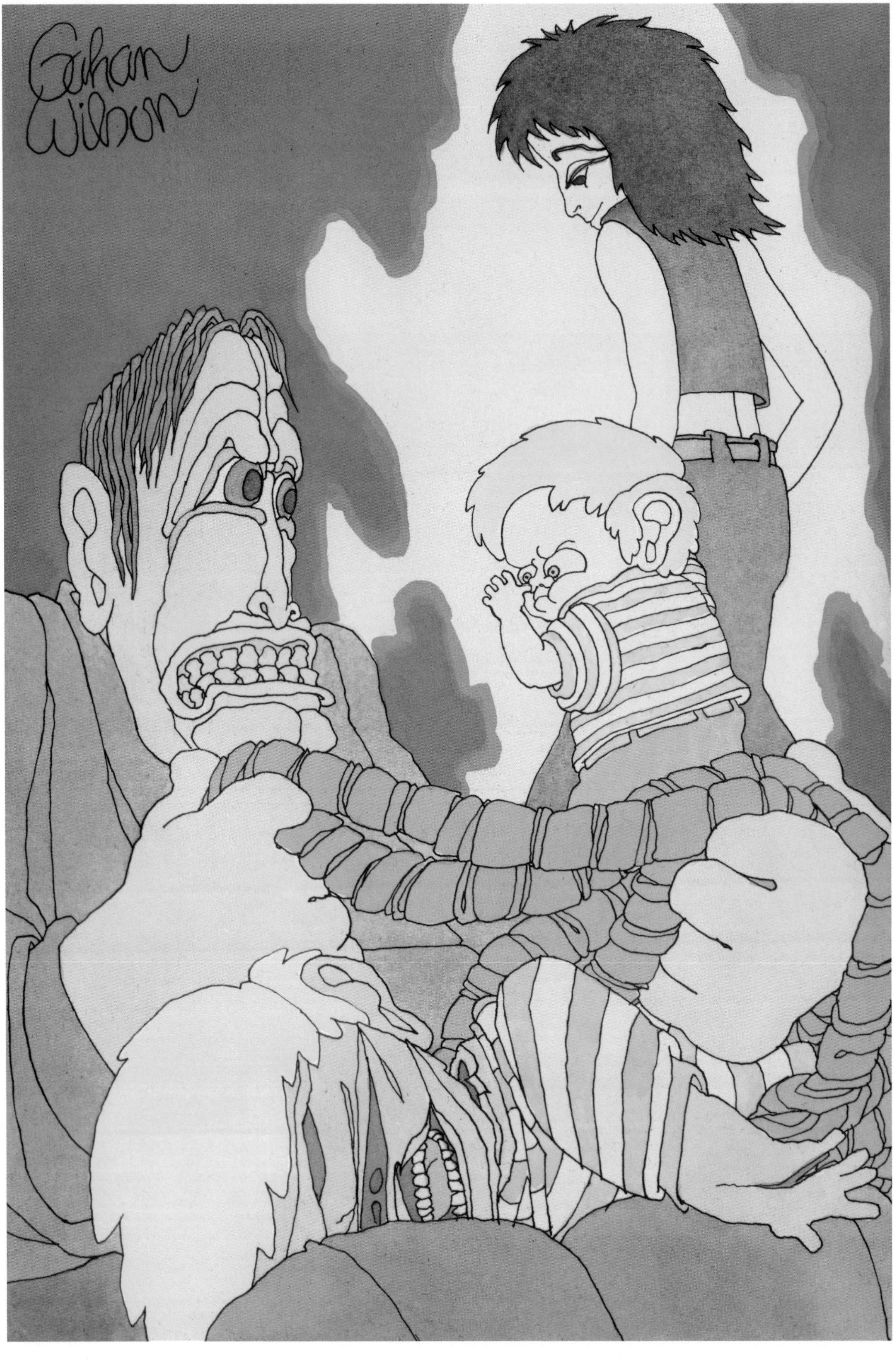
Gahan Wilson

Gahan Wilson

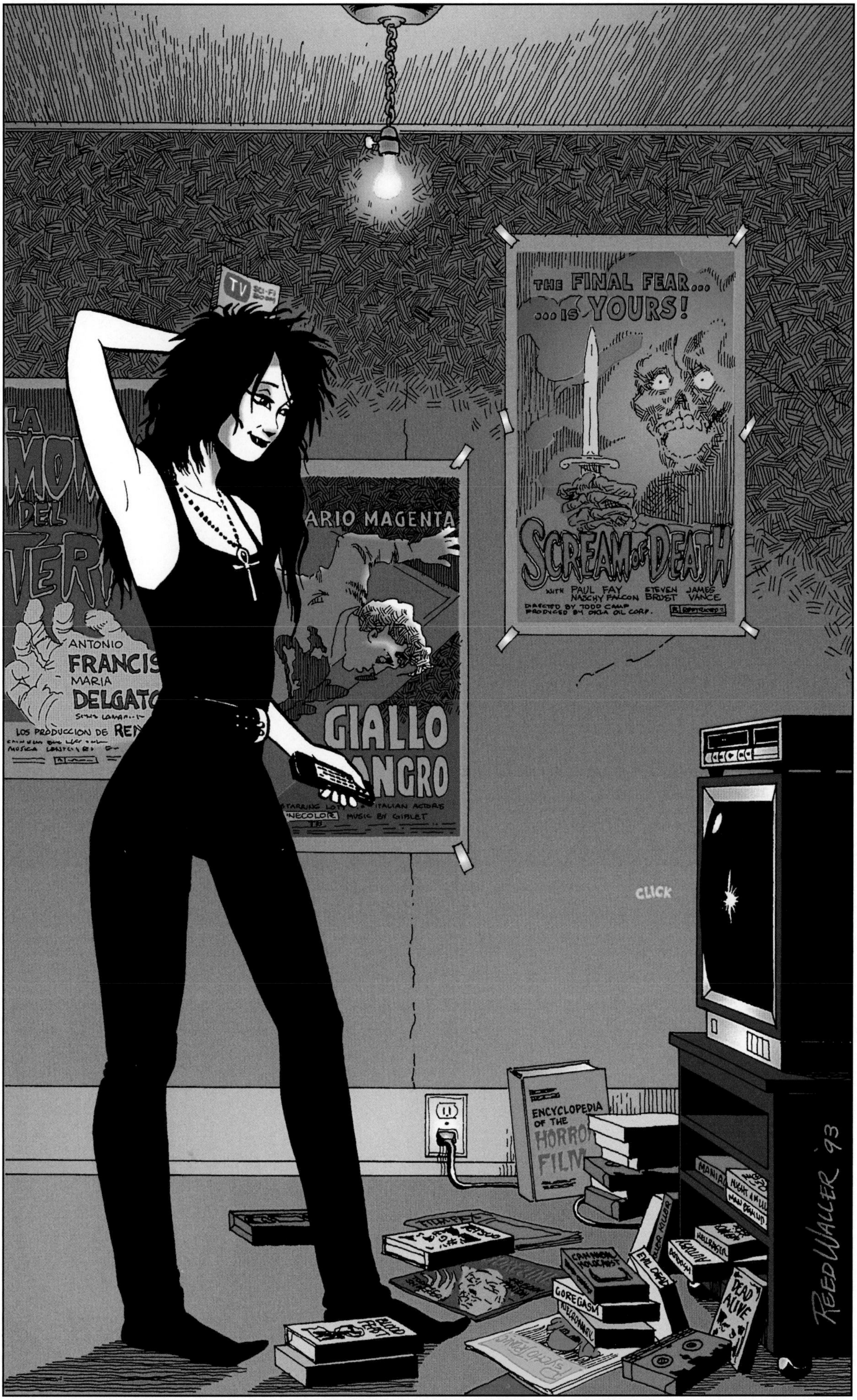
THE FINAL FEAR...
...IS YOURS!
SCREAM OF DEATH
WITH PAUL FAY NASCHY FALCON STEVEN BRUST JAMES VANCE
DIRECTED BY TODD CAMP
PRODUCED BY OKLA OIL CORP.
ARIO MAGENTA
GIALLO
ANGRO
MUSIC BY GIBLET
ANTONIO
FRANCIS
MARIA
DELGATO
LOS PRODUCCION DE
CLICK
ENCYCLOPEDIA OF THE HORROR FILM
MANIAC
HELLRAISER
CANNIBAL HOLOCAUST
GOREGASM
EVIL DEAD
DEAD ALIVE
BLOOD FEAST
REED WALLER '93

Reed Waller

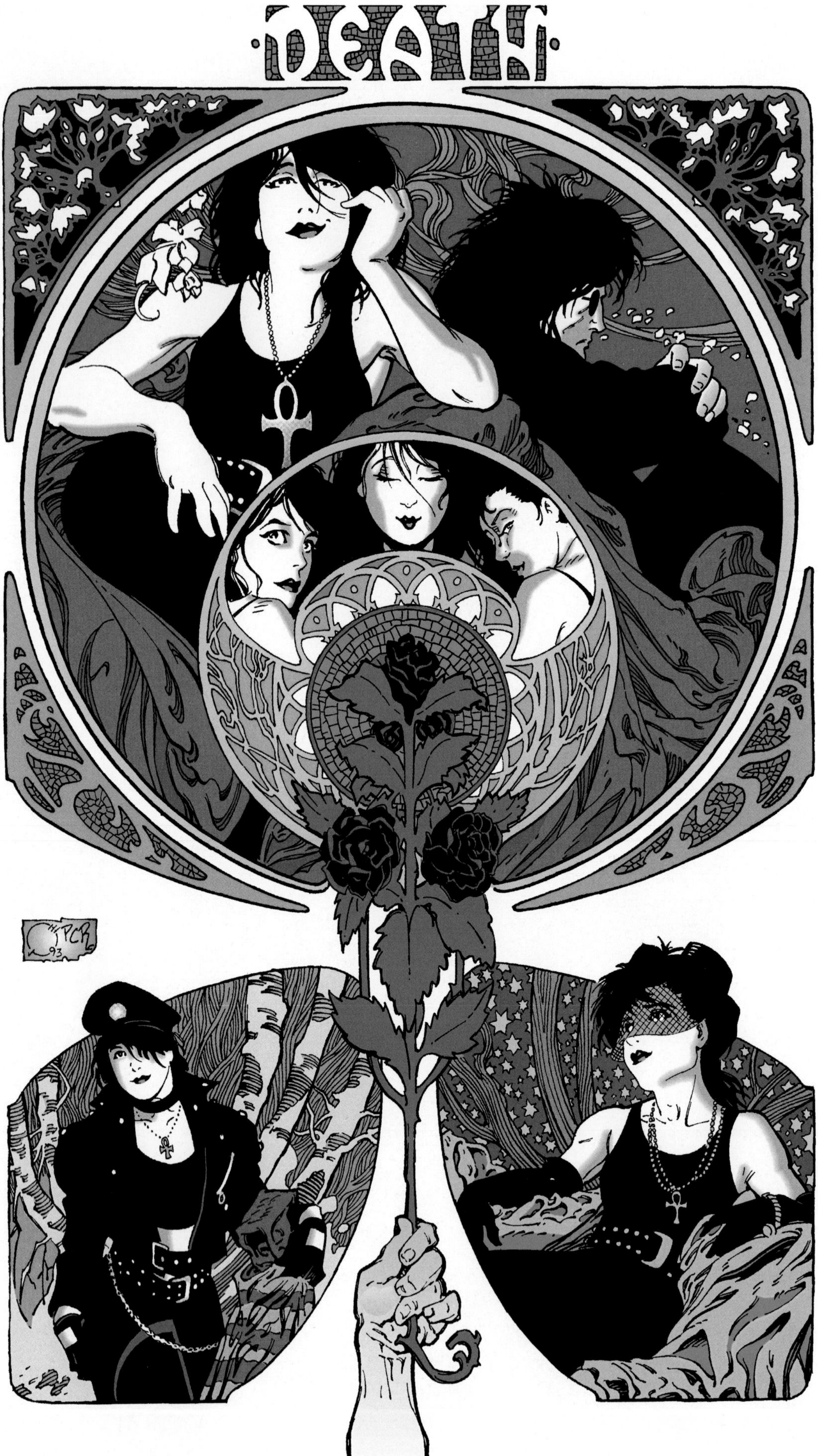
DEATH

Joe Quesada and P. Craig Russell (color by Lovern Kindzierski)

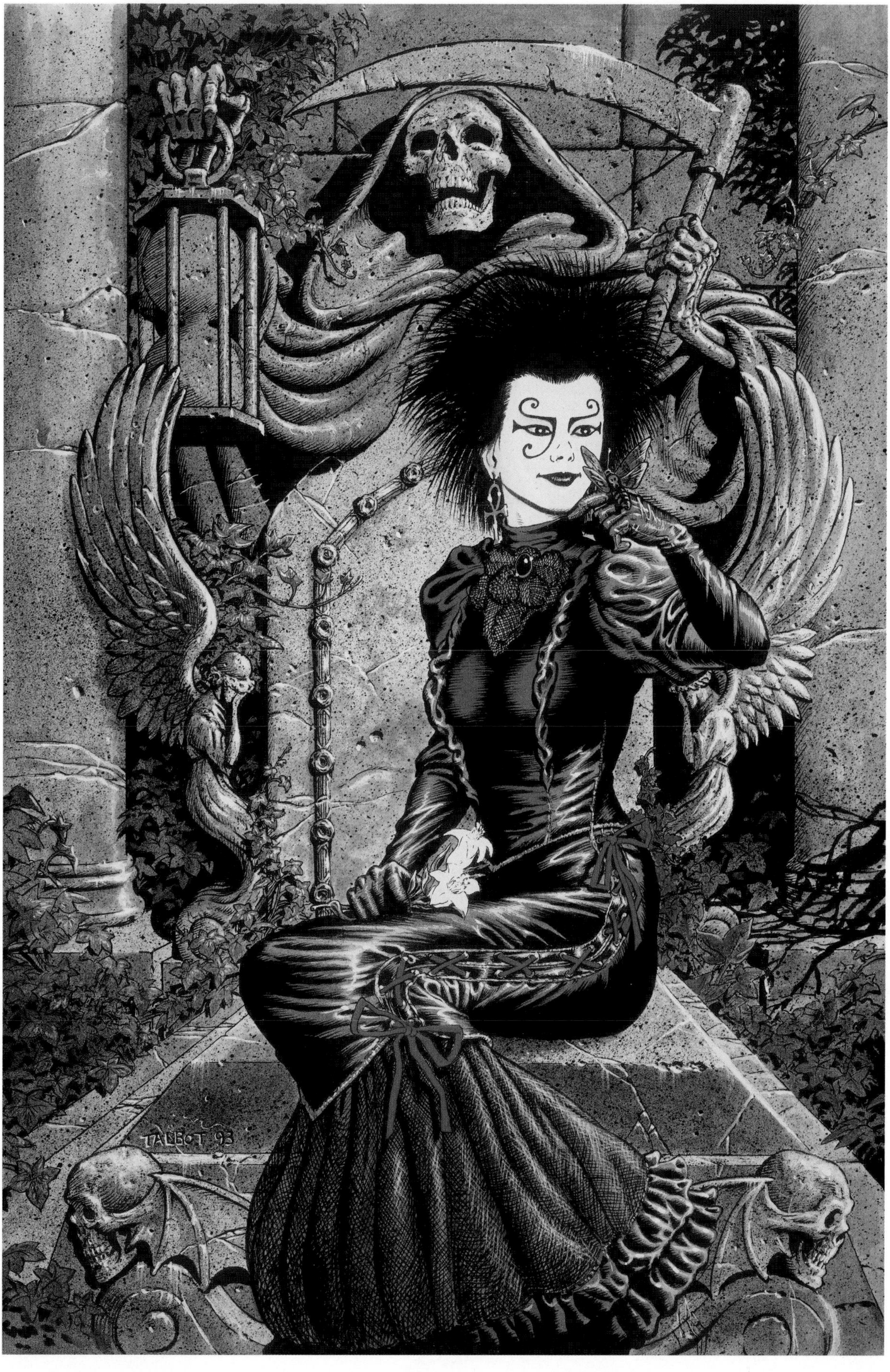
TALBOT '93

Bryan Talbot

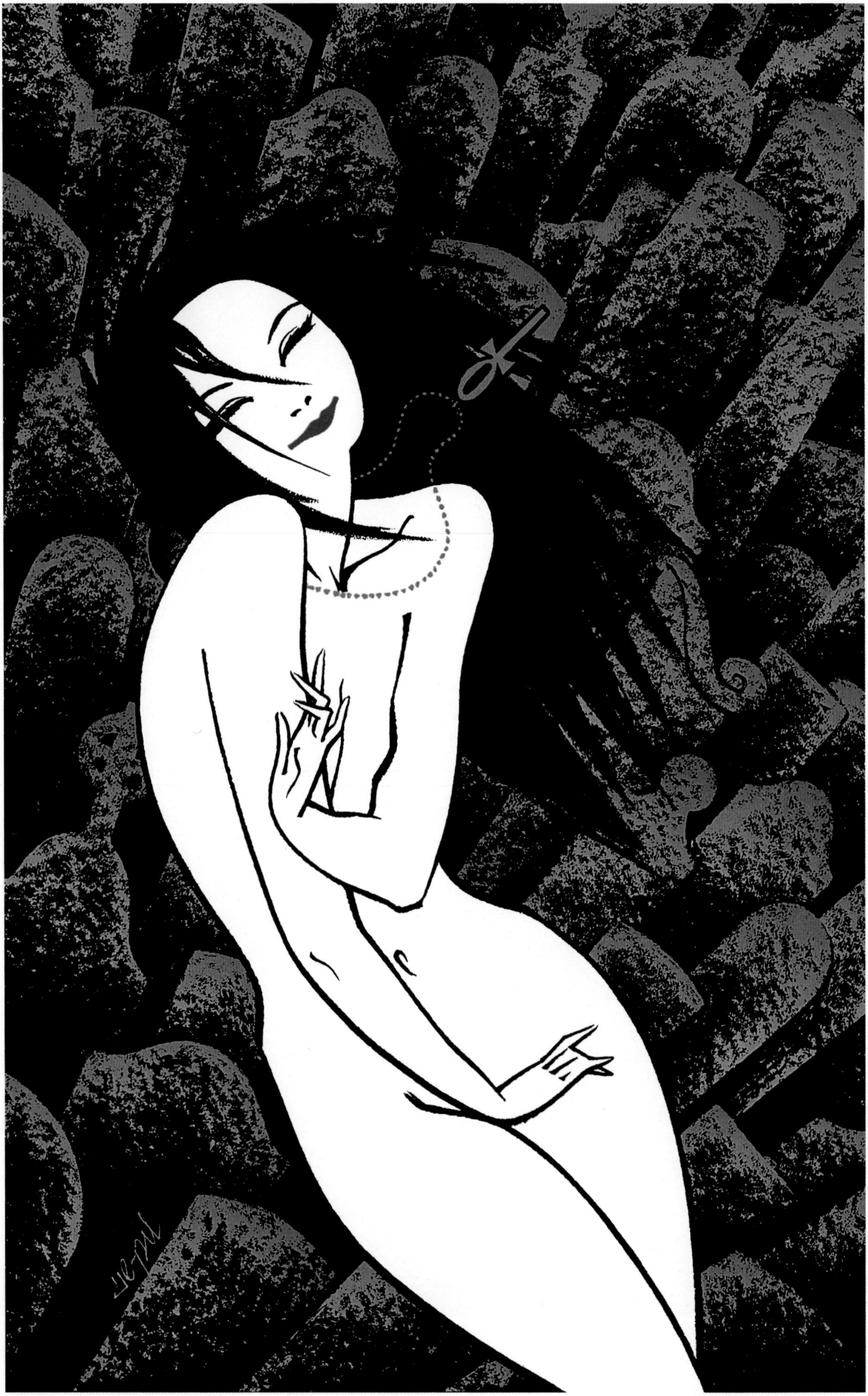

Marc Hempel (color by Daniel Vozzo)

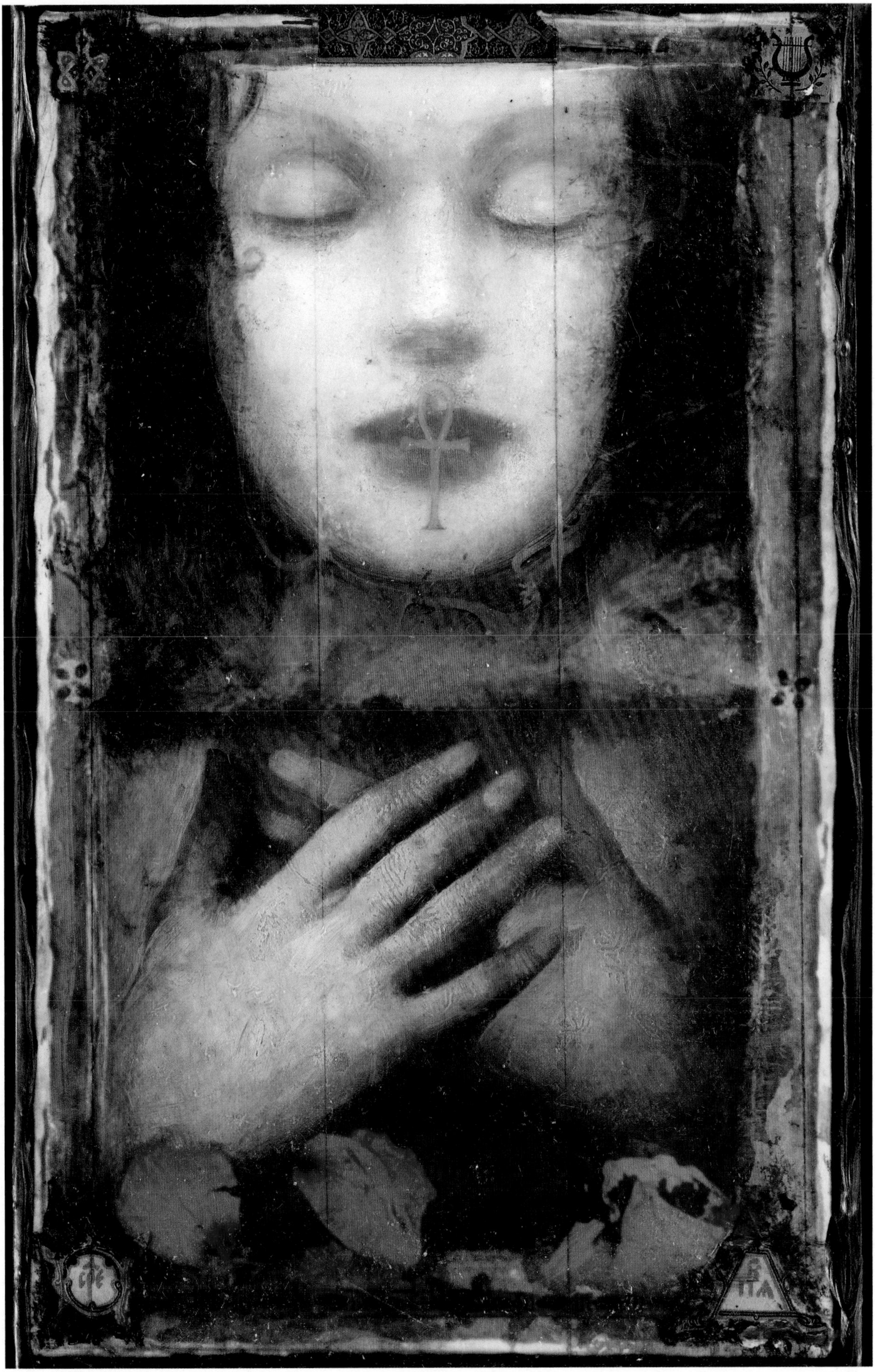

Greg Spalenka

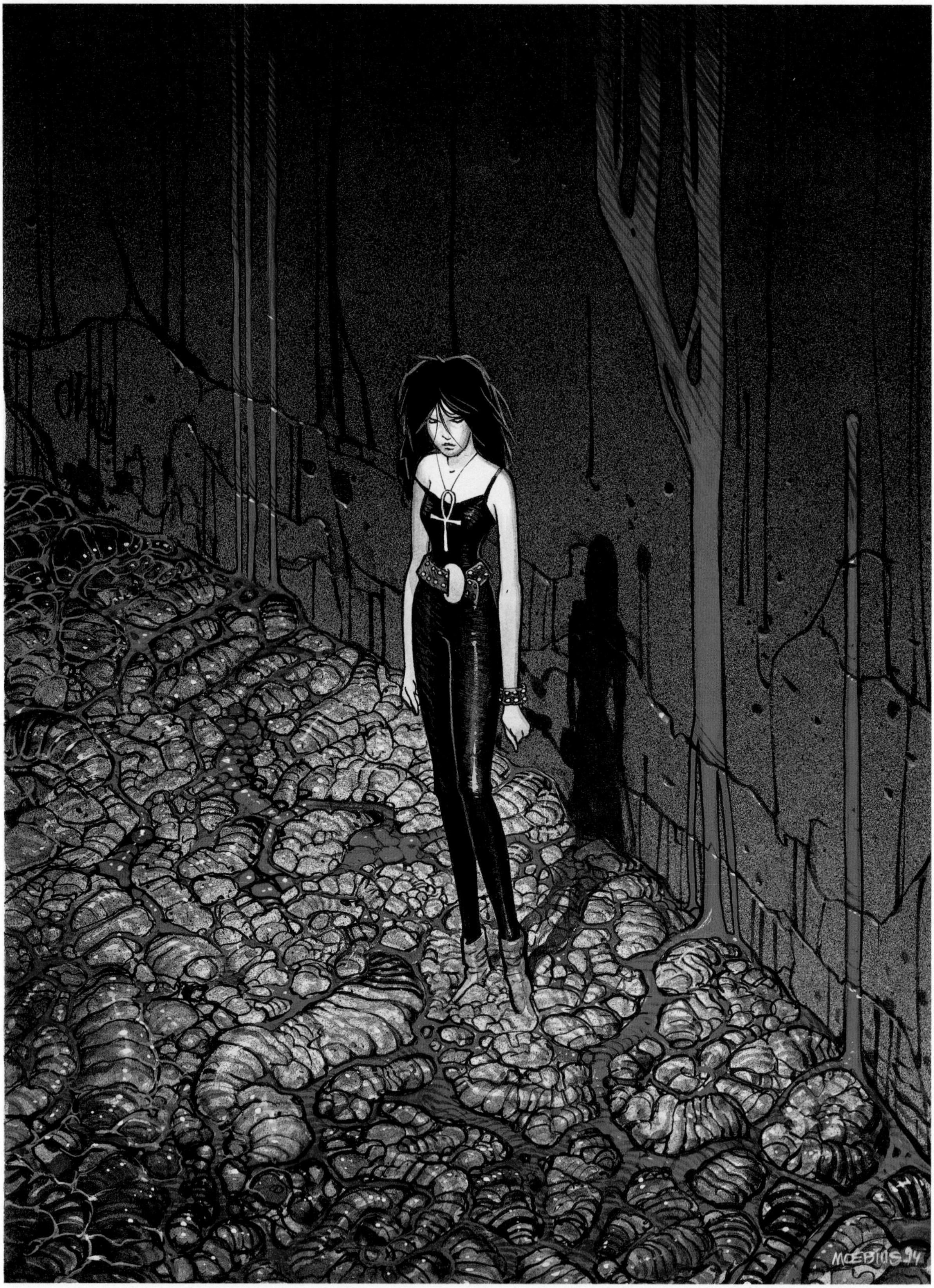
MOEBIUS 94

Moebius

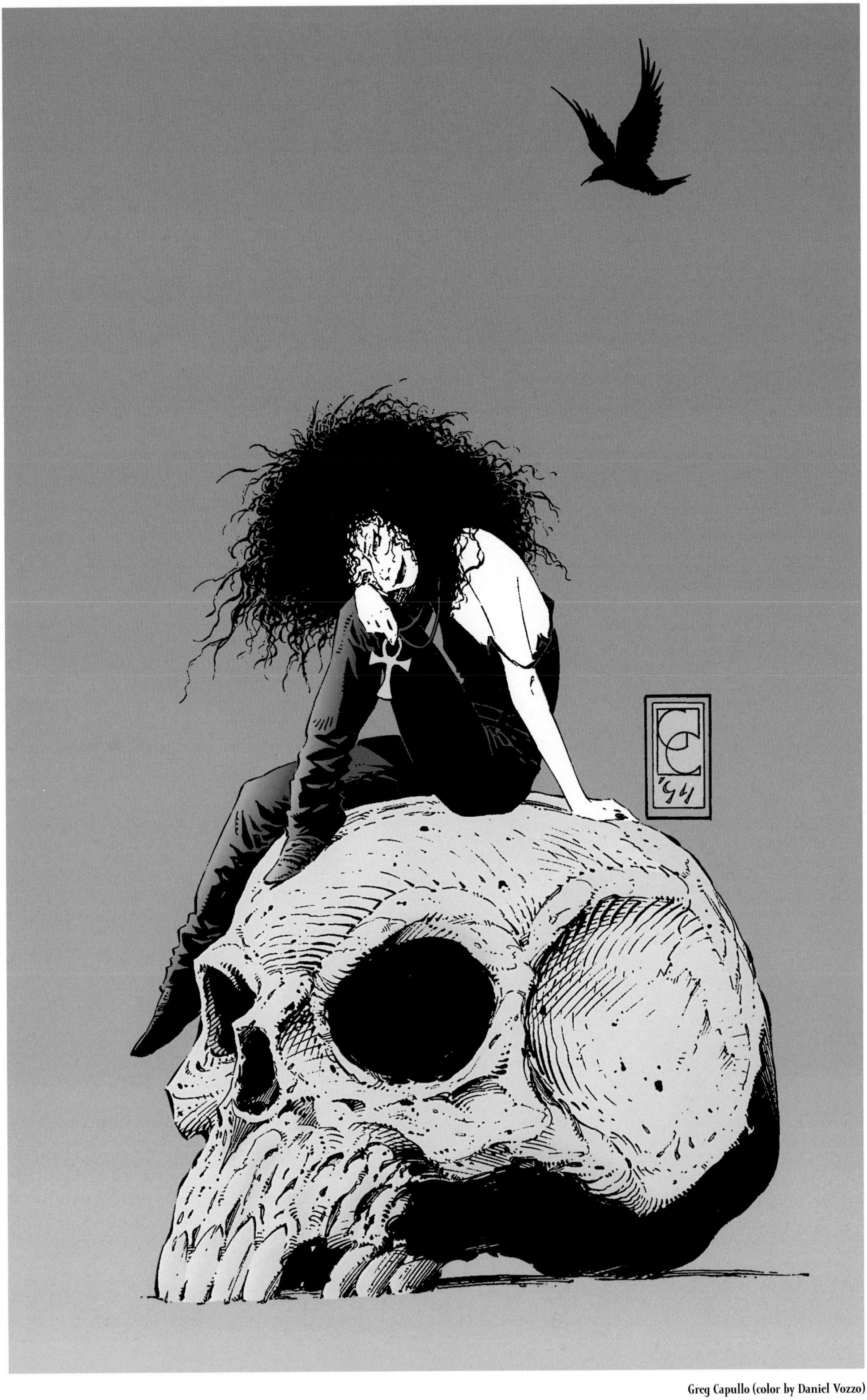

Greg Capullo (color by Daniel Vozzo)

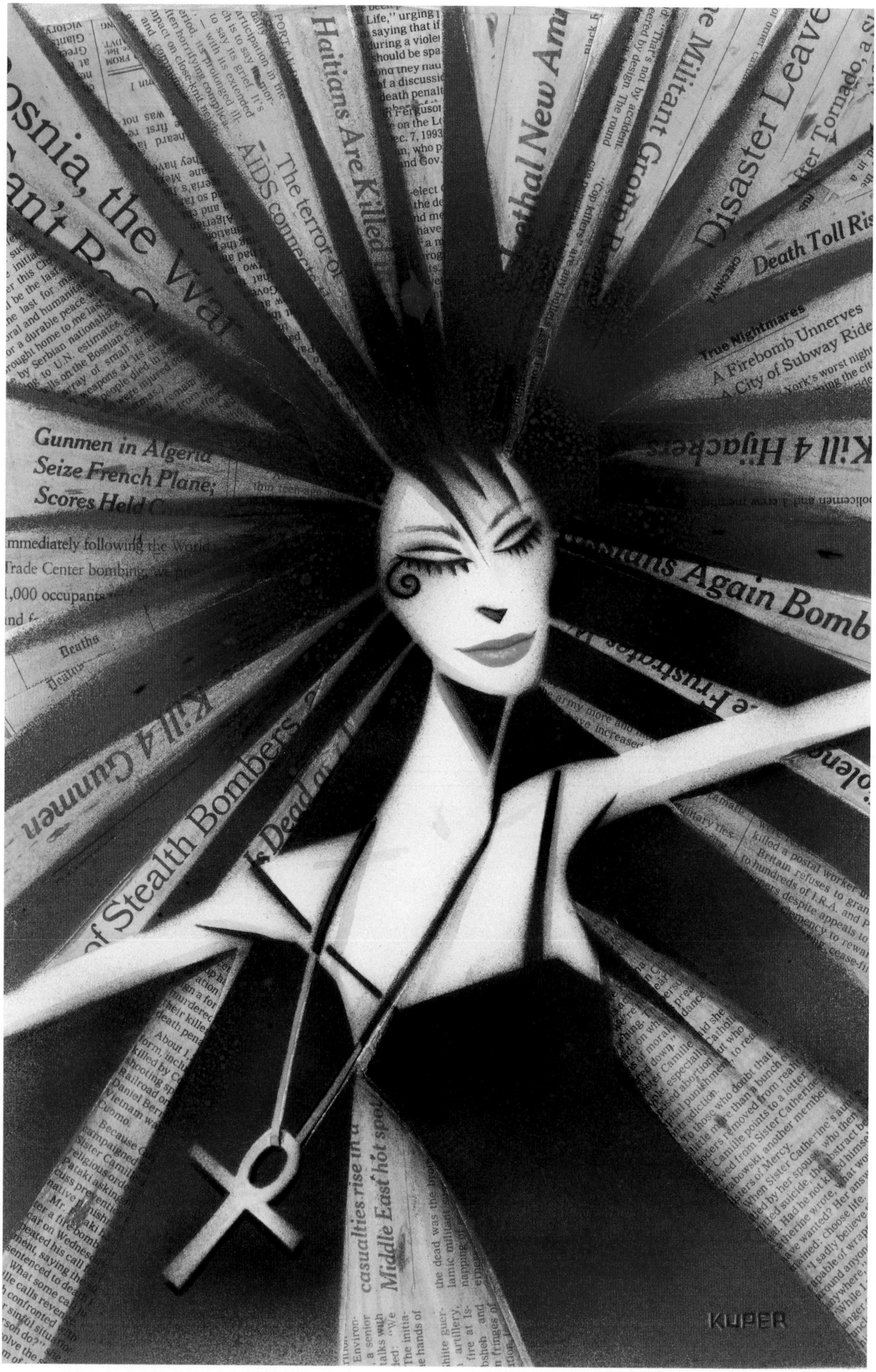
Gunmen in Algeria
Seize French Plane;
Scores Held
True Nightmares
A Firebomb Unnerves
A City of Subway Ride
Death Toll Ris
Kill 4 Gunmen
of Stealth Bombers
Kill 4 Hijackers
Again Bomb
KUPER

Peter Kuper

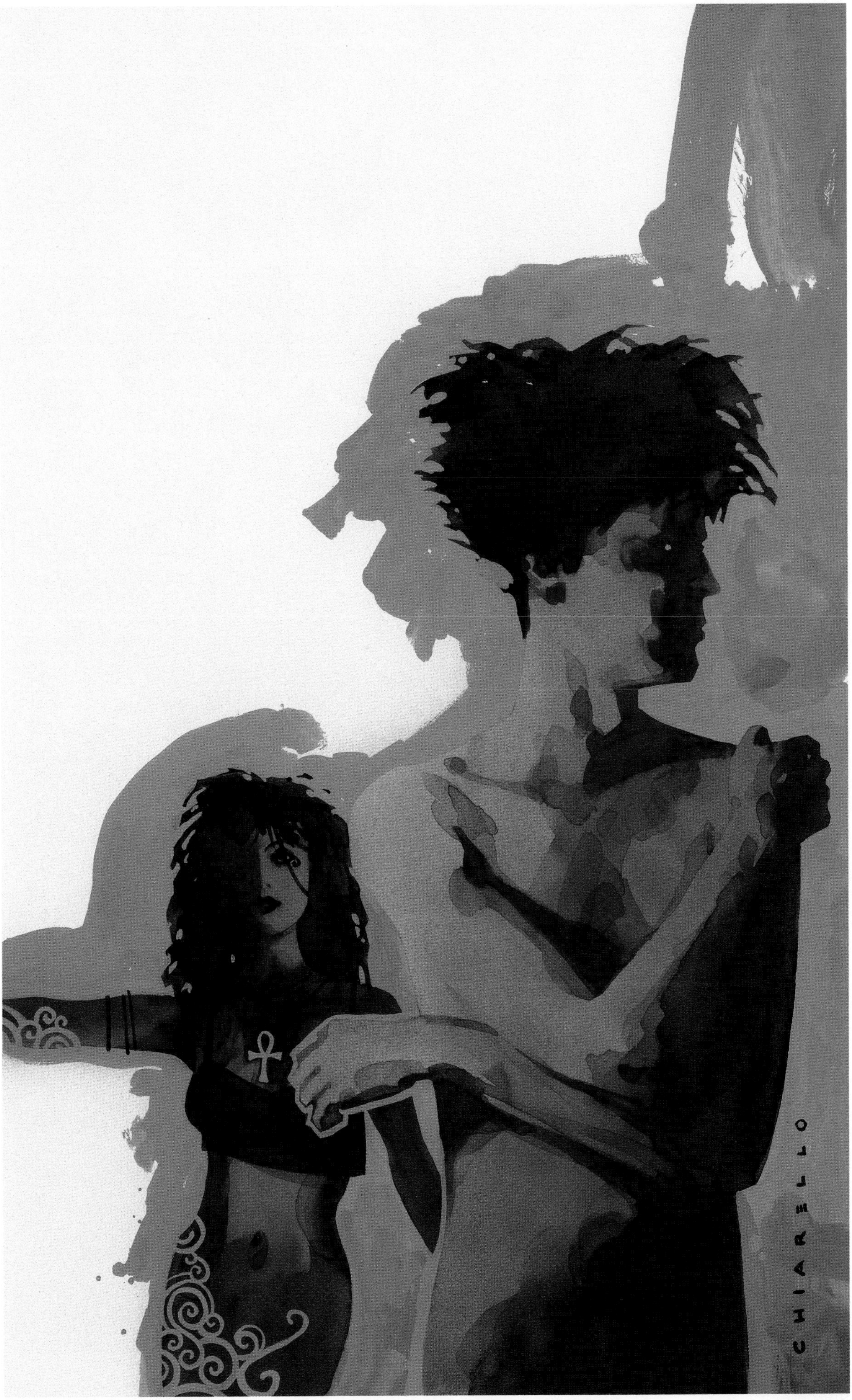
CHIARELLO

Mark Chiarello

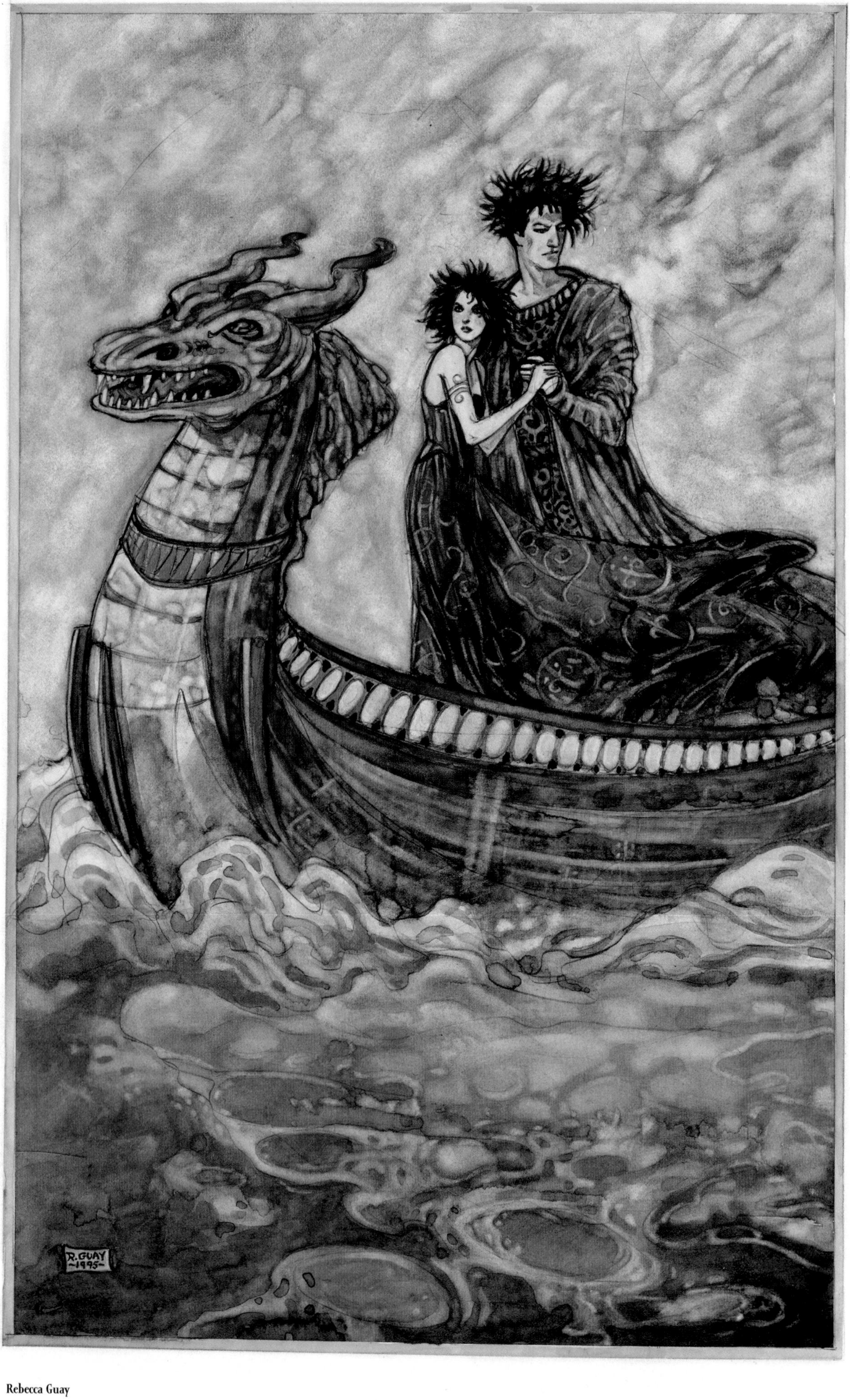
R. GUAY
1995

Rebecca Guay

FROM DREAMS I CONJURE A HANDFUL OF YELLOW GRAIN. I THROW THE GRAIN INTO THE AIR AND I HEAR THE SOUND OF WINGS

DEATH
DAVE McKEAN
1991

Dave McKean

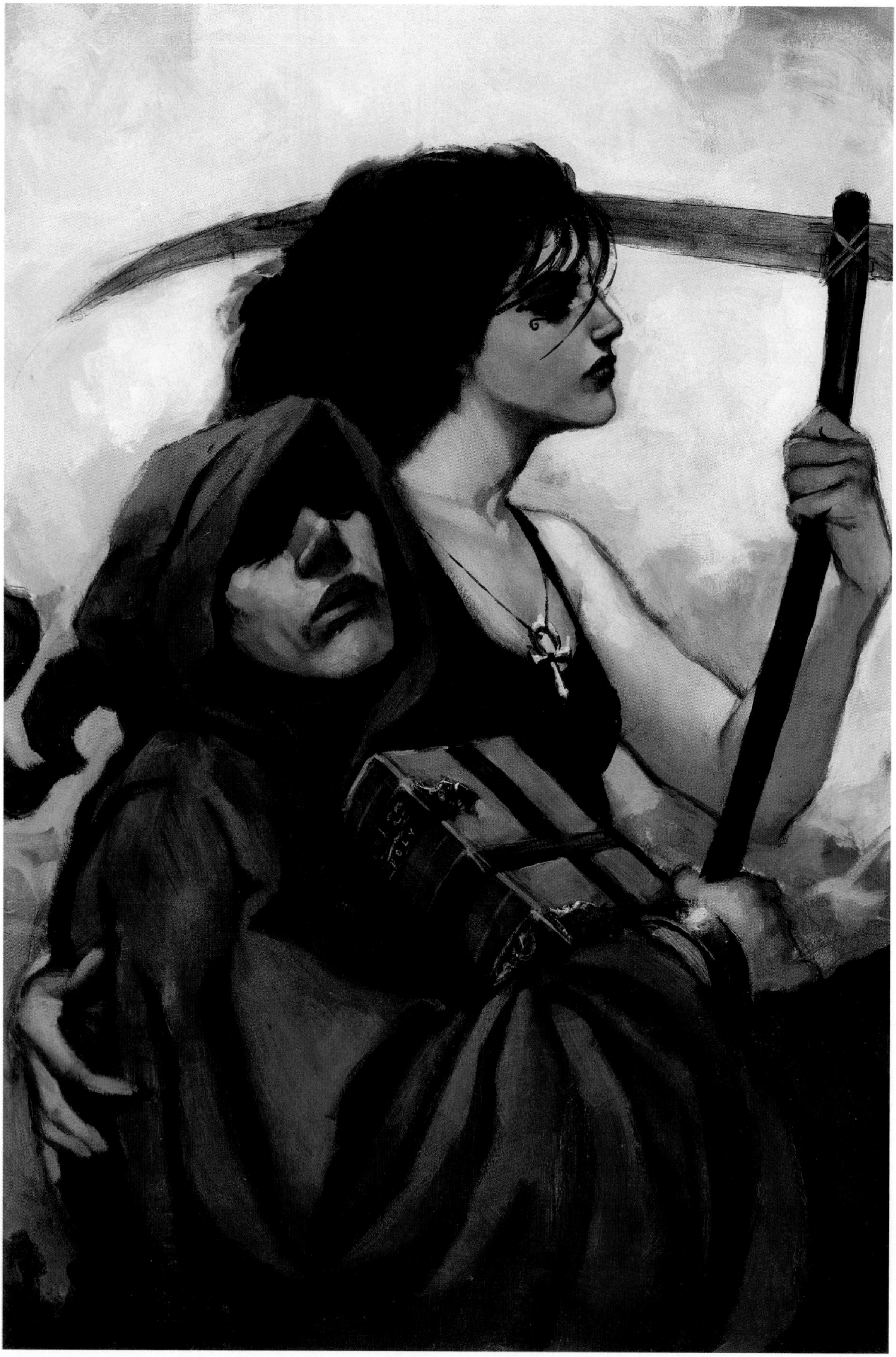

Paul Lee

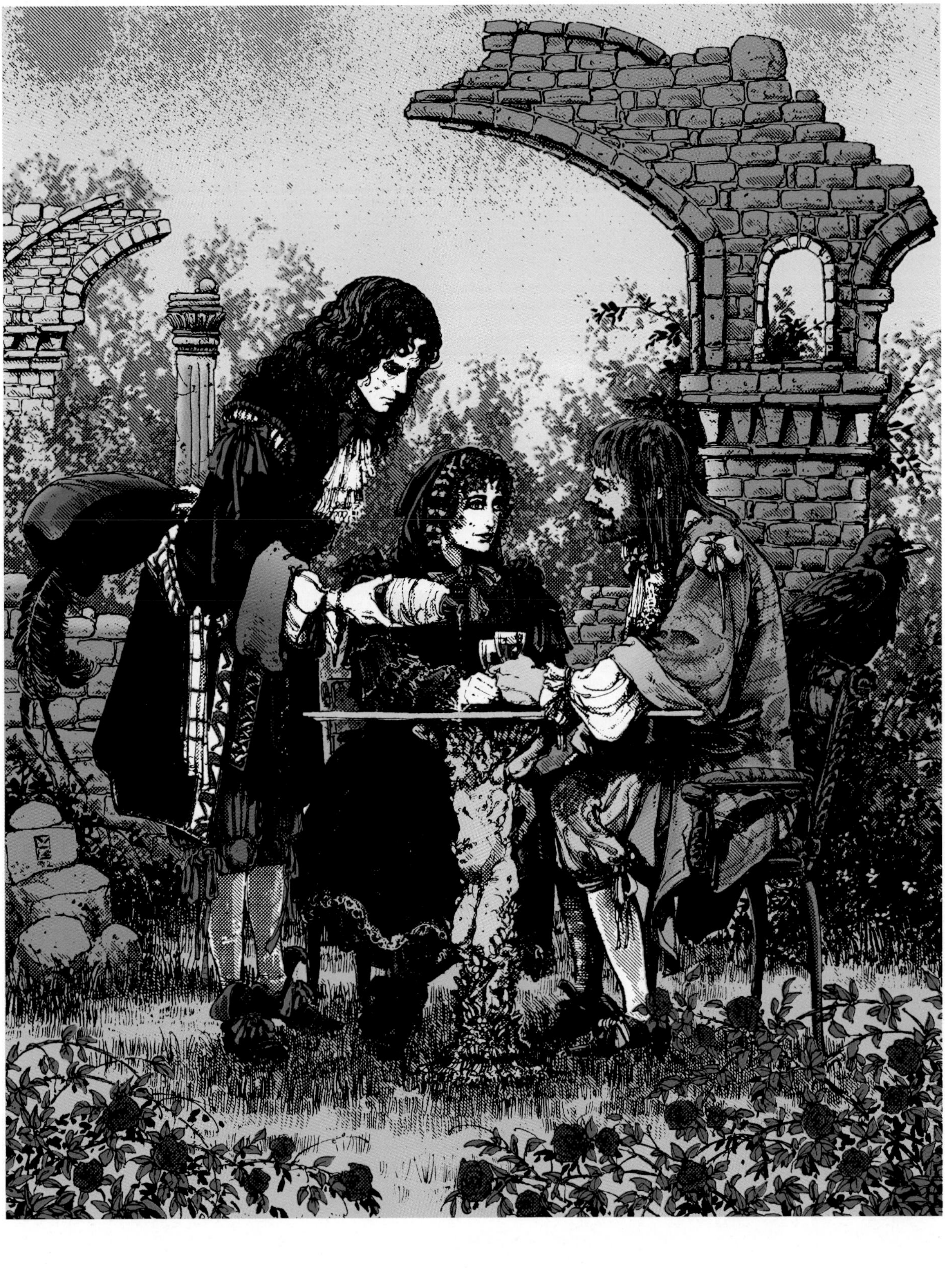

Michael Zulli (color by Lovern Kindzierski)

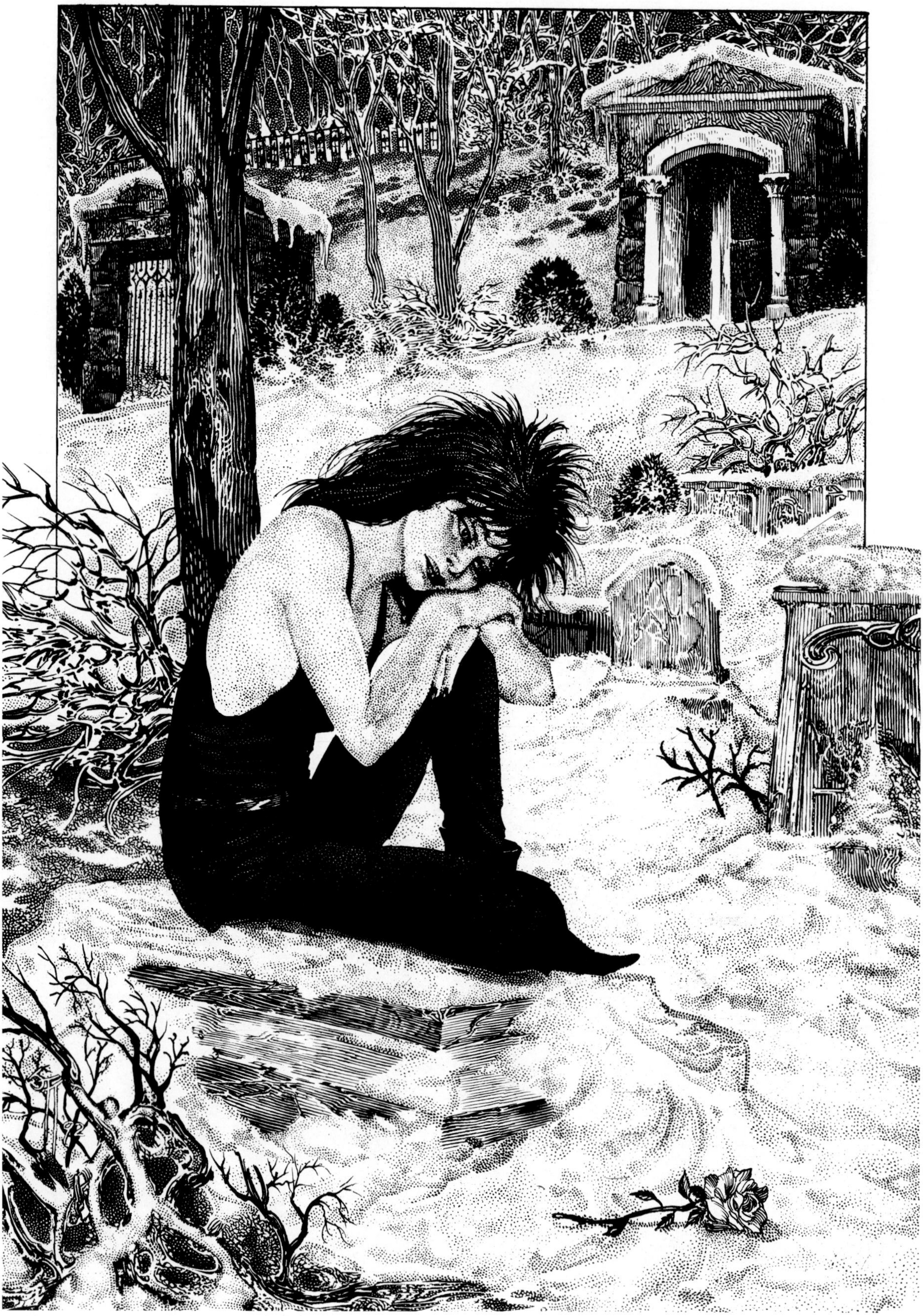

John Totleben

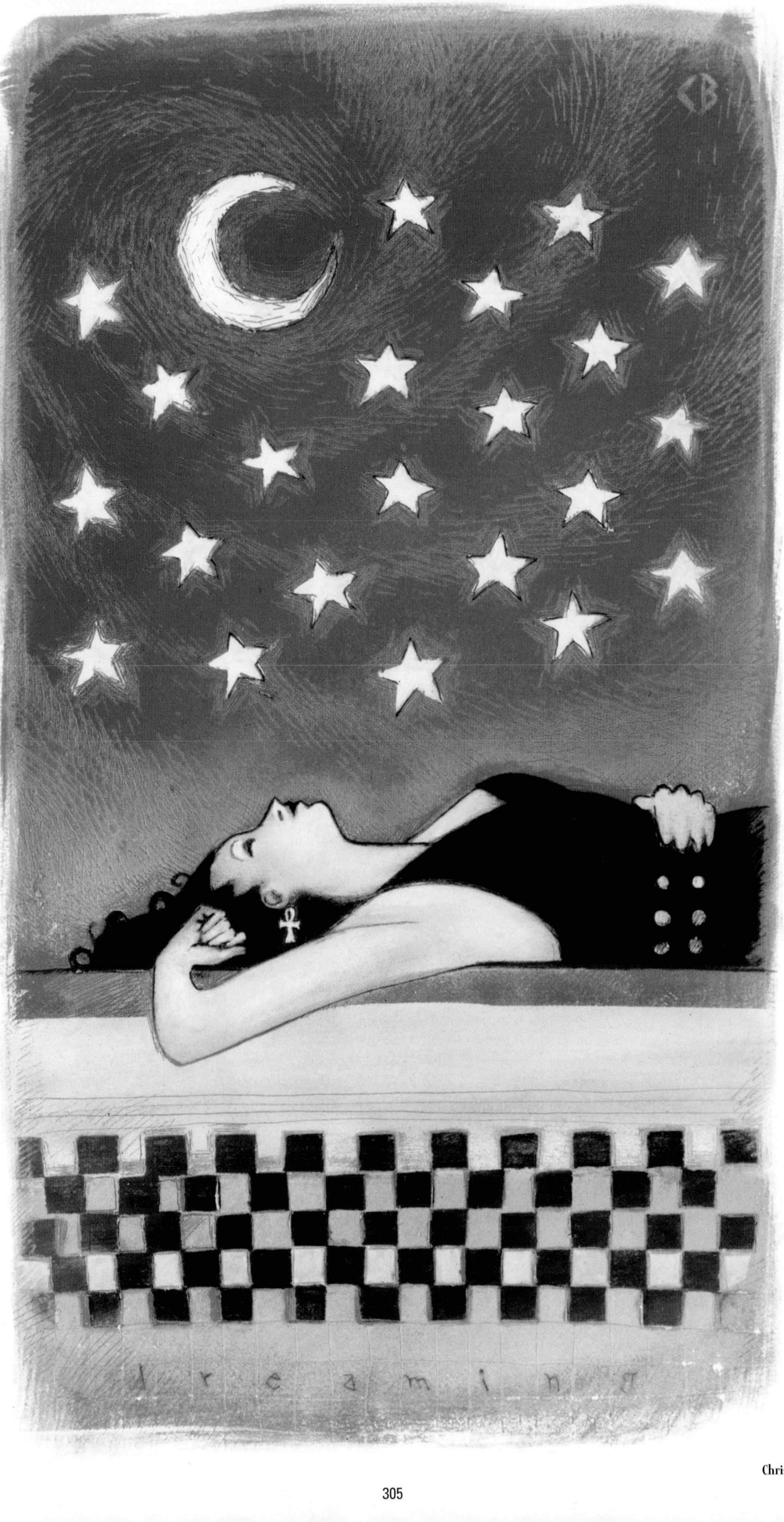
d r e a m i n g

Chris Bachalo

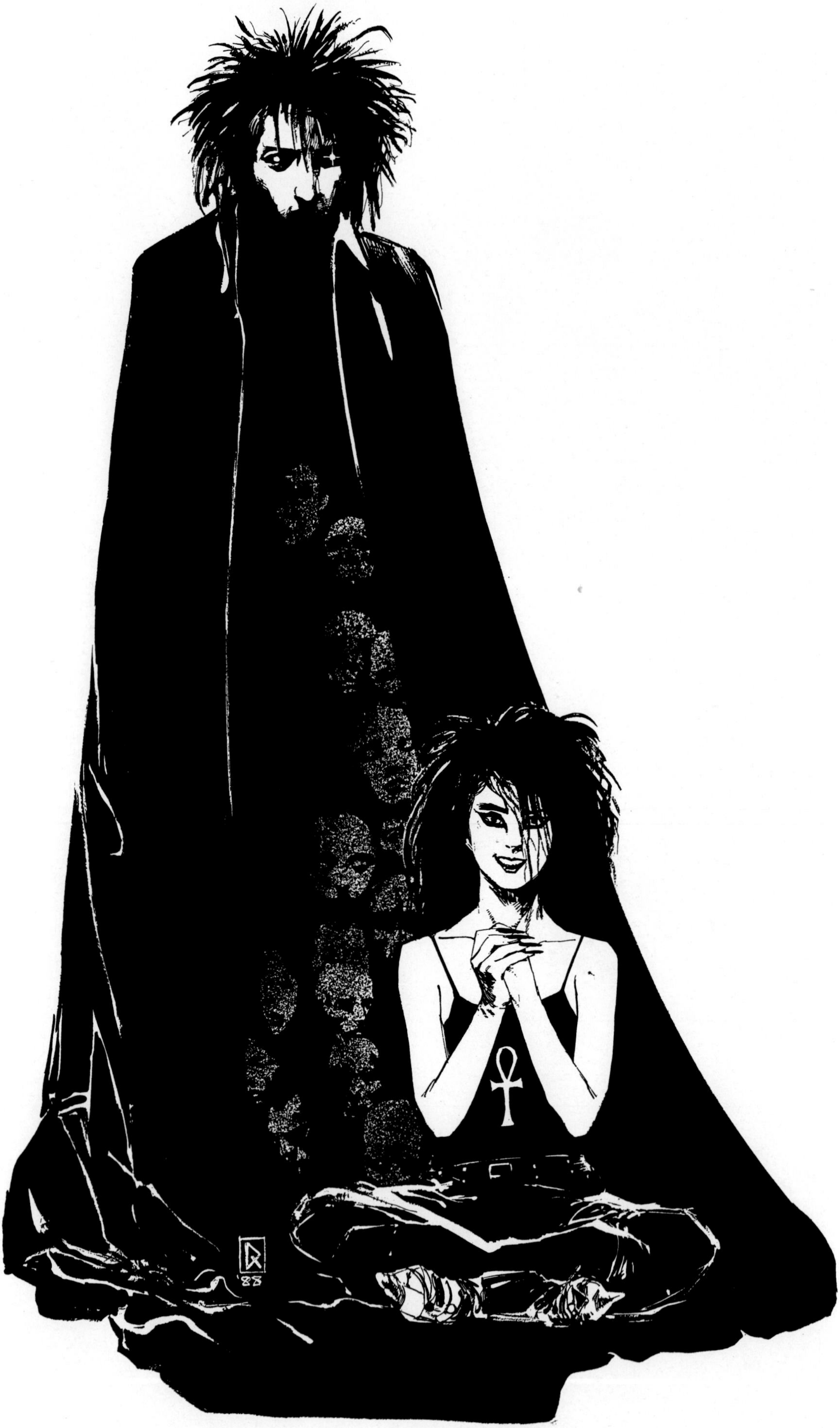

Mike Dringenberg

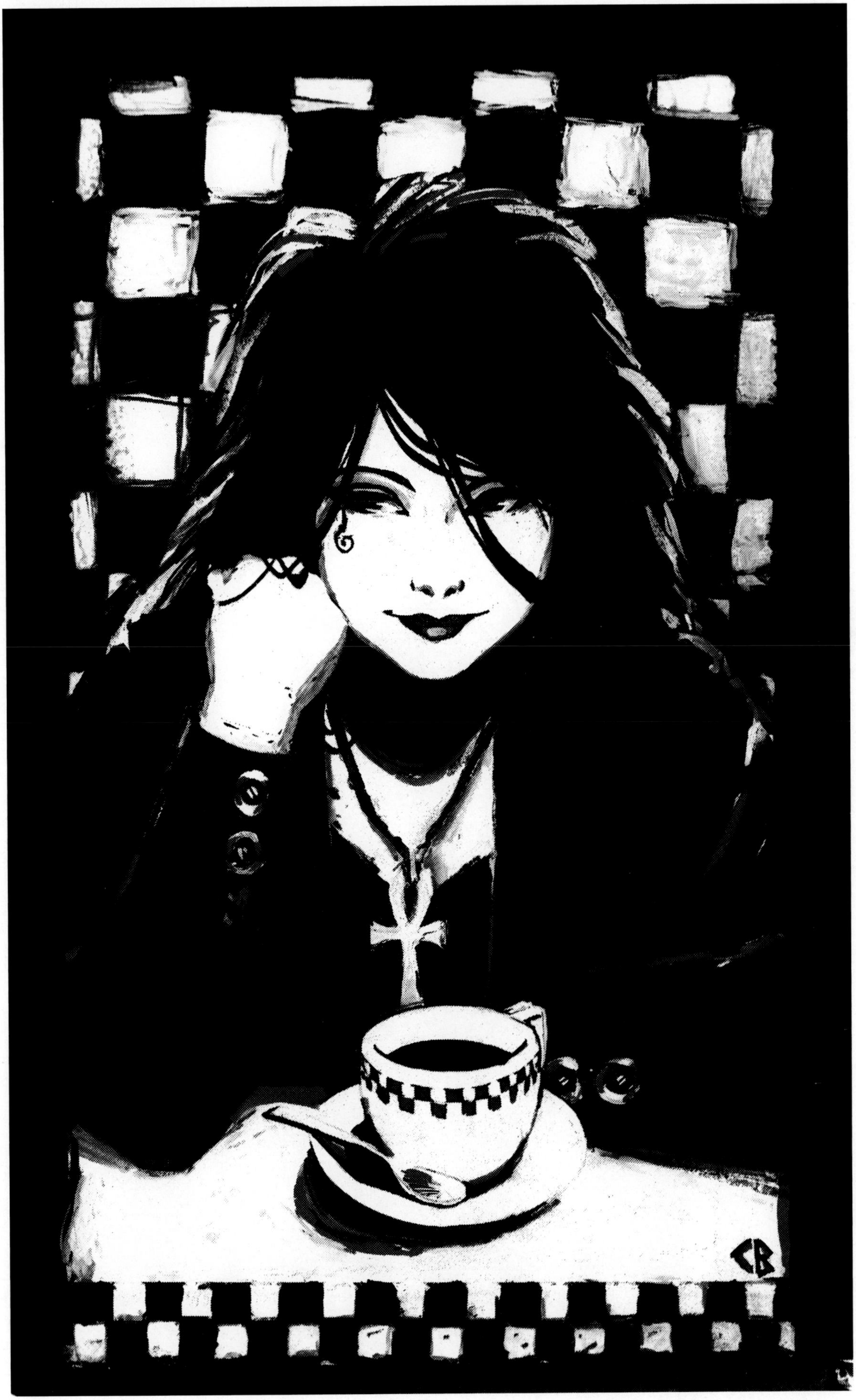
CB

Chris Bachalo

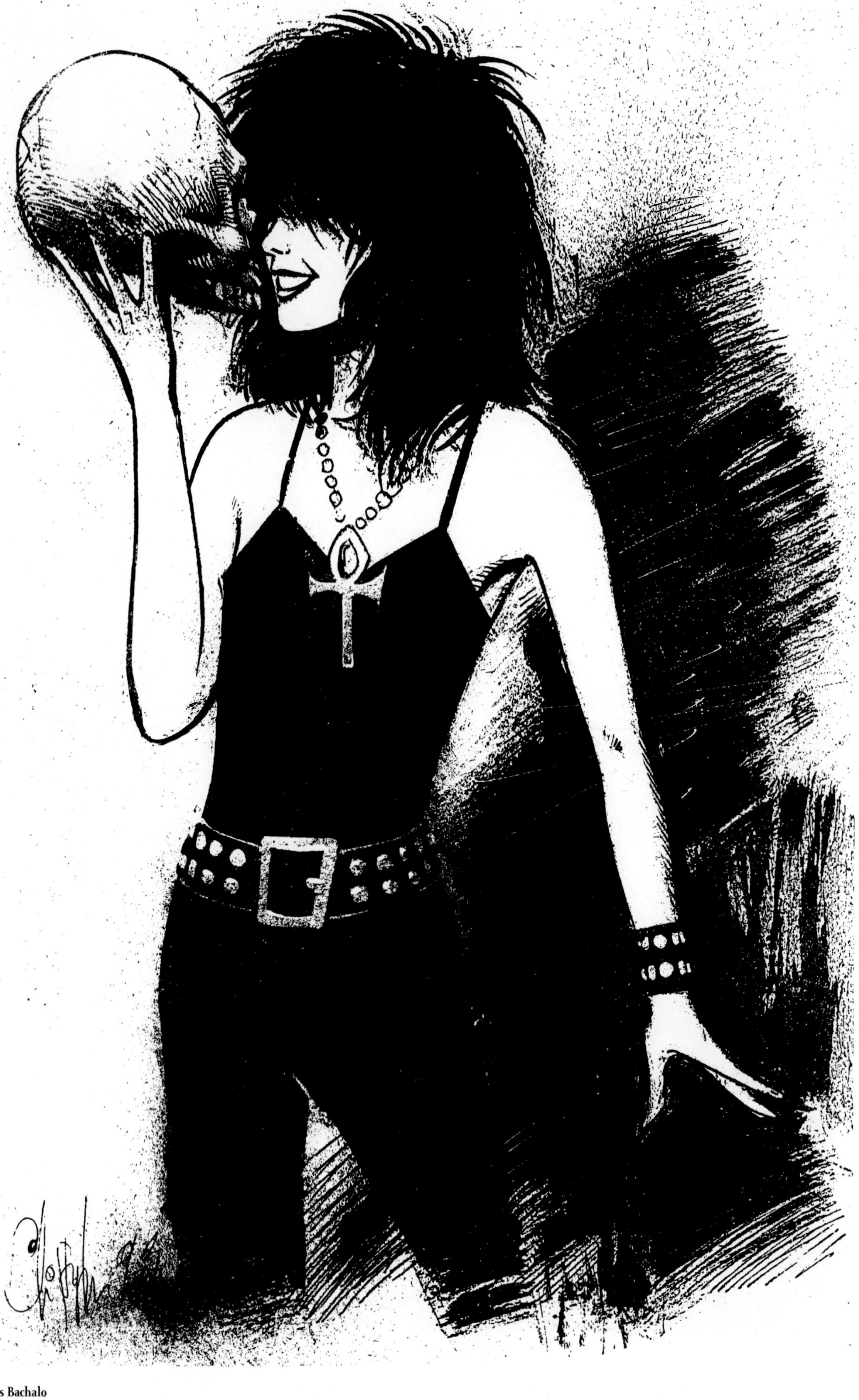

Chris Bachalo

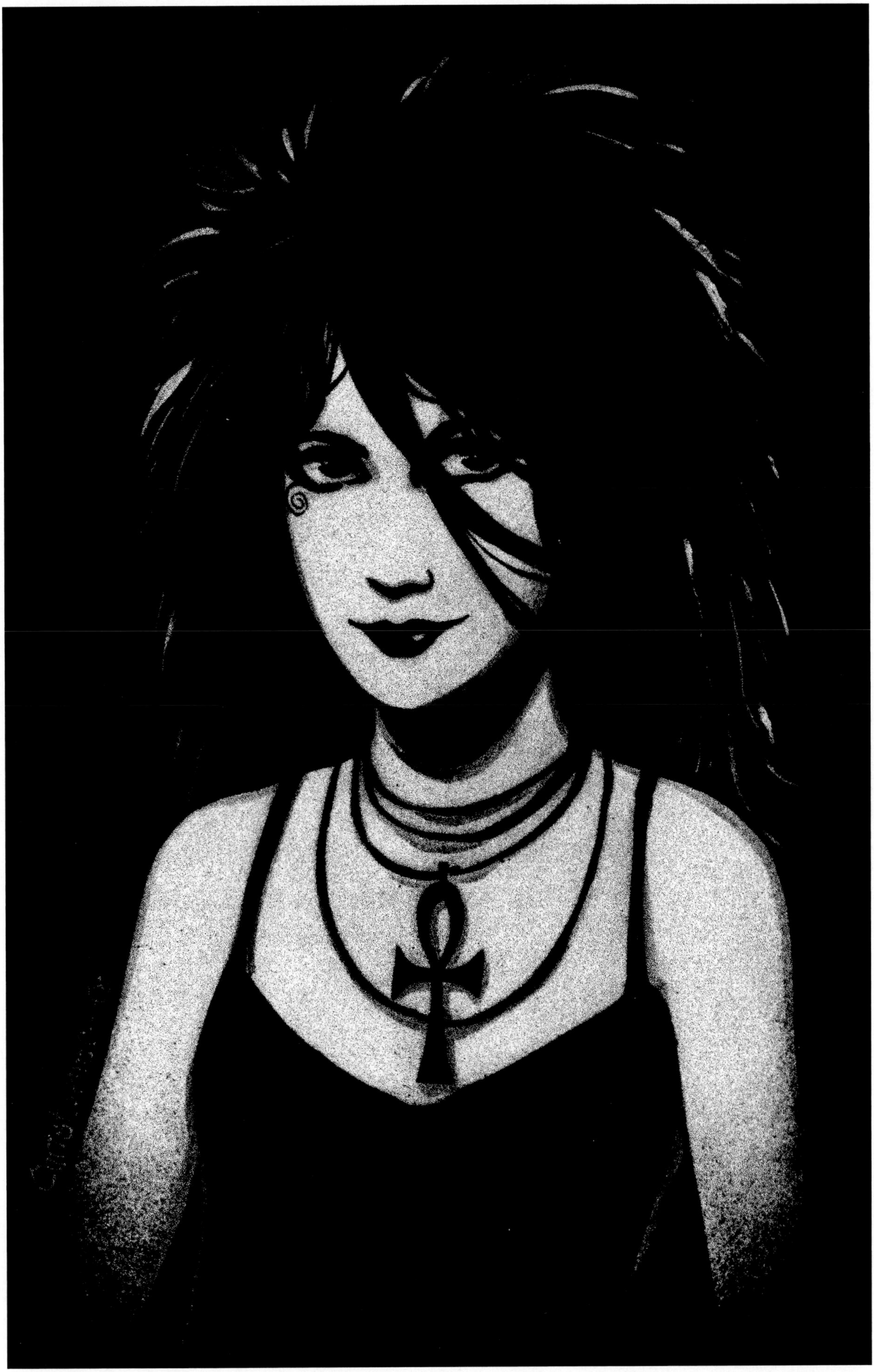

Chris Bachalo

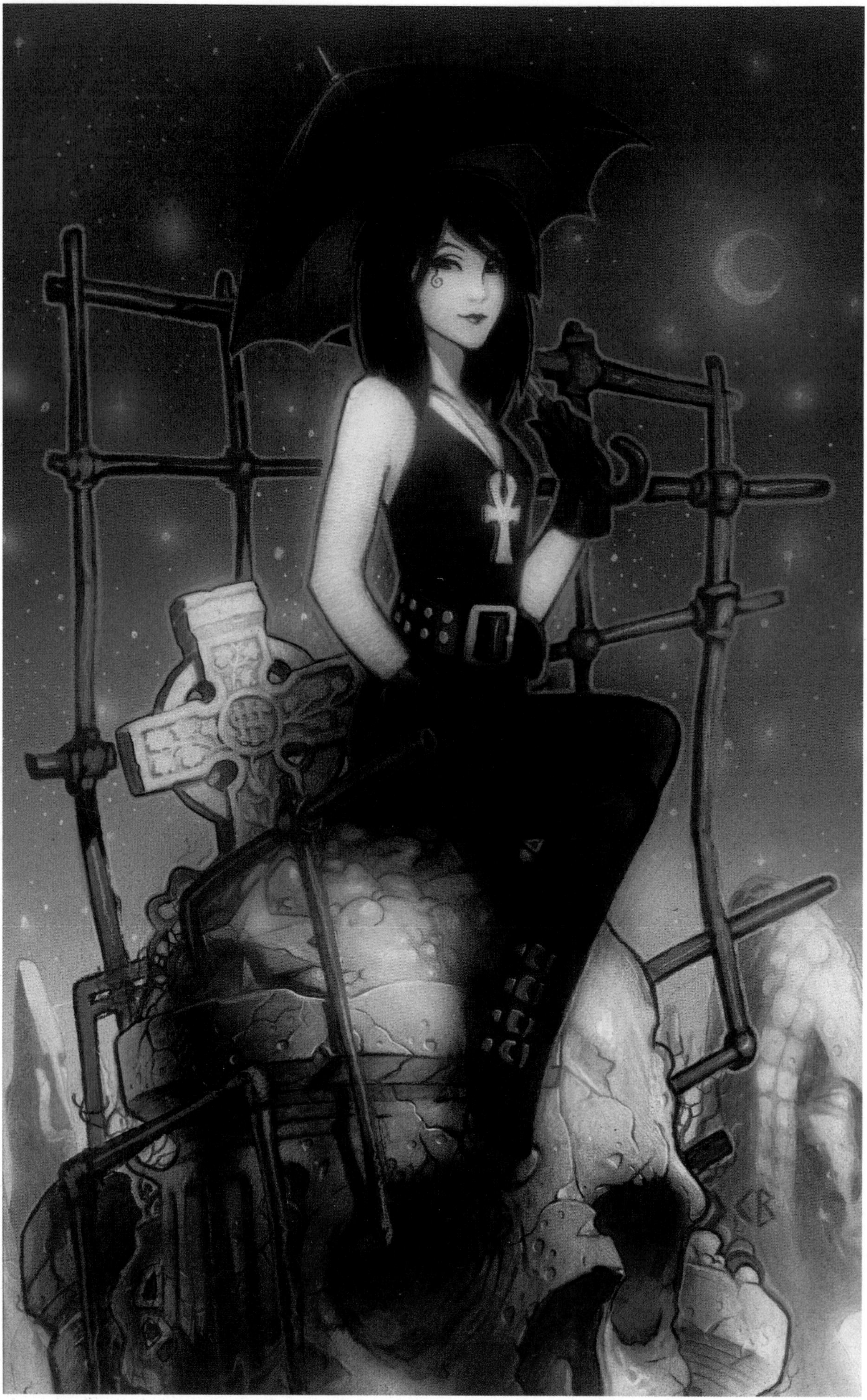

Chris Bachalo

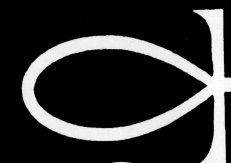

DEATH talks about LIFE

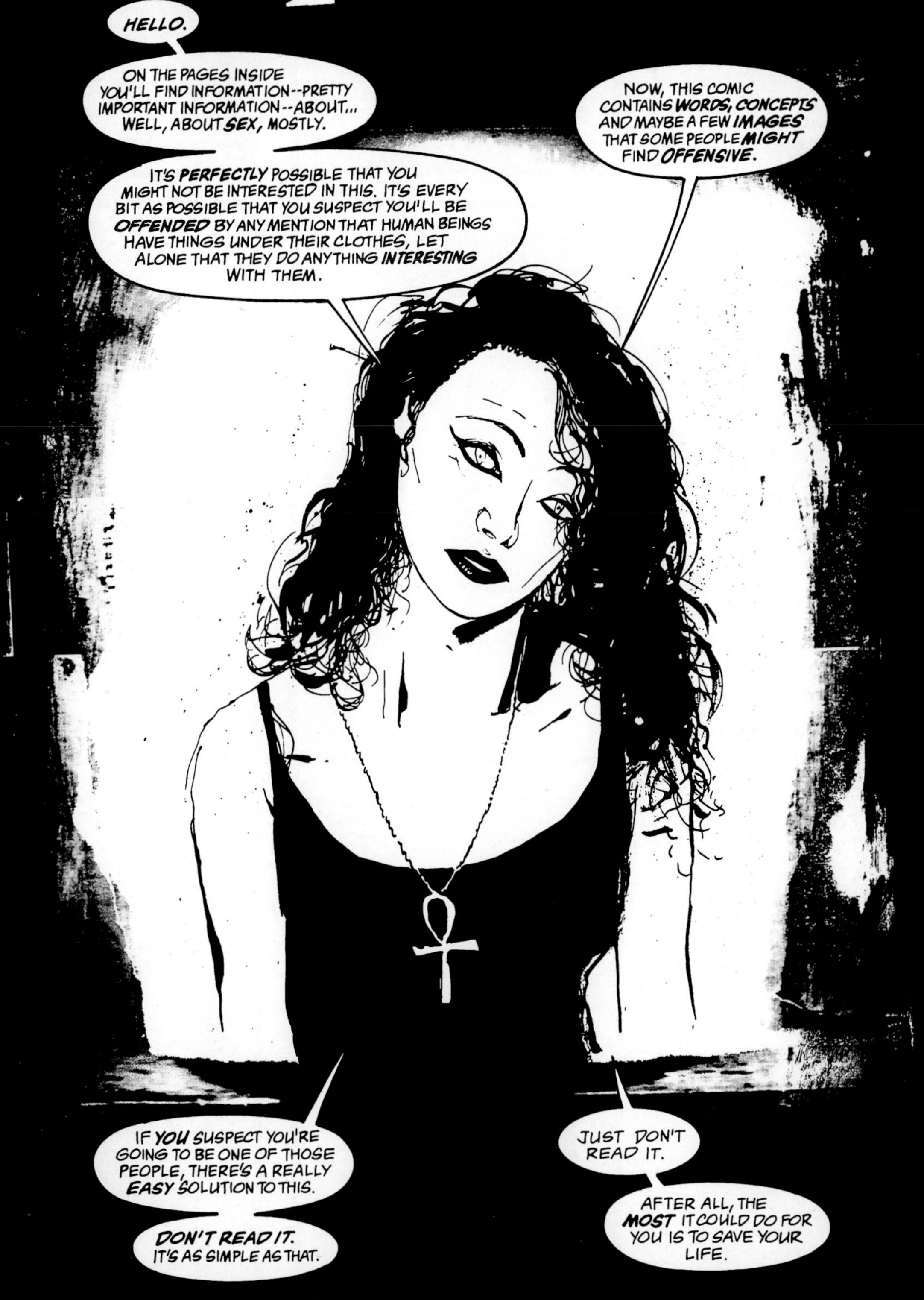
HELLO.
ON THE PAGES INSIDE YOU'LL FIND INFORMATION--PRETTY IMPORTANT INFORMATION--ABOUT... WELL, ABOUT SEX, MOSTLY.
IT'S PERFECTLY POSSIBLE THAT YOU MIGHT NOT BE INTERESTED IN THIS. IT'S EVERY BIT AS POSSIBLE THAT YOU SUSPECT YOU'LL BE OFFENDED BY ANY MENTION THAT HUMAN BEINGS HAVE THINGS UNDER THEIR CLOTHES, LET ALONE THAT THEY DO ANYTHING INTERESTING WITH THEM.
NOW, THIS COMIC CONTAINS WORDS, CONCEPTS AND MAYBE A FEW IMAGES THAT SOME PEOPLE MIGHT FIND OFFENSIVE.
IF YOU SUSPECT YOU'RE GOING TO BE ONE OF THOSE PEOPLE, THERE'S A REALLY EASY SOLUTION TO THIS.
DON'T READ IT. IT'S AS SIMPLE AS THAT.
JUST DON'T READ IT.
AFTER ALL, THE MOST IT COULD DO FOR YOU IS TO SAVE YOUR LIFE.

Art by Dave McKean

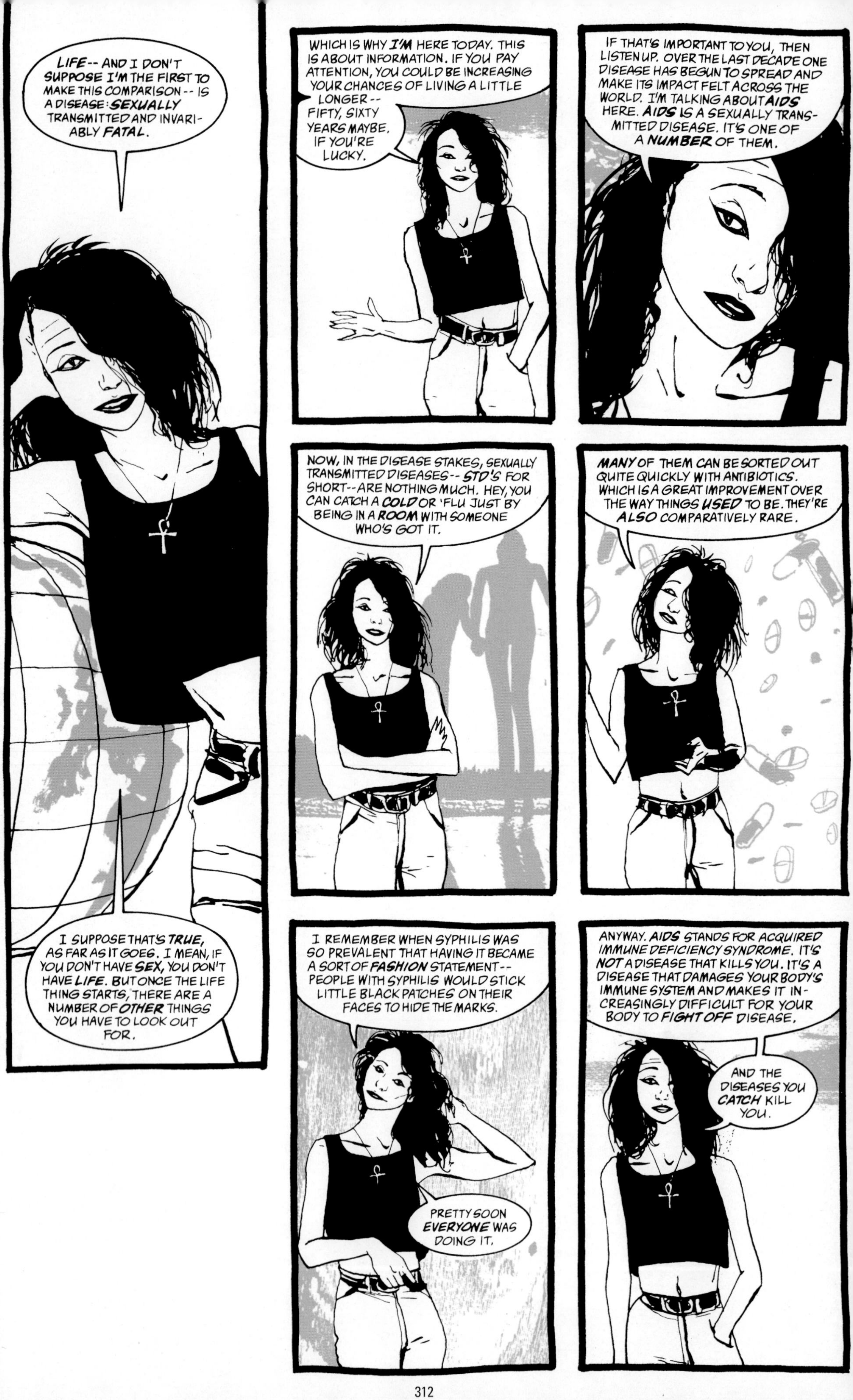
LIFE-- AND I DON'T SUPPOSE I'M THE FIRST TO MAKE THIS COMPARISON -- IS A DISEASE: SEXUALLY TRANSMITTED AND INVARI-ABLY FATAL.
I SUPPOSE THAT'S TRUE, AS FAR AS IT GOES. I MEAN, IF YOU DON'T HAVE SEX, YOU DON'T HAVE LIFE. BUT ONCE THE LIFE THING STARTS, THERE ARE A NUMBER OF OTHER THINGS YOU HAVE TO LOOK OUT FOR.
WHICH IS WHY I'M HERE TODAY. THIS IS ABOUT INFORMATION. IF YOU PAY ATTENTION, YOU COULD BE INCREASING YOUR CHANCES OF LIVING A LITTLE LONGER -- FIFTY, SIXTY YEARS MAYBE, IF YOU'RE LUCKY.
IF THAT'S IMPORTANT TO YOU, THEN LISTEN UP. OVER THE LAST DECADE ONE DISEASE HAS BEGUN TO SPREAD AND MAKE ITS IMPACT FELT ACROSS THE WORLD. I'M TALKING ABOUT AIDS HERE. AIDS IS A SEXUALLY TRANS-MITTED DISEASE. IT'S ONE OF A NUMBER OF THEM.
NOW, IN THE DISEASE STAKES, SEXUALLY TRANSMITTED DISEASES -- STD'S FOR SHORT--ARE NOTHING MUCH. HEY, YOU CAN CATCH A COLD OR 'FLU JUST BY BEING IN A ROOM WITH SOMEONE WHO'S GOT IT.
MANY OF THEM CAN BE SORTED OUT QUITE QUICKLY WITH ANTIBIOTICS. WHICH IS A GREAT IMPROVEMENT OVER THE WAY THINGS USED TO BE. THEY'RE ALSO COMPARATIVELY RARE.
I REMEMBER WHEN SYPHILIS WAS SO PREVALENT THAT HAVING IT BECAME A SORT OF FASHION STATEMENT-- PEOPLE WITH SYPHILIS WOULD STICK LITTLE BLACK PATCHES ON THEIR FACES TO HIDE THE MARKS.
PRETTY SOON EVERYONE WAS DOING IT.
ANYWAY. AIDS STANDS FOR ACQUIRED IMMUNE DEFICIENCY SYNDROME. IT'S NOT A DISEASE THAT KILLS YOU. IT'S A DISEASE THAT DAMAGES YOUR BODY'S IMMUNE SYSTEM AND MAKES IT IN-CREASINGLY DIFFICULT FOR YOUR BODY TO FIGHT OFF DISEASE.
AND THE DISEASES YOU CATCH KILL YOU.

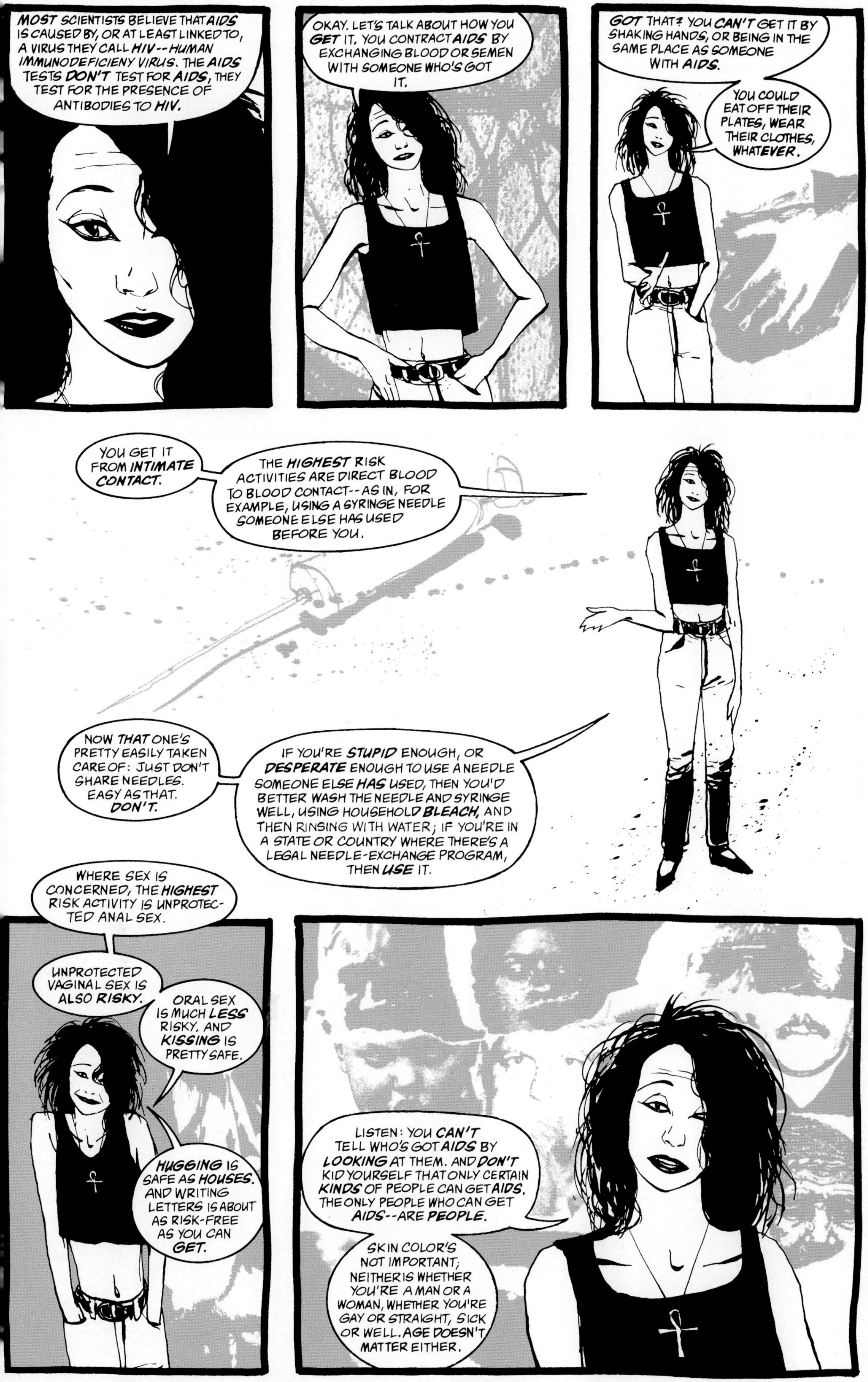
MOST SCIENTISTS BELIEVE THAT AIDS IS CAUSED BY, OR AT LEAST LINKED TO, A VIRUS THEY CALL HIV--HUMAN IMMUNODEFICIENY VIRUS. THE AIDS TESTS DON'T TEST FOR AIDS, THEY TEST FOR THE PRESENCE OF ANTIBODIES TO HIV.
OKAY. LET'S TALK ABOUT HOW YOU GET IT. YOU CONTRACT AIDS BY EXCHANGING BLOOD OR SEMEN WITH SOMEONE WHO'S GOT IT.
GOT THAT? YOU CAN'T GET IT BY SHAKING HANDS, OR BEING IN THE SAME PLACE AS SOMEONE WITH AIDS.
YOU COULD EAT OFF THEIR PLATES, WEAR THEIR CLOTHES, WHATEVER.
YOU GET IT FROM INTIMATE CONTACT.
THE HIGHEST RISK ACTIVITIES ARE DIRECT BLOOD TO BLOOD CONTACT--AS IN, FOR EXAMPLE, USING A SYRINGE NEEDLE SOMEONE ELSE HAS USED BEFORE YOU.
NOW THAT ONE'S PRETTY EASILY TAKEN CARE OF: JUST DON'T SHARE NEEDLES. EASY AS THAT. DON'T.
IF YOU'RE STUPID ENOUGH, OR DESPERATE ENOUGH TO USE A NEEDLE SOMEONE ELSE HAS USED, THEN YOU'D BETTER WASH THE NEEDLE AND SYRINGE WELL, USING HOUSEHOLD BLEACH, AND THEN RINSING WITH WATER; IF YOU'RE IN A STATE OR COUNTRY WHERE THERE'S A LEGAL NEEDLE-EXCHANGE PROGRAM, THEN USE IT.
WHERE SEX IS CONCERNED, THE HIGHEST RISK ACTIVITY IS UNPROTECTED ANAL SEX.
UNPROTECTED VAGINAL SEX IS ALSO RISKY.
ORAL SEX IS MUCH LESS RISKY. AND KISSING IS PRETTY SAFE.
HUGGING IS SAFE AS HOUSES. AND WRITING LETTERS IS ABOUT AS RISK-FREE AS YOU CAN GET.
LISTEN: YOU CAN'T TELL WHO'S GOT AIDS BY LOOKING AT THEM. AND DON'T KID YOURSELF THAT ONLY CERTAIN KINDS OF PEOPLE CAN GET AIDS. THE ONLY PEOPLE WHO CAN GET AIDS--ARE PEOPLE.
SKIN COLOR'S NOT IMPORTANT; NEITHER IS WHETHER YOU'RE A MAN OR A WOMAN, WHETHER YOU'RE GAY OR STRAIGHT, SICK OR WELL. AGE DOESN'T MATTER EITHER.

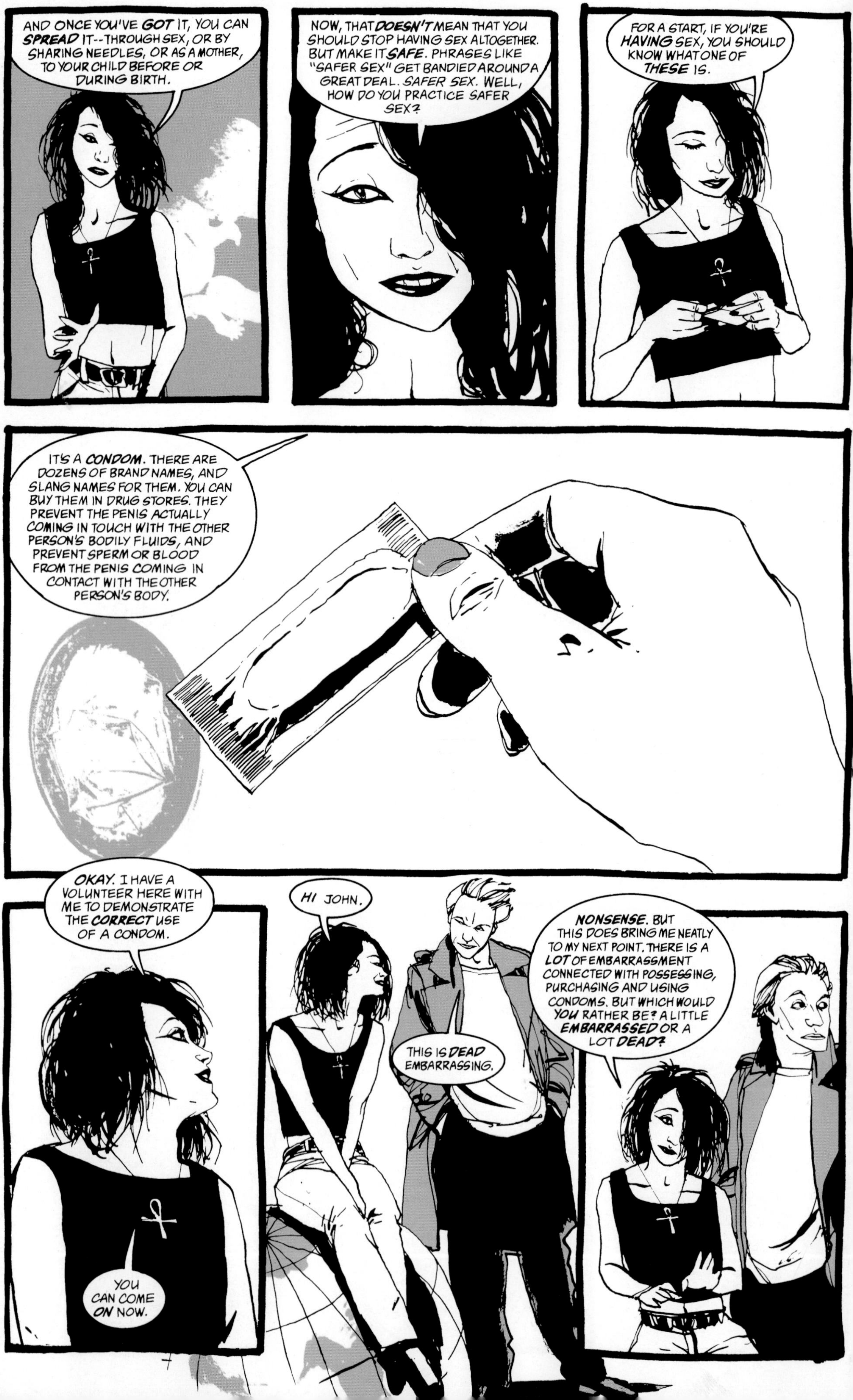
AND ONCE YOU'VE GOT IT, YOU CAN SPREAD IT--THROUGH SEX, OR BY SHARING NEEDLES, OR AS A MOTHER, TO YOUR CHILD BEFORE OR DURING BIRTH.
NOW, THAT DOESN'T MEAN THAT YOU SHOULD STOP HAVING SEX ALTOGETHER. BUT MAKE IT SAFE. PHRASES LIKE "SAFER SEX" GET BANDIED AROUND A GREAT DEAL. SAFER SEX. WELL, HOW DO YOU PRACTICE SAFER SEX?
FOR A START, IF YOU'RE HAVING SEX, YOU SHOULD KNOW WHAT ONE OF THESE IS.
IT'S A CONDOM. THERE ARE DOZENS OF BRAND NAMES, AND SLANG NAMES FOR THEM. YOU CAN BUY THEM IN DRUG STORES. THEY PREVENT THE PENIS ACTUALLY COMING IN TOUCH WITH THE OTHER PERSON'S BODILY FLUIDS, AND PREVENT SPERM OR BLOOD FROM THE PENIS COMING IN CONTACT WITH THE OTHER PERSON'S BODY.
OKAY. I HAVE A VOLUNTEER HERE WITH ME TO DEMONSTRATE THE CORRECT USE OF A CONDOM.
YOU CAN COME ON NOW.
HI JOHN.
THIS IS DEAD EMBARRASSING.
NONSENSE. BUT THIS DOES BRING ME NEATLY TO MY NEXT POINT. THERE IS A LOT OF EMBARRASSMENT CONNECTED WITH POSSESSING, PURCHASING AND USING CONDOMS. BUT WHICH WOULD YOU RATHER BE? A LITTLE EMBARRASSED OR A LOT DEAD?

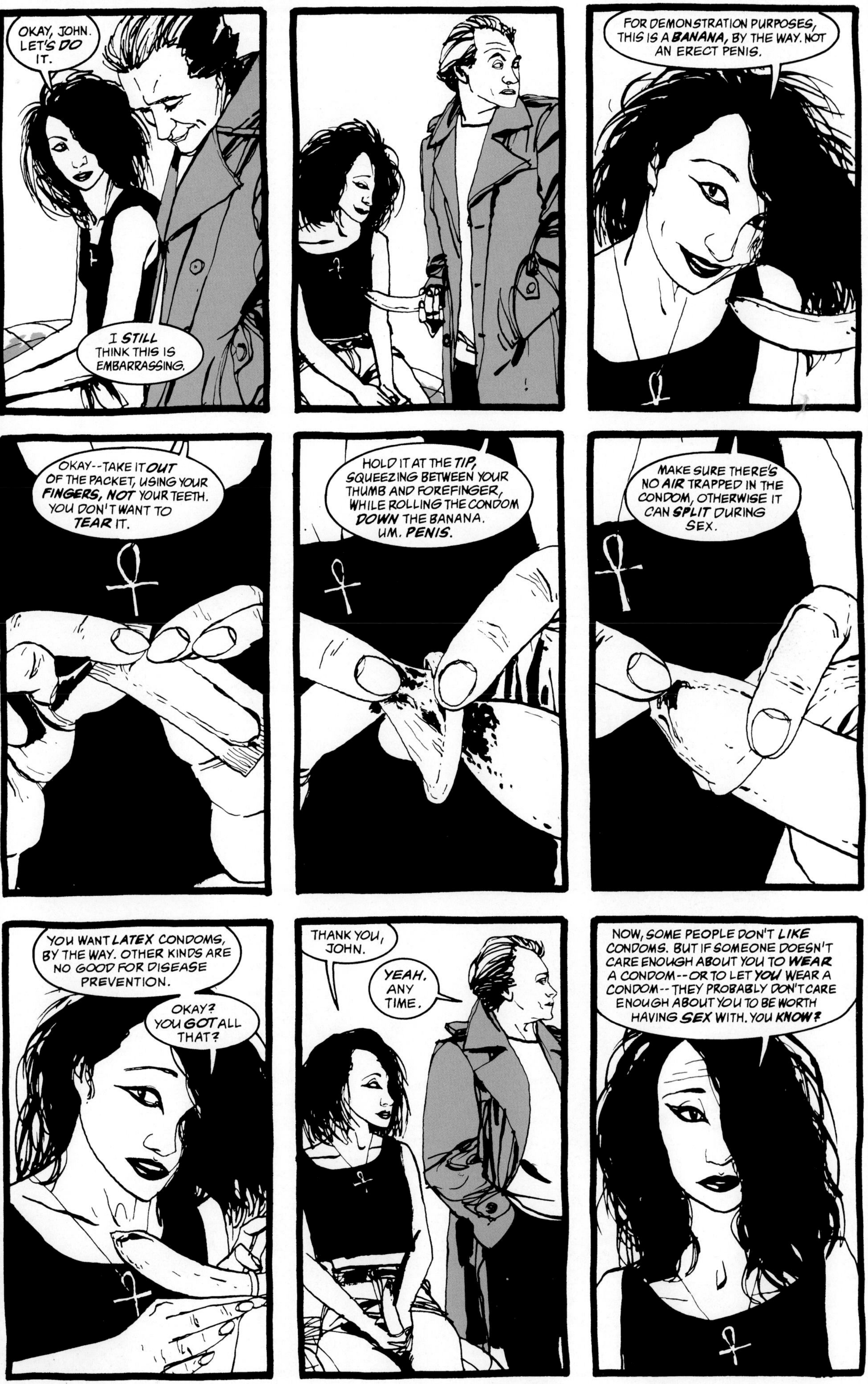

OKAY, JOHN. LET'S DO IT.
I STILL THINK THIS IS EMBARRASSING.
FOR DEMONSTRATION PURPOSES, THIS IS A BANANA, BY THE WAY. NOT AN ERECT PENIS.
OKAY--TAKE IT OUT OF THE PACKET, USING YOUR FINGERS, NOT YOUR TEETH. YOU DON'T WANT TO TEAR IT.
HOLD IT AT THE TIP, SQUEEZING BETWEEN YOUR THUMB AND FOREFINGER, WHILE ROLLING THE CONDOM DOWN THE BANANA. UM. PENIS.
MAKE SURE THERE'S NO AIR TRAPPED IN THE CONDOM, OTHERWISE IT CAN SPLIT DURING SEX.
YOU WANT LATEX CONDOMS, BY THE WAY. OTHER KINDS ARE NO GOOD FOR DISEASE PREVENTION.
OKAY? YOU GOT ALL THAT?
THANK YOU, JOHN.
YEAH. ANY TIME.
NOW, SOME PEOPLE DON'T LIKE CONDOMS. BUT IF SOMEONE DOESN'T CARE ENOUGH ABOUT YOU TO WEAR A CONDOM--OR TO LET YOU WEAR A CONDOM--THEY PROBABLY DON'T CARE ENOUGH ABOUT YOU TO BE WORTH HAVING SEX WITH. YOU KNOW?

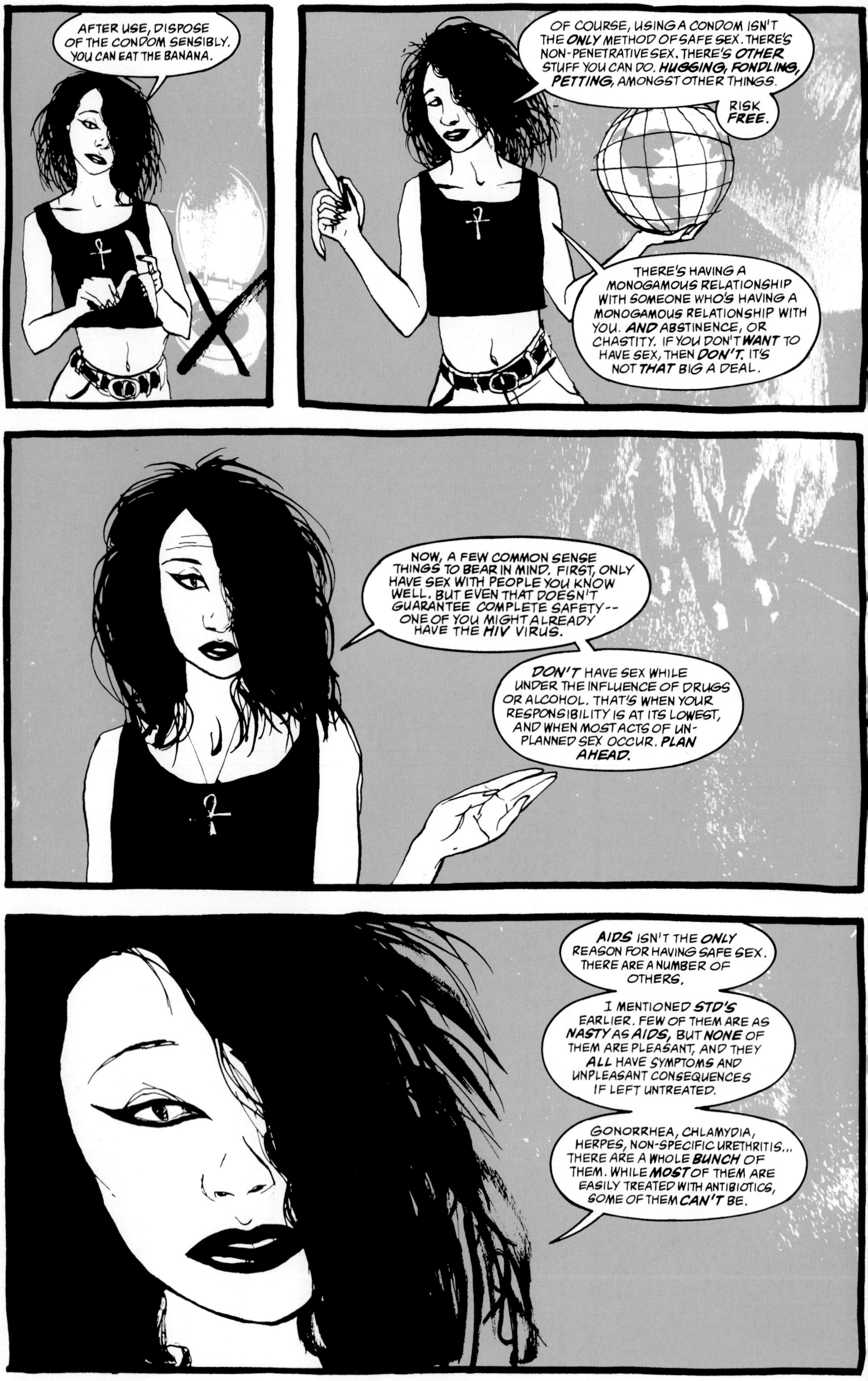
AFTER USE, DISPOSE OF THE CONDOM SENSIBLY. YOU CAN EAT THE BANANA.
OF COURSE, USING A CONDOM ISN'T THE ONLY METHOD OF SAFE SEX. THERE'S NON-PENETRATIVE SEX. THERE'S OTHER STUFF YOU CAN DO. HUGGING, FONDLING, PETTING, AMONGST OTHER THINGS.
RISK FREE.
THERE'S HAVING A MONOGAMOUS RELATIONSHIP WITH SOMEONE WHO'S HAVING A MONOGAMOUS RELATIONSHIP WITH YOU. AND ABSTINENCE, OR CHASTITY. IF YOU DON'T WANT TO HAVE SEX, THEN DON'T. IT'S NOT THAT BIG A DEAL.
NOW, A FEW COMMON SENSE THINGS TO BEAR IN MIND. FIRST, ONLY HAVE SEX WITH PEOPLE YOU KNOW WELL. BUT EVEN THAT DOESN'T GUARANTEE COMPLETE SAFETY-- ONE OF YOU MIGHT ALREADY HAVE THE HIV VIRUS.
DON'T HAVE SEX WHILE UNDER THE INFLUENCE OF DRUGS OR ALCOHOL. THAT'S WHEN YOUR RESPONSIBILITY IS AT ITS LOWEST, AND WHEN MOST ACTS OF UNPLANNED SEX OCCUR. PLAN AHEAD.
AIDS ISN'T THE ONLY REASON FOR HAVING SAFE SEX. THERE ARE A NUMBER OF OTHERS.
I MENTIONED STD'S EARLIER. FEW OF THEM ARE AS NASTY AS AIDS, BUT NONE OF THEM ARE PLEASANT, AND THEY ALL HAVE SYMPTOMS AND UNPLEASANT CONSEQUENCES IF LEFT UNTREATED.
GONORRHEA, CHLAMYDIA, HERPES, NON-SPECIFIC URETHRITIS... THERE ARE A WHOLE BUNCH OF THEM. WHILE MOST OF THEM ARE EASILY TREATED WITH ANTIBIOTICS, SOME OF THEM CAN'T BE.

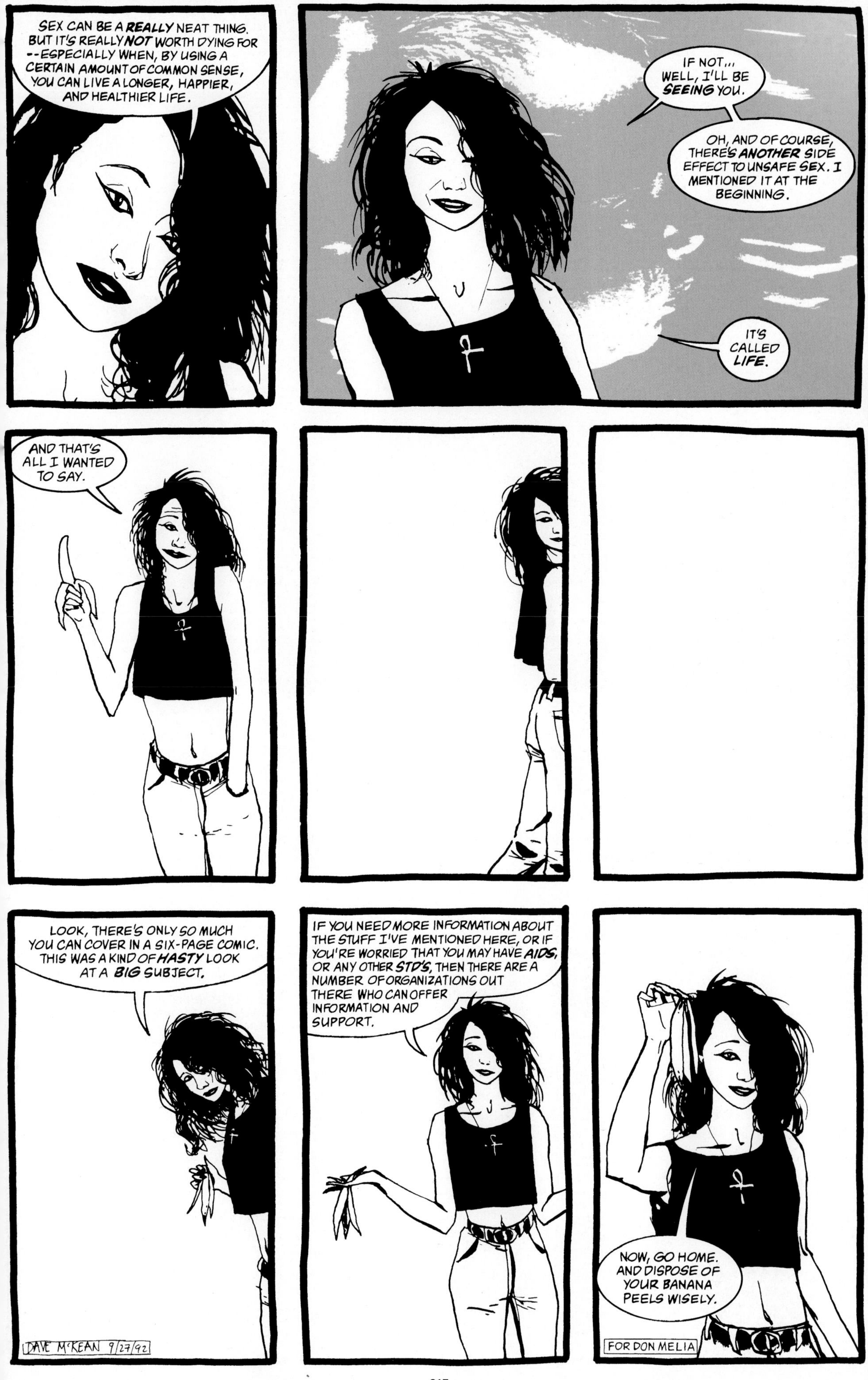
SEX CAN BE A REALLY NEAT THING. BUT IT'S REALLY NOT WORTH DYING FOR --ESPECIALLY WHEN, BY USING A CERTAIN AMOUNT OF COMMON SENSE, YOU CAN LIVE A LONGER, HAPPIER, AND HEALTHIER LIFE.
IF NOT... WELL, I'LL BE SEEING YOU.
OH, AND OF COURSE, THERE'S ANOTHER SIDE EFFECT TO UNSAFE SEX. I MENTIONED IT AT THE BEGINNING.
IT'S CALLED LIFE.
AND THAT'S ALL I WANTED TO SAY.
LOOK, THERE'S ONLY SO MUCH YOU CAN COVER IN A SIX-PAGE COMIC. THIS WAS A KIND OF HASTY LOOK AT A BIG SUBJECT.
DAVE McKEAN 9/27/92
IF YOU NEED MORE INFORMATION ABOUT THE STUFF I'VE MENTIONED HERE, OR IF YOU'RE WORRIED THAT YOU MAY HAVE AIDS, OR ANY OTHER STD'S, THEN THERE ARE A NUMBER OF ORGANIZATIONS OUT THERE WHO CAN OFFER INFORMATION AND SUPPORT.
NOW, GO HOME. AND DISPOSE OF YOUR BANANA PEELS WISELY.
FOR DON MELIA

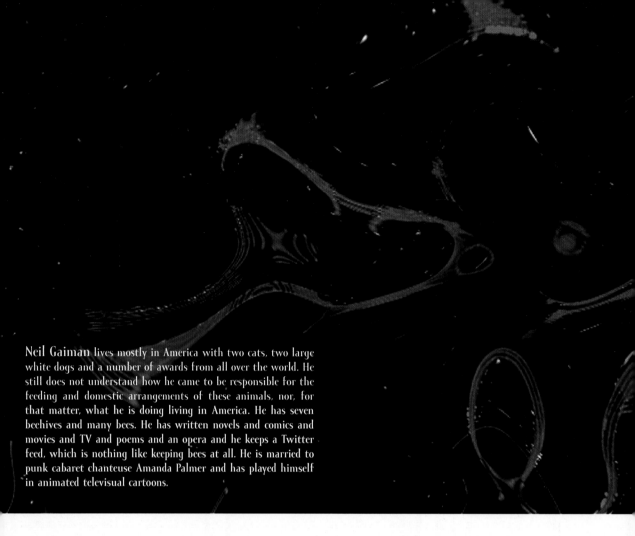

Neil Gaiman lives mostly in America with two cats, two large white dogs and a number of awards from all over the world. He still does not understand how he came to be responsible for the feeding and domestic arrangements of these animals, nor, for that matter, what he is doing living in America. He has seven beehives and many bees. He has written novels and comics and movies and TV and poems and an opera and he keeps a Twitter feed, which is nothing like keeping bees at all. He is married to punk cabaret chanteuse Amanda Palmer and has played himself in animated televisual cartoons.

Chris Bachalo is internationally recognized as one of the most popular artists in the comics industry. His body of work covers a wide spectrum of genres, ranging from the critically acclaimed series THE SANDMAN, DEATH: THE HIGH COST OF LIVING and SHADE, THE CHANGING MAN for DC to *The Amazing Spider-Man*, *The Uncanny X-Men* and the quirky pop favorite *Generation X* — which he co-created with Scott Lobdell — for Marvel. He is also responsible for the creator-owned properties THE WITCHING HOUR (with writer Jeph Loeb) and STEAMPUNK (with writer Joe Kelly), published by Vertigo and WildStorm.

Chris was born in Portage La Prairie in the western Canadian province of Manitoba, and he currently resides in southern California with his wife Helen, his son Dylan and his Siamese fighting fish Spike 2. He can also be found virtually at chrisbachalo.net.

Born in 1966 in the English seaside town of Clevedon, **Mark Buckingham** has worked in comics professionally for the past twenty years. In addition to illustrating all of Neil Gaiman's run on the post-Alan Moore *Miracleman* in the early 1990s, Buckingham contributed inks to THE SANDMAN and its related miniseries DEATH: THE HIGH COST OF LIVING and DEATH: THE TIME OF YOUR LIFE as well as working on various other titles for Vertigo and Marvel through the end of the decade. In 2002 he took over as the penciller for Bill Willingham's FABLES, which has gone on to become one of the most popular and critically acclaimed Vertigo titles of the new millennium. Buckingham returned to the world of the Dreaming with his designs for the Absolute Sandman Statue and the Sandman and Death Bookends, released by DC Direct in 2007 and 2008, and he has also reunited with Neil Gaiman to illustrate his children's book *Odd and the Frost Giants*. When not in Clevedon, Buckingham can be found with his wife Irma in the Asturias region of northern Spain.

Michael Dringenberg was born in France and grew up in Germany before emigrating to America in the early 1970s. He studied illustration and graphic design at the University of Utah and began illustrating books and comics before leaving college.

He met Neil Gaiman in 1988 and with him co-created the hugely popular and critically successful series THE SANDMAN.

Dringenberg's work as an illustrator continues, focusing on book jackets and, more recently, CD covers, exploring the relationship of sound and vision.

He likes cats and rain.

A professional illustrator since the age of fifteen, **Colleen Doran** has contributed to hundreds of comic book titles, including THE SANDMAN, LUCIFER, WONDER WOMAN, *The Amazing Spider-Man* and *Captain America*, as well as *The Book of Lost Souls* by Babylon 5 creator J. Michael Straczynski and the graphic novel adaptations of Anne Rice's *The Master of Rampling Gate* and Disney's *Beauty and the Beast*. She has illustrated two original graphic novels for Vertigo — ORBITER, written by Warren Ellis, and GONE TO AMERIKAY, written by Derek McCulloch — and she is currently working with Ellis on a third, entitled *STEALTH TRIBES*. Doran also continues to write and draw her creator-owned series *A Distant Soil*, an epic science fiction/fantasy tale that now spans some 40 issues (or four trade paperback collections).

P. Craig Russell lives in Kent, Ohio, and has been producing comic books, illustrations and graphic novels for 37 years. His work ranges from mainstream titles such as BATMAN, *Star Wars* and *Conan* to a series of adaptations of classic operas (*The Magic Flute*, *Salome*, *I Pagliacci*, *The Ring of the Nibelung*), a series of *Jungle Book* stories, and an ongoing series adapting the complete fairy tales of

Oscar Wilde. He has collaborated with Neil Gaiman on six projects, including THE SANDMAN #50, *Coraline*, and the comics adaptation of THE SANDMAN: THE DREAM HUNTERS.

Malcolm Jones III attended the High School of Art and Design and the Pratt Institute in New York City before making his comics debut in the pages of DC's YOUNG ALL-STARS. In addition to his celebrated work on THE SANDMAN, Jones contributed work to many other titles from both DC and Marvel, including BATMAN, THE QUESTION QUARTERLY, *Dracula* and *Spider-Man*. He died in 1995.

A graduate of the Joe Kubert School of Cartoon and Graphic Art, **Mark Pennington** has been active in the commercial art field for over twenty years. In the course of his prolific career he has worked for nearly every major comic book publisher, including Marvel, DC, Image, Now and CrossGen, as well as providing painted art for a wide variety of collectible card and role-playing games. He has also worked as a toy designer for Hasbro and Mattel, contributing to their G.I. Joe and Transformers product lines. When he's not chained to his drawing board, Mark likes to spend time helping his wife Cathy and playing with their three children. In his free moments he escapes into the sunshine to play golf and tennis.

Dave McKean has created designs and illustrations for hundreds of comics, books and CDs, including all of the covers for Neil Gaiman's acclaimed series THE SANDMAN. He has also illustrated the award-winning comics BATMAN: ARKHAM ASYLUM, MR. PUNCH, *Signal to Noise*, *Violent Cases* and *Cages* (which he also wrote). His short stories collection *Pictures That [Tick]* won the Victoria & Albert Museum Book of the Year Award, and his short film *N[eon]* won overall first prize at the Clermont-Ferrand Film Festival. His newest collaboration with Gaiman is the feature film *MirrorMask* from Jim Henson Productions, which he directed and co-wrote. McKean lives in England's Kent countryside.

Born in Atlanta in 1944, **Jeffrey Jones** moved to New York City in 1967 to be a professional artist — a statistically improbable goal which he nonetheless swiftly achieved. He began his career drawing for science fiction digest magazines and comics published by Warren, Gold Key and King. Learning from such master illustrators as Roy Krenkel, Al Williamson and Frank Frazetta, he soon became one of the most sought-after cover artists in the burgeoning fantasy book field, with the works of Robert E. Howard being a particular specialty.

In 1972 Jones launched the lyrical, exquisitely drawn comic strip *Idyl*, which ran monthly in *National Lampoon* until 1975. The following year he joined fellow artists Bernie Wrightson, Michael Kaluta and Barry Windsor-Smith in renting a large loft in Manhattan to serve as a four-person studio. This creative space became a legend in the fantasy art and comic book communities, and its story was immortalized in the book *The Studio*, published by Roger Dean's Dragon's Dream Press in 1979.

After the dissolution of the Studio, Jones largely abandoned the commercial art world to concentrate on his personal artistic vision. The result has been a unique body of work documented in the books *Yesterday's Lily* (1980), *Age of Innocence* (1994) and *The Art of Jeffrey Jones* (2002). He passed away on May 19, 2011.

A professional colorist for more than 25 years, **Steve Oliff** has also been a pioneer in bringing comics into the digital age. Beginning in 1989 with his Harvey Award-winning computer coloring work on Katsuhiro Otomo's *Akira* for Marvel, Oliff and his coloring house Olyoptics have revolutionized the field of comic book coloring as well

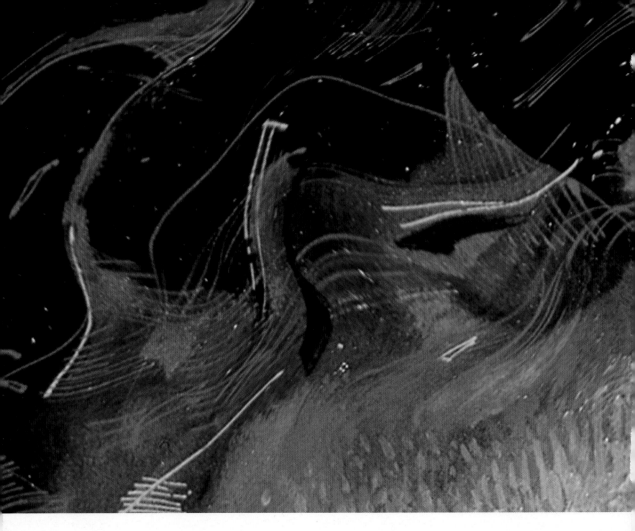

as winning over a dozen industry awards for color excellence on such titles as *Spawn*, BATMAN, THE SANDMAN and THE MAXX.

Born in southern California in 1968, **Matt Hollingsworth** began his comics career in 1991. Since then he has worked as a color artist for most of the major American comic book publishers, contributing to such titles as PREACHER, TOM STRONG, CATWOMAN, THE FILTH, *Hellboy, Iron Fist, Alias* and *Daredevil*. In 2004, while living in Los Angeles, he embarked on a two-year stint in the world of visual effects that led to assignments on seven feature films, including *Sky Captain and the World of Tomorrow*, *Serenity*, and his personal favorite, *Surf's Up*. In addition to rebuilding his home brewery, Hollingsworth spends his free time consuming massive quantities of beer, playing drums, studying genealogy, and wandering the countryside in Croatia where he lives with his fiancée and two cats.

Daniel Vozzo was born and raised in Brooklyn, New York. After spending most of the 1980s drumming for several rock-and-roll bands, he landed a job working in DC Comics' production department, where he helped develop a computer coloring department in 1989. He soon began to work freelance, coloring a number of titles for DC's Vertigo line. He sings great in the shower and always holds the door open for people. Currently living in northern New Jersey, Vozzo continues to color comics and is once again playing music. He has also been working on fine-tuning his writing skills. When asked if he thinks he's good at writing, he insists that he has always had very good penmanship.

Lovern Kindzierski has been recognized by the readers of *Comics Buyer's Guide* as one of the medium's most influential colorists. He has worked for every major publisher in the industry and has been nominated several times for both the Eisner and Harvey Awards

for Best Colorist. An accomplished painter, Kindzierski also holds a Bachelor of Fine Arts degree (with honors) from the University of Manitoba, where he now teaches a course in graphic narrative.

After working in comics for 20 years (and receiving an Eisner Award along the way), **Jon J Muth** went into the desert on a camel and came out a children's book author and illustrator. (The camel did not return calls in time for this biography.) Over the past decade, Muth's picture books have received numerous awards (including a Caldecott Honor) and have been translated into a dozen or so languages. He has interests in music, stone and spending time with his family. He lives in New York with his wife and four children.

Alex Bleyaert and **Rob Ro** began their careers at WildStorm FX, the company's in-house coloring team. In 1996 they joined with fellow FX colorist Ian Hannin to form their own studio, BAD@$$ Color, which cut its teeth on such titles as WILDC.A.T.S, WETWORKS, CRIMSON and STEAMPUNK. Initially emphasizing a punchy technique heavy on dynamic lighting and textures, BAD@$$ has since branched out to cover a wide variety of styles, with assignments ranging from DC's THE ALL NEW ATOM and SUPERMAN: TRUE BRIT to Les Humanoïdes Associés' *Marshall*. Following Ro's departure from the studio in 2003, Bleyaert and BAD@$$ are closing in on 20 years of coloring bliss.

One of the industry's most versatile and accomplished letterers, **Todd Klein** has been lettering comics since 1977 and has won numerous Eisner and Harvey Awards for his work. A highlight of his career has been working with Neil Gaiman on nearly all the original issues of THE SANDMAN, as well as BLACK ORCHID, DEATH: THE HIGH COST OF LIVING, DEATH: THE TIME OF YOUR LIFE and THE BOOKS OF MAGIC.